Developing Library and
Information Center Collections

Library and Information Science Text Series

Developing Library and Information Center Collections

Fourth Edition

G. EDWARD EVANS
University Librarian
Loyola Marymount University
Los Angeles, California

With the assistance of

Margaret R. Zarnosky
Associate Director, Learning Resource Center
Northern Virginia Community College
Alexandria, Virginia

2000
LIBRARIES UNLIMITED
A Division of Greenwood Publishing Group, Inc.
Greenwood Village, Colorado

LIBRARIES UNLIMITED
A Division of Greenwood Publishing Group, Inc.
7730 East Belleview Avenue, Suite A200
Greenwood Village, CO 80111
1-800-237-6124
www.lu.com

Library of Congress Cataloging-in-Publication Data

Evans, G. Edward, 1937-
   Developing library and information center collections / G. Edward Evans with the assistance of Margaret R. Zarnosky.-- 4th ed.
     p. cm. -- (Library and information science text series)
   ISBN 1-56308-706-5 -- ISBN 1-56308-832-0 (pbk.)
     1. Collection development (Libraries)--United States. 2. Information services--United States. I. Zarnosky, Margaret R. II. Title. III. Series.

Z687 .E918 1999
025.2'1--dc21
                                            99-059179

No Library of One Million Volumes can be all BAD!

—from a cover, *Antiquarian Bookman*

*We were told that if one put one million monkeys at one million typewriters,
they would, in time, produce the complete works of Shakespeare.
Now that we have the Internet, we know that is just not true.*

*I worry more about poor quality of information online,
and students' lack of skills for evaluating information,
than ... about frequently discussed evils like pornography.*

—John Leland
"Beyond Littleton: The Secret Life of Teens,"
Newsweek, May 10, 1999

We wish to dedicate this edition
to all the students,
who will begin developing the collections of the future,
and their instructors who will assist them in their learning.

As a personal dedication:
to the young readers
Travis and Trenton Evans

And in memory of
Clara Bower,
grandmother and special friend

Contents

6—PRINT-BASED SERIALS (*continued*)

7—ELECTRONIC SERIALS . . . . *Aug 5* 180

8—OTHER ELECTRONIC MATERIALS. . . *Aug 5* 207

Aug 8 Thurs

List of Illustrations

Figure

Table

Preface
to the First Edition

Collection development is an exciting and challenging area in which to work, and selecting the right materials for the library's community is as intellectually demanding an activity as a librarian will encounter. The selection of library materials is a highly personal process—something that takes a lifetime to learn—and the rewards are great. This book can serve as the starting point in that learning process. Any textbook that attempts to cover all aspects of collection development must give coverage to many topics. This text provides practical information on materials producers and distributors, community survey techniques, policies, materials selection, acquisition, weeding, and evaluation in order to minimize the variables involved in the selection process. Beyond the physical processes of collection development, though, are issues with which a selector should be concerned, as they influence how the collection will and can be developed. Thus, *Developing Library Collections* also delves into library cooperation, copyright (reflecting the changed statutes), and censorship as they affect the process in its entirety.

An author of a collection development textbook should acknowledge that, to a very great degree, the emphasis given each topic is based on a subjective assessment of its importance, reflecting the values and judgments of that author. Certainly, anyone with practical experience in this area knows that selection and collection development are arts, not sciences; and, as with any artistic endeavor, a person wishing to practice the art must devote years to developing the necessary skills. The basic elements of the collection development process—determining what information resources are needed, identifying the appropriate items, acquiring the items, and evaluating the collection—are rather well agreed upon. What is open to debate is how much emphasis to place upon individual steps in the process, and the interrelationship of all the elements.

A person cannot learn selection and collection development only in the classroom. A student will be able to learn the basic elements from this book; whether the student accepts the emphasis placed upon the elements is another matter. With the concepts presented in this book as a base, and using the recommended further readings, however, the student should begin to develop a solidly based, personal approach to selection and collection development.

The purpose of this book is to help library students gain an overall understanding of what is involved in building a collection for a library. Within rather broad limits, one may say that all libraries share certain general characteristics, including the need to assemble a collection of books and other library materials needed by their patrons. This book was written with the intent of emphasizing the similarities between types of libraries in the process of developing a collection.

Unlike any other book on collection development or book selection, *Developing Library Collections* provides an integrated approach to the process of building a library collection for a specific community of users—integrated in the sense that each element in the process is treated as flowing from one to another, and when something occurs in one element, it will have an impact on the others. Thus, as each element is discussed in detail, its relationship with the others will be examined as well, the underlying emphasis always being on the ultimate goal of the process—serving the library's community. To some degree, every chapter in this book has some application to any library. However, some aspects of collection development have more application, or at least are more widely used, in one type of library than another. For example, community analysis has been most widely used in public libraries, and as a result, chapter 4 tends to emphasize community analysis in the public library. Chapters 14 and 15, on weeding and evaluating the collection, deal with issues most pertinent to academic libraries, and this emphasis is reflected in the citations. Nevertheless, every chapter provides information relevant to all types of libraries.

In one sense, this is a jointly authored work. Any librarian who has written or talked about this subject has probably influenced my thinking to some degree. The further readings at the ends of the chapters reflect some of the works that have directly affected my point of view; they are but a fraction of the total waiting to be read. These writings will serve as an excellent starting point for further reading, which will need to continue as long as a librarian is involved in collection development work.

Preface
to the Second Edition

The slight change in the title of this book is a reflection of a shift in emphasis from the book and other "information packages" to the information contained in the package. Selection work has always been concerned with the contents of items being considered for a collection. What has happened over the past 15 years is that society has become aware of and concerned about the "values" of information. New systems, often computer based, offer alternative means of providing information for patrons or clients. It appears likely this trend will continue for some time.

In the first edition the first chapter was concerned with definitions and concepts, and so is the first chapter in this edition. However, more emphasis is placed on concepts of information and information transfer. It is virtually a new chapter. Most of the chapters from the first edition have been extensively revised and updated, and additions have been made. The former chapter on selection is now divided into two chapters, on theory and practice. New chapters dealing with serials, government documents, fiscal management, automation, and preservation have been added.

Suggestions for further reading are included in each chapter. Items listed were selected on the basis of ease of availability and currency. (Also, all the items mentioned in a chapter are included regardless of date of publication.) An effort has been made to provide a few references for academic, public, school, and special libraries and information centers in each chapter.

I wish to thank all the individuals who read one or more chapters of this edition and provided many helpful suggestions: Herbert Achlietner, Peter Briscoe, Alan Ericson, William Fisher, Dale Flecker, Doris Frietag, Irene Godden, William McGrath, Assunta Pisanti, Benedict Rugaas, Joel Rutstein, and Sally Williams. Naturally they are not responsible for any of the book's shortcomings. Finally, I want to thank Morris Fry for his copyediting work, Julie Wetherill for the many hours of typing, and Nancy Lambert-Brown for the figures and charts she prepared.

Preface
to the Third Edition

This edition reflects the changes that collection management has undergone during the past eight years. There is a new chapter on electronic formats. The additions, deletions, and changes in the presentation grow out of the ideas, suggestions, and comments from a number of people. I started by obtaining input from teachers who used the second edition. Their comments were especially useful. The individuals who took the time to respond in depth and with invaluable input were Robert Broadus, Donald Davis, William Fisher, Elizabeth Futas, Sheila Intner, Bill Katz, Betty Morris, Ronald Powell, James Rice, Judith Serebnick, Phyllis Van Orden, and Adeline Wood Wilkes. I also was fortunate enough to have six people from different types of library environments read the entire manuscript and comment on the material. These readers, who spent long hours reading more than 700 manuscript pages, deserve more thanks than is possible to give in writing. They were Donald Davis (University of Texas, academic libraries and teacher), Bill Fisher (San Jose State University, special libraries and teacher), David Loertscher (Libraries Unlimited, school library media centers), Nancy Pruett (Sandia National Laboratories, special libraries), Brian Reynolds (San Luis Obispo County Library, public libraries), and Margaret Zarnosky (Virginia Polytechnic Institute and State University, academic libraries). Margaret deserves an extra special thank you for her editing efforts, as well as her insightful content comments. Staff members from the Loyola Marymount Library also read many of the chapters. They were Marcia Findley (Assistant University Librarian for Collection Development), Janet Lai (Head of Acquisitions and Serials Department), Paula Nielson (Assistant University Librarian for Systems), and Sachi Yagyu (Database Services and Document Delivery). They deserve special recognition for having the courage to read the director's manuscript and make honest comments. Finally, to the others who read one or more chapters, a special thank you: Dr. Elizabeth Eaton (Director, Health Sciences Library, Tufts University), whose suggestions were of immense help in preparing the electronics chapter; Dr. John Richardson (UCLA's library school), who commented on the government information chapter; and Peter Bodell (Director, Information Services, Loyola Marymount University), who provided a computer center perspective.

All the readers' comments greatly improved the manuscript. However, they are not responsible for errors in content. I hope this edition will prove as useful to students and others as did the second edition.

Preface
to the Fourth Edition

Less than six years have passed since the issuance of the third edition. When the call came suggesting that it was time to start work on a new edition, it seemed much too soon. However, after reviewing what might require updating and thinking about new sections, it became clear that it was indeed time to get to work.

Electronic issues now pervade collection development and management activities. The underlying basics remain, but the whats and hows are changing rather quickly. As a result, this is a somewhat longer edition, and almost every chapter contains something about electronic resources, reflecting the changing environment of collection management.

As with the prior editions, I asked for user feedback to help plan the contents of the new edition. To that end, 61 instructors who used the third edition received a questionnaire/survey form. That form listed sections where I thought additions would be appropriate, as well as suggestions for dropping sections to keep the book to a reasonable length. Forty-seven individuals took the time to reply; some even included their students in the process. To all those who took the time to respond, my very sincere thanks. This edition does in fact reflect your feedback.

One of the surprises in the responses was a rather consistent reluctance to have material dropped. This posed a problem in terms of the overall length of the projected new edition. The final solution was to drop sections that 40 percent of the respondents agreed could be eliminated. Nevertheless, the final manuscript was longer than first envisioned, so much longer that major cuts became necessary in order to keep the final book to a reasonable length.

One of the biggest departures from previous editions of this text occurred as a result of all the additions. For the first time, materials from the text are now available via the Internet. Specifically, the contents of what was Chapter 4 in earlier editions (Selection Process: Theory), and the two Appendices—"Book and Electronic Collection Policies" and the International Coalition of Library Consortia (ICOLC) "Statement of Current Perspective and Preferred Practices for the Selection and Purchase of Electronic Information," are available from two web sites <http://lib.lmu.edu/dlc4> and <http://www.lu.com>. In addition, there are some examples of needs assessment forms on the web sites. We regret that space considerations prevented us from including this material in the main body of the text, but encourage you to refer to this material in your studies.

Most of the individuals who devoted some hours to reading one or more chapters for the third edition once again contributed time, thought, and critical comment for material in this edition (see the "Preface to the Third Edition"). To that list I must add: Professor F. Jay Dougherty (Loyola Law School), who provided very valuable advice about copyright material, especially on the Digital Millennium Copyright Act; Mr. Evan A. Reader (Director, CSU-Software and Electronic Information Resources, Office of the Chancellor, California State University System); Mr. Lynn F. Sipe (Associate Director for Collections, University of Southern California and 1999 Chair of the American Library Association, Association for Library Collections and Technical Services' Collection Management Section), who read many of the chapters and also provided ideas for various other chapters; and Ms. Ann Williams (American Health Care Association), who provided a special library perspective.

I also wish to thank those who provided policies for Appendix One: David R. Bender (Executive Director, Special Libraries Association); Mary Lou Calvin (Director of Library Services, Warner, Norcross & Judd); Marcia Findley (Loyola Marymount University); Paul Metz (Virginia Polytechnic Institute and State University); John Stemmer (Xavier University); Phyllis Young (Collections Development Coordinator, Los Angeles County Library System); and Ann Williams (Director, Information Resource Center, American Health Care Association).

Lastly, as one can see from the title page, I decided that it was time to bring in another person to assist in the preparation of this and future editions. Margaret Zarnosky is serving as a "junior" author on this edition, after having provided excellent comments and ideas for the last edition.

G. Edward Evans
Los Angeles, California
May 1999

This volume has provided me with a unique opportunity, and I have very much enjoyed assisting in its preparation. Beyond those individuals mentioned above, who deserve thanks for their assistance, I also wish to acknowledge several individuals for their efforts on behalf of this project. In particular, Annemarie Anderson and Sylvia Rortvedt (Northern Virginia Community College, Alexandria Campus) both deserve special thanks. Annemarie provided a critical "library student's perspective" of the work in progress, including the newly added tables in chapter 4. Sylvia, as Collection Development Officer, was always available to provide insight and suggestions for the text, as well as needed research support. Finally, a very special thank-you to my parents for their love and support.

Margaret R. Zarnosky
Alexandria, Virginia
May 1999

1

Information Age—
Information Society

*Reading is the opposite of dissipation;
it is a mental and moral practice of concentration
which leads us to unknown worlds.*

—Octavio Paz[1]

Angels of Russia, a novel by Patricia le Roy, created something of a controversy in summer 1998 when it was nominated for the Booker McConnell Prize.[2] (That annual prize is the most prestigious literary award in the United Kingdom and goes to the "best full-length novel written in English by a citizen of the U.K., the Commonwealth, the Republic of Ireland, Pakistan, or South Africa."[3]) The controversy revolved around the question of "when is a book a book?" *Angels* was not available in any bookstore, it existed solely as a virtual book. Some of the judges took the position that an electronic text is not a book, whereas others thought the emphasis should be on literary merit, not physical format. (We will revisit the concepts and issues of content versus packaging later in this chapter.) To a large degree, the *Angels* controversy reflects the same issue that libraries and information centers have been struggling with for 15 or more years—reality versus virtuality.

In recent years, there have been many developments in the electronic delivery of information. Articles about virtual libraries, or virtual knowledge centers, appear almost monthly in the professional journals (see page 3 for a discussion of virtuals). Interactive multimedia is another concept that some people claim will solve the information problems of society. Authors present images of brave new worlds in which individuals will be able to gain access to any type of information (text, numeric, graphic, or audio) from home, office, or even a traveler's hotel room. More and more, many of those scenarios are becoming reality, but they are almost always available only to those few who can afford or have access to the high-end machines required to access such material.

The technologies these authors describe—existing and projected—hold no great promise for assisting in the information transfer process. Taken to the ultimate scenario, one sees a world where one sits in one's own space and need never have direct physical contact with another human being. In fact, Raymond Kurzweil suggested that we can look forward to virtual physical relations![4] A world without face-to-face interaction does not appeal to many people, including me. One writer suggests that books and reading are something like horses.[5] That is, in the late nineteenth century, horses were the primary mode of transportation. Today, we still have horses, but primarily for pleasure use, and only a few people ride for pleasure.

Perhaps some time in the future, books and reading will be the "horses" of information. However, even if it becomes possible to deliver all information to all individuals everywhere, I believe that the interest in the technology misses a key point, as reflected in the Paz quotation, which goes on to state:

> ... to read is to discover unsuspected paths that lead to our own selves. It is recognition. In the era of advertising and instantaneous communication, how many people are able to read this way? Very few. But the continuity of our civilization lies with them.[6]

What the technologies are best at is delivering information. It takes time and personal effort to convert information into knowledge—and more time, and some luck, into wisdom.

Although reading is only one means of acquiring information, it is perhaps the most important. Presently, technologies can present on a computer screen only portions of the information that would normally appear on a printed page. Individuals must download, or have delivered, a paper copy of the material if they wish to consult the information away from the screen. There are a number of problems with this approach to reading. Two of the more significant challenges are the costs entailed in getting information from electronic sources, and users' assumptions about those sources.

As more libraries and information centers pass along some or all of the direct costs of electronic information, users will attempt to keep their costs as low as possible. This often results in the person taking only a small part of the information in a large file. Without having the full file, the individual is more likely to misinterpret or misunderstand the material. We have entered an age in which information bites could have an even greater impact on society than television's sound bites. Individuals become accustomed to instant information and subsequently demand instant facts, interpretation, and presumed understanding of complex issues in 30 seconds or less. Electronics reinforce the need for speed. (Waiting for a second becomes too long when one is working with a computer.) There is an all-too-common faith that the electronic sources are accurate, complete, and up-to-date.

Some people often assume that if they check for information in an electronic system, they have all the information on their topic. On one level they know this is a false assumption, but they operate as if it were true. A related assumption is that the information found electronically is the most current and accurate, rather like the past assumption that if the information appears in a book then it must be true. Somehow libraries and information centers must do more to educate end users about electronic sources and their limitations.

Patricia Battin stated:

> Approximately ninety percent of the information needs of academic
> and research programs rely upon an essentially nineteenth-
> century information system. It coexists with an emerging twenty-
> first century information system that currently serves only ten
> percent of those needs. The coexistence contributes to a frenetic
> schizophrenia among students and faculty, who expect the effi-
> ciency and convenience of electronic facilities from traditional library
> services, and the comprehensive literature coverage of traditional
> library collections from electronic systems.[7]

Although she wrote the above in 1990, the facts remain almost unchanged.
Paper-based resources continue to be a major source for scholarly activity.

What does all this have to do with collection development? Everything,
we believe. Even if the brave new world of electronic information comes to
pass, there will be a need for locally maintained resources, if for no other reason than cost control. Electronic information does not reduce costs, but
rather shifts them. Securing information from locally maintained databases,
for high-use sources, will most likely remain less expensive than paying for
the information plus the telecommunication charges for accessing a remote
database on an as-needed basis. Knowing who is using what, for what purposes, and how often, as well as knowing what sources exist that can supply
the information in the most cost-effective way, is the keystone of present and
foreseeable collection development work. If, however, books and reading remain crucial factors in the transfer of information, the same skills and understanding are equally necessary.

A 1998 article in *Library Journal* outlined some of the problems that
exist in finding information on the Internet.[8] The essence of the article was
who can—and how to—"tame" the Web: commercial for-profit organizations
or librarians? On the commercial side, only *Yahoo!* (http://www.yahoo.com)
even attempts to impose a semblance of order on Internet materials. Reference librarians and collection development officers have been "selecting," establishing appropriate links (acquisition), arranging (cataloging), and
periodically reviewing (evaluation) Internet sites for some time. The "collection building" of appropriate sites draws on the same skills and principles
that librarians have employed for years with print materials (see pp. 24–25).

Charles Handy, in discussing trust and the virtual organization,
touched on the issue of the volume of information, the growing dependence
on technology in peoples' daily lives, and society.[9] He described the "Three I
Economy" of information, ideas, and intelligence. His concluding remarks
dealt with society's dilemma:

> The hope for the future that is contained within the virtual or-
> ganization will end in disillusionment unless we can mobilize soci-
> ety to think beyond itself to save itself. ... [I]f business minds its
> own business exclusively or if it takes virtuality to extremes and
> becomes a mere broker or box of contracts, then it will have failed
> society. In the end, its search for wealth will have destroyed
> wealth.[10]

Our view is that the future will lie somewhere between the technologists' projections and what exists today. The idea of fiction, essays, literature, poetry, and biographies becoming the "horses" of the information future is most unappealing.

Nature of Information

Some individuals talk as if information were a newly discovered, mysterious, and natural phenomenon. For librarians and others working in information centers, information is neither new nor mysterious; it is the product they have always worked with, an old friend. Nevertheless, both perspectives have an element of truth.

Libraries and their collections (information) have existed for thousands of years. For example, the Red Temple at Uruk, dating about 3000 B.C., contained a library. People recognized the value of information, although sometimes in rather unusual ways. For example, monks in European medieval libraries chained many of their books to reading stalls. (There were several reasons for chaining the books, the value of the information being one.) Collecting and organizing information and making it more available to individuals has a long history. However, during the past 15 to 20 years, a major shift in attitude of Western societies toward information has taken place.

More organizations and people treat information as an economic product like petroleum, cardboard boxes, or automobiles. For example, there are many newsletter or special report information services that charge thousands of dollars for one year's service. (Some examples of the cost of information are *Petroleum Argus Telex,* which cost $22,198 in 1995, and the *Decima Quarterly Report* for $26,065 in 1997. The most costly of 1998 titles, *Outlook for Market Pulp Demand Supply and Prices,* was $81,729.[11]) Combined with this different attitude toward information is the variety of technological developments that affect the generation, storage, and retrieval of information.

As we near a new millennium, what is happening in the late1990s is, in many ways, similar to what happened with the widespread use of movable type. As Patricia Sabosik noted, the turmoil in today's publishing is almost the same as in the fifteenth century.[12] Just as the printing press shifted access to information from a few to many people, we are seeing a similar shift today. Sabosik suggested that the shift today is from libraries to end users. In her view, libraries are becoming intermediaries, rather than storehouses, of information. Certainly some of the shifting she described has already taken place and is likely to grow in scope; however, the process will probably take a long time to complete. That is, assuming that the virtual library, or knowledge center, of the future does become an electronic switching center service.

The net effect of the combination is a new phenomenon that creates problems for libraries and society. Many problems relate to handling the economic aspects of information and access to that information (often written about in terms of ownership versus access). Although a detailed discussion of these problems is beyond the scope of this book, I will mention them where they have an influence on collection development and resource management.

Collection development personnel and library administrators are struggling with the shift of information from print to electronic formats. For that matter, so are the producers of information. Neither libraries nor producers have decided how to resolve the access/ownership issue. Naturally, the real issue is money; vendors and producers want to profit as much as possible, and libraries need to make their limited funding go as far as possible. Not surprisingly, there has been growing tension between these parties.

In 1996, Curt Holleman examined the access/ownership issue for journals[13] in a university library setting. He found a complex mix requiring a title-by-title assessment. Even within a single field, there was no clear pattern taking into account the subscription price, usage patterns, and cost to acquire on an as-needed basis. I fully agree with his concluding comments:

> It is particularly erroneous to assume that an electronic future will offer free access to all information in all formats to all people. There are as many reasons to think that certain kinds of information will be restricted to the privileged few in an electronic environment as there are in the environment of yesterday. Librarians will be remiss if they fail to take advantage of the extraordinary offerings of the electronic revolution, but they will be equally remiss if they forsake paper products for the sake of being up to date.[14]

A year later, Payne and Burke reached a similar conclusion, this time regarding a college library environment.[15]

What are some examples of the problems and changes that have taken place? One of the challenges is how to set a fair price for electronic information. Producers and vendors realize, to a greater or lesser degree, that they cannot ignore the fact that funding is finite for libraries, and even for corporate research and development activities. Determining how to set that appropriate price is difficult, because information does not have the characteristics of other commodities, and thus traditional economic models do not work well with information. Information economics has been pondered by scholars for more than 30 years—Marshall McLuhan's *Understanding Media* (McGraw-Hill, 1964), Jean Baudrillard's *Simulations* (Semiotexts, 1983), and Cristiano and Antonelli's *Economics of Information Networks* (North Holland, 1992), to name but a few.

R. O. Mason provided a starting point for understanding what is meant by "the economic value of information." He identified three key elements:

- *Efficiency*—where information helps the user to do the job faster, more accurately, and at lower cost (i.e., how to do the job "right").

- *Effectiveness*—where information helps the performance of a task that could not be done before (i.e., how to do the "right" job).

- *Responsiveness*—where information helps to respond to customers' demands for service irrespective of efficiency or effectiveness.[16]

There is little evidence that producers have attempted to factor these concepts into their pricing decisions. The Consumer Price Index (General) increased by 89 percent between 1980 and 1997, while the academic library price index rose by 138 percent. Part of the reason for the differential is the lack of accepted standards for pricing information (paper or electronic). Carol Tenopir's article on pricing options for electronic materials identified *seven* different pricing patterns used by producers.[17] Her data came from a survey of 182 academic and public libraries. The seven methods were, in order of frequency of use: simultaneous users, flat fee, size of library, per use, potential users, type of library, and other (consortial) considerations. Vendors do change the basis for charging from time to time, making it difficult to predict costs from year to year. Libraries prefer a system that allows cost control and predictability.

What are the characteristics that are special—special enough to make information almost unique? Unlike other economic commodities, people share information even after selling it. Sellers always retain the information in some form, if only in their memories. There are two economic aspects to the sale of information: (1) the cost of packaging the information, and (2) the cost/value of information contained in the package. When the package is a book, newspaper, magazine, videotape, or audiotape, for example, people tend to think of the package *as* the information. An individual confronted with an online system where one pays for information by the "screen" and yet cannot retain a hard copy, or who is considering paying $30,000 for a quarterly newsletter subscription, quickly begins to appreciate the differences between information and package value.

Another special characteristic of information is that it is neither scarce nor depleting. In fact, the more people use and manipulate it, the more information there is. Many information problems are the result of having too much information rather than too little. The problem is locating the necessary information at the right time. To some extent, the changes discussed here are contributing to copyright problems (see chapter 18 for a discussion of copyright). *Ownership* of ideas, facts, and information is more of an issue today, unlike in the past when the issue was primarily the *expression* of ideas, facts, and information. Perhaps the ultimate in ownership is demonstrated in an electronic novel by William Gibson.[18] This book was a self-contained computer file that erased the data after the user viewed each "page." There was no going back to review the previous pages, to examine how the author expressed an idea, or to reread a passage simply because you enjoyed it—unless you bought another copy! It is frightening to think that this might become the next phase of the pricing and ownership struggle. Although such an approach solves the issue of sharing information in the traditional sense, most societies could not tolerate such an approach for the majority of the information its citizens produce.

Additional characteristics of information that make it a special commodity are transportability, intangibility, compressibility, expandability, storability (in a variety of forms and formats), and manipulability. Other characteristics that create problems in developing good pricing models include:

- Information is often developed without regard for the market (theoretical research). People create information for a variety of reasons, but not very often because they *know* there is a market for the information.

- Information is produced and consumed simultaneously—economists deal with items entering the marketplace and have a time factor between production and use.

- Information is heterogeneous, which means that no single definition covers all the variations which create multiple "commodities." It is also heterogeneous in its value; two people in the same organization performing similar work can and do value the same information differently. Also, the value of information can change over time for a person. In essence, the value is subjective, making it impossible for neoclassical economists to develop a model.

- Information is indivisible in the sense that it is difficult to determine when it is complete. Incomplete information can cause problems, but when does it become complete? In one set of circumstances, information "X" may be complete; in another circumstance, though, "X" would be incomplete.

The nature of information collections is changing, both in terms of formats collected and in ways of providing access to the information. Nevertheless, high-tech information services and databases still consist of collections of information. What to include and what to exclude from the collection must be decided. *Someone* has to acquire the information in some manner, as well as maintain the collection. Collection management usually involves making certain that the information is current; older information is discarded or stored in a manner indicating that the information is dated. If the service is fee-based, someone must monitor users' needs and interest to assure that the database reflects what the information buyers want. These are the basic steps of collection development, so collection development will not disappear when the oft-proposed high technology information center finally becomes a reality. Even Raymond Kurzweil, in spite of his suggestion about "virtual physical relations," acknowledged that the librarian will still have the function of selecting materials for the virtual collection.[19]

Whatever form the future megalibrary may take, it is certain that its basis will be a collection of information resources. Unless there is a plan for what the collection will contain, the megalibrary will have limited, if any, value. The purpose of this book is to assist individuals in gaining an understanding of the process of developing an intelligent and useful collection for the end users of that collection.

Concepts and Terms

Several concepts and terms, as we use them in this text, require definitions. Starting with some basic general terms, such as *information,* and ending with a specific concept such as *collection management,* this section provides a foundation for the remainder of the book. As in prior editions, we try to present a generic picture of collection development without tying it to any particular institutional or organizational form (e.g., the library).

Information is the recognition of patterns in the flow of matter and energy reaching an individual or organization. All flows of matter and energy have the capability of carrying patterned signals. Information is present only when a person recognizes the pattern. Each person then develops a set of recognized patterns, and not everyone recognizes the same patterns or necessarily interprets a given pattern in the same way. For example, a strange noise in an automobile may mean nothing to a driver, but to a trained auto mechanic the sound indicates that the universal joint needs servicing (information). Two other examples of pattern recognition are a well log (record of drilling operations) and spectrum analysis. To the untrained person, a well log is meaningless and of no value; to a geologist or other trained professional, these long strips of paper are an invaluable source of information about subsurface conditions and formations. Depending upon how the person interprets the information, it may save, cost, or earn thousands or even millions of dollars for a company.

For astronomers, colors in a spectrum analysis convey information about the distance, movement, and composition of stars. To the layperson, a spectrum analysis is simply an interesting or pretty display of color.

Involvement in the *information cycle* (see fig. 1.1) is a constant for everyone as matter and energy flow by us. Objects emit patterned signals that flow past us (subjects). We identify the signals and evaluate the patterns based on experience. We ignore most of the signals and act only when the pattern provides information. When a person receives an information (action) signal, he or she implements the action that will provide satisfaction.

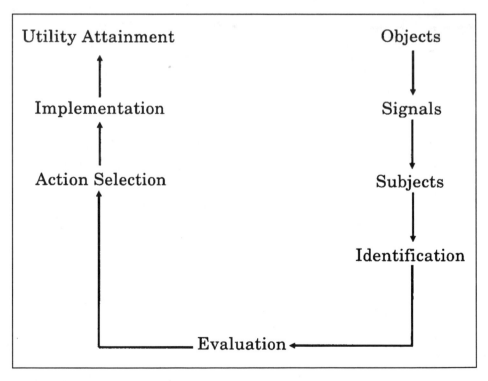

Fig. 1.1. The information cycle.

The information cycle is very similar to the human communication model that most of us learned about in one or more of our undergraduate courses. For human communication to take place, a person must express the information patterns in a symbolic form that other people know and understand. True human communication occurs only when two or more people share a symbol-referent system. Figure 1.2 illustrates the components of the communication model.

The sender, wishing to communicate with the receiver, has an idea or feeling (a meaning) that she or he encodes by selecting the appropriate symbols representing the desired meaning. This process creates the message. After encoding, the sender selects the means of delivering the message (channel)—written, oral, pictorial. On the receiver's side, the message arrives, is decoded, and a meaning is assigned to the message. When the process is completed, a communication has taken place; however, this does not necessarily imply that the sender's intended meaning is identical to the meaning the receiver assigned to the message. As is true of the information cycle, a single symbol may have multiple meanings. The more abstract the idea a person wishes to communicate, the more likely it is that "noise" somewhere in the system will distort the true meaning. Some common "noise" factors for people include differences in education, experiences, and mental

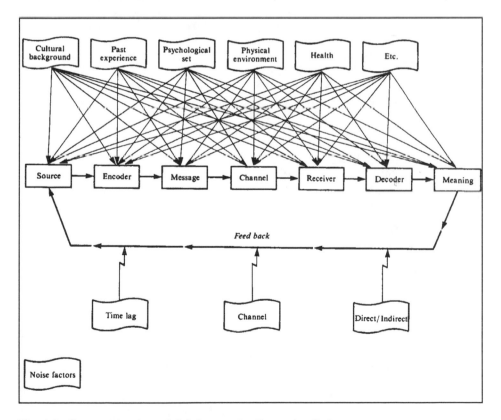

Fig. 1.2. Communication model demonstrating noise factors.

state. Normally, the general meaning will be the same, but often the general meaning is not adequate, and an identical meaning is required. The feedback loop provides a mechanism that allows people to clarify meanings, so that closer (if not identical) meaning and understanding can be achieved. Because an information center or library may work with all forms of human communication, some knowledge of the communication model is helpful in a variety of ways.

Later in this volume, such issues as conducting needs assessments, developing collection policies, evaluating collections, and handling complaints are examined. All of these activities involve the communication process (model), and remembering to use the feedback loop to verify meaning and to control system "noise" will make the library or information center a more effective service organization.

The term *organization* is used in this volume in two ways. The first meaning, and the one least often used, refers to the process of arranging information, knowledge, and materials in some logical manner for ease of retrieval. The second and more frequently used meaning relates to people and draws on work by a well-known management writer, Chester Barnard. Barnard's work on human organization is extensive, and a simplified explanation of his concept follows.

Human organization, according to Barnard, consists of five basic elements: *size, interdependence, input, throughput*, and *output*.[20] An organization can vary in *size* from one as large as the United States federal government to one as small as two people. The size factor is important for information service work because there is often a tendency not to consider two or three people working together as an organization. Barnard's model does not include any time factor; if all five elements are present, an organization could exist, whether for just a few hours or for centuries. What differentiates a group of two or more people from an organization of two or more people arises from the other elements. *Interdependence* requires recognition of the existence of one or more shared or common goals, as well as the recognition that by working together (cooperating), the achievement of these goals will be easier, faster, or in some manner beneficial to everyone in the organization. Disagreement and tension can be and usually are present, but the value of mutually shared benefits holds the organization together. Once the organization sets its goals, it must acquire the material, energy, money, and information (*input*) needed to accomplish the goals. After acquiring the resources, the organization attempts to utilize the resources (*throughput*) effectively to achieve the desired results. The end product of the processing activities is the *output* that the organization disseminates. Output can be as tangible as an automobile or as intangible as ideas that may help people to create a safer environment.

Information is one of the resources organizations acquire to accomplish desired goals. The information will be in one of four forms: *data, text, image*, or *sound*. Most organizations use all four forms of information. More new technologies are drawing these four forms closer together, and sometime in the not-too-distant future there may be an integrated information resource (see fig. 1.3). The computer is rather like the steam engine at the start of the Industrial Revolution—the power source for the integration process. Scanning equipment is becoming more sophisticated and capable of recognizing printed words and converting the recognized patterns into oral presentations (speech synthesizers). Videotext and teletext are other examples of the blending of forms taking place.

Some years ago, S. D. Neill published an article questioning the information role of the library. Neill suggested that the appropriate role is as the knowledge center.[21] Which role one selects depends largely on how one defines the concepts. In addition to information, one must define *knowledge* and *wisdom*. *Knowledge* is the result of linking together a number of pieces of

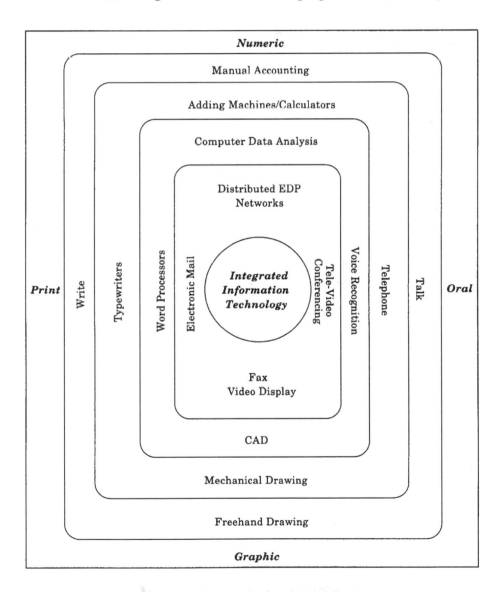

Fig. 1.3. Convergence of information technology and organizational information processing.

information into meaningful patterns. *Wisdom* is the ability to draw accurate conclusions from the available information and knowledge. Knowledge and wisdom are individual (personal) processes and what may be knowledge for one person may be wisdom for someone else. In our opinion, libraries and information centers can supply information, including recorded knowledge and wisdom. We can inform, but it is up to the users to gain knowledge and wisdom.

Robert S. Taylor proposed a more complete hierarchy. Taylor's "value added hierarchy" consists of five levels: the lowest level is *data,* followed by *information, informing knowledge, productive knowledge,* and *action.* Although his primary concern is with the means by which value is associated with information (a topic beyond the scope of this book), anyone interested in developing collections should read his article. *Informing knowledge* is similar to the definition of knowledge given earlier. *Productive knowledge* is "a judgmental process, where options are presented and advantages and disadvantages weighed."[22] Personal definitions of various terms (such as *data, information, knowledge,* and *wisdom*), as well as one's beliefs about the role of the library or information center, affect the type of collection one builds.

Another important factor is the *organizational environment* of the library or information center. Almost 30 years ago, F. Emery and E. L. Trist identified four basic types of organizational environments: *placid-randomized, placid-clustered, disturbed-reactive,* and *turbulent.*[23] Although not directly concerned with information, Emery and Trist's descriptions of these environments do indicate how the environment would affect information work. A *placid-randomized* environment, for example, is one in which the organization assumes that both the goals and the dangers are basically unchanging. (A *danger* is something that would adversely affect the viability of the organization.) Organizational goals are long-term and seldom need adjustment. Such organizations assume that changes or dangers to their well-being occur randomly, and there is little or no predictability as to when such changes or dangers will be encountered. In such an environment, the organization collects information to meet long-term goals. These goals would be considered very predictable, making collection development relatively easy. Museum collections and archives are examples of organizations operating in a placid-randomized environment; at least this was the case in the past. Today, and for the future, it does not seem likely that many organizations will be operating in such an environment.

Many libraries and information centers operate in a *placid-clustered* environment. Emery and Trist defined this environment as one where goals are primarily long-term, but the organization quickly adjusts the goals if there is a significant change in the external factors. In such an environment, the organization assumes that dangers, and to some extent opportunities, will arise in clusters. Further, the organization assumes that it will need to expend some effort in identifying and collecting information about the clusters. With collection development, this means there is a body of relatively unchanging organizational goals, but some time, energy, and money would be directed toward identifying and collecting information that might affect the goals. Most educational institutions and public libraries operate in this type of environment. They set long-term goals and rarely change those goals, although they may change short-term objectives. However, they do recognize that dangers exist, such as changing public attitudes about the value of social services generally and library services specifically. Once the questioning starts, it generally expands in scope (clustering) and does not disappear quickly. Also, new service opportunities arise as new technologies become available that may be appropriate for the institution to use. These opportunities may counteract some or all of the dangers (e.g., competition) arising from the new technologies.

Disturbed-reactive environments are those in which active competitors to the organization exist. In this environment, having prompt, accurate information about what the competitors are doing—and, when possible, what they are planning to do—is very important. Although the organization has long-term goals, it revises its goals in light of information received about competitors' activities. Business and industrial (special) libraries operate in such an environment. Here, four or five years may represent a large amount of time for long-term collection goals. However, the library or information center devotes significant resources to determining what the competition is doing.

Finally, there is the *turbulent* environment. Not only do competitors exist, but the level of competition necessitates competition for survival. As a result of knowing what others are doing or planning to do, an organization may make a radical change in its basic purposes. Anyone who reads the business section of a newspaper encounters examples of organizations that made successful basic goal changes, and those that failed because they did not change. On a slightly less extreme level, an information center or library serving a research and development team experiences occasional abrupt shifts in collecting emphasis, partly due to the knowledge gained from the information collected about competitors' work and progress. Thus, the organizational environment is also an information environment, and the nature of the environment affects the nature of the collection development activities.

With this background we can now look at how organizations and individuals process information. Figure 1.4, page 14, is a representation of how this process works; space 1 indicates the totality of matter and energy surrounding an organization or individual. The line separating spaces 1 and 2 represents the boundary between noise and patterned signals (information) as identified by a person or organization. A person or organization identifies only a small portion of the total flow as information. As the information environment changes, so does the boundary between spaces 1 and 2. A portion of what the individual or organization identifies as information is of sufficient importance to store it for a short time. Space 3 represents the short-term information storage area. Of that total, the person or organization selects a smaller amount of information for long-term/indefinite retention (space 4). The dotted line within space 4 creates an area labeled 5, which represents the information that a person or organization uses from long-term storage and disseminates to the external environment.

On an individual level, anyone in the United States who receives mail for any length of time uses this process. Almost every time a person picks up the mail (the total flow), there is an assortment of material in the delivery. The person recognizes each piece as an attempt at communication. Some material is not within the boundary of information, as defined by the person in question, and thus is noise (space 1). Items in this category go straight into the trash or recycling bin. Other pieces may be about something of interest but not of immediate high interest (space 2). Items in this category go into the bin as well, but there is a slight pause as the person completes the information cycle and selects the desired course of action. A few pieces may relate to something of some interest, and the person sets this material aside for later consideration "when there is time." Depending upon the person, days or weeks or even months go by before he or she looks at the material again. More often than not, as a result of a changed environment, this material also ends up in the wastebasket or recycling bin. A few of the items that a person or an entire organization identifies as information receive long-term retention. The person files a few items for safekeeping or later action (for example, insurance policies, legal documents, and letters from friends and family) (space 4). Of the total retained in this manner, only a few (usually bills) will require or motivate a person to process the information and respond (space 5).

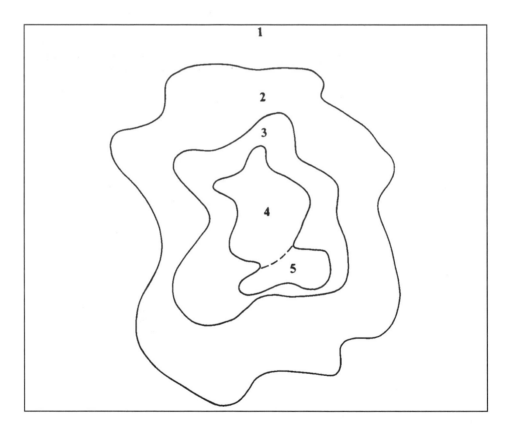

Fig. 1.4. Organizational processing of information: 1) Matter and energy surrounding an organization or individual; 2) Boundary between noise and patterned signals (information); 3) Short-term information storage area; 4) Long-term/indefinite retention of information; 5) Information that an organization or individual uses from long-term storage and disseminates to the external environment.

Libraries and information centers engage in exactly the same process. No organization can take in and process every patterned signal. They all draw some line that separates information from noise. Where the organization draws the line depends upon the nature of its activities and its information environment. The line might be drawn in terms of language, subject matter, depth of treatment, format, or combinations of factors. Even within the defined limits, only a portion of the total information is stored. Organizations acquire and store some items for short periods because their value to the organization is short-lived, due to changing interest or because the information becomes dated. Libraries and information centers normally acquire and store more information for long periods of time than the organization will use and/or disseminate to the external environment. The percentage allocated to long-term retention varies among organizations. Organizations operating in a placid-randomized environment normally have a large percentage of retained but unused or disseminated information (50 percent or more). At the other end of the spectrum (turbulent), there should be and usually is very little difference between the two categories. Archives and research libraries are at the high-retention/low-dissemination end of the spectrum, whereas information centers and libraries in for-profit organizations are usually the opposite: low-retention/high-dissemination.

The primary purpose of libraries and information centers is to assist in the transfer of information and the development of knowledge. Figure 1.5, page 16, illustrates the process involved, using nine circles to represent the transfer cycle. Information transfer is an elaboration of the basic information cycle described earlier. There is the *identification* stage, during which the organization segregates appropriate from inappropriate information. In most instances, there is more appropriate information available than the organization can handle. Thus, there is a need to *select* the most appropriate or important information to *acquire*. After acquisition, the organization *organizes* the information in some manner. Upon completion of the organizing action comes the *preparation* of the information for *storage*, which should mean the information is easily retrievable. Users often need assistance to describe their needs in a manner that leads to locating and retrieving the desired information (*interpretation*). Finally, users draw upon the secured information to aid them in their activities/work (*utilization*), and disseminate the outcome of the work to the internal or external environment, or both. If the transfer process is to function properly, there must be procedures, policies, and people in place to carry out the necessary *operational* steps. As always, there must be coordination and money for the operations to do what they were set up to do; this is the administrative and managerial aspect of information work.

The foregoing discussion helps set the stage for this book, which focuses on the process of building information collections for long- and short-term storage. Collection development, or information acquisition, is one area common to both librarianship and information resource management. As in prior editions, we define *collection development* as "the process of identifying the strengths and weaknesses of a library's materials collection in terms of patron needs and community resources, and attempting to correct existing weaknesses, if any." With only minor modifications, this definition can apply to both libraries and information collections in any organization. Thus, *collection development* is the process of meeting the information needs of the people (a service population) in a timely and economical manner using information resources locally held, as well as from other organizations. This new definition is broader in scope and places emphasis on thoughtful (timely and economical) collection building, and on seeking out both internal and external information resources. It is worth noting that Ross Atkinson suggested that the phrases *collection development* and *collection management* are being used interchangeably, and that there is no consensus on which term is more comprehensive in scope.[24]

Collection development is a universal process for libraries and information centers. Figure 1.6 illustrates the six major components of the process. One can see a relationship between figures 1.5 and 1.6, in that collection development involves three of the nine information transfer elements (identification, selection, acquisition). As implied by the circle, collection development is a constant cycle that continues as long as the library or information center exists. All of the elements in the cycle are discussed in subsequent chapters.

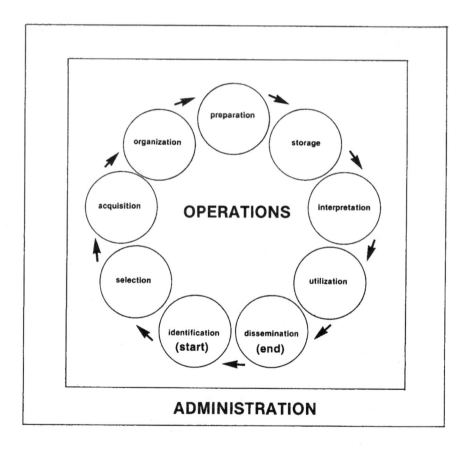

Fig. 1.5. Information transfer work.

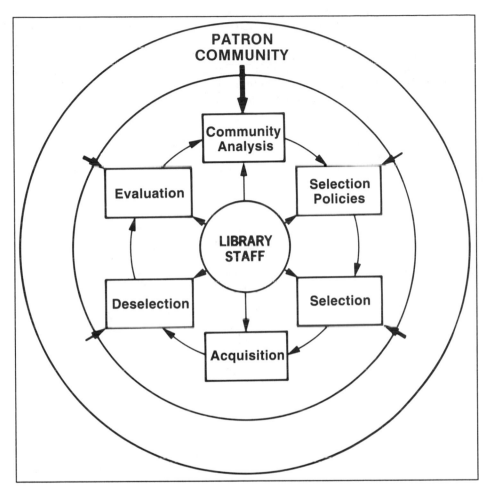

Fig. 1.6. Collection development process.

Because of our philosophy of collection development, which is a focus on meeting the information needs of the community the collection serves, we begin the discussion of collection development with the needs assessment (community analysis) element. The terms *needs assessment*, *community analysis*, or *patron community*, as used throughout this book, mean the group of persons that the library exists to serve. They do *not* refer only to the active users, but include everyone within the library's or information center's defined service limits. Thus, a community might be an entire political unit (i.e., a nation, region, state, province, county, city, or town). Alternatively, a community may be a more specialized grouping or association (i.e., a university, college, school, government agency, or private organization). Also, the number of patrons that the library is to serve may range from a very few to millions. As discussed in chapter 2, data for the analysis comes from a variety of sources, not just staff-generated material. For collection development personnel, the assessment process provides data on what information the clientele needs. It also establishes a valuable mechanism for patron input into the process of collection development. (Note the size of the arrow in figure 1.6 from the community to collection development; the size indicates the level of patron input appropriate for each element).

One use for the data collected in a needs assessment is as part of the preparation for collection development policy. Clearly delineated policies on both collection development and selection (covered in chapter 3) provide collection development staff with guidelines for choosing items for inclusion in the collection. (Note that collection policies cover a wider range of topics than just selection policies. For example, *selection* policies normally provide only information useful in deciding which items to purchase, whereas *collection* policies cover that topic in addition to such related issues as gifts, weeding, and cooperation.) Most libraries have some of the required information available for their collection development personnel, although they do not always label it "policy." Some libraries call it an *acquisitions* policy, some a *selection* policy, some a *collection development* policy, and others simply a *statement*. Whatever the local label, the intent is the same: to define the library's goals for its collection(s), and to help staff members select and acquire the most appropriate materials.

At this point, the staff begins the procedures for selecting materials (covered in chapters 4 through 10) using whatever written policies or statements the library has prepared. For many people, this is the most interesting element in the collection development process. One constant factor in collection development is that there is never enough money available to buy everything that might be of value to the service community. Naturally, this means that someone, usually one or more professional staff members, must decide which items to buy. *Selection* is the process of deciding which materials to acquire for a library collection. It may involve deciding among items that provide information about the same subject; deciding whether the information contained in an item is worth the price; or deciding whether an item could stand up to the use it would receive. In essence, it is a matter of systematically determining quality and value. Selection is a form of decision making. Most of the time it is not just a matter of identifying appropriate materials, but of deciding among items that are essential, important, needed, marginal, nice, or luxurious. Where to place any item in the sequence from essential to luxurious depends, of course, on the individual selector's point of view. It's just a matter of perception. So it is with library materials.

An individual buying an item normally does not have to justify the expenditure to anyone. However, when it is a question of spending the library community's money, whether derived from taxes or a company's budget, the problem is more complex. The question of whose perception of value to use is one of the challenges in collection development. Needs assessments and policies help determine the answer, but there is a long-standing question in the field: How much emphasis should selectors place on clientele demand and how much on content quality? Often the question of perception comes up when someone objects to the presence of an item in the collection (see chapter 19).

Once the selectors make their decisions, the acquisition work begins (see chapters 11, 12, and 13). *Acquisition work* is the process of securing materials for the library's collection, whether by purchase, as gifts, or through exchange programs. This is the only point in the collection development process that involves little or no community input; it is a fairly straightforward business operation. Once the staff decides to purchase an item, the acquisition department proceeds with the preparation of an order form and the selection of a vendor, eventually recording the receipt of the item and finally paying the bill (invoice). Though details vary, the basic routines remain the same around the world, just as they do in either a manual or automated work environment. (Note that *acquisition* does not always mean buying an item. Gift and exchange programs are also useful means of acquiring needed material.)

After receipt, an item goes through a series of internal library operations (beyond the scope of this book), such as cataloging, and is eventually made available to the patron community. Over time, nearly every item outlives its original usefulness in the collection. Often the decision is to remove these items from the main collection. The activity of examining items in the library and determining their current value to that library's collection (and to the service community) has several labels, the oldest being *weeding* (see chapter 14). Another term for this process is *deselection* (the opposite of selection). In England, the term used is *stock relegation*. When a library decides that a given item is no longer of value, it will dispose of the item (by selling it, giving it away, or even throwing it away). If the item still has some value for the library, the decision may be to transfer the item to a less accessible and usually less expensive storage location.

Evaluation (see chapter 15) is the last element in the collection development process. To some extent, weeding is an evaluation activity, but weeding is also more of an internal library operation. Evaluation of a collection may serve many different purposes, both inside and outside the library. For example, it may help to increase funding for the library. It may aid in the library's gaining some form of recognition, such as high standing in a comparative survey. Additionally, it may help to determine the quality of the work done by the collection development staff. For effective evaluation to occur, the service community's needs must be considered, which leads back to community analysis.

There is little reason to define library materials other than to emphasize that this volume covers various formats, not just books. Different authors writing about library collections use a number of related terms: *print, nonprint, visual materials, audiovisuals, a-v, other media*, and so on. There is no single term encompassing all forms that has gained universal acceptance among librarians. *Library materials* (or simply, *materials*) is a nonspecific term with respect to format that is otherwise inclusive. Thus, it is used throughout this text. Library materials may include books, periodicals, pamphlets, reports, manuscripts, microformats, motion pictures, videotapes or audiotapes, sound recordings, realia, and so forth. In effect, almost any physical object that conveys information, thoughts, or feelings potentially can be part of an information collection.

Two last terms must to be defined: *collection management* and *information resource management*. The terms cover similar activities and differ primarily in organizational context. *Collection management*, as used today, relates to a library environment (in the traditional sense) where the emphasis is on collecting materials produced by other organizations. *Information resource management*, as used today, relates to any organizational context, often without any centralized collection of materials, in which the information resource manager is responsible for identifying and making available both internal and external sources of information. Both terms incorporate all aspects of collection development discussed earlier, plus such managerial aspects as budget planning and control, staffing, and physical facilities. The goal, for both collection management and information resource management, is to provide accurate information in a timely and cost-effective manner to all members of the service community.

Collection Development and the Community

Several factors inside and outside the library influence collection development. Among these factors are the library's structure and organization, the production and distribution of the information materials, and the presence of other libraries in the area. Figure 1.7 illustrates some of the interrelationships among the library organization, the producers and distributors of materials, and other libraries.

Traditionally, libraries have organized their internal activities into public and technical services. Those activities in which the staff has daily contact with patrons are considered public services; almost all other activities are technical services. Collection development very often bridges this

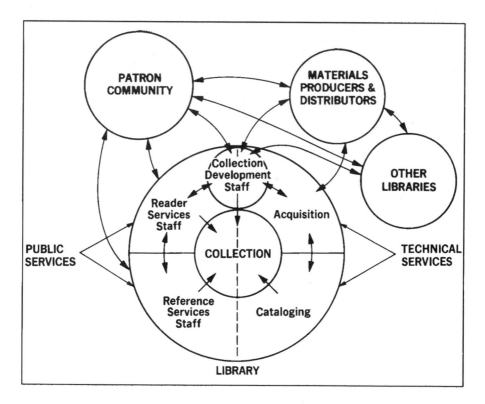

Fig. 1.7. Collection development, the library, and the community.

traditional division. With increased automation of library functions, the boundaries between public and technical services are disappearing. In fact, they are becoming so undefined that some libraries are doing away with these labels. The library staff responsible for collection development provides information to the acquisition department (usually classed as a technical service), which in turn orders the desired items from the materials producer or a distributor. After receiving the materials and clearing the records, the acquisition department sends the items on to the cataloging department for processing. Eventually, the processed items go onto shelves or into cabinets where the public can use them. Both the public service staff and the patrons using the collections provide input to the collection development staff concerning the value of individual items. The selection staff then considers the input when performing deselection and evaluation activities. The information generated from these sources may eventually influence the library's written policies for collection development.

Materials producers exert many significant influences. Obviously they control what is available for library purchase by their choice of whether or not to produce any given item. (Chapters 4 and 5 describe some of the factors in such decisions.) Furthermore, their business requirements occasionally cause libraries to modify their acquisition procedures; however, most producers and vendors are very good about accommodating unusual library requirements. Finally, producers market their products directly to the patron community, thus generating a demand. Patrons often communicate this demand to the library rather than buying the item, thus causing an indirect response to the marketing activities of the material producers.

Collections and services in other libraries and information centers used by the service population also influence collection development. Cooperative collection development programs enable libraries to provide better service, a wider range of materials, or both. Cooperative projects also can reduce the duplication of materials that results from overlapping service communities and patron influence on collection development. For example, a person might engage in business research while in the company's library. The person may take evening classes at an academic institution, using that library for class-related and business-related materials alike. That same individual may also rely on a local public library—because of its convenience—to supply information on both job-related and recreational concerns. Thus, one person's requests for job-related materials could influence three different types of libraries in the same area to collect the same material. Despite their numerous advantages, effective cooperative programs can still be difficult to work out (see chapter 16 for a further discussion of this issue).

Collection Development
and Institutional Environments

The variety of institutional settings in which one finds information services is large. However, it is possible to discuss a few general categories: education, business, government, and research. These categories share some basic characteristics. All have a specific service population, all collect and preserve materials in a form suitable for use by the service population, and they each organize materials in a manner designed to aid in the rapid identification and retrieval of desired material(s). The definitions given earlier also apply to all of these categories. Differences emerge because of both the specific service population and the limits set by the library's or information center's governing body.

Collection development is a universal process for all types of libraries. As one moves from one environmental setting to another, however, differences in emphasis on the various elements of the collection development process become apparent. For example, some education (school) and government (public) libraries tend to place more emphasis on library staff selection activities than do business and research libraries. Also, differences in emphasis occur within a type of library, so that occasionally a community college library (education) might more closely resemble a large public library (government) in its collection development activities than it does a university library (education). The approach taken in this book is to present an overview and when necessary to note the differences among and within the types.

To some extent, the chapters in this book reflect these differences in emphasis. For several reasons, needs analysis is very important in public and school libraries, as well as in information centers (in a business), but it receives less emphasis in college and university libraries. In public libraries, selection is usually the responsibility of librarians, whereas in other types of information centers patrons have a stronger direct voice in the selection process. Public libraries need the information derived from such an analysis to build an effective collection; therefore, chapter 2 on information needs assessment has a public library's slant.

The size of a library's service community has a definite bearing on collection development. Three facts of collection development are universal:

1. As the size of the service community increases, the degree of divergence in individual information needs increases.

2. As the degree of divergence in individual information needs increases, the need for cooperative programs of information materials sharing increases.

3. It will never be possible to satisfy *all* of the information needs of any individual or class of clientele in the service community.

Even special libraries and information centers, serving a limited number of persons, encounter problems in relation to these laws. Because no two persons are identical, it is impossible for their materials needs and interests to coincide entirely. In the special library environment, the interests of patrons can be and often are very similar, but even within a team of research workers exploring a single problem, individual needs will vary. The needs of a small group are not as homogeneous as they may at first appear.

The element of collection development that varies the least is collection development policy. Simply put, as the collection grows in size, the need for more complex and detailed policy statements increases. Thus, large academic and research libraries generally have the most comprehensive collection policy statements.

Selection is the element that varies the most among and within the types. Because of those many variations, it is difficult to make many generalizations. However, with that in mind, the following are some general statements about the variations:

1. Public libraries emphasize title-by-title selection, and librarians do the selecting.

2. School libraries also emphasize title-by-title selection. Although the media specialist may make the final decision, a committee composed of librarians, teachers, administrators, and parents may have a strong voice in the process.

3. Special and corporate libraries select materials in rather narrow subject fields for specific research and business purposes. Often the client is the primary selector.

4. Academic libraries select materials in subject areas for educational and research purposes, with selection done by several different methods: faculty only, joint faculty/library committees, librarians only, or subject specialists.

The size of the collection is also a factor in determining the who and the how of selection. In small public libraries, most of the librarians do some selection work. (Very often there is only one librarian to do all the professional work.) As the library system grows, adds branches, and expands services, the library director delegates work. More often than not, it is the department heads and branch library supervisors who have selection responsibilities. Large metropolitan systems frequently assign selection activities to a committee composed of representatives from all of the service programs, though not always from every branch. This committee generates a list of titles from which individual services and branches select. In essence, the book selection committee does the initial screening and identification work for the system.

A similar relationship of size and selection exists in academic libraries and some special libraries. However, the selectors in these cases more often than not are the users: academic faculty or company staff. Even when librarians are responsible for selection in libraries serving institutions with hundreds of subject specialists, the faculty members or researchers have a significant voice in the selection process. Obviously, the in-depth knowledge of a subject specialist can become the deciding factor in making a selection. A common practice in both types of libraries is to hire librarians with graduate degrees in both librarianship and one other subject area. Even then, because of the advanced and sometimes esoteric nature of the research reported in the materials, the library must draw on all of the subject expertise at the institution.

In small academic and special libraries, selection is in the hands of the subject specialist (faculty or researcher), unless the librarian is also an expert in the field. Indeed, small academic institutions often expect the teaching faculty to build the library collection. As budgets for materials increase and the collection grows proportionally, the librarians become more involved in selection activities.

Eventually a collection will fill all available shelf space. Some time before that happens, the library must decide either to reduce the collection size (deselection) or to create additional storage space. In school and public libraries, this does not present a great problem; patrons often wear out popular items, freeing up shelf space. Often such libraries buy multiple copies of items. Then, by retaining just one copy after demand drops, they regain some shelf space. Also, only exceptionally large public libraries have major archival responsibilities; thus, weeding is somewhat easier. Academic and research libraries seldom buy multiple copies and have significant archival responsibilities, making deselection an involved process. Special (business) libraries perform deselection on a regular basis because of space limitations. Often this results in rules for weeding. (For instance, discard all monographs that are five years old.) Rules of this kind help to solve one problem: lack of staff time for deselection. However, this less thoughtful approach to the problem may increase the demand for interlibrary loan of items discarded. More research has been performed on weeding/deselection in academic libraries than for all of the other types of libraries combined, and chapter 14, with its emphasis on academic libraries, includes a further discussion of this issue.

Although the final phase of the process, collection evaluation, takes place in all types of libraries, it is especially significant in libraries serving educational organizations. One form of evaluation is performed by an outside agency that determines the quality of education provided (accreditation) by schools and academic institutions. If nothing more, the agency (government or private) that funds the institution will require periodic assessments, which will invariably include the library and its collection. For such libraries, the evaluation process may have far-reaching effects. Naturally, librarians in educational institutions have a strong interest in improving the evaluation process, and they have written a great deal about the topic. Chapter 15 draws heavily upon this literature, as well as the literature on accreditation.

Every organization and person needs and uses information to survive. The way in which organizations locate, collect, and store information ranges from unstructured chance encounters to a tightly structured, carefully planned process. In the latter case, the organization usually creates a library or information center to handle the work. Collection building requires considerable resources; furthermore, the ways the library organizes, stores, and retrieves the information can be vital to the success of the organization. The definitions in this chapter and the concepts described in this book form the foundation upon which one actively develops a collection of information materials to meet the specific needs of an individual community.

Collection development is a dynamic process that should involve both the information professional and the service community. Few information professionals question the need or value of client input; the question is how much there should be. The best answer is, as much as the organization can handle and still carry out its basic functions, and as much as the community is willing to provide. The following statements are the philosophical foundations of this work:

1. Collection development should be geared primarily to identified needs rather than to abstract standards of quality; however, an identified need can be a long-term need (more than five years into the future), not just an immediate need.

2. Collection development, to be effective, must be responsive to the *total* community's needs, not just to those of the current or the most active users.

3. Collection development should be carried out with knowledge of and participation in cooperative programs at the local, regional, state, national, and international levels.

4. Collection development should consider all information formats for inclusion in the collection.

5. Collection development was, is, and always will be subjective, biased work. A periodic review of the selector's personal biases and their effects on the selection process is the best check against developing a collection that reflects personal interests rather than customer interests.

6. Collection development is not learned entirely in the classroom or from reading. Only through practice, taking risks, and learning from mistakes will a person become proficient in the process of developing a collection.

Summary

Technology is changing the way libraries and information centers do business. A term that gained popularity after 1990 is *virtual library* or *knowledge center*. Recently some writers have used the phrase in ways that negate the original meaning, which was:

> a system by which a user may connect transparently to remote libraries and databases using the local library's online catalog or a university or network gateway. Eventually, a user will be able to enter a query, get a cup of coffee, and let the computer check all the databases on the network to retrieve an answer.[25]

Some writers, as noted earlier, suggest that the virtual library means the demise of collection development. However, those who understand the concept know that the issue of selection and collection building will remain an important function in whatever environment technology brings.

One can engage in collection development in libraries and information centers that are formally or informally organized. Although organization labels will vary, the process is the same. Most large organizations now view information and its management and control to be as essential as any other resource they employ. In fact, obtaining the right information at the right time, and being able to analyze and apply it successfully, are crucial to an organization's success and survival. As a result, organizations are training and hiring people who know how to acquire and manage information resources. Though many organizations will not call these individuals librarians, and they may not work in libraries, they need and use many of the same skills librarians traditionally employ in collection building. Whatever environment one works in, collection development is an exciting challenge that requires lifelong learning. One way of keeping up-to-date is to subscribe to a discussion list, such as the Library Collection Development List (COLLDV-L@USC.VM).

Notes

1.   Octavio Paz, *The Other Voice: Essays on Modern Poetry* (San Diego, Calif.: Harcourt Brace Jovanovich, 1991), 88.

2.   Bettijane Levine, "The Cyber Book Bind," *Los Angeles Times*, September 4, 1998, at E1, E8.

3.   "Booker Prize Winners," 16 May 1998.<http://www.pond.com/~genebook/booker.htm>. (Ian McEwan's *Amsterdam* won the 1998 award.)

4.   Raymond Kurzweil, "The Virtual Library," *Library Journal* 119 (March 15, 1993): 55.

5.   James Lictenberg, "Reading: Does the Future Even Require It?," *Liberal Education* 79 (Winter 1993): 11.

6.   Paz, *The Other Voice*, 88.

7.   Patricia Battin, introduction to *Campus Strategies for Libraries and Electronic Information*, edited by C. Arms (Bedford, Mass.: Digital Press, 1990), 3.

8.   Norman Oder, "Cataloging the Net: Can We Do It?," *Library Journal* 123 (October 1, 1998): 47–51.

9.   Charles Handy, "Trust and the Virtual Organization," *Harvard Business Review* 73 (May 1995): 40–50.

10.   Ibid., 50.

11.   EBSCO personal communication.

12.   Patricia Sabosik, "Document Delivery Services: Today's Electronic Scriptoria," *Computers in Libraries* 12 (December 1992): 16–17.

13.   Curt Holleman, "Collection Issues in the New Library Environment," *Collection Management* 21, no. 2 (1996): 47–64.

14.   Ibid., 63.

15.   Valerie Payne and Mary Burke, "A Cost-Effectiveness Study of Ownership Versus Access," *Serials Librarian* 32, nos. 3/4 (1997): 139–52.

16.   R. O. Mason, "The Value of Information," in *Intellectual Foundations for Information Professionals*, edited by H. K. Achleitner (New York: Columbia University Press, 1987), 64.

17.   Carol Tenopir, "Pricing Options," *Library Journal* 123 (September 1, 1998): 130.

18.   William Gibson, *Agrippa: A Book of the Dead* (New York: Kevin Begos, 1992).

19.   Kurzweil, "The Virtual Library," 55.

20.   Chester Barnard, *Organization and Management* (Cambridge, Mass.: Harvard University Press, 1956).

21.   S. D. Neill, "Knowledge or Information—A Crisis of Purpose in Libraries," *Canadian Library Journal* 39 (April 1982): 69–73.

22. Robert S. Taylor, "Value-Added Process in the Information Cycle," *Journal of the American Society for Information Science* 33 (September 1982): 342.

23. F. Emery and E. L. Trist, "The Causal Texture of Organizational Environments," *Human Relations* 18 (1965): 21–32.

24. Ross Atkinson, "Managing Traditional Materials in an Online Environment," *Library Resources & Technical Services* 42 (January 1998): 10.

25. Laverna M. Saunders, "The Virtual Library Today," *Library Administration and Management* 6 (Spring 1992): 66.

Further Reading

General

Abel, R. "The Library Collection Crisis: What Is to Be Done?" *Publishing Research Quarterly* 10, no. 2 (June 1994): 40–44.

Adams, R. J. *Communication and Delivery Systems for Librarians.* Brookfield, Vt.: Ashgate, 1990.

Altheide, D. L. "Culture of Information." *Journal of Education for Library and Information Science* 31 (Fall 1990): 113–21.

Bailey, C. W. "Public-Access Computer Systems." *Information Technology and Libraries* 12 (March 1993): 99–106.

Blake, V. L., and T. T. Suprenant. "Electronic Immigrants in the Information Age: Public Policy Considerations." *Information Society* 7, no. 3 (1990): 223–43.

Branin, J. J. "Information Policies for Collection Development Librarians." *Collection Building* 9, nos. 3/4 (1988): 19–23.

Broadus, R. N. "History of Collection Development." In *Collection Management: A New Treatise.* Edited by C. B. Osburn and R. Atkinson, 3–28. Greenwich, Conn.: JAI Press, 1991.

Brownrigg, E. B. "Library Telecommunications and Public Policy." In *Telecommunications Networks: Issues and Trends.* Edited by M. E. Jacob. White Plains, N.Y.: Knowledge Industries Publications, 1986.

Bullard, S. R. "Collection Development in the Electronic Age." *Library Acquisitions: Practice and Theory* 13, no. 3 (1989): 209–12.

Cyzyk, M. "Canon Formation, Library Collections, and the Dilemma of Collection Development." *College & Research Libraries* 54 (January 1993): 58–65.

Hammer, D. P. *Information Age.* Metuchen, N.J.: Scarecrow Press, 1989.

Kohl, David F. *Acquisitions, Collection Development and Collection Use: A Handbook for Library Management.* Santa Barbara, Calif.: ABC-CLIO Information Services, 1985.

Leonard, W. P. "On My Mind: Libraries Without Walls." *Journal of Academic Librarianship* 20 (March 1994): 29–30.

Libraries and the Learning Society. Chicago: American Library Association, 1984.

Lopez, M. D. "Guide for Beginning Bibliographers." *Library Resources & Technical Services* 13 (Fall 1969): 462–70.

McCune, S. M. "What Is the Value of Information?" *Library Acquisitions: Practice and Theory* 13, no. 2 (1989): 161–64.

Moohan, G. "Transborder Data Flow: A Review of Issues and Policies." *Library Review* 37, no. 3 (1988): 27–37.

Osburn, C. "Collection Development and Management." In *Academic Libraries: Research Perspective*. Edited by M. J. Lynch and A. Young, 1–37. Chicago: American Library Association, 1990.

Veltman, K. "Electronic Media and Visual Knowledge." *Knowledge Organization* 20, no. 1 (1993): 47–54.

Wallman, K. "Current and Future Stresses on the Information Chain." *Information Reports and Bibliographies* 18, no. 6 (1989): 2–8.

Zink, S. D. "Will Librarians Have a Place in the Information Society?" *Reference Service Review* 19, no. 1 (1991): 76–77.

Academic

Atkinson, R. "Networks, Hypertext, and Academic Information Services." *College & Research Libraries* 54 (May 1993): 199–215.

Basch, R. "Books Online." *Online* 15 (July 1991): 13–27.

Budd, J. M. "It's Not the Principle, It's the Money of the Thing." *Journal of Academic Librarianship* 15 (September 1989): 218–22.

Dougherty, R. M., and A. P. Dougherty. "The Academic Library: A Time of Crisis, Change, and Opportunity." *Journal of Academic Librarianship* 18 (January 1993): 342–46.

Hughes, G. C. "Information Age." *Information Development* 7, no. 2 (1991): 72–74.

Johnson, M. A. "The End of Collection Development as We Know It?" *Technicalities* 12 (August 1992): 5–8.

———. "Visiting Luputa; or the Perils of Preoccupation with Technology." *Technicalities* 12 (December 1992): 5–8.

Kaufman, P. T., and T. J. Miller. "Scholarly Communications: New Realities, Old Values." *Library Hi Tech* 10, no. 3 (1992): 61–78.

St. Clair, G. "Choosing to Choose." *College & Research Libraries* 55 (May 1994): 194–96.

Public

Ballard, T. "Information Age and the Public Library." *Wilson Library Bulletin* 62 (June 1988): 74–78.

Case, R. N. "And What Do We Do Now?" *Rural Libraries* 14, no. 1 (1994): 59–69.

Curley, A. "Funding for Public Libraries in the 1990's." *Library Journal* 115 (January 1990): 65–67.

Curran, C. "Information Literacy and the Public Library." *Public Libraries* 29 (November/December 1990): 349–53.

Dowlin, K. E. "Public Libraries in the Year 2001." *Information Technology and Libraries* 10 (December 1991): 317–21.

Henry, J. D. "Public Libraries Versus the Electric Soup." *Library Association Record* 85 (July 1983): 267–68.

Nicholls, P. "The Time Has Come." *CD-ROM Professional* 7 (May/June 1994): 46–52.

Schuman, B. A. "Experience Parlor: Next Evolutionary Step for the American Public Library." *Public Libraries* 12, no. 2 (1992): 35–51.

Usherwood, B. "Privatized Public Library." *Wilson Library Bulletin* 65 (April 1991): 39–41.

Vestheim, G. "Information or Enlightenment?" *Scandinavian Public Library Quarterly* 25, no. 4 (1992): 11–17.

Weiss, M. J. "Clustered America: The Communities We Serve." *Public Libraries* 28 (May/June 1989): 161–65.

School

Aaron, S. L. "Collection Developer's Link to Global Education." *School Media Quarterly* 18 (Fall 1990): 35–43.

———. "Learner-Centered Electronic Schools of the Future." *Bookmark* 50 (Fall 1991): 15–18.

Boardman, E. M. "Don't You Have Something Newer?" *Book Report* 12 (January/February 1994): 27–28.

Brown, J. "Navigating in the 90s: Teacher-Librarian as Change Agent." *Emergency Librarian* 18 (September/October 1990): 19–25.

Callison, D. "Justification for Action in Future School Library Media Programs." *School Library Media Quarterly* 12 (Spring 1984): 205–11.

Durrance, J. C. "Information Needs: Old Song, New Tune." *School Library Media Quarterly* 17 (Spring 1989): 126–30.

Handy, A. E. "Just Do It! Collection Building for the Future." *Book Report* 12 (January/February 1994): 11–13.

Hiland, L. F. "Information and Thinking Skills and Process to Prepare Young Adults for the Information Age." *Library Trends* 37 (Summer 1988): 56–62.

Moe, L. "With Electronic Schools Will School Library/Media Centers Become Dinosaurs?" *Ohio Media Spectrum* 44 (Winter 1992): 93–95.

Saccardi, M. "Interactive Computer: Author and Reader Online." *School Library Journal* 37 (October 1991): 36–38.

Thomas, C. "Building Library Media Collections." *Bookmark* 41 (Fall 1982): 16–19.

Special

Anderson, R. K. G., and S. S. Fuller. "Librarians as Members of Integrated Institutional Information Programs." *Library Trends* 41 (Fall 1992): 198–213.

Bunting, A. "Legal Considerations of Document Delivery Services." *Bulletin of the Medical Library Association* 82 (April 1994): 183–87.

Cleveland, H. *The Knowledge Executive: Leadership in an Information Society.* New York: Dutton, 1985.

Hull, P. "Videotext: A New Tool for Libraries." *Special Libraries* 85 (Spring 1994): 81–88.

Lockett, B. A. "Scientific and Technical Librarians: Leaders of the 21st Century." *Science and Technology Libraries* 12 (Summer 1992): 51–66.

Michelson, A., and J. Rothenberg. "Scholarly Communication and Information Technology: Exploring the Impact of Changes in the Research Process on Archives." *American Archivist* 55 (Spring 1992): 236–315.

Mount, E., and W. B. Newman. "Top Secret/Trade Secret: Restricting and Accessing Information." *Collection Building* 7 (Summer 1985): 3–7.

Ojala, M. P. "Decision Points for Company Research." *Online* 17 (January 1993): 79–82.

Panko, W. B., et al. "Networking: An Overview for Leaders of Academic Medical Centers." *Academic Medicine* 68 (July 1993): 528–32.

Seidman, R. K. "Information-Rich, Knowledge-Poor: The Challenge of the Information Society." *Special Libraries* 82 (Winter 1991): 64–67.

Wolpert, A. J. "Libraries in the Year 2001." *Information Technology and Libraries* 10 (December 1991): 331–37.

2
Information Needs
Assessment

A 1998 *Library Journal* article by Patricia Schuman[1] raised some interesting and somewhat troubling issues related to the late 1990s trends in outsourcing library activities and libraries. Though libraries have engaged in some outsourcing for years, the types and extent of the outsourcing have changed. Those responsible for the area of collection development have employed vendors to handle much of the detail work involved in maintaining serial subscriptions. (To a degree, vendor approval plans are a form of outsourcing initial selection decisions.)

However, when a community decides to outsource its public library or a state decides to outsource the final selection decision, it is a very different matter. During 1997–1998, several public libraries became "privatized" (e.g., Riverside, California; Calabasas, California; and Jersey City, New Jersey), with other communities actively considering similar action. The Hawaii State Library (which also operates the public libraries in the state) outsources the entire collection development process as well as cataloging and physical processing. In the case of public libraries, the federal government's pattern was to outsource entire library functions. As for the Hawaii effort, it was a first—and one that failed.

What does outsourcing have to do with the subject of this chapter? A great deal, in our opinion. Library services, as well as their collections, must be based upon an understanding of the service community and its information wants and needs. Having a for-profit vendor make the decisions as to what should be available is risky at best. When push comes to shove and profitability is on the line, will the vendor really make a choice to meet community needs, if that will negatively affect its profits? Probably not. Any librarian who has experience with business officers or purchasing departments realizes that there is frequently a view that buying books is the same as buying a dozen pencils. If the mentality of "a book is a book" becomes the standard for the outside company that operates a library, usage by the service community will decline. Declining usage could result in a decision not to renew the contract and perhaps the community will cease to have a library. We agree with Schuman's comment: "We must draw a line between the simple purchase of products and privatization of intangible core activities like service, selection, policy setting, and management. Do we really want our libraries held hostage to the whimsy of the marketplace?"[2]

Knowledge of the service community is the key to effective collection development, which in turn is the way to effective services. It is virtually impossible, and also unnecessary, to collect information about all aspects of the lives of the customers served. However, the more the collection development officers know about the customers' work roles, general interests, education, information or communication behavior, values, and related characteristics, the more likely it is that the collection will provide the desired information at the time the service population wants it. Another reason for collecting data about the service population relates to one of the laws of collection development: no collection can meet all the information needs of any one customer or class of customer. With limited resources to serve a wide range of interests, even in a small research and development unit, one must have a solid database of client information in order to prepare an effective collection development plan. The data collected is for planning purposes; it is useful for more than collection development.

Areas in collection development affected by data about customers are policy formulation, selection, and evaluation. Selection officers should base policy formulation and modification on the data collected. Although the data will seldom provide complete help in the selection of a specific item, it will establish selection parameters. Any assessment of the collection should include a consideration of how well it meets the expectations and needs of the customers.

Researchers use several terms for the concepts and processes of learning more about a target population: community analysis, information needs analysis, needs analysis, needs assessment, role analysis, user studies, information audit, and market analysis. On a general level, the terms are identical, but they differ greatly in the specifics of application and purpose. *Community analysis* usually refers to a public library's data collection. Sometimes the term *planning process* more accurately identifies the purpose of the activity. The terms *information audit*, *needs analysis*, and *needs assessment* generally apply to the special library, information center, or information brokerage and often refer to an individual or a few individuals. (Both needs analysis and needs assessment are discussed in more detail later in this chapter.) *User studies* generally denote research projects designed to gain insight into how, why, when, and where people seek information and use information resources. *Market analyses* are studies of communities or people to assess interest in or reactions to a service or product.

There is a major problem in defining information need, information want, expressed demand, satisfied demand, information behavior, and other related terms. (A good article on this subject is T. D. Wilson's "On User Studies and Information Needs."[3]) It is far beyond the scope of this chapter to address such problems; however, the terms *needs*, *wants*, and *demands* must be defined for the purpose of this book. *Needs* are situations (community, institutional, or personal) that require solution; it does not always follow that a need is something the group or person wants. *Wants* are things that the group or person is willing to expend time, effort, or money to acquire; it does not always follow that the thing wanted is good for the group or person. *Demands* are things the group or person wants and is willing to act in concert (writing letters, making telephone calls, testifying, or demonstrating) to acquire. From a library or information center perspective, the ideal outcome of a study is identification of a need that is wanted and demanded. This topic is further explained in the discussion of analyzing survey data.

Conceptual Background

People seek information from both formal and informal systems. Informal systems are of three general types: the flow of matter and energy discussed in chapter 1; friends and colleagues; and organizations not designed as formal information sources. Without question, informal systems provide the bulk of an individual's everyday, or common, information. Daily living activities generate dozens—perhaps hundreds—of information needs, ranging from the weather report to the interest rate on loans for buying a home. Depending upon the urgency of the situation, a person locates the information with greater or lesser effort, speed, and accuracy. Most of the daily living and activities information requirements are local in nature. Mass-market sources, such as newspapers, radio, and television, answer most local information needs. However, even these sources often serve an area so large or diverse that information is not as precise as some people may require. (For example, in large urban areas major newspapers often publish regional editions.)

As the importance of the information increases, so do the amounts of money, time, and other resources devoted to securing precise, accurate information. A weather forecast (covering 18 to 24 hours) prepared and printed in a newspaper several hours before it is read is adequate for most people. For many people, the weather forecast is of marginal importance, so they expend little time, effort, or money to secure up-to-the-minute, accurate weather information. In contrast, for airline pilots and those who fly with them, weather information is much more important. As a result, airlines commit significant resources to having the latest, most accurate data. When there is a space shuttle launch, a worldwide meteorological network supplies information. From the individual to the largest organization, all information seekers place a value on each type of information used, often without being fully aware that they are doing so. Several factors influence the information's value, such as the role it plays in decision making; the type of information needed (text, numeric, graphic, or audio); and the form of information package. One important factor is accessibility and the effort required to gain access to information. This factor is governed by what may be called the "law of least effort."

According to the law of least effort, people and organizations expend as little as possible of their available resources (time, money, or effort) to secure information. Frequently when a person is preparing a document, there is a need for more accurate or current information. A typical reaction is to turn first to materials at hand, although the person knows there is only a slight chance that those materials will contain the needed information. Most people try this even when they know where they can secure the appropriate information, just because the known source is in a less convenient location than the materials at hand. In a work environment, individuals ask fellow workers before consulting formal information resources. In a variation on this method, scholars and researchers make frequent and successful use of the so-called "invisible college," which is a communication network linking people interested in particular topics. One reason for the success of informal information systems is that the formal information system is frequently slow to distribute data.

It is important for a collection development staff to know what informal sources exist within the service community. In some cases, it is possible to incorporate some of these informal sources into a formal system, thereby providing better service for all customers. Occasionally, such an incorporation improves the quality or retrievability of information. Many libraries and information centers offer referral services that supply names of people or organizations expert in an area and willing to supply information. Equally important is how people use the informal system. This may influence both the structure of a formal information system (e.g., a library collection) and the contents of that collection.

Research on both formal and informal information systems has been ongoing for some time. Generally, the studies fall into one of four broad categories: key informant, community forum, social indicators, and field or user studies. They use and examine terms such as information user (who), information need (what and why), information-seeking behavior (how), and information retrieval success and failure (why). We know that a number of variables affect the individual when he or she needs information.

Cultural background is a central factor because it creates the individual's basic values and attitudes toward information. Knowing about the service population's various cultural backgrounds and attitudes about formal information systems is essential in planning effective services and collections. Few formal information systems have a monocultural service population. It is important that collection development officers take the time to study and understand, to some extent, the cultural contexts represented in the service community.

Present and past experience with the political system also affects a person's expectations regarding formal information systems. As the degree of control (governmental or organizational) increases, there is a corresponding decrease in the variety and range of subjects contained in the formal information system. In a less controlled environment, an individual has every reason to expect the formal information systems to contain a full range of opinions on most, if not all, topics of concern for that system. As people move from one context to another, they carry with them past experiences and a set of expectations. Past experience influences information-seeking behavior just as it does other human behaviors. Again, knowledge of backgrounds in the service population can be helpful in the planning and collection building process.

Group membership, reference groups, and the invisible college all influence how an individual responds to formal information systems. In the work situation, the organization and work responsibilities also enter the picture. Organizations establish special, if not unique, values regarding information. They determine what constitutes information for them, how valuable or important information is, and how much of the organization's resources should go into providing information services. Within that context, departments and work units establish their value systems.

One influential variable is the individual's mindset. We all have days when things go right and days when nothing seems to work. We also have variations in the intensity of our own personal law of least effort. Some days we accept a close approximation for needed information, and other days no effort is too great to obtain the precise information. Personal mindset may be the most important variable in how an individual responds to a formal information system. Personal mindset is unpredictable and is not subject to control by information professionals.

Chapter 1 discusses how legal, economic, political, and technological variables affect information. In the long run, these variables have a great influence on the structure and content of formal information systems. (Chapter 18 discusses specifics concerning current laws governing formal information systems.) Economic considerations are more and more a factor in decision making in the information center environment. Twenty years ago in the United States, few people questioned the idea of a totally subsidized public library or the desirability of having such a library in every community. In the mid-1970s, there was a discussion of costs and benefits in terms of library services and materials. Now there is more and more frequent discussion of partial, if not full, cost recovery. A future may exist only for for-profit or break-even libraries, in which all public monies spent must be balanced by income from customers. This last scenario may be particularly true for public libraries if the requirement for cost recovery increases as more are privatized. In essence, there will be only neutral or positive cash flow.

Studies of users and the service community can provide information needed for effective planning. As pointed out by T. D. Wilson, studying information behavior is important because:

- our concern is with uncovering the facts of the everyday life of the service population;

- by uncovering those facts, we may come to understand the needs that push the individual into information-seeking behavior;

- by better understanding those needs, we are better able to understand what meaning information has in people's everyday lives; and

- by all of the foregoing, we should gain a better understanding of the customer and be able to design more cost-effective information systems.[4]

Though not everyone agrees on what has happened or will happen, based upon the results of several studies, we believe everyone agrees on the need for effective planning.

Some years ago Colin Mick pointed out some issues relating to the difficulties of basing plans on studies of the service population:

There is now a backlog of nearly 1,000 information needs and use studies, but they provide little information which can be applied to problems involving either the management of information work or the design of information products and services. In short, the reason information innovations are technology and content driven is because information behavior studies have failed to provide information which can be used in the design of systems and services.[5]

In the years that have passed since Mick wrote this, there has been a steady increase in the pool of useful information available. However, Douglas Zweizig, who published several pieces on community analysis, was pessimistic about the real value of such studies:

> Community analysis will not result in direct identification of community information needs. False expectation is associated with community analysis. It is raised by rhetoric that urges community analysis so we may be "responsive to the information needs of the community" ... . [B]y studying the community, we can diagnose information needs and prescribe appropriate materials and services ... . But the metaphor only serves to conceal our ignorance from even ourselves ... . "[I]nformation need" is only our idea, not necessarily something that exists in the minds of our patrons ... . [F]indings have advanced our understanding of individual information seeking but, as libraries are presently organized, the findings do not provide guidance on what programs to plan or what materials to buy.[6]

Despite his cautious view of the value of user or community studies, Dr. Zweizig realized the importance of conducting and using the results of such studies. Recognizing the limitations and dangers involved is important, and knowing what to do with the results is critical for a successful study. Using a conceptual framework is important. (Mick, Lindsey, and Callahan outline one good model for framing a study.[7])

Practical Aspects

There are several uses for the data collected in a survey, and though one may design a project to meet only one objective, the data may be of value in a later project as well. Surveys are a starting point, and when properly conducted, they provide a database that the information center can use for a variety of purposes. Through other techniques of information gathering, and by using quantitative analysis, collection development staff can more accurately assess information needs. However, first the staff must gain an accurate picture of the service community. During the years Dr. Evans taught at the University of California, Los Angeles (UCLA) library school, many students elected to do their master's thesis on some aspect of collection development, and several did some form of user/community analysis project. As a result of these projects, we identified seven areas where survey data can assist in planning and managing library or information center activities.

One obvious area is collection development. Studies for this purpose range from broad studies identifying basic characteristics of the service population to in-depth analysis of who makes the heaviest use of the collection and why, as well as how people use the materials. One student study was done in response to a statement from the Los Angeles city attorney's office that the Los Angeles Public Library (LAPL) system might be violating several civil rights laws relating to equal access and service. The city attorney's investigation noted a marked difference between branches serving white and nonwhite communities. Differences existed in all areas: staffing, service hours, collection size, amount spent on materials, and space. The branches in nonwhite communities had substantially less in all areas. The investigation showed that there was no intent on the part of LAPL to discriminate; the differences resulted from a complex series of events over a long time, primarily a budgeting system based on circulation data. Collections did not change as quickly as the service population. One finding was that some branches had decreased circulation, which translated into lower funding. Failure to consistently monitor changes in the service community also contributed to the problem. The student studied the relationship between branch collections, service area demographic data, and commercial information materials available in the service area. There was a stronger correlation between branch collections than there was between the collections of low-funded branches and their service communities (as measured by materials sold in the local retail outlets), especially in the area of non-English publications.

Frequently, librarians desire to provide innovative, or at least new, services for customers. Which services and what optimum service levels to offer are difficult questions, but data from a properly constructed survey provides decision makers with the basis for predicting user reactions to new or modified services. Should we offer computer software? Should we make computers available for public use? Should we offer online database searching? Can we charge for such searching, or printing, and how much? These are but a few of the questions that can arise, and in the absence of sound data from a survey, the decision makers can only guess at the answers. One interesting study of a public library compared four groups' ranking of desired services: the library users, part-time workers in the library (primarily students), clerical and paraprofessional staff, and the professional staff. Professional staff estimates of what would be desirable differed significantly from the users' views, but the part-time employee rankings were very similar to those of the community. Although this study was too small in scope to generalize beyond one community, it does suggest that a cautious approach to instituting new services would be wise, especially in the absence of user input.

Two related uses of assessment studies are determining service points and changing physical facilities requirements. With an ever-increasing ability to deliver information electronically, the questions of whether there should be service points and, if so, where to locate them, become very important. Commitments from funding authorities for capital expenditures for new facilities or long-term leases of space will be harder to secure. Many individuals question mobile delivery services (bookmobiles or media mobiles) because of high energy and maintenance costs. These factors, along with other economic concerns, often suggest that electronic delivery will or would be the best solution. However, electronic delivery has long-term cost implications and raises questions regarding how the library will provide access to electronic systems, and to whom. Data from an assessment project will be helpful in making informed decisions. Sharon Baker devoted an entire chapter to the question of service points, in her book *The Responsive Public Library Collection*.[8]

Many older buildings were not designed with the needs of the disabled and elderly in mind. With steadily improving health care and increased longevity, an increasing number of individuals in the service population will be in one or both of these categories. The passage of the Americans with

Disabilities Act of 1990 (ADA) has implications for services in all types of libraries and information centers. Knowing the size of the affected population can help in planning budgets, services, and equipment needs. Complying with ADA regulations will require changes in public access areas. Modification of existing structures is often more expensive per square foot than new construction. Even the process of making decisions about modifying the library or information center is costly. Data about how many and what types of disabilities are present in the service population will assist in making effective decisions. An article about assessing needs of library users who have various physical challenges appeared in *Public Libraries* (March/April 1995). A library conducted a survey of staff and users and found, as did the study mentioned earlier, that there were both similarities in and differences between professional staff and user priorities. Not surprisingly, users preferred more and better of what they already had available.[9]

The service community clearly varies by type of library. For educational institutions, the primary groups are faculty and students, followed by staff and the general public. Special libraries have a variety of missions that determine the primary clientele, which may range from the entire organization to a single project team. Public libraries have the largest customer base, which presents a great challenge for collection builders.

All libraries and information centers depend on the good will of their customers. Complaints to funding authorities, be they profit or nonprofit, cause those authorities to question the effectiveness of the library or information center. A regular assessment program can be helpful in gauging the service population's attitudes about services and collections. Having current information readily available may make the difference between receiving quick approval of a project or budget and undergoing a long, possibly painful, review and justification process.

As community demographics change, there may be a need to adjust the staffing pattern of the library or information center. Changes in subject expertise (in an academic or business setting); a need for bilingual skills; attention to special population groups (e.g., children, the institutionalized, or the elderly); a need for more technical skills in various electronic fields or in indexing, abstracting, or information consolidation—all of these may require the library or information center to have more staff with different skills and knowledge.

Hiring staff always takes more time than one expects; if you add to the hiring process redefining or restructuring an existing position, the process takes even longer. Survey data about the shifts in the service community can assist in projecting when one should start planning for staff changes. Such projections will allow the library or information center to respond in a timely manner.

All of the areas discussed have cost and budget implications. Funding authorities look with greater favor on budget requests that the library supports with objective data and that come from individuals whose past requests were generally accurate. Survey data can prove useful in the budgeting process.

The preceding list of possible uses of survey data is not exhaustive, but illustrates the many processes that can benefit from assessment studies. Again, such surveys can serve multiple purposes, not just collection development.

Needs assessment projects for libraries and information centers and market research for profit organizations share several characteristics. Both types of studies often seek the following types of information:

- why a person does or does not use a particular product or service
- how the person uses the product or service
- where the person acquires and uses the product
- what is good and bad about the product or service
- what new products or services would be of interest
- occasionally, how much the person would be willing to expend, in terms of time, money, or effort, for a product or service.

When considering an assessment project, some basic concerns about the outcome will arise. Careful planning using sound research methods will take care of technical issues, such as sample size, pre-testing requirements, question bias, and interviewer influence. Questions that can be difficult to answer include:

1. Is the target population knowledgeable or interested enough to respond to complex questions? Would several simple questions covering a complex question be better?

2. Is the cost, in time and energy, of providing adequate background information to individuals lacking the necessary research experience balanced by more or better research data?

3. To what extent will the data accurately reflect the attitudes, opinions, needs, and issues important to respondents instead of information that the respondent thinks the data collectors want?

4. Will the survey process result in unrealistic expectations in both respondents and staff?

Answers to these questions are never fully known until one starts to analyze the survey results. However, by thinking them through in advance, the researchers and library can avoid some of the pitfalls of the process.

It is sometimes possible to locate a recent study conducted for another purpose—unrelated to the library—that contains data useful for the library's current project. In such cases the risk of having data biased by respondents giving answers they think the current project planners want does not exist (although it may have existed for the original study). An example of finding information useful to libraries in an existing nonlibrary study was a survey about lifestyles, done by a large advertising agency and analyzed by Madden.[10] One of the more than 200 questions the marketing firm asked was, "How frequently did you use the library in the last year?" Because the survey was performed by an advertising agency, more people answered honestly than would have had a library sent the survey. Still, some bias undoubtedly exists in the data, because people tend to think that using the library is a good thing to do, and they respond in a way that will make them look good. Though some librarians did not agree with Madden's conclusions based on the reanalyzed data, no one questioned the data. Being aware of studies like this one can save time and effort.

More often than not, you or a consultant will have to develop a customized user or community study. Several sources can assist in formulating a project. Almost any basic textbook on research methods outlines the fundamental techniques of survey research, and many marketing books are helpful. Beyond the fundamental research methodology level, more specific aids exist. In this area, currency is less an issue than having adequate information to assist in formulating a study. Some useful titles include:

Horton, Forest W. *How to Harness Information Resources*. Cleveland, Ohio: Association for Systems Management, 1974. *Information Management Workbook*. Washington, D.C.: Information Management Press, 1983. Of great interest to special libraries, information brokers, and others in less traditional information center environments.

Kaufman, Roger, and Fenwick English. *Needs Assessment*. Englewood Cliffs, N.J.: Educational Technology Publications, 1979. A useful book that provides an excellent overview of the process.

Lauffer, Armand. *Assessment Tools for Practitioners, Managers and Trainers*. Newbury Park, Calif.: Sage Publications, 1982. A practical guide to assessment methods.

Nickerns, J. M., A. J. Purga, and P. P. Noriega. *Research Methods for Needs Assessment*. Washington, D.C.: University Press of America, 1980. A sound work for developing a needs assessment project.

Rossman, Marlene L. *Multicultural Marketing*. New York: American Management Association, 1994, Rpt. 1996, 1997. Written for businesses wishing to become more effective in marketing products to a wider base, this book provides excellent insights that apply to library needs assessments. Particularly good for public libraries.

Warren, Roland L. *Studying Your Community*. New York: Russell Sage Foundation, 1955. This is an old but useful book for those planning a public library assessment project.

Full-scale studies are expensive and time-consuming, but they must be done occasionally. Between large-scale projects, libraries and information centers can conduct small-scale projects. Small studies cost less, produce reliable data, and may lengthen the time between large studies. The following section contains suggestions for the content of both large- and small-scale projects, focusing on how collection development activities may be improved as a result.

Elements of the Study

As soon as the library decides to conduct an assessment project, it must answer several questions, including: (1) Who is to collect the information? (2) What information do the planners want? (3) What methods will produce the desired data? (4) How will the planners use the data?

Who Will Do the Study?

Who or how many people will be responsible for supervising and running the study depends on several factors: financial support (library budget or supplemental funds), the number and qualifications of personnel available (staff members or outside consultants), and the depth and breadth of the study.

Any survey of major proportions must have financial backing sufficient to hire a consultant to assist in planning the study. This is true even if one or more staff members have expertise in designing assessment projects. An outsider's view can be helpful in catching problems insiders are too close to see.

Occasionally, because of limited funding, the survey must be carried out by a committee made up of paid and volunteer workers. In this case, whether or not the library hires a consultant, the involvement of collection development personnel and other staff is essential to the project's success.

Regardless of whether a consultant or volunteers are used to plan the survey, the library must weigh the advantages and disadvantages of using staff to carry out the project. An inexperienced team of staff members can waste inordinate amounts of time and energy. Furthermore, staff members would normally work on the survey during regular working hours, which could cause service and scheduling problems. Also, a staff team may draw conclusions based upon individual members' personal biases concerning a particular area or aspect of the service community, rather than from the research data.

A compromise solution is to hire an outside consultant to formulate a plan, which the library staff then implements. A problem with this approach is that the consultant must divide the tasks into units small enough so that personnel who have little experience in conducting surveys can accomplish them. Each project will require weighing the staffing problem against the consequences of failing to conduct any survey.

One way to overcome lack of staff time and experience in assessment work is to build the project into the regular collection development activities. Many larger academic libraries have started moving in this direction by using subject specialists. To some degree this movement is accidental, because the literature about the reasons for and functions of subject specialists gives little indication that formalized survey work is or ever was a primary concern. Instead, the literature suggests that subject specialists' activities are contact with faculty, work in conjunction with faculty and specialized users, development of subject areas in the light of institutional and patron needs, syllabus analysis, and citation analysis. In essence, such libraries have laid the foundation for subject specialists to conduct ongoing assessments. A meeting once a year with each faculty member whose subject interest touches on the area of responsibility will maintain close contact with community needs.

Including assessment work in the job description for collection development staff assures an ongoing assessment program. Naturally, it may be difficult to convince funding authorities that adding a major task to existing operations creates a need for additional staff. Incorporating assessment activities in job descriptions may, in effect, increase the staff size by at least one full-time position. In the past, most libraries did not view needs assessment work as a major issue. Now, with stable or shrinking materials budgets, all types of libraries are concerned with making the most effective use of the funds available. Needs assessment data is a key factor in establishing collection priorities and, occasionally, choosing among specific items for the collection.

Using the library staff as the assessment team does offer several advantages. The staff members collecting the data fully understand how the results will be used. A staff team comes to the task armed with useful information about needs gained through day-to-day work. For example, the staff members have taken requests for or attempted to locate information for customers that is not available in-house.

Another benefit of using employees is that the staff on the team gain or increase their commitment to the assessment process and its value as they learn more about the service community. Generally, staff involved in a project show greater willingness to accept and implement the results and to use them daily. In addition, when one uses a staff project team, they need less time to inform the rest of the staff about the results, because staff social interaction cuts across departmental boundaries. Using an outside person or firm to conduct the study normally results in one or two presentations to the staff or circulation of draft documents for comment. Because of time constraints, the process often leads to staff misunderstandings and, occasionally, resistance to the entire project.

A useful step, especially to secure community support, is to establish an advisory board for the project. The board should represent all the major groups covered by the assessment project (e.g., students, faculty, researchers, administrators, young people, adults, and various ethnic groups). Though the committee must be advisory in nature, it can provide invaluable insight into problems the project team may encounter in collecting data. For example: What are some of the pressing information needs of the target populations? When and where should data gatherers make contact with the sample group? What are some ideas about how to approach people to enlist their full cooperation? In addition to helping answer these questions, the advisory board can help set project priorities and assist in interpreting the collected data. Ideally, the board members and the project team will discuss the project and its goals.

After the library decides who will run the project, it can move on to other issues. This includes developing a clear statement of the study's objectives and a detailed list of the steps to take and the questions to ask. Unclear goals lead to disastrous results and open the way for self-serving interpretations of the data.

What Will Be Studied?

Each type of library or information center will have a slightly different definition of the word *community*. In the context of the public library, *community* means the political jurisdiction that the library serves. For academic and school libraries, the community is the parent institution. In the case of special libraries, it is the company, business, institution, or foundation that provides the operating library's funds. In the corporate setting, the community may be a division or unit of the parent company. With these distinctions in mind, it is possible to identify 11 broad categories of data that apply to all types of libraries.

Historical data is useful in several ways. Understanding a community's historical development may lead to a better, and sometimes quicker, understanding of where that community stands today. Although corporate libraries may not have any long-term collection preservation functions, an understanding of the history of the library or information center and its service community can help clarify or restructure current collection development objectives. Historical background information also provides clues about areas of the collection to weed or areas in which it is no longer necessary to acquire material.

Geographical information may be used to answer questions such as: In which physical directions is the community growing? (This is an issue for large academic campuses as well as for public libraries.) What is the distribution of population (or departments or offices) over the geographic area? This type of information helps the library staff determine service points, which, in turn, influences the number of duplicate titles the library needs to acquire. (In most instances, purchasing duplicate copies cuts into the number of titles the library can buy.) This assessment should consider geographic and transportation data, which, because of their interrelatedness, are discussed next.

Transportation availability data, combined with geographic factors, is important in the library's decision-making process regarding how many service points to establish and where to locate them. Merely noting the existence of a bus or shuttle service does not provide enough information for a meaningful analysis. How often is the service provided? What does it cost? What are the hours of service? What is the level of use? Answers to these questions are vital in determining service points and service hours. As noted in the previous paragraph, the number of service points affects plans for developing the collection. Often, large academic and industrial organizations provide their own internal transportation systems, especially in urban areas. The existence of a good internal transportation system may help a library to build a more varied collection. A courier or document delivery system may help alleviate the need for as many (or as large) branch operations. Reduction in the number of branches, while still maintaining the same level of service, can reduce the need for duplicate materials.

Legal research will not be too difficult to do, nor will the amount of data accumulated be large. Nevertheless, there may be legal implications for collection development. In some academic institutions, the teaching faculty has the legal right to expend all book funds. Although there is no longer any American university where the faculty fully exercises this legal authority, cases of limited implementation do exist. Also, this right may exist, but most persons—including the librarians—will have forgotten about it until a problem arises. Preparing for a possible problem is less difficult than dealing with an existing one or with an unexpected surprise. Clear policies about the delegation of selection authority and responsibility may help to avoid a problem and will certainly help to solve those that do arise.

Knowledge of how a community's legal system functions can also be important. Where does authority lie? To which bodies is the library accountable, especially for collection development? Are there any legal restrictions on what the library may buy with monies allocated for collection development? Some jurisdictions, until a few years ago, had regulations making it illegal to buy anything except books, periodicals, and newspapers; other media were supposed to be off-limits. In addition to purchasing, there may be legal restrictions on how long a library must keep material and regulations regarding disposition of the material. Libraries that are depositories for government publications are subject to a substantial body of regulations regarding the retention, usage, and disposal of the material. In a corporate information center or archives, government regulations as well as professional guidelines may affect records retention. Some regulations not only specify how the organization must retain the records but in what format (paper, microfilm, or electronic). How does one go about changing the regulations? Knowledge of the library's legal position will help answer this question.

Political information, both formal and informal, has a relationship with legal data, much like the link between geographic and transportation information. On the formal level, questions include: To what extent is the library a political issue? If political parties exist, how do their attitudes toward library and information services differ? What is the distribution of party affiliations in the community? Are some areas of the community more politically conservative or liberal than others? Should library service-point collections reflect these philosophical differences? On the informal level, some questions to consider are: How do the politics of the community work? Who influences fiscal decisions? In an academic or special library, what are the politics of the allocation of collection development funds? Answers to most of these questions will not have a direct bearing on which titles go into the collection, but they may influence the way in which the library secures and allocates funds and how much money is available for collection development.

Demographic data is essential in formulating an effective collection development program in all libraries. Basic changes in the composition of the population are inevitable, but only by monitoring the community can collection development staff anticipate changes in the composition of the population. Waiting until change takes place creates an image of an institution that is slow to adapt. For example, United States academic institutions and their libraries operated for years on the premise that their student bodies would continue to grow in size. However, Census data in the 1960s indicated a sharp drop in the birth rate, which time translated into a smaller pool of potential students. This fact, combined with widespread discontent with the higher education system, should have been a clear indication that continued growth was at least problematic. However, only after several years of declining or stable enrollment did academic institutions and their libraries react to the "news," which had been available for more than 18 years.

Census data should be the starting point for any public or school library assessment projects. For the 1990 census data, the CD-ROM of the Summary Tape Files 3-A (STF3-A) is probably the most reasonable starting point. One of the factors making this a good starting point is that it provides a number of geographical levels of analysis—county, city/town, tract, and block. (Dr. Evans used this product to collect the data for the map in figure 2.5.) Another useful file is the County-to-County Migration Flow Files (SP312). What makes this a good resource is that it provides information on where the respondent lived five years prior to the census. Because it includes countries as well as U.S. counties, one can also gain a sense of the countries of origin of recent immigrants to one's service area. If one has access to a Geographical Information System (GIS), one can make even greater use of census tract data. C. Koontz has written extensively about GIS techniques that can be useful to library managers, as well as collection development officers (see the "Further Readings" section for references to her work).

Public libraries, in contrast, must deal with shifts of population out of inner cities. Occasionally such shifts can change the city's tax base, which affects library revenues. Other changes in the population (e.g., age, education, nationality, and health) have serious implications for developing a collection.

Although Los Angeles is not representative of many cities, the 1990 U.S. Census data suggests that its experience may be typical of what is occurring in many cities, at least in terms of ethnic and cultural diversity. The city's experience with demographic shifts illustrates the need to monitor shifting community composition and information needs. One group to become involved with when building an ethnic collection is the Ethnic Materials Information Exchange.[11]

One indication of the cultural diversity of Los Angeles comes from data from the school district (a good source of data for many types of community assessment projects). The district's 1992 data indicated that one in six students spoke limited English; among the homes of 30 percent of the students, 95 different languages were regularly spoken.[12]

Shifts in composition and location of population groupings in Los Angeles affected library service as the city tried to respond to the changes. In 1950, 86 percent of the Los Angeles population was Anglo; by 1990, the Anglo percentage was 37 percent. Meanwhile, the Hispanic percentage rose from 7 percent to 40 percent. Other "minority" groups grew in size during this time as well. The 2000 census is very likely to demonstrate further shifts in the "West L.A." areas.

Figures 2.1 through 2.5 (on pages 46–47) illustrate the shift in the West Los Angeles area. The maps were developed using census tracts from the Santa Monica, Westwood, Venice, and Marina del Rey areas. (Note: The racial and ethnic terms used in this discussion and on the maps are those used by the Census Bureau in earlier census reports. The 1990 map uses the same terms for the sake of consistency.)

Fig. 2.1. Los Angeles/Santa Monica distribution of ethnic populations, 1950. Map drawn using data from the U.S. Census, 1950.

Fig. 2.2. Los Angeles/Santa Monica distribution of ethnic populations, 1960. Map drawn using data from the U.S. Census, 1960.

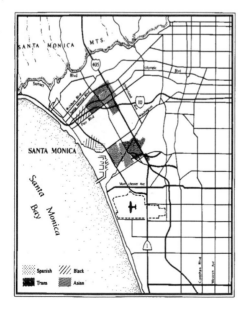

Fig. 2.3. Los Angeles/Santa Monica distribution of ethnic populations, 1970. Map drawn using data from the U.S. Census, 1970.

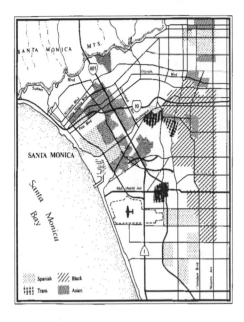

Fig. 2.4. Los Angeles/Santa Monica distribution of ethnic populations, 1980. Map drawn using data from the U.S. Census, 1980.

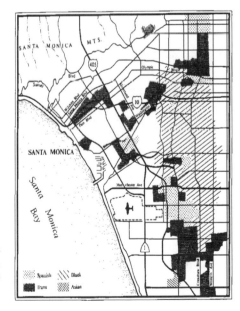

Fig. 2.5. Los Angeles/Santa Monica distribution of ethnic populations, 1990. Map drawn using data from the U.S. Census, 1990.

In 1950, only a few tracts were transitional, that is, with no ethnic grouping dominating. By 1960, the tracts that had been transitional in 1950 were predominantly Asian, and a number of new transitional tracts had appeared. Ten years later, additional transitional areas appeared, along with three Black, one Hispanic, and another large block of Asian tracts. Most dramatic is the change between 1970 and 1980, when non-Anglo groups became the majority in Los Angeles. Note that by 1990, many of the areas had become Anglo once again. This occurred after large sections of small, single-family homes were replaced by expensive condominiums. Not shown on the maps is the shift of the Anglo population to the suburban areas of Los Angeles, to housing developments on what had been agricultural land.

As the city grew out from the core, the Los Angeles Public Library (LAPL) built new branch libraries to serve the new residential areas. Old branches remained in place; unfortunately, so did the original collections. In charging LAPL with discrimination against minority groups, the Los Angeles city attorney's office produced a series of charts showing the great differences in almost all aspects of library service between Anglo and minority areas. To a large extent, the problem arose from a failure to monitor changes in the service community and to adjust the collection to the changing interests and needs of the service population. Like many public library systems, LAPL used circulation data as a major factor in allocating money to branch libraries. That is, as circulation goes up or down, so does the branch's budget. If there is a major shift in the service population and there is no corresponding shift in the collection, there can be a drop in circulation and thus a drop in funding. When this happens, a library can be caught in a cycle that is difficult, if not impossible, to break. Even if the staff recognizes the problem, there is too little money to effect a change that would adequately reverse the trend. Flexibility in funding is necessary to help break the cycle when the situation has gone on for any length of time.

Two things are clear from this example. First, monitoring the service community and adjusting to the changes are important. Second, major shifts can take place almost overnight, even in a large community. (Ten years in the history of a city of millions of people is almost overnight.) In the case of Los Angeles, an official agency did alert city agencies to the trends and in 1976 predicted quite accurately the 1980 census results. (Predicted Anglo population 49 percent, actual 48 percent; predicted Black population 16 percent, actual 16 percent; and predicted Hispanic population 28 percent, actual 29 percent.) Making use of data from such agencies saves time, money, and work. Unfortunately, budget problems caused Los Angeles to close this office in the late 1970s. However, in most governments there is a planning agency that can supply useful information about community trends. If no such agency exists, it is even more important for the library to undertake community analysis. In such cases, the library may be able to locate a university geography or sociology department that has an interest in demographics and can provide data for an assessment project.

Economic data are useful for both general planning and collection development. Knowledge of the existing economic base of the community and of possible changes may help the library better plan its collection development activities. That is, anticipating increases or decreases in funding can lead to a more even collection, especially for serial publications. An economy based on semiskilled or unskilled workers calls for one type of collection, a skill-based economy calls for another, and an economy based on knowledge workers calls for still another. Communities with a seasonal economy or a predominantly migrant population face several problems. What type of service and which formats would best serve the seasonal population? When you know the answers to these and similar questions, you can begin to build a useful collection.

Communication systems available to the community are important to the library's service mission. Closed-circuit and cable television, as well as telecommunication systems, have become valuable resources for delivering information directly to customers. Long important in primary and secondary schools, television is becoming a factor in higher education and in the education of the whole community. Public access to cable television—one channel reserved for community use—has had an impact on some libraries. Community reference services combining cable television and telephone are becoming more common, and some libraries offer story hours on cable. Cable television as well as interactive video and teletext will open up new areas of service and patron access, as well as collection development needs. Another developing phenomenon is electronic villages—for example, Blacksburg, Virginia, where the entire community is connected to the Internet.

Social and educational organizations reflect community values. Though social patterns are slower to change than individual attitudes, the library must consider such pattern shifts in planning an integrated collection building program. Social clubs, unions, and service organizations affect and reflect community interests. The most important group of organizations is educational. An academic institution no longer offers only two-year, four-year, and postgraduate degree programs. Evening adult education classes, day and night degree programs, off-campus classes, and even some remedial high-school-level courses create complex instructional programs, each facet having different information needs. A public library's concern must be broader than public and private primary and secondary schools; it should also consider adult vocational programs and higher education. Special libraries in business exist to serve research and development and planning needs; however, other areas, such as in-house training and development, may require library support.

Cultural and recreational organizations also reflect community interests. As with social organizations, these formal groups provide useful clues to highly specialized interest areas with enough community interest to sustain a formal group. Many of these groups, when given library service, join the library's most solid and influential supporters. This category does not apply to special libraries, as there is seldom a question about who their customers are. (For a discussion of cultural diversity and needs assessment, see an article by Dr. Evans in the journal *Collection Building*.[13])

Other *community information services* are, in some respects, the most important elements in the collection development program. If the library identifies several community information sources, and if the various sources can develop a working cooperative agreement, everyone will benefit. All too often public, school, and academic libraries in the same political jurisdiction operate as if they existed in isolation. When a group of publicly supported libraries in a local area fails to develop cooperative programs, considerable resources and services go to waste. The first step in achieving a cooperative arrangement is to know what resources each library holds. In addition to knowing what library resources exist in the community, the librarian should know about other information resources, such as bookstores, video and music stores, newspapers, radio and television stations, and motion picture theaters. Some writers have suggested that fewer recreational materials are necessary in the library if other recreational outlets are available to the community.

How and Where Is Data Collected?

Knowing what you need to know is only one-third of the battle. Knowing how to get the information and how to analyze it represent the remaining two-thirds. The fields of social welfare and sociology have developed a number of methods for systematically studying a community. One may divide community studies into four primary types: (1) key informant, (2) community forum, (3) social indicators, and (4) field survey. Libraries can use all of these methods, singly or in combination, depending on the specific project. Combining approaches is a good technique because it helps to ensure that valid, unbiased data is obtained. (A good book to review for planning a combined approach is Jack McKillip's *Needs Analysis*.[14])

Key Informant

Key informants are individuals who are in a position to be aware of the needs of the people in the community. Included in this group are public officials, officers of community organizations, business leaders, the clergy, and certain unofficial leaders (those who do not hold office) in the community who are influential and whom other people view as knowledgeable about community affairs. The project team interviews these individuals to ascertain their opinions and ideas concerning the community's information needs. Another term that is sometimes used for key informant is *gatekeeper*. (A particularly good article on gatekeepers and libraries is by Cheryl Metoyer-Duran.[15])

To be effective, a tested interview schedule must be established. A tested interview schedule uses questions that the team develops and tests with individuals who have backgrounds or positions similar to the people who will be part of the study. The purposes of pre-testing are to learn what types of responses the researcher may expect to receive and whether the answers address the issues covered by the project. Frequently researchers get unexpected results from the pre-test and find they must develop new questions to collect the designated data. Individuals differ in their understanding of what a question really means. Pre-testing questions allows a team to reduce the range of interpretation by rewording ambiguous or confusing questions. There should not be too many interviewers, and unless they have already had extensive experience in interviewing, they must receive thorough training before they begin.

Potential shortcomings of the key informant approach include the fact that key informants do not fully represent the community. Because their selection is not random, the researchers cannot treat the data as if it represents the community population. The opinions of key informants reflect personal biases; their perceptions of a community's information needs may differ from the perceptions of people who do not hold positions of influence. In essence, this type of data supplies subjective but useful information about how people of influence perceive the community information needs.

The key informant approach is relatively easy to prepare and implement. It requires the least amount of time to collect data, and it is very helpful in making key people aware of the information problems of a diverse community. However, when using this approach, one must supplement data from key informant interviews with published (objective) data and, when possible, with a representative cross-section of community opinion.

Community Forum

The community forum is a type of town meeting. Again, the advisory committee can be useful in setting up such meetings and encouraging community members to attend. This approach avoids selection bias by the researcher, as anyone in the community can express his or her opinion at a number of public meetings. The key to success for this approach lies in extensive publicity. Libraries may use several mechanisms to encourage people to attend community forums, such as letters to individuals and selected organizations or use of mass media, including newspapers, radio, and television. In a large community, a number of meetings may be necessary in order to keep the groups small enough so people will feel comfortable expressing their opinions. Smaller, more numerous meetings also allow for adequate time to fully hear all points of view. To make these meetings useful, the research team must provide some structure for the meetings. A typical approach is to design sets of questions to raise at all the meetings. The team must also leave time to handle questions from the audience. It is usually desirable to have the entire survey team present at all meetings, or at least to tape all the meetings.

Two advantages of the community forum are that it is easy to arrange and inexpensive. Forums also help identify individuals who have an interest in improving the quality of library service in their community. When it comes time to implement new programs, the library can call on these people to assist in the work. One glaring disadvantage of the community forum is that people who do not use the library probably will not attend the meetings. If they feel they have no need for the library, why should they spend time talking about its services? Another major disadvantage is that the data obtained are impressionistic and subjective. These data are extremely difficult to categorize and are not readily amenable to systematic analysis. Although these disadvantages are serious, the community forum is useful as a major grassroots democratic process for soliciting opinions, ideas, and criticism from the general population. When exploring options for starting a service to an unserved cultural or ethnic group, the community itself is an essential part of the process.

Social Indicators

Social scientists have developed a method that makes use of social indicators to determine the needs of various segments of a community. "The notion of the city as a constellation of 'natural areas' has ... proven useful as a method of describing social subdivisions within communities."[16] A natural area is a unit within the community that can be set apart from other units or areas by certain characteristics. Those characteristics, or social indicators, may be geographical features, such as rivers or transportation patterns; sociodemographic characteristics, such as age, sex, income, education, and ethnicity; population factors, including distribution, density, mobility, and migration; the spatial arrangements of institutions; and health and social well-being characteristics, such as condition of housing or suicide rates.[17]

By using descriptive statistics found in public records and reports, the library involved in community analysis can deduce certain information needs of the community's population. By selecting factors that researchers think are highly correlated with those groups in need of information, surveyors may be able to extrapolate the information needs of the whole community. What these social indicators (also called factors, variables, or characteristics) may be is a point of much disagreement among researchers in library and information science. Some social indicators are age, health, sex, employment, education, marital status, income, and location of domicile or work site.

What are the implications of those indicators for library users? The following are some broad generalizations based on library research.

- Use of libraries and information centers tends to decrease with age, especially among adults over the age of 55. (One reason for decreased use is deteriorating vision and other health problems.)

- Senior faculty, researchers, and organization officials tend to use libraries and information centers less as they increase in status and age. (They still use information; however, the actual gathering is done by junior or support staff, who tend to be younger.)

- Women make greater use of libraries and information centers than men, regardless of the library's institutional environment (public, academic, or corporate).

- As the number of years of education increases, so does use of libraries, up to about 16 years of formal education. After earning a bachelor's degree, a person's library use curves downward. (Apparently, graduate and postgraduate education moves the person into the invisible college network, so there is less need to use formal information systems.)

- Income level and use of formal information systems also show a J-shaped curve. That is, low income usually translates into low use; use rises through middle and upper-middle income levels; and use sharply decreases at high income. (Apparently, persons with high incomes can purchase a large percentage of the information they require.)

- Generally, as health declines, there is a decrease in the use of formal information systems. (However, with proper equipment and special services, libraries can reverse this tendency.)

- Persons employed in manual labor tend not to use formal information systems. Information use tends to increase in direct relationship to increased levels of skills required to perform the work.

- The law of least effort is clearly evident in the finding that as the distance of the residence or workstation from the information center increases, there is a corresponding drop in use.

- Single persons and married couples with no children tend to use formal information systems less than couples with children, and as the number of children rises, so does use.

After researchers select the indicators, they can start to collect data from a variety of existing sources. The most detailed and accurate source of demographic data is the national census. In the United States, census tract data (a unit for data collections based on geographic areas of a few thousand people) are resources. The major drawback with census data is that it is a complete study done only once every 10 years in the United States. (The Census Bureau does an annual population estimate, but it covers only the county and state levels.) In rapidly changing communities, this is a problem because the statistics are misleading after a few years. However, other sources are available for up-to-date local data. Regional, county, or city planning agencies gather statistics and make projections that can be useful. In addition, school boards, chambers of commerce, social service agencies (public and private), and police departments compile data useful to library researchers.

For actual investigation, the research team must select a unit of analysis, such as census tracts or *block groupings*. Census tracts are one of the most widely used units of analysis for community studies. One obvious reason is that some of the desired data are readily available, and in most cases the geographic area is relatively small. Though the ease of data collection can serve as a basis for selecting the study unit, the team should never allow ease of data collection to jeopardize the integrity of the study.

Field Surveys

The field survey approach to community analysis depends on the collection of data from a sample or entire population of people living within a given area. The most common means of collecting data is through interview schedules or questionnaires. The methods most frequently used are telephone interviews, person-to-person interviews, and mailed questionnaires. Each of these methods employs a series of questions. In a community survey for public libraries, questions often elicit data from an individual or household regarding frequency of use of the library, reading habits, economic and/or educational background, or any other information that the library believes will provide insight into need, use, and especially nonuse of the library.

Researchers must be careful when designing questions so as not to violate an individual's right to privacy. If the person or group designing the questionnaire is not certain of the legality of the questions, advice from reliable legal counsel is required. The questions should have a direct relationship to the objectives of the survey. Questions that elicit peripheral information lengthen the questionnaire, raise the cost of the survey, overburden the respondent, and create unrealistic expectations. This, in turn, may decrease the response rate and reduce the validity of the findings.

One choice the team must make is between a structured or unstructured format for the questionnaire. Open-ended questions (unstructured format) take more time to answer than fixed-alternative, or closed, questions (structured format). The type of question asked can affect both the response rate and data analysis. Open-ended questions are much more difficult to code and analyze, and there are fewer methods of statistical analysis that one can apply to them. With the structured format, data are homogeneous and are more easily coded and analyzed. The structured format is much easier to use, especially when volunteers are conducting interviews or coding and analyzing the data. However, even when using the structured format, the researcher must carefully prepare instructions to volunteers to assure accurate results.

If the target population does not speak English, it is helpful to have the questionnaire translated into the language of the target population. This can increase participation by showing respondents that the team wants their input. Respondents should be offered both versions of the questionnaire; offering only the translated version may be interpreted as an insult. The translation should be done by a native speaker; slang or local usage may not follow formal speech patterns that nonnative speakers tend to use.

The next step in the field survey is to select a sample. According to Warheit, "The selection of the sample depends largely upon the information needed: the unit for analysis, i.e., individuals, households, etc.; the type of data gathering techniques used; and the size it must be to adequately represent the population from which it is drawn."[18]

Cost must be taken into account when selecting a sample. A large sample may call for complex selection methods, and more time will be required to complete the survey. Of course, the use of volunteers can keep the cost down, but the survey method, including sampling, is not a simple procedure. This is an area where the services of a paid consultant are valuable.

A popular method of obtaining information from respondents is through the personal interview. This permits face-to-face contact, stimulates a free exchange of ideas, and usually has a high response rate. The telephone interview, though popular, has the disadvantage of a limit to the amount of time that the interviewer can hold the interest of the respondent. Twenty minutes is about the maximum length for telephone interviews that have a good response rate. With a highly structured interview schedule and a well-trained interviewer, the research team can gather the necessary data efficiently.

Mail surveys require less staffing and training than surveys that depend on personal or telephone interviews. These two advantages can significantly reduce the cost, in both time and money, of conducting a survey. However, there are two significant disadvantages to the mailed survey. First, most mailed surveys have a low response rate. Organizations conducting mail surveys have reported a response rate as low as 35 percent, and such rates can seriously affect the validity and reliability of the collected data. Even with repeated mailings the response is frequently low, and the cost of keeping track of who has or has not responded is high. Second, some persons in the community are unable to respond to anything but the simplest of questions. This may be especially true in bilingual or multilingual communities. Of course, the problem of language can be overcome by printing the questionnaire in all the appropriate languages, but there will still be the problem of literacy level, regardless of the language used. With an interview, a trained interviewer can detect, from the respondent's verbal and nonverbal signals, when there is something not quite right about a question. One lacks this feedback with the mailed questionnaire. Because of these disadvantages, libraries using the mail survey must carefully design the questionnaire and use the simplest and most succinct language possible while still meeting the established objectives. The libraries should also attempt to determine what an acceptable response rate will be before expending the time and money for a survey that could be of questionable value.

The survey approach, like the other needs assessment approaches, has certain advantages and disadvantages. The primary disadvantage is its cost. Designing a survey of a large sample, extensive interviewing, and advanced statistical analysis, for example, tend to cost more than other methods. Another disadvantage is that many individuals refuse to supply information about themselves or other family members. In many communities, the refusal or nonreturn rate may be so high as to make the data of questionable value.

However, one important advantage of the survey approach is that, if carefully designed and administered, it will produce the most accurate and reliable data for use in determining the information needs of the service community. The other community needs assessment approaches are useful, but they have drawbacks. The key informant approach is not fully representative of the community. The community forum does not attract nonusers. Variables indicating library use and the benefits derived from that use are not fully established for the social indicators approach. When one combines the field survey with one or more of the other methods, the shortfalls of each individual method are mitigated. The combined approach allows the team to compare results from the different methods; especially valuable is the comparison of data from a user study with the data gathered by a field survey.

How Is Data to Be Interpreted?

In some respects, collecting the data is the easy part of the process. Analyzing the data takes time and skill. Analysis begins with tabulating the data. The tabulation method selected depends on how the team collected the data and the capabilities of the agency or group performing the analysis. Tally sheets are one way to start the process. These sheets list each aspect or question of the study, its value or range of responses, and overall totals. After tabulating the data, one can perform elementary statistical analysis, such as averages and standard deviations.

One simple and inexpensive method of analysis is to prepare maps indicating the study units (e.g., census tracts) and the variables or responses analyzed. Adding map overlays improves this method, as they can illustrate distributions of and relationships among the selected variables. This produces the most useful results when there are a small number of variables. Analysis involving a large number of variables requires more sophisticated techniques. Today computers allow the team to employ more sophisticated types of analysis that were costly to perform in the past. However, the team must have sound reasons for using each type of analysis. The ability to do something is not reason enough to do it. It can be just as difficult to draw conclusions from a mass of statistical test results as it is from raw data if one has not planned for each test.

Most assessment projects yield large quantities of data that one can manipulate statistically. However, statistics give only one level of probability and statistical significance. The main question—how to interpret the data— remains.

One way to interpret data is in terms of social needs. Some years ago, J. Bradshaw discussed four types of social needs: normative, felt, expressed, and comparative.[19]

Normative needs often are based on expert opinion. One commonly cited normative need is the need to increase the literacy level. Teachers, librarians, and others, in their professional roles, express this normative need. To some degree, the general public accepts this need, but little funding is available to meet it.

Felt needs come from the population or community based on its insight into its problems. How appropriate or realistic felt needs may be is not the issue; they are a reflection of a problem. However, just as normative needs are not always what the community wants, felt needs do not always reflect what is good for the community. Where normative and felt needs conflict, interpretation and compromise come into play.

Expressed needs reflect behavior. Individuals often say they want or need something, but their behavior shows they really want or need something else. Libraries and information centers respond well to expressed needs; that is, they are more likely to meet a greater percentage of the information needs of active customers than the needs of infrequent users. Libraries react to expressed needs by adding more material about the subject to the collection. Though that is not wrong, it does risk unbalanced spending or failure to respond to real, though unexpressed, information needs. The needs assessment project can reveal whether the library is overresponding to active users' needs.

Comparative needs are the result of comparing the target population to other populations. One such comparison might be the number of items checked out, per capita, by the target group versus overall usage by registered borrowers. When making such comparisons, the services for the two groups must be the same. One advantage of focusing on comparative needs is that they usually result in some quantitative measures that can be useful in setting goals for new services or programs according to the results of the assessment project.

The project team and its advisory board can begin analysis and interpretation by considering a series of questions. Following is a sample of the types of questions these groups might review before preparing a draft report. Each project generates its own set of questions.

- What are the most important felt needs within the community?
- What are the most important normative needs as identified by the experts?
- Which needs are the most relevant to the mission and experience of the library or information center?
- How can you reconcile the multiple and conflicting needs?
- What is a realistic expectation for resources to respond to the needs?
- What are the clients' costs for each alternative?

- What are the direct and indirect costs to the institution or parent organization for each option?
- What impact or outcome is likely for each alternative? Are they measurable?
- Are timelines feasible to set up an effective program?
- Are the materials available to provide the service?
- How will the option(s) fit into the existing service structure?[20]

To present the findings of the study, the team must choose the most suitable format for the community. The selection factors relate to the character of the community, the type of survey, and the intended audience. Advanced statistical analysis may be a suitable format for audiences that can understand the assumptions and implications of such tests (e.g., academic and corporate environments). For public libraries, the target audience is more varied, from highly literate to illiterate. Thus, the team must present the results in such a way that individuals in the community, in public office, and in the library can easily understand the implications. One way to achieve such broad coverage is by employing descriptive summaries, charts, diagrams, and other visual aids.

The examination of the data by several individuals and groups helps the team identify action areas. This can be done by providing the opportunity for group discussions of the preliminary results. For instance, meetings such as those discussed in the section on community forums provide citizen feedback. If the preliminary conclusions are weak or unsubstantiated, group discussion will reveal it. These discussions will also indicate to the community the areas where action must be taken to improve library services. This type of public discussion can help create a strong commitment among all interested parties to seeing that action is taken to improve services. Another advantage of involving several groups in the analysis is the identification of certain unmet needs and interests of the community that are not the responsibility of the library. Public disclosure of such community problems will bring them to the forefront and possibly motivate an agency or group to assume responsibility for taking corrective action. In this matter, the study will not only help to improve community access to information, but can also benefit all aspects of community life. After the project staff gathers all the comments, suggestions, and other feedback, it should analyze the conclusions once more in preparation for the final report. The final report should include the objectives of the study, the methodology used to collect the data, a list of the identified problem areas, and a prioritized list of recommendations.

The most important question to ask following a needs assessment is: Do the present objectives of the library coincide with its new knowledge of the community? Are the objectives in line with the current needs of the community, do they reflect a past need, or are they merely self-serving? The findings of the study should answer these questions, and if the objectives of the library do not reflect the needs and interests of its community, staff recommendations should ensure that the proper changes will occur.

The study may reveal segments of the community that should receive better service. The findings should indicate what areas of library service contributed to the failure to achieve the desired level of service. Hours of service, location or lack of service points, attitude of staff, and citizens' lack of knowledge about library programs may all be causes of failure. Ways to solve the problems should be recommended. For example, an extensive publicity campaign, using newspapers, radio, posters, and bulletins, may be effective in informing the community of existing programs.

Recommendations should include those that can be easily and economically implemented as well as those that call for extensive programming changes, but all recommendations should be realistic and economical. "Blue sky" reports, in which recommendations are uneconomical or unfeasible, seldom receive favorable consideration by those who are responsible for resource allocation. Present and future resources should be a factor in formulating the recommendations. In most countries during the 1990s, most libraries had little prospect of receiving large infusions of additional funds. Thus, establishing new services necessitates reducing existing services, making it all the more essential that recommendations be realistic.

After a final report is drafted, each unit of the library should examine it for implications for the work unit. Only after all units have completed the review can the selection staff start to assess the impact of the report. After the staff identifies all of the needs and desired changes in programs, it can start formulating a realistic collection development program.

Adjusting the collection development policy is easy to do after the research team identifies the information needs and interests of the community. For example, more older people may have moved into the community, requiring large-print books and materials dealing with living on a limited income. Justifying a change in the collection development policy to reflect the change in service population is easy given accurate survey data.

As soon as the library completes a major needs assessment project, it should establish an ongoing analysis program. Statistical information is easy to keep current, and staff can gather additional information using smaller samples than employed in the original survey. The amount of time and staff effort needed for continuing analysis will be a fraction of that devoted to the original study. This means that the staff can continuously adjust the library's objectives, programs, and collection to meet the changing information needs and interests of the service community.

Community Participation

The need for customer participation in needs analysis is substantiated in both the literature of library science and that aspect of social work called *community organization*. "Community organization refers to various methods ... whereby a professional ... helps a community ... composed of individuals, groups or organizations to engage in planned collective action in order to deal with social problems within a democratic system of values."[21] Practitioners in community organization see "the participation of service users in institutional decision making [as] one means of promoting consumer needs and protecting consumer interests."[22] In other words, in community organization the people of a community are seen as having a definite role in determining the type and quality of services that institutions provide.

Participation of citizens in the operation of public institutions is part of the democratic heritage. Citizens must share in the decision-making process of the institutions that exist to serve them. To do otherwise is to undermine the foundations of a free society. However, a select few often try to dictate what they think is best for the general welfare. Consequently, if not mandated by legislation, citizens will demand participation. Libraries are not exempt from this phenomenon. They are beginning to see the writing on the wall regarding community participation in policymaking. Lowell Martin expressed it this way:

> Policy-making for libraries has been mainly in the hands of the professionals; the administrator and staff determine aims and programs for the most part, with trustees furnishing the stamp of approval. This may not be the structure of the future. Our institutions are being questioned, as is the role of professionals within them. If and as libraries become more essential, people will seek a more direct and active voice in what they do.[23]

Ensuring citizen participation in library affairs, especially in community analysis, is not an easy task, and the library will encounter several problems when initiating a program of community participation. For example, it is difficult to find citizens who are both representative of the community and willing to participate. Nevertheless, the greatest problem lies with librarians themselves. Most library administrators, as professionals, believe they have the expertise to run the library without the help of citizens in the community. Not infrequently, library publications report differences of opinion between lay governing boards and librarians. Such individuals contend that citizen participation is extremely time-consuming and actually may hinder the library's overall operation. They also believe that the general population does not have enough knowledge about libraries and librarianship to participate in decision-making functions concerning them.

These objections do have some validity. They can be overcome if the library administration believes that community service is the library's primary function and that citizen input can help improve service. Of course, citizen participation is time-consuming, but most library programs do require large amounts of time to initiate.

The traditional routes of citizen participation, such as library boards, friends of the library groups, and volunteers, often overlook the disadvantaged and the nonusers. These traditional methods do not encourage participation from all segments of the community. By relying on citizens from all segments of the community (as opposed to one or more experts) to participate in the community study, the library solicits diverse opinions and ideas. This broad approach solicits views the library might not learn if it relied solely on users.

Libraries have a democratic responsibility to utilize citizen participation to provide improved library services. By combining citizen participation and community analysis, the library reaches out to the community and fulfills its democratic obligations while at the same time determining what information the community needs and desires. Community study is an essential element in providing sound data which, with other data, can lead to library services that fulfill the information needs of the community. In addition, by utilizing citizen participation in community analysis, the library fulfills the four-fold purpose of gaining publicity, acquiring voluntary help, encouraging the direct expression of needs, and securing the involvement of the people in library affairs. This democratic process will benefit both the library and the community.

Type of Library

Much of the focus in the preceding section was placed on the public library, in part because public libraries have a long history of assessing community needs. Today, any library hoping to maintain—not to mention increase—its funding must know its service community.

Public Libraries

King County Library System (KCLS) in Washington has an extensive and ongoing community assessment program that must be the envy of all public library systems.[24] With a service area of more than 2,000 square miles, the system has been studying its service areas for some time. Between 1991 and 1997, 24 of 40 service areas had in-depth studies done. The plan is to conduct four such studies each year, and I hope they will continue to fund the work to make it an ongoing cycle.

KCLS uses a variation of a method Dr. Evans employed when consulting on needs assessment—a visualization of the service area. In their case, they drive the team through the area, making stops at various points. (Dr. Evans would also drive the area, then return to photograph "typical" areas. In working with the branch staff, he would mix the photographs with some from other service areas and determine just how well the staff knew their service area.)

KCLS uses its data for more than collection development purposes, just as suggested earlier in this chapter. They plan services, collections, hours, programs, etc. around, at least in part, the data gathered during the survey/ assessment activities. A sample of the type of data their studies generate, as well as other needs assessment forms, can be found at <http://lib.lmu.edu/dlc4> or <http://www.lu.com>.

Academic Libraries

Some years ago, Norman Roberts and Thomas Wilson wrote, in reference to academic libraries and assessment, "such studies should be a normal method of obtaining management data at regularly repeated intervals."[25] One university library that has engaged in studying its service population is the University of Michigan.[26] They employed a methodology often used in marketing studies—focus groups. These are seldom used to generalize to a larger population group because often they are self-selected. (Dr. Evans has used focus groups of undergraduate and graduate students to assist in evaluating services at the Loyola Marymount libraries.)

At the University of Michigan, the focus group information led to the formulation of a telephone survey. With the assistance of a marketing firm, the library designed a study to assure that there would be statistically reliable and valid data. (In an academic or special library environment, the telephone survey can be an effective and time-saving method.) The primary focus was five open-ended themes/questions:

- When you need information for your work or studies, what do you do?
- What role does the library play in your work or studies? How does the library compare to other sources of information you may use?
- Are you comfortable with your level of awareness of the library and its services?
- When you come to the library, does the facility assist you or impede you in your work?
- In your wildest dreams, what does the library of the future look like to you and how do you see it serving you?[27]

In today's atmosphere of technology and "virtual" environments, academic libraries might specifically focus on aspects such as:

- What electronic databases do you use more than once a month?
- When preparing the results of your research, do you prefer print or electronic "notes" and resources?
- What are the major or critical problems you encounter when using digital resources?
- What type(s) of assistance would you like to have available when using electronic resources?

Special Libraries/ Information Centers

Normally, in the special library or information center environment, the focus is on small groups and individuals. Thus, the techniques used by larger academic or public libraries do not always apply. Corporations, research institutes, professional organizations, and the like seldom have a sound knowledge of the basic issues related to acquisition and use of information within themselves, unless there are regular information assessments/audits. Some of the key issues are:

- What information resources are currently in use?
- How are these resources used?
- What are the outcomes, if any, of their use?
- What equipment is required to use the information, and who uses that information?
- What is the cost of the information and its associated equipment?
- What is the "value" of the results? That is, what is the cost/benefit of information acquisition and use within the organization?

A 1994 article by Ann Peterson Bishop explored some of these issues in the aerospace engineering environment.[28] Although the primary focus was on technology usage and its impact on research, productivity, and information exchange, the article also touched on preferred forms of information gathering. It demonstrated that individuals in the same organization doing basically the same work value information differently. For example, 63 percent of the respondents "valued" journal and trade magazine articles as "great" or "some," which suggests that the remaining 37 percent valued these resources as little or none. One expected result was that, like other scholars, aerospace engineers' most preferred channel of communication was face to face (69 percent). Something of a surprise was that the second-place channel was print media (37 percent). (*Note:* each respondent could select up to three channels.) Third place was the telephone (36 percent). Surprisingly, the electronic means (6 possibilities) were all below 20 percent![29]

Currently, information centers employ five basic methods to assess the needs of individuals and small groups: activities, data analysis, decision making, problem solving, and empirical analysis. (F. W. Horton's books, listed on page 40, provide detailed information about these assessment techniques.)

The *activities* approach uses an in-depth interview with an individual or group and has as its objective the outlining of all the activities of a typical day or project. The focus is on decisions made, actions taken, topics discussed, letters or memos written and received, and forms processed. The approach is based on the assumptions that daily activities fall into a regular pattern and that once a pattern is identified, the information officer can translate the activities into specific information requirements. One problem with the method is that people often forget important but infrequently performed tasks. Another drawback is the tendency to overemphasize the most recent problems or activities.

Data analysis is a method in which the investigator examines information sources used and materials produced by the person or study group. This approach circumvents the problems of forgetfulness and overemphasis on recent work. Reports, files, letters, and forms are the focal point of the study. The documents are studied to determine what information was used in creating them. After finishing the examination, the researcher discusses each item in some depth with the person(s) concerned to determine which resources they consulted in preparing the documents. Through this process, it is possible to identify unnecessary information sources and to determine unmet needs.

The *decision-making* approach is similar to data analysis, but it focuses on the decision-making process. Again, the researcher is interested in the information used to formulate decisions and the origin of that information. The researcher also looks at the information received but not used. During the interview the researcher explores how the cost of not having the right information, or not having it as soon as required, affected the decision-making process. In the profit sector, either or both factors can have serious financial implications for the organization.

The *problem-solving* approach is similar to the decision-making approach, except the focus shifts to problem solving. Frequently, a problem-solving activity cuts across several departments or units and takes more time to complete than a decision-making process. The problem-solving approach provides a better organizational picture more quickly than the decision-making approach does.

All of the preceding approaches depend on the user providing accurate information about what she or he did or did not do. *Empirical studies,* in contrast, are based on observations of what is done (expressed needs), how users act, and information sources used. If a formal information center exists, it might conduct experiments, such as varying the location of information sources or removing them, to determine whether the users' perceptions of the value of an item translate into use.

Summary

Effective collection development is possible only when it is based on sound knowledge of the service community. All types of libraries should engage in needs assessment. The methods covered in this chapter, though emphasizing the public library environment because of its complex service population, can be modified for use in any type of library or information center environment.

Notes

1.   Patricia Glass Schuman, "The Selling of the Public Library," *Library Journal* 123 (August 1998): 50–52.

2.   Ibid., 52.

3.   T. D. Wilson, "On User Studies and Information Needs," *Journal of Documentation* 37 (March 1981): 3–15.

4.   Ibid.

5.   Colin Mick et al., "Toward Usable User Studies," *Journal of the American Society for Information Science* 31 (September 1980): 347–56.

6.   Douglas Zweizig, "Community Analysis," in *Local Public Library Administration,* 2d ed., edited by E. Altman (Chicago: American Library Association, 1980): 38–46.

7.   Mick et al., "Toward Usable User Studies."

8.   Sharon L. Baker, *The Responsive Public Library Collection* (Englewood, Colo.: Libraries Unlimited, 1993).

9.   Cynthia Holt and Wonda Clements Hole, "Assessing Needs of Library Users with Disabilities," *Public Libraries* 34 (March/April 1995): 90–93.

10.   Michael Madden, "Marketing Survey Spinoff: Library User/Nonuser Lifestyles," *American Libraries* 10 (February 1979): 78–81.

11.   Ethnic Materials Information Exchange, David Cohen, director. Graduate School of Library and Information Studies, Queens College of the City University of New York.

12.   In such an environment, communication becomes complex, and we are all prone to some cultural biases that can further hinder communication. A good article to read, even if one is not involved in a multicultural assessment project, is Patrick

Hall's "Peanuts: A Note on Intercultural Communication," *Journal of Academic Librarianship* 18 (September 1992): 211–13.

13. G. Edward Evans, "Needs Analysis and Collection Development Policies for Culturally Diverse Populations," *Collection Building* 11, no. 4 (1992): 16–27.

14. Jack McKillip, *Needs Analysis: Tools for the Human Services and Education* (Beverly Hills, Calif.: Sage Publications, 1987).

15. Cheryl Metoyer-Duran, "Information-Seeking Behavior of Gatekeepers in Ethnolinguistic Communities," *Library and Information Science Research* 13 (October-December 1991): 319–46.

16. G. J. Warheit et al., *Planning for Change: Needs Assessment Approaches* (Rockville, Md.: Alcohol, Drug Abuse and Mental Health Administration, n.d.), 48.

17. Ibid.

18. Ibid.

19. J. Bradshaw, "The Concept of Social Need," *New Society* 30 (1972): 640–43.

20. Evans, "Needs Analysis and Collection Development Policies," 18.

21. R. M. Kramer and H. Specht, *Readings in Community Organization Practices,* 2d ed. (Englewood Cliffs, N.J.: Prentice-Hall, 1975), 6.

22. G. Brager and H. Specht, *Community Organizing* (New York: Columbia University Press, 1973), 34.

23. Lowell Martin, "User Studies and Library Planning," *Library Trends* 24 (January 1976): 483–96.

24. Jeanne Thorsen, "Community Studies: Raising the Roof and Other Recommendations," *Acquisitions Librarian* 20 (1998): 5–13.

25. Norman Roberts and Thomas Wilson, "The Development of User Studies at Sheffield University, 1963–88," *Journal of Librarianship* 20 (October 1988): 271.

26. Margo Crist, Peggy Daub, and Barbara MacAdam, "User Studies: Reality Check and Future Perfect," *Wilson Library Bulletin* 68 (February 1994): 38–41.

27. Crist, Daub, and MacAdam, 37.

28. Ann Peterson Bishop, "The Role of Computer Networks in Aerospace Engineering," *Library Trends* 42 (Spring 1994): 694–729.

29. Bishop, 726.

Further Reading

This list presents references for each type of library. Many of the works apply to more than one type of library. To find ideas, methods, or techniques for doing an assessment study, review the entire list.

General

Babbie, E. R. *Practice of Social Research.* 6th ed. Belmont, Calif.: Wadsworth, 1992.

Biggs, M. "Discovering How Information Seekers Seek: Methods of Measuring Reference Collection Use." *Reference Librarian* 29 (1990): 103–17.

Billings, H. "Bionic Library." *Library Journal* 116 (October 15, 1991): 38–42.

Bremer, T. A. "Assessing Collection Use by Surveying Users at Randomly Selected Times." *Collection Management* 13, no. 3 (1990): 57–67.

Creelman, J. A., and R. M. Harris. "Coming Out: The Information Needs of Lesbians." *Collection Building* 10, nos. 3/4 (1989): 37–41.

Curly, A., and D. Broderick. "Studying the Library's Community." In *Building Library Collections,* 6th ed., 10–23. Metuchen, N.J.: Scarecrow Press, 1985.

Devin, R. B. "Who's Using What." *Library Acquisitions: Practice and Theory* 13, no. 2 (1989): 167–70.

Donahugh, R. H. "Questioning the Questionnaires." *American Libraries* 19 (May 1988): 402–3.

Gabriel, M. R. *Collection Development and Collection Evaluation: A Sourcebook.* Metuchen, N.J.: Scarecrow Press, 1995.

Hannabuss, S. "Importance of User Studies." *Library Review* 36 (Summer 1987): 122–27.

Koontz, C. *Library Facility Siting and Location Handbook.* Westport, Conn.: Greenwood Press, 1997.

Koontz, C., and M. Gluck. *Public Sector Market Research: A Continuing Education Course for Public Librarians Utilizing Geographic Information Systems.* Tallahassee, Fla.: Florida State University, 1998.

Koontz, C., and D. Jue. *Market-Based Adult Lifelong Learning Performance Measures for Public Libraries Serving Lower Income and Majority-Minority.* Washington, D.C.: U.S. Department of Education, 1996.

Lawton, B. "Library Instructional Needs Assessment: Designing Survey Instruments." *Research Strategies* 7 (Summer 1989): 119–28.

Newhouse, R. C. "A Library Essential Needs Assessment." *Library Review* 39, no. 2 (1990): 33–36.

Quinn, J., and M. Rogers. "122 Million Library Users Ask for More Technology." *Library Journal* 116 (April 15, 1991): 14–15.

Verhoven, S. M. "User Survey." In *Encyclopedia of Library and Information Science,* vol. 45, 373–99. New York: Decker, 1990.

Academic

Allen, B. "Effects of Academic Background on Statements of Information Need." *Library Quarterly* 60 (April 1990): 120–38.

Broadus, R. N. "Information Needs of Humanities Scholars." *Library and Information Science Research* 9 (April 1987): 113–29.

Chaudhry, A. S., and S. Ashoor. "Comprehensive Materials Availability Studies in Academic Libraries." *Journal of Academic Librarianship* 20 (November 1994): 300–305.

Crist, M., P. Daub, and B. MacAdam. "User Studies: A Reality Check and Future Perfect." *Wilson Library Bulletin* 68 (February 1994): 38–41.

Ford, N. "Psychological Determinants of Information Needs: A Small-Scale Study of Higher Education Students." *Journal of Librarianship* 18 (January 1986): 47–61.

Gothenberg, H. "Library Survey: A Research Methodology Rediscovered." *College & Research Libraries* 51 (November 1990): 553–59.

Hardesty, L. "Use of Library Materials at a Small Liberal Arts College: A Replication." *Collection Management* 10, nos. 3/4 (1988): 61–80.

Pasterczyk, C. E. "Checklist for the New Selector." *College & Research Libraries News* 49 (July/August 1988): 434–35.

Richardson, J. M. "Faculty Research Profile Created for Use in a University Library." *Journal of Academic Librarianship* 16 (July 1990): 154–57.

Schlichter, D. J., and J. M. Pemberton. "Emperor's New Clothes? Problems of the User Survey As a Planning Tool in Academic Libraries." *College & Research Libraries* 53 (May 1992): 257–65.

Schloman, B. F., R. S. Lilly, and W. Hu. "Targeting Liaison Activities: Use of a Faculty Survey in an Academic Library." *RQ* 28 (Summer 1989): 496–505.

Slater, M. "Social Scientists' Information Needs in the 1980s." *Journal of Documentation* 44 (September 1988): 226–37.

Thompson, R. K. H. "Evaluating Academic Library Service." *Technical Service Quarterly* 5, no. 4 (1988): 27–39.

Public

Anderson, L., L. Luster, and P. Woolridge. "Reading Needs of Older Adults: A Survey." *Wilson Library Bulletin* 67 (November 1992): 41–44.

Davies, A., and I. Kirkpatrick. "To Measure Service: Ask the Library User." *Library Association Record* 96 (February 1994): 88–89.

Davis, M. B. "Developing a Native American Collection." *Wilson Library Bulletin* 67 (December 1992): 33–37.

Dillman, D. "Community Needs and the Rural Library." *Wilson Library Bulletin* 66 (May 1991): 31–33.

Farmer, L., and S. J. Farmer. "Using Research to Improve Library Services." *Public Libraries* 26 (Fall 1987): 130–32.

Fish, J. "Responding to Cultural Diversity: A Library in Transition." *Wilson Library Bulletin* 67 (February 1992): 34–37.

Gaydosh, L. R. "Planning Collection Development in Relation to Community Population Growth." *Public Library Quarterly* 10 (Fall 1991): 3–19.

Kern, S. "Older Adult Needs Assessment Survey." *New Jersey Libraries* 20 (Spring 1987): 18–20.

Marchant, M. "Motivators and User Characteristics: Effects on Service." *Public Libraries* 30 (July/August 1991): 218–25.

Panz, R. "Library Services to Special Population Groups in the 21st Century." *Journal of Library Administration* 11, nos. 1/2 (1989): 151–71.

Smith, B. "Strategies of Collection Development: The Public Library." In *Collection Development: Options for Effective Management*. Edited by S. Corrall, 45–55. London: Taylor Graham, 1988.

Spiller, D. J., and M. Baker. "Library Service to Residents of Public Housing Developments." *Public Libraries* 28 (November/December 1989): 358–61.

Vavrek, B. "Assessing Rural Information Needs." In *The Bowker Annual*, 35th ed., 472–78. New York: R. R. Bowker, 1990.

School

Day, C. "Open Discussions As a Market Research Method." *Library Association Record* 93 (June 1991): 389–92.

Dowd, F. S. "Public Library and the Latchkey Problem: A Survey." *School Library Journal* 35 (July 1989): 19–24.

Durrance, J. C. "Information Needs: Old Song, New Tune." *School Library Media Quarterly* 17, no. 3 (1989): 126–30.

Eaton, G. "What the Public Children's Librarian Needs to Know About Location Skills Instruction in Elementary Schools." *Journal of Youth Services in Libraries* 2 (Summer 1989): 357–66.

Feehan, P. "Youth Services: Collection Development Issues." *Collection Building* 10, nos. 1/2 (1990): 55–60.

Grover, R. "A Proposed Model for Diagnosing Information Needs." *School Library Media Quarterly* 21 (Winter 1993): 95–100.

Locke, J. L., and M. M. Kimmel. "Children of the Information Age: Changes and Challenges." *Library Trends* 35 (Winter 1987): 353–68.

Willet, H. G. "Changing Demographics of Children's Services." *Journal of Youth Services in Libraries* 2 (Fall 1988): 40–50.

Wilson, C. M. "Output Measures Identify Problems and Solutions for Middle Schools." *Public Libraries* 29 (January/February 1990): 19–22.

Special

Bichteler, J., and D. Ward. "Information-Seeking Behavior of Geoscientists." *Special Libraries* 80 (Summer 1989): 169–78.

Bowden, V. M., M. E. Kromer, and R. C. Tobia. "Assessment of Physicians' Information Needs." *Bulletin of the Medical Library Association* 82 (April 1994): 196–98.

Covell, D. G., G. C. Uman, and P. R. Manning. "Information Needs in Office Practice: Are They Being Met?" *Annual of Internal Medicine* 103, no. 4 (1985): 596–99.

French, B. A. "User Needs and Library Services in Agricultural Sciences." *Library Trends* 38 (Winter 1990): 415–41.

Jester, R. E. "To the Ends of the Earth: Librarians and Management Information Needs." *Special Libraries* 83 (Summer 1992): 139–41.

Johnston, M., and J. Weckert. "Selection Advisor: An Expert System for Collection Development." *Information Technology and Libraries* 9 (September 1990): 219–25.

Krikelas, J. "Information-Seeking Behavior: Patterns and Concepts." *Drexel Library Quarterly* 19 (Spring 1983): 5–20.

Kuhlthau, C. C. "Inside the Search Process: Information Seeking from the User's Perspective." *Journal of the American Society for Information Science* 42 (June 1991): 361–71.

Lundeen, G. W., C. Tenopir, and P. Wermager. "Information Needs of Rural Health Care Workers." In *Proceedings of the 56th Annual Meeting of the American Society for Information Science,* 253–69. Medford, N.J.: American Society for Information Science/Learned Information, 1993.

Sy, K. J., and P. Walther. "Tracking Issues and Meeting Information Needs in Government Agency Libraries." *Special Libraries* 80 (Summer 1989): 157–63.

Wilson, T. D. "Tools for the Analysis of Business Information Needs." *Aslib Proceedings* 46 (January 1994): 19–23.

3
Collection Development Policies

Textbooks on management, including those specific to libraries, all have one or more chapters that address issues of planning—short-term, long-term, and strategic plans. Most of those chapters identify a variety of plans, one of which is usually called "policy." It is important to keep that fact in mind: a policy is a plan. A collection development policy, when properly prepared, is in fact the library's master plan for building and maintaining its collections. Like all good plans, the collection development policy must reflect and relate to the library's other plans, especially those that are long-range and strategic in character.

Collection development policies, selection policies, acquisition policies—are they all one and the same? Given their functions, it is obvious they are not. However, many librarians use the terms interchangeably, perhaps because some of the same information is included in policies which are variously identified as collection development, selection, or acquisition policies. This assumes, of course, that the library has a written policy. One library school professor who taught collection development told her classes, "On the first day you go to work in collection development, ask to see the written policy so you can study it. When they tell you they don't have one, faint. By the way, you need to practice fainting and falling so you don't hurt yourselves—not many libraries have written collection development policies." This is less and less true as we near the end of the 1990s than it was in the 1970s and 1980s. Pressures to engage in various types of resource-sharing activities have created an environment where it is almost essential for libraries to put into writing how they go about developing their collections.

One of the factors leading to increased emphasis on collection policies is the complexity arising from electronic resources. A discussion of the issues related to e-materials and policies appears on pages 84–85.

What Are Collection
Development Policies?

Although selection and acquisition policy statements may contain most of the same information found in a good collection development policy, they do not cover some important topics. Selection policies often omit references to evaluation, deselection, and intellectual freedom. Acquisition policies tend to focus on the mechanics of acquiring materials instead of the selection process or collection building.

As we discussed in chapter 1, *collection development* is the process of making certain the library meets the information needs of its service population in a timely and economical manner, using information resources produced both inside and outside of the organization. Effective collection development requires creating a plan to correct collection weaknesses while maintaining its strengths. A collection development policy is the written statement of that plan, providing details to guide the library staff. Thus, a policy statement is a document that represents a plan of action and information used to guide the staff's thinking and decision making. Specifically, the staff consults the collection development policy when considering which subject areas to augment and determining how much emphasis to give each area. At the same time, the policy should be a mechanism for communication with the library's service population, as well as with those who provide its funding.

Why Have a Collection Development Policy?

Hundreds of libraries and information centers have no written policy and yet have sound collections. Luck plays a strong role in having a sound (much less an excellent) collection without also having a written policy—that is, the luck of having had individuals charged with the responsibility of building the collection who were highly intelligent and motivated by a deep commitment to the library and its collections. As a result, these individuals stayed at that library for most, if not all, of their careers and had extensive knowledge of the collections' content as well as the needs of the library's service community. In talking to these people, one often finds that they do have a plan and a policy, although it is not on paper.

Today, it is improbable that a librarian will devote an entire career to a single library. In the United States, career development in librarianship involves moving from one library to another and occasionally changing from one type of library to another.

Electronic resources create new challenges that cannot be left to chance. If nothing else, e-materials have finally broken down the idea that library collections can and should be solely print-based. As Dan Hazen suggested, there is a need to be flexible in our collection policies, whether a single comprehensive document or, as he proposed, a series of shorter descriptions.[1] It is also clear that we must embrace all the appropriate formats for the collection and the service population.

Another argument for a written collection development policy is the problem of lack of continuity in both staff and funding. A written policy helps assure continuity and consistency in the collecting program despite changes in staff and funding. Collection development policies are even more important for school libraries because of the many attacks on materials from individuals and groups who seek to limit children's access to certain materials. Further, collection development policies can be used as the foundation for the development of a practical manual or handbook to assist librarians in the selection of materials for the library. One such handbook, developed by the Library of Congress, is available online at <http://lcweb.loc.gov/acq/colldev/handbook.html>.

An interesting article that places some of these reasons in a public library context is Merle Jacob's "Get It in Writing."[2] One technique that she employed in proposing the policy was to issue a questionnaire to the selectors to complete. To complete the survey, selectors had to look at the materials in the collection within their areas of responsibility, as well as review past selection decisions. It should be noted, however, that comprehensive plans are never short; for instance, the Skokie policy is 115 pages long.

Even large research libraries are developing written collection development policies, after years of operating successfully (or with the appearance of success) without them. One call for written collection development policies stated:

> I am calling on you to formulate written collection policies to articulate the rationale that guides your decisions in the selection, preservation, transfer, and deselection of library materials. At the UCLA Collection Development Forum in June 1988, collection policy statements were identified as a high priority. As a result, the Collection Development Council distributed a format to assure the key components would be included. Some of you have submitted excellent statements since then. This year we need to complete statements for all areas and subjects.[3]

Arguments Against Writing a Collection Development Policy

Why did so many libraries fail to formulate or update a collection development policy? One of the major reasons was that a good policy statement requires large quantities of data. It is necessary to know (1) the strengths and weaknesses of your collection; (2) the community you are serving and how it is changing; and (3) other resources available to your patrons locally or accessible through interlibrary loan. Only when you have all of this knowledge in hand are you ready to start developing a collection development policy.

Another reason policies are lacking is that they require a great deal of thought. A policy must change to reflect the changing community; therefore, collection development staff never finishes collecting data and thinking about the changes. Some librarians say it is not worth the trouble: As soon as the plan is on paper, the situation changes so much that the plan is almost immediately out of date. Of course, after the library completes the basic work and writes the policy, updating the policy should not be a monumental problem. Updating does take time, but if it is done annually, it is almost painless.

Uses of a Collection Development Policy

A policy statement provides a framework within which individuals can exercise judgment. Unless the library is highly atypical, its collection development work will involve several persons at any one time and a great many persons throughout the library's history. Whenever a number of persons set a policy without written guidelines, slightly different views of the library's purpose will probably emerge. Without written statements, the divergence of opinion can cause confusion. With a collection development policy statement, everyone has a reference point. A written policy allows discussions of differences of opinion based on a common document. In such situations, working agreements are possible even when total agreement is impossible. In a school media center setting, differences of opinion about what should or should not be in the collection can and do lead to the courtroom rather than the classroom.

In an academic situation, with faculty in charge of selection, many points of view come into play. For example, four different anthropology professors might be selectors in four successive years. Lacking a policy statement, each professor would be free to, and sometimes would, buy heavily in a particular area of personal interest. The result might be one year of almost exclusive purchasing of North American ethnology, one of Bantu studies, one of physical anthropology, and one of Oceanic material. Given enough changes in professors and their personal interests, it might be possible to cover the entire field. Still, many fields would receive little or no attention during most years. A professor might not stay long enough to fully develop a collection in an area, with the result being that the library cannot claim strength in any one area. If the professors have full authorization for the selection process, the library can do little to keep a bad situation under control.

Special libraries may or may not have a written collection development policy. One reason many do not have a policy is that the mission statement of the library is so specific—as to service community, formats, and subject areas collected—that a collection policy would be redundant. Where the service population and areas of interest diversify, there is a need to develop a written policy covering all or some of the topics discussed in this chapter.

Admittedly, a written policy statement will not solve all problems, because selectors normally have authority to make the final decisions. However, if the library has a document outlining the fields requiring coverage, the policy can serve as a reminder that areas other than the selector's favorites need consideration. Even the small public library will find a written collection development policy useful, especially if there is community involvement in its approval or preparation. Among its many uses, the collection development policy:

- informs everyone about the nature and scope of the collection
- informs everyone of collecting priorities
- forces thinking about organizational priorities for the collection
- generates some degree of commitment to meeting organizational goals

- sets standards for inclusion and exclusion
- reduces the influence of a single selector and personal biases
- provides a training and orientation tool for new staff
- helps ensure a degree of consistency over time and regardless of staff turnover
- guides staff in handling complaints
- aids in weeding and evaluating the collection
- aids in rationalizing budget allocations
- provides a public relations document
- provides a means of assessing overall performance of the collection development program
- provides outsiders with information about the purpose of collection development (an accountability tool).

Some people suggest that a collection development policy would be more practical if it also incorporated material that allowed the document to serve as a bibliographer's manual. Others suggest preparing mini-policies for specialized service programs. The additional information needed to make the policy a bibliographer's manual will not make the document too lengthy. Providing information about the characteristics of the user population, in addition to simply identifying who the library will serve, will assist newly hired bibliographers in understanding the customer base. Data about what and how the primary customer groups use information materials aids in selecting the right material at the right time. Outlining the character of the various subject fields the library collects, as well as information about the major producers of the materials collected, will assist individuals taking over a new subject responsibility. Including data about review sources will further enhance the usefulness of the manual. Statements about subject and format priorities also are beneficial, especially when combined with an indication of the percentage of the materials budget normally expended on a subject.

Elements of a Collection Development Policy

In addition to the advantages outlined earlier, a collection development policy statement can provide a useful means of communicating with patrons. Though a complete policy statement runs to many pages, longer than most patrons care to read, a summary of its major points can be valuable. This is especially true if the patrons have had some say in the policy formulation.

What elements belong in a good collection development statement? The following discussion of the three major elements—overview, details of subject areas and formats collected, and miscellaneous issues—illustrates why policy formulation is so time-consuming and why it is critical to success. Certainly all American libraries should consult two American Library Association (ALA) publications: *Guide for Written Collection Policy Statements* (2d ed., 1996) and the earlier *Guide for Writing a Bibliographer's Manual* (1987,

O.P.). The following discussion parallels the latter document, but includes additional considerations not covered in the manual.

Element One: Overview

The first element consists of a clear statement of overall institutional objectives for the library. Statements such as "geared to serve the information needs of the community" have little value or concrete meaning. To ensure that the statement will help selectors and has specific meaning, all of the following factors should be present in the first section:

1. A brief general description of the service community (town, country, school, or business). What is the composition of the community and what changes are occurring? If you have done a thorough job of community analysis (see chapter 2), this part of the policy and many of the following sections will be easy to prepare.

2. Specific identification of the service clientele. Does this include anyone who walks in the door? Probably not, or at least not at the same level as the primary clientele. Who are the primary clients? Does this group include all local citizens, all staff and students of the educational institution, all employees of the business? Will you serve others? If so, to what degree? Will the service to others be free, or will there be a fee? Are there other differences in service to various groups (for example, adults, children, faculty, or students)? Must patrons come to the library? Will there be service for the disabled, the institutionalized, and users with below-average reading ability or other communication problems? These are but a sample of the questions one might ask about the service population. There are no universal answers; there is a right answer for a particular library at a particular time, and this answer will change over time.

3. A general statement regarding the parameters of the collection. In what subject fields will the library collect? Are there any limitations on the types of format that the library will acquire (e.g., only printed materials, such as books, periodicals, and newspapers)? What are the limits in audiovisual areas? This section should provide an overview of the items covered in detail in the second major element of the policy.

4. A detailed description of the types of programs or patron needs that the collection must meet. In a public library, to what degree is the collection oriented toward educational purposes, that is, toward the support of formal educational programs and self-education? Will the library meet recreational needs? If so, to what degree? Will the collection circulate, or is it for on-site reference only? (For public libraries with specialized service programs, this is the place to outline service goals. When developing an ethnic collection, the goals can be different for different groups.)

Dr. Evans developed the following list, based on the book *Understanding You and Them*, to illustrate different service goals one could have for various purposes. (The target population will decide which goal will be most desirable.)

- The root culture, to help maintain its heritage and social values.
- The experiences of the ethnic group in the United States.
- Survival skills and general information about life in the United States.
- The changing nature of society, with an emphasis on social changes in the root culture.
- Relations with other ethnic groups.
- Materials that reflect the current situation of the group in the United States.
- The future of the group in American society.
- Educational materials that will help adults and children in various formal and informal educational programs.[4]

Academic libraries need to consider how much emphasis to place on research material in comparison to instructional material. Again, statements about collection goals are appropriate. Gale Hannigan and Janis Brown suggested five collection development goals in the area of microcomputing. These guidelines can be used in either academic or special libraries. The suggested goals are:

- to provide computer-based instructional programs to support the clinical years of the medical school curriculum.
- to provide a central facility for expensive resources needed by individuals on an occasional basis, such as interactive videodisc.
- to provide productivity tools (for example, word processing) to increase student computer literacy.
- to provide a facility for evaluation of clinically oriented software.
- to provide end users with access to computerized databases, either online or CD-ROM.[5]

These goals may appear unrelated to the collection; however, by changing the wording to relate the goals to the service population, they could apply to most academic or special libraries or information centers. In special libraries, the question tends to focus on which classes of users to serve.

1. The general limitations and priorities, including an outline of how the library will develop the collection. To what degree will the library collect retrospective materials? One important issue to cover in this section of the policy is whether the library will buy duplicate copies of an item. If so, what factors will the library use to determine the number of copies to acquire and how long to retain

them? One excellent book on the topic of duplicate copies is Michael Buckland's *Book Availability and the Library Users*.[6] This book provides information essential to members and potential members of a collection development staff.

2. A detailed discussion of the library's role in cooperative collection development programs. To be effective, this section must leave no doubt in a reader's mind as to whether the basic philosophy is one of self-sufficiency or cooperation. If the reader is in doubt, it means the policy writers either did not want to make a decision on this critical issue, or wanted to avoid taking a public stand. Furthermore, when the library is part of one or more cooperative programs, this section should identify those programs and identify the subject areas for which the library has a major collecting responsibility. For subject areas that the library does not collect, the policy should list the libraries that do collect them.

Element Two: Details of Subject Areas and Formats Collected

In this section of the policy, the policy writers must break down the collections into constituent subject areas, identify types of material collected, and specify the primary user group for each subject. This may sound like a lot of work—it is. Collection development officers must spend hours talking to customers about what subject areas they use and spend many more hours thinking about what they have learned. After collecting the data, someone must assign priorities to each area, perhaps by format within each area. All of this work is done with the goals of achieving a proper balance of subjects and supplying the information needs of the service community. A complete listing of patron groups and formats could run to several pages if each of the major categories is subdivided. The following list provides the major categories.

Patrons

Adults
Young adults
School-age children
Preschool children
Physically disabled (e.g., the blind, visually impaired, and persons who use wheelchairs)
Shut-ins and persons in institutions (e.g., hospitals, residential care facilities, and prisons)
Teaching faculty
Researchers
Staff and administrators
Undergraduate students
Graduate students
Postgraduate students
Alumni

Formats

    Books (hardbound or paperback)

    Newspapers

    Periodicals (paper, microform, and electronic)

    Microforms

    Slides

    Films and videos

    Pictures

    Audio recordings

    Online resources (Internet and other services)

    Musical scores

    Pamphlets

    Manuscripts and archival materials

    Maps

    Government documents

    CD-ROMs and laser discs

    Realia

    Games and toys

    Specimens

    Software, databases, and other electronic formats

The lists provide a clear picture of the magnitude of the project, especially when one adds in subject-area considerations and changing formats. Although this may seem too time-consuming, remember that few libraries collect all categories, formats, or subjects. Libraries set priorities, or levels of collecting intensity, in several ways. The ALA guidelines suggest a five-level system: comprehensive, research, study, basic, and minimal. The Research Library Group (RLG), an organization of large research libraries in the United States, developed a multipurpose conspectus that identifies collecting levels. The Association of Research Libraries (ARL) also adopted the conspectus model. European and Canadian academic libraries have or are considering engaging in a conspectus assessment project.

Nonacademic groups have modified the conspectus concept to meet the needs of all types of libraries. Some of these groups include Alaska Statewide Inventory Project, Colorado State Library Project, Illinois Statewide Collection Development Project, Metropolitan Reference and Research Agency of New York, and, most notably, the Pacific Northwest Collection Assessment Project. The conspectus model has become the de facto standard for assigning a numerical value to the existing collections and the level of collecting the library wishes to maintain or achieve. It serves as a tool for both collection policy development and assessment.

The conspectus model helps in formulating a collection policy because it forces collection development staff to engage in detailed subject analysis. Normally, it uses the Library of Congress Classification System, with conversion tables for the Dewey Decimal Classification numbers, as the basis for subject analysis.

The Pacific Northwest model has been successfully employed by more than 200 libraries of all types. It employs the basic conspectus structure, but provides a coding system that all types of libraries can use. There are four possible subject level approaches a library may select from:

- 20 major LC divisions (the least detailed and most appropriate for small and medium-sized nonspecialized libraries);
- 200 subject level (this is the level many colleges use);
- 500 field level (the most common level for medium-sized academic and most large public libraries); and
- 5,000 topic level (this is the level one needs to employ with a research collection).

In most of the models, a collection development officer assigns a numerical value to each subject area in terms of both current collecting levels and existing collection strength. With some models the library may also indicate the desired level of collecting, if it differs from existing values. The RLG system of coding employs five values: 0—out of scope; 1—minimal; 2—basic information; 3—instructional level; and 4—research level. The *Pacific Northwest Collection Assessment Manual* offers a more detailed division of the coding: 1a, 1b, 2a, 2b, 3a (basic), 3b (intermediate), and 3c (advanced).[7]

One of the major concerns or criticisms about the conspectus method relates to how different selectors, in the same or different libraries, apply the codes. It is important that all selectors apply the codes in the same way to ensure some degree of consistency among libraries. Until the *Pacific Northwest Manual* appeared, the process of assigning values was highly subjective. However, the *Pacific Northwest Manual* offers quantitative guidelines to help selectors assign consistent values. The following are the major points:

1.   Monographic Coverage in a Division (will vary according to publishing output)

   1a = out-of-scope
   1b = (or less) fewer than 2,500 titles
   2a = 2,500–5,000 titles
   2b = 5,000–8,000 titles
   3a = 8,000–12,000 titles representing a range of monographs
   3b = (or more) more than 12,000 titles representing a wider range than 3a

2.   Percentage of Holdings in Major, Standard Subject Bibliographies

   1b (or less) = 5% or below
   2a = less than 10%
   2b = less than 15% holdings of major subject bibliographies
   3a = 15–20%
   3b = 30–40%
   3c = 50–70%
   4 (or more) = 75–80%

3. Periodical and Periodical Index Coverage

　1b = some general periodicals + *Readers' Guide to Periodical Literature* and/or other major general indexes

　2a = some general periodicals + *Readers' Guide to Periodical Literature* and other major general indexes

　2b = 2a + wider selection of general periodicals + 30% or more of the titles indexed in the appropriate Wilson subject index + access to the index

　3a = 50% of the titles indexed in the appropriate Wilson subject index and access to the index(es)

　3b = 75% of the titles indexed in the appropriate Wilson subject index and/or other appropriate major subject indexes + access to the indexes + a wide range of basic serials + access to non-bibliographic databases

　3c = 3b + 90% of the titles indexed in the appropriate Wilson subject indexes + access to the major indexing and abstracting services in the field.[8]

Because the categories are not mutually exclusive, there is a wide margin for interpreting what value one might assign. However, the system is much tighter than the RLG system, which provides no such guidelines.

Elizabeth Futas's interesting article about genre literature suggests that one might use categories called recreational, informational, instructional, and reference for genre materials when preparing a policy statement:

The level that makes the most sense for genre literature is the recreational level, which indicates the best current titles on the market. Some of the better known and still read genre authors might fall into one of two other levels available for public library selection, general information level, indicating a large number of current titles, or instructional level, a good selection of current titles and a good selection of retrospective titles. As an example of authors in each, take the Mystery genre:

Level	Author
Recreational	Lillian Jackson Braun, Joe Gores
Informational	Mary Higgins Clark, Ed McBain
Instructional	P. D. James, Elmore Leonard
Reference	Dorothy Sayers, Dashiell Hammett[9]

After the detailed subject information (a complete conspectus) is available, a selector can focus attention on the items appropriate for the collection. Policy statements are only guidelines, with ample room for individual interpretation, but they do narrow the scope of a person's work. Combine the subject intensity section with the patron list and format listing, and the result is a solid framework on which to build a sound collection.

Most subject areas fall into one of the middle intensity ranges. Few libraries have more than one or two topics at the upper levels; libraries usually restrict such categories to a person (e.g., Goethe, or Sir Thomas More) or a narrow topic (e.g., pre-Columbian writing systems or nineteenth-century Paris theater).

The next part of the policy is short but important. It identifies where responsibility for collection development lies. Ultimately, responsibility lies with the head of the library, as it does for all library activities. However, unless the library is very small, no one expects the head librarian to personally perform all the tasks for which she or he is responsible. Because the collections are important to the success of the library's programs, the question of who will actually develop them is vital. The answer requires a careful examination of the needs of the library and the nature of the service community. This section of the collection development policy should contain a clear statement of who will be responsible for selection, what guidelines the selectors are to use in making their decisions, and the basis for evaluating the selectors' performance. Media center selection responsibility can be particularly troublesome because of possible conflicts about who controls collection content—parents, teachers, media specialists, or the school board. The United States Supreme Court ruling in *Board of Education, Island Trees Union Free School District v. Pico*[10] limited the power of school boards to add, remove, or limit access to materials. (Chapter 19 contains additional information about the *Island Trees* case.)

Who Shall Select?

Potential selectors include:

- patrons or users;
- librarians from public service areas, with no special background or training beyond basic library education;
- librarians from technical service areas, with no special background or training beyond basic library education;
- subject or service specialists with advanced training in a subject or service area;
- department heads; and
- the head librarian.

A library may utilize one or more of the groups listed here.

How Shall They Select?

Delegation of selection responsibility in any given library depends on the type of library and local conditions. Whatever the decision regarding who will select, it must be in the policy so there will be no question where the responsibility and accountability lie. Selection decisions may be made by:

1. independent selectors, with or without a systematic alerting program from the library;
2. committees; and

3. individuals or groups using a centrally prepared list from which selections are made.

One can make a few generalizations about differences in where selection responsibility lies in different types of libraries. Many exceptions to these generalizations exist, but broad patterns are apparent in most areas. Educational institution libraries usually have more patron (teachers and students) involvement and greater use of subject specialists than is seen in public libraries. Special or technical library staff often have advanced training in the field in which their library specializes. That staff, with substantial input from the primary customers, is responsible for selection. Public libraries normally use librarians, often department heads from public service areas, as selectors, working through selection committees or from lists prepared by a central agency.

When nonlibrarians have an active voice in the selection process, most of their input relates to the working collection. Usually, members of the library staff have primary responsibility for the reference collection. Thus, users recommend current books and monographs, and librarians do most of the retrospective buying and selecting of serials and other media for the collection.

In addition to specifying how selectors will select, this section of the policy should provide general guidelines concerning what, and what not, to select. Normally, such written guidelines are more important in public libraries and school library media centers than in academic or special libraries. This is because there are more groups with an interest in the content of the collection and concern about its impact upon the children and young adults using it. Following are some sample selection guideline statements:

- Select items useful to clients.

- Select and replace items found in standard lists and catalogs.

- Select only those items favorably reviewed in two or more selection aids.

- Do not select items that received a negative review.

- Try to provide both, or all, points of view on controversial subjects.

- Do not select textbooks.

- Do not select items of a sensational, violent, or inflammatory nature.

- Select only items of lasting literary or social value.

- Avoid items that, though useful to a client, are more appropriately held by another local library.

The list could go on and on. See chapters 6, 7, and 8 for additional discussion about selection criteria. Whatever criteria the library chooses, the collection development policy must clearly state the criteria to answer questions that may arise about why something is or is not in the collection.

Element Three: Miscellaneous Issues

This section of the collection development policy statement deals with gifts, deselection and discards, evaluation, and complaints and censorship. Each topic is important. However, each can stand alone, and some libraries develop longer, separate policy statements for each. Because they do have some relationship to collection development, the collection policy writers incorporate an abstract or summary of those policies instead of preparing something new.

Gifts

The golden rule for gifts is: Do not add a gift unless it is something the library would buy. Selectors must resist the temptation to add an item because it is free. No donated item is ever "free." Processing costs are the same for gifts and purchased materials. Expending library resources to add something to the collection just because it was a gift, when it does not match the library's collection profile, is a very poor practice. Applying the same standards to gifts as you do to purchased items will also reduce later weeding problems.

A written gift policy must make it clear whether the library accepts only items matching the collection profile, or accepts anything with the proviso that the library may dispose of unwanted items in any manner deemed appropriate. Equally important is a statement regarding conditional gifts. Will the library accept a private collection and house it separately, if the donor provides the funds? Will it accept funds earmarked for certain classes of materials and use them to acquire new materials? If the library is trying to expand the collection through gifts and endowment monies, who will be responsible for this activity? How will the library coordinate the activities? These are some of the major questions that the policy writers should address in a section on gifts.

Gifts and endowment monies are excellent means of developing a collection, provided the library has maximum freedom in their use. Naturally, the library must answer an important public relations question regarding gifts: Is it better to accept all gifts, regardless of the conditions attached to them, or should the library avoid conditional gifts? If there is a clearly reasoned statement as to why the library does not accept conditional gifts, there should be no public relations problem.

Deselection and Discards

Deselection programs vary from library to library, but all libraries eventually must face the issue. Even the largest libraries must decide what materials to store in less accessible facilities; all large libraries have some type of limited-access storage facility. (Chapter 14 provides a detailed discussion of this issue.) The policy statement records staff decisions regarding the criteria, scope, frequency, and purpose of a deselection program.

At present, deselection questions seldom arise for anything but books and periodicals. In media centers and public libraries where other media are in high demand, especially audio and video recordings, there is a greater need for replacing worn-out items than for weeding unused materials.

Multiple copies of bestsellers and other books in high demand are issues in most public and educational libraries. The questions are, how many copies should the library purchase, and for how long should the library retain multiple copies? To some extent, the McNaughton Plan, which provides for short-term rental, can help reduce the cost of popular titles and reduce long-term storage of books in high demand for short periods of time. However, rental plans do not resolve the question of how many extra copies to retain or what the retention period should be.

Questions about multiple copies are not limited to popular or mass-market titles in public libraries. Similar issues arise concerning textbooks in academic libraries. There are no easy solutions to the problem of extra textbooks in educational settings, unless the library operates a rental system. Some policy guidelines for academic libraries are:

- Buy one copy for every 10 potential readers during a six-month period.
- Buy one copy for the general collection and acquire one copy for every five readers during X months for the high-use or rental collection.
- Buy one copy for every 10 students for required reserve reading use.

The length of time, number of readers, nature of use, and local conditions influence how many textbooks are purchased and how long they are retained.

Evaluation

Evaluation is essential to collection development. Chapter 15 outlines the major issues and needs the policy should cover. The policy should indicate whether the evaluation process is for internal purposes (e.g., identifying collection strengths and weaknesses), for comparative purposes, or perhaps for reviewing selectors' job performance. Each purpose requires different evaluation techniques or emphases. Making decisions about the how and why of evaluation ahead of time, putting them in writing, and getting them approved will save time and trouble for staff, patrons, funding agencies, and governing bodies.

Complaints and Censorship

The final section of the collection development policy statement outlines the steps to be taken in handling complaints about the collection. Eventually, every library will receive complaints about what is or is not in the collection. It is easier to handle questions about what is not there. (The library can always try to buy a missing item.) The major problem will be complaints about what is in the collection or questions as to why the policy limits collecting areas in a certain way.

When faced with a patron who is livid because of an item's inclusion in the collection, how does one defuse the situation? Passing the buck to the supervisor will only increase the patron's frustration. However, without guidelines for handling this type of situation, it is dangerous to try to solve the problem alone.

Usually the patron wants the offending item taken out of the collection. The librarian should not promise to remove the item, but instead should agree to review it, if the library has an established review procedure. It is necessary to identify who, how, and when the library will handle the review process. Usually the process begins by asking the patron to fill out a form. Though this response may appear bureaucratic to the patron, it does help identify the exact nature of the complaint. Complaint forms should consist of two parts, one explaining the library's review procedure, the other asking the patron to identify the offending sections or qualities of the item. Because the staff is offering to take action, the patron becomes less angry. (Chapter 19 explores the issues of censorship and intellectual freedom.)

It is important that the library establish procedures for handling complaints *before* the first complaint arises. Ad hoc decisions in this area can cause community relations problems for the library. In this instance, the merits of consistency far outweigh the drawbacks. Whatever system for handling complaints the library chooses must become part of the written collection development policy.

There are books of policies one can use as models; for example, E. Futas's *Collection Development Policies and Procedures,* 3d ed. (Oryx Press, 1995) and D. H. Morse and D. T. Richard's *Collection Development Policies for Health Sciences Libraries* (Medical Library Association, 1992). One can also find examples on the Internet, such as at Wellesley College's site (<http://www.wellesley.edu/Library/pol-menu.html>) and the University of Wyoming Libraries site (<http://www-lib.uwyo.edu/cdo/cd_pol.htm>).

Electronic Resources

Turning now to e-materials and policies, there are both similarities and differences in the structure of the policy(ies). In many ways the similarities are such that a single comprehensive policy would be the best approach. However, given the length of most print policies, incorporating more material into them might make them too complex to use effectively on a day-to-day basis. Two other factors in favor of separate policies are the current concern about e-resources and the relative ease of creating a separate document. (Appendix 1, on the server, contains some examples of electronic resource policies.) Some libraries make a distinction on the basis of "ownership"— print equals ownership and one type of policy; leased equals e-resources and another policy. That leaves a variety of electronic resources without a policy home.

Like the print policy, there ought to be an overview section that defines terms and outlines the context of the policy. What does the policy cover? Does it include one-time purchases of CD-ROM products, only ongoing subscription services, or both? What about data sets? Does it cover the library's linking to various Websites?

When there is agreement on the scope of the policy, just as with the print policy, there should be a statement about users. There are some thorny issues related to Internet access and certain classes of users, in particular children (see chapter 19). There are also some user issues associated with some companies' license agreements. Some libraries, especially U.S. government depositories, provide different levels of service to different types of databases. Both the differences in service levels and, if appropriate, the type(s) of user eligible to receive the service should be in the policy.

Content is, of course, a factor. Therefore, some type of statement about comparing print and electronic versions, when both exist, should be part of the policy. The policy is probably the best place to have a statement regarding the role of electronic materials: whether they are replacements for print, supplements to print, duplicates of print, or some variation on the theme. Although policies are guidelines rather than ironclad rules, outlining expectations for electronic materials is often easier at the abstract policy level than in a heated debate about a given product. Related to the question of role is an assessment of how an electronic version of a title compares to a print version—is it a total or partial duplication, or is it complete with added features? If the e-version duplicates a paper one, is there a time delay between them? Sometimes (more often than one would expect based on the popular press about technology) the print version appears months ahead of the electronic one.

Because the cost associated with electronic materials is high, and the items involved are often packages of titles rather than the print single-title approach, the policy ought to have a section devoted to cost assessment. Technology upgrades, both hardware and software, may be "hidden" costs of a product. Statements about how many, if any, upgrades are acceptable could go into this section. A related cost factor is whether the library is to buy or lease the product. If an annual lease is used, does the library get to retain anything when it ceases to pay the annual fee? Some guidelines about the preferred approach will help the selectors.

Training and support issues and how to assess them should be part of the policy as well. A list of factors to investigate will help avoid surprises later. For instance, does the product use a search interface already in use by other products in the library? What level of online/telephone vendor support (days and hours available) exists? If the product is Web-based, how stable and reliable is the host site? Erratic or uneven connection rates can cause the staff extra work and stress because they must handle users who are upset by being locked out or disconnected or by other problems that don't allow the search to be successfully completed.

A section that is particular to electronic resources is one on technical issues and license agreements. Many libraries do not have enough staff and expertise to support all types of e-resources. The policy is the place to outline what is and is not supported. A few libraries, especially those with limited staff or expertise, appear to be limiting themselves to Web products and few, if any, networked CD-ROMs. (As more and more products become Web-based, the decision not to support local tape mounting and/or networking of CD-ROMs is less problematic.) Decisions about licensing—who signs, what changes to seek, who is responsible, etc.—should be part of the policy.

Getting the Policy
Approved

Having invested considerable staff time to preparing a comprehensive collection development policy, it is important that the library's governing board approve that policy. With board approval, everyone agrees on ground rules for building a collection that will serve the community.

An ideal policy approval process might consist of the following:

1. The director appoints a staff committee to draft a basic policy statement for submission to the director.

2. The director reviews and comments on the draft and distributes it to the library staff for comments and suggestions.

3. The original committee incorporates the comments and suggestions into a interim draft. Perhaps the committee will call a general meeting to discuss the interim draft before preparing the final version.

4. The director presents the final draft statement to the governing board for review, possible revision, and approval.

5. Between board review and final approval, the library holds an open meeting for community feedback about the proposed policy. At the meeting, members of the drafting committee, the director, and representatives of the governing board explain, describe, and, if necessary, defend and modify the statement.

6. The final step is to prepare multiple copies of the final statement for the library staff and patrons who request a copy. A good public relations device is to prepare a condensed version for distribution to each new user of the library.

Following these steps ensures community, staff, and administrative consensus about issues before a problem arises. It is much easier to agree on evaluation procedures, review procedures, levels and areas of collecting, and so on in advance than to try to handle them in the heat of a specific disagreement. An approved policy makes it easier to resolve disagreements, because it provides a body of established and agreed-upon rules.

Summary

Collection development is a complex process that is highly subjective, rife with problems and traps for the unwary. A comprehensive written policy, developed with the advice and involvement of all parties concerned, helps regulate the process and makes it less problematic.

Notes

1. Dan C. Hazen, "Collection Development Policies in the Information Age," *College & Research Libraries* 56 (January 1995): 29–31.

2. Merle Jacob, "Get It in Writing: A Collection Development Plan for the Skokie Public Library," *Library Journal* 115 (September 1, 1990): 166–69.

3. Karin Wittenborg, *Collection Policy Statements* (Internal Document, University Library, University of California, Los Angeles, January 14, 1992).

4. For a more complete discussion of items in the list, see G. Edward Evans, "Needs Analysis and Collection Development Polices for Culturally Diverse Populations," *Collection Building* 11, no. 4 (1992): 167. The list was based on C. E. Cortes, F. Metcalf, and S. Hawke, *Understanding You and Them* (Boulder, Colo.: Social Science Education Consortium, 1976).

5. Gale Hannigan and Janis F. Brown, *Managing Public Access Microcomputers in Health Sciences Libraries* (Chicago: Medical Library Association, 1992), 90.

6. Michael Buckland, *Book Availability and the Library Users* (New York: Pergamon Press, 1975).

7. *Pacific Northwest Collection Assessment Manual*, 4th ed. (Lacey, Wash.: Western Library Network, 1992).

8. Ibid., 48.

9. Elizabeth Futas, "Collection Development of Genre Literature," *Collection Building* 12, nos. 3/4 (1993): 39–45.

10. 457 U.S. 853, 102 S. Ct. 2799 (1981).

Further Reading

General

Boge, K. D. "Integrating Electronic Resources into Collection Development Policies." *Collection Management* 21, no. 2 (1996): 65–76.

Bostic, M. J. "A Written Collection Development Policy: To Have and Have Not." *Collection Management* 10, nos. 3/4 (1988): 89–103.

Branin, J. J. "Information Policies for Collection Development Librarians." *Collection Building* 9, nos. 3/4 (1989): 193.

Bryant, B., ed. *Guide for Written Collection Policy Statements*. Chicago: American Library Association, 1989.

Bullard, S. R. "Read My Lips: The Politics of Collection Development." *Library Acquisitions: Practice and Theory* 13, no. 3 (1989): 251–53.

Cassell, K. A., and E. Futas. "Collection Development Policies." *Collection Building* 11, no. 2 (1991): 269.

Farrell, D. "Policy and Planning." In *Collection Management: A New Treatise*. Edited by C. B. Osburn and R. Atkinson, 51–66. Greenwich, Conn.: JAI Press, 1991.

Ferguson, Anthony W. "Interesting Problems Encountered on My Way to Writing an Electronic Information Collection Development Statement." *Against the Grain* 7 (April 1995) 16.

Futas, E. *Collection Development Policies and Procedures.* 3d ed. Phoenix, Ariz.: Oryx Press, 1995.

Gorman, G. E. "An Embarrassment of Riches, or Just an Embarrassment?" *Australian Library Review* 8 (November 1991): 381–88.

Harloe, B., and J. M. Budd. "Collection Development and Scholarly Communication in the Era of Electronic Access." *Journal of Academic Librarianship* 20 (January 1995): 29–31.

Hattendorf, L. C. "Art of Reference Collection Development." *RQ* 29 (1989): 2199.

LaGuardia, C., and S. Bentley. "Electronic Databases: Will Old Collection Development Policies Still Work?" *Online* 16 (July 1992): 60–63.

Losee, R. M., Jr. "Optimality and the Best Collection: The Goals and Rules of Selectors and Collection Managers." *Collection Management* 14, nos. 3/4 (1991): 21–30.

Martin, K. F., and K. F. Rose. "Managing the CD-ROM Collection Development Process." *Collection Management* 21, no. 2 (1996): 77–102.

Serebin, R. "Video: Planning Backwards into the Future." *Library Journal* 113 (November 15, 1989): 33–36.

White, G. W., and G. A. Crawford. "Developing an Electronic Information Resources Collection Development Policy." *Collection Building* 16, no.2 (1997): 53–57.

Academic

Atkinson, R. "Old Forms, New Forms: The Challenge of Collection Development." *College & Research Libraries* 50 (Summer 1991): 507–20.

Boyarski, J. S., and K. Hickey, eds. *Collection Management in the Electronic Age: A Manual for Creating Community College Collection Development Policy Statements.* Chicago: ACRL, 1994.

Buis, E. "Collection Development Policies: Coordinating Teaching Faculty and Library Staff Interests." *Collection Management* 13, no. 3 (1990): 116.

Carpenter, E. J. "Collection Development Policies Based on Approval Plans." *Library Acquisitions: Practice and Theory* 13, no. 1 (1989): 39–43.

Fedunok, S. "Hammurabi and the Electronic Age." *RQ* 36 (Fall 1996): 86–91.

Hamilton, P., and H. Feis. "A Model of Cooperative Collection Development Policies for Academic Libraries." *Technicalities* 9 (1989): 9–11.

Hazen, D. C. "Collection Development Policies in the Information Age." *College & Research Libraries News* 56, no. 1 (January 1995): 29–31.

Shreeves, E. "Between Visionaries and the Luddites." *Library Trends* 40 (Spring 1992): 579–95.

Smith, L. "Interactive Multimedia and Electronic Media in Academic Libraries— Policy Implication." *Reference Librarian* 38 (1993): 229–44.

Public

American Library Association. "Guidelines for Developing Beginning Genealogical Collections and Services." *RQ* 32 (Fall 1992): 31–32.

Feehan, P. "Youth Services Collection Development Issues." *Collection Building* 10, nos. 1/2 (1990): 55–60.

Hamilton, P. A., and T. L. Weech. "Give 'em What They Want or Give 'em What They Should Have." *Illinois Libraries* 69 (April 1987): 284–89.

Jackson, M. E. "Library to Library." *Wilson Library Bulletin* 64 (February 1989): 88–89.

Jacob, M. "Get It in Writing: A Collection Development Plan for the Skokie Public Library." *Library Journal* 115 (September 1, 1990): 166–69.

Little, P. "Collection Development for Bookmobiles." In *The Book Stops Here*. Edited by C. S. Alloway, 59–73. Metuchen, N.J.: Scarecrow Press, 1990.

Pettas, W. A. "Cooperative Collection Development: The Northern California Experience." *Collection Building* 9, no. 2 (1988): 3–6.

School

Callison, D. "Evolution of School Library Collection Development Policies." *School Library Media Quarterly* 19 (Fall 1990): 27–34.

Caywood, C. "Nonprint Media Selection Guidelines." *Journal of Youth Services in Libraries* 2 (Fall 1988): 90–94.

Gerhardt, L. N. "Matters of Policy." *School Library Journal* 39 (January 1993): 4.

Hopkins, D. M. "Put It in Writing." *School Library Journal* 39 (January 1993): 26–30.

Mancall, J. "(Un)changing Factors in the Searching Environment: Collections, Collectors and Users." *School Library Media Quarterly* 19 (Winter 1991): 84–89.

Special

Beglo, J. "Today Is for Tomorrow." *Art Libraries Journal* 19, no. 1 (1994): 13–15.

Hodge, S. P., D. Calvin, and G. E. Rike. "Formulating an Integrated Library Government Documents Policy." *Government Information Quarterly* 6, no. 2 (1989): 199–213.

Hoolihand, C. "Collection Development Policies in Medical Rare Book Collections." *Collection Management* 11, no. 3/4 (1989): 167–69.

Ionesco, M. "Regional Cooperation for Research Collections." *Collection Building* 9, no. 2 (1988): 7–11.

Lein, E. "Suggestions for Formulating Collection Development Policy Statements for Music Score Collections." *Collection Management* 9 (Winter 1987): 69–101.

Okpokwasili, N. P., and M. L. Bundy. "A Study of Selection and Acquisition Policies of Agricultural Libraries in the United States." *Libri* 39 (December 1989): 319–30.

Singerman, R. "Charting the Course: University of Florida's Collection Management Policy for Jewish Studies." *Judaica Librarianship* 6 (Spring 1991): 115–19.

Thomas, V. C. "Formulating a Federal Depository Collection Development Statement." *Legal Reference Services Quarterly* 11, nos. 1/2 (1991): 11–16.

Wykle, H. H. "Collection Development Policies for Academic Visual Resources Collections." *Art Documentation* 7 (Spring 1988): 22–26.

4

Selection Process in Practice

Chapter Four in prior editions addressed the theory of selection work as presented in a number of textbooks. Due to the need to add substantial material to this edition and to keep the book a reasonable length, we had to drop that chapter from this edition. One can find the material in older editions and on two Web sites (<http://lib.lmu.edu/dlc4> and <http://www.lu.com>). However, we were able to include in this edition a summary table of the key points for six of the authors (table 4.1, pages 92–93). This chapter presents the practical side of the process by exploring what takes place in the real world of libraries and information centers. It also examines how different environmental settings influence selection work, and describes the major categories of selection and acquisition aids. First, however, a few more basic points about selection are covered.

What Happens in Selection

No matter what type of library one works in, there are several steps in the selection process. First, selectors must identify collection needs in terms of subjects and specific types of material. (This is especially important in the absence of a written collection development policy.) The next steps involve determining how much money is available for collection development and allocating a specific amount for each category or subject; developing a plan for identifying potentially useful materials to acquire; and finally, conducting the search for the desired materials. In most situations, the identification of potential acquisitions draws heavily from published lists, catalogs, flyers, announcements, and bibliographies. After securing the list, a person or group assesses the worth of various titles on the same topic. In some cases, only one title is available. When that occurs, only two questions remain. First, is the price reasonable for the level of use that the item will receive? Second, is the item physically suitable for the proposed use? If the answer to both questions is the same (yes or no), the issue is resolved. When the answers are different, one must secure more information about the level of need before ordering the item.

Table 4.1   Selection theory process compared.

McColvin	Drury	Haines
Theory of Book Selection (1925)	Book Selection (1930)	Living With Books (2d. ed., 1950)
1. Information should be as accurate as possible.	1. Establish suitable standards for judging all books.	1. Know the community's character and interests.
2. Items should be complete and balanced regarding subject and intended scope.	2. Apply criteria intelligently, evaluating the book's content for inherent worth.	2. Be familiar with subjects of current interest.
3. Authors should distinguish between fact and opinion.	3. Strive to get the best title on any subject, but add mediocre titles that will be read rather than superior titles that will be unread.	3. Represent subjects applicable to these conditions.
4. Information should be current. (Frequently *the* determining criteria for selection.)	4. Duplicate the best rather than acquire the many.	4. Make the collection of local history materials useful and extensive.
5. Writing style and treatment of the subject should be appropriate to the type of demand the book will answer.	5. Stock the classics and standards.	5. Provide materials for organized groups whose activities and interests can be related to books.
6. The title should reflect the cultural values of its country of origin.	6. Select for positive use.	6. Provide materials for both actual and potential readers.
7. Consider physical characteristics are when deciding between two books with similar content.	7. Develop the local history collection.	7. Avoid selecting books that are not in demand; withdraw books that are no longer useful.
	8. Be broadminded and unprejudiced in selection.	8. Select some books of permanent value regardless of their potential use.
	9. Do select fiction.	9. Practice impartiality in selection. Do not favor certain hobbies or opinions. In controversial or sectarian subjects, accept gifts if purchase is undesirable.
	10. Buy editions in bindings suitable for circulation and borrowing.	10. As much as possible, provide for the needs of specialists.
	11. Know publishers, costs, and values.	11. Strive not for a "complete" collection, but for the best: the best books on a subject, the best books by an author, the most useful volumes of a series.
	12. Know authors and their works.	12. Prefer an inferior book that will be read over a superior one that will not.
		13. Keep abreast of current thought and opinion.
		14. Maintain promptness and regularity in supplying new books, especially for books that are both good and popular.

Ranganathan	Broadus	Curley & Broderick
Library Book Selection (1952; Rpt. 1990)	Selecting Materials For Libraries (2nd ed., 1981)	Building Library Collections (6th ed., 1985)
1. Books are for use.	1. Be aware of the impact of publicity that may stimulate demand.	1. Large public libraries with both a heterogeneous community to serve and a reasonable book budget can in theory apply most collection principles with little modification within the total library system.
2. Every reader his book.	2. Consider the duration as well as the intensity of the demand.	2. Medium-sized libraries are similar, except that funding usually forces greater care in selection. Mistakes are more costly.
3. Every book its reader.	3. Weigh the amount of possible opposition to a title. Controversy stimulates demand.	3. Small public libraries are the most limited. Most can only hope to meet the most significant community demands, and they may lack both the professional staff and the money to do more.
4. Save the reader's time.	4. Include a reasonably high percentage of standards and classics in the collection.	4. College libraries serve a more homogeneous population. In most cases, demand is the operative principle: college libraries acquire materials needed to support the instructional program. No one questions the quality of the material if the request originated with a faculty member or department.
5. A library is a growing organism.	5. Consider past loans of specific titles and subjects. Past use is one of the most reliable predictors of future use.	
	6. Make some provision for serving the needs of potential users in the community. Having made such a provision, advertise it.	
	7. Weigh the differences between true demand (which reflects individual needs) and artificial demand (resulting from organized propaganda efforts).	

More often than not, one makes the assessment using published information rather than a physical examination of the book. An item-by-item physical examination and reading, listening, or viewing is the ideal. However, most libraries lack the staff resources or the time to secure examination copies and review each title. Typically, school and public libraries devote more time to looking over approval copies than do academic libraries, although university and research libraries do use approval plans.

Most wholesalers and jobbers will provide examination copies if they can reasonably expect that the libraries will purchase most of the titles sent or will order multiple copies of some of the titles. For example, if a librarian requested 100 titles on approval and kept 90, the jobber would probably send other titles on approval. However, if the library kept only 65 titles, it would become necessary to convince the jobber that there was good reason for this high rejection rate, or the firm might cancel the program. (If the library orders multiple copies of most of the retained titles, most vendors would continue to ship approval materials.) The reason is simple: it costs as much to select, pack, and ship an approval order as it does a firm order. (This is true for both the library and the vendor.) Thus, the more a library can depend on published selection aids to reduce the need for examination copies, the better off everyone will be. Many academic libraries use a jobber approval program, but the principle remains the same for all types of libraries: the return rate must be low. Vendors will want to reassess a plan if the return rate rises much above 10 percent.

This is a good place to note some common terms used in selection and acquisition work. Four related terms are *standing order, blanket order, approval plan,* and *Till Forbidden.* Although some people use these terms imprecisely, each has a specific meaning. Serials librarians frequently use *Till Forbidden* to indicate that the publisher or supplier of a journal should automatically renew a subscription without any further approval from the library. This system saves time and money for both the library and publisher or supplier by reducing the amount of paperwork required to maintain subscriptions. (This is discussed in more detail in chapter 6.) *Standing orders* and *blanket orders* are similar; in both cases, the library commits to purchasing everything sent by a publisher or vendor, provided the materials match the terms of a formal agreement. (From a collection management point of view, such orders create a high degree of uncertainty in terms of the total annual cost, although some libraries do set an upper limit on total cost of materials a jobber may send without permission. Using the prior year's cost and an inflation factor is the best one can do to make an estimate, but variations in publishing schedules do cause marked variations in actual costs.) A *standing order* is normally placed for a series (for example, Academic Press's Studies in Archaeology series). A *blanket order* is placed for a subject field, grade level, or country's publications (for example, all books about politics in Latin America, all books for undergraduates, or all the books published in Finnish in Finland). *Approval plans*, as noted earlier, allow the library to examine items before deciding to buy; they are not firm orders. (*Note:* A firm order is a legal contract.)

Each of these mechanisms plays a role in effective and efficient collection development, and each clearly affects selection activities. When selectors know the library needs everything on a subject or all of one type of information material, or when selectors can satisfactorily define the scope and depth of need, a standing or blanket order is best. Such orders free selectors' time for more difficult decision-making activities. If selectors have less precise information about needs, but know the library will need large numbers of titles, an approval plan may be best. However, the approval plan requires selectors to examine each shipment to decide which titles to keep and which to return.

Variations in Selection

This section covers some of the variations that occur in selection activities due to the different institutional environments in which the activities occur. Given the universal nature of information and the diversity of institutional settings in which an information specialist may work during a career, no single method of categorizing institutional environments is completely satisfactory. For convenience of presentation, this section employs the traditional categories of libraries: academic, public, school, and special. There are great differences even within each category, and what follows provides only a broad overview of the thousands of variations that may exist.

Academic Libraries

Community or Junior Colleges

In the United States and many other countries, there are at least two broad types of postsecondary schools: vocational and academic. People usually refer to publicly supported vocational programs in the United States as community or junior colleges. However, most of these institutions have both vocational and academic programs. The academic program is roughly equivalent to the first two years in a college or university and serves as a transfer program to a four-year college or university. Frequently, the quality of education is just as good as that of a four-year college. If the transfer program is to succeed in providing the equivalent of the first two years of a four-year undergraduate degree, then the scope of the program must be just as comprehensive as that of the university program.

Collection development officers in a community college library have a challenging job. Not only must they focus on the academic programs, but they must also give equal attention to a wide range of vocational programs—and do so with a modest budget. Unfortunately, from a cost perspective, it is seldom possible to find materials that are useful in both programs. Also, many vocational programs need more visual than print materials, which accounts in part for the fact that American community college libraries tend to be leaders in the use of audiovisual (AV) materials. Strength in the AV collection means that the selection staff must know more about AV selection than their colleagues in other types of academic libraries. Community college librarians normally have other duties assigned to them aside from their collection development responsibilities, such as reference and instruction, which prevent them from devoting their entire focus to collection development.

In addition, most community or junior colleges offer extensive adult education or continuing education programs, which all too often have little or no relationship to the degree programs. It is true that most academic institutions offer some form of adult, or nondegree, courses and programs. However, in most community colleges the library, or learning resource center (LRC), must handle all programmatic information needs. Many universities provide a separate library to support the nondegree program. Given the diversity of subjects and levels of user ability, the community college library more resembles the public library than it does its larger relation, the university library.

Some help in establishing collection scope and size is available to the LRC. In 1979, the Junior College Library Section of the Association of College and Research Libraries (part of the American Library Association) published a "Statement on Quantitative Standards for Two-Year Learning Resources Programs."[1] This statement has been revised over time and the current version was approved in 1994 by the Association of College and Research Libraries, ALA, and the Association for Educational Communications and Technology (AECT).[2]

Though the statement does not indicate what to buy, it does help set some limits for what could be a bottomless pit. Distributing copies of such standards may generate more interest in selection and collection building among both faculty and administration. Faculty involvement in LRC selection work is desirable, just as it is in other educational settings, and such support is just as difficult to secure in LRCs as it is in other educational settings.

LRCs serve a heterogeneous community, and their collections must often reflect a diverse population with varying levels of language skills. Given space restrictions, selection is usually item by item, with less use of blanket orders and approval plans than in other types of academic libraries. Collections generally contain at least a few items in all the standard educational formats. Selection personnel generally use a greater variety of selection aids than their colleagues in other types of libraries.

College Libraries

Though college libraries serving primarily bachelor's degree programs are diverse, each serves a highly homogeneous user group. Only the small special library that caters to a company or research group is likely to have a more homogeneous service community. One characteristic of bachelor's degree programs is that, within a particular college, all the students who graduate, regardless of their major, complete some type of general education program. A program of core courses means that students select from a limited number of courses during their first two years. Less variety in course offerings makes selection work for that aspect of the institution's activities less complex. Support of the curriculum is the primary objective of the college library collection. College libraries may offer some collection support for faculty research, but, unlike universities, colleges seldom emphasize research. With the curriculum as the focus for collection development activities, selectors have definite limits within which to work. Faculty members frequently play an active role in selection, more so than in the LRC or university context.

Most of the items selected for the American college library are current works in English. College libraries in general have fewer AV materials than do LRCs, but there is a growing trend to include all formats in the collection. Most institutions have a music audio collection and art slides or CDs to support the core curriculum survey courses in music and art. Retrospective collection building (identifying and acquiring out-of-print items) is not a major activity in the college library. Many college libraries have rare book rooms and spend a small percentage of their materials budget on rare items. A few college libraries have a strong special collection in a narrow subject field. Even without a rare book or special collection, some retrospective buying takes place. Most of the out-of-print searching and buying activities are to replace worn-out and lost books.

Because of their numbers (more than 900 in the United States) and their long history, college libraries have developed a series of standards, some quantitative and some qualitative. A particularly good review of the standards and the issues surrounding them appears in an article by David Kaser in *Library Trends*.[3] As was the case with junior colleges, the Association of College and Research Libraries developed standards for college libraries, which were approved in 1995.[4] Though standards are of some help in determining collection size, they do not have any influence in selection work, at least on a day-to-day basis.

Without question, the most widely used selection aid in American college libraries is *Choice* (published by the American Library Association). ALA created *Choice* to meet the specific needs of college library collection development officers by reviewing publications aimed at the undergraduate market. Subject experts, including librarians, write the reviews with an emphasis on the subject content and the title's overall suitability for undergraduate, rather than research, use. With small staffs (typically 10 to 15 people), few college libraries have sufficient subject expertise to evaluate all the potentially useful titles published each year, even with help from the teaching faculty. Because *Choice* annually reviews more than 6,000 titles of "potential use by undergraduates,"[5] and because of its widespread use as a selection aid, several librarians have studied *Choice* to determine whether it is an effective selection aid. For example, do items receiving positive reviews receive more use than titles receiving neutral reviews? One such study concluded that *Choice*

> reviews appear helpful in identifying the most worthy titles, as those most likely to be used repeatedly ... . [T]itles appealing primarily to a more elite audience of specialists ought to be scrutinized if the selector is concerned about maximum use. The question of the level on which the book is written is an important one ... . [S]electing strictly on the basis of probable popularity runs the risk of developing a collection which could be categorized as "lightweight" academically.[6]

The authors also noted that a collection based on *Choice*'s so-called worthy titles may or may not address the needs of the particular institution.

University Libraries

University and research libraries' interests and needs dominate the professional literature, judging by the number of books and articles published about academic collection development in recent years. This domination arises from several types of numerical superiority. Though these libraries are not as numerous as libraries of other types, the size of their collections and the number of their staff, as well as monies expended per year on operations, far surpass the combined totals for all the other types of libraries. University and research libraries have collections ranging from a few hundred thousand to more than 10 million volumes. As an example, Tozzer Library (Harvard University) is a research library of about 211,000 items, a small library in the world of research libraries. However, it collects only in the fields of anthropology and archaeology. It is, as a result, one of the two largest anthropology libraries in the world. Like all research libraries, Tozzer spends a good deal of money on materials each year, does much work that is retrospective, and collects in most languages.

Collection development and selection work requires more time and attention in university research libraries than in other academic libraries. Typically, there are full-time collection development officers. In other academic libraries, collection development is one of many duties a librarian performs. Looking at the history and development of United States academic libraries, one can see a changing pattern in regard to who does the book selection. In small libraries with limited funds, there is strong faculty involvement; sometimes the faculty has sole responsibility for building the collection. As the collection, institution, and budget grow, there is a shift to more and more librarian involvement and responsibility. At the university and research library level, subject specialists come back into the selection picture, but they are members of the library staff rather than the teaching faculty. Many, if not most, of the persons responsible for collection development in research libraries have one or more subject graduate degrees in addition to a degree in library science. Such individuals are usually responsible for developing the collection in a specific subject or language. There is no single method by which academic libraries divide the universe of knowledge among subject specialists. Local needs and historical precedents determine how the library divides the responsibilities. Some universities use broad areas (social sciences or humanities), others use geographic divisions (Oceania or Latin America), and still others use small subject fields (anthropology or economic botany) and languages (Slavic or Arabic). It is not uncommon to find a mix of all methods.

A significant problem in large university and research library systems with departmental or subject libraries is coordinating collection development activities. Budgets may be large, but there is always more material than money. Unintentional duplication is always a concern, but the biggest problem is determining whose responsibility it is to collect in a given subject. As the number of persons involved goes up and the scope of each person's responsibility diminishes, the danger of missing important items increases. Working together, sending one another announcements, and checking with colleagues about their decisions becomes a major activity for university collection development officers. (Joint collection development activities with the "conspectus" approach were covered in chapter 3.)

University libraries tend to depend heavily on standing and blanket orders, as well as approval plans, as means of reducing workloads while assuring adequate collection building. Using such programs allows selectors more time for retrospective buying and for tracking down items from countries where the book trade is not well developed. Knowledge of one or more foreign languages is a must if one wishes to be a collection development officer at the university level.

Public Libraries

As is the case for junior or community college library clientele, diversity is the primary characteristic of public libraries' selection practices (arising from the heterogeneous nature of the communities they serve). Communities of a few hundred people, with a small library open only a few hours per week with no professional or full-time staff, do not follow the same practices that large urban libraries follow. Collection sizes range from several hundred items (Mancos, Colorado) to large research collections of millions of volumes (New York City).

Despite this variety, some generalizations apply to most public libraries. The service population normally consists of many unrelated constituencies: persons from various ethnic groups, of all ages, with various educational backgrounds and levels of skill and knowledge, and with a variety of information needs. All these groups fall within the public library's service population. Community need is the dominant factor in selection, all too often because funding and good sense permit no other choice. Though librarians do the selecting, occasionally they employ a committee format with patron involvement. Growth of the collection is modest because of limited stack space and the removal of worn-out or outdated materials. Most selections are current imprints, with retrospective buying generally limited to replacement titles. Medium and large public libraries commonly collect audio and video recordings as well as a variety of other AV formats. Perhaps the main difference in collection development between public libraries and libraries of other types is the strong emphasis on recreational needs, in addition to educational and informational materials. Trade publishers count on a strong public library market for most of their new releases. Without the library market, book buyers would see even higher prices, because only a fraction of the new books published would become strong sellers, much less bestsellers.

For larger libraries, there are two important issues in selection: speed and coordination. Most of the larger libraries are systems with a main library and one or more branches. The reading public likes to read new books while they are new, not six to nine months after interest wanes. Often interest is fleeting, especially in fiction. So, having the new books on the shelf and ready to circulate when the demand arises is important. With several service points, a system must control costs. One way to help control cost is to place one order for multiple copies of desired items rather than ordering one now, another later, and still more even later.

Anticipating public interest is a challenge for the public library selector, and it probably would be impossible without several aids. Unquestionably, the most important aid is the selector's inquiring, active mind and the commitment to read, read, read. In addition, one of the most useful aids is *Publishers Weekly* (*PW*). Reading each issue cover-to-cover provides a wealth of information about what publishers plan to do to market new titles. Clues such as "30,000 first printing; major ad promo; author tour"; "BOMC, Cooking and Crafts Club alternative"; "major national advertising"; "soon to be a

TV miniseries"; or "author to appear on the *Tonight Show*" can help the selector to identify potentially high-interest items before demand arises. *PW* bases its information on publishers' stated plans, and the information appears well in advance of implementation, so there is time to order and process the items before patron requests begin to materialize. Needless to say, not all the highly promoted titles generate the interest the publisher hopes for. Occasionally *PW* has an article that covers publishers' successes and failures.[7] Additionally, *Library Journal* and *Booklist* provide "Prepub alerts" and "upfront preview" listings. All three publications include such information in both their print and online publications.[8] By knowing the community and the publishers, a selector can, in time, predict with reasonable accuracy the high-interest titles. The McNaughton Plan (rental plan) is one way to meet high, short-term demand for multiple copies.

The need to coordinate order placement is one reason many public libraries use selection committees. Such committees, especially if they include a representative from each service location, reduce the problem of order coordination. In large systems with dozens of branches and mobile service points, such as the Los Angeles Public Library, total representation is impractical. In such cases, the selection committee develops a recommended buying list, and the service locations have a period of time to order from the list. Though not a perfect system, it does help achieve some degree of coordinated buying and cost control.

Small public libraries do not experience the problems of large libraries. Instead, their problems involve finding the money and time to buy materials. Reviews play a vital role in helping selectors at the small library locate the best possible buys with limited funds. More and more public libraries, including the smallest, depend on some type of cooperative network to help with collection development. Thus, small libraries sometimes can draw on the expertise of the network for identifying appropriate materials and can use selection aids they could never justify having if they were on their own. Some cooperatives engage in joint purchasing to gain discounts on high-volume purchases. In such cases, the smaller libraries use the purchasing list approach that large systems use. Even for small U.S. public libraries that are part of a cooperative, *Booklist* is the most important selection aid. Though *Booklist* contains only recommended titles, it identifies highly recommended titles (called "the best buys"). *Booklist* also reviews a wide range of nonprint materials and reference items.

Another distinctive feature of public library collection development is an emphasis on children's materials. In many public libraries, children's books get the highest use. Most libraries depend on positive reviews when making selection decisions about children's books. Often, the staff members examine the title when it arrives to make certain it fits collection guidelines. One of the first specialist positions a growing public library tries to create is for children's materials and services.

(*Note:* Although there is some overlap between children's materials in schools and those in public libraries, it is not large. Throughout the United States and in other countries as well, requirements for being a school librarian and for being a children's librarian in a public library vary.)

Two other special features of public library collection development are noteworthy. First, the public library, historically, has been a place to which citizens turn for self-education materials. Self-education needs range from basic language and survival for the recent immigrant, to improving skills gained in schools, to maintaining current knowledge of a subject studied in college. In addition to the true educational function of the preceding, there is the self-help and education aspect exemplified by learning how to repair a car, how to fix a sticky door, how to prepare a special meal, or how to win friends and influence people. Selecting materials for the varied educational wants and desires of a diverse population can be a real challenge and a specialty in itself.

The last feature of note is the selection of genre fiction, a staple in most public library collections. Most people read only a few types of fiction regularly. One of the problems for the selector of genre materials is the lack of reviews; learning about types of fiction and the authors can be a problem. (It might be a good idea for all public librarians to have a course in genre novels while in library school.) A good book that can be of help in learning about such fiction is *Genreflecting: A Guide to Reading Interests in Genre Fiction.*[9] Although one may think that all westerns are the same, *Genreflecting* lists 40 distinct themes and the names of authors who specialize in each one. Some readers will devour any western about range wars but will not touch a title about mountain men. Learning about the different categories and their authors is not only fun but useful for anyone developing a public library collection. Senkevitch and Sweetland found that certain "core" fiction items remain in the collection from year to year, so the entire genre collection would not likely have to be replaced from year to year.[10]

School Library Media Centers

Curriculum support dominates school library media center (LMC) collection development. Some similarities exist among community college, college, and school media center selection and collection development. Each emphasizes providing materials directly tied to teaching requirements, and each uses instructor input in the selection process. An emphasis on current material, with limited retrospective buying, is common. Community college and school media centers share the distinction of having the greatest number and variety of AV materials in their collections. Both school and community college media centers must serve an immense range of student abilities.

Although similarities do exist, the differences between school media centers and other educational libraries far outweigh the similarities. Take curriculum support, for example. School media centers have limited funds for collection development, in this matter resembling the small public library. With limited funds and limited staff (often there is only one professional on the staff), most of the money goes to purchasing items that directly support specific instructional units.

Library media specialists often build a core collection that provides some breadth and then concentrate on building emphasis collections that target curricular goals. For example, the media specialist might combine textbook and LMC funds to build rotating classroom and LMC collections of fiction and literary nonfiction to support a literature-based reading program. A hands-on math collection of manipulatives and fun math-oriented literature might be used to support a move to meet the National Council of Teachers of Mathematics curriculum standards. Science department and LMC funds could be combined to access the Internet or National Geographic's KIDNET.

In some schools, teachers and LMC staff must plan effectively to assure that scarce funds meet topical requirements and that cooperation with other school, public, and academic libraries will maximize student access to needed materials. School libraries in particular realize that excellent access for children builds expectations for the future and a willingness to fund all types of libraries as intellectual needs expand.

Normally, teachers and media specialists serve on committees that review and select items for purchase. Some parent representation on the committee is desirable. Whatever the committee composition, the media specialist must take the responsibility for identifying potentially useful items, preparing a list of suggestions, and securing examination or preview copies for group consideration. Most importantly, the committee must have a clear sense of collection emphasis, of how the items under consideration support current curriculum, and of how the collection will grow as the curriculum evolves.

More and more schools are equipping entire buildings with new technologies so that each classroom teacher has access to telecommunications, audio, video, and computer equipment. Next on the horizon is the further integration of these technologies to expand multimedia access and presentations. In these cases, library media specialists must do more than build a centralized collection. In addition, they must continue to expand areas in the school for instant access (high-tech teaching stations) or on-call access (we will get the material if you give us advance warning), or they must help get students to a location where the materials or technology can be used (the school's LMC, the public library, or an academic library).

The need for a collection development policy may be more acute in school media center operations than in other types of libraries. Although selection responsibility lies with the library media specialist, parents and others have legitimate concerns about both formats and content of materials to which children have access. Some parents and religious groups have strong objections to certain ideas in books and journals. Clearly stated, written collection goals and selection criteria allow everyone to operate as efficiently (and safely) as possible.

School library media centers are probably the most closely monitored of all types of libraries. However, public libraries receive their share of monitoring, especially in the area of children's materials. Media centers handle an ongoing flow of questions about and legal challenges to the content of the collection. An illustration of this scrutiny was the tongue-in-cheek *Reader's Guide to Non-Controversial Books* published by the National Committee for Good Reading. This publication listed items that would not be "offensive to any of the cultural or religious values in our society." Its proposed users were to be children, young adults, and "discriminating" adults in the United States. The publication contained 10 blank pages.[11] Concern about controlling, influencing, developing, or expanding (or a number of other labels) children's minds generates challenges. At times, both liberal and conservative pressure groups question why a certain item is or is not in a collection. Written policies and advisory committees are two means of answering such questions.

Published reviews play a significant role in media center selection. Often, school districts secure published reviews and also inspect items before making purchase decisions. The reasons for this are parental and school board interest in the collection's content and the need to spend limited funds on materials that will actually meet teachers' specific needs. The most widely used review sources are ALA's *Booklist*; H. W. Wilson's catalogs, such as the *Children's Catalog*; *School Library Journal*; and Brodart's *Elementary School Library Collection*. To a lesser degree, school libraries also use *Library Journal* and *Wilson Library Bulletin*. Finding reviews that provide adequate coverage of nonprint formats is a challenge; although *Booklist*, *Library Journal*, *School Library Journal*, and *Wilson Library Bulletin* all contain some AV reviews, they cover only a small percentage of the total output. Information about grade level and effectiveness in the classroom are two crucial concerns for the media specialist. Grade level information is generally available, but it is very difficult to locate data about classroom effectiveness. Usually, the time involved in gathering effectiveness data is too great to make it useful in media center collection development.

The term *library media specialist* denotes a person who knows about all types of information formats and the equipment necessary for using the formats. Today, at least in the United States, many school library media centers also serve as computer centers. Selection of instructional computer software is a common responsibility and, not infrequently, so is teaching students and staff how to use computers and software.

Building the school media center collection is probably the most rewarding and the most frustrating of all types of collection building. Normally, the center serves a relatively small population, and each customer is known on a personal level seldom found in other types of libraries. Frustration comes from having too little money to buy all the needed material, understaffing, and the difficulty in finding both appropriate material and necessary reviews.

Special Libraries
and Information Centers

Almost any general statement about special libraries and information centers is inaccurate for any individual special library, because of the diversity of environmental settings. In a sense, this is a catchall category. As a result, this category may be the largest and the least homogeneous. Dividing this category into three subclasses—scientific and technical, corporate and industrial, and subject and research—allows some useful generalizations. However, even these subclasses are not always mutually exclusive. A hospital library can have both a scientific and a corporate orientation if it has a responsibility to support both the medical and the administrative staff. In teaching hospitals, there is an educational aspect to collection building as well. There may even be a flavor of a public library, if the library offers a patient-service program. Some corporations establish two types of information centers, technical and management; others have a single facility to serve both activities. A geology library in a large research university may have more in common with an energy corporation library than it does with other libraries in its own institution. Large, independent, specialized research libraries, such as the Newberry, Linda Hall, or Folger libraries, fall into a class by themselves, yet they have many of the characteristics of the large university library.

Depending on which commercial mailing list one examines, the count of special libraries in the United States and Canada ranges from 12,000 to more than 19,000. Despite their substantial numbers, special libraries have not influenced professional practice as much as one would expect. This does not mean that special libraries have not made important contributions or developed innovative practices; it merely means that circumstances often make it difficult or impossible for special libraries to share information about their activities in the same manner as other libraries. Their diversity in character and operational environment is one reason for special libraries' modest influence. Another reason is that libraries and information centers in profit-oriented organizations frequently limit the reporting of activities and new systems for proprietary reasons; knowing what a competitor is working on may provide a company with an advantage. Such concerns often limit the amount of cooperative activities in which corporate libraries may engage. One way to learn about an organization's current interests is to study the materials in its library.

One widely shared characteristic of special libraries is lack of space. Limited space for all services, but particularly for collection storage, is a frequent complaint of the special librarian. Although all libraries eventually experience lack of space, a special library seldom expects to expand beyond its assigned area. Deselection becomes, more often than not, a regular part of the special library's cycle. Sound information about the most useful core items for the collection and how long these items will remain useful aids the librarian in providing cost-effective service. Special librarians and information officers make good use of data generated by bibliometric techniques in selecting and maintaining collections of the most needed serials. Bradford's law, Lotka's law, Zipf's law, and citation analysis have contributed to the effective operation of special libraries. Two examples illustrate the use of bibliometric data. Researchers have identified the half-lives of journals for many scientific fields. For example, the half-life of a physics journal is 4.6 years. This means that half of the references in a current physics journal carry a publication date within the last 4.6 years. In addition to half-life, researchers also study journals' impact, importance, or influence. When one knows which journals receive the most bibliometric citations, one can decide which titles to acquire and keep. Like any statistical data, information from bibliometric studies is approximate. Therefore, though helpful in collection building and management, these studies assist only in decision making and cannot serve as a substitute for professional judgment. (An excellent review of bibliometrics appeared in the Summer 1981 issue of *Library Trends*.[12]) Other libraries will likely make increasing use of these techniques as they come under the economic and space pressures faced by special libraries.

Most special libraries have very current collections and, in terms of collection policy, would be level 4 (research), but without the retrospective element. Despite the heavy emphasis on current materials, the best-known selection aids provide little help to persons responsible for collection building in special libraries. Most of the material acquired for special libraries is very technical and of interest to only a few specialists; as a result, no meaningful market exists for review services. Recommendations of clients and knowledge of their information needs become the key elements in deciding what to buy.

Information center is a reasonable label for most special libraries, because they collect many information formats seldom found in other libraries. For example, special libraries frequently acquire patent and trademark information. In some cases, the library conducts regular searches for new information that may be of interest to the organization; most typically, it makes occasional searches for specific items. Two other classes of unusual information collected by some special libraries are well logs and remote sensing data. Well logs are records of drilling operations and are of interest to most energy companies involved in exploration. Remote sensing data take many forms, but are normally from satellite sources; these data, depending on their specific content, can be of interest to farmers, archaeologists, mining engineers, geologists, military officials, and others. Both formats are secured from specialized sources. Most are generally expensive (normally, cost is less important than access and speed of delivery) and require special handling. Some special libraries also handle restricted information. The restricted material may be labeled as classified by law or government agency, or it may take the form of internal documents that are important or sensitive. Staff members working with classified information are usually investigated and given clearances before they begin handling classified material. An interesting book on the handling of special materials is Ellis Mount's and Wilda B. Newman's *Top Secret / Trade Secret: Accessing and Safeguarding Restricted Information.*[13]

Special library collections tend to be *now* collections. Their purpose is to meet immediate needs, not future needs. When needed, the library secures historical material through interlibrary loan. Order placement takes place by telephone, and librarians use credit cards to pay for the items. Some special librarians place international telephone calls to order a single item for next-day air express delivery, with the costs of the telephone call and special delivery equaling or exceeding the cost of the item ordered. When that happens— and certainly it is not an everyday occurrence—it does give one a sense of how valuable information is in some organizations.

Online database access is something that most special libraries provide. Unlike other libraries, which tend to emphasize bibliographic databases, special libraries access numeric, bibliographic, and full-text services. A particular concern for today's special librarian is deciding when to join a database service for occasional access to information and when to acquire a hard copy of the same data. Indeed, this type of cost-benefit question confronts all types of libraries to some degree.

Needs assessment activities are also a regular part of the special library program, to a greater degree than in other types of libraries. Selective dissemination of information (SDI) is a technique often used in special libraries. By developing and maintaining user interest profiles, the library can continually monitor the information needs and interests of its service population, allowing more effective collection building. The technique also serves as a public relations activity. Every SDI notification serves as a reminder of the library's existence and value. Usually, SDI services are ineffective for large service populations, because the services are too costly to operate; however, several commercial firms offer SDI-like services. The Institute for Scientific Information (ISI) is one commercial organization that offers SDI-like services; it also publishes several indexing and abstracting tools to which many special libraries subscribe (e.g., *Science Citation Index* on paper or online).

These firms also provide bibliometric data, including information about half-lives and impact, about the titles they cover.

Selection Aids

Everyone involved in collection development recognizes the importance of bibliographies and review sources in building a library collection, even if they are rarely used. One can imagine a situation in which published aids are not used, but in such cases, the size of the library staff would have to increase dramatically or the number of items acquired would drop. The aids provide, to some degree, an overview of the output of publishers and media producers. Imagine the problems a library staff would have if no bibliographies or review sources existed. Each publisher and media producer would flood the library with catalogs and announcements of products; the filing and retrieval system for that material would add significantly to the library's workload. Finding the answer to the question, "How many books exist on vegetable gardening?" would entail going through thousands of catalogs and announcements to cull all relevant items. This merely underscores the fact that, despite their shortcomings and librarians' complaints about specific selection aids, they are time-saving tools essential to the efficient function of the library.

This section describes several categories of selection aids and mentions a few representative titles. All of the aids save time and frustration if one takes the time to study the titles in each one. As with any reference tool, the first step is to read the introductory material that the publisher or producer provides.

This chapter covers seven general categories of selection aids for books, which are summarized in table 4.2. Serials and government documents selection aids appear in the chapters about those formats. The categories covered in this chapter are:

1. current sources for in-print books

2. catalogs, flyers, and announcements

3. current reviews

4. national bibliographies

5. online databases

6. best books, recommended lists, and core collections

7. subject bibliographies

The examples within each category are selective at best. To give complete, worldwide coverage to all the titles in each group would require one or two books at least as long as this one.

Table 4.2   Selection aids.

Type of Selection Aid	Characteristics	Advantages	Disadvantages	Example
Current sources for in-print books	Contain citation information.	Identify new materials as they become available; particularly useful in large libraries attempting to achieve broad coverage.	Usually only provide for author searches; subject searches are time-consuming; do not contain review/content information	*American Book Publishing Record (ABPR)* *Books in Print*
Catalogs, flyers, and announcements	Marketing material designed and distributed by publishers.	May contain more information than in-print lists.	Advertising copy tends to present the item in its most favorable light	Some catalogs collected in: *Publishers Trade List Annual (PTLA)*
Current review sources	Designed to promote or evaluate works. Three types of reviews: 1. Reviews for persons making their living buying books 2. Reviews for subject specialists 3. Reviews for the general public.	Save staff time in locating/reviewing newly published works.	"Differential marketing" may affect promotion of titles; only a small percentage of total book output reviewed; delay in review's appearance in print; reviewer competence varies; reviews tend not to be critical in nature	*Library Journal* *Wilson Library Bulletin* *Choice* *Booklist* *New York Times Sunday Book Review*
National bibliographies	A listing of books published in or about a country. Usually nonprofit origin. Contain citation information.	Means for identifying out-of-print materials for retrospective collection development.	Main entry and subject entries can vary among sources; little consistency in listing series.	*British National Bibliography* *National Union Catalog* (complemented by OCLC and RLIN)
Online databases	Cooperative and individual library catalogs; serve as partial replacement for national bibliographies.	Access to millions of records worldwide; usually do not need separate access to national bibliography; useful for verification work; information can be downloaded and serve as bibliographic record in online catalog.	Not all countries well represented in online systems.	OCLC RLIN

(Table 4.2 continues on page 108.)

Table 4.2—*Continued.*

Type of Selection Aid	Characteristics	Advantages	Disadvantages	Example
Recommended, best, and core collection lists	Lists of items recommended for purchase.	Useful when used carefully.	Impractical to strive to collect every item listed; list becomes dated immediately upon publication.	*Public Library Catalog* *Books for Junior College Libraries*
Subject bibliographies	Listings prepared by subject experts and including critical evaluations.	Can exist for virtually any subject.	Currency and selectivity issues exist.	J. P. Lang, *Reference Sources for Small and Medium-Sized Libraries*, 5th ed. (Chicago: ALA, 1992)

Current Sources for In-Print Books

New books (those acquired during the year they are published) represent the majority of the materials acquired by most libraries. In some large research or archival libraries, this may not be the case, but even in such libraries, new books represent a large percentage of the total annual acquisitions. Every country in the world with any significant amount of publishing has a publication that attempts to list that nation's books in print. (One source of information about selection aids and dealers in countries in which English is not the native language is *Books in Other Languages*.[14]) Naturally, the degree of success varies, and access to such lists may be easy or difficult. For countries with a high volume of publishing (such as the United States, Great Britain, and other industrialized countries), there may be weekly lists of new books. (An example is Whitaker's *Bookseller.*) Most listings of in-print books provide information about the author, title, publisher, place of publication, date of publication, and price. In addition, the listing may offer information about length; special features; series information; International Standard Book Number (ISBN); and cataloging information, including subject headings. Cataloging information can be helpful in selection because, too often, the title of a book does not provide enough information to allow anyone to make an informed judgment about its content. More often than not, weekly lists facilitate only an author search; a subject search is time-consuming. Monthly lists are also common, offering either first listings or cumulations of weekly lists. Monthly cumulations include *American Book Publishing Record* (R. R. Bowker) and *Books of the Month* (Whitaker). Monthly lists that cumulate weekly lists offer the same information contained in weekly listings. In addition, monthly lists provide several means of access, usually subject, author, and title. In a few countries, prepublication announcements appear in a single source, such as *Forthcoming Books* (R. R. Bowker). *Books of the Month and Books to Come* (Whitaker) combines current and future items for a three-month period. Though such aids can be of some value in planning purchases of new books, two major factors limit their use: first, announced books do not always appear on schedule; and second, a few announced titles never appear.

In many countries, an annual list is the only list, or at least the only one that a library outside of the country can acquire. Annual lists range from a few hundred pages to multivolume sets. All contain the basic bibliographic information required to order a specific book (author, title, publisher, date); most include many of the features included in weekly or monthly lists, including author, title, and subject access. Examples of annual lists are *Books in Print* (R. R. Bowker); *Cumulative Book Index* (H. W. Wilson); *British Books in Print, Paperbacks in Print*, and *Whitaker's Cumulative Book List* (Whitaker); *Les Livres Disponibles* (Editions du Cercle de la Librarie); *Libros Españoles en Venta* (Instituto Nacional del Libro Español); and *Verzeichnis Lieferbarer Bucher* (Verlag der Buchhandler-Vereinigung GmbH). There is an in-print book list corresponding to almost every major language in which there is active publishing.

Most comprehensive in-print lists issued by commercial publishers are not complete. In most cases, the comprehensiveness of the list depends on information submitted by book and media publishers. The in-print list publisher has neither the staff nor the time to attempt to track down all possible titles for inclusion. Thus, if a publisher forgets or does not wish to submit data about a title or group of titles, nothing appears for those items. Because libraries and retail outlets use in-print lists as a buying tool, most larger publishers send in the information, but many smaller publishers do not. One should never assume that, because a specific title does not appear in the national in-print list, that item is out of print or does not exist. Even if other titles by the same publisher do appear, it is wise to write to the publisher to inquire about the availability of the missing item. Some persons have suggested that a few publishers do not appear in commercial in-print lists because of commercial competition. To date, no evidence shows that this did or does happen. However, an annual list that is based on copyright deposit data is more likely to be complete than is a commercial list.

National in-print lists are key tools in selection because they identify new materials as they become available. To be effective, individuals involved in selection and acquisition work must be familiar with these tools.

Weekly and monthly lists play a major role in the selection process of large libraries, regardless of type, because reviews are less important in making selection decisions. Reviews are less important because the collecting goal is to achieve broad coverage rather than a selection of the best available items. For small libraries, semiannual and annual listings are the key selection tools because they allow the selector to see a broader spectrum of the current output and help assure a better expenditure of limited funds. There is a slight danger that some items appearing in a less frequent list will be out of print, but for most small libraries, this is hardly a concern, because their "wish lists" far exceed the funds available.

Catalogs, Flyers, and Announcements

Publishers market their products through catalogs and other forms of promotional material. Some publishers use direct mail almost exclusively. They believe that national in-print lists bury their publications among too many others and that such in-print lists do not provide enough information to sell their books. Such publishers distribute catalogs listing all their available products and send out flyers and announcements of new titles. Even publishers who participate in combined in-print lists employ these sales methods.

Generally, such announcements contain more information about a book and its author(s) than do national in-print lists. When one cannot secure a review copy or find a published review, catalogs and flyers can provide useful selection data. It is necessary to use such information with caution. The purpose of the catalogs and flyers is to sell merchandise; though few publishers would lie about an item, advertising copy will present the item in its most favorable light. As the selector becomes familiar with publishers, she or he learns which publishers are objective and which puff their products more than the content warrants.

There are a few unscrupulous individuals who attempt to deceive libraries and individual book buyers. Here is an example: The senior author has a large personal collection of Native American reference works, of which two titles illustrate our point. One is a three-volume set (5-x-8 inches) titled *Dictionary of Indians of North America,* with the imprint Scholarly Press, St. Clair Shores, Michigan (1978). The other is a two-volume set (7-x-10 inches) titled *Biographical Dictionary of Indians of the Americas,* with the imprint American Indian Publishers, Newport Beach, California (1983). The content of both works is identical. The owners of these and many other imprints were convicted of fraud. However, their convictions did nothing to help the many libraries that paid for materials that were never delivered or that duplicated existing material. All one can do when confronted with information about what appears to be a title of high interest from an unfamiliar publisher is to ask for an examination copy and to ask selectors in other libraries if they know the firm. In time, one may associate a company name or location with potential problems. Flyers from unknown publishers offering large discounts for prepaid orders deserve second, third, and fourth looks before committing funds. One may never see the publication or get the money back.

An article suggesting that Mellen Press is a vanity publisher (rather than a trade publisher) generated a subsequent discussion on a collection development discussion list and illustrates the need to know publishers.[15] The discussion list exchange also shows how quickly information about a problem publisher can spread among selectors.

Libraries that make heavy use of announcements, flyers, and catalogs for selection must set up an efficient storage and retrieval system. In the past, commercial firms have attempted to collect publishers' catalogs and sell the collections to libraries (for example, R. R. Bowker's *Publisher's Trade List Annual* [*PTLA*]). The process has become cumbersome and the collections incomplete. Some years ago, Bowker's *Books in Print* was limited to information from the catalogs in *PTLA*. This is no longer the case. Too many publishers could not afford to be in *PTLA*. Thus, fewer and fewer libraries buy it, depending instead on their own filing system. Of course, the library keeps catalogs only from publishers and dealers that it uses on a regular basis.

Another source of information, available in an electronic format, is the Brodart TIPS program. TIPS is an acronym that stands for **T**itle **I**nformation **P**review **S**ervice, which provides reviews, customized to the profile of the subscribing library, of new and forthcoming titles. Information about this service is available on the Brodart home page (<http://www.brodart.com/BOOKS/b_tips.htm>).

Current Review Sources

Wherever a flourishing book trade exists, so does an equally strong book reviewing system. One can divide book reviews into three types: 1) reviews for persons making their living buying books (trade and professional book-sellers and librarians), 2) reviews for subject specialists, and 3) reviews for the general public. Book selectors use all three types, but those of greatest utility are the trade and professional reviews. Some differences in emphasis do exist among types of libraries. Special libraries make the least use of re-views, but when they do need a review, the first two categories receive the greatest credence, with a preference for the specialist reviews. Academic and school collection development personnel make extensive use of the first two types of reviews but seldom examine popular reviews. Public libraries fre-quently consult mass-market review sources along with the other types of sources.

Trade and professional reviews are of two types: those designed to pro-mote and those designed to evaluate. Although the primary market of such trade journals as *Publishers Weekly* (Cahners) and *Bookseller* (Whitaker) is booksellers (both wholesale and retail), librarians can and do make effective use of their reviews. The reviews alert booksellers to new titles that will receive heavy promotion. Publishers have a reasonably good grasp of which titles will sell well and which will not. Because of this, not all titles are pro-moted in the same manner, nor with equal funding; this is called *differential marketing*. In differential marketing, each title's marketing "allowance" var-ies based on its anticipated sales, as does the approach taken for the promo-tion of that title. A potentially good seller may receive extra promotional effort and funding to cultivate the book into a bestseller. Bookstore owners want to know about such titles ahead of time so they can order enough copies to meet the demand at its peak (usually no more than one or two months). Like book buyers, library patrons want to read bestsellers when they are bestsellers, not after demand subsides. Like bookstore owners, selection per-sonnel read trade reviews to assure that bestsellers are in the collection by the time interest peaks. Trade reviews may miss an unexpected bestseller or predict greater popularity than some books achieve, but they do help selec-tors identify which items will be in top demand.

Evaluative reviews prepared by librarians or by specialists for librari-ans are also extremely important in selection, especially in public and school libraries. One will find these reviews in almost all library publications (*Li-brary Journal*, *Wilson Library Bulletin*, and *LA Record*, for example). Nor-mally, such reviews are descriptive and evaluative; occasionally, they are comparative. Reviews of this type are particularly useful because the reviewers prepare them with library needs in mind.

As useful as they are, current review sources are not without their problems. One of the biggest problems is lack of comprehensive coverage. Although many library publications contain book reviews, only a small percentage of the total annual publishing output is reviewed. Some titles appear to garner more reviews than their content warrants; others never receive a single review. Each *Bowker Annual: Library and Book Trade Almanac* contains information about the number of titles reviewed. The 1998 volume shows the following pattern for 1997 books:

Booklist	7,569 (up 380 from 1996)
Bulletin of the Center for Children's Books	800 (unchanged)
Choice	6,788 (up 60 from 1996)
Horn Book Guide	3,312 (up 312 from 1996)
Library Journal	5,955 (up 402 from 1996)
*New York Review of Books**	410 (up 2 from 1996)
New York Times Sunday Book Review	2,200 (up 115 from 1996)
Publishers Weekly	6,600 (down 1,300 from 1996)

*Not all *New York Review of Books* reviews concern new books.

The Bowker Annual lists 14 review sources that published a total of 42,599 reviews, 6,408 of which appeared in newspapers.[16] The magnitude of the problem of coverage is clear when one realizes that at least 52,599 titles appeared in 1996.[17] If even only minimal overlap existed (and everyone knows that overlap is fairly extensive), the average number of reviews would be less than one per title.

Choice covers the largest percentage of new books of primary interest to academic libraries. However, during 1996 publishers released 10,494 titles in the fields of sociology and economics. If one adds history (3,559 new titles), there is a total of more than 14,000 new titles in those three fields alone. With only 6,788 reviews in 1997, *Choice* could not have completely reviewed even those three fields, to say nothing of other fields of academic interest.

Another sign of the problem in review coverage of new titles is found in *Book Review Digest* (*BRD*). Each year *BRD* publishes citations to and summaries of 5,000 to 6,000 new books. A nonfiction title must receive at least two reviews to be included in *BRD*. To find the reviews, *BRD* editors examine leading journals and newspapers that have large book review sections. Even with this large pool of potential sources, only 5,000 to 6,000 new books, out of an annual output of more than 40,000 titles, meet the inclusion criteria. What are the implications of incomplete review coverage? First, no one source of book reviews covers more than a fraction of the total output. Second, even if every book did get reviewed, there would be only 1.25 reviews per title. Third, many new titles never receive even one review. Even in Great Britain, where there is very high interest in the book trade and a strong tradition of reviewing, most books seldom receive more than one review, and a fairly large number of new books get none.

Another limit on the usefulness of reviews is the speed with which they appear. Most trade reviews appear on or before the publication date, whereas most professional (library) reviews appear several months after publication. One reason for the delay is that librarians and subject specialists write the reviews—one of the strong points of this approach. But first, the title must get to a review editor, who decides which titles ought to be reviewed and identifies an appropriate reviewer. The reviewer may or may not be able to review the item immediately. Eventually, the reviewer returns a review to the editor, who then edits the text and fits the review into the publishing schedule. This is a complex process, but it is necessary to disseminate professional opinions about new titles. For most journals, the only compensation a reviewer receives is the title she or he reviews. Using unpaid reviewers minimizes costs to the journals; hiring professionals to review books would greatly increase the journals' expenditures.

Some professional journals focus on a particular type of library, for example, *School Library Journal, Choice* (academic), and *Booklist* (public and school). Some materials are useful in more than one type of library, and journal editors try to make their publications useful to several types of libraries. Nevertheless, each journal has a primary emphasis, focusing on certain classes of books and using qualified reviewers who make value judgments about the materials covered.

A few journals (for example, *Booklist*) publish only positive reviews. This approach leaves one wondering why a certain title failed to appear. Was it because of a negative evaluation, or did the editors decide not to review it? Just as the general professional review sources cannot cover every new title, neither can the specialty sources. If a library depends on published reviews, this drawback can be important. One can wait a long time before being reasonably certain that no review will appear, and even then there are nagging questions as to why no review appeared.

When reading reviews, one must consider reviewer competence. Nonfiction titles require reviewers with subject expertise. For general trade books (titles intended for the general reader), it is not essential that the reviewer have in-depth subject knowledge for every book reviewed. When one gets beyond introductory texts and average readers' guides, the need for depth in background increases, until one reaches the level where one expert is reviewing another expert's publication for a few other experts in the field. Most academic disciplines have one or two journals that publish scholarly reviews for the field. Expert reviews of this type could be, but seldom are, of great assistance in developing a collection. A major reason for their lack of usefulness is that the reviews are slow to appear; often books are one or two years old by the time a review is published. Such delays are unacceptable in libraries with patrons who need up-to-date material. Adding to the problem are scholarly publishers' small press runs (small quantities printed); the item may be out of print by the time a librarian sees its review. Some online bookstores (such as Amazon.com) include reviews of titles carried, but the credibility of the reviewer must be carefully considered, as any reader may be a "reviewer."

The best source for the broadest coverage of academic titles from the United States is *Choice. Choice* reviewers are subject experts, and the reviews normally appear within a year of publication, often within three or four months after the title's release. To provide wide coverage, the reviews are relatively short, one or two paragraphs; thus, one sacrifices depth to gain coverage and speed.

A final category of review sources focuses upon the interests of the general reader or user of a format (for example, *The New York Times Book Review*, *Times Literary Supplement, High Fi*, and *Video Review*). Anyone concerned with building a collection geared to current popular interests must examine these publications as a normal part of the selection process. Editors of popular review sources must keep in touch with current interests and tastes to hold their readership. Because they can review only a small percentage of the new titles, their selections are made with great care and an eye on popular current interests. One knows that thousands of people will read the reviews, and demand for the reviewed titles will likely increase. Because of the need to be up-to-date, and the fact that most popular press reviewers are paid, reviews of most titles appear within a month or two after the title's release.

It is important to note that many reviewers who write for the popular press are friends of the authors they are reviewing.[18] Thus, one needs to be careful when using popular press reviews for anything more than identifying titles that may experience high demand.

Data about the number of book reviews published each year makes it clear that one will probably face a search problem (Where has that book been reviewed?) if one must use reviews for selection purposes. To some extent, indexing services that cover book reviews help, but they provide little assistance in tracking down the most current titles (from publication date to about eight months old). Two factors account for the problem. First, it takes time to produce and publish a review; second, after the review appears, it takes the indexing service time to prepare and publish its index. However, for older titles, the indexes can be major time savers. *Book Review Digest* (*BRD*) and *Book Review Index* (*BRI*) are two major American tools of this type. *BRI*, which does not include any annotations, lists the reviews that appear in about 325 journals and provides citations to more than 40,000 reviews each year. (Again, one might think that number means every title receives at least one review; not so, as some books receive as many as 20 reviews.) The price of gaining access to review citations is time. Certainly, *BRI* is a useful tool, but only for older titles.

In addition to the index publications devoted solely to book reviews, many general periodical indexes include book review citations. Selectors need to maintain at least a mental list of these sources, especially if reviews drive the selection process.

A final limit of book reviews is that, as a whole, they are not very critical. A reviewer does not work from the assumption that a book is bad. Rather, the expectation is that the book will be good, if not great. As a result, the vast majority of reviews are positive or noncommittal. One indexing product on CD-ROM (and used for checking citations for this book) allows one to search "review—favorable" and "review—unfavorable." Of the reviews in the database, 118,923 were favorable and only 11,521 were unfavorable; 32,903 were "mixed," and 3,107 offered "no opinion."

Certainly reviews are helpful when used with care. Book reviews can and do save libraries valuable staff time; no library has staff with enough time to read and review all of the potentially useful new titles that appear each year. However, a library should not employ reviews as a substitute for local judgment. Just because review *X* claims that an item is great does not mean that the item fits local needs. Reviews aid in the selection process, but they should never be the sole basis for selection. When selectors gain familiarity with book review editors and reviewers' biases, these tools become more valuable.

National Bibliographies

From time to time, most libraries will need to add some out-of-print books. Retrospective collection development is a normal part of academic and research library collection-building programs. School and public libraries buy replacement copies of the books that are lost or worn out from use. Special libraries do the least retrospective buying, but they do, on occasion, acquire out-of-print materials. (Chapter 12 discusses sources for acquiring out-of-print books.)

Before buying out-of-print material, it must first be identified. There are various sources for identifying authors, titles, publishers, and dates of publication of out-of-print items. One major source is the national bibliography network. Most countries with a book trade (except the United States) have some form of national bibliography. For purposes of this book, a *national bibliography* is a listing of books published in a country or about a country. One common characteristic of most of these bibliographies is their nonprofit origin. In many cases, the national library or a large research library publishes the bibliography. Some examples are the *British National Bibliography*, *Bibliographie de la France*, *Deutsche Bibliographie*, and *Gambia National Bibliography*.

Frequency of publication varies from weekly to yearly; in some cases, it occurs whenever there is enough material to warrant issuing a volume. In a few countries, the bibliography is based, in part, on books received by the country's copyright office. One bibliography of this sort is the *British National Bibliography* (*BNB*). If such bibliographies also include out-of-print titles added to the library's collection, the bibliography serves as both an in-print and retrospective aid. Several of the national and large research libraries have published or are publishing their public catalogs in multivolume sets (the British Library, Library of Congress, Bibliothèque Nationale). If selectors have access to a full set of the public catalog, plus the updated material, they have an almost complete record of the official holdings of the library. Because of the size of these libraries, they collect almost everything produced in and about their countries. As a result, their published catalogs serve as national bibliographies. Selectors use them to verify the existence of a particular work and as a source for interlibrary loan (usually as a last resort).

The *National Union Catalog* (*NUC*), published by the Library of Congress, contains entries for libraries other than the Library of Congress. The *NUC* contains information about other libraries that hold a particular book;

in some cases, the book is not even in the Library of Congress collection. The *NUC* is not a true national bibliography because its coverage is not comprehensive. For comprehensive coverage of current titles published in or about the United States, the best sources are national bibliographic utilities such as OCLC or RLIN, the online version of *Books in Print*, and the Library of Congress CDS Alert Service.

A searcher can learn all of the following information from any national bibliography: author, full title, publisher, place and date of publication, pagination, and form of main entry for the book in the library. In most cases, one can locate information about special features of the book, such as whether it contains bibliographies, illustrations, charts, or maps; series information; scope notes; and subject information, including the classification number and subject heading tracings. A few national bibliographies provide the original price of items.

Many large academic and research libraries use the current issues of *NUC*, *BNB*, and other national bibliographies as selection aids. For most libraries, national bibliographies, when they are used at all, are used for verification rather than selection. No matter what the purpose, selectors must use national bibliographies with care. For example, several years ago, the senior author searched three titles in the then-basic American and British bibliographies: *Publishers Weekly (PW)*, *American Book Publishing Record (ABPR)*, *Publisher's Trade List Annual (PTLA)*, *Books in Print (BIP)*, *Subject Guide to Books in Print*, *Paperbound Books in Print*, *Cumulative Book Index (CBI)*, *National Union Catalog (NUC)*, *Bookseller*, *British Books in Print (BBIP)*, *Whitaker's Cumulative Book List (CBL)*, *British National Bibliography (BNB)*, and *British Museum Catalog of Printed Books*. All three titles were monographs that had personal author entries. Two of the titles were available in both hardbound and paper covers; two of the books were American and one was British.

As indicated by the list of bibliographies searched, both the United States and Great Britain have reasonably comprehensive bibliographic networks for new books. However, despite searching each title through all available approaches (author, title, and sometimes subject) in each bibliography, only two of the fourteen bibliographies listed all three books. This study showed

- American titles are slow to appear in British sources and vice versa.
- When a publisher releases a title in England and the United States at the same time, it appears in the trade bibliographies of both countries.
- Subject entries varied even within the same bibliography.
- There is little consistency in the listing of series.
- When searching a library's catalog, one must know that library's rules for establishing the main entry.

Though most of the sources searched have undergone various changes since the study, there are still many factors to keep in mind when using national and trade bibliographies.

Online Databases

Online databases, in the form of both cooperative and individual library catalogs, are, in a way, replacements for national bibliographies. With organizations such as OCLC and RLG providing access to databases of millions of records from thousands of libraries around the world, most libraries do not need access to national bibliographies for collection development. Certainly for retrospective work, national bibliographies are important, and for countries not well represented in the online systems, they are essential. However, for most libraries in the United States, the online databases are much more useful.

For verification work, online databases often prove to be the best single source. Not only can searchers verify the existence of a title, but, with proper equipment, they can also download the information to the library's acquisition system, thus eliminating the need to key in entries. Further, once the library receives and catalogs the item, the information from the online service can serve as the bibliographic record in the library's online public catalog. Another use of the online databases is in selection. Because systems like OCLC and RLIN provide information about which libraries hold certain titles, it is possible for a selector to determine which local libraries already hold an item under consideration. If resource-sharing agreements are in place, and the selector thinks the item will have low use, the decision may be to not purchase the title.

Yet another use of the databases is for collection evaluation. A library can buy CD-ROMs that contain holdings information about a particular group of libraries, as well as its own holdings. The data comes from one of the large bibliographic utilities. Using this data, the library can make a variety of comparisons of its holdings against other libraries on the disk. (Chapters 9 and 10 discuss the uses of online databases in more detail.)

Best Books, Recommended Lists, and Core Collections

The material on the server touches on the problem of generating "best of" lists or lists of items recommended for purchase. Such lists are useful when selectors employ them carefully. A brief examination of the amount of material in such lists will dispel any doubts about the subjectivity of the selection process. Titles such as *Public Library Catalog* (H. W. Wilson), *School Librarians' Sourcebook* (R. R. Bowker), *Books for Junior College Libraries* (Books on Demand), or *Handbook of Contemporary Fiction for Public Libraries and School Libraries* (Scarecrow Press) show some overlap but also some differences. The differences arise from the purposes of the lists and the individuals who make the selections. Personal opinions vary, and these lists reflect either one person's opinion or a composite of opinions about the value of a particular title.

Few specialists in collection development would claim that a library ought to hold any title just because of its presence on two or more recommended lists. Consider a list that contains basic books for undergraduate programs in mathematics, published by a national association of mathematics teachers. One would expect a library that serves an undergraduate mathematics program to hold a high percentage of the listed titles, but even in such a case, one should not expect to find every title. Why not? A major reason is the emphasis of the school's program; there may be no need for a particular title. Another reason is that, often, several equally good alternatives exist. A final reason is that the list is out of date on its publication date; almost immediately, new titles supersede the titles listed. Also, trying to get a copy of every title on a list can be extremely time-consuming. Unless there is agreement that it is important to secure every title, do not spend the time; retrospective buying requires much more time than buying in-print titles.

Subject Bibliographies

Subject bibliographies suffer from many of the same limitations as lists of best or recommended items: currency and selectivity. When subject experts prepare a bibliography and they write critical evaluations for the items listed, such publications provide useful information for both selection and collection evaluation activities. Only the imagination of the compilers limits the range of subject bibliographies. A quick review of some publishers' catalogs proves that compilers have unlimited imagination. (Two good reviews of subject selection aids for academic libraries are McClung's *Selection of Library Materials in the Humanities, Social Sciences and Sciences*[19] and Shapiro and Whaley's *Selection of Library Materials in Applied and Interdisciplinary Fields.*[20]) In most broad fields, at least one such bibliography exists, and for most fields several are available. When there have been multiple editions, it is advisable to check on the amount of change between editions. Do new editions merely add more titles, or is there a real revision, with older, superseded titles dropped and new assessments made of all the items? One should not depend on published reviews but do one's own checking before using such a bibliography as a selection aid.

Using Citation Information for Selection

Many selection aids provide only the basic bibliographic information about an item. Selectors using only citation information select thousands of titles to add to library collections each year. How do they make their decisions from such limited data? Ross Atkinson proposed a model that, in time, may prove useful for neophyte selectors. He based his model on the citation, that is, "any string of natural language signs that refers to or represents, regardless of its textual location, a particular information source or set of sources."[21] Atkinson noted that every selector begins work with a personal "I," the biases and knowledge base that each of us develops over time. The "I" is one element in his model. The citation is a "text" that the "I" reads and judges both from past experience and from the context of the citation. Atkinson proposed three general contexts: syntagmatic, supplemental, and resolution.

Most bibliographic citations follow a convention for the presentation— the content and order—of the entry. (More and more, ANSI Z39.29-1977, American National Standard for Bibliographic References, is the convention selection aids use.) The standard means that the selector can expect to see the same pattern in entries in various selection aids. That order provides "information" regarding the item cited (Atkinson's syntagmatic context). With experience, one's judgment about an item may change as one examines each element of the citation.

A selector reading a citation about conditions on the Dakota reservations in South Dakota would make different judgments about the content of the cited item depending on whether the citation read "Washington, D.C., 1986" or "Pine Ridge, S.D., 1977." Similarly, the selector's judgment of a title about apartheid would depend on whether its imprint was "Johannesburg, 1993" or "Maseru, 1993." Another example of how an element could modify a judgment is a title implying comprehensive or comparative treatment of a broad or complex subject, with pagination indicating a much shorter book than would be reasonable for the topic. Who authored the title is a key factor in the selection process. Certainly, this context relates to all the factors writers on selection have discussed for years: accuracy, currency, bias, style, and so on; what Atkinson did was provide a framework for understanding how the process operates.

When the citation string includes subject descriptors, profound modification in judgment can occur (Atkinson's supplemental context). An entry in a selection aid may seem appropriate for Tozzer Library (Harvard University) until one encounters the subject heading *juvenile*. Without the supplemental context, it is possible and even probable that the library would order some inappropriate items because of inadequate information. (This is a good reason to follow Ranganathan's rule to know the publishers; even then one may be fooled occasionally.)

As aptly noted by Metz and Stemmer, "even the best bibliographers can be expected to be familiar with only a minority of authors in their fields, and because titles provide limited information, knowledge of the publisher often furnishes the decisive element in selection decisions."[22] The authors surveyed collection development officers at ARL and Oberlin group institutions as to their perceptions of the reputations of academic and larger commercial publishing firms. Their research indicated that "although not the most important factor in selecting a book, the reputation of the publisher does play a significant role in collection development."[23]

John Calhoun and James Bracken[24] proposed an index of publisher quality. (See also a follow-up study by Goedeken,[25] and the definitions of *quality* and *relevance* offered by Metz and Stemmer.[26]) Although their article describes an index or model for an academic library, it is easy to apply to any type of library. Their concept was very straightforward:

1. Determine the top 50 to 75 producers/publishers from which the library buys. Select a number of book awards, such as the Caldecott or a best-of-the-year award (e.g., *Choice*'s annual Outstanding Academic Books); or select a frequently updated list of recommended titles (e.g., Bill Katz's *Magazines for* ...) that are appropriate for the library.

2. Develop a table of award-winning titles by publisher based on the award lists. Total the number of award winners for each publisher over a period of time (e.g., two, three, or five years).

3. Calculate a ratio based on each publisher's average output (during the time period covered by the award lists) and the number of award-winning titles published during that time.

The authors suggested that using this index could improve one's chances of selecting the best books without seeing reviews. For example, a person who blindly selected books from Academic Press stood a 1 in 46.67 chance of picking an award winner; the odds with Basic Books were 1 in 10.97. The effort to collect the data to create the index, though considerable, would familiarize selectors with the publishers from which the library frequently buys as well as with the publishers' track records in producing highly recommended titles.

As long as individuals and not machines assign subject headings and classification numbers in selection aids, selectors must realize there is a large element of subjectivity in the process. Normally only one class number appears; the problem is that another person might reach a different opinion about the item and assign other headings and classification numbers. If a selector uses several sources with overlapping coverage and they also supply subject assignments, the selector may gain some additional insight as to subject content. However, more often than not, the selector makes her or his decision on only one source of information. One seldom has time to track down entries in several sources, especially if the initial findings are positive.

To return to Atkinson's model (supplemental context), another type of supplemental information is the source in which the citation appears. In national bibliographies, compilers make no value judgments regarding the merits of an item, whereas in a publication like *Booklist*, one knows it contains only recommended items. Thus, each selection aid carries with it a form of supplemental context. And, as Atkinson notes, a patron request may be the supplemental information that determines the selection decision, regardless of any other contextual information. This is especially true in special libraries.

Atkinson's last category, the context of resolution, ties in the selector's personality. This context consists of three elements—archival, communal, and thematic—that relate to a selector's attitudes, knowledge, values, perceptions, and personality. Atkinson defined *archival* as the selector's knowledge of the collection and its strengths and weaknesses. *Communal* refers to the knowledge of the clientele and its interests, and *thematic* refers to the selector's knowledge of the total current output on a topic (theme) area. How these three elements interact is a function of the selector's background, values, and personality as well as of the information environment in which the selector works. Atkinson suggested that one of the elements will dominate most of the time. For a school media center or industrial center, the communal context would most likely dominate. In research libraries, the archival context is the most important. For a public library, where funds are scarce and getting the best materials for the available monies is essential, the thematic context is usually the most influential.

The Atkinson model is useful as a way of thinking about selection, and in time, with more research, it may become part of a true theory of selection. Every beginning selector should read his article. (Two other good sources are Schwartz's "Book Selection, Collection Development, and Bounded Rationality"[27] and Rutledge and Swindler's "The Selection Decision."[28])

To conclude this chapter, we will outline the steps we follow when using selection aids that supply subject information. Most of the time, Dr. Evans selects in the area of anthropology and sociology. One quickly learns that, for anthropology, appropriate material can appear under a wide variety of class numbers or subject headings. If one confines one's search to the anthropology class numbers, one will miss important new titles. Thus, one must scan long lists of titles to identify the appropriate title for the library. To do this quickly and effectively, one needs a system for thinking about the titles scanned.

Whenever possible, start by looking at the subject information with this question in mind: Does this fall within the areas of our collecting? If the answer is yes, then consider whether the material is of interest to the library's clientele. An affirmative answer to that question raises the third consideration: How much do we already have on this subject (what formats, how old)? If the title remains under consideration at this point, think about the cost of the item: Can the library afford to acquire it? Also consider quality, taking publisher and author track records into account. If the item is not a one-time purchase, think about the library's ability to maintain the acquisition. Occasionally, you may encounter a reprint of a title already in the collection. Then you must attempt to determine whether there is new material in the reprint (frequently there is a new introduction or other additions); the question is, How much new material is there? Another question is, What is the condition and use pattern of the item in the collection? More and more frequently, there is a question about the need for special handling, as is the case with CD-ROMs or floppy disks that come with traditional books. Two final questions to consider are: What is the source of the information under consideration, that is, review media, publisher's flyer, vendor announcement, trade or professional publication, national bibliography, or other? and, Will the acquisition of the item cause a problem, such as objections, mutilation, or theft?

This approach requires selectors to know the user population, collection content, collection priorities, materials budget status, primary authors and publishers or producers in the selector's areas of responsibility, and review sources and general production levels in the selector's areas of responsibility.

Summary

Although this has been a lengthy discussion, it covers only the high points and basic issues of book selection. Selectors must know their service population, what exists in the collection, types of formats and materials that meet the needs of a given situation, and vendor sources that can supply appropriate materials. In addition, selectors must be able to choose among a variety of items and formats to get the most cost-effective items for a given situation; determine quality and its many variations; balance quantities, qualities, and costs; and recognize the real value or nonvalue of gifts. Learning to be a book selector is a lifelong process, and the items listed in the bibliography provide leads to material about various aspects of this challenging, exciting, and rewarding area of information work.

Notes

1. Junior College Library Section, Association of College and Research Libraries, "Statement on Quantitative Standards for Two-Year Learning Resources Programs" (Chicago: American Library Association, 1979).

2. "Standards for Community, Junior and Technical College Learning Resources Programs," *College & Research Libraries News* 55, no. 9 (October 1994): 572–85.

3. David Kaser, "Standards for College Libraries," *Library Trends* 31 (Summer 1982): 7–18.

4. "Standards for College Libraries, 1995 Edition," *College & Research Libraries News* 56, no. 4 (April 1995): 245–57.

5. "Introduction," *Choice* 1 (March 1964): ii.

6. J. P. Schmitt and S. Saunders, "Assessment of *Choice* as a Tool for Selection," *College & Research Libraries* 44 (September 1983): 375–80.

7. "The Red and the Black," *Publishers Weekly* 227 (April 19, 1985): 26–30.

8. Readers are encouraged to visit the following Websites to view how each of the three publishers has provided reviews of current works: *Booklist,* <http://www.ala.org/booklist/index.html>; *Library Journal,* <http://www.ljdigital.com>; and *PW Interactive,* <http://www.bookwire.com/PW/pw.html>. Accessed 4 October 1999.

9. Betty Rosenberg and Diane Tixier Herald, *Genreflecting: A Guide to Reading Interests in Genre Fiction*, 4th ed. (Englewood, Colo.: Libraries Unlimited, 1995).

10. Judith Senkevitch and James H. Sweetland, "Public Libraries and Adult Fiction: Another Look at a Core List of 'Classics,' " *Library Resources & Technical Services* 42, no. 2 (April 1998): 102–12.

11. National Committee for Good Reading, *Reader's Guide to Non-Controversial Books* (Castle Rock, Colo.: Hi Willow Research and Publishing, 1986).

12. *Library Trends* 30 (Summer 1981). Edited by William Gray Potter.

13. Ellis Mount and Wilda B. Newman, *Top Secret / Trade Secret: Accessing and Safeguarding Restricted Information* (New York: Neal-Schuman, 1985).

14. *Books in Other Languages* (Ottawa: Canadian Library Association, 1970).

15. Warren St. John, "Vanity's Fare: The Peripatetic Professor and His Peculiarly Profitable Press," *Lingua Franca* 3 (September/October, 1993): 1, 22–25, 62.

16. *The Bowker Annual Library and Book Trade Almanac,* 43d ed. (New York: R. R. Bowker, 1998), 539.

17. Ibid., 522.

18. Katherine Dalton, "Books and Book Reviewing, or Why All Press Is Good Press," *Chronicles* 18 (January 1989): 20–22.

19. Patricia A. McClung, *Selection of Library Materials in the Humanities, Social Sciences and Sciences* (Chicago: American Library Association, 1985).

20. Beth Shapiro and John Whaley, *Selection of Library Materials in Applied and Interdisciplinary Fields* (Chicago: American Library Association, 1987).

21. Ross Atkinson, "The Citation as Intertext: Toward a Theory of the Selection Process," *Library Resources & Technical Services* 28 (April/June 1984): 109–19.

22.   Paul Metz and John Stemmer, "A Reputational Study of Academic Publishers," *College & Research Libraries* 57 (May 1996): 235.

23.   Ibid., 245.

24.   John Calhoun and James K. Bracken, "An Index of Publisher Quality for the Academic Library," *College & Research Libraries* 44 (May 1983): 257–59.

25.   Edward Goedeken, "An Index to Publisher Quality Revisited," *Library Acquisitions: Practice and Theory* 17 (Fall 1993): 263–68.

26.   Metz and Stemmer, "A Reputational Study of Academic Publishers," 238.

27.   Charles A. Schwartz, "Book Selection, Collection Development, and Bounded Rationality," *College & Research Libraries* 50 (May 1989): 328–43.

28.   John Rutledge and Luke Swindler, "The Selection Decision: Defining Criteria and Establishing Priorities," *College & Research Libraries* 48 (March 1987): 123–31.

Further Reading

General

Atkinson, Ross. "Managing Traditional Materials in an Online Environment: Some Definitions and Distinctions for a Future Collection Management." *Library Resources & Technical Services* 42, no. 1 (January 1998): 7–20.

Batt, F. "Folly of Book Reviews." In *Options for the 80s*, edited by M. D. Kathman and V. F. Massman, 277–89. Greenwich, Conn.: JAI Press, 1981.

Blake, V. P. "Role of Reviews and Reviewing Media in the Selection Process." *Collection Management* 11, nos. 1/2 (1989): 1–40.

Cline, G. S. "Application of Bradford's Law to Citation Data." *College & Research Libraries* 42 (January 1981): 53–61.

COLLDV-L@USC.EDU. Library Collection Development Discussion List. To subscribe to the list, send the following message to LISTSERV@USC.EDU:
SUBSCRIBE COLLDV–L Your–First–name Your–last–name.

D'Aniello, C. "Bibliography and the Beginning Bibliographer." *Collection Building* 6 (Summer 1984): 11–19.

Dickinson, G. K. *Selection and Evaluation of Electronic Resources*. Englewood, Colo.: Libraries Unlimited, 1993.

ECOLL@UNLLIB.UNL.EDU. Collection Development of Electronic Resources Discussion List. To subscribe to the list, send the following message to LISPROC@UNLLIB.UNL.EDU:
SUBSCRIBE ECOLL Your–First–Name Your–Last–Name.

Eisenberg, H. "So Many Books, So Little Space: What Makes a Book Review Editor Pick up a Book?" *Publishers Weekly* 231 (April 10, 1989): 25–30.

Furnham, A. "Book Reviews as a Selection Tool for Librarians: Comments from a Psychologist." *Collection Management* 8 (Spring 1986): 33–43.

Katz, B. "Who Is the Reviewer?" *Collection Building* 7 (Spring 1985): 33–35.

Ryland, J. "Collection Development and Selection: Who Should Do It?" *Library Acquisitions: Practice and Theory* 6, no. 1 (1982): 13–17.

Sandy, John H. *Approval Plans: Issues and Innovations* (New York: Haworth Press, 1996).

Stiffler, S. A. "Core Analysis in Collection Management." *Collection Management* 5 (Fall/Winter 1983): 135–49.

Academic

Atkinson, R. "Humanities Scholarship and the Research Library." *Library Resources & Technical Services* 39, no. 1 (January 1995): 79–85.

———. "Old Forms, New Forms: The Challenge of Collection Development." *College & Research Libraries* 50 (September 1989): 507–20.

Carrigan, D. "Data-Guided Collection Development: A Promise Unfilled." *College & Research Libraries* 57, no. 5 (September 1996): 429–37.

Chu, F. T. "Librarian-Faculty Relations in Collection Development." *Journal of Academic Librarianship* 23 (January 1997): 15–20.

Dickinson, D. W. "Rationalist's Critique of Book Selection for Academic Libraries." *Journal of Academic Librarianship* 7 (July 1981): 138–43.

Jenkins, P. O. "Book Reviews and Faculty Book Selection." *Collection Building* 18, no. 1 (1999): 4–5.

Luchsinger, D. "Developing the Reference Collection." In *Community College Reference Services*. Edited by Bill Katz, 106–12. Metuchen, N.J.: Scarecrow Press, 1992.

MacLeod, B. "*Library Journal* and *Choice*: A Review of Reviews." *Journal of Academic Librarianship* 7 (March 1981): 23–28.

Miller, W., and D. S. Rockwood. "Collection Development from a College Perspective." *College & Research Libraries* 40 (July 1979): 318–24.

Pasterczyk, C. E. "Checklist for the New Selector." *College & Research Libraries News* 49 (July/August 1988): 434–35.

Rea, J. W. "A Core Collection Strategy for Protecting Undergraduate Education at a Comprehensive University." *Journal of Academic Librarianship* 23 (March 1998): 145–50.

Schmitt, J. P., and S. Saunders. "Assessment of *Choice* as a Tool for Selection." *College & Research Libraries* 44 (September 1983): 375–80.

Public

Baker, S. L. *The Responsive Public Library Collection*. Englewood, Colo.: Libraries Unlimited, 1993.

Clewis, B. "Selecting Science Books for the General Reader." *Collection Building* 10, nos. 1/2 (1990): 12–15.

Cuesta, Y. J. "From Survival to Sophistication: Hispanic Needs = Library Needs." *Library Journal* 115 (May 15,1990): 26–28.

Haighton, T. *Bookstock Management in Public Libraries*. London: C. Poingley, 1985.

Pearson, J. C. "Sources of Spanish-Language Material." *Library Journal* 115 (May 15, 1990): 29–33.

Sariks, Joyce G. "Providing the Fiction Your Patrons Want: Managing Fiction in a Medium-Sized Public Library." Co-published simultaneously in *Acquisitions Librarian,* no. 19 (1998): 11–28; and *Fiction Acquisition / Fiction Management: Education and Training.* Edited by Georgine N. Olson, 11–28. New York: Haworth Press, 1998.

Scheppke, J. B. "Public Library Book Selection." *Unabashed Librarian,* no. 52 (1984): 5–6.

Serebnick, J. "Book Reviews and the Selection of Potentially Controversial Books in Public Libraries." *Library Quarterly* 51 (October 1981): 390–409.

Swope, D. K. "Quality Versus Demand: Implications for Children's Collections." In *Festschrift in Honor of Dr. Arnulfo D. Trejo,* 66–73. Tucson, Ariz.: Graduate Library School, University of Arizona, 1984.

School

Altan, S. "Collection Development in Practice in an Independent School." *Catholic Library World* 54 (October 1982): 110–12.

Ekhaml, L. "Peer Review: Student Choices." *School Library Journal* 37 (September 1991): 196.

England, C., and A. M. Fasick. *ChildView: Evaluating and Reviewing Materials for Children*. Englewood, Colo.: Libraries Unlimited, 1987.

Miller, M. L. "Collection Development in School Library Media Centers: National Recommendations and Reality." *Collection Building* 1 (1987): 25–48.

Patrick, Gay D. *Building the Reference Collection: A How-to-Do-It Manual for School and Public Libraries* (New York: Neal Schuman, 1992).

Reeser, C. "Silk Purse or Sow's Ear: Essential Criteria in Evaluation of Children's Literature." *Idaho Librarian* 34 (October 1982): 157–58.

Van Orden, P. J. *The Collection Program in Schools: Concepts, Practices, and Information Sources*. 2d ed. Englewood, Colo.: Libraries Unlimited, 1995.

White, Brenda H., ed. *Collection Management for School Library Media Centers*. New York: Haworth Press, 1986.

Special

Bell, J. A., et al. "Faculty Input in Book Selection: A Comparison of Alternative Methods." *Bulletin of the Medical Library Association* 75 (July 1987): 228–33.

Byrd, G. D., et al. "Collection Development Using Interlibrary Loan Borrowing and Acquisitions Statistics." *Medical Library Association Bulletin* 70 (January 1982): 1–9.

Dalton, L., and E. Gartenfeld. "Evaluating Printed Health Information for Consumers." *Medical Library Association Bulletin* 69 (July 1981): 322–24.

Elder, N. J., et al. "Collection Development, Selection, and Acquisitions of Agricultural Materials." *Library Trends* 38 (Winter 1990): 442–73.

Hurt, C. *Information Sources in Science and Technology*. Englewood, Colo.: Libraries Unlimited, 1988.

McCleary, H. "Practical Guide to Establishing a Business Intelligence Clearing House." *Database* 9 (June 1986): 40–46.

Parker, R. H. "Bibliometric Models for Management of an Information Store." *Information Science* 33 (March 1982): 124–38.

5

Producers of
Information Materials

Producers of information materials are grappling with technology issues just as are libraries. Chapter 1 noted two of the issues facing producers. First, in the opening paragraph about the Booker Prize, the question of what *is* a book was raised; second, later in the chapter, the issue of how to handle pricing of electronic materials was introduced. Richard Cox addressed some of the issues in his article "Taking Sides on the Future of the Book,"[1] in which he commented on the Internet, books-on-demand, electronic books, and other nonprint/nonlinear electronic resources. At one point he wrote, "I still read books as well as navigate the Internet. I still write books as well as upload electronic texts on the World Wide Web. I still browse bookstores as well as scan electronic library catalogs."[2] Those words are probably reasonable descriptors of the behavior of a great many of us and, in our opinion, will remain so for some time to come. They are also probably good indicators for what a great many producers of information materials are and will be doing for some time: producing a mix of traditional and electronic products.

In the past, one could categorize information producers by product: 1) those who produced printed matter (books, periodicals, newspapers, and the like), and 2) those who produced audiovisual materials. Seldom did a producer work in both areas. Today the situation is different. Though some companies are solely devoted to the production of print or audiovisual materials, most trade book publishers also have one or more electronic and audiovisual lines. University presses and other scholarly publishers are also moving into electronic publishing. An example is the University of North Carolina Press's CD-ROM *Excavating Occaneechi Town*.[3]

Writers have been predicting a paperless society, office, or library for some time. (For example, Frederick W. Lancaster has written extensively about this topic. One of his more wide-ranging titles is *Libraries and Librarians in an Age of Electronics*.[4]) Despite such predictions, printed materials are still very much with us and probably will be for some time. Print materials still comprise the largest percentage of items available through most libraries and information centers.

Some sense of the staying power of print is found in sources such as *Books in Print (BIP)*. The 1988 edition of *BIP* listed 781,292 titles; by 1998 that number had more than doubled to over 1.6 million. (*Note:* These numbers are based upon unique ISBNs; thus, many titles would be double-counted if there were both hardcover and paper versions in print. Some popular titles might even be triple-counted, if there was also an audio version available.) Certainly electronic products are being produced, but as of 1999 they had not noticeably slowed the production of print materials.

A major reason for the staying power of books is that paper copies still provide the least expensive means of distributing large quantities of timely information to a large number of people. Certainly one can mount a long document (300 or more pages) on the Internet; many people do. Further, it is obvious that any number of individuals can simultaneously read that document. However, very few individuals using that material attempt to read it off the computer screen. Rather, they print some portion or the entire file and read the material in a printed form. (Anyone with experience in a reference department is well aware of the volume of printing being done of electronic data, most of which is in relatively short files.) Also, some people are uncomfortable with technology-based information sources. There is always some question, with electronic files, about the integrity of the material: is what one sees on the screen what the author originally input? Finally, many people still like to read in bed, on the subway, at the beach, and other places where technology-based systems are inconvenient, if not impossible, to use. (Try reading a CRT screen in full sunlight at the beach.)

The first portion of this chapter examines publishing, that is, the production of printed material, with comments about the changing nature of the field. The second portion discusses audiovisual production. (The chapters on serials, government documents, Web resources, and electronic materials, as well as others, all touch on issues related to the electronic information environment of today.) The chapter provides an overview of the important production characteristics of both types of products, with enough depth for one to begin to understand how information producers operate.

What Is Publishing?

What is publishing? That question has been with us, at least in the United States, for almost 300 years. Publishers and others have debated whether publishing's purpose was/is cultural or commercial, or both.

In the abstract, and to some degree in the real world, "the book" is a cultural artifact as well as an essential means of recording and preserving the culture of a society. Certainly libraries of all types have, to a greater or lesser degree, some role to play in preserving and passing on their society's cultural values and heritage. Thus, books have taken on a special aura of importance—some might even say sacredness—that is very different from that of, say, clothes, cars, or cameras. Discarding worn-out items like the latter may bring some scowls from a few people. However, there is widespread disapproval of doing the same with a book. From early childhood one hears, "don't bend the pages," "wash your hands before using your books," "treat your books with respect"—and being labeled a "book burner" is something no one wants.

Because of the cultural and literary aspects involved in the production of books, there is some sense that a literate society *must* have a publishing program of some type. Further, that publishing *must* produce books for the good of society. Sometimes supporters of the cultural purpose seem to paint a picture of noble people—from writer, to editor, to owner—who are free of the concerns of economics and profit. (A less flattering view might be that they act as the gatekeepers to or controllers of knowledge.) Does that mean, then, that there should be no concern with costs? Clearly not. The romantic view of publishing is nice but unrealistic; even most government publications have a price. (As we will see in chapter 9 on government information, the cost of that information is rising.) The fact is, the bottom line of publishing is the bottom line. Without an expectation of a reasonable return, why would anyone invest time and money in publishing? Certainly one can debate what "reasonable" means, but no one should question the need for a return beyond that of survival. The return ought to be greater than that of putting the money in an insured savings account, as there are substantial risks in publishing—not everything sells as fast as one might hope, if it sells at all. Publishers are in the commercial world, and often they have stockholders to take into account as well as the interests of readers and society.

Albert Greco summed up the present situation in U.S. publishing as follows:

> Many industry analysts believe that publishing is in disarray, dangerously weakened by steep returns, stark sales figures, fickle and price sensitive customer base, the "rise" of chains and super-stores and price clubs and the concomitant "decline" of independent book store[s], a population more interested in watching television than in reading books, paper thin profit margins, staggering technological challenges, and author advances that dumbfound even seasoned industry veterans ... . Its best days are indeed ahead, a fact that excites tens of thousands of people every day about this wonderful, funny, and, at times, hard business.[5]

Publishing is both a cultural and a commercial activity, but without the commercial there would be no cultural purpose. Librarians should be among the first to discard the stereotype of the publisher as a retiring, highly sophisticated literary person interested only in creative quality, just as publishers should abandon the view of the librarian as a woman with her hair in a bun, wearing horn-rimmed glasses, with a constant "shush" on her lips.

When one is going to work day in and day out with an industry, even if one is just buying its products, some knowledge of that industry will make everyone's life a little easier. An understanding of the trade's characteristics—such as how producers determine prices, how they distribute products, and what services one can expect—can improve communication between producers and buyers. Under the best of circumstances, a great deal of communication exists between the library and the trade regarding orders.

This knowledge provides the librarian with some understanding of, if not sympathy for, the problems of producers. Publishers who depend on library sales know (or should know) a great deal about library problems and operations. They often joke about how uninformed librarians are about the trade. The present strained relationship between libraries and publishers developed, in part, because neither group fully understood nor tried to understand the other's position. (For instance, copyright and pricing are areas of controversy.) Yet, we also know that when two parties discuss problems with mutual understanding of the other's position, the working relationship will be more pleasant. Each is more willing to make an occasional concession to the other's needs; this flexibility can, in turn, foster mutually beneficial alliances.

Book selection and collection development courses in library schools usually touch only lightly on publishers and their problems, as teachers often claim there is insufficient time to give more coverage to this important topic. Further, courses in the history of the book trade seldom have time to deal with the contemporary situation, because it is not yet history. Most schools' curricula do not have a place for a course in contemporary production. Even if they did, most students would not have time for it in their one-year course of study. For this reason, students lack information that could prove invaluable, because knowing what happens in publishing can affect the selection process. First, knowing something about publishing helps selectors identify the most likely sources of materials; that is, which among the thousands of producers are most likely to produce the needed material. Second, by keeping up-to-date with what is happening in publishing, one can anticipate changes in quality and format. Third, librarians may be able to influence publishing decisions, if the publisher is aware that the librarian is knowledgeable about the issues involved in developing profitable books.

How Publishing Works

Publishers supply the capital and editorial assistance required to transform an author's manuscript into books and electronic products. (Two exceptions to this are vanity and subsidy presses, discussed later in this section.) Generally, publishers in Western countries perform six basic functions:

1. Tap sources of materials (manuscripts).

2. Raise and supply the capital to make the books.

3. Aid in the development of the manuscript.

4. Contract for the manufacturing (printing and binding) of books.

5. Distribute books, including promotion and advertising.

6. Maintain records of sales, contracts, and correspondence relating to the production and sale of books.

A thumbnail sketch of the basic publishing development pattern is pertinent. The pattern seems to be worldwide, and it does have an impact on acquisition and selection work. In the history of publishing, there appear to be three stages of development. These stages have occurred in both Europe and America. They also appear elsewhere in the world.

In stage one, the publishing, printing, and selling of the product are all combined into one firm. The early giants of printing in Europe acted as publisher, printer, and retail bookseller. These publishers included Froben, Schoffer, Manutius, Caxton, and others. When one examines American publishing history, the same pattern appears on the eastern seaboard and moves west with the frontier; names like Franklin, Green, and Harris crop up during this period. Elsewhere in the world, publishing exhibits a similar evolutionary pattern, which is largely a function of how societies organize economic, educational, and human resources. In countries with limited resources, technical skills, and small markets, it is unfeasible, and in many cases impossible, to have specialty publishers in all fields.

From a collection development point of view, a publishing industry in stage one presents many interesting challenges. Research libraries buy materials from around the world, but countries with weak economies and low literacy rates seldom have anything resembling a national bibliography or trade bibliography (mainstays in identifying important titles). As if this were not enough of a challenge, most publishers operating at this level print a limited number of copies of each book. In many cases, they take orders before printing the book. When they do this, they print just a few more copies than the number ordered. Many collection development officers have experienced the frustration of having an order returned with the comment "unavailable, only 200 copies printed." Some books are, in fact, out of print on the date of publication; this frequently occurs in areas where publishing is at the stage-one level.

In stage two, specialization begins, with firms emphasizing publishing or printing. New firms, many with a single emphasis, appear. The factors creating this situation relate to available economic, educational, and human resources. Better education creates a greater market for books among both individual and institutional buyers. The retail trade develops at the same time, because the reading public exists countrywide and a single outlet in the country's major population center is no longer adequate. Publishers from this period in American publishing history include John Wiley, George Putnam, and the Lippincott Company. In 1807, Charles Wiley joined George Putnam in a bookstore operation in New York City. During the following 150 years, the heirs of the two men built two of the leading publishing houses in the United States. The Lippincott Company started in 1836 as a bookstore; over the years it shifted its emphasis to publishing.

Often, when bookstores begin to develop, a company will decide to create a listing or publication through which publishers inform bookstores about new and existing titles. Collection development librarians expend time and energy trying to track down such systems in countries where the book trade is in stage two. The usual procedure is to establish a good working relationship with a large bookstore, with that shop functioning as a purchasing agent. This may entail signing an agreement to spend a certain amount of money each year with the store, but it normally results in much better coverage, and usually better service, than trying to buy directly from the publishing houses.

The third stage is the complete separation of the three basic functions, as publishers discontinue printing activities. For example, John and James Harper started as printers in 1817. Today, HarperCollins is one of the leading publishers in the United States. It ceased printing years ago. (Two of the last major publishers to retain printing plants are McGraw-Hill and Doubleday.) When publishing reaches stage three, all the trappings we see in contemporary U.S. publishing are evident: specialty publishers, literary agents, trade journals, sales personnel, jobbers and wholesalers, and so forth. Normally, there is something resembling a national bibliography as well as a trade bibliography, both of which are essential for collection development work.

Canadian, U.S., and European publishers have undergone two other changes since reaching the third level of development in publishing. Before 1950, most publishing houses existed as family-owned or privately held firms. With the rapid expansion of the educational market, especially in the United States, most publishers found it impossible to raise enough capital to expand adequately. Slowly at first, and then with increasing frequency, publishers sold stock in the firm to the public. Going public generated several changes in the publishing field, some good and some bad. On the positive side, publishers issued more new material and offered more services. On the negative side, publicly held companies placed an increased emphasis on profitability, with, perhaps, a decline in overall quality. The problems were neither as great nor as bad as the doomsday prophets predicted.

As governments spent more and more money on education in the late 1950s and early 1960s, educational publishing became increasingly profitable. High profitability made publishing an area of interest for large conglomerates looking for diversification, so large electronics and communication firms began to buy publishing houses. The 1980s were known as a time of "merger mania" in the publishing industry; in the 1990s mergers continued, albeit at a somewhat slower rate. Two dated but relevant articles about mergers are Celeste West's "Stalking the Literary-Industrial Complex" and "The Question of Size in the Book Industry."[6]Another older, but still valid, article that covers all media is Ben Bagdikian's "The Media Brokers."[7] A more recent, and balanced, assessment of mergers is chapter 3 in Albert Greco's 1997 work *The Book Publishing Industry* (Allyn & Bacon). According to one study, in 1987 the top 12 U.S. publishing houses accounted for 56 percent of all domestic and international publishing sales.[8] The data covered all distribution channels: trade, mass-market, school textbook (elementary through high school, also called el-hi), and so forth. In the mid-1990s, if one could get accurate data, the results would probably be much the same.

Bagdikian offered the following amusing but worrisome thought:

> Is it possible, we're heading
> Towards one great climactic wedding
> When all but two remain unmerged,
> The rest absorbed, acquired or purged.[9]

Late in 1998, Bertelsmann, a German media conglomerate, announced plans to buy Barnes & Noble's online division for $200 million. Barnes & Noble, in turn, raised eyebrows in late 1998 when it announced plans to invest in Ingram Book Group, at the time the nation's leading wholesale book distributor.[10] Thus, the merger interest is still present in the late 1990s. The potential effect of these new combinations is great. If nothing else, it will mean that market potential will take on even greater importance when publishers select manuscripts to publish. Anyone with a little imagination can envision a future publishing industry that controls what the public may know. To date, little evidence indicates any real change in the quality of books being produced. However, the threat of too few information producers with access to a free market still exists. Selection and acquisition librarians, if they are aware of what is happening in the publishing field and of the implications of changes, should be among the first to note any significant changes.

A fourth stage—electronic publishing—is quickly developing. Some publishers offer information in two or more formats (for example, print and electronic), and others offer some information only in an electronic format. For example, in 1992 Random House entered into a joint venture with Voyager Company (software) and Apple Computer.[11] The group publishes both electronic and paper versions of Random House's Modern Library series. The group projects press runs of 7,500 to 15,000 books and 500 to 5,000 discs. Digital devices are creating a variety of opportunities for publishers. In a sense, the devices are almost as revolutionary as the introduction of movable type. Digitization is especially useful in the production process; submission of electronic manuscripts containing digitized images also speeds editorial work. The implications of electronic publishing for the bottom line are clear to most publishers, as suggested by Gayle Feldman: "Whether it be CD-ROM opportunities for scholarly presses, document delivery revenue for journal publishers, or multimedia packages for the reference crowd ... the coffee breaks buzzed with conviction that publishers who ignore new technology do so at their peril."[12] As the next millennium begins, few publishers are risking being left behind in a print-only world.

Insight into the impact of technology on the published bottom line appeared in a *Publishers Weekly* (*PW*) report showing that a completely digital publisher spends an average of $13.60 per page to prepare material for printing. A traditional approach costs slightly over $43 per page.[13]

Types of Publishers

The publication *Book Industry Trends* employs a nine-category system for grouping books:

- Trade
- Mass market
- Book clubs
- Mail order (including e-mail)
- Religious
- Professional
- University presses
- El-hi
- College textbook

Because its interest is in primarily economic/statistical data and publishers can and do have several "lines," this grouping is slightly different from the one we will use here. The following listing provides an overview of 12 types of publishing firms, some of which mirror the categories used by *Book Industry Trends*, and some more specific to the library world.

Trade publishers produce a wide range of titles, both fiction and nonfiction, that have wide sales potential. HarperCollins; Alfred A. Knopf; Doubleday; Macmillan; Little, Brown; Thames & Hudson; and Random House are typical trade publishers. Many trade publishers have divisions that produce specialty titles, such as children's, college textbooks, paperback, reference, and so forth. Trade publishers have three markets: bookstores, libraries, and wholesalers. To sell their products, publishers send sales representatives to visit buyers in businesses or institutions in each of the markets.

Specialty publishers restrict output to a few areas or subjects. Gale Research is an example of a specialty publisher. Specialty publishers' audiences are smaller and more critical than trade publishers' audiences. The categories of specialty publishers include reference, paperback, children's, microform, music, cartographic, and subject area.

Textbook publishers, especially those that target the primary and secondary schools (el-hi), occupy one of the highest-risk areas of publishing. Most publishers in this area develop a line of textbooks for several grades, for example, a social studies series. Preparation of such texts requires large amounts of time, energy, and money. Printing costs are high because most school texts feature expensive color plates and other specialized presswork. Such projects require large upfront investments that must be recouped before a profit can be realized. If enough school districts adopt a text, profits can be substantial, but failure to secure adoption can mean tremendous loss. Larger textbook firms, such as Ginn or Scott, Foresman, & Company, produce several series to help ensure a profit or to cushion against loss. Why would a company take the risk this type of publishing involves? Consider the amount of money spent on textbooks each year: more than $2.345 billion in 1995.[14] Because of the scheduling practices in school textbook adoption (usually occurring once a year), textbook publishers can reduce warehousing costs, thus adding to the margin of profit. During the 1990s U.S. el-hi publishers faced increased pressure to change the content of their publications from a variety of special-interest groups[15] (see chapter 19). This pressure adds yet another element of risk to textbook publishing.

Subject specialty publishers share some of the characteristics of textbook houses. Many have narrow markets that are easy to identify. Focusing marketing efforts on a limited number of buyers allows specialty publishers to achieve a reasonable return with less risk than a trade publisher takes on a nonfiction title. Specialty houses exist for a variety of fields; examples include art (Harry N. Abrams), music (E. C. Schirmer), scientific (Academic Press), technical (American Technical Publishers), law (West Publishing), and medical (W. B. Saunders). Many specialty books require expensive graphic preparation or presswork. Such presswork increases production costs, which is one of the reasons art, music, and science and technology titles are so costly. Another factor in their cost is the smaller market as compared to the market for a trade title. A smaller market means that the publisher must recover production costs from fewer books. Although the risk level is greater for specialty publishing than for trade publishing, it is much lower than that of el-hi publishers.

Vanity presses differ from other publishing houses in that they receive most of their operating funds from the authors whose works they publish. An example is Exposition Press. Vanity presses always show a profit and never lack material to produce. They offer editing assistance for a fee, and they arrange to print as many copies of the book as the author can afford. Distribution is the author's chore. Although such presses provide many of the same functions as other publishers, they do not share the same risks. Many authors who use vanity presses give copies of their books to local libraries, but such gifts usually arrive with no indication that they are gifts. Books arriving in the acquisitions department without packing slips or invoices cause problems. By knowing local publishers, persons in the acquisitions department can make their work easier.

Private presses are not business operations in the sense that the owners expect to make money. Most private presses are an avocation rather than a vocation for the owners. Examples are Henry Morris, Bird, and Poull Press. In many instances, the owners do not sell their products, but give them away instead. Most private presses are owned by individuals who enjoy fine printing and experimenting with type fonts and design. As one might expect, when the owner gives away the end product (often produced on a hand press), only a few copies are printed. In the past, many developments in type and book design originated with private presses. Some of the most beautiful examples of typographic and book design originated at private presses. Thus, large research libraries often attempt to secure copies of items produced by private presses.

Scholarly publishers, as part of not-for-profit organizations, receive subsidies. Most are part of an academic institution (University of California Press), museum (Museum of the American Indian Heye Foundation), research institution (Battelle Memorial Institute), or learned society (American Philosophical Society). Scholars established these presses to produce scholarly books that would not be acceptable to most for-profit publishers. Most scholarly books have limited sales appeal. A commercial, or for-profit, publisher considering a scholarly manuscript has three choices: 1) publish it and try to sell it at a price that ensures cost recovery; 2) publish it, sell it at a price comparable to commercial titles, and lose money; or 3) do not publish the item. Because of economic factors and a need to disseminate scholarly information regardless of cost (that is, even if it will lose money) the subsidized (by tax exemption, if nothing else), not-for-profit press exists. As publishing costs have skyrocketed, it has been necessary to fully subsidize some scholarly books, almost in the manner of a vanity press.

The role of the scholarly press in the economical and open dissemination of knowledge is critical. Every country needs some form of this type of press. Without scholarly presses, important works with limited appeal do not get published. Certainly, there are times when a commercial house publishes a book that will not show a profit simply because the publisher thinks the book is important, but relying on that type of willingness, in the long run, means that many important works will never appear in print.

Like their for-profit counterparts, scholarly presses are making evergreater use of electronic publishing techniques. Two good survey articles about how electronics are changing scholarly publishing are William Arms's "Scholarly Publishing on the National Networks"[16] and Ann Okerson's "Publishing Through the Network."[17] Though the networks hold promise, they also hold the possibility of higher information costs. As Freeman noted,

If profit rather than commitment to scholarly communication becomes the primary goal of those controlling access to the Internet,
university presses would find themselves unable to afford to publish the scholarly works that are the core of their activities. Thus
the public nature of the Internet must be carefully guarded if we
want to realize the true benefits of a democratic networked environment: broad access to scholarly research and information not
driven by financial concerns. A diverse range of independent, nonprofit publishers is critical to that goal.[18]

Government presses are the world's largest publishers. The combined
annual output of government publications—international (UNESCO), national (U.S. Government Printing Office), and state, regional, and local (Los
Angeles or State of California)—dwarfs commercial output. In the past,
many people thought of government publications as characterized by poor
physical quality or as uninteresting items that governments gave away. Today, some government publications rival the best offerings of commercial
publishers and cost much less. (The government price does not fully recover
production costs, so the price can be lower.) Most government publishing
activity goes well beyond the printing of legislative hearings or actions and
occasional executive materials. Often, national governments publish essential and inexpensive (frequently free) materials on nutrition, farming, building trades, travel, and many other topics. (See chapter 9 for more detailed
information about government publications.)

Paperback publishers produce two types of work: quality trade paperbacks and mass-market paperbacks. A trade publisher may have a quality
paperback division or may issue the paperbound version of a book through
the same division that issued the hardcover edition. The publisher may publish original paperbacks, that is, a first edition in paperback. Distribution of
quality paperbacks is the same as for hardcover books. Mass-market paperback publishers issue only reprints, or publications that first appeared in
hardcover. Their distribution differs from other book distribution. Their low
price is based, in part, on the concept of mass sales. Therefore, they sell anywhere the publisher can get someone to handle them. The paperback books
on sale in train and bus stations, airline terminals, corner stores, and kiosks
are mass-market paperbacks. These books have a short shelf life compared
to hardcovers.

People talk about the paperback revolution, but it is hard to think of it
as a revolution. Certainly the paperback has affected publishers' and a few
authors' incomes. Also, some readers are unwilling to accept a hardcover
when the smaller, more compact paperback is more convenient for use. The
low price of a paperback also appeals to book buyers.

Books with paper covers are not new. In some countries all books come
out with paper covers, and buyers must bind the books they wish to keep.
The major difference is that most people think of only mass-market paperbacks as paperbacks. The emphasis on popular, previously published titles
issued in new and colorful covers and sold at a low price is apparent. Those
are the elements of the paperback revolution, not the paper cover nor even
the relatively compact form. Nor has the paperback created a whole new
group of readers, as some overenthusiastic writers claim. It has merely
tapped an existing market for low-cost, popular books.

Contrary to popular belief, using a paper cover rather than a hard cover does not reduce the unit cost of a book by more than 20 or 30 cents. Original paperbacks incur the same costs, except for the cover material, as a hardcover title, which is why their cost is so much higher than reprint paperbacks. The reason the price of paperbacks is so much lower than hardcovers is that most first appeared as hardcovers. The title already sold well in hardcover, or there would be no reason to bring out a paper version, and so the book probably has already shown a profit. This means that the publisher has already recovered some of the major production costs. Having recovered most of the editorial costs, it is possible to reduce the price. In addition, releasing a paperback version of a hardcover title allows the publisher to benefit from marketing efforts expended on the hardcover version. Marketing efforts for the hardcover carry over to the paperback, which further reduces publishing costs. Economies of scale, or high sales volume and low per-unit profits, also reduce the price.

Newspaper and periodical publishers are a different class of publisher. Usually, book publishers depend on persons outside their organization to prepare the material that they publish. Newspaper and periodical publishers retain reporters or writers as members of their staffs. Of course, there are exceptions to the exception. For instance, some popular (and most scholarly) periodicals consist of articles written by persons not employed by the organization that publishes the journal. In general, in newspaper or periodical publishing, one finds the same range of activities found in book publishing. In other words, there are commercial publishers of popular materials, specialty publishers, children's publishers, scholarly or academic publishers, and government publishers. All subcategories share the characteristics of their book publishing counterparts; some are divisions of book publishing organizations.

Supplying current information is the primary objective of newspaper and journal publishers. With books, one can assume that most of the material published is at least six months old at the time of publication. The newspaper or periodical format provides the means for more rapid publishing, from two or three months to less than one day. (A major exception are some scholarly and academic periodicals, which frequently are one, two, or more years behind in publishing accepted articles.) To provide the most current information available, the library must acquire the newspapers or periodicals that suit the community's needs and interests. (Chapter 6 discusses problems concerning control and selection of these materials.)

Two other types of publishing activities deserve mention: *associations* and *reprint houses*. Professional and special-interest groups and associations frequently establish their own publishing houses. The American Library Association is one such organization. These organizations may publish only a professional journal, but they also may issue books and audiovisual materials. The operating funds come from the association, but the association hopes to recover its costs. Professional associations are often tax-exempt, and thus their publishing activities are similar to those of scholarly presses: limited-appeal titles, small press runs, relatively high prices, and indirect government subsidies. Some associations do not have paid publication staff and use volunteer members instead; they contract with a commercial publisher to print the group's journal, conference proceedings, and other publications. Association publications, whether published by the organization itself or by contract, can provide the library with numerous bibliographic control headaches. For example, they announce titles as forthcoming, but the items never get published. Many publications are papers from meetings and conventions (called "Transactions of ..." or "Proceedings of ..."); the titles of such publications frequently change two or three times before they appear in hardcover. Many of these publications do not find their way into trade bibliographies.

Reprint publishers, as the name implies, focus on reprinting items no longer in print. Most of the sales by reprint houses are to libraries and scholars, and many of the titles that these publishers reprint are in the public domain (that is, no longer covered by copyright). The other major source of reprinted material is the purchase of rights to an out-of-print title from another publisher. Although many of the basic costs of creating a book do not exist for the reprint house (editing, design, and royalties, for example), reprints are expensive because of their limited sales appeal. (In the past, some publishers would announce a new release with a prepublication flyer that included an order form. Later, the company would announce the cancellation of the title. Some suspicious librarians suggested that such cancellations were the result of insufficient response to the prepublication announcement.) Sometimes reprints cause as many or more bibliographic headaches for libraries than do association titles. Despite the many problems, reprint houses are an essential source of titles for collection development programs concerned with retrospective materials.

Small presses are important for some libraries. Small presses are thought of as literary presses by some people, including librarians. Anyone reading the annual "Small Press Round-Up" in *Library Journal* could reasonably reach the same conclusion. The reality is that small presses are as diverse as the international publishing conglomerates. Size is the only real difference; in functions and interests small presses are no different from large trade publishers.

Small Press Record of Books in Print (*SPRBIP*) annually lists between 15,000 and 17,000 titles from about 1,800 small publishers.[19] Many of these presses are one-person operations, done as a sideline from the publisher's home. Such presses seldom publish more than four titles per year. The listings in *SPRBIP* show the broad range of subject interests of small presses and shows that there are both book and periodical presses in this category. Some people assume that the content of small press publications is poor. This is incorrect, for small presses do not produce, proportionally, any more worthless titles than do the large publishers. Often, it is only through the small press that one can find information on less popular topics. Two examples of very popular books that were originally published by small presses are *Ruby Fruit Jungle* by Rita Mae Brown and the Boston Women's Health Book Collective's *Our Bodies, Ourselves.*

Another factor that sets small presses apart from their larger counterparts is economics. Large publishers have high costs and need substantial sales to recover their costs, but small presses can produce a book for a limited market at a reasonable cost and still expect some profit. Small presses also can produce books more quickly than their larger counterparts.

From a collection development point of view, small presses represent a challenge. Tracking down new releases can present a variety of problems. Locating a correct current address is one common problem. Another is learning about the title before it goes out of print. With *SPRBIP*, Len Fulton of

Dustbooks tries to provide access, and he has succeeded to a surprising degree, given the nature of the field. However, waiting for his annual *SPRBIP* may take too long, because small presses frequently move about and their press runs are small (that is, only a limited quantity of books is printed). In essence, few small presses are part of the organized trade or national bibliographic network.

Very few of these presses advertise, and even fewer of their titles receive reviews in national journals. There are two publications that focus on small press titles, *Small Press Review* and *Small Press Book Review*. Lack of reviews is not the result of book review editors discriminating against small press publications. Rather, it is a function of too many small press operators not understanding how items get reviewed and failing to send out review copies.

Collection development librarians interested in small presses have had some commercial help. Quality Books of Northbrook, Illinois (a vendor that in the past was known primarily as a source of remainder books), has become active in the distribution of small press publications. Although it stocks books from only a small percentage of the presses listed in *SPRBIP* (about one-fifth), the fact that it does stock the items is a major feature. Most jobbers say they will attempt to secure a specific title for a library if they do not stock the publication. A librarian could easily devote too much time to an effort to track down a single copy of a $10.95 item from an obscure small press. Librarians interested in small presses, collection development, and access to information need to keep their collective fingers crossed in the hope that Quality Books will find its operation sufficiently profitable and that it will continue to offer the service. (For more information about distributors and vendors, see chapter 12.)

Functions of Publishing

Publishing consists of five basic functions, which apply equally to print and nonprint materials: administration, editorial, production, marketing, and fulfillment. A publisher must be successful in all five areas if the organization is to survive for any length of time. Just because the organization is not for profit does not mean it has any less need for success in each of these areas. Administration deals with overseeing the activities, ensuring the coordination, and making certain there are adequate funds available to do the desired work. It is in the editorial area that publishing houses decide what to produce. Acquisition and managing editors discuss and review ideas for books or articles. Large book publishers develop *trade lists* (a combination of prior publications, manuscripts in production, and titles under contract) to achieve a profit while avoiding unnecessary competition with other publishers.

Book selectors ought to learn something about the senior editors in the major publishing houses with which they deal. As with reviewing, the view of what is good or bad material is personal, so knowing the editors will help in planning selection activities. The editors' opinions about what to accept for publication determine what will be available.

Securing and reviewing manuscripts is a time-consuming activity for most editors. Based on a range of guesses concerning the number of unsolicited manuscripts reviewed for each one accepted, the average suggests that editors reject approximately 90 percent of all unsolicited manuscripts after the first examination. After the first complete reading, still more manuscripts are rejected. Even after a careful review by several people, all of whom have favorable reactions, the editor may not accept the manuscript. Three common reasons for this are: 1) the title will not fit into the new list, 2) the sales potential (market) is too low, and 3) the cost of production would be too high.

The *annual list* is the group of books that a publisher has accepted for publication and plans to release during the next 6 to 12 months. The *backlist* comprises titles published in previous years that are still available. A strong backlist of steadily selling titles is the dream of most publishers. Editors spend a great deal of time planning their lists. They do not want to have two new books on the same topic appear at the same time unless those books complement one another. They want a list that will have good balance and strong sales appeal as well as fit with the titles still in print.

Librarians and readers often complain that commercial publishers are exclusively, or at least overly, concerned with profit and have little concern for quality. What these people forget is that publishing houses are businesses and must show a profit if they are to continue to operate.

In 1998, *The New York Times* published an article about rising book production, loss of editors, and the increase in errors in books. This article noted there was a 16 percent drop in the publishing workforce in New York City between 1990 and 1998 and that the decrease was primarily in the editorial category. It also speculated about the role mergers played in the situation. One editor was quoted as saying, "It's all become a big, fat, screaming, mean, vicious, greedy, rude, and crude feast … . So little of your time is spent doing creative work that I'm seriously considering leaving."[20] Editors are critical to the publishing process, so one hopes that the New York City situation is not representative of the field as a whole.

Production and marketing join with the editorial team to make the final decisions regarding production details. Most publishers can package and price publications in a variety of ways. Some years ago, the Association of University Publishers released an interesting book entitled *One Book Five Ways* (for a full citation, refer to the bibliography at the end of this chapter). The book provides a fascinating picture of how five different university presses would handle the same project. In all five functional areas, the presses would have proceeded differently, from contract agreement (administration), copyediting (editorial), physical format (production), pricing and advertising (marketing), to distribution (fulfillment).

Production staff consider issues such as page size, typeface, number and type of illustrative materials, and cover design, as well as typesetting, printing, and binding. Their input and the decision made regarding the physical form of the item play a major role in how much the title will cost. Although electronic and desktop publishing are changing how and who performs some production activities, the basic issues of design, layout, use of illustrations, and use of color remain unchanged.

Marketing departments are responsible for promoting and selling the product. They provide input about the sales potential of the title. Further, this unit often decides how many review copies to distribute and to what review sources. Where, when, or whether to place an ad are the responsibility of the marketing department. All of these decisions influence the cost of the items produced. Many small publishers use direct mail (catalogs and brochures) to market their books. Publishers' sales representatives visit stores, wholesalers, schools, and libraries. When salespeople visit the library or information center, they keep the visits short and to the point. Each visit represents a cost to the publisher, and the company recovers the cost in some manner, most often in the price of the material. One activity for which most marketing units are responsible is exhibits. For library personnel, convention exhibits are one of the best places to meet publishers' representatives and have some input into the decision-making process. From the publishers' point of view, if the conferees go to the exhibits, conventions can be a cost-effective way of reaching a large number of potential customers in a brief time. Librarians should also remember that the fees exhibitors pay help underwrite the cost of the convention.

Fulfillment activities are those needed to process an order, including warehousing of the materials produced. In many ways, fulfillment is the least controllable cost factor for a publisher. Libraries and information centers sometimes add to the cost of their purchases by requiring special handling of their orders. Keeping special needs to a minimum can help keep prices in check. Speeding up payments to publishers and vendors will also help slow price increases, because the longer a publisher has to carry an outstanding account the more interest has to be paid. Ultimately, most increases in the cost of doing business result in a higher price for the buyer, so whatever libraries can do to help publishers control their fulfillment costs will also help collection development budgets.

For various reasons, despite strong marketing efforts, some publications do not sell as well as expected. When this happens, sooner or later the publisher has to dispose of the material; many times, these become remaindered items. A decision by the Internal Revenue Service has influenced press runs and the speed with which publishers remainder slow-moving warehouse stock (the *Thor Power Tool* decision; see chapter 18). Remaindered items sell for a small fraction of their actual production cost. Prior to the *Thor* decision, businesses would write down the value of their inventories, or warehouse stock, to a nominal level at the end of the tax year. The resulting loss in the value of the inventory (which was, by and large, on paper only) then became a tax deduction for the company, increasing its profit. Since *Thor,* publishers can take such a deduction only if the material is defective or offered for sale below actual production cost. Under the previous method, publishers could find it profitable to keep slow-selling titles in their warehouses for years. Thus far, efforts to get an exemption from the ruling for publishers have been unsuccessful. At first, the ruling increased the number of remaindered books, but now most publishers have cut back on the size of their print runs in an attempt to match inventories to sales volume. More often than not, this means higher unit costs and retail prices. Despite all the problems for the field, total net sales income for book publishing has increased steadily, from $14.1 billion in 1989 to an estimated $22.1 billion in 1998.[21]

Several times in this chapter we mention the publisher's goal of profit or reasonable return. What is "typical" for a 250-page trade book selling for $25.00? Let's take a look at a hypothetical first press run (see page 142):

Suggested Retail Price	$25.00	
Printing/binding	- 2.00	(a cost no matter the number of items sold)
	23.00	
Warehouse/Distribution	- 2.00	(also a given "at best" warehousing)
	21.00	
Discount to retailer	-12.50	
	8.50	
Overhead (including editorial)	- 2.00	
	6.50	
Marketing	- 1.50	(This is a high number as it represents 10% of list price. Most royalties are based on net sales income which is always lower.)
	4.00	
Author royalty (10%–15%)	- 1.25	
	2.75	

Werner Rebsamen published some percentages of costs he was provided by a major New York publisher to use at his presentation at the Book Manufacturing Institute[22]:

- 24.1% Royalties and Guarantees
- 5.7% Editorial Production
- 16.4% Marketing
- 24.2% Manufacturing
- 9.2% Returns
- 8.4% Fulfillment
- 9.3% General Administration

One can find data on annual sales in a variety of sources: *PW, The Bowker Annual of Library & Book Trade Almanac,* Standard and Poor's *Industry Surveys,* and so forth. Anyone concerned with collection development must make use of statistical data about publishing to develop intelligent budgets and work plans. Statistical data about the number of new titles available as paperbacks, reprints, and so forth, can be useful in planning the workload for the next fiscal year. For example, perhaps the library will need to hire more staff or redirect efforts of existing staff if the volume of acquisitions increases. Knowing the pricing patterns over a period of years and the expected acquisitions budget allows one to project the workload. The two most accessible sources of publishing statistics for the United States are *PW* and *The Bowker Annual.* Data in both sources, and almost all other printed statistical data about publishing, come from the American Book Producers Association (ABPA). Remember that the statistics represent information drawn from ABPA members, and not all publishers belong to that group. In fact, a great many small and regional publishers do not.

Publishers use a variety of distribution outlets, selling directly to individuals, institutions, retailers, and wholesalers. Distribution is a major problem for both publishers and libraries because of the number of channels and the implications for acquiring a specific publication. Each channel has a different discount, and one accesses them through different sources. Figure 5.1 illustrates in a general way the complexity of the system. Production and distribution of information materials, whether print or nonprint, consist of several elements, all interacting with one another. Writers and creators of the material can and do distribute their output in several ways: directly to the community or public, to agents who in turn pass it on to producers, or directly to the producers. Producers seeking writers often approach agents with publication ideas. The figure illustrates the variety of channels publishers use to distribute their publications to the consumer.

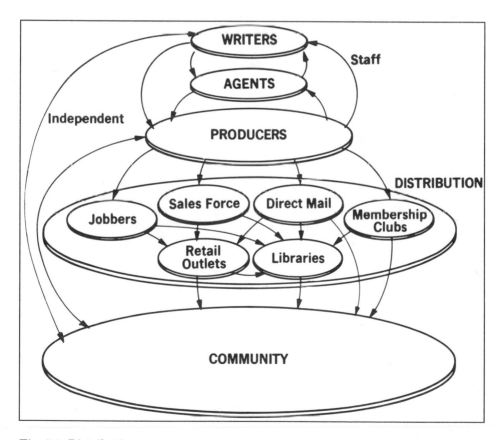

Fig. 5.1. Distribution system.

Most publishers use all these sales channels. Wholesalers, direct mail companies, and retail store operators act as middlemen; a retailer may buy from the jobber or directly from the publisher. Each seller will have different discounts for different categories of buyers, ranging from no discount to more than 50 percent. Not only are there a great many choices available to the buyer, but the sources also compete with one another. These factors combine to push up the cost of distributing a publication, which in turn increases its list price. With multiple outlets, different discounts, and different credit conditions, the publishing industry has created a cumbersome, uneconomical distribution system.

Selling practices vary by title and publisher; however, one can make a few generalizations. Advertising will help a good book, but it seldom, if ever, makes a success out of a poor book. Publishers use both publicity and advertising, which are two different marketing devices. An interview with the author or a review of the book on a national radio or television program are examples of publicity. Normally free, publicity will do a great deal for the sales of a book. However, the book's topic, or at least its author, must be of national interest or the title will not attract attention. Changes in current events can change a slow-moving book into a bestseller overnight, something that no amount of advertising can accomplish.

Publishers advertise in several ways. First, they use trade advertising directed toward retail outlets and institutional buyers. Second, they make an effort to get items reviewed in major professional and general review media. (Reviews are technically promotion rather than advertising, because one does not pay to have a title reviewed. However, a lead review can be worth more than a full-page advertisement.) Third, they place announcements and ads in professional journals, where the emphasis is on reaching individual buyers, both personal and institutional. Fourth, they employ cooperative advertisements (co-op ads) in the book review sections of many newspapers. A co-op ad is one in which the publisher and a retail store share the cost of the advertisement. The publisher determines which titles are eligible for cooperative advertising. Finally, for books with a defined audience for which there is a good mailing list, the publisher often uses a direct mail campaign, again with individuals and institutional buyers as the targets.

This brief overview outlines the most basic elements of publishing. Its purpose is to start a collection development novice thinking about the trade. The next section presents a discussion of audiovisual producers. Unfortunately, because of their diversity, it is not possible in this limited space to parallel the discussion of print publishing.

Producers of Audiovisual Materials

Media producers are a diverse group working with a variety of formats (audio recordings, film, filmstrips, video, models, and so on), making it difficult to generalize about their operations. The following discussion is an attempt to cover all of those audiovisual formats, but it would require a full-length book to describe all the individual variations and exceptions.

Media producers enjoy substantial annual sales to schools and libraries. Indeed, this market is almost the sole sales outlet for the majority of media producers. Two major exceptions are audio and video recordings. The audio and video recording industries are the major sources of "other media" for most libraries. Recorded music, as part of a growing audio collection that includes talking books, is a common feature of libraries, reflecting the fact that a large segment of the general population buys or listens to music. In terms of sales, however, libraries and other institutions represent only a fraction of the music industry's income.

When one considers average circulations per title, video recordings are often the top circulation format, especially in public libraries. Video collections in libraries contain both educational and theatrical film recordings. The sales of motion picture videocassettes to the general public are far larger than those to libraries, but libraries (including school media centers) are the largest market for educational video.

One important fact to remember about most media, with the exception of books and filmstrips, is that they require the user to follow the material at a fixed pace—the pace of the machine involved. Certainly, the equipment allows for rewinding and reviewing a section of special importance, and video players can freeze a frame, but the formats make it difficult to skip around as one can do with a book. Selectors must keep this fact in mind when considering these formats for the collection. Will our typical user be able to benefit from the material, given the pace of presentation? is a question for selectors to ponder. Interactive video and hypermedia allow for easy random access, and these technologies are most likely to replace many of the traditional media formats libraries have made available. What newer format and technology will replace interactive systems is impossible to guess. Virtual reality is, to many people who follow developments in the field, an enhancement of interactive systems and not really a new "system."

Most media producers design products for the average ability or level of knowledge of the target audience. In the case of educational media, the producer assumes that the item is for group presentations, with a teacher adding comments and creating a context for the material. Though individuals working alone can benefit from the material, many will gain less from use of the item without some interaction with an instructor. More and more teachers in schools and higher education are assigning media use outside the classroom in the same way they have traditionally employed print material to supplement the instructional program. This translates into libraries and media centers receiving requests for bigger and more diverse media collections.

The first major difference between book publishers and media producers is that media producers market a product designed primarily for group use, and book publishers market a product designed primarily for individual use. This difference has an influence on how media producers market and distribute their products. Media producers place heavy emphasis on direct institutional sales. Also, there is less use of wholesalers. Though some book jobbers do handle audio and video recordings, a large percentage of media acquisitions are made directly from the producer.

One characteristic of media production that is frequently overlooked is authorship. Most books are the result of the intellectual effort of one or two persons. Textbook publishers frequently commission books. (Perhaps in the age of mergers, this approach will become more common for trade publications as well.) For media, the process is the opposite. Normally, the producer generates the ideas and seeks the necessary persons to carry out the project if the company's staff cannot handle the project. *This means that the producers have almost total control over the final product.* It is true that book publishers have the final say in what they will publish. The difference is that the book publisher receives hundreds of manuscripts and ideas for books to consider each year, and thus has exposure to ideas and projects that otherwise might not receive consideration. In addition, even if one publisher rejects a manuscript, there is always the chance that another may pick it up. Book publishing has a tradition of being a free marketplace for ideas, whereas this concept is almost nonexistent in the media field. Although this may seem to be a subtle difference, it does have an effect on the type of material produced and, in turn, on the library's collection.

Despite the producers' control, people often think of the media field as one of independence and freedom. One reason for this view is, at least in the past, the relatively low cost of entering it. One hears stories about the individual who started off with a few thousand dollars and some equipment and is now a major producer. One does not hear about the thousands of others who tried and failed. Mediocre equipment and a low advertising budget usually mean a mediocre product and few, if any, sales. The opportunity is there, but the chances of success are only slightly better than for any other business venture. Almost anyone may become a media producer; for example, to become a producer of 35mm slides (educational, art, travel, and so forth), one needs only a 35mm camera, a stock of master images to use to produce slides on demand, and some money for advertising. Success is not likely, but this is all that one needs to become a media producer and be listed in a directory of media sources. In general, the start-up capital (money required to begin operations) is much lower than would be necessary for a book publisher. Good-quality professional media production equipment is exceedingly expensive; however, many of the so-called producers do not invest in quality equipment. They depend on commercial laboratories and hope for the best.

Because of a lack of materials and the pressure to have media in schools and libraries, it has been and still is possible to sell copies of extremely poor-quality materials, because they are all that is available. All too often a selector must purchase an item on the basis of curriculum needs rather than on the basis of quality.

Another characteristic of media producers is that their products have a fairly high cost per unit of information conveyed. Many media items are single-concept materials. (Single-concept films are a special class of educational films that deal with a very narrow concept, such as cell division, and are usually very short, 3 to 4 minutes long.) Books, in contrast, have a low cost per unit of information. For example, no single film, videotape, audiotape, or set of 35mm slides can convey the same amount of information about Native Americans as one 300-page book. This feature of the media has great importance for selection, because not every medium is ideal for every purpose. Librarians must know the advantages of each medium and select and acquire items on this basis.

Generally, media products cost more per copy than do books. Today educational videocassettes range from $200 to $300 for educational videos to theatrical cassettes that are less than $20. Sets of 35mm slides range from $5 to more than $100. In general, the kit combinations of media are high-profit items. Prices on such combinations run from $20 to more than $100. Also, they are the perfect medium for building-level materials, that is, developing media collections around curriculum needs over time. Because of the cost factor, selectors normally can buy only a few items each year, thus making the selection process important.

Though book publishers use a multitude of outlets to sell their products, media producers use few outlets. With the exception of audio and video stores and a few map shops, there are no retail outlets for "other media." There are no media-of-the-month clubs (except for music recordings and videos), few mail-order houses, and no remainder houses (except for recordings and some videos). Even wholesalers dealing with all media are few and far between. The main source, and in some cases the only source, is the producer. Because the producers are the basic source, collection development personnel must spend an inordinate amount of time and energy maintaining lists of producers' addresses. Without such records, schools and libraries would almost have to halt their acquisition of "other media." Because many producers are small and move frequently, updating of addresses is a constant problem for the library. It means that directories more than 12 months old are likely to be out of date.

The one advantage to this situation is that the market for media is clearly identifiable: schools and libraries. Like the specialty publisher, the media producer is better able to focus advertising and sales activities on a small area with a high probability of success. Trade book publishers use a broad spectrum of advertising sources: newspapers, periodicals, flyers, radio, and television. In general, the trade publisher must take a shotgun approach, but specialty publishers and media producers should have a much better idea of their market.

Both books and other media are easy to copy. The difference is in the cost of the item. Most institutions capable of using media also have the capability to duplicate that material. That capability is a concern for producers because it was, and still is, common to request to preview the material before placing a firm order. Previewing can be an opportunity for copying. Awareness of this potential danger may be one factor accounting for the general absence of media wholesalers. The media for which this danger is greatest are tapes (video and audio) and 35mm slides.

The majority of media producers are small business owners without a large capital reserve. For the small media producer, cash flow is a real problem. Anything that the library can do to help the small media firm control its costs will help to control the unit cost of products as well (for example, using cooperative previewing and keeping ordering and billing procedures simple).

One other important characteristic of the media field is the speed with which its technology changes. This characteristic is a central problem for everyone concerned, both producers and consumers. Improvements in equipment constantly make existing equipment almost obsolete; occasionally, a new format may, in fact, make equipment obsolete. Given the volatile nature of the field, many users, with good reason, are reluctant to invest heavily in equipment. For the producer, the problem is greater; it means deciding rather quickly whether to go with the new or stay with the old. On the one hand, staying with the old too long may cut the producer out of the field because of licensing, franchising considerations, or simply not keeping up-to-date. On the other hand, moving too soon may use up capital on a change that does not last.

Table 5.1 provides an overview of the basic differences between book publishers and media producers, differences that affect collection development. The table presents broad generalizations to which there are many exceptions.

Table 5.1   Differences between media producers and book publishers.

	Media Producers	Book Publishers
Audience	Individual as part of a group	Individual
Idea Authorship	Company generated	Agent generated
Use	Group and sequential, equipment paced	Single and nonsequential, self-paced
Cost per concept	High	Low
Selection process in library	Usually group	Individual
Cost to enter field	Relatively low, except for interactive formats	Moderately high, desktop publishing low
Inventory	Low	High
Market	Clearly defined	Highly variable
Potential sales volume	Low (except audio and video recordings)	Medium
Cost per copy to buy	Moderate	Relatively low
Ease of copying	Easy to copy, high sales price	Easy to copy, low sales price
Distribution	Mostly single source	Multiple source
Changes in format and equipment	Very rapid with high rate of obsolescence	Relatively slow

Producers' Problems and Collection Development

Collection development personnel need to understand some of the important issues and problems facing producers, because those factors inevitably have an impact on their collections. Rising costs create problems for everyone, but publishers and media producers have some special problems. Information producers experience pressure from two sides. On the one hand, the rising costs of materials and labor put pressure on them to raise the prices of their products. On the other hand, if they do raise prices, they must realize that this may cut into sales, thus cutting into their profits more than the cost increases themselves. The consumer must meet basic needs first, and during periods of inflation, meeting basic needs cuts into funds available for luxury items. For most individual buyers, books and media are among the first items to be cut.

Producers are likely to continue increasing their prices as the personal buyer market continues to shrink. Institutional buyers will continue to buy materials, but a static materials budget over two or three years, in combination with increasing costs of materials, means that the library buys fewer items each year. Most libraries do not receive large budget increases even during inflationary periods. The increases they do receive do no more than keep pace with inflation; thus, for all practical purposes, the budget is static. These two factors effectively limit the number of items purchased, and producers must carefully weigh these concerns before raising prices. This, in turn, forces them to be more and more selective about the items they produce. They will carry few, if any, materials that do not show a profit.

If producers could simplify their distribution system, they could achieve significant savings. Why should the general consumer (individual or institution) be able to purchase an item directly from the producer or from a wholesaler or retailer? The distribution system as it now operates is cumbersome and costly. For book publishers, it is a matter of having a typical marketing system (producer to wholesaler to retailer), but at the same time the system allows any individual customer access to any level of the system to make a purchase. Media producers, in contrast, use direct sales. Both systems are costly for everyone. The book system requires complex handling procedures at each level because of different classes of customers. For the media system, shipping single-item orders to numerous locations increases the cost of placing and filling an order. The impact on collection development is that more money goes into paperwork and administrative procedures and less is available to collection development. Both producers and librarians must strive to solve this problem.

Perhaps the most difficult question concerns the right to use knowledge resources, or rather, how one may use them. As noted earlier, copyright has become a central issue among librarians, educators, and other users of knowledge resources on the one hand and the producers on the other. Yet, without copyright, there is little incentive for anyone to produce a work. The problem is how far society can go to provide and protect such incentives and still ensure adequate access to material at a fair price. Libraries want open, free access and use, and producers want limited free access. This issue, of course, has an important role to play in determining how one develops a collection, with electronic information making the issue ever more complex.

Notes

1. Richard J. Cox, "Taking Sides on the Future of the Book," *American Libraries* 28 (February 1997): 52–55.

2. Ibid., 53.

3. R. P. S. Davis, P. C. Livingood, H. T. Ward, V. P. Steponaitis, *Excavating Occaneechi Town* (CD-ROM) (University of North Carolina Press, 1998).

4. Frederick W. Lancaster, *Libraries and Librarians in an Age of Electronics* (Arlington, Va.: Information Resources Press, 1982).

5. Albert N. Greco, *The Book Publishing Industry* (Boston: Allyn & Bacon, 1997): x–xi.

6. Celeste West, "Stalking the Literary-Industrial Complex," *American Libraries* 13 (May 1982): 298-300; and "The Question of Size in the Book Industry," *Publishers Weekly* 214 (July 31, 1978): 25–54.

7. Ben Bagdikian, "The Media Brokers: Concentration and Ownership of the Press," *Multinational Monitor* 8 (September 1987): 7–12.

8. John R. Secor, "Growing Crisis of Business Ethics," *Serials Librarian* 13 (October-November 1987): 70.

9. Bagdikian, "The Media Brokers," 12.

10. Yahlin Chang, "Books Caught in the Web," *Newsweek* 132, no. 22 (November 25, 1998): 85; Julian Barnes, "Independent Bookstores Say Big Deal Is a Big Deal," *New York Times* (January 3, 1999): 5.

11. "Modern Library Relaunch to Include Electronic Books," *Publishers Weekly* 239 (May 11, 1992): 10.

12. Gayle Feldman, "Professional Publishing Goes Electronic," *Publishers Weekly* 239 (May 11, 1992): 31.

13. Sally Taylor, "The Joys of Electronic Togetherness," *Publishers Weekly* 240 (March 29, 1993): 24.

14. Greco, *The Book Publishing Industry*, 26.

15. "State Board of Education Approves New Texts Despite Groups' Protests," *San Fernando Valley Daily News* (October 13, 1990): 1, 23.

16. William Arms, "Scholarly Publishing on the National Networks," *Scholarly Publishing* 23 (April 1992): 158–69.

17. Ann Okerson, "Publishing Through the Network: The 1990s Debutante," *Scholarly Publishing* 23 (April 1992): 170–77.

18. Lisa Freeman, "Big Challenges Face University Presses in the Electronic Age," *Chronicle of Higher Education* (April 28, 1993): A44.

19. *Small Press Record of Books in Print* (Paradise, Calif.: Dustbooks, 1975–).

20. Doreen Carvajal, "The More Books, The Fewer the Editors," *New York Times*, Monday, June 29, 1998, at B1, B3.

21. Greco, *The Book Publishing Industry*, 22.

22. Werner Rebsamen, "Trends in Publishing, New Technologies and Opportunities," *New Library Scene* 16 (December 1997): 10–12.

Further Reading

General

Baker, J. F. "Reinventing the Book Business." *Publishers Weekly* 241 (March 4, 1994): 36–40.

———. "Selling to Libraries: Publishers Learn About a Billion-Dollar Market." *Publishers Weekly* 233 (December 18, 1987): 14–15.

Britt, B. "What Thou Lovest Well Remaindered." *Small Press* 10 (Winter 1991): 52–55.

Carter, R. A. "Taking Aim at the Library Market." *Publishers Weekly* 237 (June 8, 1990): S6–S12.

Dave, R. *The Private Press*. 2d ed. New York: R. R. Bowker, 1983.

Finn, M. "Everything You Need to Know About Trademarks and Publishing." *Publishers Weekly* 239 (January 6, 1991): 41–44.

Graham, G. "Publishers, Librarians and the Eternal Triangle." *Library Acquisitions: Practice and Theory* 15, no. 3 (1991): 261–64.

Grannis, C. B. *What Happens in Publishing?* 2d ed. New York: Columbia University Press, 1967.

Greco, Albert N. *The Book Publishing Industry*. Boston: Allyn & Bacon, 1997.

Hoffert, B. "Getting Published." *Library Journal* 115 (February 15, 1990): 153–56.

Hunter, K. A. "Making the Commercial Transition from Paper to Electronic: Or Publishing in the 'Twilight Zone.' " *Collection Management* 15, nos. 1/2 (1992): 129–39.

Kopka, M. "Backlist: How to Use It." *Publishers Weekly* 240 (October 4, 1993): 24–25.

Loe, M. K. H. "Book Culture and Book Business: U.K. vs. the U.S." *Journal of Academic Librarianship* 16 (March 1990): 4–10.

Newlin, B. "Traveling the New Information Superhighway." *Small Press* 12 (Spring 1994): 26–29.

One Book Five Ways. Los Altos, Calif.: William Kaufmann, 1977.

Posel, N. R. "High Priced or Over-Priced: They're Every Library's Problem." *Reference Librarian* 19 (1987): 257–67.

Rettig, J. "Do Publishers Have Ears?" *Wilson Library Bulletin* 62 (January 1988): 15–22.

Salace, J. "Video Distribution: The Maze Made Manageable." *Library Journal* 115 (July 1990): 42–44.

Sexton, M. "Replacing the Myths About Marketing to Libraries." *Publishers Weekly* 236 (March 10, 1989): 56–57.

Taylor, S. A. "Joys of Electronic Togetherness." *Publishers Weekly* 240 (March 29, 1993): 24–28.

Weisberg, J. "Rough Trade: The Sad Decline of American Publishing." *New Republic* 204 (June 17, 1991): 16–21.

Academic

Baker, J. F. "Beyond the Ivory Tower." *Publishers Weekly* 239 (June 1, 1992): 26–28.

Berry, J. N. "A New Alliance Aborning?" *Library Journal* 112 (August 1987): 56–60.

Byrd, G. D. "An Economic 'Commons' Tragedy for Research Libraries: Scholarly Journal Publishing and Pricing Trends." *College & Research Libraries* 51 (May 1990): 184–95.

Graham, G. "Adversaries or Allies?" *Scholarly Publishing* 14 (July 1983): 291–97.

Henon, A. L. "Publish and Perish." *Serials Librarian* 17, nos. 3/4 (1990): 35–41.

Hutton, F. *Early Black Press in America, 1827-1860.* Westport, Conn.: Greenwood Press, 1993.

Lewis, D. W. "Economics of the Scholarly Journal." *College & Research Libraries* 50 (November 1989): 674–87.

McGinty, S. "Political Science Publishers: What Do the Citations Reveal?" *Collection Management* 11, nos. 3/4 (1989): 93–102.

Moore, T. W. "Believe It or Not, Academic Books Are a Bargain." *Scholarly Publishing* 24 (April 1993): 161–65.

Public

Burroughs, R. "Book Publishers Focus on Librarian Focus Groups." *Library Journal* 114 (March 15, 1989): 48–49.

———. "Fitting into the Conglomerate Picture (Children's Imprints)." *Publishers Weekly* 236 (July 28, 1989): 138–40.

Dahlin, R. "Category Closeup: Mystery." *Publishers Weekly* 240 (March 8, 1993): 51–52.

Eaglen, A. B. "Publishers' Trade Discounts and Public Libraries." *Library Acquisitions: Practice and Theory* 8, no. 2 (1984): 95–97.

Epstein, H. M. "Strengthening the Partnership." *Publishers Weekly* 238 (May 31, 1991): 33–34.

Hays, K. H. "Sleepy Library Market Awakes." *Library Journal* 115 (November 1, 1990): 22.

Hoffert, B. "Getting People to Read: A Talk with Librarians, Publishers and Booksellers." *Library Journal* 116 (February 15, 1991): 161–65.

———. "A Publisher Checks out Libraries." *Library Journal* 116 (September 1, 1991): 146–48.

———. "Striking a New Balance of Power." *Library Journal* 117 (February 15, 1992): 124–28.

Nixon, W. "Art of Publishing Popular Science Books." *Publishers Weekly* 238 (August 23, 1991): 32–35.

Strussy, S. A. "Librarians and the Salesperson: Allies or Enemies?" *Catholic Library World* 57 (May/June 1986): 274–77.

School

Eaglen, A. "Publishers' Sales Strategies: A Questionable Business." *School Library Journal* 34 (February 1988): 19–21.

———. "Shell Game: Publishers, Vendors and the Myth of the Backlist." *School Library Journal* 38 (November 1992): 24–28.

Kayden, M. "Out of Print and Back in Print." *Journal of Youth Services in Libraries* 6 (Spring 1993): 265–69.

Lasky, K. "Creativity in a Boom Industry." *Horn Book Magazine* 67 (November/December 1991): 705–11.

Lodge, S. "Making of a Crossover: One Book, Two Markets." *Publishers Weekly* 239 (November 23, 1992): 38–42.

Lotz, J. W. "Here Today, Here Tomorrow: Coping with the OP Crisis." *School Library Journal* 35 (July 1989): 25–28.

Nilsen, A. P. "Speaking Loudly for Good Books." *School Library Journal* 37 (September 1991): 180–83.

Roback, D. E., and S. Maughan. "Children's Books." *Publishers Weekly* 240 (February 15, 1993): 26–32.

Tangorra, J. "Publishers Refining Strategies for Children's Audio Market." *Publishers Weekly* 237 (February 23, 1990): 186–89.

Special

"Cost Effectiveness of Science Journals." *Publishing Research Quarterly* 8 (Fall 1992): 72–91.

De Kerckhove, D. "What Makes the Classics Classic in the Sciences?" *Bulletin of the American Society for Information Science* 18 (February/March 1991): 13–14.

Hunter, K. A. "Through a Kaleidoscope Darkly." *Science and Technology Libraries* 12 (Summer 1992): 91–98.

Kawula, J. D. "Similarities Between Legal and Scientific Literature." *Special Libraries* 84 (Spring 1993): 85–89.

Krupp, R. G. "Issues in Acquisition of Science Literature." In *Special Librarianship*, 492–99. Metuchen, N.J.: Scarecrow Press, 1980.

Thornton, J. L. *Thornton's Medical Books, Libraries and Collectors: A Study of Bibliography and the Book Trade*. 3d rev. ed. Andershots, England: Gower, 1990.

Walker, R. D., and C. D. Hurt. *Scientific and Technical Literature*. Chicago: American Library Association, 1990.

White, H. S., and B. M. Fry. "Economic Interaction Between Special Libraries and Publishers of Scholarly and Research Journals." *Special Libraries* 68 (March 1977): 109–14.

6

Print-Based
Serials

The 21st century will, in all likelihood, be one in which we see a steady decrease in paper-based serials and a rapid rise in the number of electronic titles. Such a trend is already underway and the role of electronic serials has grown quickly since the third edition of this book went to press. Internet/ Web-based, CD-ROM products, and online services create customer expectations that present a challenge for collection development officers as well as all the library staff. Providing access to electronic resources—serials or other material—is costly and complex for a variety of reasons. Though the foregoing is true, it is also true that print-based serials are still very much a part of a library's resource base. Thus, there is the challenge of providing the most cost-effective mix of serials that will come as close as fiscal limits permit to meeting customer needs and desires. (Anyone with experience with serials knows that no matter how many titles one has, users always seem to want more!)

In chapter 7 we explore the new dimension of serial management: electronic journals and full-text journals available electronically. At this point we merely wish to note that the issue exists and is rapidly becoming another major cost concern for libraries. *Note:* Electronic journals are "publications" that exist only in an electronic format, whereas "full-text" identifies the availability of the text of paper-based journals in an electronic format. At present (1999), full-text often does not guarantee that one will find the graphic material and photographs from the print version accompanying the online text. This will change over time, but it should be noted that graphics often require high-end computers and laser-quality printers to handle the material.

Serials, regardless of their format, are important sources of current information for the public. Libraries attempt to maintain as large a collection of serials as their budgets will allow, but costs and space considerations have significantly modified the "all and forever" retention philosophy that many serials departments employed in the past.

Serial work is interesting, challenging, and frustrating. The following quote sums up the work nicely:

The Publisher is my Tormentor. I shall not smile:
He maketh me to work all day at my desk.
He leadeth me astray with misnumbered issues:
His Roman numerals confound me:
He changeth titles over and over for His own sake.
Yea, when I walk through the shadow of missing or irregular
   issues, I can find no respite, for He has moved
He answereth not my letters, nor useth the correct mailing label;
He starteth not when I ask and quiteth before it is time;
My work never endeth.
Rising prices and duplicate issues shall follow me all the days
   of my life; and
I shall moan and groan in the library forever.[1]

What Is a Serial?

Individuals (customers and librarians alike) frequently use the words *journals, magazines, periodicals*, and *serials* interchangeably, with no great misunderstanding resulting from the imprecise usage. Thomas Nisonger, in his fine book on serial management,[2] devoted more than six pages to how different groups have attempted to define the material covered in this and the next chapter.

The following definitions are adequate for the purposes of this chapter. The *ALA Glossary of Library and Information Science* provides the following definitions of two key terms:

Serial—"a publication issued in successive parts, usually at regular intervals, and, as a rule, intended to be continued indefinitely. Serials include periodicals, annuals (reports, yearbooks, etc.) and memoirs, proceedings, and transactions of societies."

Periodical—"a publication with a distinctive title intended to appear in successive (usually unbound) numbers of parts at stated or regular intervals and, as a rule, for an indefinite time. Each part generally contains articles by several contributors. Newspapers, whose chief function it is to disseminate news, and the memoirs, proceedings, journals, etc. of societies are not considered periodicals."[3]

Definitions in general dictionaries have more overlap:

Journal—"a periodical publication especially dealing with matters of current interest—often used for official or semi-official publications of special groups"

Magazine—"a periodical that usually contains a miscellaneous collection of articles, stories, poems, and pictures and is directed at the general reading public"

Periodical—"a magazine or other publication of which the issues appear at stated or regular intervals—usually for a publication appearing more frequently than annually but infrequently used for a newspaper"

Serial—"a publication (as a newspaper, journal, yearbook, or bulletin) issued as one of a consecutively numbered and indefinitely continued series"[4]

We use the term *serials* because it represents the broadest spectrum of materials.

Some years ago, Fritz Machlup and others developed an 18-part classification system for serials.[5] The following discussion uses their classification system because it covers all types of serials, including serials "not elsewhere classified." We have yet to encounter a serial that does not fit into one of his other 17 categories. Because the system appears to be comprehensive, we will describe the categories.

Institutional Reports

The first category is "annual, semiannual, quarterly or occasional reports of corporations, financial institutions, and organizations serving business and finance." Academic libraries serving business and management programs frequently need to acquire this type of serial. Some corporate libraries also actively collect this serial category. Most of the reports available to libraries and information centers are free for the asking. Some organizations will add a library to their distribution lists, but others will respond only to requests for the current edition. Collecting in this area is labor-intensive because it requires maintaining files and correspondence, especially if one collects much beyond the large national corporations. Without question, having a computer system that has both word-processing and mailing list capabilities will make collecting less tedious, but it will not reduce the need to constantly monitor the program. Corporate annual reports are issued every month. Many companies issue an annual report for the annual meeting of the management board, owner, or stockholders, which normally occurs in the month the organization was established. It had been difficult to find a satisfactory vendor for this serials category, except for 10-K reports to the Securities and Exchange Commission, which had previously been available on microfiche from Disclosure, Inc. Thanks to the advent of electronic full-text resources, EDGAR- (SEC) filings are now available from a number of sources, including *Dow Jones Interactive* and *Moody's Company Data Direct*. (A good discussion of the vendors that offer annual report assistance appears in Judith Bernstein's "Corporate Annual Reports: The Commercial Vendors."[6])

Yearbooks and Proceedings

A related category is "annuals, biennials, occasional publications, bound or stapled, including yearbooks, almanacs, proceedings, transactions, memoirs, directories and reports of societies and associations." Many libraries collect serials in this class, especially academic, special, and large public libraries. The more libraries that collect a particular society's or association's publications, the more likely it is that a commercial vendor would handle a standing order for the material. Although it is possible to secure some of these serials through a vendor, there are a significant number that one must secure directly from the society or association.

Superseding Serials

Two other labor-intensive collecting categories are 1) "superseding serial services (each new issue superseding previous ones, which are usually discarded) including telephone directories, airplane schedules, catalogs, loose-leaf data sheets, etc.," and 2) "nonsuperseding serial services bound, sewn, stapled, or loose-leaf, including bibliographic and statistical data." One must acquire most of the materials in these classes directly from the publisher. Superseding serials are important but problematic: important because people need the correct or current information, problematic as they can be difficult to track and sometimes to secure. Airline schedules, current hotel guides, and other travel-related serial sources have been something of a problem for libraries to acquire. In the past, the publishers would sell the material only to qualified travel agencies. As more and more corporations handle staff travel on their own, it has become easier for libraries to subscribe to such services. In many corporations, the library or information center maintains current travel information. In the United States, since the break-up of AT&T, libraries have found it more difficult and expensive to secure telephone directories outside their immediate area.

Loose-leaf services are particularly important in U.S. law libraries and accounting firms (two examples, *Labor Relations Reporter,* from the Bureau of National Affairs, and *Standard Federal Tax Reporter,* from Commerce Clearing House). Proper filing and discarding of material is of critical importance in such an environment, because incorrect information can be very costly to a firm (perhaps the clearest way to demonstrate the cost of not having the right information at the right time). With a loose-leaf service, one must make certain that all sections released are received. Many publishers of loose-leaf services make their services available through the Internet/Web and some also offer CD-ROM versions. Naturally, there is a substantial cost for the electronic versions; however, one needs to weigh the value of reducing staff labor in filing the material as well as the greater assurance that what is available is in fact correct. (The problem of misfiling or even not filing material can be costly for a organization such as a law firm.)

Nonsuperseding serials are less of a problem, and some are available from serial jobbers. However, the materials in this class tend to be expensive, and one must order them directly from the publisher. Indexing and abstracting services fall into one of these two classes. All types of libraries need a few of these reference serials. As the serial collection grows, there is an increasing demand from patrons for more indexing and abstracting services.

Newspapers

All types of libraries, with the exception of elementary school media centers, collect newspapers, another serial category. Almost every small public library receives the local newspaper and one or two newspapers from nearby communities. Large public and academic libraries try to have some national and foreign newspaper coverage. Serial jobbers handle subscriptions to major newspapers for libraries. Thus, it would be possible to place one order with a jobber, such as Faxon or EBSCO, for almost all the major newspapers from around the world. At the time the order is placed, selectors and collection development officers must establish the value of the newspapers' content, in the sense of the demand or need to have the latest issue in the shortest time. For example, one can receive the *London Times* in a variety of packages, each with a different cost: daily airmail edition by air freight, daily airmail edition by airmail (the most expensive option), daily regular edition by air freight, daily regular edition in weekly packets (the least expensive option), or microfilm edition. The *New York Times* offers a wider variety of editions: city edition, late city edition, national edition, New York edition, large-type weekly, same day, next day, two-day, weekly packets, and microfilm.

As is clear, subscribing to a newspaper is no simple matter. Depending on the library's clientele, a certain edition and delivery method will provide the right service at the least cost, but determining the right combination takes more time than selecting a book.

Like other serials, newspapers present special storage and access problems. When a library subscribes to several newspapers, a display of recent issues can occupy a large portion of a current issues area. For research libraries, long-term storage is a problem. Bound newspapers tend to be large, heavy, and awkward to handle. The poor quality of newsprint presents preservation problems. Today, most libraries use a microformat for back issue storage, but this adds to the overall subscription cost, because most newspaper companies control the microfilming of their publication. Access is another problem, except for the largest newspapers, because most indexing services cover only the best-known papers.

A number of the major newspapers are now available online—some from a vendor (for example, LEXIS-NEXIS), some only through the publisher. According to Wallys Conhaim, 600 daily newspapers (about one-third of the U.S. total) were operating some level of online service in early 1998.[7] Electronic versions may solve some of the storage issues associated with newspaper backfiles, at least to a point. They also work well for many readers, as the articles are not very long and people are more willing to read an article without wanting to print a hard copy. Often, however, people demand good-quality printing capability for electronic journal articles because of their length. If one subscribes to a sizable number of regional or local newspapers that are available electronically through a service such as *Newsbank*, it may be more economical to choose this option. In any event, choosing the electronic version would lessen the "housekeeping" (storage, reshelving, claims) costs for the print versions held. These costs can be difficult to track.

Newsletters

Newsletters, leaflets, news releases, and similar materials represent yet another serial category of major importance for some libraries. Special libraries are the most likely to become involved in the ongoing collection of this class of serial. Many of the items in this class are very inexpensive or free. Others, especially newsletters, can cost thousands of dollars. In either case, someone must put in the time and effort to identify the sources and get on the appropriate mailing lists. Libraries in marketing and public relations firms are likely to be active collectors of this type of material. Any library operating in a disturbed-reactive or turbulent information environment (see pages 12–13) is likely to collect heavily in this class.

Magazines

What are the most common serials? Eleven of Machlup's categories cover the variations in the common serials—magazines and journals (scholarly publications). According to Machlup's definition, magazines are mass-market serials, the ones that almost any serial jobber will handle for a library. His magazine categories include:

- Mass-market serials, weekly or monthly news magazines (such as *Newsweek*)

- Popular magazines dealing with fiction, pictures, sports, travel, fashion, sex, humor, and comics (an example is *Sports Illustrated*)

- Magazines that popularize science, social, political, and cultural affairs (*Smithsonian*)

- Magazines focusing particularly on opinion and criticism—social, political, literary, artistic, aesthetic, or religious (an example is *Foreign Affairs*)

- "Other magazines not elsewhere classified" category. An example of an item in this last category is an organization publication (governmental or private) that is really a public relations vehicle, sometimes called a *house organ*. These publications often contain general-interest material, but there is usually some clearly stated or implied relationship between the subject covered and the issuing organization (e.g., *Plain Truth*). Another type of publication in the "other" category is the magazine found in the pocket of airline seats. These publications contains interesting short articles about people, places, and things. Many contain advertising, so the magazine not only helps distract the nervous traveler, but also provides an additional source of revenue for the airline.

Libraries may receive a substantial number of house organs, as their publishers give them away. We do not know of any library collecting airline magazines, but perhaps, somewhere, in a research or corporate library, some collection development officer is trying to work out a plan for doing just that. Who knows when some sociologist may wish to study the reading habits of airline passengers? Vendors seldom handle this type of magazine.

Journals

Machlup similarly divided journals into four subcategories, with one category divided into two smaller units:

- nonspecialized journals for the intelligentsia well-informed on literature, art, social affairs, politics, etc. (*Science* is an example)

- learned journals for specialists—primary research journals and secondary research journals (*American Indian Culture and Research Journal,* for example)

- practical professional journals in applied fields, including technology, medicine, law, agriculture, management, library science, business, and trades (*RQ*)

- parochial journals of any type but addressed chiefly to a parochial audience, whether local or regional (*Kiva*).

Again, most titles in these categories are available through vendors, although one must place direct orders for some of the more specialized learned journals. Most parochial journals must be purchased directly from the publisher; local history and regional archaeological publications are examples of this class of serial.

The final serial category identified by Machlup was "government publications, reports, bulletins, statistical series, releases, etc. by public agencies, executive, legislative and judiciary, local, state, national, foreign and international." Because we cover this group in chapter 9, no further discussion is offered here.

With the preceding variations in serials in mind, you can understand why there is confusion about terms and challenges in collecting and preserving them. Each type fills a niche in the information dissemination system. Although they do create special handling problems, they are a necessary part of any library's collection, and the public service staff must deal with them.

Several characteristics unique to serials make this format useful. For many patrons, serials are the most important source of printed information. Serials contain the most current information about a topic, other than what may be available on an electronic bulletin board or discussion list. Some professional-society serial publications are very slow to appear, and scholars in the field will know about the material before it is published in the journal; nevertheless, the journal article will be the first published source of information. (Given the importance of currency, providing a system that allows patrons to determine the latest issue received is important.) Related to currency is the frequency with which serials update information. For serials, the update interval can be short; for example, newspapers are updated daily. (In contrast, few monographs get updated, and for those titles that go into second or subsequent editions, the update interval may be several years.) Serial articles can be short and tend to focus on narrow subjects; thus, readers with a specific information need frequently find that serials provide the desired information more quickly than monographic publications. Finally, serials are often the first printed source of information about a new subject or development. People use serials to learn about new ideas, concepts, and information, and they use monographs to gain a broader or deeper knowledge of a subject.

Selection of Serials

Selection and deselection of serials focus on three basic issues: titles currently in the collection, titles not in the collection, and new titles. One uses slightly different criteria in assessing each group. When reexamining titles in the collection, subscription price and use patterns are the two primary issues (see page 165 for an explanation of why periodic reexamination is necessary).

Looking at interlibrary loan (ILL) data and citation analysis information helps one decide whether an existing title that is not in the collection ought to be. For new titles, the subject area, cost, and—when available— reviews are the key elements in deciding whether to place a subscription. As with books, one can incorporate some macro selection decisions into the collection development policy for serials. Some possible macro decisions are:

- Subscribe to any titles requested by users that match collected subject areas (this rule is often used in special libraries).
- Subscribe to any title borrowed through ILL more than X number of times.
- Subscribe to all core titles, as identified through citation analysis, in subject areas collected.
- Do not subscribe to unindexed titles.
- Do not subscribe to journals that contain unrefereed articles.

The list could go on; the point is, the more macro decisions there are, the easier serials management becomes.

One can also make other broad generalizations about serials selection. The fields of science, technology, and medicine (commonly abbreviated as STM in the literature) are very dependent on serial publications. At the opposite end of the spectrum are the humanities, which depend more on books than on serials. Between these two are the social sciences, some of which are more similar to the science disciplines (e.g., psychology, linguistics, physical anthropology), and others of which are more similar to the humanities (e.g., political science, education, and social anthropology).

A decision to subscribe to or place a standing order for a serial is a much bigger decision than similar decisions for monographs. Several factors account for the difference. Because serials are ongoing, they can become a standing commitment for the library or information center and thus become a more-or-less fixed element in the materials budget. Because serials arrive in the library or information center in parts, there must be an ongoing process for receiving the parts and maintaining records about what did or did not arrive. Unfortunately, few serials arrive in a form that allows for easy long-term storage or heavy use; therefore, libraries must bind or otherwise develop a means to preserve them. In addition, serials occupy large amounts of storage space, which over time becomes scarce. Gaining access to the contents of most serials usually requires use of indexing and abstracting services, which are in themselves serials. Adding a new indexing or abstracting service typically results in additional work for the ILL unit, unless the library subscribes to all of the titles covered by the service. A serials collection that does not provide for quick, easy, and inexpensive photocopy services will quickly become a collection of covers and advertisements; the articles will disappear. When adding a title that has been published for some time, one must consider the question of backfiles. Finally, serials change over time. These are the most important differences between selecting a book and a serial.

Unlike a monograph, a serial normally implies a long-term commitment. Subscriptions require renewals, but with most vendor plans the renewal process is automatic, requiring no action on the part of the collection development staff. When the subscription renewal requires a positive decision by the library staff, the serial holdings are more likely to reflect the current interests of the library's customers. With automatic renewal, there is a substantial chance that the library will continue inappropriate serials long after the serial ceases to meet community needs.

A long-term commitment to a serial results in subscription costs becoming a fixed feature of the budget. With rapidly rising prices and small budget increases, each year serials take up an increasing proportion of the total materials budget. Chapter 13 on fiscal management provides more information about this problem, but in general, serial prices have been increasing at a much faster rate than general inflation. Thus, each year the amount of money required to maintain the present serials subscriptions increases at a rate greater than many libraries are able to sustain.

Another fixed cost is processing. When ordering and receiving a monograph, the library incurs a one-time cost. Serials have ongoing receiving and renewal costs, in addition to the cost of placing the initial order. Claiming missing issues is a normal part of maintaining a serials collection. A staff member records each issue when it arrives in the library. When the person notes that an issue is missing or that a number has been skipped, the library contacts the publisher or agent to attempt to secure the missing material. (This is called *placing a claim*.) Acting promptly on claims is important, because serial publishers print only slightly more copies than the number of subscribers. Serial publishers know that a certain percentage of issues sent will go astray in the mail, and they print extra copies to cover the expected claims. However, at times the number of claims is greater than the number of available copies. When that happens, a number of unlucky libraries receive out-of-print notices. The closer the claim is made to the publication date, the greater the chances are of receiving the missing issue. (The consequences of small print runs appear again when it is time to bind the volume and the library discovers that one of the issues is missing. Locating a copy can be time-consuming, if not impossible.) Daily serial check-in is a must to avoid missing issues. Automated serial systems help speed routine serials work, including providing automatic claiming, but in a library with a large serials list, one or more full-time staff may work exclusively on processing serials. Clearly, each new serial adds to the workload on an ongoing basis.

By their nature, serials arrive in successive issues, normally as paperbacks. If the library maintains serials for long periods of time or the titles receive relatively heavy use, the library must repackage the serial for more convenient handling. One method is to store the loose issues in a cardboard or metal container (sometimes referred to as a Princeton File) that keeps a limited number of issues together in a vertical position. This makes it easier to shelve the loose issues alongside bound materials. The container must have room on its outfacing side to record the title and issue or volume number of the items in the box. The most common long-term storage treatment is binding. A third alternative, microformat storage, represents an additional cost. Whatever choice is made, there is an ongoing cost to package each serial year after year.

Eventually, finding storage space for collections becomes a problem for all libraries and information centers. Storing long runs of serials can consume large quantities of limited shelf space. Using microforms as the long-term storage format for long runs of low-use serials will help with the space problem for a time. However, microforms also present some problems. Customers usually resist and complain about using microforms, so there is a public relations issue to address when shifting to microforms. Microforms also mean acquiring equipment: microform readers at a minimum, with reader-printers being the best solution. Libraries usually have at least two types of microform readers, film and fiche. Most machines have several lenses to accommodate various reduction ratios. The library must maintain the equipment and provide users with assistance as needed, especially when it is necessary to change lenses. As the size of the microform collection increases, more equipment will be needed to meet user demands. Finally, microform storage cabinets are heavy when empty and very heavy when full. Libraries may face problems in locating a growing collection of such cabinets if the floor cannot sustain their combined weight. Clearly, microform brings with it new costs and concerns.

Another solution for storage is to move low-use items to a less accessible and less costly facility. Yet another solution is to deselect some titles. As space becomes scarce, decisions about what to keep and for how long become more and more difficult. Given the current nature of most serials, older holdings are prime candidates for remote storage. After making the first, relatively easy decisions about which titles to store, weeding decisions become increasingly complex, take more time, and can lead to conflicts between staff and patrons. This is discussed in more detail in chapter 14.

An important consideration in serials selection is how the patron gains access to the information each issue contains. Going through each issue is not efficient, and few patrons are willing to do this. Many serials produce an annual index, but this is of no help with current issues. An entire industry has developed around providing access to serials. A variety of indexing and abstracting companies now provide services that assist in locating information in serials. Naturally, most of these services are expensive and are a hidden cost of building a serials collection. Though Harvard's Tozzer Library (an anthropology library) is atypical, it illustrates the nature of the problem. That library receives more than 1,200 anthropology serials each year. If it did not do its own indexing, the library would have to spend more than $30,000 per year for indexing and abstracting services to achieve only 83 percent coverage of its serial holdings. Tozzer's solution to the indexing problem is to index all the serials it receives. It publishes the index as *Anthropological Literature*, which helps offset the indexing costs.

One selection question is, "Should one subscribe only to commercially indexed serials?" If a library subscribes to an unindexed title, does the library do anything to help patrons locate information in the new serial? Specialized (subject) indexing services lead to patron requests for titles indexed in the service but not held by the library. The library must then decide whether to add yet another title to the serials list, increase the interlibrary loan (ILL) department's workload, or make patrons unhappy. Copyright law limits the library's ability to use ILL in place of subscribing to a particular title; copyright law imposes legal constraints on the frequency with which one may borrow articles from a single serial title (see chapter 18).

Document delivery services for journal articles are changing the nature of the selection decision. These systems, such as CARL Uncover (originated by the Colorado Alliance of Research Libraries), allow libraries and information centers to offer customers access to thousands of serial titles and their tables of contents. Not only can one identify articles through an index service (presently search capabilities are not very sophisticated), but one can also order the items. The services have taken care of copyright, and the patron receives the full text. There are substantial costs ($10 to $20 per article on average) which the library or customer must pay. Mode of delivery varies from postal service to facsimile, with corresponding price differences. For low-use titles, document delivery (DD) services may be the most cost-effective way to provide service. As of 1993 in the United States, the DD business was small ($60–$70 million) compared to the subscription business (about $1 billion).[8] Today the gap is much narrower and will, in all likelihood, continue to lessen in the future.

Selecting a document delivery or full-text vendor requires as much consideration as selecting a serial title. One must assume that funds to pay for the documents, unless the users are to pay the full costs, are likely to come from collection development allocations. Like all aspects of collection development, one must have a clear understanding of the purpose of and need for the service. Some of the possible reasons for employing a service are:

- To provide faster service than through traditional ILL service
- To reduce the overall cost of ILL by having less mediation
- To reduce subscriptions to high-cost, low-use journals
- To provide a supplement to course reserve usage.

Other issues include the type of equipment required to implement the service and what, if any, remote access is available. The factors one uses to evaluate possible vendors are the same as for other library vendors (see chapter 12), such as service and size. As popular as document delivery services are electronic indexing and full-text delivery services. These are discussed in greater detail in chapter 7.

Serials tend to increase the volume of photocopying activities. Serial articles are short (seldom more than 25 pages); as a result, many people prefer to photocopy the article and consult the material at their leisure. Also, many libraries do not allow serials, or at least journals, to circulate, which further encourages photocopying. The amount of library or information center photocopying is another copyright issue. Although the copyright law covers photocopying of monographs, it is the serials photocopying that is the major issue among serial publishers, librarians, and users.

When a library does not start a subscription with volume 1, number 1, the librarian must decide whether and to what extent to acquire back issues or volumes. Are backfiles needed? Some serial publishers have full runs available, but most do not. Titles widely held by libraries may be available from reprint houses. Backfiles are expensive, they may be difficult to find, they may require binding, they certainly take up valuable shelf space, and many receive little use. Libraries also cannot assume that vendors handling online full-text serials will maintain backfiles or make them available for all titles.

Serials can and do change over time. New editors, governing boards, or owners make major and minor shifts in the content and orientation. A major shift in emphasis usually is well publicized. As selectors become aware of such shifts, they can reassess the serial. A title change is something librarians frequently complain about, primarily because of internal concerns (see articles by Foggin[9] and Nelson[10]). From a collection development point of view, a title change should be welcome because it probably signals a significant change in the serial's content. For that reason, the selectors should review the changes in content to determine whether the item is still appropriate for the collection. More difficult to identify is a slow shift over a number of years. The final result may be a greater difference in content than a well-publicized major change, but few people will notice the shift. Periodic examination of incoming serials by the selection officers is an excellent method for checking on changes in emphasis.

Given all of these factors, one can see why serial selection is a major decision. Yet, all too often, libraries treat it as being no different from the decision to acquire a monograph.

Selection Models

There are five basic approaches to selection: cost, citation analysis, worth or use, polling, and core lists. There are many variations, but the five listed form the basis for models for selecting serials. Much of the work done in this area is relatively recent and more the result of having to cancel rather than to start subscriptions.

Cost models of selection are the oldest and have the greatest number of variations. One of the most complex models deals with the real annual cost of a serial. The annual cost consists of six elements: acquisition cost, processing cost, maintenance cost, storage cost, utility or use cost, and subscription price. *Acquisition costs* include such things as selection, order placement, and time spent in working with the subscription agent or publisher. *Processing costs* cover check-in, claiming, routing, cataloging or other labeling, adding security strips, and shelving in public service for the first time. *Maintenance costs* involve binding, microfilming or acquiring microform, selecting for remote storage, and possibly discarding. *Storage costs* entail calculating the linear feet of storage space (either or both shelf and cabinet space) used by the title and the cost of the space. *Utility* or *use costs* are the most complex to calculate. They incorporate costs of time for such things as retrieval from a storage location (library staff only), pick-up and reshelving, answering questions about the title ("Do you have ...?", "I can't find ...", and "What is the latest issue you have?"), and all other required assistance (assistance with microform readers, for example). The last, and often the lowest, cost is the subscription price. The sum of these costs represents the real annual cost of the title for the library. Looking over the list of costs makes it clear that it will take some time to calculate the individual cost centers. However, once one determines the unit costs (for example, the average time to shelve an issue), it is fairly easy to calculate the cost for a given number of issues of a title. With an annual cost for each title, selectors can determine which titles to continue or discontinue. Several articles describing variations on this approach are included in the "Further Reading" section at the end of this chapter.

Like cost models, citation analysis paradigms take several forms. The main objective, from a selection point of view, is to identify frequently cited titles. Citation analysis can help identify a core collection for a field and provide a listing of titles ranked by the frequency with which they are cited. Another collection development use of citation analysis is in evaluating a collection. (Could a set of papers/reports have been done using this collection?) Citation analysis information is most useful in large or specialized research collections, although core collection information is valuable to smaller and nonspecialized collections as well.

It is important to understand certain assumptions about citation analysis before deciding to use this approach. The underlying assumption is that the subject content of the cited document relates to that of the citing document. A second assumption is that the number of times a document receives a citation is proportional to the value or intrinsic worth of the document. Another assumption is that all the publications an author cites were, in fact, used. (A related assumption is that authors list all the sources they used.) One other major assumption is that the sources used to secure the citation data are representative of the field under investigation. These are the major assumptions; others do exist. However, many people do not accept all the assumptions. If one cannot accept the assumptions, one should not use citation data for collection building.

There are two major sources of citation data: research reports and articles in the professional press, and data from the publishing firm Institute for Scientific Information (ISI). ISI publishes *Science Citation Index (SCI), Social Sciences Citation Index (SSCI)*, and *Humanities Citation Index (HCI)*. These publications provide citation information for many journals. For example, *SSCI* covers almost 1,500 social science titles and provides selective coverage of about 4,500 nonsocial science journals that contain some social science material. On an annual basis, ISI also produces *Journal Citation Reports (JAR)*, which provides a useful analysis of the journals ISI covers. Some of the major features of *JAR* are:

- a listing of the number of articles a title contained for the year
- how many citations were made to articles that appeared in the title through time
- a ratio of articles published to articles cited (impact factor)

- a ratio of articles published during the year to citations to those articles (immediacy index)

- a cited half-life, that is, how far back in time one needs to go to retrieve 50 percent of all citations appearing during a year to all articles that ever appeared in the title.

Such information can be helpful in making continuation and storage or deselection decisions.

Using the Bradford Distribution, one can rank titles to develop information for collection policy use as well to make decisions regarding current subscriptions.[11] The goal of this ranking is to identify all journals containing articles relevant to a given subject and to rank them in order based on the number of relevant articles they publish in a year. The pattern, according to Bradford's Law of Scattering, will show that a few journals publish the majority of articles and a large number of journals publish only one or two cited articles. If one equates a basic collection (level 2 in the conspectus concept, see pages 78–79 with holding journals that contain 20 percent of the relevant material, one might subscribe to only three or four titles. For libraries with a comprehensive collection (level 5), the subscription list may contain several hundred titles. For example, Tozzer Library has a current subscription list of more than 1,200 titles for its coverage of anthropology. Journal worth models usually involve some information about title usage along with other data. An article by Dawn Bick and Reeta Sinha described one of the many worth models,[12] one that is reasonably easy to implement. The model involves cost, use, impact factor, and information about the nature of the publication (core subject, for example) to calculate a cost-benefit ratio.

As one might assume, most of the models require a substantial amount of data collection. If their only utility lay in making selection decisions, few libraries would use them. Their major value comes into play when the library must cut subscriptions. Having collected data that is similar for all the titles makes the unpleasant task a little easier. What librarians hoped would be a rare occurrence has, for some libraries, become an almost annual task. Each time the task becomes more difficult, and the models demonstrate their value.

Polling experts and using lists of recommended journals are other methods for identifying what to buy or keep. Both suffer from being less directly linked to the local situation, unless the experts are local users. One can find lists of journals in relatively narrow subjects, often listed with recommendations, or at least comments, in journals like *Serials Librarian* and *Serials Review*.

Maria Janowska described a rather complex model to use when making the choice between paper and electronic materials.[13] She drew on a publishing method known as Multiple Criteria Evaluation (MCE). Her approach used content, publication cycle, number of subscribers, overall cost, and price as the criteria. She then used a matrix that allows one to compare the criteria against one another, which allows consistency in the decision-making process. The process is somewhat complex but is worth considering when making a series of decisions regarding paper or electronic journals.

Identifying Serials

Serials employ a different bibliographic network than that used for monographs. Few of the selection aids for books cover serials. However, there are several general and specialized guides to serial publications. Reviews of serials are few and far between. Bill Katz's column in *Library Journal* is one regular source of serial reviews. In the past, when publishers would supply several free sample copies of a title for the library to examine, the lack of reviews was not a problem. Today, many publishers charge for sample issues, and though it depletes the funds for subscribing to serials and adds to the time it takes to acquire them, it is useful to get sample issues before committing the library to a new serial.

Four useful general guides are *Ulrich's International Periodicals Directory* (R. R. Bowker), *Irregular Serials & Annuals* (R. R. Bowker), *Serials Directory* (EBSCO), and *Standard Periodical Directory* (Oxbridge Communications). All employ a subject arrangement, and entries provide all necessary ordering information. Bowker updates the annual *Ulrich's* with *Ulrich's Update*. Another resource, *Standard Periodical Directory,* covers American and Canadian titles and has a reputation for providing the best coverage of publications with small circulations, lesser-known organizations, and processed materials.

Newspapers, newsletters, and serials published at least five times a year are identifiable in guides like *Gale Directory of Publications and Broadcast Media* (Gale Research) and *Willings' Press Guide* (Thomas Skinner Directories). For literary publications, one should use *International Directory of Little Magazines and Small Presses* (Dustbooks), *MLA International Bibliography* (Modern Language Association), and *L'Année Philologique* (Société International de Bibliographie Classique).

All of the above, with the exception of *Ulrich's Update,* have limited value in identifying new titles, because they are annuals and the information is therefore at least several months old. (As noted earlier, serials change in a variety of ways—titles, frequency, editorial policy, and so on—and keeping up with existing titles is enough of a problem without adding the need to identify newly created serials.) The best source of information about serials acquired by American libraries is the Library of Congress's *New Serial Titles (NST),* which reflects data in OCLC. The data in *NST* is the result of a cooperative effort called Cooperative Online Serial Program (CONSER). One gains a useful sense of the number of existing serial titles when one considers that in 1981, there were 339,000 CONSER records in OCLC; in 1997–1998, there were 856,618 records, with the addition of almost 34,000 new records. If one can justify costs, online systems provide the most current information. Certainly OCLC is one source, as are BRS and DIALOG. The latter services have information from *Ulrich's.* Such services are current but costly; $75 per hour is not an uncommon charge, so one must be certain that the speed and currency are essential. Some serial vendors also supply new serial titles information online.

Using a review of serials presents certain difficulties. Most serials that receive reviews are popular magazines rather than scholarly journals. Given the propensity of serials for change, a completely accurate assessment of a title is possible only when the serial ceases publication and the reviewer can examine all the issues. All that one should expect from a review of a serial is an accurate description of the content of the issue(s) available to the reviewer, usually not more than six issues. What a selector wants from the review is as much information about the purpose, audience, and editorial policy as the reviewer can identify; information about publisher, price, frequency, and other technical matters; and, if appropriate, comparisons to other related serials. Unfortunately, some of those limited data may be lacking, because it is sometimes difficult to determine purpose and editorial policy, even with the volume 1, number 1, issue in hand. Information about the publisher is less important in serials selection than in monograph selection because many times the serial is the publisher's only publication, and only time will reveal the publisher's reliability.

Serials Review (Pierian Press) publishes some reviews prepared by serials librarians and, occasionally, subject experts. The journal started as both a reviewing journal and a professional journal for serials librarians. Today it is primarily a professional journal, with only a few pages of serials reviews in each volume. Occasionally, Serials Review reviews an established serial. Such reviews help librarians monitor changes in the editorial policy of titles to which the library subscribes.

Library Journal (R. R. Bowker) offers a regular section focusing on new periodicals. Each issue contains brief annotations describing 6 to 10 new titles. Because of the breadth of coverage, most types of libraries will find some titles of interest covered in the course of a year. Every few years, Bill Katz and Linda Sternberg Katz compile Magazines for Libraries,[14] in which they list 6,000 to 7,000 recommended titles.

New Magazine Review (New Magazine Review) covers titles of particular interest to public librarians. Choice (Association of College & Research Libraries) features a column, "Periodicals for College Libraries." An additional way to see new titles is to check at book and serial exhibitor booths at professional association meetings.

One can also use "core" or recommended lists for a variety of subject fields. Two examples are: A. Brandon and D. Hill's "Selected List of Books and Journals for the Small Medical Library," Bulletin of the Medical Library Association 83 (April 1995): 151–75; and Selma Richardson's Magazines for Children, 2d ed. (Chicago: American Library Association, 1991). Some caution is in order when using core lists; one must understand the methodology employed to generate the list and know that it fits the needs of the library.

Serial Vendors

For most libraries, it is not economical to place serial subscriptions directly with the publisher. As we have seen, the amount of work required to monitor expiration dates, place renewals, and approve payments repeatedly for each title is too great. In any sizable serials collection, a few titles will be direct orders to the publisher; however, if a library uses a serials vendor for most orders, there will be more time for other problem-solving activities related to serials.

Serials jobbers tend not to handle monographs, just as book jobbers tend not to handle serials. Tend is the key word here, given the variety of serials; in the area of annuals and numbered monograph series, lines become blurred and jobbers overlap. Given the nature of serial publications, one is better served by an experienced serials jobber than by a friendly and willing book jobber who offers to handle the serials list along with book orders. Many serials librarians find it best to use domestic dealers for domestic serials and foreign dealers for foreign titles. Choosing a foreign dealer can be a challenge; for American libraries, the American Library Association's *International Subscription Agents: An Annotated Directory* is helpful. The 1994 edition lists agents and provides information about countries and regions covered, types of material serviced, catalogs or listings provided to customers, notes about special services (standing orders for monographs, for example), and name and address. It is advisable to ask other librarians about their experience with the dealers one is considering. If the librarian cannot identify anyone using a dealer, he or she might start by placing one or two subscriptions with the dealer and increase the volume of business if service is satisfactory.

Service is what one is looking for in a serials vendor. To provide service, the company must make a profit. How does it do that? In the past, vendors offered discounts. Today, libraries pay a service charge based on a percentage of the total subscription price. Serial vendors have one minor and two major sources of income. One major source is the discount publishers offer vendors. (Publishers offer these discounts because it is more convenient for them to deal with one billing/ordering source rather than subscriptions to many individual subscribers.) Recently, librarians have blamed publishers for rising subscription costs, but a few publishers claim that vendors share the blame because vendors are not passing on a share of the discount they receive from the publishers. Whatever the case may be, vendors depend on publishers' discounts to make a profit.

The second major revenue source for vendors is the service charge they add to their invoices to libraries. The service charge varies from library to library, depending on several factors. It often requires a good deal of work to determine just what the service charge is. When a subscription list contains thousands of titles, it is unlikely that there will be only one invoice, if for no other reason than that prices change during the year; supplementary invoices will arrive. Sales representatives may not know all the factors involved in calculating the charge and can give only an overview explanation. There may be various rates for various types of publications: in part, the service charge depends on the size of the discount the vendor receives.

Another variable in the calculation of a library's service charge is what services the library uses. Often, there is an extra charge for handling unusual serials, such as government publications. The types and number of management reports the library receives from the vendor also affect the service charge. Title mix is another factor, just as it is with book jobbers. For serial vendors, it is more a matter of knowing which titles generate additional work for the vendor, rather than a bookseller's pricing concerns with popular titles (low price/high discount) versus scholarly titles (high price/low discount). If a library has a high percentage of problem titles, its service charge may be somewhat higher than for another library with a similar number of subscriptions, costing about the same, but with fewer problem titles.

The setting of the service charge is an art, and the service charge is open to negotiation. A good book on the acquisition aspects of serial work is N. Bernard Basch and Judy McQueen's *Buying Serials.*[15] A growing source of income comes from a variety of extra services most agencies offer, such as automation packages, publishing and electronic services (CD-ROMs, for example), or custom lists.

What does the customer receive beyond the basic advantage of one order, one invoice, and one check for multiple subscriptions? Automatic renewal by a vendor saves library staff time, and when the invoice arrives, there is the opportunity to cancel titles no longer needed. Jobbers may offer multiple-year subscription rates that will save the library money. Notifying libraries about discontinuations, mergers, changes in frequency, and other publication alterations is a standard service provided by a serials jobber. The jobber is more likely to learn of changes before a library does, especially if the jobber has placed hundreds of subscriptions with the publisher.

Vendors also provide some assistance in the claiming process (missing issues, breaks in service, and damaged copies). Several of the larger American subscription agents (for example, EBSCO and Readmore) have fully automated serial systems that libraries use to handle their serials management programs, including online claiming. (Faxon supports a backfile service, *SerialsQuest*, that includes data from libraries and dealers.) For libraries with manual claiming systems, most vendors offer two forms of claims: one by which the library notifies the vendor, which in turn contacts the supplier; and one by which the vendor supplies forms for the library to use to contact the publisher. Assistance in claiming has become more important in the past 10 to 15 years as more and more popular-market publishers use fulfillment centers. These centers serve as a publishers' jobber; that is, a center handles a number of different publishers' titles by receiving, entering subscriptions, and sending copies to subscribers. (For such centers, the mailing label is the key to solving problems; until recently, few libraries worried about serials' mailing labels.) Often the subscription vendor is more effective in resolving a problem with a fulfillment center than is a single library.

Management information is another service serial vendors offer. Their information regarding price changes can be most useful in preparing budget requests. (A sample of this type of data appears in figure 12.1, page 344).

Other types of management information that may be available (at an extra cost) are reports that sort the subscription list by subject or classification category, accompanied by the total amount spent for each group or (if there are several groups) a record of how many titles and how much money were charged to each group.

A good place to learn about the variety of services available, and who offers which services, is at the national meetings of various library associations. For example, representatives of most national serial vendors, as well as a number of foreign vendors, attend the ALA annual conventions. They will supply more than enough promotional material to fill a suitcase. Collect the information (including a formal request to quote), make comparisons, and talk with other librarians about their experiences with various vendors; this is the best way to go about selecting a vendor for one's library.

Cooperation in Serials Work

No library can acquire and keep all the serials that its patrons need or will at some time request. Knowing who has what serial holdings is important to serials librarians and anyone involved in interlibrary loan activities. The CONSER project and *NST* help to identify holdings in American and Canadian libraries. It is interesting to note that, despite the long-time concern about serial holdings, it was not until early 1986 that a national standard for serials holding statements was adopted in the United States (ANSI Z39.44). The standard provides for the same data areas, data elements, and punctuation in summary holding statements in both manual and automated systems.

Although the Center for Research Libraries (CRL) is much more than a cooperative serials program, CRL serial holdings have been effective in holding down the amount of duplication of low-use serial titles in American and Canadian research libraries. Bibliographic utilities such as OCLC and RLIN, whose databases include serial holdings, provide a type of union list service that H. W. Wilson's *Union List of Serials* provided so well in the past. To some extent, even vendor-based systems offer a form of union listing. Though it is possible to use such union lists and shared holdings to cover some low-use serial requirements, the librarian must be certain to comply with copyright regulations before deciding not to buy.

Many libraries using the same serials vendor are able to acquire union lists from the vendor. For example, the four largest Catholic universities in California (University of San Francisco, Santa Clara University, Loyola Marymount University, and the University of San Diego) use EBSCO and have a union list produced each year to coordinate serial holdings. The libraries have agreed that when only one institution holds a title, there will be consultation with other libraries before the library drops the title.

Issues and Concerns

Several major issues face libraries today in regard to their serial collections. Cost is perhaps the major concern (cost of subscriptions, processing, storing, changing value of currencies, and tight budgets). Another issue is the delivery of serial information to customers without subscribing to the title by using document delivery or, as some librarians phrase it, "just in time rather than just in case." Related to document delivery are questions about copyright and traditional ILL services; on a percentage basis, ILL does more work with serials than monographs.

Continued growth in the number of serials and their spiraling costs are two issues of grave concern, especially for scholarly journals. Areas of knowledge are constantly being divided into smaller and smaller segments; at the same time, these smaller audiences want more information about the narrower topic. An example of the problem may be seen from the journal department of Academic Press, which announced one new journal, *Applied Computational Harmonic Analysis*; one journal dividing into two parts: *Journal of Magnetic Resonance—Series A* and *Series B*; and seven titles increasing the number of issues per volume. All these changes carried price increases with them.

Costs of producing a special-interest journal will rise, no matter how many or how few people are interested in reading about the subject. When a journal reaches a certain price level, the number of individual subscribers drops quickly. More often than not, any price increase to individual subscribers only makes the problem worse. Increasingly, journal publishers have adopted a dual pricing system, one price for individuals and another, higher price (often double or triple the individual rate) for institutions (read: libraries). The publishers' premise is that an institutional subscription serves the needs of many readers, which justifies the higher price. An interesting ethical question for librarians in general, and collection development personnel in particular is: Is it ethical for a library to regularly accept an individual's gift of a journal that has a high dual-rate subscription? (Our view is no, the library should not do that. If not for ethical reasons, there are practical concerns about the regularity with which the person delivers the issues, as well as with securing missing issues.)

If publishers take the dual-pricing concept to its logical conclusion, publishers will demand that libraries track the use of each serial and pay an annual service fee based on that number. Or, as one occasionally sees in the literature, publishers will make the title available only on a site-licensed basis. Before dismissing the idea as unrealistic, one should consider two things. First, for years libraries subscribing to H. W. Wilson's periodical indexes have been paying an annual service fee or subscription fee based on the number of journals indexed to which the library subscribes. Second, some countries, including Canada, now have a lending fee, that is, a fee paid to the author for each circulated use of his or her book in a public library (see chapter 18).

There are two types of journal price studies with which collection development staff should become familiar: macro pricing and micro pricing. Macro information deals with subscription prices, rates of increase, and projections of coming price increases. One can obtain this type of data about the library's subscription list from the library's serials vendor (see fig. 13.4, page 385). Information about overall price changes appears in several sources for U.S. serials, including *Library Journal* and *American Libraries*. One problem for many libraries is that data about projected price changes appears at a time when it is of little help in preparing the budget request for the next fiscal year. The data may be useful, but it is about a year behind the budget. That is, one uses 2001 projections for preparing the 2002–2003 budget request. (See chapter 13 for more information about budgeting.) What was clear at the time we prepared this edition was that no relief is in sight in terms of price increases. (One serials vendor issued an information sheet in late 1998 indicating that the price escalation had not really slowed. The vendor projected the 1999 increases in prices to range from 9.5 to 11.5 percent.) This pattern has been facing libraries for many years. Publishers don't understand why libraries cut their subscription lists and libraries and users don't understand why the prices must rise by so much more than the consumer price index.

Micro studies examine cost of the information in the journal, number of articles per volume, number of pages, page size, and cost per thousand words or characters. Such studies are helpful in the retention and cancellation activities in which more and more libraries must engage on an annual basis. (Finding micro studies takes a little effort; one good article dealing with the subject and presenting some examples is by Barbara Meyers and Janice Fleming.[16]) Not all publishers are pleased to see micro studies published, but such studies do provide useful data for building a cost-effective serials collection. Naturally, one must use these data in conjunction with other information, such as local use patterns.

Robert Pikowsky published a good article outlining both the history of journal price problems and the potential for electronic journals' solving the problem, at least for academic and special libraries.[17] Not surprisingly, he did not see how e-journals would change the picture, and presently it appears that he was correct.

As journal prices rise and serial budgets fail to keep pace with the increases, collection development staff face the unpleasant task of deciding what to keep and what to drop. No one likes the process, especially the customers. Everyone has her or his favorite candidates for keeping and dropping. A library's first cancellation project may be relatively easy, but after the initial round of cuts, the process becomes progressively more difficult. The usual response is to assist decision makers by developing a model that takes price and use information into account. Price data are easy to acquire, at least at the macro level, but use data are more difficult to come by. Many libraries do not circulate journals, so circulation data analysis is not an option. In such cases, the library must establish some process for collecting the data. Though one can find a number of articles about journal use data and cancellation work,[18] the true task is to find a method that will work in the local situation.

For the most part, serials will continue to escalate in price, and budgets may or may not keep pace. Clearly, serials will continue to play a major role in meeting customer information needs, and likewise may command a growing share of a limited collection development budget. How far can a library or information center go in cutting back on the acquisition of other formats to maintain the subscription list? Will switching to electronic sources for on-demand material really help with the budget problem, or just make matters worse? Answers to such questions vary from institution to institution. Electronic services and document delivery may or may not be a viable answer (more about e-serials/journals in the next chapter).

Many libraries and information centers face the problem of buying the journal twice, in paper and electronic formats. Even in a networked environment, it is likely that some potential users will not have network access. Does the library ignore these users and provide only the electronic version, or does it offer both versions? One thinks twice about dropping the paper version, because some publishers (*Biological Abstracts*, for example) charge a higher fee for the CD-ROM version if the library does not have a paper subscription as well. Often the higher fee is equal to the price of both subscriptions. With the ADONIS product (biomedical titles), the price of each article printed is based on whether the library has a paper subscription to the journal. Networking the material also entails extra expenses, such as license fees, that can equal or surpass the basic subscription price. Additionally, some products have a per-page or per-view charge that increases the overall cost. For example, Bell & Howell Information and Learning Company has a 10 cents per printed page copyright charge for its full-text material on

CD-ROM. Libraries should not expect to save money by shifting from paper to electronic formats, unless they also shift some of the costs to the users.

Short of providing full text in electronic form, the library can provide document delivery services backed by indexing and abstracting and table of contents access in electronic form. (A summary article about these services and their costs is by Ronald Leach and Judith Trible.[19] Although the specific information in this article is outdated, the issues and considerations they raise remain valid.) Commercial services, such as Bell & Howell Information and Learning Company's Article Clearinghouse and ISI's Genuine Article, provide documents based on those companies' indexing and abstracting services. Newer services are based upon the tables of contents of a large number of titles (11,000 to 12,000 titles). Subject searching is generally limited with the table of contents approach; basically, searching is keyword in title. In essence, with table of contents services, one gives up depth of subject access for broader scope in title coverage. Most table of contents services have also entered the document delivery field. CARL *UnCover 2* is the oldest such service, with OCLC's *ContentFirst* and *ArticleFirst* and RLG's *CitaDel* also available to users. As with full text, there are a variety of charges to consider before one can decide to drop a paper subscription.

Summary

Serials are a vital part of any information collection. They are complex and costly, regardless of their format. Cost is probably going to remain the primary concern for some time. For the past 15 years, serial prices have had double-digit rate increases, higher than anything else a library adds to its collection. Thus, serials continually take a larger and larger share of the materials budget, or the library must begin to cancel titles and provide access to the information in some other manner. Technology is changing the way libraries handle serials and is making it possible to provide access to more titles. However, technology will not solve the economic concerns of either the publishers and producers or the consumers. How the two groups will solve the problem is impossible to predict. It is likely that the serials price problem will be present for some time.

Notes

1.   The quotation is from a friend's letter. The poet is unknown.

2.   Thomas Nisonger, *Management of Serials in Libraries* (Englewood, Colo.: Libraries Unlimited, 1998).

3.   Heartsill Young, ed., *ALA Glossary of Library and Information Science* (Chicago: American Library Association, 1983).

4.   *Webster's Third New International Dictionary* (Springfield, Mass.: G & C Merriam, 1976).

5.   Fritz Machlup et al., *Information Through the Printed Word* (New York: New York University, 1978).

6.   Judith Bernstein, "Corporate Annual Reports: The Commercial Vendors," *College & Research Libraries News* 47 (March 1986): 178–80.

7. Wallys Conhaim, "Linking up to the Global Network," *LinkUp* 15 (January/February 1998): 5–11.

8. Janice Kuta, "AAP Seminar Explores Document Delivery," *Publishers Weekly* 239 (November 30, 1992): 20.

9. Carol Foggin, "Title Changes: Another View," *Serials Librarian* 23, nos. 1/2 (1992): 71–83.

10. Nancy Nelson, "Serials Title Changes: What's in a Name?" *Computers in Libraries* 13 (February 1993): 4.

11. Robert Sivers, "Partitioned Bradford Ranking and the Serials Problem in Academic Libraries," *Collection Building* 8, no. 2 (1986): 12–19.

12. Dawn Bick and Reeta Sinha, "Maintaining a High-Quality, Cost-Effective Journal Collection," *College & Research Libraries News* 51 (September 1991): 485–90.

13. Maria A. Janowska, "Printed Versus Electronic: Policy Issues in the Case of Environmental Journals," *Serials Review* 20 (Fall 1994):17–22.

14. William Katz and Linda Sternberg Katz, *Magazines for Libraries,* 9th ed. (New York: R. R. Bowker, 1997).

15. N. Bernard Basch and Judy McQueen, *Buying Serials* (New York: Neal-Schuman, 1990).

16. Barbara Meyers and Janice Fleming, "Price Analysis and the Serial Situation: Trying to Solve an Age-Old Problem," *Journal of Academic Librarianship* 17 (May 1991): 86–92.

17. Robert Pikowsky, "Electronic Journals as a Potential Solution to Escalating Serials Costs," *Serials Librarian* 32, nos. 3/4 (1997): 31–55.

18. Marifran Bustion, John Eltinge, and John Harer, "On the Merits of Direct Observation of Periodical Usage," *College & Research Libraries* 53 (November 1992): 537–50; Anna Price and Kjestine Carey, "Serials Use Study Raises Questions About Cooperative Ventures," *Serials Review* 19 (Fall 1993): 79–84; Christie Degener and Marjory Waite, "Using an Automated Serials System to Assist with Collection Review and Cancellations," *Serials Review* 17 (Spring 1991): 13–20; Maiken Naylor, "A Comparison of Two Methodologies for Counting Current Periodical Use," *Serials Review* 19 (Spring 1993): 27–34, 62.

19. Ronald G. Leach and Judith E. Trible, "Electronic Document Delivery: New Options for Libraries," *Journal of Academic Librarianship* 18 (January 1993): 359–64.

Further Reading

General

Anderson, B. "CONSER on the Internet: Facilitating Access to Serials Information." *Serials Librarian* 31, no. 1/2 (1997): 77–94.

Clasquin, F. F. "Financial Management of Serials and Journals Through Core Lists." *Serials Librarian* 2 (Spring 1978): 287–97.

Diodato, L. W. "Serials Claims: Three Perspectives, Library/Publisher/Vendor." *Serials Librarian* 21, nos. 2/3 (1991): 201–3.

Enserink, M. "Libraries Join Forces on Journal Prices." *Science* 278, no. 5343 (1997): 1558.

Harrington, S. A. "Serials Specialists Are Hard to Find." *Serials Librarian* 21, no. 1 (1991): 1–11.

International Subscription Agents. 5th ed. Chicago: American Library Association, 1986.

Katz, William W., and Linda Sternberg Katz. *Magazines for Libraries.* 5th ed. New York: R. R. Bowker, 1986.

Keating, L. R. "Replacement Issues: Where Do You Find Them and at What Cost?" *Serials Librarian* 21, nos. 2/3 (1991): 165–68.

Marcinco, R. W. "Issues in Commercial Document Delivery." *Library Trends* 45, no. 3 (Winter 1997): 531–50.

Nisonger, T. *Management of Serials in Libraries.* Englewood, Colo.: Libraries Unlimited, 1998.

Prabha, C., and E. C. Marsh. "Commercial Document Suppliers: How Many of the ILL/DD Periodical Article Requests Can They Fill?" *Library Trends* 45, no. 3 (Winter 1997): 551–58.

Quint, B. "Document Delivery Field Continues to Shrink with Demise of EBSCO Document Services." (September 21, 1998). *Information Today NewsBreaks.* March 1, 1999. <http://www.infotoday.com/newsbreaks/nb0921-2.htm>.

Stein, L. L. "What to Keep and What to Cut?" *Technical Services Quarterly* 10, no. 1 (1992): 3–14.

Wilkas, L. *International Subscription Agents.* Chicago: American Library Association, 1994.

Woodward, H. M. "Impact of Electronic Information on Serials Collection Management." *IFLA Journal* 20, no. 1 (1994): 35–45.

Academic

Alexander, A. W., and J. L. Smith. "Annual Survey of Serials Collection Assessment Programs, Practices, and Policies in Academic Libraries." *Journal of Library Administration* 17, no. 2 (1992): 133–48.

Chrzastowski, T. E., and K. A. Schmidt. "Surveying the Damage: Academic Serial Cancellations—1987/88 through 1989/90." *College & Research Libraries* 54 (March 1993): 93–102.

Davis, D. "FirstSearch: Collection Management and Academic Libraries." *OCLC Systems and Services* 9 (Fall 1993): 43–45.

Dow, R. F., et al. "Commentaries on Serials Publishing." *College & Research Libraries* 52 (November 1991): 521–27.

Houbeck, R. L. "Locked in Conversation: College Library Collections and the Pluralist Society." *Journal of Library Administration* 17, no. 2 (1992): 99–131.

Kingma, B. R., and P. B. Eppard. "Journal Price Escalation and the Market for Information." *College & Research Libraries* 53 (November 1992): 523–35.

McCain, K. W. "Some Determinants of Journal Holding Patterns in Academic Libraries." *Library & Information Science Research* 14 (July 1992): 223–43.

Welsch, E. K. "Measures of Social Science Collection Development Costs." *Behavior and Social Science Librarian* 10, no. 2 (1991): 9–26.

Public

Boyer, R. E. "Serials in the Small Public Library." *Library Resources & Technical Services* 29 (April/June 1985): 132–38.

Falk, G. "Increase Your Budget by Convincing Users to Adopt-a-Magazine." *Library Journal* 110 (June 15, 1985): 34.

Fyfe, J. "History Journals for a Public Library." *Serials Librarian* 13 (December 1987): 69–75.

Lenahan, N. M. "Use of Periodicals and Newspapers in a Mid-Sized Public Library." *Serials Librarian* 16, nos. 3/4 (1989): 41–47.

Ostling, E. "Periodicals in Libraries—A Democratic Right." *Scandinavian Public Library Quarterly* 25, no. 2 (1992): 16–17.

Stout, M. A., and B. Stunz. "Creating Core Serial Lists in a Public Library." *Reference Librarian*, nos. 27/28 (1989): 367–78.

School

Buboltz, D., and R. Ling-Louie. "A Treeful of Good Reading (Magazines as a Way to Promote Reading)." *Book Report* 10 (January/February 1992): 16–18.

Bury, J. M. "Management of Periodicals in a Small School LMC." In *Collection Management for School Library Media Centers.* Edited by Brenda White, 313–49. New York: Haworth Press, 1986.

Clark, M. P. "Young Adult and Children's Periodicals: Selections for the School Media Center." *Serials Review* 7 (October 1981): 7–24.

Drott, M. C., and J. Mancall. "Magazines as Information Sources." *School Media Quarterly* 8 (Summer 1980): 240–44.

Estes-Ricker, B., and J. Johnson. "Relevant Resources: Periodicals in Elementary Schools." *School Library Media Quarterly* 19 (Fall 1990): 53–56.

Richardson, S. K. "Magazine Collections in Elementary School Library Media Centers." In *Library Education and Leadership.* Edited by S. Intner and K. Vandergrift, 373–85. Metuchen, N.J.: Scarecrow Press, 1990.

Swisher, R., et al. "Magazine Collections in Elementary School Media Centers." *School Library Journal* 37 (November 1991): 40–43.

Special

Anderson, D. C. "Journal for Academic Veterinary Medical Libraries." *Serials Librarian* 18, nos. 3/4 (1990): 73–86.

Battistella, M. S. "OCLC-SERHOLD Connections: An Evolution in Health Sciences Union Listing." *Bulletin of the Medical Library Association* 79 (October 1991): 370–76.

Cawkell, A. E. "Evaluating Scientific Journals with Journal Citation Reports." *American Society for Information Science Journal* 29 (January 1978): 41–46.

Cooper, E. R. "Simplified Approaches for Serials Management." *Serials Review* 18, no. 4 (1992): 17–20.

Freehling, D. J. "Cancelling Serials in Academic Law Libraries." *Law Library Journal* 84 (Fall 1992): 707–24.

Humphreys, B. L., and D. E. McCutcheon. "Growth Patterns in the National Library of Medicine's Serials Collection." *Bulletin of the Medical Library Association* 82 (January 1994): 18–22.

Morton, D. "Making the Most of Your Serials Budget." *College & Research Libraries News* 53 (November 1992): 630.

Shalini, R. "Journal Acquisition and Cost Effectiveness in Special Libraries." *International Library Review* 13 (April 1981): 189–94.

Triolo, V. A., and D. Bao. "A Decision Model for Technical Journal Deselection." *Journal of the American Society for Information Science* 44 (April 1993): 148–60.

White, B., and J. Tomlinson. "Library Subscription Scheme at the Institute of Advanced Legal Studies." *Law Librarian* 23 (March 1992): 29–34.

7
Electronic Serials

In chapter 6, we discussed a variety of issues related to print serials in general. Most, if not all, of them apply to digital serials as well. One reason for having a separate chapter on electronic versions of serials is that they are becoming more and more important in collection building. There is also a very large body of literature about this format, which we attempt to summarize in the following pages. Also, there is no question about the popularity of such materials with library customers. They often prefer the electronic version, especially for indexing and abstracting capabilities. One advantage of the electronic index is the capability to perform complex searches quickly, such as a Boolean search. Another advantage is the ease of printing or downloading the search results. Most of the serials that are currently digitized fall into one of five of Machlup's categories (which we discussed in chapter 6): journals, magazines, newspapers, newsletters, and loose-leaf services.

Digital or Paper?

Just as there are several terms for paper-based serials, so there are for the digital format: *electronic journals*, *online journals*, *digital journals*, and the more all-embracing *electronic resources*. According to Thomas Nisonger, there is no standard accepted definition of an electronic journal/serial.[1] *E-journal* is a reasonably short term and the one we will use, simply to save space. Producers take three broad approaches with e-journals: an electronic-only version of a new title, an electronic-only version of a title converted from a paper version, and both an electronic and paper version.

In the past decade or so, libraries and producers have struggled with how to migrate from a print-only world to one that is a mix of paper and electronic resources. As we stated in chapter 6, the electronic side is becoming more and more dominant and will continue to do so in the future, at least in some serial categories. One of the first forays into the digital world that is still widely used is the CD-ROM product. Those first seen in libraries were primarily DOS-based, and have since evolved to a Windows environment.

Starting principally with indexing and abstracting services, the CD-ROM products quickly became popular in reference departments. Proprietary software and differing search engines created and continue to create challenges for the library's public service staff. Stand-alone systems were satisfactory at first, but it was not long before there was significant pressure to "network" the stations and allow users to select from a number of products from any station. Making CD "jukeboxes," network software, servers, and user computers all work together is a continuing challenge for libraries.

When the producers moved into full-text products, the issues of compatibility became even more complex. Naturally, more and more people wanted more and more access and variations in computer platforms and equipment became increasingly complex. Full-text products were created by scanning printed pages. Producers then converted the scanned data into bit-mapped images, put them on optical discs, and manufactured and distributed the CD-ROMs. Early scanners had fairly high error rates, so a step had to be interposed between scanning and creating the bitmap images, namely, comparing the scan results against the original. All these steps took time, resulting in products that were electronic in character, but appeared some weeks or even months after their paper-based counterparts. (One still encounters this problem, at the beginning of the third millennium, with some Web-based products from e-journal aggregators.) Essentially, the CD-ROM products complement traditional paper-based ones, even if end users seem to have a misplaced faith that electronic products are always the most current and complete. What CD-ROMs are best at is solving the problem of misplaced, misshelved, and mutilated journals, as well as "at the bindery" issues.

Another, somewhat later, approach was to have libraries load tapes on their local computer system. This basically transferred a number of producer/publisher problems and costs to the libraries. Libraries quickly found that this approach took up ever-growing amounts of staff time and created demands for more and more computer memory. Neither CD-ROMs nor local tape loads completely solved the problem of users having remote access to e-resources when the individuals had different computer platforms (PCs and Macs). Most libraries struggled, and some still do, with how to provide equal access for each group. "Black boxes" of various types were produced that were supposed to emulate one or the other system—most often to emulate the PC. Very few of these systems really provide complete equality in access, and one often heard (and still hears) complaints from Mac users that their needs are ignored.

Today the move to Internet/Web-based products has helped to bring a balance to the access issues. Up to a point, any "authorized" user who has access to the Web will have the same access to a product, regardless of the computer platform. The "up to a point" assumes that all users have equivalent computer systems, which is of course not true except perhaps in a special library situation where all employees have the same equipment. In the rest of the world, libraries have a few users with the very latest high-end configurations, many with the current "average" setup, and a fairly large number with rather old, slow machines. Nevertheless, Web-based e-journals and indexing/abstracting services do provide much more equal access for end users. Where the next stage in the migration will come from and take us to is impossible to predict with any degree of assurance. What we do know is that print is still with us, and it is likely to be for some time to come.

Hazel Woodward and her colleagues[2] outlined what they called 15 myths about electronic journals. Although they based their article on research they conducted in the United Kingdom (primarily at Loughborough University), we believe the myths they discuss are universal in nature. These myths are:

1. Electronic journals will provide better access to journal articles.

2. Academics and researchers read journals at their office desks.

3. Readers want electronic journals.

4. Electronic journals are quick and convenient to access.

5. Readers know and care who publishes a journal.

6. Readers want page integrity.

7. Electronic journals will bypass libraries and make them redundant.

8. Electronic journals will save libraries money.

9. Storage and dissemination of electronic journals is inexpensive or free.

10. Electronic journals will save paper.

11. Publishers care about readers.

12. Electronic journals will save publishers money.

13. Electronic journals will make subscription agents redundant.

14. Only recent issues of journals are required.

15. All scholarly journals will be available electronically in a few years.

To that extensive list we would add several more "myths":

- Electronic journals are always more current than their print counterparts.

- Electronic journals provide all graphic materials of their print counterparts.

- Electronic journals are always accessible.

- All readers have equal access to required computers at any time.

- Electronic journals will save library staff time and effort in handling serials.

We point out these myths not to suggest that electronic serials are unimportant, but rather to note that they are *not* the final answer to the issues of providing readers with access to the most current and accurate information in the most timely manner. They certainly are important and are the next step in the process, but they arc not the ultimate solution as they now exist. Many of the myths exist because the popular press and somewhat overenthusiastic technology people promote the concept beyond its current actual capabilities.

Academic and special librarians have, all too often, encountered a chief financial officer who believes at least one of the myths—that electronic journals will save the library money. We have not found that e-serials save the library money; in fact, they add to the cost of operations, as they are almost always add-ons rather than replacements. Several years ago the senior author's library tried to cover the cost of an aggregator's product, which offered the full text of a large number of journals online, by canceling the paper subscriptions to the titles that would be available electronically. After one year the library reinstated all but five of the paper subscriptions.

A number of reasons (the aforementioned myths) caused this to happen. First of all, full text means just that: full text, but not necessarily including graphics. Some products claim to include tables and charts, but in this particular case data was too difficult for users to interpret, so a number of paper subscriptions were quickly restarted. The library had not even thought about ending paper subscriptions for journals that arc highly dependent on graphics. (Even in the future, when graphics are consistently available electronically, the library will probably continue the paper subscriptions, as many of the users who want and have remote access to the material do not have computers that can effectively handle graphics.) Another reason was the staff's discovery that a surprising number of the electronic titles were a month or more behind the paper versions. That proved unacceptable to several academic departments as well as individual users. Yet another factor was network issues, both on and off campus. Because users were accustomed to finding certain titles on the library's shelves, they still expected the materials to be there when the networks were slow or down. Finally, the volume of printing from the library's public-access printers skyrocketed, even after installation of network printers and charging as much per printed page (without any volume discount) as for the photocopy machines. (Clearly users were *not* reading the material on the computer screens.) What the product did accomplish was to give PC and Mac users equal access to the material, as well as providing easier remote access as long the networks were operating properly.

There are a number of issues to ponder in the interplay between digitized and paper-based serials. One issue is how to provide access. Digital serials, in theory, are accessible anywhere, anytime, as long as there is a connection between a computer and the database containing the desired material. Many customers and technology supporters see this as the ideal future: anywhere at any time. Library literature generally approaches this issue in terms of ownership versus access.

When a library subscribes to a paper journal, the library owns the copies of those titles, for which it paid the appropriate fee. Electronic formats are often a different matter. Producers of electronic material usually include a license agreement that limits the library's ability to use the material and normally states that the library has access rights only so long as the annual fee is current. In essence, the library only leases the data. If a library has any responsibility for long-term retention of information, leasing is a problematic policy even if the producer says it will archive the files and gives the library the right to access the files for the years for which it paid a lease fee.

Other aspects of serials are the issues of "just-in-case" and "just-in-time." Long-term preservation is, in a sense, "just-in-case." That is, someone at some time will require the information. "Just-in-time" is locating the desired material at the time the user needs it, most often from somewhere other than the home library collection. Digitized data makes just-in-time delivery a realistic option. One reality is that fewer and fewer libraries can continue to subscribe to thousands of serial titles just-in-case. If there is a paper subscription, it must be for high-demand items, not the seldom-used titles.

Leasing and just-in-time delivery work well, but one cannot help but wonder (as we did in chapter 6), about how far profit-oriented producers will go to maintain backfiles, or, for that matter, who will still be in business 20 years in the future. There are serious concerns about who, how, and for how long electronic data will be available (archived).

Without a doubt, digitized serials are a mixed blessing. They are very popular, they provide more flexibility in searching than their paper-based counterparts, and remote access at any time is a possibility. Although they do not reduce library operating costs, they do present new challenges for public service staff. Electronic systems can fail, as do power supplies, causing customer and staff frustration. Also, as anyone who has spent much time with Internet-based services knows, "electronic" does not always translate into "fast." On the one hand, waiting for files to download, waiting to have a server "accept" your query, or being abruptly cut off in mid-session are sources of frustration that do not exist with paper-based serials. On the other hand, torn-out articles, misshelved or missing volumes, or holiday library closures are not problems with the electronic serials (provided offsite access to the required systems is available). Without question, e-serials will be increasingly important in any overall collection development plan for any type of library. Thus, one must understand their benefits as well as their limitations.

Selecting E-Serials

Is the process of selecting e-serials different from that that followed for print serials? The answer is no, not really; however, there are some additional steps. (*Note:* One good source for identifying electronic serials is *Books and Periodicals Online: 1997.*[3]) We believe that all the factors that apply to selecting paper titles also apply to e-journals. One factor that differs is that often, at least in the case of journal aggregator services, the purchasing decision is made for a package of titles rather than title by title. (We return to this issue later in the section on aggregators.) That in turn means that the cost being considered is substantially higher than for any single typical library paper subscription. Thus, one adds factors of new costs, vendor support, and a "package" of titles.

Another factor complicating the decision is that electronic resource decisions involve more staff than is typical for paper-based selection decisions. If nothing else, there are questions about technology requirements and capabilities that systems staff must answer. In addition, more of the public service staff are involved in supporting users of electronic resources. Few users need assistance in opening a paper journal, but many may need it when locating and using an electronic title. Packages from either producers or other vendors often employ different search engines; this requires staff to remember which database operates in which manner. Thus, public service staff often want a voice in deciding what, if any, new electronic products to add to the service program.

Mary Jean Pavelsek outlined a set of 11 "guidelines" for evaluating e-journals and their providers[4] (we modified some of her phrasing slightly):

- Economics
- Ease of use/User flexibility
- Archival implications
- Future accessibility
- Access
- Licensing, copyright, and distribution restrictions
- Single or multiple publisher
- Print vs. electronic comparisons
- User support
- If a package, is it "all or nothing"?
- Planned enhancements.

To her list we would add cost per user, technological issues, and aggregators.

We have mentioned the two typical methods for securing e-serials: direct from the publishers/producers or from so-called aggregators. An *aggregator* is an organization that develops "packages" of electronic serials. The aggregator enters into contracts with a number of publishers/producers to offer their titles as a group. Producers gain by not having to invest as much in marketing, programming, and technology. Then the aggregator adds value to the package by providing a consistent search engine for searching all the titles. Naturally, aggregators then add a charge for their services on top of what the cost was from the producers, often in the 30 to 40 percent range. Some of the large aggregators are OCLC, Bell & Howell Information and Learning Company, Lexis/Nexis, and EBSCO.

Deciding on aggregator packages usually entails accepting a number—sometimes a substantial number—of titles one would never subscribe to in print. Few of the aggregators allow a library to take only the titles of interest. Naturally, that means the library pays for titles it does not want. Thus, one question to consider is if the overall cost is really appropriate for the number of titles the library *does* want. One interesting effort in 1999 was the California State University System's issuance of a Request for Proposal (RFP) to aggregators to supply access to a list of 1,279 journals on what the System calls the "Journal Access Core Collection."[5] The titles on the list are those in highest demand in the System's 23 libraries. At the time we prepared this edition, there was no indication of how successful the RFP would be in providing access to just the titles desired rather than titles to which the aggregators have easy access.

One system for evaluating aggregator as well as publisher/producer titles is the weighted system developed by the California State University Libraries (CSUL) for deciding on system-wide purchases. CSUL has a committee of 12 members, representing the 23 campuses of the system, who each serve for two years. Evaluations are made independently by each committee member, using the weighted system, during a two-week trial period. Results of their evaluations are available on the system's Web page (<http://www.co.calstate.edu/irt/seir/>).

The form used by the CSU system, which is submitted online, contains the elements shown in figures 7.1, pages 187–89 and 7.2, pages 190–94. (The figures were slightly reformatted for this book; this original forms are available online.)

Figure 7.2 is an example of the type of evaluation that the system produces and posts for all staff to read. Keep in mind that what the figure shows is only an example stating the assessment as of the date shown. Databases can and do change over time; sometimes changes are due to critical reviews. This example is for JSTOR (Journal STORage).

Most of the basic issues to be considered when selecting e-serials were visible in the JSTOR example. Financial concerns are high, and it is highly improbable that a library will save any money by subscribing to electronic serials. Thus, the real question becomes: How much value/benefit does the library gain as a result of the expenditure? How does that benefit compare to benefits from spending the same amount on something else? Pricing models vary widely from vendor to vendor. (When one looks at both single-institution and consortial purchasing, one can identify more than 50 variations in pricing models. A cynical person might think the producer has an amount needed in mind and will work up any model the library wants—but the final price will always be the same.)

Staff and customer comfort level with a chosen product is important. Outstanding content in a product that is complex or difficult to use, even if the cost is relatively modest, may not be the most cost-effective purchase. An unused resource is a waste of funds.

Technical issues of network capability, stability, and compliance with general standards are all key factors. Also, how much support is available from the vendor, and during what hours? If required, how is authentication handled? Domain access—recognizing IP ranges—is a low-cost option for the library; however, remote users with private Internet service providers will not have access without special arrangements such as a proxy server.

Content concerns relate to the usual subject issues and also to how complete the material is, assuming there is a print counterpart. Another concern should be whether there are "additions" to the product, and whether they are necessary or beneficial. Some vendors/producers add some form of multimedia—sound or video clips—to their material. Often this is of the "gee whiz, look what technology allows us to do" variety rather than being a true added value. Such additions create hardware and software compatibility problems for some library-owned and certainly for some remote users' machines.

(Text continues on page 195.)

THE CALIFORNIA STATE UNIVERSITY
Electronic Access to Resources Committee

Review Reply Form (RRF)
Item under review:
Response due date:
EAR Committee Member Name:
EMail Address:
Campus:
Date of this review:
I am unable to respond to the review at this time: Unable to respond
Reason (Please enter your reason in the spaces provided below AND
click on the SEND button at the end of this document.)

INTRODUCTION

Each EAR committee member is expected to review and evaluate
formal proposals as they are submitted. The review process is initiated
by either the Chair of the EAR committee or the IRT/SEIR (Software &
Electronic Information Resources) representative. This Electronic Access to Resources Review Reply form is the vehicle designed for you to
submit your assessment. You may find it necessary to consult with others in order to complete this form, however, the completion of this form
constitutes your review and evaluation and may not be transferred to
another or others. The rating should be based upon the potential value
of the proposal to the CSU as a whole, and not solely on the needs of
your specific campus. Please telephone or contact the Chair of the EAR
committee or the IRT/SEIR representative on the EAR committee if
there are items regarding a specific review and evaluation that you do
not understand.

COMMITTEE PROCESS AND PHASES

Each item to be reviewed must pass several phases before it may be
submitted to library directors for their acceptance or rejection. An item
may be withdrawn from the review and evaluation process at each
phase. The phases are:

1. Opening
Anyone may request the committee to examine an item. However, either the Chair of EAR or the IRT/SEIR representative may reject an
item and therefore eliminate it from further consideration.

2. Preparatory
Items are then subject to fact finding and prepared by the IRT/SEIR
representative in written form for the formal review process by the
EAR committee. This initiates the Review Reply Form.

(Figure 7.1 continues on page 188.)

Fig. 7.1. CSUL committee form. Reprinted with permission from California State
University.

Figure 7.1—*Continued.*

3. Proposal or Withdrawal
Tabulation of the RRF responses determines whether or not the item is further prepared and issued as a Proposal or Withdrawn. Withdrawn items may be recycled via the subcommittee route on the basis of new fact finding. Recycled items start over as new items. An overall border-line response may or may not result in a proposal. If such a proposal is issued, the specific detail of the overall evaluation shall be provided.

4. Implementation
Implementation is based upon acceptance of the proposal by a predetermined number of library directors.

Please place a check mark in the appropriate box. Enter comments in the spaces provided below, if necessary, for rationale for ratings and comments.

I have/have not consulted with others in responding to this formal review.

PROPOSALS MAY REQUIRE YOU TO SCORE ONE OR MORE OF THE FOLLOWING CATEGORIES. FOR THE ITEM SUBJECT TO THIS REVIEW, PLEASE PLACE A SCORE IN EACH APPLICABLE CATEGORY.

The score to be assessed is 1–4, with 1 representing the "least value" and 4 representing the "most value". *Note:* The product is to be evaluated on its potential value to the CSU and not solely on the needs of your individual campus.

INFORMATION DATABASE

Consider its functionality, the appropriateness of format (bibliographic/full-text), the content of the information, the adequacy of coverage (retrospective, current), and its value to the CSU system as a whole.

Rationale for rating:

SEARCH INTERFACE

Consider the functionality and ease of use of the interface. Is it intuitive, or is an excessive amount of training required? Are any crucial features missing from the search interface?

Rationale for rating:

USER SUPPORT SERVICES

If documentation is required for successful use of product, is it available, comprehensive, and well written? Is online help adequate and user friendly? Does vendor supply training if it is needed? Is a telephone helpline available?

Rationale for rating:

COST

If cost is available, does it seem reasonable in terms of comparable products?

Rationale for rating:

ACCESSIBILITY OF SERVICE

Is access/connection to product reliable and stable? Is response time adequate?

Rationale for rating:

OVERALL ASSESSMENT

#1 — No Support
#2 — No Support at this time. Future support conditional upon
    enhancements noted below in Comments Section.
#3 — Support and Recommend proposal be forwarded to Library
    Directors for their acceptance or rejection. Would like to see
    enhancements in product noted below in Comments Section.
#4 — Outstanding offer and opportunity. Recommend proposal be
    forwarded to Library Directors for their acceptance or rejection.

COMMENTS:
What would your rating be if product was evaluated based on utility for your home campus only?

COMMENTS:

The California State University
EAR Committee Review of JSTOR
January, 1997

The CSU Libraries Electronic Access to Information Resources Committee (EAR) undertook a two-week "hands-on" study of JSTOR, an electronic archive of core scholarly journal literature with an emphasis on the retrospective conversion of the entire backfiles of key journals. JSTOR, the "journal storage" project, was initiated as a demonstration program sponsored by the Andrew W. Mellon Foundation in the Spring of 1994. It began as an effort to ease the increasing problems faced by libraries seeking to find appropriate stack space for the long runs of back issues of scholarly journals. Collaborating with developers at the University of Michigan, JSTOR has built a fully searchable database accessible with standard browsers via the World Wide Web.

JSTOR intends to build its collection in separate phases that will include clusters of journals in specific fields. The first phase, expected to be completed within 3 years, will contain the complete runs of a minimum of 100 important journal titles in 10–15 fields. At the time of the EAR Committee's review JSTOR had 17 of these journals converted in their entirety and available.

Each EAR committee member independently, or in concert with other qualified professionals on their campus library staff, reviewed and evaluated JSTOR on the Web. Assessments were submitted on a Review Reply Form specifically designed by the Committee for this purpose. Though other staff may have helped in the review process, completion of the form was the responsibility of the EAR committee member only and not transferred to another. Ratings were based upon the potential value of the proposal to the California State University system as a whole and not solely on the needs of any specific campus.

Attributes of the information resource are assessed on a scale of 1 to 4, with 1 representing the "least value" and 4 representing the "most value". The following attributes were examined:

INFORMATION DATABASE
Consider functionality, the appropriateness of format (bibliographic/full-text), the content of the information, the adequacy of coverage (retrospective, current), and its value to the CSU system as a whole.

SEARCH INTERFACE
Consider functionality and ease of use of the interface. Is it intuitive, or is an excessive amount of training required? Are any crucial features missing from the search interface?

USER SUPPORT SERVICES
If documentation is required for successful use of the product or service, is it available, comprehensive, and well written? Is online help adequate and user friendly? Does the vendor supply training if it is needed? Is a telephone helpline available?

Fig. 7.2. Sample JSTOR evaluation. Reprinted with permission from California State University.

USER SUPPORT SERVICES
If documentation is required for successful use of the product or service, is it available, comprehensive, and well written? Is online help adequate and user friendly? Does the vendor supply training if it is needed? Is a telephone helpline available?

COST
If cost is available, does it seem reasonable in terms of comparable products?

ACCESSIBILITY OF SERVICE
Is access/connection to the product or service reliable and stable? Is response time adequate?

OVERALL ASSESSMENT
#1 — No Support
#2 — No Support at this time. Future support conditional upon enhancements noted below in Comments Section.
#3 — Support and Recommend proposal be forwarded to Library Directors for their acceptance or rejection. Would like to see enhancements in product noted below in Comments Section.
#4 — Outstanding offer and opportunity. Recommend proposal be forwarded to Library Directors for their acceptance or rejection.

Following are the results of the Committee's review as well as comments taken from the Review Reply Forms of individual members:

INFORMATION DATABASE (3,1,3,2,4)
This database has the potential to be of great value. There are a limited number of titles available now.

Retrospective only. Doesn't allow for cancellation of current subscriptions.

Unable to test how multiple pages, illustrations and references are handled.

Not knowing CSU's holding status for these particular titles, I can't say how valuable it would be to have them online.

Given that these are archival copies and to complete the run we'd have to get access to current issues elsewhere, it could become very awkward having to explain that to students and faculty who need these journals.

Insufficient coverage to really test this aspect currently.

(Figure 7.2 continues on page 192.)

Figure 7.2—*Continued.*

SEARCH INTERFACE (3,3,2,2,3)

There is a lot of jumping back and forth between windows that is time consuming.

Response time also seems a bit sluggish.

There appear to be some very serious problems with the seemingly easy to use interface. The boxes lead a user to believe that filling in the blank and choosing the right parameters is all that is necessary, but it appears that the search engine cannot deal effectively with searches that require more than one 'AND' or 'OR' statement, or a combination 'AND/OR' statement (see example). This is neither explained on the screen or in the help files. For example, searching full-text of economics, history, and political science databases, the search statement "united states" and "trade" and "japan" or "china" finds 3622 hits. However, the search statement "china" or "japan" and "united states" and "trade" finds 18,219 hits. Based on minimal documentation, it should find the same number of hits as the first search. On the other hand, searching "united states" and "trade" and "china" or "japan" yields 132 hits, but it is unclear whether the search engine is finding all documents with either "china" or "japan" in them or the phrase "china or japan".

Online searchers know this as "first-in, first-out" order to the boolean operators, but students and faculty who don't deal intimately with these databases would never know this and it leads to a lot of confusion when trying to go through the hits.

Printing is unnecessarily difficult and time-consuming. I was never able to get a complete document printed due to vague "postscript" errors, even though I have a postscript 2 printer in my office. In addition, many libraries do not have postscript capable printers in their public areas due to the expense. Browse function is similar to that used for CARL UnCover. Easy to use but time consuming. Can specify field searching, but limit features appear on second screen. Not good for ADA compliance: no text only, names on buttons, tab between boxes possible but return doesn't work. Have to click on search button. Sensitive to singular and plural word forms in keyword search. Unable to locate an item during subject search that was found during a browse search. Couldn't get it to consistently enlarge type size for display.

The search interface is quite easy. However, it is cumbersome to have to close the window to exit help. A link back to the search screen would be a great improvement. Also, I found no help regarding author entries. I also wondered if there is authority control on author names. This seems critical for a database such as JSTOR.

USER SUPPORT SERVICES (2,2,3,2)

Has potential. Numerous help screens. Unclear how to get back to article from help window. Instruction to close window doesn't work. Couldn't find instructions on emailing. Print option described but not available for testing.

Many of the features discussed are not mentioned at all in the documentation. Nor are the software/hardware requirements for printing given up-front.

I like the outline under "about JSTOR". It is well done and a time saver.

ACCESSIBILITY OF SERVICE (2,4,4)

No problems in accessing service. Speed ok. Response time ok. Unable to test retrieval for complete documents or graphics.

It appears to be very stable and accessible.

I was able to reach the site every time I tried it and response time was fine.

COST (1,2,1)

Cost is very high for what we would get. JSTOR's goals are valuable but unclear how much faculty would use it. Most CSU libraries have back volumes in print. Would cost too much as an option for replacement of stored volumes. Faculty not wired enough. Topical areas covered represent areas of low enrollment and use. A significantly reduced price would allow CSU to subscribe and offer each library an option to replace print with electronic storage.

For the CSU to have to pay that amount up front with no guarantees of additional titles or software enhancements seems to be too much. There are obvious advantages due to the ability to gain shelf space by using online journals, but with our current lack of enough public Web stations and our status as a "public" university, we have been reluctant to pull anything off the shelf due to online access.

I fear that cost will preclude the CSU's entering into an agreement during the development phase.

(Figure 7.2 continues on page 194.)

Figure 7.2—*Continued.*

OVERALL ASSESSMENT (1,3,3,2)

While faculty often request more access to research materials electronically, the CSU is not a PHD-granting institution. Journals and subject areas are low use for the time periods covered. Too expensive as an alternative method of storage.

Even though I don't think we could afford JSTOR, I like the concept. This seems like a good answer to accessing retrospective collections. Perhaps we could find a benefactor.

In order to print the results, both quick and high quality printing options require applications to be downloaded to handle 'TIF' file format. Having to deal with PDF file format is difficult enough for our users, especially the remote access users, let alone having to deal with another format. JSTOR should make the "quick" printing option work with Netscape printing so that a special application is not needed.

I'm pleased to see an effort to provide retrospective coverage of scholarly journals, especially in the humanities. I'm not sure, however, if this is the best place to put fiscal resources, since print collections and document delivery are adequate. But, as a way of expanding access to remote users to a wider array of resources, this is an exciting initiative.

COMMENTS ON UTILITY FOR HOME CAMPUS USE ONLY (Each member responds as to how they would feel with respect to the use of this product or service at their home campus only):

Offers alternative for current storage problems, but price is too high.

Many selectors feel that buying an archive of a journal without access to current issues is too confusing for both users and cataloging.

Wonderful product that I doubt we could afford.

Another issue to consider is what the library can or cannot do with the electronic material. Some vendors place restrictions on who can use the material, even in a public access setting. Such restrictions create problems for the public service staff—how to identify user types and monitoring what is being used. For example, *Academic Universe*® from Lexis/Nexis is contractually limited to the students, staff, and faculty of the purchasing institution. Individuals not affiliated with the institution are not permitted to use the service. What happens if the purchase was through a consortium and a person is visiting another campus that is part of the consortium? Can the visitor use the service without violating the license agreement, since the home institution also has the service? Logically, one would think that such use would be acceptable; however, unless the consortium's agreement so indicates, there is a chance that such use would be a violation. Another concern is that all contracts call for the purchaser to be responsible for copyright violations. The whole question of license agreements is complex, and we will discuss these matters more fully in chapter 18 on legal issues.

Finally, long-term access to and preservation of material is usually a concern. Who will archive the material? How will it be archived, and for how long? These are questions one needs to consider at the point of making a selection decision. Programs operated by libraries, such as JSTOR, are more likely to provide the electronic long-term archiving that both librarians and scholars expect with print materials. Commercial ventures are profit-driven and are unlikely to maintain a service that loses money for very long. Although the current purpose of JSTOR—a not-for-profit organization—is the selective digital conversion of retrospective files of print journals of scholarly interest, it seems likely that it, or a similar organization, will begin archiving e-serials.

Handling E-Serials

Handling e-serials? What does that mean? Unlike a print subscription, after the appropriate recordkeeping files are in place, e-serials require more set-up steps. Generally a new print subscription merely goes into its appropriate place with the other current issues of the print journals.

In the case of e-serials, as we mentioned in the section on selection, someone must assure that the technical issues have been addressed before the service is implemented. If the access is Web-based and domain in nature, providing IP ranges is fairly straightforward. However, password verification is still a requirement of some systems, and libraries must decide who will have access to these passwords. Will patrons be logged on individually, or will certain patrons (such as faculty members) be given the password to use as needed? There must be testing to determine compatibility with other services (changes in hardware or software configurations, for example). Libraries must also consider what, if anything, will appear in the library's OPAC about the product. If a package of, say, 1,000 full-text journals is purchased, will the library add a note to the holdings statements for titles the library also has in a print format? What about entries for the "new" titles, even those that may not be important to the library's customer base? Will the OPAC reflect just title, electronic address only, or both? Will there be a "hot link" in the OPAC or on the library Website? If images are included in the package, does the library need "helper" applications (such as Adobe's Acrobat Reader) installed on its public machines?

Every library using electronic materials needs one person or office that handles and maintains a file of license agreements. Someone must review the agreement and notify staff of any new requirements.

Public service staff will need time for familiarization and training in using the new product. Vendor support telephone numbers and/or Internet addresses should be available to staff. End users may also need assistance, especially if they want to print, e-mail, or download an article from the product for the first or second time. If the journals are accessible from offsite, whether through a proxy server or other means, what support exists in the library and at the institution for offsite patrons who have trouble using the resource? A good article outlining all the steps and issues in implementing a new e-serial is Cindy Stewart Kaag's "Collection Development for Online Serials."[6]

In 1998, Janet Hughes and Catherine Lee published an interesting article[7] that can serve as a case study of the process of selecting, acquiring, and implementing a full-text journal package. Part of what makes this article interesting is that it addresses issues related to multiple service points. The authors described the process used at Pennsylvania State University and its statewide 23-campus system. They concluded by stating, "Overall, although the experience of implementing the first networked full-text databases at Penn State was a positive one, its success depended upon careful planning and dedicated inter-departmental and campus cooperation. These qualities will be needed to make future forays into full-text equally successful."[8]

Up until this point, our discussion of print and electronic serials has focused upon some of the more standard entries: scholarly journals, magazines, newspapers, and the like. There is a type of literature that does not receive much discussion, the so-called grey literature. In the past, some research and special libraries made an effort to collect this type of material. Today, with electronic "publishing" on the Internet a fact of life, grey literature takes on a new meaning. Grey literature was and is primarily of scholarly interest, particularly in the sciences, and tends to be the output of the "invisible college." A widely accepted definition of grey literature has yet to be formulated. *Harrod's Librarians' Glossary* defines these items as "semi-published material, for example reports, internal documents, theses, etc. not formally published or available commercially, and consequently difficult to trace bibliographically."[9] Julia Gelfand stated, "The definition of grey literature has changed rather drastically since the First International Conference, held in Amsterdam, four years ago [1993]."[10] One of the reasons for the changing nature of the concept of grey literature is electronic publishing.

To some degree, what we now call the Internet was developed so that scientists and scholars could more quickly share results (grey literature) and work together from different physical locations (the invisible college). Today, technology and the Internet are creating new types of grey literature, not just online preprint services and technical report access. Perhaps the most striking change is the ability to describe phenomena in other than textual terms—modeling online, movement, sound, and true interactive collaborative work. Julia Gelfand suggested,

Learning about this new grey literature is in itself a non-traditional role for librarians and scholars ... . Training and bibliographic familiarity in this age is indeed quite different, because one does not follow a curriculum or set of readers or textbooks, but instead studies by doing, engaging in online time, discovering what the digital literati in different fields contribute as resources for good, appropriate, critical, sought after information. Usually, a strong needs assessment for the information, coupled with this new facility in making it readily available without enhanced packaging, encourages its use.[11]

Is grey literature a serial? As it tends to be ongoing in nature, one can consider it at least a semi-serial. To what degree the library tries to provide access to such material is very much a matter of local need and close collaboration between the library and its users.

Document Delivery

We debated where to put this discussion, as it could fit into several chapters. We first touched on this issue in chapter 6, and finally settled on this chapter as the place for this section because many of the services draw on electronic serials to provide the "document." In the past, traditional inter-library loan (ILL) services often provided the only access to materials not owned, especially to grey literature. Today libraries have a choice in how to provide customers with needed but unowned materials.

There are at least seven broad types of document delivery services in addition to the traditional ILL: general commercial services, specialized commercial services, direct from publisher/producer, aggregator services, national library collections, information brokers, and fee-based services in a large research library.

Why are libraries turning to this approach, and how does it relate to collection development? The answer to the relationship question resides in how a given library decides to address the issues of access or ownership. The more material a library knows it must own, the greater the work for the collection development officers. Even when employing document delivery to provide "just in time" access to very low-use materials, there is a need for collection development staff to coordinate their activities with those of document delivery. Essentially, there must be ongoing planning and coordination of both activities.

The answer to why use services other than traditional ILL is more complex. Certainly a major factor is the escalating costs of serials, which far outpace inflation in other areas of the economy and library budgets that are hard-pressed to do more than maintain constant collection levels, much less increase their size. Almost every library of any size has had to implement at least one journal reduction exercise some time in the last 15 years. Many libraries have had to undertake several such cutting efforts in the recent past. The first such program is relatively easy, as there are usually a number of titles that were acquired for the "just-in-case" need and show little or no use over time. Depending upon the size of the necessary reduction, perhaps the first time will only have to "hit" very low-use titles; in those cases, depending on ILL to fulfill the rare request may be an adequate alternative.

Unfortunately, most of the reductions in serials collections have cut more deeply, which required thinking about how to supply the wanted material more quickly than traditional ILL. Also an issue is how much of an increase in ILL requests the existing staff can handle. If there are alternatives that allow the requestor to have direct access to the document-supplying service, there will be little or no increase in the ILL workload.

Another factor, at least for a few libraries, relates to space and money. Libraries have had difficulty maintaining their operating budgets; when it comes to securing funding for additional space to house the ever-growing collections, the track record is even bleaker. One way to gain space in an existing facility is to look at long back runs of journals, especially those that have very little usage. Withdrawing the physical volumes will provide shelving space. The question then becomes how to provide access to the withdrawn titles. Certainly, buying microfiche/film versions is one option; however, microfilm storage cabinets take up space, and the cost of the microforms and the equipment to use them must be considered. Going with a document delivery option saves space and the cost of requested materials may never equal the cost of the microforms.

Gale Etschmaier and Marifran Bustion discussed the pro and cons of such services in an article about the experience of Gelman Library at George Washington University in implementing a document delivery service. The situation they described was a major journal cancellation project in which the library cancelled 1,031 journal titles in 1993–1994. One of their interesting findings was that, as of early 1997, only 35 of those titles (roughly 3 percent) had been the subject of any requests for articles.[12] They concluded by stating, "The data gathered through monitoring direct requests through document delivery and interlibrary loan services can be monitored and analyzed as an aid to collection development."[13]

When evaluating possible document delivery services, one should use most of the factors one employs to assess any vendor (see chapter 12). The additional elements to consider are similar to those for choosing an e-journal vendor:

- Type of access provided
- Quality/content of the database
- Ordering options (user, library)
- Costs and what is covered (copyright fees)
- Delivery options (fax, e-mail, overnight mail)
- Reliability (does the service meet advertised delivery times?)
- Payment options (credit card, invoices, prepaid deposit)
- Customer service availability (end users, staff only)

As Suzanne Ward stated in her article evaluating delivery services, "The only certainties in document delivery today are that the number of requests will increase exponentially and that tomorrow there will be even more suppliers and methods for ordering from them."[14]

Pricing

As we noted in the myths section, e-serials do not save either the producer or the library money. Perhaps at some point in the past there was a reasonable expectation of such savings. However, by the mid-1990s it was clear to both vendors and libraries that this would not be the case. For example, as Robert Marks noted, the American Chemical Society estimated that its CD-ROM journals cost 25 to 33 percent more to produce than their print versions. The higher cost was attributed to the need to provide and maintain a search engine.[15] In another article, Tom Abate reported the American Institute of Physics' estimate that providing both a print and electronic copy of a title cost between 10 and 15 percent more than just offering a print version of the same title.[16] Conversations with publishers of electronic-only serials indicate that they see no difference in costs; they claim it costs just as much for an e-only version as it does for print-only. Janet Fischer of MIT Press indicated that the reason producers of e-only serials see costs as equal was not so much a function of production costs as it was an overall loss of revenue—no back-issue sales, no renting of subscriber mailing lists, and, perhaps most importantly, the loss of advertising income.[17]

The dual pricing one found and still finds with many scholarly print serials (that is, one price for individuals and a higher price for institutions) continues in the electronic environment, if in a slightly different guise. Individuals do not face the same licensing issues as libraries and do not pay for more than one user, nor are they asked about number of potential users in the household or office. Libraries usually have to pay extra fees, rather substantial at times, for more than one simultaneous user license. Different producers use different increments, such as 1 to 4 users at one rate, 5 to 9 another rate, and so on to a rate for unlimited access.

Another pricing mechanism is by size of the service population, frequently based upon the number of full-time students or staff (full-time equivalent or FTE) at an institution. This is probably one of the most costly approaches for libraries when it comes to specialized serials and products. For example, say a fictitious university (we will call it ICU) has an anthropology department with 10 faculty, 68 graduate students, and 129 undergraduate majors, and its course offerings each year enroll a total of 1,400 different students. The library considers subscribing to an electronic version of a print product in the field of anthropology that has a record of modest use. The producer, using the FTE pricing model, sets the price at 50 cents per FTE. Unfortunately, typically the vendor calculates the cost on the basis of the institutional FTE, not that of the department or even a realistic estimate of the potential users. Thus, if the institutional FTE (staff/faculty/students is the typical request) is 12,000, then the cost becomes $6,000 for a product that has had only modest use in the print format. Certainly there is the prospect that the electronic version will have greater use, assuming the product comes with a reasonably good search engine, but there is no reasonable expectation that every person at the institution will access the database at some point during the year.

Transaction-based fees are another pricing mechanism that can drive up the cost of electronic serials for a library (this is the model that OCLC was using for FirstSearch in the late 1990s). In some ways, this approach is less costly than the FTE model, as actual usage determines the price. One draw-back of this model is that the library is never certain what its costs will be until after the fact. With FirstSearch, OCLC (at least with consortiums) sets an annual fee that includes a fixed number of searches. The fee is paid in advance, and at the end of the year there may be additional charges if the search limit was exceeded. The amount may be something of a shock for the library, if it has not been carefully monitoring usage. (The Loyola Marymount University library belongs to a consortium that purchased access to FirstSearch, and members discussed what databases they could "turn off" to control the year-end charges. Somehow it seems strange to buy access to a database and then have to discuss which ones we should restrict public access to in order to save money.) Part of the problem with the transaction-based approach is that every search *counts*, even those in which the searcher has misspelled a word or does not understand how to search the database. It is difficult to know how much value for money expended one actually receives from this model. At least with paper formats user and staff mistakes do not cost the library additional money.

When buying a package from an aggregator, the library knows it will be paying an extra fee for the "added value" of having a single source and search engine for journals from a variety of producers. However, one often is buying access to titles of little or no interest to the library's service population, because a package truly is all or nothing. This effectively drives up the cost of the titles that are of interest to the library users.

Some publishers/producers, at least in 1999, have not decided which model to follow. As a result, some offer free access to an electronic version of a title if the library has a subscription to the print format. Others offer such access for a modest fee (10 to 15 percent) above the print subscription cost.

Where the pricing will go is difficult to predict beyond the fact that prices will continue to escalate. As Bill Robnett stated, "The complexities of online serials pricing may increase as more publishers enter the electronic publishing market. ... One consideration is that serials budgets will be redefined as libraries purchase access in units of articles, an open-ended concept quite different from the now prevalent subcription."[18]

Summary

Electronic serials are probably the "wave of the future," but perhaps a more distant future than technology enthusiasts would have us believe. Despite the advantages of having materials available in such formats, it appears that there is little prospect of either producers or libraries realizing any cost savings as a result of migrating to an electronic environment. How libraries will handle the ever-escalating costs of serials, regardless of format, is something to ponder seriously.

Notes

1.   Thomas Nisonger, "Electronic Journal Collection Development Issues," *Collection Building* 16, no. 2 (1997): 58.

2.   Hazel Woodward et al., "Electronic Journals: Myths and Realities," *OCLC Systems and Services* 13, no. 4 (1997): 144–51.

3.   Nuchine Nobari, *Books and Periodicals Online: 1997* (Washington, D.C.: Library Technology Alliance, 1997).

4.   Mary Jean Pavelsek, "Guidelines for Evaluating E-Journal Providers," *Advances in Librarianship* 22 (1998): 39–58.

5.   Michael Rogers, "Cal State Proposes New E-Journal Buying Model," *Library Journal* 124 (February 15, 1999): 107.

6.   Cindy Stewart Kaag, "Collection Development for Online Serials: Who Needs to Do What, and Why, and When," *Serials Librarian* 33, nos. 1/2 (1998): 107–22.

7.   Janet Hughes and Catherine Lee, "Giving Patrons What They Want: The Promise, the Process, and the Pitfalls of Providing Full-Text Access to Journals," *Collection Building* 17, no.4 (1998): 148–53.

8.   Ibid., 153.

9.   R. Prytherch, comp., *Harrod's Librarians' Glossary* (Aldershot, U.K.: Gower, 1995): 285.

10.   Julia Gelfand, "Teaching and Exposing Grey Literature," *Collection Building* 17, no. 4 (1998): 159.

11.   Ibid., 160–61.

12.   Gale Etschmaier and Marifran Bustion, "Document Delivery and Collection Development: An Evolving Relationship," *Serials Librarian* 31, no. 3 (1997): 24.

13.   Ibid., 26.

14.   Suzanne M. Ward, "Document Delivery: Evaluating the Options," *Computers in Libraries* 17 (October 1997): 26.

15.   Robert Marks, "The Economic Challenges of Publishing Electronic Journals," *Serials Review* 21 (Spring 1995): 85–88.

16.   Tom Abate, "Publishing Scientific Journals Online," *Bioscience* 47 (March 1997): 175–79.

17.   Janet Fischer, "True Costs of an Electronic Journal," *Serials Review* 21 (Spring 1995): 88–90.

18.   Bill Robnett, "Online Journal Pricing," *Serials Librarian* 33, nos. 1/2 (1998): 68.

Selected Websites*

Back Issues and Exchange Services
        <http://www.uvm.edu/~bmaclenn/backexch.html>
    A source of missing issues and exchange of serials and other materials. Maintained by Birdie MacLennan; her main site (<http://www.uvm.edu/~bmaclenn/>) is "Serials in Cyberspace," a collection of resources and services of use to serials librarians.

CJS/E—Doc Home Page
        <http://www.edoc.com>
    CREN's (originators of www) "WWW Virtual Library." One of the top Websites.

CONSER Program Home Page
        <http://lcweb.loc.gov/acq/conser/>
    The Library of Congress's Website for information about the Cooperative Online Serials Program (CONSER).

The Daily Press
        <http://www.docuweb.ca/sispain/english/media/press.html>
    An English Website providing information about print and electronic newspapers in Spain.

Ejournal SiteGuide
        <http://www.library.ubc.ca/ejour>
    Joseph Jones's Website with annotated links to sites for e-journals.

Electronic Journal Access
        <http://www.coalliance.org/ejournal>
    The Colorado Alliance of Research Libraries site that provides information on almost 3,000 e-journals. Provides LC subject heading, an abstract, URL, contact data, ISSN, and other useful information.

enews.com
        <http://www.enews.com>
    A list of more than 2,000 commercial magazine resources available on the Web.

e-zine list:John Labovitz's e-zine-list
        <http://www.meer.net/~johnl/e-zine-list/>
    John Labovitz's site for electronic 'zines available via the Web, FTP, or otherwise electronically.

Serials discussion list site.
        <http://uvmvm.uvm.edu>
    Subscribe by e-mailing to
        <LISTSERV@uvmvm.uvm.edu>.
    Type message SERIALST and then your name.

ICOLC Statement on Electronic Information
        <http://www.library.yale.edu/consortia/statement.html>
    Site for information on the International Coalition of Library Consortia (ICOLC), which deals with consortial purchases of electronic resources.

The Journal of Electronic Publishing
        <http://www.press.umich.edu/jep/>
    A good source of information about e-publishing from the University of Michigan Press.

Liblicense: Licensing Digital Information
        <http://www.library.yale.edu/~llicense/index.shtml>
    Archive for LIBLICENSE-L discussion list.

NewJour
        <http://gort.ucsd.edu/newjour/>
    List of archived networked e-journals.

North American Serials Interest Group
        <http://nasig.ils.unc.edu/nasigweb.html>
    NASIG is an important group in serial management programming and information. A site worth bookmarking.

Scholarly Electronic Publishing Bibliography
        <http://info.lib.uh.edu/sepb/sepb.html>
    References on electronic publishing.

Scholarly Journals Distributed Via the World-Wide Web
        <http://info.lib.uh.edu/wj/webjour.html>
    A University of Houston libraries Website that lists more than 120 free Web-based academic journals.

UK Serials Group WWW Page
        <http://www.uksg.org>
    An excellent source of information about U.K. and European serial vendors and services.

Web Tools for Serialists
        <http://toltec.lib.utk.edu/~serials/sertools.htm>
    Kathy Ellis's site that lists Websites related to serials work. Three major divisions: General Serials Resources, Serials Acquisitions, and Cataloging and Online Publications.

Welcome to JSTOR
        <http://www.jstor.org>
    The home page of Journal Storage (JSTOR).

Welcome to United States Book Exchange
        <http://www.usbe.com/>
    USBE has been a mainstay for serials librarians as a source of missing journal issues and exchange of serials.

*These sites were accessed 4 October 1999.

Further Reading

General

Abate, Tom. "Publishing Scientific Journals Online." *Bioscience* 47 (March 1997): 175–79.

American Library Association. "Directory of Union Lists of Serials." *Serials Review* 14, nos. 1/2 (1998): 115–59.

ARL/OMS. *Electronic Journals in ARL Libraries: Issues and Trends.* SPEC Flyer 202. Washington, D.C.: ARL/OMS, August 1994.

———. *Electronic Journals in ARL Libraries: Policies and Procedures.* SPEC Flyer 201. Washington, D.C.: ARL/OMS, August 1994.

Barnes, J. H. "One Giant Leap, One Small Step: Continuing the Migration to Electronic Journals." *Library Trends* 45 (Winter 1997): 404–15.

Cameron, R. D. "Not Just E-Journals: Providing and Maintaining Access to Serials and Serials Information Through the World-Wide Web." *Serials Librarian* 29, nos. 3/4 (1996): 209–22.

Cline, N. M. "Local or Remote Access: Choices and Issues." *Collection Management* 22, nos. 3–4 (1998): 21–29.

Cole, J. E., and J. W. Williams, eds. *Serials Management in the Electronic Era*. New York: Haworth Press, 1996.

Davis, T. "Evolution of Selection Activities for Electronic Resources." *Library Trends* 45 (Winter 1997): 391–403.

Donnice, C., and E. F. Jurries. "An Idea Whose Time Has Come: The Alliance Electronic Journal Access Web Site," *Colorado Libraries* 22 (Summer 1996): 15–19.

Duranceau, E. F. "Beyond Print: Revisioning Serials Acquisitions for the Digital Age." *Serials Librarian* 33, nos. 1–2 (1998): 83–105.

Fritseh, D. "A Capital Idea: Electronic Serials from Acquisition to Access." *Serials Review* 23 (Winter 1997): 83–88.

Gadd, E. "Copyright Clearance for the Digital Library." *Serials* 10 (March 1997): 27–32.

Gilbert, N. "Aggregators of Electronic Journals." 1997. Available via e-mail from <LIBLICENSE-L@pantheon.yale.edu>.

Gordon, B., and M. A. Sheble. "Archiving Electronic Journals." *Serials Review* 21 (Winter 1995): 13–21.

Guernsey, L. "Library Groups, Decrying 'Excessive Pricing,' Demand New Policies on Electronic Journals." *Chronicle of Higher Education* 44, no. 31 (1998): A33–34.

Guthrie, K. M., and W. P. Lougee. "The JSTOR Solution: Accessing and Preserving the Past." *Library Journal* 122, no. 2 (1998): 42–44.

Harter, S. P., and H. K. Kin. "Accessing Electronic Journals and Other E-Publications." *College & Research Libraries* 57 (September 1996): 440–56.

Hawbaker, A. C., and C. K.Wagner. "Periodical Ownership Versus Fulltext Online Access: A Cost-Benefit Analysis." *Journal of Academic Librarianship* 22, no. 2 (1996): 105–9.

Hawkins, L. "Network Accessed Scholarly Serials." *Serials Librarian* 29, nos. 3/4 (1996): 19–31.

Homan, J. M. "Precocious Dinosaur or Preeminent Electronic Resource?" *Bulletin of the Medical Library Association* 85 (January 1997): 59–60.

Hruska, M. "Remote Internet Serials in the OPAC?" *Serials Review* 21 (Winter 1995): 68–70.

Ingoldsby, T. C. "Electronic Publishing from the Producers' Point-of-View." In *National Online Meeting Proceedings—18th*. New York: Information Today, 1997.

Jeapes, B. "Learning to Live with E-Journals." *Electronic Library* 15 (February 1997): 27–30.

Ketcham, L., and K. Born. "Projecting Electronic Revolution While Budgeting for the Status Quo." *Library Journal* 121 (April 15, 1996): 45–53.

Ketcham-Van Orsdel, L., and K. Born. "E-Journals Come of Age." *Library Journal* 123 (April 15, 1998): 40–45.

Knight, N. H. "Electronic Pubs Pricing in the Web Era." *Information Today* 15 (September 1998): 39–40.

Kreitz, P. A., et al. "The Virtual Library in Action." *Publishing Research Quarterly* 13 (Summer 1997): 24–32.

Lancaster, F. W. "Evolution of the Electronic Publishing." *Library Trends* 43 (Spring 1995): 518–27.

Lynch, C. A. "Technology and Its Implications for Serials Acquisition." *Against the Grain* 9 (February 1997): 34, 36–37.

Machovec, G. S. "Electronic Journal Market Overview—1997." *Serials Review* 23 (Summer 1997): 31–44.

———. "Pricing Models for Electronic Databases on the Internet." *Online Libraries and Microcomputers* 16 (March 1998): 1–4.

———. "User Authentication and Authorization Challenges in a Networked Library Environment." *Online Libraries and Microcomputers* 15 (October 1997): 1–5.

McKay, S. C. "Partnering in a Changing Medium." *Library Acquisition: Practice and Theory* 22, no. 1 (1998): 23–27.

McMillan, G. "Technical Processing of Electronic Journals." *Library Resources & Technical Services* 36 (October 1992): 470–72.

Metz, P., et al. "A Standardized Form for Evaluation and Description of Electronic Resources Under Consideration by the Virginia Tech University Libraries." *Technicalities* 18, no. 10 (November/December 1998): 9–10.

Miller, W. "Electronic Access to Information Will Not Reduce the Cost of Library Materials." *Library Issues: Briefings for Faculty and Administrators* 15, no. 6 (July 1995): 1–4.

Moothart, T. "Providing Access to E-Journals Through Library Home Pages." *Serials Review* 22 (Summer 1996): 71–77.

Mouw, J. "Changing Roles in the Electronic Age." *Library Acquisitions: Practice and Theory* 22, no.1 (1998): 15–22.

Pikowsky, R. A. "Electronic Journals as a Potential Solution to Escalating Serials Cost." *Serials Librarian* 32, nos. 3/4 (1997): 31–56.

Rowland, J. F. "Electronic Journals: Delivery, Use, and Access." *IFLA Journal* 22, no. 3 (1996): 226–28.

Schottlaender, B. "Development of National Principles to Guide Licensing Electronic Resources." *Library Acquisition: Practice and Theory* 22, no. 1 (1998): 49–54.

Simser, C. N., and M. A. Somers, eds. *Experimentation and Collaboration: Creating Serials for a New Millennium.* New York: Haworth Press, 1998.

Sonberg, P. "Partnering in a Changing Medium: Challenges of Managing and Delivering E-Journals." *Serials Librarian* 34, nos. 3/4 (1998): 295–99.

Strangelove, M. "Current and Future Trends in Network-Based Electronic Journals and Publishing." In *The Evolving Virtual Library: Visions and Case Studies.* Edited by L. M. Saunders, 135–45. Medford, N.J.: Information Today, 1996.

Tenopir, C. "The Complexities of Electronic Journals." *Library Journal* 122 (February 1, 1997): 37–38.

Ward, S. M. "Document Delivery: Evaluating the Options." *Computers in Libraries* 17 (October 1997): 26–30.

Woodward, H. "Electronic Journals: Issues of Access and Bibliographic Control." *Serials Review* 21 (Summer 1995): 71–78.

Wusteman, J. "Electronic Journal Formats." *Program* 30 (October 1996): 319–43.

Yocum, P. B. "Libraries and Electronic Journals in Science." *IFLA Journal* 22, no. 3 (1996): 181–247.

Youngen, G. K. "Citation Patterns to Traditional and Electronic Preprints in the Published Literature." *College & Research Libraries* 59 (September 1998): 448–56.

8
Other Electronic Materials

The opening sentence of the Library of Congress's publication *Collection Development and the Internet* concisely states the reason for this chapter: "The Internet has the potential to change radically much of our work, whether it be as reference specialists or as recommending officers."[1] Today that statement might best be phrased as "The Internet *has* radically changed ... ." Libraries are making ever-increasing use of Internet resources in their service programs and as part of their "virtual collections." Certainly the electronic environment goes well beyond just Internet/Web resources, but those resources are becoming more and more dominant factors.

In the preceding chapter we discussed electronic serials, and many of the issues we raised there apply to any type of electronic material. What we will cover in this chapter are some of the collection development concerns with other electronic resources, particularly Internet material. Chapter 9, which examines government information, also contains substantial information about electronic access. All of the materials covered in these chapters do carry legal concerns for the library, and to avoid duplication as much as possible we provide a detailed discussion of these concerns in chapter 18.

A question often asked is: Are electronic materials merely another type of storage medium, like microforms? They are, indeed, another storage format in one sense, because digitized data does allow compact storage of large quantities of information. However, digital formats also allow data manipulation in ways that are not cost-effective in other formats. Further, the electronic environment allows both free-text and Boolean searching. Downloading information from electronic resources to a user's computer and being able to cut, paste, move, add, and delete as much as desired is now possible. (Note: This is possible either with or without complying with copyright; the new copyright law has special implication for libraries in this regard, see chapter 18.) Such capabilities make electronic information the preferred information format for many users.

Electronic formats cause libraries and information centers to concentrate their attention on overall operations and rethink systems and services in a way never before required. To some degree, it may be a question of the survival of our field. Electronic information producers can deliver the product directly to the end user at home or in the office, and increasingly they are doing so. Proper planning, realistic goals, and intelligent reorganization of operations will ensure that libraries play an ever-expanding role in the information transfer process in the electronic age.

Electronic delivery of information requires delivery platforms, equipment, software, substantial user support, and time to assess the various services and products that producers offer. Few users have the time, energy, inclination, or funds to handle all these activities effectively. Libraries can and should undertake these tasks. If we do not, someone else will.

Background and Needs Assessment

The electronic environment creates several dichotomies for libraries and information centers: print versus electronic; ownership versus access; user need versus institutional need; free versus fee; and gatekeeper versus user selection. It is not a matter of either/or; rather, it is a matter of determining the proper local mix. Clearly, one cannot make the necessary judgments about these issues without knowing the local users, what information they want and need, how and where they use the information, what type of equipment they have, what network capabilities exist, and what monetary and equipment resources are available to the library or information center.

Print and electronic information sources are both complementary and competitive. Users with an interest in historical information and data certainly will require, in most cases, collections of older print material. Few of the electronic products or services provide pre-1970s information. This may change in time, but at the moment recent information is in highest demand, and it is on the highest-demand areas that commercial providers focus. (One example of a change in backfile access is JSTOR; however, it is worth noting that this is a library-initiated rather than commercially run project.) One obvious advantage of print sources is that they do not malfunction, and one can use them in a variety of locations without having to consider power, network connections, and similar technical issues. However, electronic sources have a clear advantage in terms of locating and manipulating information. In any case, it is imperative to have an understanding of the service community's preferences for end users of print and electronic information.

Traditionally, libraries and information centers depended on an ownership-of-materials model as the primary means of meeting customer information needs. Interlibrary loans (ILL) for books and photocopies of journal articles more or less filled any gaps between the local collections and local needs. Interlibrary loan adheres to the ownership-of-materials model in that it requires other libraries to own the loaned material. Customers check out ILL materials from their home library and return the materials to the local library when finished; the local library then ships the materials back to the lending source. For all practical purposes, this system operates as if the local library owned the items. Another form of ownership is photocopied ILL journal articles that the user gets to keep. The ILL process is slow, but it preserves the sense of ownership.

Taking the ownership model to an extreme, research libraries once attempted to acquire everything their service community actually did or might need: the goals were impossible to achieve and the attempt was costly. Even in a cooperative collection environment, it was not possible for libraries to own everything their customers wanted or might conceivably want.

Electronic materials and methods of information dissemination present the opportunity for libraries and information centers to provide access to more resources than they can realistically expect to acquire and house. Access can be directed to a user's home or workplace, allowing end users to make independent choices about what they want, from what source, and how quickly. Access may be a more cost-effective option for the library or information center, even if the organization pays for all searches and documents ordered. (Cost issues are covered later in this chapter.)

The balancing of individual and institutional needs raises the issue of free versus fee services. There is the long-standing tradition of free library service. Though maintaining this tradition is the goal of many information professionals, it has been some time since all services were free. Charging for services began with charging for photocopying, and the practice has expanded steadily over the years. In the electronic environment, it is easy to associate service costs with individual customers, and there are a greater variety of costs (for example, charges for per-page or per-screen viewing, connect time, printing, or copyright or royalties). Because it is easier to associate costs with an individual in the electronic environment than it is in the print environment, it is possible to pass the charges on to the customer. To some degree, the new costs are not new; they were merely hidden or too time-consuming to track in the print world. Again, how far one goes in charging fees depends on the local situation and service community.

Libraries supporting educational programs are more likely to absorb the costs for electronic information that directly supports instruction and pass on charges for noninstructional uses. Some institutions, like Loyola Marymount University, have a sliding scale, allowing for a base level of free access and some form of cost sharing as the individual's use increases. Public libraries must consider the economic differences in the community with the goal of assuring that those who cannot afford to pay the fees do not become information-poor. Special libraries may pass costs to project teams or departments to answer an organization's desire to track actual operating costs of various units; in other situations, the costs are considered overhead and are not assigned to any unit other than the information center.

The roles of the library, computing services, telecommunication services, and customers in electronic information transfer is a topic of debate in electronic discussion groups and conferences, as well as in the literature and in the institution. Who has primary responsibility? If shared, how is it shared? Who decides what will be available? Who supports and maintains the service(s)? None of these questions, nor many related ones, have clear answers. We are in the process of developing models based on experience. Efforts to merge the various institutional players have not proven successful. However, as noted in chapter 1, it is clear that text, numeric, voice, and image data technologies are becoming integrated and, at some point, the institution must come to grips with the need to coordinate the various activities.

One aspect of the debate is whether there should be preselection of electronic materials. In preselection, the library or information center plays the role of gatekeeper, rather than letting users search independently. Although the terms are different, the fundamental issue is as old as libraries and collection development. Years ago, a favorite examination question in collection development courses was, "Is collection development selection or censorship?" On one side are those who believe that no one should predetermine what resources best fit the organization's mission and profile. Their position is, let the user find what she or he needs without preselection by someone else. The opposite view is that preselection and guidance are in the best interests of both the users and the organization. As in the past, libraries, information centers, and organizations cannot provide access to everything. Thus, choices are inevitable; someone or some group must function as a gatekeeper or, at least, as a cost controller (that is, an information manager).

Refusing to perform the gatekeeper function is akin to putting a person in the middle of a multimillion-volume storehouse, with only a floor plan keyed to broad classification groupings, and saying to this person, "You are on your own." That will waste not only the individual's time, but also the institution's resources. In a sense, this view is a return to the research library philosophy of the 1950s, 1960s, and early 1970s: "Get everything possible, just in case." A gatekeeper who points the way to potentially useful materials, perhaps by adding pointers on the library's Web home page, aids the user in the long run and maximizes the benefit of the institution's funding for information services. When the library or information center provides such assistance, it does not deny the user access to other electronic resources available through other services, such as the Internet (assuming the individual has network access and the ability to explore it effectively). The case for some assistance and evaluation is summed up in the following:

> Still in its infancy—with only a hint of its future richness—networked information is currently anarchic and pretty much "use at your own risk." One writer characterized the Internet as "awash with information, both useful and banal." Data files are incomplete and unverified, there is little or no documentation or support, it is difficult to pin down author responsibility, and there are few evaluative resources.[2]

One advantage of electronic collection building, compared with building print collections, is more effective tracking of the person using the information and what resources she or he used that one could supply with electronic materials. (Although state-of-the-art online circulation systems allow one to easily get similar information about circulated items, for in-house use the best one can do is track the items used, not who used them.) Many of the better commercial electronic products have management report software that allows one to learn how and when the users accessed the material. One gets more accurate and complete data with less effort in the electronic environment. It is up to librarians to make effective use of the data to provide the right information at the right time at the right cost.

Issues in Electronic Collection Building

One issue that makes processing some e-materials, especially Web/Internet materials, challenging is that they do not usually remain "fixed" in the way print materials do. Anyone with any amount of experience with Web/Internet materials has at least once encountered a message indicating that the URL one bookmarked is no longer operative. Sometimes a new address is provided on a "transition page," but often there is no referring link. Not only are addresses variable, but so is the content of the site. "This document last modified on ..." is a message found on many Internet/Web sites; another message is "under construction." Both messages make it clear that what you see today may not be what or all you will see tomorrow.

Some individuals believe that, as we stated in the opening paragraph of this chapter, electronic materials and the Internet have indeed radically changed collection development. Kathleen Kluegel wrote, "it is time to see if the traditional models of technical processes, collection development, and collection management still fit the needs of the library and its users."[3] Certainly she is correct that electronic resources require different cataloging processing (we address some of these views later in this chapter). The basic question, though, is whether they are really so different as to require radical changes in processing activities. The fact that libraries are leasing or renting the data does not really change the acquisition process. Certainly there are echoes of the old approval plan in the free trial that many e-materials vendors generally offer. (The major concern with trials is whether one has access to the full product or just a sample. Needless to say, only a full product should be reviewed.)

An aspect of e-materials that is seldom addressed is how to deal with bytes rather than books. This is an area where we *do* need to make radical changes in how we deal with collection statistics. Many agencies that collect data about libraries do not ask about electronic resources—in some cases they only ask about "volumes." Volumes are also something funding bodies understand; they can see and hold them. The fact that one "rents" rather than owns the material, at least in many instances, also raises questions in funders' mind about what they and the library have to show for expending substantial amounts of money on e-materials.

With packages of e-materials, the vendors and producers decide what is or is not included, as well as for how long. It is not uncommon for packages' content to change even during a single lease period. That, of course, raises the question of what to count. For example, is a package such as FirstSearch one package or N number of databases? If one counted just the packages, one could not compare libraries very accurately, because libraries can turn off access to individual databases. Why do that? Because the OCLC pricing model is per-search-based; libraries can and do turn off databases that are least useful to local users but may generate a significant number of searches.

In the past, library "status" was, at least in part, a function of the size of collection—the more volumes, the higher the status. Changeable packages make for variable counts, assuming that one counts databases, and create fluctuating statistics that are difficult to quickly explain to nonlibrarians.

When adding a printed item into one's OPAC, one has a reasonable expectation that the only time a change to the record will be needed is if the item is withdrawn. (*Note:* We know that subject heading and authority records do change and can cause additional changes to the item's "bibliographic record" in the system; however, such changes generally affect only a small percentage of items. Also, some libraries do not make the changes unless it is clear that users know and will use the new form.) The lack of a "final" contact, if one adds a record for an electronic product to the OPAC, means either that someone must check the site on a regular basis and make any needed adjustments in the OPAC record, or that the library must accept the fact many such records no longer reflect reality. Although it is possible to "automate" the process of checking links, it still requires people power to check content, make decisions about any needed changes, and input the new information.

Types of Electronic Materials

Full Text

Of the major types of electronic resources, at present full text is the most challenging and replete with options. We covered the issues of e-serials in chapter 7. Here we will just remind readers there are two categories—electronic only and electronic/print—of interest in this chapter. E-only journals present a decision point: the library must decide how to provide access (that is, through the library or other gatekeeper or gateway or through direct access). It also must decide whether to include a record of those titles in its OPAC. Certainly the technical, legal, and financial issues addressed later in this chapter must be considered, but collection development issues are easily dealt with.

Full-text material comes in three formats: online, CD-ROM, and print. In some cases, there are cost differences when both print and electronic formats are available. As we mentioned in chapter 7, the vendor or publisher frequently has one price for the print version and a different price for the electronic version. If one orders just the electronic version, there is a third price, roughly equal to the sum of the print and electronic rates. An advantage to having both formats becomes obvious during, for example, a power outage when users still have access to the print version.

Another question is the definition of *full text*. Often, in the online version, it means text without graphics. As of 1999, online databases offered some limited graphical interfaces and imaged information. The reason for the limits is that images (charts, tables, and other illustrations) require substantial amounts of disk space and delivery time, as well as delivery platforms capable of handling images. CD-ROMs, in contrast, provide a wide range of imaging area, including full-motion video. Windows interfaces, now available with many CD-ROM products, will probably be available soon for online services. Graphics require megabytes of memory and powerful PCs (currently, mid- to high-end Pentiums), more powerful than many PC owners own. In addition, even if an end user's modem is capable of transmitting data at 56KB, online imaging is a slow process. Because of imaging issues, it will probably be some time before online services follow in the footsteps of OCLC's *Clinical Trials* journal.

Although we devoted an entire chapter to e-serials (chapter 7), we also need to give some attention to e-books. We opened this edition with a brief discussion of the controversy surrounding the 1998 Booker award and the question of "when is a book a book." Just as there are variations in e-serials, so there are with e-books. Some, like Patricia le Roy's *Angels of Russia*, are available only in an electronic version. One Website for e-books is "Alex: A catalog of Electronic Books on the Internet" (<http://www.lib.ncsu.edu/whatsnew/index.htm#ebook>).

One of the oldest efforts in digitizing existing books is Project Gutenberg. A goal of that Project is to have 10,000 titles available in its "Project Gutenberg Electronic Public Library" (<http://promo.net/pg>). Titles in the project are all public domain (no longer covered by copyright) items. At a different level, the Oxford Text Archives is of primary interest to academics. The Archives contains about 2,000 literary works as well as collections of unpublished field notes of linguists. This is a noncommercial service available to scholars to archive their electronic texts (<http://firth.natcorp.ox.ac.uk/ota/public/index.shtml>).

Other projects include the University of Michigan Libraries' "UM Press" (<http://www.press.umich.edu/>), and the School of Library and Information Studies' "Humanities Text Initiative" (<http://www.hti.umich.edu>), which focuses on Middle English materials and American poetry, as well as recent releases from the UM Press. From Brown University there is "The Woman Writers Project" (<http://www.wwp.brown.edu>). This project's goal is to create a full-text database of the publications in English written by women between 1330 and 1830. Since 1992, the "Electronic Text Center at the University of Virginia (<http://etext.lib.virginia.edu>) has been working to create a unique collection of online materials. By early 1999, the collection included "45,000 on- and off-line humanities texts in twelve languages with more than 50,000 related images (book illustrations, covers, manuscripts, newspaper pages, page images of Special Collections books, museum objects, etc.)."[4]

With any full-text material, whether book or serial, one issue to consider is the way the text was digitized: ASCII, Adobe, HTML, or SGHL. ASCII is the oldest and in many ways the easiest approach. However, one loses most of the formatting of the original document, as well as any images. Adobe Acrobat PDF (Portable Document Format) is an approach that retains formatting and images and is frequently encountered on the Internet. HTML (Hypertext Markup Language) is probably the most common method used on the World Wide Web. It is in fact a sub-language of SGML (Standard Generalized Markup Language). Many organizations use SGML to digitize their internal documents. There are several advantages to using SGML; it is an international standard, it is device independent, and it is system independent. Having documents in SGML makes it easier to change systems without incurring significant document conversion costs.

Music

Music, in recorded form, is available on the Internet, but almost nothing exists for musical scores. The only site of which we are aware is Stanford University's Center for Computer Assisted Research in the Humanities (<http://musedata.stanford.edu>), and there are fees to access the material. This site does have full electronic scores of many of the classical works. A controversy was brewing in early 1999 regarding the availability of MP3 files. This compression format allows for digitization and copying of music files, which are easily posted on the Internet, rarely legally. In February 1999, Leonardo Chiariglione, who invented the format, was named to head the "Secure Digital Music Initiative" to standardize the way songs and albums are distributed on the Internet.[5] This is obviously an issue that concerns the music industry, and until the issue can be addressed, one's best bet to find legal recordings is at recording company sites. We address electronic access to other nonprint formats, such as photographs, maps, and videos, in chapter 10.

Numeric Databases

Numeric databases have been part of library or information center collecting activities for at least 25 years. Generally, libraries acquired these data sets, such as the U.S. Census, as tapes that were mounted on a mainframe. Today, researchers can gain access to such sets online. A disadvantage is that downloading large data sets takes a long time; an advantage is that local ownership speeds the work.

A source for numeric data sets is the Inter-University Consortium for Political and Social Research (ICPSR) at the University of Michigan (<http://www.icpsr.umich.edu>). Hundreds of universities in 22 countries around the world are members of ICPSR. This consortium serves as a central repository and dissemination service for social science electronic data sets. Since its establishment in the early 1960s, ICPSR has collected data sets that cover a broad range of topics. Beginning with a few major surveys of the American electorate, the holdings of the archive have now broadened to include comparable information from diverse settings and for extended periods. Data ranging from nineteenth-century French census materials to recent sessions of the United Nations, from American elections in the 1790s to the socioeconomic structure of Polish *poviats*, from characteristics of Knights of Labor Assemblies to expectations of American consumers, are contained in the archive.[6]

When considering numeric collection building, one must remember that these tend to be very large files, and format or compatibility may be issues to consider, as well as the quality of the documentation. In the case of ICPSR, data sets are available as round tapes, 9-track, or diskettes. It is also possible to FTP files online using CDNet (Consortium Data Network) on the Internet. Users electing this mode might pay telecommunication charges, as well as University of Michigan computer services charges. Though avoiding the potential conversion costs, the online approach leaves open the possibility of surprisingly large and unpredictable service and telecommunication charges.

Occasionally, one may encounter a conflict between how long users wish to have access to the data and how long the organization's computing service is willing to make the tapes accessible through the campus network. This may result in pressure on the library not only to acquire the data sets, but also to have in-house CPU capacity to operate statistical software packages, as well as mount the tapes.

Support depends both on people with the skills and knowledge to do the technical work and on sound documentation. Anyone who has seen the documentation that accompanies many commercial products can imagine the quality of documentation for data sets from researchers whose primary purpose was their own project. If the library is already mounting bibliographic or full-text tapes, it may have staff with appropriate computer operations background. Probably, however, the staff will not have experience with all the various statistical packages on the market (such as SPSS and SAS). Support means institutional costs. Again, there are costs associated with either mode of access (online or tape). Careful consideration of both options and how to handle the charges is essential before moving into the business of acquiring data sets.

"Traditional" Reference Materials

Bibliographies, indexes, abstracts, and tables of contents are the traditional types of reference materials. As with full text, one has the option of electronic or print for each of these. The debate about CD-ROM versus online access is particularly applicable to these reference materials. Because licensing agreements allow greater legal control over the use of their products, producers tend to prefer to distribute information in the CD-ROM format. With the data in electronic form, the publishers or producers can generate more and more specialized products. An example is SIRS's *Discover* CD-ROM for the school market, which draws on SIRS's larger CD-ROM database *Researcher*. Public service users frequently prefer online or CD-ROM products over print versions.

User expectations or beliefs about electronic information also create challenges for the staff. Too often, users think the electronic data is both the most current and the most comprehensive. A few years ago the senior author reviewed a book, a revised doctoral dissertation, about the image of Native American women in nineteenth-century American literature. The author made several statements to the effect that her conclusions were *proven* by the fact that she had done several searches of DIALOG. Needless to say, it took little time to locate more than 25 citations, from print sources specific to Native American literature covering the nineteenth century, that disproved her conclusions. Both the author and her doctoral committee failed to recognize the limits of electronic databases. If doctoral-level researchers and their committees fail to understand the nature of electronic information, what can one expect from undergraduate students and less sophisticated users?

Software

Few libraries actively collect software because of copyright problems and the difficulty of maintaining the integrity of the software. (Chapter 18 discusses copyright and circulation issues related to software.) Though it is possible to collect operating systems, few, if any, libraries maintain collections of these programs for public use. Programming tools and languages are two other types of software that are rarely collected. The two areas where some collecting occurs are applications and, as discussed earlier, data files. Libraries are acquiring more and more books that come with software that is integral to use of the printed material. School media centers, if they have responsibility for computing services, are the most likely to maintain collections of educational application programs. (Perhaps the safest software to collect is so-called shareware.)

Without a doubt, libraries and collection development officers will face increasing pressure to add electronic formats. Cost, legal, and selection issues each will become more complex as time goes by. Balancing the various needs will present challenges for all concerned.

Selection Issues

Loyola Marymount University considers four broad categories of issues when evaluating a new electronic product: content, access, support, and cost. The approach is similar to what other libraries do in this area (see fig. 8.1, pp. 217–19).

Content

As with any format, content issues should be the first consideration. There is some temptation to acquire an electronic format because it is new, because others have it, because it is attractive or entertaining, because it is multimedia-based, or because it will interface with existing equipment. None of these are valid reasons for adding a title. Instead, care should be taken to make certain the item matches up with both library and institutional goals. In an ideal situation, the item will match several goals.

Given the relatively high cost of electronic formats, it is important that the material be useful to a large number of potential users. It is not unreasonable to purchase a $50 or $75 book for a single known user and a few potential users. Similarly, a library might subscribe to a $1,000 journal to serve the needs of a department and, in an academic environment, the needs of departmental majors. However, in today's tight budget environment, with the exception of specialized research environments, most libraries would think long and hard about committing $2,000 or more to any product that did not meet multiple user needs.

(Text continues on page 220.)

Boston College Library's
Checklist for CD-ROM Products and Subscriptions

Name of Vendor _____ Date _____

Vendor _____ Phone _____

Address _____

Suggested by _____

Product Description

1. What subject area(s) does the product cover? _____

2. How often is the data updated? _____

3. How accurate is the data? _____

4. How thorough is the indexing? _____

5. How will the product support the curriculum? _____

6. Explain why the product is appropriate for an academic library. _____
   _____

7. Is the content suitable for ready reference, basic inquiry, or in-depth research?
   _____

8. What other patron information needs will this source fill? _____
   _____

9. What is the printed counterpart of this product? _____
   _____

10. What other sources now available in the library cover this subject?
    _____

Technical Considerations

1. Does the software meet High Sierra Group NISO standards for the
   CD-ROM drive? _____

2. Does the product run on hardware presently owned? _____
   If not, what hardware is needed? _____

3. Will the product's operating system be compatible with those systems
   already loaded on the same machine? _____

(Figure 8.1 continues on page 218.)

Fig. 8.1. Sample checklist for CD-ROMs.

Figure 8.1—*Continued.*

Administrative Considerations

1. Is the product available through outright purchase (data is owned) _____ or lease (data is rented and returned on cancellation)? _____

2. Can this product be networked? _____ If yes, what are the costs? _____

3. Is this information available from other vendors? _____

    What is the cost? _____

    Vendor _____ Cost _____

    Vendor _____ Cost _____

    How does the content of this product compare? _____

4. In what other electronic formats is the product available? _____

    What is the cost? _____

Product Costs

1. What is the initial subscription cost of the product? _____

2. What are the annual costs, if any, for updates? _____

3. What are the costs, if any, for current and archival disks?

    Current _____

    Archival _____

4. What are the licensing costs? _____

5. How much of a discount is applied to the cost if the product is already being purchased in a different format (print, microfiche, etc.)? _____

6. What is the cost of the print product? _____

    Do we currently subscribe to the print product? _____

    How many subscriptions? _____

Related Issues

1. Presently, are there enough workstations to support the projected use of the product? _____

2. Will any additional hardware be needed? _____ Cost? _____

3. How many compact discs will be received with this product? _____ _____

4. How many additional compact discs will be added each year? _____

5. What sources could this product replace? _____
   _____

   What are content comparisons? _____
   _____

6. What percentage of the material covered is owned by Boston College?
   _____

7. Are there any access restrictions imposed on this product? _____
   _____

Vendor Support and Staff Impact

1. What user documentation is available? _____
   _____

2. Is there a toll-free hotline and/or other forms of user support? _____
   _____

3. Who will provide training and user aids? _____

4. What impact will the purchase have on online searching costs and staff time? _____
   _____

Other Considerations

1. Include basic technical specifications for the product.

2. Include a copy of any published evaluation of the product.

3. Include the names of institutions that already own the product.

4. Attach any supporting material available.

Though popularity, or high demand, is a basic reason for selecting an item, it also creates some public service concerns. One can lease or buy multiple copies of bestseller books, develop request lists, and have a few rental copies of high-demand items. Few libraries or information centers circulate their journals, which usually means that current journals are available when a user seeks them. A single-user license for a CD-ROM product, however, can create queues and substantial paper and ink/toner costs (if there is a printer attached to the computer) as well as a need for equipment maintenance of heavily used hardware. Thus, though multiple users are an important factor in the selection decision, the consequences of that popularity also must be taken into account. A popular item may require purchasing a multiple-user license or several single-user copies to handle the workload. All these options add to the cost.

Content of the product is the key issue, as it is for any addition to the collection. If the product is bibliographic or statistical in nature, one must consider how far back in time the data goes. What use characteristics of the subject field are represented in the product? The myth that older literature in the sciences is obsolete has little research documentation.[7] Though it is true of all fields that use declines with age, that does not mean that use, or importance to the field, ceases entirely. Understanding local use patterns will be a key issue in making the selection decision.

More and more full-text and image CD-ROMs are spin-offs of print publications. Some of the products incorporate only a portion of the print version, but others contain everything. The question is, "How complete or comprehensive is the product?" Here's a rough rule of thumb: if the price is less than $200, chances are it is not the full print version, especially if there are extensive graphics in the print edition.

In addition to these questions, there are other considerations. For instance, how often is the product updated? Are there plans to add to the backfiles? If so, how soon will they be added and how far back will they go? These are key questions for products that incorporate bibliographic and abstracting data. Occasionally vendors advertise greater coverage than the product actually offers. In 1992, Loyola Marymount University reviewed the initial offering of a bibliographic CD-ROM product that claimed coverage from 1520 to 1990. The search data capabilities were used to check the number of items included for several sets of years (1986 to 1990 and 1520 to 1526), and the results were surprising. There were more items for the sixteenth century than for the most recent. In fact, there were an equal number of items for 1520 and 1990. By checking 1989 and 1990 issues of a quarterly journal covered by the database, it became clear that there was only limited coverage of the late 1980s and 1990s. Indexing of that particular journal ended in mid-1989. The producers did have 93 items from 1990 in the database, so the claim of coverage from 1520 to 1990 was not exactly false. Nevertheless, it was not completely accurate either, because there were at least 1,000 items from 1990 that should have been in the database. The annual updates to the product would have improved coverage of the most recent five-year period, but would not cover the most recent years, if the first offering was indicative of future indexing practices.

Problems like this make it important to seek out reviews *and* require at least a 30-day trial for new products. Clearly, the public service staff will need to be fully aware of the various product limitations, so that they can make the end users equally aware of the situation. This is one excellent reason why library and information center staffs need to continue to serve as interpreters and guides to information services, whether electronic or print.

In selecting any product for the collection, aspects like quality, accuracy, authoritativeness, and currency of data are factors any collection development officer will consider. With electronic products, these factors can be even more significant than with other formats. Many people have great respect for anything in print (see chapter 1) and transfer that faith to electronic products, which they believe always contain the most current, complete, and accurate information available. This almost-blind end-user acceptance of electronic information means that selection personnel must be careful in their decisions about electronic formats.

As mentioned previously, long-term availability is another concern. On-line material sometimes disappears overnight. The person operating a discussion list or Website may simply stop maintaining the service, or may make a significant change in a server; some users don't learn of the change, and they lose that connection. With a print version in the collection, there is a reasonable degree of certainty that the data will always be available, as long as the book remains a part of the collection.

A real concern is how long the CD-ROM format will be with us. Will full text on CD-ROM become the next "problem" format, rather like sound recordings? How many times must a library or information center acquire the same information? Will *Time* become available on multiple formats, like the sound recordings of Handel's *Water Music*—first a 78-rpm disk, then a 33 1/3-rpm disk, then 8-track tape, then cassette, and now CD and MP3? (See chapter 10 for more about this issue.) If one of the library's or information center's goals is to preserve information for future generations, then format viability and support must be a concern. Technologists claim there is nothing to worry about. They say once the information is digitized it can be preserved. What is to say that digitization is the final process? Will systems 50 years in the future have the capability to handle "ancient" material in an ASCII format? More to the point, who will own that data, and what will it cost to have access? These questions have no ready answers. We do know that print has served humankind very well for centuries and that it can continue to do so without regard to operating systems or hardware delivery platforms.

A final item on the list of content considerations is whether the product offers some value-added advantage over existing print versions. Especially important is any type of customization the producer offers that more closely links the product's content to the local collections. For example, indexes that are customized to show which indexed titles are locally available would have added value. Almost all electronic products offer easier searching, more search options, and generally faster results than their print counterparts. Because of this, it is important to try to find some other value-added feature before committing funds. As Matthew Ciolek[8] suggested, a danger exists that electronic material, especially on the Web, will move from WWW to MMM (Multi-Media Mediocrity). We must always focus first on content.

Access

Being able to customize a product to indicate local holdings brings us to the second major category of selection issues: *access*. One aspect of access is availability of materials. This issue applies primarily to the indexing, abstracting, and table of contents products. As noted in chapter 6, when the library adds a new indexing or abstracting service, users will see citations to some publications that are not in the local collection. A decision to give users access to the tables of contents of thousands of periodicals will, for most libraries, generate numerous requests for articles from titles not available locally. One should not ignore the impact on ILL service when making this decision.

Returning to other access issues, one question that requires an answer is: how compatible is the product with the local network or library automation system? Related to compatibility is the question of licensing; that is, what is the difference in cost between single-user and multiple-user or networking licenses? Also of concern is the type of search engine or interface used by the product. One must consider how different it is from other electronic products already locally available. In the past, one could assume Boolean logic searching, but today some vendors are using statistical searching or weighted terms. (*Weighted term searching* is a system that retrieves on the basis of word-frequency matches of search terms to words in the document and presents the user with the most frequent matches first.) The popularity of the latter system in commercial text imaging and retrieval systems (for example, a records management application) is causing companies like Westlaw and Mead Data Central to use statistical searching engines. Strategies for a successful search are very different for the two search engines. This will translate into extra training for staff and patrons alike.

The overarching access issue is the user. Where (library, office, home), when (during library operating hours, 24 hours per day) and how (local network, Internet, commercial service) does the end user gain access to the information? As a general rule, as accessibility goes up, so does the cost. An as-yet-unavailable ideal solution is having everything available 24 hours a day, from any authorized location, with full cost control capability, and no need for local support.

Support

Support should be a prime consideration during the selection process. How much training does a user need to successfully use the product? Having only similar products, or having only a few variations in how one can use products, means that the public service staff will have less support activity. This leads to another question: how much initial and ongoing staff training is necessary to provide customer support? The answers to these questions depend on the quality of the documentation that accompanies the product. Usually, a toll-free telephone number for vendor support works well only when the caller has good to fair technical knowledge of the product. Usually, this means that staff members rather than end users must make the call.

Anyone with public service experience knows that most people follow the directions only when everything else fails. Reading introductory material

about how to use print resources was never a strong point with general users. They are no more likely to take the time to read instructions for electronic products, some of which come with extensive user manuals. A rule of
thumb is: the bigger the manual, the more help the public service staff will
have to provide. Information about ease of use and size or usefulness of
manuals may appear in product reviews (if a review can be found). Some
review sources to consult are *Database: Magazine of Electronic Database
Reviews, Online and CD-ROM Review,* and *American Reference Books Annual (ARBA).* Often, information about ease of use and size of the manual is
available only after the library receives the product. Calling a library that
has the product is worthwhile, especially for products costing more than
$500. However, your library may receive a later version of the product that
incorporates significant changes, so the experiences of libraries with previous versions may not apply to the new version.

Questions about vendor/producer reliability are important support considerations. Reliability of the producer is a more significant issue with electronic products than it is with print products. Will the toll-free telephone
number for customer help remain active, and is help available at times when
it would likely be needed? What are the systems (computing resource) requirements? Will new versions result in retraining users or reconfiguring
the local system? What is the relationship between vendor support service
hours and the library's hours? Just because the producer of the electronic
product is one the library staff knows from its nonelectronic products does
not mean that the transition to the new format will be smooth. It also does
not mean that the producer will stay with the format or support existing
products if the company decides to drop the format. Just as technology
changes rapidly, so do the producers of electronic materials.

Some software can be unreliable and troublesome. Invariably, some
products have one or more bugs that take time and effort to eliminate. A few
seem to have bugs in each new release, although, in a sense, this is better
than the occasional bug. When there is a consistent pattern, one can plan
how to do the debugging, instead of encountering unexpected problems.
Compatibility of hardware and software is also a key issue in selecting a format for mounting electronic information.

Support issues affect the impact new products have on existing services
and activities. Some new products reduce pressure on the staff (for example,
the full text of materials frequently requested through ILL). In some instances, it may be possible to reduce staff work by giving end users thorough
training in using a product and assigning users their own accounts and passwords. Other times, there will be a substantial increase in the staff workload. In those cases, staff discussions about the impact and the value of the
product are an essential part of the decision-making process.

This section could have appeared in pieces in various chapters, but we
thought that bringing them all together would make the information stand
out more clearly. There are a variety of Websites that are useful to collection
development officers. A very good article on this area is by Shelley Arlen and
her colleagues.[9]

A starting point for anyone interested in collection management is the
COLLDV-L@usc.edu discussion list. Another source is the Internet, where
most major publishers as well as vendors and suppliers have Websites. Examples are the Yankee Book Peddler (<http://www.ybp.com>) and EBSCO

(<http://www.ebsco.com>). Generally, these sites are digitized versions of the catalogs and promotional materials that one can secure in a paper format. What one usually gains from looking at the Websites is the most current pricing information, as well as information about recent releases or new services. Something akin to the print version of *Publisher's Trade List Annual* is a site maintained by Northern Lights Internet Solutions, titled "Publisher's Catalogs Home Page" (<http://www.lights.com/publisher>). Obviously, the ability to go to one site to access multiple publisher catalogs can save selection staff time.

Probably the most comprehensive site for acquisitions is AcqWeb, maintained by the staff at the Vanderbilt Law School Library (<http://www.library.vanderbilt.edu/law/acqs/acqs.html>). This site also has an excellent directory of publishers and vendors. We mentioned a number of sites to consult for serials in chapter 7; however, we wish to note here our favorite serials site: <http://toltec.lib.utk.edu/~serials/sertools.htm>. For government documents, a good starting point is GPO Access (<http://www.access.gpo.gov/su_docs/db2.html>).

Many types of libraries use reviews in their selection processes. A useful site for schools and public libraries is *Booklist* (<http://www.ala.org/booklist/index.html>);a notable addition in the electronic version, not available in the print edition, is a cumulative index to its reviews. One interesting site of special interest to public libraries is "Chapter One" (<http://www.dialabook.inter.net/>), which provides the full text of the first chapter as well as the table of contexts for the titles covered. Selectors can also locate book reviews published in many U.S. newspapers: for example, *New York Times Book Review* (<http://www.nytimes.com/>), which requires user registration to gain access to this file; or *Los Angeles Times Book Review,* which has free access (<http://www.latimes.com/HOME/NEWS/BOOKS>).

Cost

After addressing questions of content, access, and support, the selection process must also deal with cost. The most obvious costs are the initial cost of the product and ongoing charges for updates. Though the most obvious, these may not be the largest costs in the long run. Networking fees, which are almost always in addition to the base fee or annual fee, may equal or surpass the base fee. Information is an economic good that does not follow traditional pricing models. As we noted in earlier chapters, producers employ a variety of pricing strategies. This makes it more complicated to calculate what electronic information will really cost the library or information center and makes it difficult to accurately compare prices of various products offering similar information. Likewise, it is a time-consuming task to attempt to compare the unit cost of a print periodical subscription and full-text CD-ROM or Web service to the cost of securing the article from one of several document delivery services. As an example, how does one compare McGraw-Hill's *Multimedia Encyclopedia of Mammalian Biology* with the five-volume set *Encyclopedia of Mammals*? Can cost really be a factor in the comparison? To assign a logical monetary value to ease of use and speed of access is difficult. It depends on local circumstances. At best, one can look at the expected use or cost of each format and decide whether the value is reasonable for the library. The sample form developed by Bart Harloe for the Claremont Colleges, shown in figure 8.2, page 226, provides some assistance in making the needed comparisons.

Additional cost considerations for one or more electronic formats may include connection and telecommunication charges; display or print charges; downloading charges; customization charges; optional features, such as saved searches; and charges for management reports or software. Even CD-ROM products have imposed printing charges; for example, UMI's full-text CD-ROM *Business Periodicals Ondisc* (BPO) imposed a 10-cent royalty charge for each page printed. This leads to a very pertinent question: when you buy a CD-ROM product, what do you *buy*? Do you own the material, or do you own only a license to use the material for a period of time? If equipment is included as part of the contract, does it revert to the library after a stated number of years, or must it be returned when and if the subscription is canceled? Is a service contract available for this equipment? If so, is the cost of this less than an independent service contract that the library might purchase? The answers vary by product and vendor. In the past, libraries did not send back quarterly issues of print indexing services when the annual volume arrived. However, with most CD-ROM indexing products, the library only leases the product and must return superseded discs or make a cut in the edge of the disk to prevent use. This is the route staff at the Northern Virginia Community College Alexandria Campus Library had to take when they canceled their subscription to the CD-ROM version of *ProQuest Direct*. Staff had to destroy more than 500 individual discs and send an affidavit to UMI after this was done. Occasionally, the library can arrange to continue to use the earlier discs in another area of the library. For example, technical services might use the current version of *BIP* while reference uses the preceding version. With a paper subscription, the library retains all the paper copies after canceling the subscription; with a CD-ROM subscription, the library may have nothing to show for its investment after it cancels the service.

In addition to vendor costs, local costs are a factor in the decision-making process. The computers and other hardware required to use electronic materials are generally more expensive to buy and maintain than other media playback equipment. As programmable units, they are susceptible to system failure, to loss of information because of power fluctuations and inadvertent user error, to tampering by computer hackers, to viruses, and to theft. All of these factors generate additional costs (equipment; security devices; service contracts and maintenance; and, all too often, replacement).

An estimate of the amount of printing or downloading activity the product will generate is another cost factor that cannot be ignored. Even without a royalty fee, there are printing costs, assuming that the decision is to allow users to print information. Paper, ink, ribbon, and toner cartridge costs can and do mount quickly, if there is no effort to control them. Libraries and information centers employ several techniques to control such costs. One obvious method is to assess a printing charge. (There are coin and debit-card units that work with printers.) Another method is to allocate a number of free copies per user, with the staff providing the appropriate number of sheets of paper and charging for additional paper. This approach generates a cost in staff time to provide the paper and, occasionally, to put the paper into the printer or troubleshoot paper jams. Some libraries allow downloading to disk instead of printing. There are several drawbacks to this approach. First,

Discipline/Title	Print $	CD-ROM $	CD-ROM Network $	TOTAL	First Search Y/N	Coverage	Lexis/Nexis Y/N	Online* Y/N	Keep Selection Decision Y/N	Sys/Ver
SOCIAL SCIENCES-Group 3										
Eric	271	1,195	---	1,195	Y	(1966-)	N	Y (CDE)		
Education Index	809	1,489	---		Y	(1983-)	N	Y (E)		
Dissertation Abstracts	1,700	1,995	---		N		N	Y (CDES)		
SOCIAL SCIENCES-Group 4										
P.A.I.S.	535	1,600	800	2,400	Y	(Last 10yr)	N	Y (CDE)		
GPO	-	1,495	-		Y	(1976-)	N	Y (DE)		
Index to Legal Per.	225	1,495	250+		Y	(1981-)	Y	Y (E)		
ASI/Statistical Master File	6,490	2,595	250+		N		N	N		
CIS/Cong. Master File	4,610	1,845	250+		N		N	Y		
FBIS	2,200	2,550	-		N		N	N		
Popline	-	790	395				N	Y?		
Total	16,840	14,070	1,195	3,595	7,000 +		3,500 +	3,500 +		

*C = Classmate D = Dialog   E = Epic   S = STN

$ Bold highlights Title/Database available at Claremont in 92/93 fiscal year

Fig. 8.2. Sample worksheet to guide decision making. Courtesy of Bart Harloe, St. Lawrence University. Matrix developed at The Libraries of the Claremont Colleges in 1993.

the library must keep on hand a stock of disks to sell. Second, some products do not allow downloading. Another serious disadvantage is that not all customers can use downloaded data, which means that the library *must* allow some printing or risk having a single user tie up a product for extended periods. Plus, allowing patrons to download opens the risk of them inserting a virus-infected disk into the computer—if arrangements have not been made to scan disks before use.

For popular products, libraries want to keep the customer turnover rate as high as possible, which means offering both printing and downloading. Shareware programs, such as PRNAFILE, provide a way of printing to disk rather than to paper, which is useful for programs that are not set up for downloading. Another method for handling printing costs is to locate a system printer, perhaps connected to a local area network, in a staff area, making it possible to monitor and charge for printing activities. This option generates staff costs but establishes a distribution system that assures that each customer gets the right printout. If the institution is networked and has sophisticated software, printing charges, as well as other costs of use, could become automatic debits against individual user accounts. An additional option, which is becoming more and more popular for Web-based resources, is to e-mail articles to the patron's own account. This assumes that users have the capability to send and receive e-mail—but free options such as HotMail do exist. This can transfer printing costs to the individual user and save valuable library resources.

In 1994, Peter Young stressed the need to create a paradigm for libraries and librarians, addressing the need to evaluate resources as quantifiable commodities and products.[10] In that same year, a team of British researchers outlined a scenario in which information as a commodity was examined not only in terms of the set price of the commodity (such as an online database), but also in terms of the total cost of all the elements of an electronic resource.[11] Karen Svenningsen wrote a very good survey article on this topic and provided several models one can employ for conducting cost analysis.[12]

The overall goal is to select the most cost-effective format that will meet the needs of a large number of users. This is no easy task, given the cost and pricing variables that exist. By seriously considering the factors outlined in the preceding sections, one has a better chance of successfully achieving this objective.

Other Issues

The legal, financial, and technical issues relating to electronic acquisitions and processing work, as well as to other activities and services, are important enough to merit extra emphasis.

One question that becomes increasingly important as one moves further and further into the arena of electronic collection development is how users know the material is available. Providing lists of possible Internet sites, with addresses, or even creating and maintaining a library Web page with direct links to the available resources, works reasonably well as long as the list is manageable and resources are available to create and maintain the Website. As the listing grows in length, grouping by subject is a frequent next step. In a sense, libraries begin to develop another online catalog, but why have two online catalogs?

OCLC began looking at Internet resources in 1991, and by 1993 was testing the suitability and usefulness of the MARC format and AACR2 for cataloging sites and materials found. By 1995, it was apparent that "traditional" cataloging systems would work for most Internet resources and that linking the catalog record to the resource site was highly desirable. After some discussion, the USMARC record added the 856 field (Electronic Location and Access). That field is now the location of URL (Uniform Resource Locator) information.

Erik Jul, in a 1997 article, noted that: "Cataloging Internet resources raises many critical questions, among which three stand out as fundamental: (1) Are Internet resources worth cataloging? (2) Is traditional MARC/AACR2 cataloging appropriate for Internet resources? (3) What about resources that change location?"[13] One might add to his last question the phrase "or that simply disappear?" Certainly it seems reasonable, since we employ cataloging methods for other information formats in our collections, that we do the same with Internet materials deemed appropriate for our service population.

Jul suggests that the answer to his first question is clearly yes. However, the question of whether they *should* be cataloged remains somewhat at issue. Some public service staff strongly resist adding electronic resources that are not also added to the OPAC. This is not the book in which to explore this complex issue. We note it here because it is and will continue to be a growing concern for collection managers, library staff, and end users alike.

Great difficulty arises in attempting to answer Jul's last question about changing (or disappearing) locations or resources. Anyone with even limited experience using Internet resources has encountered the message "Error 404, File Not Found" at least once. According to data from the OCLC Inter-Cat project, an average of 3 percent of URLs could not be accessed during any given test.[14] The time and effort necessary to check and update records are considerable. There are products that can assist in checking URLs, but when there is a change in address for an item in the OPAC, someone has to make the required changes. One good Website for valuable Internet resources is the Internet Scout Project, which is funded by the National Science Foundation and operated by the Computer Science Department at the University of Wisconsin-Madison (<http://scout.cs.wisc.edu>). The Scout Report is prepared on a weekly basis, and a daily "Net-Happenings" report is available via e-mail.

In addition to the other issues we have addressed, there are legal issues involved in the use of electronic resources that cannot be ignored. These issues encompass both copyright and licensing agreements. Copyright involves several topics: fair use, preservation, and production. Electronic (digital) material is easy to transmit, manipulate, and duplicate. These features make the medium popular, but also raise copyright questions. According to Mark McGuire:

> One of many challenges in the digital realm is the problem of ensuring appropriate compensation in transactions involving intellectual property. Other considerations include: ascertaining and

proving liability in information malpractice; safeguarding information integrity; ensuring respect for privacy; and maintaining equitable access to information.[15]

Achieving compliance with these copyright requirements and standards provides ongoing challenges for library and information center staffs. Some of the use issues are addressed by the licensing agreements accompanying the product or contract for online services. Rather like photocopying services, the library takes no responsibility for what users do with downloaded data after they leave the library. Whether posting signs regarding copyright in the electronic work area(s) will prove adequate to protect libraries and information centers remains to be seen. In any case, the staff must know what use rights exist for each product.

The entire question of preserving print material by converting it to a digital format is slowly being resolved. (See chapter 18 for a discussion of how this issue relates to copyright.) In all likelihood, if the digital material is not publicly accessible, except through the group preserving the material, that will be acceptable to everyone. The ease with which electronic data is manipulated and duplicated is one of the concerns regarding preservation of materials that are becoming too brittle or fragile to handle.

A complex area is that of author responsibility or ownership. Perhaps the idea put forward by McGuire,[16] or something similar—embedding codes in the data to link various information elements to their original producers, thus identifying authorship as well as assigning responsibility for content—will solve the problem. In addition, such coding could ensure that economic value is equitably attributed to the originators. Such a system would avoid the fair use concerns that Robert Kost identified as the key problem: "We have lost the control necessary for copyright law to be effective. Control over copies is hopeless."[17]

When the library or information center provides equipment or assists with multimedia production, under copyright law, it has some responsibility for assuring that the copied material is public domain or that permission is granted to reproduce the material. (See chapter 18 for a discussion of the 1998 Digital Millennium Copyright Act and library/institutional liability, especially regarding electronic resources.)

Copyright law requires libraries and information centers that supply public access equipment to post signs reminding users about the need to comply with copyright law. One further step to consider, if the equipment is in a secure area or locked cabinet that requires users to get a key from library staff, is for a staff person to have the user sign a statement assuming full responsibility for complying with copyright law. Obviously, if the library is producing products, it can make certain that compliance occurs. A question arises about accepting multimedia courseware from instructors without some type of protection for the library in the event the developer failed to get the required permission(s).

Licensing agreements are a relatively recent issue for libraries and collection development staff. Initially, library staff paid little attention to such agreements. Acquisition staff signed the agreements and returned them without fully understanding what they were signing. As Edward Warro stated,

> When is the last time you stood at the counter of a rental car agency and quibbled over various clauses on your rental agreement? ... To make them even more unappealing to read, the agreements are normally printed in fine gray type on pink paper to maximize eyestrain. There is good reason for the fine print: the people who wrote these agreements would sooner have you die than read them. But if you do read them, you will probably die anyway when you realize what you have been signing.[18]

Anyone involved in the selection or acquisition of electronic materials should read Warro's article.

Financial and technical considerations are what staff talk about most after they address other concerns. In times of tight budgets, which seem to be the norm, budgeting for high-priced electronic materials represents a challenge. Balancing quality, quantity, and cost is the fundamental task of collection development staff. The fact that electronic materials tend to be expensive for single-user agreements, and even more expensive for multiple-user agreements, makes it even more difficult to answer the question: how much benefit to how many users? Does enhanced searching capability justify the purchase? What must be given up in other areas?

Shifting resources from monographs, to serials, to electronics is a finite game for most libraries and information centers. Sometimes, additional funding is available for electronic materials, particularly when funding bodies view it as enhancing the image of the parent institution. As the glamour of electronic material delivered to individual workstations fades, so does the additional funding. Sometimes, the tradeoff involves canceling low-use serials to gain enough money to cover the DDS costs for acquiring both the occasionally needed article from the canceled titles and a few articles from titles never held. The question of formats is also a question of technology and money. Realistically, additional funding will come from direct and indirect charges paid by end users. These charges will, at best, cover only the cost of the information, not the support, training, staffing, equipment, and maintenance costs, thus creating an overall net cash drain and cost shift from other areas—often print collection funds.

Because electronic information access offers the potential of end users having full control of their searches and acquisition of data, cost containment will likely become an important consideration. For example, initial costs will vary depending on how the organization decides to handle its connections with electronic services, such as the Internet. There are three basic options for handling such service: terminal access, SLIP or PPP, and leased line. Terminal access employs someone else's host computer. This approach eliminates host computer overhead and operating costs. Institutional costs are a registration fee, a monthly access charge, and hourly connect charges. (This approach is similar to the one employed by Prodigy, America Online, CompuServe, and other online services.) A major disadvantage of this option is that the hourly connect charges are unknown until the monthly bill arrives. It is not uncommon for active users employing this option to accumulate monthly charges in excess of $700. Unsophisticated searchers, or experienced searchers without software that permits them to do some of the search formulation offline, can run up large bills. If users do not have to pay the costs, they have little incentive to improve their searching methods or to limit use time.

Employing the serial line Internet protocol (SLIP) or point-to-point protocol (PPP) option provides more control over the connect costs. Many suppliers of these services charge an annual fee for unlimited connect time and no hourly charges. The disadvantage is that the annual fee will vary depending on the number of users. Additional charges are for local host capability for TCP/IP (transmission control protocol/Internet Protocol) as well as the technical expertise to manage the host. Though this capability and expertise probably exist in most academic and other large organizations, a question may arise as to whether the people with the capability have the time and willingness to take on the extra work.

The third access option, with even higher operating costs, is a leased-line connection. With this approach, the organization operates a full-time host connection. The speed and bandwidth of service selected (for example, a T1 line) determines the annual service charge ($10,000 is not uncommon). However, the real cost in this method is that it requires significant staff support as well as a solid computing program.

As one can see, the question of how to provide access is not just a library or information center decision; it involves substantial technical and financial resources. All options have implications for cost. One cost that is sometimes overlooked is user education, training, and support. That cost is ongoing, and depending on the turnover rate of users, can result in a large or small annual cost for training.

Collection Development and the Web

As most librarians are aware, Web materials are a mixed bag ranging from solid, scholarly material to junk. Developing an appropriate collection of Websites brings to mind, at least for older librarians, the efforts to create and maintain the "vertical file pamphlet" collection. Print vertical files contained free or inexpensive items, but were labor-intensive to maintain. Website collections are the same in those two regards. The difference is in usage: vertical files seldom did and certainly now do not receive as much use as one would like. Because the Web is popular with the public, usage is higher, and if the library provides network access to its electronic material, the material is probably available 24 hours a day, which will further increase use.

In a presentation at the 1997 Internet Librarian conference in Monterey, California, Hope Tillman suggested that the Web and print-world publishing are much the same in the range of material (<http:www.tiac.net/users/hope/findqual.html>). That is, both range from vanity pieces to the very scholarly. She made the point that personal home pages are a form of vanity publishing. Experienced collection development officers know that not all self-publishing is poor quality or without value. What is different is that self-publishing does not go through the "vetting" process that takes place with other forms of publishing. The vetting/review process of print publishing serves the very useful purpose of imparting at least some degree of quality assurance. Websites that one knows are equally vetted are the equivalent of the scholarly print publications. The key is that one "knows" this to be the case. The Web also allows people to make any type of representations about themselves and what they are putting on the Web.

The following example illustrates many of the concerns that should be addressed when considering Websites as information resources. A surprising number of people are what Native Americans call "wanabes," people who are not but for some reason want to be identified as or with true Native Americans. Just because a Website author claims to be Native American does not necessarily make it so. Sites filled with sophisticated graphics, sounds, and perhaps video clips, and claiming to represent Native American views, ideas, or affiliation, should raise questions. A great many Native Americans, especially those living on reservations, do not have access to such high-end technology and software. By itself, the sophistication of a site does not mean that the site is incorrect or exploitive—but it should suggest that further checking is in order. The URL can provide a useful clue: does it contain a nation name such as Navajo, Oneida, or Blackfeet? Even the address information does not necessarily mean that it is an official site or that the tribal government knows of its existence. The best approach is to locate a telephone number or mailing address for the tribal government and contact them (guides such as Barry Klein's *Reference Encyclopedia of the American Indian,* or *The Native American Almanac,* edited by Duane Champagne, provide such information).

One should be particularly wary of supposed Native American Websites that suggest they are providing information of a spiritual, religious, or mystical nature. Almost all true Native Americans would not think of publicly sharing such information. This does not mean that some Native peoples are unwilling to share such information with a nonnative person whom they believe has a serious interest in the subject. The print world has done a thriving business promoting pseudo-Native American spirituality, and that activity has spread to the Web.

One should be wary of sites that present a picture of *the* American Indian/ Native American. There is no such group. There are more than 500 different Native American groups with different languages, values, and traditions. Even the "urban Indian" is not a single entity.

The essentials of Website evaluation are the same as for print. The challenge arises from the fact that there are fewer quick clues to quality in the Web environment. Where Web and print publishing differ is in the amount of promotional/advertising material. Not that print is not also filled with similar material, but it can be much more difficult to determine whether Web data is actually promotional and advertising material. It is not too difficult to determine when something on television or a printed page is advertising, even the so-called television "infomercials." With self-published material on the Web, it is often hard to tell where information ends and advertising begins. Thus, determining Web quality is a bit more challenging than with printed material.

Determining quality is challenging for several reasons. First, there is the changing nature of Web material. What was good yesterday may be poor or bad today, and vice versa. This requires one to look for a last revised, modified, updated statement that one finds on quality Websites ... as well as some not-so-good sites. At least one gets some sense of the age of the material;

naturally, a current date does not necessarily guarantee that the material was in fact modified.

Another factor making evaluation more challenging is lack of knowledge about the "publisher." With a book from a commercial or university press, selectors have a history of quality of prior publications to draw upon. (See pp. 119–20 for a discussion of publisher reputation.) The best indicator one has for Websites is information contained in the URL. If it implies it is from an academic institution, ".edu," one has a little stronger sense the material is at least not promotional or advertising. Though most educational institutions do not closely monitor the content of pages posted, most do have rules against using the institutional resources in a manner that would harm the institutional image, as well as forbidding individuals from engaging in commercial activity.

An excellent site dealing with evaluation of Internet resources is Nicole Auer's "Bibliography on Evaluating Internet Resources" (<http://www.lib.vt.edu/research/libinst/evaluating.html>).

Summary

Electronic materials will be an ever-growing part of collections and user expectations. According to Mary Morley and Hazel Woodward,

> In an era of restricted funding, decisions have to be made between the provision of printed and electronic information; between local holdings of material and remote access to external information; between "just in case" as opposed to a "just in time" strategy. Librarians dealing with electronic information are constantly confronted by questions about equipment requirements; pricing polices; bibliographic control; archival access; staffing implication; and user needs.[19]

Balancing these various elements demands constant adjustments in how libraries think about services and the most cost-effective approach. One must keep up-to-date on changing technology, changing players in the marketplace, and user needs and wants. Further, libraries must do what they can to maintain a balance between producers' economic interests and rights and users' rights to fair use. It will be an ongoing challenge to libraries and information centers for years to come. By engaging in careful planning (including the preparation of an electronic collection policy), employing sound selection criteria, and monitoring the use of the resources, libraries will meet the challenge.

Notes

1.   *Collection Development and the Internet: A Brief Handbook for Recommending Officers in the Humanities and Social Sciences Division at the Library of Congress.* Compiled by A. Yochelson et al. (Washington, D.C.: Library of Congress, 1997). Available at <http://lcweb.loc.gov/acq/colldev/handbook.html>. Accessed 4 October 1999.

2.   Peter Jasco, "Tomorrow's Online in Today's CD-ROM: Interfaces and Images," *Online* 18 (March 1994): 41–47.

3.   Kathleen Kluegel, "From the President of RUSA: Redesigning Our Future," *RQ* 36 (Spring 1997): 330.

4.   "Electronic Text Center Holdings," Electronic Text Center, University of Virginia Library, Internet Home Page, <http://etext.lib.virginia.edu/uvaonline.html>. Accessed 4 October 1999.

5.   Neil Strauss, "Expert to Help Devise Format for Delivering Music on Net," *New York Times*, March 1, 1999, at A1; Collin Levey, "New Technology Calls the Tunes," *Wall Street Journal*, March 8, 1999, at A18.

6.   Inter-University Consortium for Political and Social Research, *Guide to Resources and Services 1993-1994* (Ann Arbor, Mich.: ICPSR, 1993), vii.

7.   Thomas W. Cokling and Bonnie Anne Osif, "CD-ROM and Changing Research Patterns," *Online* 18 (May 1994): 71–74.

8.   Matthew Ciolek, "Today's WWW—Tomorrow's MMM?," *Computer* 29 (January 1996): 106–8.

9.   Shelley Arlen, Nanji Lindell, and C. Seale, "Web Tools for Collection Managers," *Collection Building* 17, no. 2 (1998): 65–70.

10.   Peter Young, "Changing Information Access Economics," *Information Technology and Libraries* 13 (1994): 103–14.

11.   D. Badenoch et al., "The Value of Information," in *The Value and Impact of Information,* ed. M. Feeney (London: Bowker, 1994).

12.   Karen Svenningsen, "An Evaluation Model for Electronic Resources Utilizing Cost Analysis," *Bottom Line* 11, no. 1 (1998): 18–23.

13.   Erik Jul, "Cataloging Internet Resources: Survey and Prospectors," *Bulletin of the American Society for Information Science* 24 (October/November 1997): 6–9.

14.   Ibid., 8.

15.   Mark McGuire, "Secure SGML: A Proposal to the Information Community," *Journal of Scholarly Publishing* 25 (April 1994): 146.

16.   Ibid.

17.   Robert Kost, "Technology Giveth ... Electronic Information and the Future of Copyright," *Serials Review* 18, nos. 1/2 (1992): 69.

18.   Edward A. Warro, "What Have We Been Signing? A Look at Database Licensing Agreements," *Library Administration and Management* 8 (Summer 1994): 173.

19.   Mary Morley and Hazel Woodward, eds., *Taming the Electronic Jungle* (Horsforth, U.K.: National Acquisitions Group and U.K. Serials Group, 1993), xiii.

Further Reading

General

Antelmon, K., and D. Lagenberg. "Collection Development in the Electronic Library." *Association for Computing Machinery SIGUCCS* 21 (1993): 50–56.

Davis, T. L. "The Evolution of Selection Activities for Electronic Resources." *Library Trends* 45 (Winter 1997): 391–404.

Demas, S., P. McDonald, and G. Lawrence. "The Internet and Collection Development: Mainstreaming Selection of Internet Resources." *Library Resources & Technical Services* 39, no. 3 (July 1995): 275–90.

Eaton, E. K. "Information Management Systems Planning: A Process for Health Sciences Libraries and Institutions." In *Advances in Librarianship*, vol. 18. Edited by I. Godden, 131–57. New York: Academic Press, 1994.

Fedunok, S. "Hammurabi and the Electronic Age: Documenting Electronic Collection Decisions." *RQ* 36 (Fall 1996): 86–90.

Flanagan, M. "Database Licensing: A Future View." *Computers in Libraries* 13 (January 1993): 21–22.

Gammon, J. A. "EDI and Acquisitions." *Library Acquisitions: Practice and Theory* 18 (Spring 1994): 113–23.

Hastings, S. K. "Selection and Evaluation of Networked Resources." *Acquisitions Librarian* 20 (1998): 109–22.

Hunter, K. "National Site License Model." *Serials Review* 18, nos. 1/2 (1992): 71–72+.

Johnson, P., and B. MacEwan, eds. *Collection Management and Development: Issues in an Electronic Era*. Chicago: American Library Association, 1994.

Martin, K. F., and R. F. Rose. "Managing the CD-ROM Collection Development Process: Issues and Alternatives." *Collection Management* 21, no. 2 (1996): 77–101.

Pack, T. "Electronic Books: A New Spin on the Great American Novel." *CD-ROM Professional* 7 (March 1994): 54–56.

Sasse, M. L., and B. J. Winkler. "Electronic Journals: A Formidable Challenge for Libraries." In *Advances in Librarianship,* vol. 17. Edited by I. Godden, 149–73. New York: Academic Press, 1993.

Sutherland, L. "Copyright and Licensing in the Electronic Environment." *Serials Librarian* 23, nos. 3/4 (1993): 143–47.

Woodward, H. M. "Impact of Electronic Information on Serials Collection Management." *IFLA Journal* 20, no. 1 (1994): 35–45.

Valauskas, E. J. "Reading and Computers: Paper-Based or Digital Text: What Is Best?" *Computers in Libraries* 14 (January 1994): 44–47.

Zarnosky, M. "Knowledge Served on a Silver Platter: Planning and Paying for CD-ROMs." *RQ* 32 (Fall 1992): 75–84.

Academic

Atkinson, R. "Crisis and Opportunity: Reevaluating Acquisitions Budgeting in an Age of Transition." *Journal of Library Administration* 19, no. 2 (1993): 35–55.

———. "Networks, Hypertext, and Academic Libraries." *College & Research Libraries* 54 (May 1993): 199–215.

Brett, G. H. "Networked Information Retrieval Tools in the Academic Environment." *Internet Research* 3 (Fall 1993): 26–36.

Cassel, R. "Selection Criteria for Internet Resources." *College & Research Libraries News* 56 (February 1995). 92–93.

Dougherty, R. M., and A. P. Dougherty. "Academic Library: A Time of Crisis, Change, and Opportunity." *Journal of Academic Librarianship* 18 (January 1993): 342–46.

Forth, S. "Emerging Technologies." *Journal of Library Administration* 17, no. 4 (1992): 15–23.

Kaufman, P. T., and T. J. Miller. "Scholarly Communication: New Realities, Old Values." *Library Hi Tech* 10, no. 3 (1992): 61–78.

Lenzini, R. T. "New Partners for Collection Development." *Journal of Library Administration* 24, nos. 1/2 (1996): 113–24.

Pratt, G. F., P. Flannery, and C. L. D. Perkins. "Guidelines for Internet Resource Selection." *College & Research Libraries News* 57 (March 1996): 134–35.

Rutstein, J. S., et al. "Ownership Versus Access: Shifting Perspectives for Libraries." In *Advances in Librarianship*, vol. 17. Edited by I. Godden, 33–60. New York: Academic Press, 1993.

Schwartz, C. A. "Scholarly Communication as a Loosely Coupled System." *College & Research Libraries* 55 (March 1994): 101–17.

Wilson, D. L. "Creating Electronic Texts: Scholar Believes New Encoding Guidelines Will Spur a Wave of New Research." *Chronicle of Higher Education* 40 (June 15, 1994): A19, A23.

Public

Batt, C. "Cutting Edge." *Public Library Journal* 7 (July/August 1992): 103–6.

Dervin, B. "Information—Democracy." *Journal of the American Society for Information Science* 45 (July 1994): 367–85.

LaRue, J. "Library Tomorrow." *Computers in Libraries* 13 (Fall 1993): 14–16.

McCune, B. "Leading Technology by the Nose: Denver Public's Booktech 2000." *Wilson Library Bulletin* 68 (November 1993): 33–35.

Newhagen, J. E. "Media Use and Political Efficacy." *Journal of the American Society of Information Science* 45 (July 1994): 386–94.

Rogers, E. M., L. Collins-Jarvis, and J. Schmitz. "The PEN Project in Santa Monica." *Journal of the American Society of Information Science* 45 (July 1994): 401–10.

Valauskas, E. J. "Using Internet in Libraries." *IFLA Journal* 20, no. 1 (1994): 22–28.

School

Bard, N. "Networking CD-ROMs." *Journal of Youth Services Libraries* 6 (Winter 1993): 185–89.

Burleigh, M., and P. Weeg. "KIDLINK: A Challenging and Safe Place for Children Across the World." *Information Development* 9 (Spring 1993): 47–57.

Callison, D. "Impact of New Technologies on School Media Center Facilities and Instruction." *Journal of Youth Services Libraries* 6 (Summer 1993): 414–19.

Caywood, C. "Tunneling Through the Internet." *School Library Journal* 40 (March 1994): 164.

"Hooked on Technology." *Book Report* 11 (November/December 1992): 20–23.

Hughes, D. R. "Appropriate and Distributed Networks: A Model for K–12 Educational Telecommunications." *Internet Research* 3 (Winter 1993): 22–29.

Martinez, M. E. "Access to Information Technologies Among School-Age Children." *Journal of the American Society of Information Science* 45 (July 1994): 395–400.

Sutton, R. E. "Equity and Computers in Schools." *Review of Educational Research* 61 (1991): 475–503.

Special

Ashdown, B. G. "Managing Information as a Corporate Asset." In *Looking to the Year 2000: Papers from the 84th Annual Conference of the Special Library Association* 21–49. New York: Special Library Association, 1993.

Aston, J. "The Selection Dilemma." *Law Librarian* 27 (December 1996): 238–41.

Bennett, V. M., and E. M. Palmer. "Electronic Document Delivery Using Internet." *Bulletin of the Medical Library Association* 82 (April 1994): 163–67.

Brudvig, G. L. "Managing the Sea of Change in Science and Technology Libraries." *Science and Technology Libraries* 12 (Summer 1992): 35–50.

Ertel, M. "Electronic Challenge: Providing and Evaluating Information Services." In *Online / CD-ROM '92, 14th Conference Proceedings*, 68–72. Wilton, Conn.: Eight Bit Books, 1992.

Hoffman, M. M. "Document Supply Service of the AT&T Library Network." In *Looking to the Year 2000: Papers from the 84th Annual Conference of the Special Library Association*, 123–30. New York: Special Library Association, 1993.

Kreizman, K. "Optimizing and Enhancing Information Resources: Development of a Corporate Library Network." In *Looking to the Year 2000: Papers from the 84th Annual Conference of the Special Library Association*, 51–59. New York: Special Library Association, 1993.

Prime, E. "Virtual Library: A Corporate Imperative." *Information Technology and Libraries* 12 (June 1993): 248–50.

Tyler, J. K., and F. A. Brahmi. "Effect of a Local Area MEDLINE Network on Online End-User and Mediated Searching." *Medical Reference Services Quarterly* 12 (Winter 1993): 1–6.

Weinstein, L. "Lifenet/Internet and the Health Science Librarian." *Special Libraries* 85 (Winter 1994): 16–23.

9
Government Information

People who have access to accurate information make more informed, if not necessarily better, decisions. When it comes to understanding governmental actions and processes, having free access to information is essential, if the people are to respond effectively. Further, as we noted in chapter 5 on producers, commercial publishers need to make a profit on the majority of their publications. There is a host of information, data, and other materials that is useful, if not essential, to individuals and organizations, but that is not commercially viable, due to the cost of collecting and compiling the material as well as its relatively limited sales appeal. Government publications fill the gap between no profit and no information.

As James Madison wrote in 1832,

> A popular government without popular information, or the means of acquiring it, is but a prologue to a farce or a tragedy; or perhaps both ... . And a people who mean to be their own governors, must arm themselves with the power that knowledge gives.[1]

As this quotation shows, interest in and concern about society's access to government information has a long history in the United States.

All types of libraries acquire some kinds of government information. Without question, governments are the world's number one producers of information and publications. Despite major efforts stemming from the U.S. Paperwork Reduction Act (1980) and the Government Printing Reform Act of 1996, the U.S. federal government still produces more publications than the combined total from U.S. commercial publishers. The relationship between the volume of government and commercial publications is probably the same in every country. In many countries, all levels of government generate information and publications, not just the national level.

Government documents and information form a mysterious and frequently misunderstood part of a library's collection. Because of their unique nature, these materials can frighten and confuse staff and user alike. Yet they also constitute an important, current, and vital part of any collection, and they can provide a wealth of information on almost any topic. People use various labels for this type of material, such as government publications, government information, official documents, federal documents, agency publications, legislative documents, or presidential documents. Libraries house the materials in several ways, ranging from a separate collection containing nothing but government material to complete integration into the general collection. How the library houses these materials affects their processing, from fully cataloged to partially cataloged to uncataloged.

Documents may be classified using anything from the Library of Congress Classification System or the Superintendent of Documents (SUDOCs) system to local classification systems. Finally, libraries handle access in several ways. The materials may be included or excluded from indexes, card catalogs, and online catalogs; and there may be separate files for government information.

To add to the confusion created by their diverse management, the documents themselves have only one common trait: they are all official publications of some government or international body. Thus, all of them have corporate rather than personal authors, which makes it difficult for users to locate material. If the item is included in an online catalog that has subject or keyword searching, clients will identify and use more government information than they will if the material is cataloged in manual files. Government information comes in a variety of sizes, shapes, and media formats. There are books, technical reports, periodicals, pamphlets, microforms, posters, films, slides, photographs, CD-ROMs, online databases, and maps, to name but a few of the possibilities. They have no special subject focus, because they are the product of many diverse branches and agencies of government. Normally, they reflect the concerns of the agency that produced them. Predictably, a document produced by the U.S. Department of Agriculture (USDA) probably deals with a subject related to agriculture, such as livestock statistics, horticulture, or irrigation. The relationship may be less direct, because USDA also publishes information about nutrition, forestry, and home economics. However, as remote as the connection may seem, most government publications do have some connection to the issuing agencies' purpose and function.

Compounding the confusion about the nature of government information is the fact that any level of government may issue an official document. Although national government documents are frequently the only official publications easily identified or treated as government publications, all other levels of government—local, regional, state, foreign national, and international—also produce official publications that are government documents. Though national government documents are the most numerous and important in the library's collection, other levels of government publications are also valuable and useful. A library may choose to include only one type or level of document in its government documents section, or it may include several.

Defining what is government information is not always easy. Are reports prepared by nongovernmental agencies but required by a government agency truly government publications? What about the publications produced by short- and long-term multijurisdictional groups? Usually discussions of government information include materials published by the United Nations, which is clearly not a governmental body in the usual meaning of the term. Rather, countries contribute funds to operate the United Nations, including the information/publications program. We take a broad view of this and, for our purposes, any information that has government involvement, with or without direct government funds, is included in this chapter.

The inherent diversity of government agencies and their publications combines with the diverse library management techniques concerning government documents to create bibliographic schizophrenia about government information. However, this immense body of information, available at a modest cost, makes government publications and services a worthwhile collection development information resource.

The cost of government publications varies among the levels of government and according to purchase plans or depository agreements. However, most government publications cost very little. For example, U.S. law states that the federal government may not make a profit from selling documents. The price, by statute, may only recover publication and overhead costs. This can lead to remarkable bargains for collection development officers. Where else can one purchase a major reference tool like the annual directory of the federal government, which includes names, addresses, organizational charts, and brief descriptions of the mission and activities of each agency, for $30?[2] Other levels of government follow a similar philosophy concerning pricing and distribution of documents. This makes government publications an inexpensive means of expanding segments of a collection.

Though price and subject coverage are attractive features, the variety of target audiences of documents within any subject area also offers many advantages for collection development. The USDA may publish information on nutrition, ranging from bilingual pamphlets to nutritional research studies. The National Aeronautics and Space Administration (NASA) likewise publishes a variety of documents, ranging from space science for school children to extremely technical studies of space flight and the possibilities of extraterrestrial life. Some CD-ROMs issued by federal agencies include the Department of Defense's *Hazardous Materials Information System*, the Department of Commerce's *U.S. Imports of Merchandise*, and the Central Intelligence Agency's *World Factbook*. Information about most subjects related to government is available at a surprising number of reading and use levels that can serve the needs and interests of most age groups. Perhaps the most attractive feature of government documents is their timeliness. Frequently, they provide the most current information available about popular topics.

Background

Some scholars suggest that society's right to government information, at least in the English-speaking world, has its origin in the English Magna Carta of 1215.[3] The U.S. Constitution requires that Congress shall "keep a journal of its proceedings, and from time to time publish same, excepting such parts as may in their judgment require secrecy; and the yeas and nays of the members of either house on any question shall, at the desire of one-fifth of those present, be entered on the journal."[4] By 1813, selected libraries were part of a depository program that covered congressional materials. Later, in 1857, the program expanded to cover items produced by the executive branch. The program continued to grow over the next 120 years, both in types of material distributed and in the number of libraries receiving all or some of the available material.

At some point, in small steps, the government decided that citizens needed easy access not only to information about government activities, but also to information that would improve the economy or enhance daily living. How-to publications, such as those on gardening and carpentry, became part of the government's publication list. Thus, a second purpose of a government publication program is to help people improve their quality of life. As Bruce Morton wrote, "The consumption of information, like the consumption of food, is vital to the nourishment of the pursuit of life, liberty and happiness in a democratic society."[5]

Some people question the role the government should play in producing such publications. Morton summarized the situation in the following:

> The first information obligation of the government of the United States is to produce the information it needs to effectively govern, and in so doing provide accurate information about its activities for itself and so it can be held accountable to, and by, its constituents.
>
> To accomplish this, the government, libraries, and the press all must, and do, play important roles. The government, however, is neither obliged (nor should it feel so) to produce, let alone provide it, based on the needs of the researchers who occupy the nation's libraries. One neither disputes the needs of these researches nor their researches.
>
> Indeed, their needs are compelling, as is the need for government information in meeting those needs. However, it must be understood that what is called government information describes not necessarily a source of information, but rather the point of collection and data origination.[6]

By the time of the Reagan administration, there were more than 1,300 U.S. government document full and partial depository libraries. During President Reagan's first term, the Office of Management and Budget (OMB) received authorization to develop a federal information policy as the result of the passage of Public Law 96-511 (The Paperwork Reduction Act of 1980). OMB had the responsibility to minimize the cost of "collecting, maintaining, using, and disseminating information."[7]

One of OMB's initiatives supported the concept of disseminating federal information as raw data in an electronic format, often without software for using or searching for the desired data.[8] Certainly OMB's role in shifting the emphasis from paper to electronic means of dissemination has been significant. In 1996, Congress began debating the Government Printing Reform Act of 1996, the core concept of which was to provide easy access to government information by electronic means.

A major problem, which remains at the time we wrote this chapter, is that the national (much less local) technological infrastructure necessary to make the concept viable does not exist. Another significant issue was the lack of government-wide standards for making information available electronically. Experience in the late 1980s and early 1990s with the electronic dissemination of federal information demonstrated the necessity of a single government-wide standard. Some departments employ two or more software programs with their various databases. Even the most experienced computer user has difficulty securing the desired information. Very, very few individuals who want such information have the skills to retrieve what they need without assistance. Realistically, until there is a single standard, most people will have to depend upon either their place of employment or libraries to provide the needed assistance.

From a public service point of view, providing such assistance for all the variations in U.S. government databases is a challenge that few libraries can fully meet. Even if the library confines itself to assisting with CD-ROM products, the challenge is great, due to variations in approach and the generally minimal documentation accompanying these products. The products also have a history of changing without adequate information, in a printed form, about the changes. This results in discovery of the changes only when one tries to use the product in the same manner as one did in the past.

As for the Internet, the Government Information Locator Service (GILS) is a federal-wide standard for describing information. However, even this "standard" does, and will continue to, present complexities, for public service staff as well as for end users. GILS consists of two basic elements. One is the centrally maintained "GILS Core," which is for "general" access to information. The second element relates to the fact that agencies maintain a GILS designed to meet the special requirements of their primary constituencies. Specialized GILS are linked back to the Core, but there are a host of variations within GILS.

GILS provides for two search modes, intermediated and direct. The government appears to expect that intermediated use will be through libraries, schools, and places of employment, or information brokers. Direct users, according to the plan, "must have network access, and be literate in English to at least the secondary-school level, capable of using a personal computer, *and aware, if any, of limitations of their own hardware and software environment* [emphasis added]."[9] How many individuals are aware of what limitations may be relevant or even what exactly is meant by the last clause?

Philosophy of Library Government Information Service

It is unlikely that the founders of the depository system envisioned the federal government becoming the country's largest publisher, or really debated which documents should or should not be available to the public. Today, there is a debate about what information should be available, and this debate has had (and continues to have) some effect on public service staff.

Access to scientific and technical information, provided by the National Technological Information Service (NTIS), is one focal point of the debate. The government discussed and to some extent acted to limit access to its information, particularly scientific and technical material. Walter Blados reviewed the pros and cons of providing unrestricted access to unclassified government information in *Information Management Review*.[10] Many people, including most librarians, think that complete freedom of access to unclassified government information is vital to scholarship and to the well-being of society. Others think that access to scientific, but unclassified, information leads to increased security risks for the country. A few people even suggest that "the individual abstracts or references in government and commercial databases are unclassified, but some of the information, taken in aggregate, may reveal sensitive information concerning U.S. strategic capabilities and vulnerabilities."[11]

From the library point of view, government publications still provide a means of inexpensively expanding a collection. Given the range and content of government information packages, all types of libraries can acquire useful, authoritative materials at minimal cost. The Smithsonian Institution, for example, is issuing a 20-volume set, the *Handbook of North American Indians*. The published volumes range in length from 700 to 930 pages, have extensive illustrations (maps, line drawings, and photographs), and contain text prepared by leading scholars. Prices for the volumes range between $23.00 and $74.00 (averaging $37.43). As a rough comparison, the average price for the 20 Native American reference books listed in the 1994 and 1999 volumes of *American Reference Books Annual* ranged from $6.95 to $795.00, with an average price of $93.74. None of the commercial publications matched the length and overall quality of the Smithsonian volumes. Although the government did not create its publication program for the purpose of building library collections, it is a real, if unanticipated, benefit of the program.

Free, unrestricted access is the cornerstone of library public service programs, at least for the library's primary service population. In the case of information in depository libraries, there is a legal requirement that the documents collection be open to *all* persons, not just the primary service population. Thus, privately funded libraries that have depository status must allow anyone to come in and use the government material, even if the library limits access to its other collections. This requirement can create some problems for public service staff, especially if the library requires the patron to show a valid identification card to enter the library. Lacking that practice, the library may decide to escort such individuals to and from the government documents area. Staff operating the entrance control desk must understand that they have to admit anyone requesting access to the depository collection. Most private institutions that have depository status do not attempt to monitor entrances and in-house use of the collection.

We will return to the depository system later in this chapter. We just wish to note here that as agencies move to electronic means of dissemination, there are questions about the need for such a system or what its role may be in the dissemination process.

Staff members who work regularly with government information also believe that better and more frequent use of government material would benefit most library customers. They believe that if individuals understood the broad range of information and subjects available, usage would increase. Two factors work against increased usage. First, in depository collections, the lack of full cataloging for all received items means that even patrons interested in using government material often cannot use the public catalog to identify specific items. The high volume of material received is a major reason why depository items are not fully cataloged. Even though the items in the *Monthly Catalog* are now being listed in OCLC, the size of uncataloged older collections keeps the old uncataloged system in place. Second, if depository items are not fully cataloged, libraries normally establish a separate area to house the items. Frequently the government documents room is in a corner or basement of the library with a low volume of traffic. The old saying "out of sight, out of mind" is all too true about government documents. To some extent, even the public service staff forgets to direct patrons to government information. The forgetfulness is due not only to the location of the material but also to the difficulty in identifying appropriate material. This is true for both print and electronic information.

In nondepository libraries, government publications usually receive full cataloging, because the material goes into the general or reference collection. This may be particularly true in special library collections, where government information is fully integrated into the collection alongside their commercial print counterparts. Undoubtedly, many people in such libraries use government publications and never realize it. Thus, a government publication represents no unique problem for public service staff, if government material receives the same treatment as other formats—that is, if they are housed in the general reference or circulating collection. What follows applies primarily to libraries that maintain independent government publication collections.

During congressional consideration of the Government Printing Reform Act (1996), various library associations (including the American Library Association, American Association of Law Libraries, and Association of Research Libraries) actively attempted to influence the final form of the legislation. One of their efforts was to create a list of basic principles:

- The public has a right of access to government information;

- The government has an obligation to guarantee the authenticity and integrity of its information;

- The government has an obligation to disseminate and provide broad public access to its information;

- The government has an obligation to preserve its information; and

- Government information created or compiled by government employees or at government expense should remain in the public domain.[12]

There is a concern on the part of libraries that the federal government will change the "rules." What will happen was unclear at the time we prepared this chapter; however, OMB guidelines indicate that Websites and electronic dissemination fall under current policies governing the dissemination of federal information. Some of the unresolved issues include such things as storage and retention in the National Archives; what goes to depository libraries; when and how to charge for information; and the need for quality assurance. Current federal policy is essentially to maximize the usefulness of information while minimizing costs and recovering some of the costs of developing the information. How these issues are resolved will have implications for public service staff.

A hint of where the process may be going appeared in a 1998 article in *Library Journal,* written by Wayne P. Kelly.[13] Mr. Kelly served as Superintendent of Documents from 1991 to 1997. In the article, he discussed the question of privatization of traditional Government Printing Office (GPO) publications. His case study was the sale of one of the best-selling titles produced by GPO, *U.S. Industrial Outlook,* to McGraw-Hill. Kelly raised several points: (1) that there was no empowering legislation allowing the privatization of government-produced information; (2) that there has been no debate about the new policy; and (3) that agencies are becoming more restrictive in their distribution arrangements or are charging use fees. One of his concerns about privatization is the fact that what one could use in the past without permission is now copyrighted—is this in the public interest? Another concern is accountability; he noted that McGraw-Hill printed a disclaimer of responsibility for the accuracy and completeness of the material, apparently even for the work compiled by McGraw-Hill. (The new work, entitled *U.S. Industry & Trade Outlook*, is almost one-third larger than the GPO publication, with McGraw-Hill supplying the additional data.) His final concern was about who profits from such activities, in the sense of how much revenue is actually coming back to the government. Citing the experience surrounding the privatization of *The Journal of the National Cancer Institute* in 1997 as an example, Kelly expressed concern that such privatization activities create the potential for conflicts of interest, especially if the details of the transaction are secret.

A 1998 article by Charles Seavey[14] suggested three steps to improve accessibility. One suggestion was for the GPO to add LC and Dewey numbers to the MARC records for all government publications in its catalogs. Such a step might well increase the number of government publications receiving cataloging and representation in OPACs and thus increase usage. His second suggestion was to expand the number of libraries in the depository system (as of 1998, there were 1,400 libraries in the program). He addressed electronic issues and the problems of access in his third suggestion. His idea was to have someone create "a well-thought out subject thesaurus for searching the Web … . We badly need somebody, anybody, at the federal level to grasp the nettle of access to the Web before we get more committed to a dissemination system that shows every sign of breaking down under its own complexity."[15]

Reference service in this "new age" of electronic government information presents some challenges for the staff. There is much to learn about the idiosyncrasies of the various agency databases, even in terms of such basics as how to search, display, and print or download. Also, some agencies provide different or more information in the electronic format than in the print version. That means remembering which version supplies which type of information.

Some depository libraries (for example, Duke University) have or are creating "tiered-service" for electronic government information. Essentially, the library collects data about local usage patterns of the electronic products and factors in information about each database (ease of use, type of data, search methods, etc.) to establish various tiers of service. Libraries are using two-, three-, and four-tier systems. The purpose of the tiering is to provide staff with guidelines for what they need to know about the content and search characteristics of different databases.

Ann Miller described the four-tier system at Duke as follows:

> The highest level is expected for products loaded into our CD tower (content knowledge, search characteristics, display, download/print), the second level for products on individual machines in the department (locate, searching, display, download/print). The third level is for products that will need to be loaded. Users

are required to allow two working days for the product to be installed and will receive minimal support. Finally, we circulate some CD products for a week.[16]

As have others writing on the subject, Miller noted the lack of formal training available for federal electronic products. The result is additional time and effort by already overextended staff to develop the necessary knowledge within the library. Certainly there are training opportunities at some library conferences, but most are presented by other librarians who have used their time to develop the knowledge. Yes, the GPO does offer some training programs through its Institute for Federal Printing & Electronic Publishing; however, the titles of the courses listed for 1998 and 1999 indicated that the emphasis was on producing rather than using federal electronic information (for printing and electronic publishing technology, systems, and processes). The statement introducing the course schedule indicated that depository librarians may attend the courses.[17] Looking through the schedule, it would appear that librarians could gain some information about how to use the products by learning about the way they are produced, but it is a rather indirect method of gaining the needed information.

Furthermore, as might be expected, the vast majority of courses are given in Washington, D.C. Not many libraries have sufficient travel and staff development funds to send all the staff who could benefit from such training to these workshops. In a sense, one could consider this as an example of the federal government shifting costs to other institutions. Some of the Web-sites, such as *GPO Access,* do have online "user manuals" that are no better or worse than other such commercial training products, and may be used as a substitute for attending formal training programs.

One of the major arguments from the federal government is that the move to electronic formats is reducing costs. The reality is that it does *not* reduce costs, but rather shifts the burden to end users and organizations such as libraries that support the end user. Customers/end users face the loss of their favorite print publications as well as the challenge of learning new formats—often with less than complete instructions from the producer on how to use the product. Few commercial ventures would last long following the methods used by some federal agencies in producing their electronic products.

Library staff must struggle to learn the new and seemingly endless changing formats. In addition, the library must address equipment issues, such as multiple-disk CD-ROM products that really require the availability of all the disks on a tower to assure complete or at least somewhat efficient searching. Extra equipment equals extra expense as well as support and maintenance costs. Moving to Web-based products will reduce the CD tower cost, but will generate greater computer cost as more and more graphics are added to the products, and low-end machines will lead to customer complaints. High-end machines seem to require more "care and feeding" from a maintenance point of view. (In addition, no one takes into account staff and end-user time lost when access to the Internet is down.)

Another cost passed on to the end user is printing. Certainly it is not just government information that has driven printing up to the point that many libraries are charging printing fees just as they do for photocopying— but it has added to the load. Like some other electronic products, downloading is a possibility for government information. However, this is not always a practical option, as the customer may not have a home computer or may have one that is too old to handle the necessary software and file sizes. Charging for printing is yet another cost for both the end user and the institution providing access to government information, even though very few libraries attempt to recover all the indirect costs associated with providing public printing capability.

Finally, there are hints that subscription fees for the databases are in the near future. Depository libraries may be able to avoid some or all of these fees, but that is not certain. The question that remains unanswered is: will these fees be as low as their former print versions were (and are)? A concern is that, as yet, there is no generally accepted model for pricing electronic materials. Commercial producers approach the pricing in a seemingly ad hoc manner; some use size of service population, some use size of collection budget, others link it to having the print version ... the variations go on and on. The worry is that the federal interest in reducing and recovering costs will result in substantial fees, and that agencies will use a myriad of ways of setting the fees.

Evaluating government electronic resources is actually no different from evaluating other electronic sites. Assessment of the content should include both ease-of-use issues and technical concerns. From the earlier discussion, one might expect the technical aspects to be highly important, given the variations in approach by different agencies. Also, unlike commercial information producers, government agencies have little interest or need to respond to complaints about access problems.

Types of Documents

U.S. Federal Documents

The executive, judicial, and legislative branches, as well as executive cabinet-level agencies and independent agencies, all issue documents. However, it appears that presidential statements, reorganization plans, and executive orders are the publications most users want. Sources used to identify such publications are the *Code of Federal Regulations—Title 2 (President)* and the *Weekly Compilation of Presidential Documents,* and *GPO Access* (<http://www.access.gpo.gov/su_docs/>). Presidential commission reports belong to this class of publications, as do the *Budget of the United States Government* and *Economic Report of the President Transmitted to the Congress.* Such documents are valuable for academic and general-interest purposes, and most large and medium-sized public and academic libraries collect some or all of them. School media centers may collect a few publications that relate to curriculum concerns.

A relatively new source of presidential information is *White House Briefing Rooms* (<http://www.whitehouse.gov/WH/html/briefroom.html>), which also has good statistical summaries, especially for economic data. *POTUS: Presidents of the United States* (<http://www.ipl.org/ref/POTUS>), sponsored by the Internet Public Library, provides bibliographical data on all the U.S. presidents, including election results, cabinet members, memorable events, inaugural addresses, and a host of other information.

Cabinet-level departments (Department of Agriculture or Department of the Interior, for example) include administrative units, such as agencies and bureaus. Most of these units issue reports, regulations, statistics, and monographs; many issue educational and public relations materials as well. Some sample titles include: *U.S. Statistical Abstract of the United States, Yearbook of Agriculture, Handbook of Labor Statistics,* and *The Smokey the Bear Coloring Book.* All types of libraries will find publications of interest from the various units. Special libraries collect many of the technical publications. Most academic libraries collect heavily in this area, but media centers and public libraries are rather selective in their acquisition of such materials. In addition to cabinet-level agency publications, many independent agencies publish a similar range of items. The Tennessee Valley Authority, Federal Reserve Board, and Central Intelligence Agency are examples of independent agencies that publish documents.

Cabinet-level and independent agency publications constitute the core of the widely collected federal documents. Many departments and subunits publish general-interest periodicals that are very popular with library users. Media centers also find these agencies a good source of inexpensive, high-quality visual materials.

Judicial documents (aside from case law reports) are not as numerous as those from the other two branches of government. A good starting point for judicial information available electronically is a site maintained by Administrative Office of the U.S. Courts (<http://www.uscourts.gov>). This is essentially a clearinghouse for information from and about the judicial branch of the U.S. government. It also contains links to a variety of documents. The best known and most important title is the *Supreme Court Reports,* which contain Supreme Court opinions and decisions. (Note: Private commercial publishers issue the decisions of lower federal courts; these are not normally considered government documents.) Although large law libraries must have a set of the *Supreme Court Reports,* other libraries' patrons may find them useful for historical, political, or personal reasons. As a result, many larger public and academic libraries acquire a set for the general collection, even when there is a good law library nearby.

Users often seek information about members of Congress and their activities. One very sound starting point for electronic access to information is *CAPWEB: Internet Guide to the U.S. Congress* (<http://www.capweb.net/classic/index.morph>). This site includes biographical data, records of Web addresses, staff member information, and home district contacts.

Congressional publications are second in number and popularity only to executive publications. In addition to the text of proposed and passed legislation, these publications include materials documenting House and Senate deliberations. Floor debates appear in the *Congressional Record;* assessments of the need for legislation are available in congressional committee reports; testimony before congressional committees appears in documents that bear the words *Hearings of* or *Hearings on.* There are also several important reference books: *Official Congressional Directory*, *Senate Manual*, and *House Rules.*

The *Congressional Record* provides a semi-verbatim transcript of the proceedings on the floor of each house of Congress—semi-verbatim, because it is possible for a congressperson to add or delete material in the *Congressional Record.* Thus, it is not an accurate record of what actually transpired on the floor of Congress. Many libraries, including large public libraries, see a strong demand for the *Congressional Record.*

House and Senate committee hearings offer a surprising wealth of material for libraries, because most hearings address controversial issues. The reports become a source containing the pros and cons about the subject, as well as information about what groups support or oppose proposed legislation. Often the hearings contain the first detailed reporting of topics under consideration in Congress. Though such hearings may have immediate general interest for library clients, they also are important for scholars of legislative history.

Reports that accompany bills out of committee form another important information resource for libraries. These reports document recommendations concerning the proposed legislation and background on the need for it. Often these reports are central in interpreting the law after the bill becomes law. Many of the current practices regarding copyright law are the result of interpretation of such reports (see chapter 18 for a discussion of this topic).

Laws of the United States first appear as "slip laws." They next appear in the chronological list *Statutes at Large,* and finally they are published in codified form in the *United States Code.* For most nonlegal libraries, the *United States Code* is the more useful publication, because it provides access by subject and popular name, in addition to placing a specific law in the broad context of other laws on the same subject.

The *Congressional Directory* provides biographical information and current addresses for members of Congress, plus useful information about the executive and judicial branches of government. It is a basic reference work, and many libraries acquire it. Any library with patrons having an interest in the federal government or in doing business with the federal government should have a copy. Fewer libraries collect congressional procedure manuals, but these publications do help the public and scholars better understand how the federal legislative process works and assist them in following legislation of interest.

Some collection development officers think of the special congressional publication methods and formats in terms of "all or nothing." Certainly it is possible and appropriate for many libraries to acquire all the items mentioned in this discussion, plus many others. But it is also reasonable and possible to select one or two series, such as *Reports* or *Hearings.* It also is possible to collect by subject; for example, all congressional publications about the elderly or Native Americans. In many cases, especially in smaller libraries, it may be appropriate to acquire only a few items of high local interest.

Federal publications are an important source to consider for current information at a modest price. It is not a matter of all or nothing, any more than it is a matter of acquiring all or none of the books and serials on a given topic. Learning more about federal publications and their contents will pay dividends in meeting the information needs of a library's community in a timely and cost-effective manner.

The Government Printing Office home page (<http://www.access.gpo.gov/su_docs>) allows one to search the *Monthly Catalog* (the online version has a shorthand title of *MOCAT*) for recent publications, as well as which depositories selected the item. It also provides access to *Pathfinder,* which identifies government Websites and provides links to other federal agency home pages. Table 9.1, page 250, is a list of all titles available by *Access* as of March 29, 1999.

Table 9.1 Databases available online via GPO *Access*.

The Budget of the United States Government, FY 97 Forward
Catalog of U.S. Government Publications
Code of Federal Regulations (CFR)
List of CFR Sections Affected
Commerce Business Daily
Congressional Databases:
    Campaign Reform Hearing
    Congressional Bills 103d Congress–forward
    Senate Calendar 104th Congress–forward
    House Calendar 104th Congress–forward
    Congressional Directory (Interim), 104th Congress–forward
    Congressional Documents, 104th Congress–forward
    Congressional Reports, 104th Congress–forward
    Congressional Record 1994–forward
    Congressional Record Index (CRI) 1983–forward
    Congressional Hearings
    Economic Indicators
    Economic Report of the President
    Final House Calendar, 104th and 105th Congress
    Final Senate Calendar, 104th and 105th Congress
    History of Bills Documents (Historical 1983–1996)
    History of Bills (1996–forward)
    House Calendar, Daily 106th Congress
    House Rules Manual, Historical, 103d Congress
    House Rules Manual, 105th Congress
    International Space Station Hearing
    Public Laws, 104th Congress–forward
    Senate Calendar, 106th Congress
    Senate Manual, 104th Congress
    United States Code, 1994 (Supplements 1, 2, 3)
    Ways and Means Committee Prints, 104th Congress–forward
    U.S. Constitution, Analysis and Interpretation: 1992 Edition
        and 1996 Supplement
Federal Register, 1994–forward
GAO Reports 1994–forward
GAO Comptroller General Decisions
Government Information Locator Service (GILS) Records
Government Manual, 1998/1999
Interior Department—Reports of the Office of the Inspector General
Privacy Act Issuances, 1995 and 1997 Compilation
Sales Product Catalog
Supreme Court Decisions (1937–1975)
Unified Agenda (Semiannual Regulatory Agenda) 1994–forward
Weekly Compilation of Presidential Documents, 1995–forward

An example of the variations one will encounter within the databases is found in a brief guide to *Access:*

> All databases are available as ASCII text files. Most databases provide Adobe *Acrobat* Portable Document Format (PDF) files. Users with the appropriate Internet connection and free Adobe *Acrobat Reader* software can display and print typeset pages, including embedded graphics. For some 1994 databases and those with no equivalent printed product, graphics are provided as individual TIF files.[18]

Access also includes a *Federal Bulletin Board* that allows access to files from more than 25 agencies in all three branches. Some examples are the White House, Supreme Court, Department of the Treasury, the Environmental Protection Agency, and Federal Labor Relations Authority.

Earlier we mentioned that end users face the prospect of losing their favorite print publications as federal agencies move into electronic dissemination of their information. Joe Morehead, who is certainly one of the most preeminent, if not *the* leading, scholars of government publications and their distribution, wrote an article in 1997 about the migration of federal periodicals from print to electronic formats.[19] He labeled the electronic versions "govzines." His baseline was the Congressional Information Service's *U.S. Government Periodical Index* and information taken from the University of Memphis Government Documents Department's Website, in particular its database of "migrating government publications." In all, he discussed 14 govzines. When describing *The Third Branch* he noted, "with this govzine (and others, especially *FDA Consumer*, encountered in my cybersurfing expedition), the print version turned out to be considerably more current than the electronic version, a refutation of a guiding Internet principle, the rapid access to information."[20] (Some agencies, such as the General Accounting Office (GAO), no longer automatically send out printed GAO reports. It is now up to the user to monitor the GAO's site, at <http://www.gao.gov>, and either download in Adobe Acrobat form or request a print copy.)

An ongoing concern about electronic resources, whether government or commercial, is how permanent is permanent. Who will archive and assure continued access to electronic information as operating systems, software, and hardware change time and time again? In classic Moreheadian prose, he concluded his sermon with:

> It seems that while the GPO gets a grand makeover, the using public suffers a bad hair day. To change the metaphor, the migration to the Internet and the concomitant extirpation of print-equivalent sources will falter if it proceeds with the frenetic exigency exhibited by the thundering herds of wildebeest across the Serengeti plains.[21]

When the public service staff is aware of the variety of information contained in federal information sources, especially those that are not reporting on government activities, they can direct the public to these useful sources. All types of libraries can find some useful material for patrons in the annual pool of federal publications. Even at higher prices, these materials not only enrich the collection but also help stretch the collection development funds. The extra material in turn will benefit the individual and the institution or community being served.

State and Local Governments

Several differences exist between state and federal information. One difference is that there is still a very strong print orientation at the state level. Certainly there is a movement to having more and more state information available through the Web; however, it was not until 1996 that all states had a presence there, and even then not all the sites were "official." Very few states produce audiovisual materials; thus, *state publication* or information refers to textual material, whether printed, mimeographed, or occasionally in microformat or some type of electronic format. A second and often overlooked difference is that states can and frequently do copyright their publications. Some shared characteristics of state and federal information are diversity of subject matter, relatively low purchase price, and increasing difficulty in identifying "official" publications.

Many people, including librarians, erroneously believe that state publications are public domain (not copyrighted) items, similar to federal publications. Though many state publications are in the public domain, states do have the right to copyright some or all of their publications. Some states elect to use this option, whereas other states do not, so there is some confusion in this area. In Michigan, for example, the state *may* copyright materials, whereas in Pennsylvania state law *requires* copyrighting. Undoubtedly one major reason for securing copyright is the hope that the material will generate revenue. From a library point of view, state documents are no different from any other copyrighted material. The staff and the public should assume that the concept of fair use, rather than the concept of public domain, applies to state publications. Staff need to understand the copyright differences in order to provide effective advice and service.

Like the federal publishing program, most state programs now produce materials mandated by law; that is, they record government activities and release a variety of statistical data and general information about the state. Many of the federal statistical publications are compilations of state data, which means the most current information, by as much as two or three years, is in the state publications. The volume of general information and how-to publications from states is low compared to federal output.

The availability of documents of state and local government agencies is limited in most libraries and information centers. In the last 20 years, most states established or passed legislation to establish depository programs that roughly parallel the federal depository program (see pages 257–64).

Access to state publications is often difficult and the most comprehensive source is the *Monthly Checklist of State Publications* printed by the U.S. Government Printing Office, based on material received by the Library of Congress.[22] No one claims that the publication is a complete listing, but it is all that exists, and with the addition of a subject index in 1987, it is a useful reference tool. Some states do publish lists of their new titles (for example, *California State Publications*); however, not all states do so. Two Web resources that help locate state and local information are "State and Local

Government on the Net" (<http://www.piperinfo.com/state/states.html>) and Yahoo!'s "Government: State Government (<http://dir.yahoo.com/U_S_Government/State_Government/>).

Variations in access to electronic state information are as wide as for federal agencies. In terms of Websites, some states have well-organized and well-coordinated home pages. Some examples are Minnesota's North Star page (<http://www.state.mn.us>) and North Carolina's (<http://www.state.nc.us>) and Utah's (<http://www.state.ut.us>) Websites. Others take a more *laissez-faire* approach. Many of these tend toward just promoting state tourism and why one should move one's business to their state. In other instances, the legislators appear more interested in marketing and selling state data than in providing public access to information.

The Council of State Governments (<http://www.csg.org>) has provided states with products that assist in governing. It also publishes items such as *The Book of the States*, and *State Trends* (based on 50 state surveys as well as historical data). Most of their products are available in print, disk, and online.

State and local governments tend to take greater advantage of the Web's interactive and graphic potential than does the federal government. For example, for a time the California site (<http://www.state.ca.us>), in addition to providing information from more than 30 departments, featured an interactive "game" that allowed the public to see what would happen to the state budget when one employed different strategies and assumptions. Maryland's home page (<http://www.mec.state.md.us>) not only contains state information, but also data about all counties and many cities, as well as some video clips about the state.

Depository practices and requirements differ from state to state. The statutes of any particular state set the frequency of deposit and the framework of the depository program. The state library can provide more detailed information about its state depository program, including a list of depositories, sales and acquisition information, and information about which materials are available from a central source and which are available only from individual agencies.

Historically, the most effective method for acquisition of state and local documents has been through direct agency contact. Like the federal government, most state agencies produce and sell publications at or near cost. Often, complimentary copies are available to libraries. One problem in acquisition of state documents has been their short press runs, which results in state documents being out of print practically before they are off the press. Although state and local agencies are usually willing to provide copies of their available publications, they rarely accept standing orders, deposit accounts, and other convenient methods of library acquisition. Usually, acquisition is possible only on a case-by-case basis, which is time-consuming and frustrating. Frequently, the only way a library learns about a timely document is through a newspaper article or a patron request.

Privately published indexes provide additional guidance. CIS's *Statistic Reference File (SRF)* contains a large section of state-government-published statistics. The *Index to Current Urban Documents (ICUD),* published by Greenwood Press, offers both bibliographic control of state and local documents and an optional microfiche collection. Given the poor bibliographic control of state and local documents, these sets, though expensive, sometimes offer the most cost-effective option for collection development.

Local Government Publications

Collecting local documents is something almost all public and academic libraries do, if not through intent then by accident. Even if there is nothing about acquiring local documents in the library's collection development policy, local governments often view the library as a distribution mechanism. A better approach is to plan on collecting local documents, as they are often high-interest items for the community. Perhaps the major question to answer is how long to retain such documents.

In general, local government publications offer even fewer selection tools and less bibliographic control than state publications. However, some major publications of special interest, such as long-range county plans, demographic studies, or almost anything with local impact, get local publicity. Often, inexpensive or free copies are available to local libraries. The problems of acquisition roughly parallel those for state documents; that is, no agency mailing lists or standing orders and no effective acquisition options (such as deposit accounts). Furthermore, there is the need to negotiate individually with agencies to acquire reports and short-run publications. The strategic problems are almost identical to those for state documents, but without the advantage of the state documents depository programs. In many communities, the central public library becomes an unofficial local documents depository, and it may offer support to other libraries seeking local documents.

Collecting and retaining local city and perhaps county documents are reasonable for a central public library and perhaps one local academic library. Collecting from more than two or three local governments becomes expensive in terms of staff time. Very few libraries attempt to collect from more than 20 local governments, unless they are buying microforms through the Greenwood Press program, through which documents listed in *Index to Current Urban Documents (ICUD)* are made available on microfiche.[23]

Normally the public learns about local government publications through newspaper articles or local news broadcasts, not from indexes. Almost all local governments produce budgets, minutes of meetings, annual reports, and so on, but the problem for both the public and library staff is learning what and when something appeared. Bibliographic control of these publications is almost nonexistent, except for *ICUD*. *ICUD* covers cities of greater than 100,000 in population, but does not cover county publications. Very few cities or counties set up depository programs and most do not have a central publications office. Tracking down reports of various departments and programs is obviously time-consuming. Adding to the problem are various short- and long-term associations formed by several local governments. Where would you go to get a copy of the 1987 survey of visitors to the Monterey Peninsula, produced by AMBAG (Association of Monterey Bay Area Governments)? For that matter, how would anyone learn about such a publication? We found our example in an article about the Monterey Peninsula published in the February 1990 issue of United Airlines' magazine *Vis à Vis*. Local-area documents can be high-interest items. They also will represent the biggest challenge for library staff to find.

As one might expect, local and regional government use and organization of electronic information are highly varied. One early effort took place in

Santa Monica, California, in 1989 with the development of PEN (Public Electronic Network). The name PEN suggests the fact that the initial purpose of the network was conferencing and e-mail service, to provide electronic interaction between the citizens and local government. Today, that concept is embedded in a much larger system linking all major city departments, including the public library's online catalog. The site of Riverside County, California, provides links to 60 county, city, and school agencies. Another well-publicized site is the Blacksburg Electronic Village (BEV) in Virginia (<http://www.bev.net>), which provides access to government and commercial material.

International Documents

National governments in almost every country issue at least a few publications each year and a great many now have Internet sites. In many countries, the government publication program equals the U.S. program in volume and complexity. The good news is that these large-scale programs generally use an agency, like the U.S. GPO, as the primary distributor of the publications. Although dated, Cherns's *Official Publications: An Overview* provides a good starting place for information about the 20 countries with the largest publishing programs.[24] Very few countries offer a depository program to foreign libraries. Only the large research libraries actively collect foreign documents, because few patrons need the material. If the public service staff knows the location of the nearest foreign document collection, they can adequately serve the few patrons with an interest in or need for these publications. The University of Michigan maintains a Website about national government information, called *Foreign Government Resources on the Web* (<http://www.lib.umich.edu/libhome/Documents.center/foreign.html>). Another source of information is the *World Fact Book* (<http://www.odci.gov/cia/publications/factbook/index.html>), which is prepared by the Central Intelligence Agency.

International documents, especially United Nations publications, however, have a wider appeal. The major source of international publications and information are IGOs (intergovernmental organizations). An IGO may be defined as a group of three or more member countries working together on one or more long-term common interests. Without doubt, the largest IGO is the United Nations. There are also nongovernmental organizations (NGOs), such as the World Health Organization, that issue publications and information of interest to a fairly large number of library users. A good starting point for such organizations are *Geneva International* (<http://geneva.intl.ch/g:/egimain/edir.htm>) and Northwestern University's *International Organizations* (<http://www.library.nwu.edu/govpub/resource/internat/index.html>) sites. Another starting point is Yahoo!'s *Government:Countries* listing (<http://dir.yahoo.com/Government/Countries>), which provides links to Internet sites of 100-plus countries. Though some of these sites have little information, they may contain links to other helpful electronic resources.

The United Nations has an extensive publications program, and like other governmental bodies is beginning to issue material in electronic formats. The U.N. Website provides a variety of information about the organization, including the *UN Publications Catalogue* (<http://www.un.org/publications>), which contains ordering information. The site also has a listing of all U.N. depository libraries worldwide. For most libraries that have some U.N. documents, the material is part of the regular collection, circulating or reference, rather than held in a separate document area, simply because they do not acquire very many titles.

Another interesting activity that few librarians are aware of is the UNESCO Collection. This collection of representative works from various countries comprises more than 900 titles, most in English and French. Each year, the UNESCO director and member countries select the best titles in all genres from each country. UNESCO then underwrites translation costs and selects a commercial publisher to issue the inexpensive edition. The following gives one a sense of what the collection contains:

> upcoming additions to the collection will include an anthology of Ukrainian contemporary poetry in Spanish, complete short stories of Gael Cortazar in French, an anthology of contemporary short stories from South Africa in English, "memory poems" of America in Spanish, an anthology of contemporary short stories by Turkish women in French, and new Albanian poetry in English.[25]

This UNESCO series can be useful to smaller libraries seeking to expand their collections of international authors. Many of the authors included in the series are Nobel Prize winners.

In addition to the UNESCO Collection, UNESCO also publishes some excellent reference titles, such as *Statistical Yearbook, World Education Report, World Science Report,* and *Study Abroad*. Some other titles published by agencies related to the U.N. are the International Labor Organization's *Year Book of Labour Statistics*, the UNICEF *State of the World's Children Report,* the Food and Agriculture Organization's (FACE) *State of Food and Agriculture*, and the U.N.'s *Yearbook of the United Nations*.

The international document collection development situation has benefited from the existence of UNIPUB, a private distributor that collects international documents, creates catalogs, and offers the documents for sale from a central facility. This vendor offers a unique opportunity to build an international documents collection from a variety of agencies; UNIPUB provides all the conveniences found in the trade book field, such as standing orders, sales catalogs and subject pamphlets, deposit accounts, and a central sales office. An important fact to keep in mind is that UNIPUB handles many intergovernmental agency publications, such as those of FACE, the International Atomic Energy Agency, the United Nations University Press, the General Agreement on Tariffs and Trade (GATT), the World Bank, and the International Monetary Fund.

Like state and federal documents, international documents profited from inclusion in computerized bibliographic databases. Privately published indexes, such as CIS's *Index to International Statistics (IIS),* are among the tools creating some degree of bibliographic control and collection development assistance. As with CIS's state and federal documents program, *IIS* offers companion fiche collections.

As in the case of U.S. federal materials, libraries can elect to collect legislative, judicial, or executive materials from other national governments.

Generally, for legislative material, it is all or nothing for a particular series; for example, the British parliamentary papers or France's *Journal Official*. Frequently, one can acquire, in microformat, sets of retrospective legislative material from commercial vendors or the originating government. Like the U.S. executive branch, foreign executive branch material can be a challenge to collect. More often than not, it is a matter of title-by-title selection from each agency, office, bureau, or other entity. Standing order programs are few and far between.

Very few countries offer depository arrangements for foreign libraries. Some do allow libraries to establish a deposit account; however, variations in exchange rates often cause problems. One method that works, if one wishes to buy a substantial number of publications from a country, is to have a book dealer or vendor in the foreign country purchase the documents. This approach may result in a higher volume of acquisition than the library can handle. As one might expect, there is a wide variation in bibliographic control, from almost total to nonexistent. Anyone involved in an extensive foreign publications collection development program should read the bimonthly *Government Publications Review* published by Pergamon Press (see the bibliography at the end of this chapter). Pergamon Press also publishes a series, *Guides to Official Publications*, that is steadily increasing its coverage on a country-by-country basis. Books in this series provide useful acquisition information.

Each type of document has its own place in a collection development program, and each has special acquisition problems, collecting methods, and advantages. Depository programs offer free documents, but may pose problems resulting from depository status requirements, such as being open to the public. A library may also not wish to assume depository responsibilities in order to acquire documents, especially given the wide variety of items available to nondepository libraries.

Public Access and the Federal Depository Library Program

We briefly discussed depository libraries earlier in this chapter, noting that national, some state, and international bodies have depository programs. Here we focus on the U.S. federal program, because it is so widespread. The Federal Depository Library Program (FDLP) has a long history, as noted earlier. It has been successful in getting government information to the public. At the 1998 ALA convention in Washington, D.C., the GPO representative indicated that there were 1,365 depository libraries in the United States. (*Note:* the number has been declining over the past 10 years; many libraries that were "selective" members dropped out of the program as collection space and staffing problems grew in magnitude and electronic resources became more available.)

There are two types of depository libraries, full and selective. A full depository agrees to accept all items available to FDLP participants, whereas selective institutions take only a portion of the material. The selective libraries are encouraged to take at least 15 percent of the items available—the depository program does *not* include all publications issued by federal agencies and organizations. All the items in MOCAT are part of the program, so locating an entry in that product means that the item should be available at the closest full member library and might be available at a selective member. (To locate the nearby members electronically, use <http://www.gpo.gov/libraries>.) The GPO provides government information products at no cost (at least at present) to members of FDLP. Member institutions are, in turn, required to provide local, no-fee access in "an impartial environment" to the public and to provide professional assistance in using the material.

The composition of FDLP is heavily weighted toward academic libraries (50 percent), with public libraries a distant second (20 percent). (Earlier we mentioned Seavey's suggestion that the FDLP expand; his idea was that this expansion would be in terms of public libraries rather than academic.) The breakdown for the balance of members is: 11 percent academic law libraries, 5 percent community college libraries, 5 percent state and special libraries, 5 percent federal and state court libraries, and 4 percent federal agency libraries. As one can determine from the preceding data, the academic and law libraries dominate the program in terms of numbers. Many people view academic libraries as intimidating, so increasing the number of public libraries in the program might well increase usage by the general public.

As the federal government moves toward greater and greater dependence on electronic dissemination of information, some people raise questions such as:

- Is the FDLP still necessary?

- Is the FDLP a remnant of the nineteenth century?

- Is the FDLP really the best way to get information to people in the twenty-first century?

- Is there a way to change the system to make it more cost-effective?

A good article that explores the challenges facing FDLP is Patrick Wilkinson's "Beyond the Federal Depository Library Program." Wilkinson concluded, "The traditional FDLP is dead … . The new entity will be created to fill the country's need for free and open access to government information in the twenty-first century."[26] In contrast, Prudence Adler believes that FDLP "has stood the test of time because of the role that it has played in promoting access to government information, and in support of teaching and learning and in stimulating economic development. That role continues and, indeed, should be strengthened and reaffirmed."[27]

Earlier we mentioned that, all too often, separate government documents collections are housed in low-use areas of the library. The primary issue is not the physical location but rather integration versus separation of government information and the general collections. In essence, intellectual access is the primary concern.

On the one hand, those who favor integration argue that greater use of government information will take place if all the material on a subject is in the general circulating collection, regardless of who produces it. Further, many users, especially those interested in popular how-to material, don't care who published the material, and separating such material on the basis of publisher adds an unnecessary retrieval step. On the other hand, it is true that intensive reference service from highly experienced staff is necessary to exploit *fully* the wealth of information in government publications. Expert reference assistance is especially important for large collections, such as those found in depository and even many partial depository libraries. It is also true that many of the finding aids for government publications, including the *Monthly Catalog*, are complex and difficult to use effectively if they are not consulted regularly.

Another consideration is that few libraries have enough catalogers to catalog all the books, journals, other media, and government publications, at least in those libraries on depository programs. Most of the depository collections use the Superintendent of Documents number (SUDOC number) to organize their U.S. document collection. A 1996 survey of private academic depository libraries showed that 88 percent employed SUDOC numbers to organize their collections.[28] (The survey covered 285 libraries.) A service of OCLC, called GOVDOC, has helped to reduce this problem:

> The service was created to enable libraries, whether they are OCLC members or not, to rapidly but accurately catalog government documents without straining the budget or staff's time. Each month GOVDOC will generate OCLC-MARC tapes or catalog cards for everything distributed through the federal depository program, e.g., posters, charts, audiovisual materials, and machine readable files. Libraries will then use a customized order form to select the materials they want.[29]

The service makes integrating federal documents into the general collection less of a problem, at least in terms of cataloging and classification issues.

For the majority of libraries that do not actively collect government documents, the integrated approach is the only reasonable option and is the one most libraries employ. If the library is a partial depository, taking 25 percent or less of the items available, and there is no full-time public service documents staff, we believe the integrated approach is best. (*Note:* the GPO expects partial depository libraries to take 25 percent or more of available items, but many do not do so.) The reason is that, without experienced public service documents staff, the separate collection is too often forgotten and vastly underused for the shelf space occupied. Undoubtedly the large separate collection with a full-time staff will be more effective if the general reference staff remembers to direct patrons to the document collection. There is no problem when a person asks about government documents. The public service staff, however, often forget to suggest the government documents collection when responding to a general subject request. It is vital that *all* the public service staff remember to suggest this source of information when there is a separate collection.

As governments move toward ever greater dependence on electronic formats for the dissemination of information, the issue of how to handle print materials is less critical to increasing usage. Nevertheless, at least in the near term, FDLP members will continue to receive some material in print formats. Even when, or if, all government information is available only in electronic format, there will be the question of what to do with more than 185 years' worth of print publications. Thus, there will still be a few challenges for depository libraries regarding traditional formats.

A good, if dated, discussion of the advantages and disadvantages of integrated and separate collections appears in Yuri Nakata's 1979 book, *From Press to People*. Although the following duplicates some of our preceding discussion, it provides additional points and an excellent summary:

Integration of Documents and the General Collection

Advantages are:

1. Integration places government publications on various subjects with other related works.
2. There is one classification system for the library.
3. The public catalog permits access by author, title, and subject.
4. There is minimum duplication of materials.

Disadvantages are:

1. The reference staff cannot become as knowledgeable about government publications as can documents librarians who specialize in this area.
2. There is delay in cataloging and classification of materials; and the cost of full cataloging is often cited as a disadvantage.
3. There is lack of compatibility between entries in printed indexes of government publications and the entries in the card catalog. LC subject cataloging offers only limited subject access to government publications. Monthly Catalog subject headings are not compatible with LC subjects (prior to 1976).

Separation of the Collection

Advantages are:

1. If the Superintendent of Documents classification scheme is used, it is ready made and thus can save some costs in traditional cataloging and classification. Major indexes, such as *CIS* and *ASI*, include the Superintendent of Documents classification number.
2. A special staff of documents librarians and support staff handle all publications and become intimately aware of the content of materials, whether the data are in a single-page news release, periodicals, or monographs.
3. Acquisition of materials, with or without charge, is facilitated by direct handling.

4. The patron is better served by a special collection, where staff becomes aware of user needs and can respond to them.

5. Document librarians can make maximum use of special catalogs and indexes to government publications.

Disadvantages are:

1. Materials in subject area are separated from related materials in other parts of the library.

2. Users of the separate collection must deal with a separate classification scheme.

3. Heavy reliance must be placed on staff in other areas of the library to refer patrons to the separate unit.[30]

One obvious way to achieve greater utilization of government publications is through the online catalog, even when there is a separate collection that uses SUDOCS or some other system to organize its holdings. Zink made a strong case for this approach, while acknowledging the technical service concerns.[31] Perhaps the new GOVDOC service mentioned earlier will help alleviate the problems of access to the content of government documents. With more and more libraries having online public catalogs that allow patrons to search a variety of files using the same search methods, patrons should begin to increase their use of government documents, if we remember to or can afford to add a documents database to the system. The Blazek article cited earlier indicated that the majority of private depositories had less than 25 percent of the depository titles in their OPACs.[32]

A reminder about public access to federal documents is appropriate here. Any depository library, partial or full, *must* allow anyone access to the federal documents, regardless of the library's policies about public use of its other collections. (The *U.S. Code* states, "Depository libraries shall make government publications available for free use of the general public."[33] In the *Instructions to Depository Libraries*,[34] "free use" is further defined, and the *Federal Depository Library Manual*[35] [FDLM] addresses issues of access to electronic materials.) If the library restricts public access to its general collections and few people request access to the documents collection, staff members, especially new staff, may unknowingly deny legally required access. It is important that all public service staff understand this legal requirement.

Another requirement is that there be a library staff member primarily responsible for handling the depository material, but this does not necessarily mean a public service person. Very often, when there is just one person, that staff member is part of the technical services section, because of the high volume of recordkeeping and processing associated with maintaining a documents collection. In such cases, occasional mini-workshops for the public service staff on use of government publications and access tools (indexes, abstracts, and so forth) will help increase use of the material.

FDLP members have an obligation to promote their federal information collections and services. The *FDLM* states that when it comes to promotion, the "most important group to target for public awareness is the general public."[36] In essence, the library's primary service population may not be the target group GPO is interested in reaching. A survey by David Heisser[37] and another by Charles McClure and Peter Hernon[38] demonstrated a lack of public awareness about FDLP and the service available through the program. Heisser surveyed nonprofit and small business organizations and found that 77 percent were unaware of the existence of depository libraries. McClure and Hernon looked at users of depository libraries. Their findings showed that only 12 percent of all academic depository users were from outside the institution.

Another aspect of the depository program is mandated retention. Adequate collection space is a chronic problem in most libraries. One method for gaining space is deselecting material from the collection. A traditional weeding/deselection technique is to remove the lowest-use items and either store them in less expensive space or discard the material. Government publications more often than not fall into the low-use category, yet the depository may not be as quick to remove these items as it might be with low-use purchased materials. All depository libraries must retain items for at least five years after receipt. Regional (full) depositories *must* retain their collections, and selective depositories must offer items identified as discards to the regional library and local partial depositories before discarding. On the plus side, periodic reviews of the documents collection may also encourage a review of the general collection's low-use items, which also occupy valuable shelf space.

Preservation problems are the same as found in the general collection. Paper-based government publications are just as likely to be printed on acidic paper as their commercial cousins. There was, in 1990, a congressional resolution under consideration to encourage, if not require, all publishers to use acid-free paper for important publications. Nonprint government materials also suffer from the same problems as their commercial counterparts; for example, poor processing—especially microformats—and poor bonding of the emulsion layer to the carrier film base in both photographs and motion picture film. All the materials need the same care in handling by staff and patrons, as well as the appropriate environmental controls (temperature and humidity) as discussed in other chapters (see especially chapter 17).

Use of microformats for distribution of government information, which was a significant factor in the recent past but decreasingly so now, presents another challenge for service and access. All the issues about microforms outlined in chapter 10 are present with government use of these formats, with three additions.

First, most commercial firms that publish microforms as their primary business must produce reasonably consistent, quality products to ensure repeat sales. Often when a governmental body issues material in a microformat, it contracts with an outside firm to do the production work. Because the contractor's profit comes from the contract, not the sale of the product, quality control can be a problem. The firm may also distribute the material for the agency. It can be some time before corrective actions solve the problems of quality and even timely distribution if the agency does not carefully monitor the contractor. Several instances of these problems have occurred in the past few years, primarily with federal documents. Public service staff who file or refile microforms should be alert to damage to items being filed as well as items already in the file.

The second factor is also a staffing issue. One of the requirements for processing depository items is that *each* item is to carry a stamp indicating that it is government property and the date it became part of the depository collection. That requirement also applies to the microforms. Staff time is involved in carrying out this procedure and staff time is needed to ensure that the microform is returned to the proper storage box or envelope carrying the appropriate date stamp.

A third factor is where to house government microforms, especially when there is a separate documents collection. Duplicating microform readers and printers may be too costly an option in view of the relatively low use government publications receive. If all microforms are in one location, should they be in the documents collection area or elsewhere in the library? The decision will depend upon local conditions such as space available, staffing patterns, and the size of the nondocument microform collection and its use patterns. A major reason for trying to have the government microforms with other government information materials is the complexity of indexing and access tools mentioned earlier. As more government information becomes available in an electronic format, most of these problems will likely become less troublesome.

The preceding discussion provides an overview of access issues in a depository environment. A thoughtful reader may wonder about the costs associated with being a depository library. A 1993 study by Duggan and Dodsworth indicated that the Georgetown University library expended $217,970 in direct, support, and overhead costs on its depository program.[39] For smaller depository programs, the dollar costs would be much smaller, but we wonder if the proportions of depository costs to total operating expenses might not be very similar. There is no question but that substantial dollar and staff costs are associated with depository status. For at least some selective depositories in southern California, those costs and related issues are causing second thoughts about the value of being a selective depository.

There are competing factors at work in the FDLP system. On the one hand, it is thought that more depositories would increase awareness and use of government information. Of course, most of the promotional activity for the program resides with the libraries, not the GPO. On the other hand, library budgets have shown modest, if any, real growth beyond inflation in recent years. Taking on a new activity/service program is difficult to justify when existing services have valid claims for additional funding. It becomes very problematic when the service is likely not one of high demand with the primary service population.

Some existing depository libraries are thinking about dropping or have dropped out of the program. Loyola Marymount University (LMU) library was a selective depository that decided it would not be cost-effective to remain in the program. Several other southern California private academic libraries are also considering withdrawing. The GPO inspection reports were one of the factors that triggered the LMU decision to drop out of the program.

FDLP onsite inspections, conducted by GPO personnel, allow both the federal government and the library to assess how well the site is meeting program requirements. For the library, it is also an opportunity to think about the actual value of the program in meeting the library's primary mission and goals, as well as the service needs of the primary service population.

At LMU, several factors were involved in the decision to withdraw. Two of the primary issues were lack of collection space and staffing concerns. The university was in the process of building up the overall library collections and was (and is) providing very generous funding support for collection development. That, in turn, created the problems of collection space and increasing staff workload. In the late 1980s, the library was removing user stations from any area that could accommodate a few stack ranges, to try to keep storage space close to collection size. (Jokes about requiring all students and faculty to check out 50 books and keep them for a year were close to being serious.)

A third factor was the 1987 inspection report indicating that the library should select more items. The faculty/student library committee discussed the report with the possibility of withdrawing in mind. However, after consulting with the campus community, the group decided to wait for the next inspection report, due in 1992, and to ask the library to collect data on use of the material and who the users were. The decision to drop out of the depository program was made that same year.

Bibliographic Control

United States federal publications have good but incomplete bibliographic control. For retrospective purposes, *Poore's Descriptive Catalogue of Government Publications, 1774–1881*; *Ames' Comprehensive Index of Publications of the United States Government, 1881–1893*; *Checklist of United States Public Documents 1789–1969*; and *Congressional Documents: Tables and Indexes, 1789–1893* provide pre-twentieth-century coverage. Since 1898, the *Monthly Catalog of United States Government Publications* has been the basic listing of GPO output. Unfortunately, the GPO does not produce all government agency publications. Some of the agencies regularly issue sales catalogs. If a library desires to have almost comprehensive coverage, it must consult a number of sources and write numerous letters. However, for most libraries, the *Monthly Catalog* is adequate. Publications for sale appear in the GPO's *Publication Reference File (PRF)*. Any library buying federal publications should probably buy *PRF* (on microfiche) and use it the same way as *Books in Print* is used. For each publication, *PRF* provides price, Superintendent of Documents classification number, stock number (essential for purchase from the GPO), bibliographic information, and a brief description. Thorough indexing makes it easy to use for selection and acquisition. Other sources of information about materials include the daily depository shipping lists and *Resources in Education*.

Libraries that buy only a few popular titles will probably find *New Books* or *Government Books* (both free) sufficient to identify appropriate items for the collection. Public libraries will find the *Consumer Information Catalog (CIC)* an excellent source for rapid identification of government consumer information. Many of the items listed in *CIC* are free and available from the Consumer Information Center in Pueblo, Colorado. (The center charges a processing fee for two or more free titles.)

The National Technical Information Service (NTIS) issues *Government Reports Announcements and Index*. The NTIS is the source for most reports prepared under government contract, including many reports listed in the *Monthly Catalog*. It is also, on occasion, able to provide copies of out-of-print GPO publications. The future of NTIS as a source of inexpensive government publications is uncertain. There have been extensive discussions about the possibility of converting it to a commercial (for-profit) organization. If that happens, many libraries, particularly special libraries, may find their acquisition funds stretched too far to meet the essential needs of their collections. Perhaps of greater concern is the likelihood that a commercial publisher will not keep the reports available for as long as NTIS currently does.

Acquisitions

Libraries acquire government documents in a variety of ways. Some assume the responsibilities of depository collections, if they can. Others purchase documents to match a collection profile. Some have standing orders through official or commercial vendors; others purchase documents individually or acquire most of their documents free of charge.

Another common method of acquisition is purchase through the agency's official sales program. The agency may or may not offer a standing order program. Some commercial jobbers and bookstores do deal in documents, and some booksellers, especially used or rare booksellers, may stock some documents.

One large vendor of government documents is Bernan Associates of Maryland. Bernan Associates handles federal documents; through UNIPUB, a library may acquire UNESCO, U.N., and other international organization publications. One reason for using UNIPUB, rather than the U.N. sales office in New York, is that UNIPUB handles materials that the sales office does not, such as those published by FACE and the International Atomic Energy Agency. Bernan Associates offers several standing order programs.

Of course, many documents are available free of charge from issuing agencies and congressional representatives. They also are available as gifts or exchanges from libraries that have held them for the statutory period and wish to dispose of them or from libraries with extra nondepository or gift copies.

Retrospective Collections

Much of the value of a larger, long-established documents collection revolves around its historical research significance. A historical collection containing old congressional serial set volumes, Smithsonian American Ethnography Bureau publications, early Army Corps of Engineers reports and surveys, State Department surveys, and countless other documents of the United States offers a rare treasure for the scholar, subject specialist, statistician, or curious researcher. Such a collection contains valuable and fascinating primary documents of great public and scholarly merit. However, most functioning documents collections are not in this category, nor should they be.

Most depository libraries collect current documents. This is appropriate, because the primary use of documents focuses on timeliness. In fact, "selective" status allows a collection to be exclusively a current documents collection. Libraries may weed unwanted depository documents after a statutory period of five years, provided they follow proper procedures. This is neither an uncommon nor a bad policy, when the library deselects on the basis of community needs, clientele, space, money, and geographic or regional availability of historical resources. However, for the library that chooses to develop retrospective historical collections, the rewards are substantial.

The major bibliographic tools necessary to deal with pre-1962 publications (chosen because this date marks the beginning of the modern depository program) were listed earlier in the section about bibliographic control. Each source serves a different function. *Poore's Descriptive Catalogue* and *Ames' Comprehensive Index* both describe historical documents, but provide little more than bibliographic verification information. *Poore's Descriptive Catalogue* purports to be comprehensive, but it is an incomplete catalog of nearly a century's worth of government publishing. *Ames' Index* offers bibliographic identification and serial set identification where possible, which makes it at least marginally functional as a bibliographic finding tool as well as for verification. The *Monthly Catalog* in its pre-1962 format is difficult to use. However, it is the basic catalog for GPO publications. It began as a sales catalog and in the 1920s, when the Superintendent of Documents added classification numbers, it became a valuable finding tool as well as a verification tool. The *Documents Catalog (1898–1940),* originally envisioned as the basic bibliographic catalog for U.S. government publications, eventually ceased publication, and was replaced by the faster appearing *Monthly Catalog.* Cumulative subject and title indexes for the *Monthly Catalog* are available from commercial publishers.

The GPO and Sale of Government Publications

Only publications chosen for the sales program are available from the GPO. These are documents that the GPO has screened and evaluated for sales potential and public interest. The GPO produces these documents in quantities sufficient for sale and adds them to the sales program. The GPO operates regional bookstores as well as a sales office in Washington, D.C. Publications in the sales program are available for purchase from the central GPO sales office or the regional bookstores. The bookstores are located in several cities, including Atlanta, Denver, Houston, and Los Angeles.

One can order publications listed in *PRF* individually or collectively from the GPO's sales office or through the regional bookstores. GPO deposit accounts are available to minimize purchasing problems. These accounts also apply to NTIS purchases, and NTIS accounts also work for GPO purchases. Additionally, the GPO accepts major credit cards for purchases of GPO publications from Washington, D.C., or regional bookstores. Items may also be ordered online at <http://www.access.gpo.gov/su_docs/sale/prf/prf. html>.

The GPO sales office offers a series of subject bibliographies based on the current *PRF*, which is republished regularly, adding new publications and deleting out-of-print items. The subject bibliographies are particularly useful as acquisition tools for libraries that have particular subject interests or strengths or for libraries with limited access to the *PRF*. The bibliographies provide patrons with ordering information and an idea of the availability of documents that they might wish to acquire. The GPO sales office also creates a series of sales brochures and catalogs. These range from catalogs to flyers and are available through the GPO sales office and bookstores. Because mailing lists are expensive to maintain, the GPO requires occasional purchases to assure continued receipt of the catalogs.

Other Sources of Federal Documents

Some congressional publications, such as hearings and committee prints, and a few agency publications, may be obtained by contacting the local or Washington, D.C., offices of congressional representatives. Obviously, this is not an appropriate acquisitions technique for large quantities or standing orders, but it can be quite effective for current issues or special subject publications. It is especially effective for acquisition of information about current legislation or information covering a wide range of subjects. School and media centers should take advantage of this source of free government documents. The best method for acquiring recently out-of-print or nonsales publications is to contact the issuing agency directly. The annual *United States Government Manual* provides a list of addresses and telephone numbers for the major and minor agencies of the federal government. Individual contact can produce copies of many federal documents, often free of charge.

Summary

Government information is an important element in any collection development program. It is fundamentally important for society to have such information easily available, even if people do not use it heavily. All types of libraries can acquire useful information from government agencies at a reasonable cost. The idea that private, for-profit firms would provide the variety and depth of information and keep the costs reasonable seems naive. One has only to look at the cost of scholarly serials to see how privatization might affect the cost of government information.

Notes

1. James Madison, letter written in 1832.

2. *U.S. Government Manual* (Washington, D.C.: Government Printing Office, 1999).

3. Michael White, "The *Federal Register*: A Link to Democratic Values," *The Record* (January 1996): 7.

4. U.S. Constitution, Art.1, § 5.

5. Bruce Morton, "The Depository Library System: A Costly Anachronism," *Library Journal* 112 (September 15, 1987): 54.

6. Ibid., 53.

7.   Charles McClure, A. Bishop, and P. Doty, "Federal Information Policy Development," in *United States Government Policies: Views and Perspectives,* edited by C. McClure, P. Hernon, and H. Relyea (Norwood, N.J.: Ablex, 1989), 54.

8.   U.S. Congress, Office of Technology Assessment, *Informing the Nation* (Washington, D.C.: Government Printing Office, 1988), 9.

9.   E. J. Christian, "Helping the Public Find Information: The U.S. Government Information Locator Service," *Journal of Government Information* 21, no. 4 (1994): 307.

10.   Walter R. Blados, "Controlling Unclassified Scientific and Technical Information," *Information Management Review* 2 (Spring 1987): 49–60.

11.   Ibid., 51.

12.   "Statement on H.R. 4280, The Government Printing Reform Act of 1996," *Documents to the People* 25 (March 1997): 11.

13.   Wayne P. Kelly, "Keeping Public Information Public," *Library Journal* 123 (May 15, 1998): 34–37.

14.   Charles Seavey, "On My Mind: Accessible Government Information: Three Step Proposal," *American Libraries* 29 (February 1998): 34–35.

15.   Ibid., 35.

16.   Ann E. Miller, "U.S. Government Publications in a Time of Change," *North Carolina Libraries* 55 (Spring 1997): 24.

17.   U.S. Government Printing Office, Institute for Federal Printing and Electronic Publishing, *Course Schedule* (January 1998).

18.   U.S. Government Printing Office, *The Pathway to Federal Information* (no paging, no date).

19.   Joe Morehead, "Govzines on the Web: A Preachment," *Serials Librarian* 23, nos. 3/4 (1997): 17–30.

20.   Ibid., 25.

21.   Ibid., 29.

22.   *Monthly Checklist of State Publications,* vols. 1– (Washington, D.C.: Library of Congress, 1970– [monthly]).

23.   *Index to Current Urban Documents* (Westport, Conn.: Greenwood Press, [quarterly]).

24.   S. J. Cherns, *Official Publications: An Overview* (Oxford: Pergamon Press, 1979).

25.   www.un.org/publications.

26.   Patrick Wilkinson, "Beyond the Federal Depository Library Program," *Journal of Government Information* 23, no. 3 (1996): 411–17.

27.   Prudence Adler, "Federal Information Dissemination Policies and Practice," *Journal of Government Information* 23, no. 4 (1996): 441.

28.   Daniel Blazek, "Private Academic and Public Depositories," *Journal of Government Information* 24, no. 4 (1997): 288–89.

29.   "OCLC Introduces New Service," *Library Journal* 115 (Feb. 1, 1990): 14.

30. Yuri Nakata, *From Press to People* (Chicago: American Library Association, 1979), 34–35.

31. S. D. Zink, "For Collection Development Officers: An Introduction to Government Publications," *Collection Building* 6 (Fall 1984): 4–8.

32. Blazek, "Private Academic and Public Depositories," 289.

33. 44 U.S.C. § 1911 (1944).

34. "Physical Facilities," in *Instructions to Depository Libraries* (Washington, D.C.: Government Printing Office, 1992).

35. "Reference Service and Policies for Electronic Publications," in *Federal Depository Library Manual* (Washington, D.C.: Government Printing Office, 1993).

36. Ibid., 112.

37. David Heisser, "Marketing U.S. Government Depositories," *Government Publications Review* 13 (January/February 1986): 58.

38. Charles McClure and Peter Hernon, *Users of Academic and Public GPO Depository Libraries* (Washington, D.C.: Government Printing Office, 1989), 61.

39. Robert Duggan and Ellen Dodsworth, "Costing a Depository Library," *Government Information Quarterly* 11 (1994): 268.

Further Reading

General

Adler, P. S. "Legislative and Institutional Changes—New Approaches." *Vantage Point* (EBSCO, 1999): 5–8.

Brown, G. E. "Federal Information Policy." *Government Information Quarterly* 4, no. 4 (1987): 349–58.

Government Publications Review. New York: Pergamon Press, 1974– .

Higden, M. A. "Access to Government Information." *Texas Library Journal* 67 (Spring 1991): 9–10.

Huls, M. E. "Access to Federal Audiovisual Productions." *RQ* 27 (Winter 1987): 184–89.

Kidd, Y. M. "The Federal Government: Your Virtual Servant." *Inform* 8 (March 1994): 14–16.

Lane, M. T. *Selecting and Organizing State Government Publications*. Chicago: American Library Association, 1987.

Lynch, C. "Institutional Response to the Networked Environment." *Vantage Point* (EBSCO, 1999): 9–11.

Morehead, J., and M. Fetzer. *Introduction to United States Government Information Sources*. 6th ed. Englewood, Colo.: Libraries Unlimited, 1999.

Ryan, S. M. "Recent Literature on Government Information." *Journal of Government Information* 21 (March/April 1994): 149–74.

Schuman, P. G. "Making the Case for Access." *RQ* 29 (Winter 1989): 166–70.

Sears, J. L., and M. K. Moody. *Using Government Information Sources*. Phoenix, Ariz.: Oryx Press, 1994.

Seavey, C. A. "Fixing the Depository Library System." *Journal of Government Information* 21 (March/April 1994): 77–81.

Smith, D. H., ed. *Management of Government Document Collections*. Englewood, Colo.: Libraries Unlimited, 1993.

Snowhill, L., and R. Meszaros. "New Directions in Federal Information Policy and Dissemination." *Microform Review* 19 (Fall 1990): 181–85.

Stierholtz, K. "U.S. Government Documents in the Electronic Era: Problems and Promise." *Collection Management* 21, no.1 (1996): 41–56.

Academic

Arnold, D. S., and J. M. Benovetz. "Building a Bridge from Academe to City Hall." *Scholarly Publishing* 18 (October 1986): 59–71.

Danks, L. E. "The Public Affairs Service at UCLA." *Government Publications Review* 14, no. 1 (1987): 89–101.

Hallewell, L. "Government Publishing in the Third World." *Government Publications Review* 19 (January/February 1992): 23–58.

Heir, K. M., and M. Moody. "Government Documents in the College Library." In *College Librarianship*. Edited by W. Miller and D. S. Rockwood, 214–32. Metuchen, N.J.: Scarecrow Press, 1981.

Hernon, P. "Academic Library Reference Service for Publications of Municipal, State and Federal Government." *Government Publications Review* 5, no. 1 (1978): 31–50.

Keith, D. J. "Introducing Governmental Documents in Academic Libraries and School Media Centers." *Reference Services Review* 15 (Spring 1987): 51–66.

Ruhlin, M. T. "The Gathering Storm: Government Information in CD-ROM Format." *New Jersey Libraries* 24 (Summer 1991): 18–21.

Schmidt, C. J. "Rights for Users of Information: Conflicts and Balances Among Privacy, Professional Ethics, Law, and National Security." In *Bowker Annual of Library and Book Trade Almanac*, 83–90. New York: R. R. Bowker, 1989.

Shil, H. B., and S. K. Peterson. "Is Government Information in Your Library's Future?" *College & Research Libraries News* 50 (September 1989): 649–57.

Public

Documents to the People. Chicago: American Library Association, 1972.

Jones, D. E. "Serving Everyone: Government Documents to Serve the Physically Handicapped." *Illinois Libraries* 72 (April 1990): 355–59.

Lesko, M. "In Our Information Society, Why Isn't the Public Library the Most Important Building in Our Community?" *Public Libraries* 31 (March/April 1992): 85–87.

Lowe, J. L., and S. Henson. "Government Publications for School and Small Public Libraries." *Collection Management* 11, nos. 3/4 (1989): 141–50.

Moody, M. K. "Source of First Resort." *Library Journal* 117 (May 15, 1992): 36–45.

Morehead, J. H. "Between Infancy and Youth: Children and Government Serials." *Serials Librarian* 4 (Summer 1980): 373–79.

School

Dickmeyer, J. N. "U.S. Government Documents Belong in School Media Centers." *Indiana Media Journal* 3 (Spring 1981): 23–26.

Ekhaml, L., and A. J. Wittig. *U.S. Government Publications for School Library Media Centers*. 2d ed. Englewood, Colo.: Libraries Unlimited, 1991.

Gonzales-Kirby, D. "Reading with Uncle Sam." *Behavioral and Social Sciences Librarian* 11, no. 2 (1992): 1–38.

Hardie, L. "Depository Versus Nondepository Status." *RQ* 28 (Summer 1989): 455–58.

Jay, H. L. "Government Documents and Their Use in Schools." In *Collection Management for School Library Media Centers*. Edited by Brenda White, 295–312. New York: Haworth Press, 1986.

Keith, D. J. "Introducing Government Documents in Academic Libraries and School Media Centers." *Reference Services Review* 15 (Spring 1987): 51–66.

Spencer, M. D. *Free Publications from U.S. Government Agencies*. Englewood, Colo.: Libraries Unlimited, 1989.

Swartz, B. J., and K. J. Zimmerman. "Hidden Treasure: Government Documents for Children and Teens." *School Library Journal* 35 (August 1989): 40–43.

Special

Larsgaard, M. L. "Government Cartographic Materials for Earth Sciences/Energy Resources Research." *Information Bulletin* [Western Association of Map Libraries] 21 (June 1990): 172–74.

Morehead, J. H. "Corporate and Government Annual Reports." *Serials Librarian* 5 (Winter 1980): 7–14.

Rockwell, K. "Privatization of U.S. Geological Survey Topographic Maps." *Government Publications Review* 17 (May/June 1990): 40–43.

Sauter, H. E., and R. H. Rea. "Place of Research/Classified Reports in a Special Library." In *Special Librarianship*. Edited by E. B. Jackson, 509–20. Metuchen, N.J.: Scarecrow Press, 1980.

Schmidt, F., and H. W. Welsch. "Acquisition Guide: Technical Reports and Other Non-GPO Publications." *Government Publications Review* 8, no. 4 (1981): 175–79.

Taylor, S. N. "Technical Reports and Non-Depository Publications." *Government Publications Review*. [This article, an annual survey, is usually in the November/December issue of *Government Publications Review*.]

10
Audiovisual
Materials

Over the past 20 years, librarians and those who fund libraries have become more and more accepting of the idea that libraries should include nonprint materials in their collections. In fact, formats other than print on paper have an important role to play in providing the level of service the community expects and wants. Certainly some libraries have had media collections for much longer than just 20 years. However, the advent of cable television, home videocassette recorders (VCRs), cassette and CD players in motor vehicles, computers, and the Internet have created an environment where most libraries have some type of nonprint collection. Though there are some individuals, librarians and nonlibrarians alike, who agree with Will Manley's views about videos in libraries, their ranks are shrinking. (Will Manley wrote an opinion piece several years ago in which he suggested that videos were the "Twinkies" of library collections: expensive, draining much-needed funding from the important materials, only attracting nonreaders, creating more potential censorship issues, and acting as unnecessary competition for video rental operations.[1]) Essentially, libraries have recognized that they are in the information rather than just the book and magazine business.

The library's most important products are information and service. If one accepts this philosophy, then the library collection must consist of more than print materials. Books are, and will be for some time, the least expensive method of conveying large amounts of detailed information to many people at a given time. Television may reach millions of people at one time, but it does not convey detailed information, except in the most exceptional circumstances. A major consideration in building an information collection is how to convey the right information at the right time to the public at the lowest cost.

Why Audiovisual Collections?

Books are useful only to persons who are literate. Depending where in the world one is, the percentage of persons who are literate ranges from 1 to 100 percent. Throughout a large portion of the world, less than 50 percent of the population is literate. Even in countries with apparently high literacy rates, such as the United States, there is a difference between the reported and the actual literacy rates. In the United States, many people express concern about functional illiteracy, which refers to persons who may have gone through the required education (12 years of schooling), but are unable to read beyond the level reached by the third or fourth year of schooling. Because of functional illiteracy and the many immigrants entering the United States recently, many communities have established literacy programs outside the formal educational system. Many of these programs operate out of, and with the support of, the public library. Many colleges and universities worry about the inability of matriculating students to read and write effectively. There is a growing difference in the United States between young people's ability to use and understand the spoken, as opposed to the written, word.

For many purposes, textual material is not the most effective or most reasonable method of conveying a particular message. For teaching, research, and recreation, more and more people consider collections of graphic and audio materials appropriate and useful. Some people still consider these materials less intellectually sound than print—as "toys," or fit only for recreational purposes—and they resist adding such formats to a collection. However, as the number of people who have used various formats to learn about a subject increases, so does the pressure to have all appropriate formats in a collection. Librarians need to remind the public, and sometimes themselves, that libraries are in the information business, not the book business. Certainly, publishers one might consider primarily book publishers now consider themselves to be in the information business.

With each passing year, as multimedia computer systems combine text, graphics, audio, and video clips, the distinction between books and audiovisuals becomes more and more blurred. Information that once was available only in printed formats is now available in several forms, including books, microfiche, CD-ROM, and online. Book publishers, especially publishers of scholarly journals, are thinking about and (in more and more cases) actually publishing their material electronically (see chapter 5). Many publishers expect to use, and are using, CD-ROM packages to distribute reference material. Almost all software mail-order catalogs include one or two CD-ROM packages of reference material. The Library of Congress is experimenting with the use of laser discs (a technology related to CD-ROM) to store the contents of brittle books.

Certainly anyone reading *Publishers Weekly* (*PW*) knows that publishers and booksellers no longer limit themselves to just books and magazines. Regular columns in *PW* on audio as well as video releases indicate that both producers and vendors view themselves as being in the information business. Articles on compact and laser disc technologies provide additional evidence of their thinking about any economical and marketable format for delivering information. The use of computerized typesetting and scanning equipment, which produces a record of the text in a digital format, opens up a number of options for delivering the information, including the Internet. If libraries confine themselves to just the traditional paper and print formats, they will quickly lose ground to organizations that define their business in the same manner as the producers.

Primary, secondary school, and community college libraries took the lead in incorporating all formats into their service programs. In these library settings there existed the instructional aspect to media and the recognition that many ideas are best expressed using a form other than the printed word. Further, the media were integrated into the library's collection. Undoubtedly one reason for this, at least in the case of schools, was the relatively small size of the organization and the need to keep things simple from an administrative point of view. Why have two units, one for books and magazines, and one for media, when one unit could handle the workload for both? Use of media in classrooms has been a longstanding tradition in these institutions, unlike four-year colleges and universities.

In academic institutions, the pattern was to establish separate units to handle media needs. Academic institutions tended to view media, essentially films, as solely classroom material; even then there were doubts about its real instructional value. Some professors believed—as some few still do today—that use of media in classroom the lazy persons' way of not "doing" the teaching themselves. Certainly, art, film, music, and theater departments were exceptions, but they tended to create their own departmental collections for staff and majors use only.

The notion of media only in the classroom resulted in the creation of a "media services department" that usually operated during classroom hours, basically 8:00 A.M. to 5:00 P.M. Monday through Friday. The reason was that the department provided the equipment, the material/film, and the operator for the instructor. Given the complexity of operating the equipment, as well as potential damage to the material from mishandling, neither the instructor nor the department were too interested in having the material used outside the classroom. With the relative ease of using VCRs and laser disc players, both in the classroom and in a media department, there has been a change in attitude. This is partly due to technological developments and partly due to the views of younger faculty, who grew up in a "multimedia" environment and who see nothing out of the ordinary in using a variety of formats to convey material.

Today it is not uncommon for a student to have an assignment to review several scenes from *Hamlet*, which requires both reading the text and watching how different actors and directors handled the scenes. That is, faculty now make use of media both in and out of the classroom and often the assignment requires the combined use of print and nonprint items. It will be less costly for the institution, as well as less time-consuming for the student, to have a single service point. Additionally, the two services are increasingly being integrated; more often than not, in or as an administrative part of the library. Integration of all formats will be what most people will demand and expect in the future.

Public libraries were early collectors of sound recordings, and a number developed large film collections. Sound recordings circulated and over time the collections expanded from just classical music to all forms of music and the spoken word. Motion picture films attracted groups for in-house showings and were also available for loan to groups such as Scouts, churches, and occasionally schools. Today, few libraries collect films except in a video format, but the number of public libraries doing so is growing.

Media play an important role in meeting the educational and recreational needs of the service community. Some people are print-oriented, whereas others prefer audio or graphic presentations of information. For many types of information, a print format is inappropriate. Limiting a collection to one or two formats seldom provides the range of services appropriate to the service community's needs.

Sally Mason, although specifically addressing public libraries, summed up the situation for all types of libraries when she wrote: "Clearly, the visual media will only become more important to library service in the future …. It is not enough for librarians to 'capitulate' on the issue of visual media. We must become leaders and advocates … helping the public to learn what is available, to sort through multiple possibilities, and offering guidance in the use of media to obtain needed information."[2]

A 1998 *Library Journal* article on media services and collections in public libraries indicates that many are acting on Sally Mason's recommendation.[3] Between 1993 and 1998, media collection budgets grew by 53 percent, compared to just 36 percent for books (based on the 486 public libraries included in the survey). Audiobooks are a major factor in the escalation of both demand for and circulation of media resources. Like bestselling books, audiobooks can be leased by libraries—the major sources for leasing are Landmark and Brodart's McNaughton Service, which also leases books.

Issues in Media Service

Some type of equipment is necessary to use most of the media that we cover in this chapter. One goal of media services is to make use of the equipment so simple that it is "transparent." This means that the customers can focus their attention on the information presented rather than on operating the equipment. In the past, using the equipment was so complex that some people refused to learn how. Now most of the equipment is easy to use, as long as all one wants to do is play back the information. One important issue in keeping equipment simple to use is maintaining it in good working order.

In addition to making operations simple, most media specialists recommend integrating media with other services. This ideal is not often fully achieved. The ideal OPAC would reflect the total holdings of the library, regardless of format. Thus, a subject search for Native American basketry would produce a listing of books, journals, films, and videotapes, oral histories, and, perhaps, in a museum setting, even some indication of holdings of actual baskets. One reason for the separation of media and print formats in catalogs of the past was the result of administrative and work patterns. Having a book catalog, a serials catalog, a government documents catalog, a microform catalog, and, perhaps, a media catalog was common not too many years ago. Also, until relatively recently, there were no generally accepted rules for cataloging all the different media formats so as to allow an integrated catalog. Another factor, at least in academic institutions, was that media were not part of the library. With more and more libraries collecting all formats, along with greater administrative integration, there is a strong need for a single integrated catalog. Fortunately, OPACs make this process more feasible and less demanding on staff time.

A third goal is to collect and provide access to all the appropriate formats. Thus, collection development officers must know and appreciate the value of all the formats collected. Also, the staff must know how to operate the appropriate equipment and be able to assist the public. Recognizing that some individuals have strong preferences for a particular format is also important, as is not letting the staff's personal preferences influence the service provided. Ranganathan, a leading figure in librarianship (see <http://lib.lmu.edu/dlc4> or <http://lu.com>), proposed five laws of librarianship to which media services staff might add a sixth law—or perhaps modify his law "Each book its user," to "Each format its user."

Media Formats

Media formats, like print formats, exist in a variety of sizes and shapes. Unlike the print forms, each media format requires special equipment or handling for an individual to gain access to its information. Thus, a decision to add sound recordings to a collection requires additional decisions about which type of recordings to acquire:, CDs, tape, audio files on the Internet, or all of these? In this chapter, we discuss only 14 of the most commonly collected media formats and some of their implications for public service. We devote more space to video and spoken-word recordings in this edition, as those formats have had the greatest growth in use and impact on media services. Today videotapes are part of almost all library collections; even special libraries are building their collections.

Any list of current media formats quickly becomes dated as new technologies and new combinations of older forms appear. Just when one thinks one has identified the latest developments and decides to invest money in the equipment and software, a new, even more exciting and potentially valuable format appears. With this in mind, the following list provides a snapshot of media formats of interest to librarians at this writing:

- Audio recordings (single- and multiple-track, CDs, and audiobooks)
- CD-ROM multimedia products
- Computer programs
- Films (8mm and 16mm, primarily for older titles not available in a video format)
- Filmstrips (with or without sound; this is a declining format)
- Flat pictures (photographs, illustrations, original artwork, posters, and the like)
- Games (usually educational, but some libraries offer a variety of recreational games)
- Globes (terrestrial and celestial)
- Maps (flat and relief)
- Microforms (all types)

- Mixed-media packages (kits)
- Printed music (performance and study scores)
- Slides (35mm and 4-x-4)
- Video formats (including games)

Considering the range of material, and remembering the special aspects of the media trade, one can understand why collection development in media areas presents some special problems.

General Evaluation Criteria

To a degree, the same factors that determine inclusion or exclusion of books apply to other formats. Obviously, one omits factually incorrect items unless there is a sound reason to buy them. Poorly organized and badly presented material seldom becomes part of the collection. If the quality of a book is difficult to assess, assessing the quality of other media is even more difficult. All of us have seen a film we enjoyed only to hear a friend claim that it is "absolutely *the* worst film" ever made. Thus, subjectivity is a major concern. Though bias is also a problem with literature, we receive more training or exposure to good literature through formal schooling. Few of us receive formal training in evaluating nonprint materials. Basically, the issues of authority, accuracy, effectiveness of presentation or style, and value and usefulness to the community are as valid for all other formats as they are for books.

Before embarking on a program to develop a media collection, one should carefully evaluate each format in terms of its unique utility to the service community. Each format has its strong and weak points, and similar information may be available in a variety of formats. The following paragraphs offer general guidelines for assessing the strengths and weaknesses of various forms.

Formats that involve motion (such as 8mm, 16mm, and 35mm films, videotapes, and video discs) are among the more expensive formats to purchase. Therefore, an important question to ask is whether motion really adds information. There are films in which there is no motion at all, or, if there is motion, it may not be relevant to the content. For example, many educational films and videotapes simply alternate shots of one or two persons talking to one another or to the viewers (so-called "talking heads"); there are no other graphics (or, at least, no graphics that require this expensive mode of presentation). In contrast, one can read hundreds of pages and look at dozens of still photographs of cell division and still not fully understand how it occurs. A short, clearly photographed film combined with a good audio track can sometimes produce a more accurate understanding than one can achieve through hours of reading.

Detailed study is sometimes most effectively carried out with the use of still pictures, charts, or graphs. Another advantage is that the cost of producing and acquiring these formats is much lower than for those that involve motion.

With both motion and still graphic formats, color is an important consideration. Full-color reproduction is more costly than black-and-white reproduction; the question is whether the color is necessary or merely pleasing.

In some instances, color is necessary. Certainly, anything that attempts to represent the work of a great artist must have excellent color quality, as is also the case with medical and biological materials.

Audio formats also can provide greater understanding and appreciation of printed material. One's own reading of a poem is never the same as hearing the poet's recitation of the work. Tone, emphasis, inflection, and so forth can change the meaning of a printed text dramatically. On a different level, there are literally millions of people in the world who cannot read music scores and yet get enormous enjoyment from listening to music. Audio recordings are a must in any collection serving the visually impaired. Spoken-word recordings can be an important service for such persons as well as for commuters who want to listen to a book as they travel.

Other general selection factors include cost, flexibility and manipulation, and patron preference. Audiovisual formats frequently require expensive equipment in addition to rather costly software. When thinking about cost factors, one needs to know what types of equipment patrons own (for example, slide projectors, videotape players, CD or tape players, or even record players). If patrons do not own the necessary equipment, can the library supply it free of charge or on a rental basis? Should the library buy the equipment and allow its use only in the library? The librarian also must consider what patrons like and use. Libraries ought not to get into the position of attempting to change patron format preferences. Thus, both cost and patron preference become significant in deciding what to buy or not to buy.

Flexibility and manipulation are inseparable. How and where can one use the format and equipment? With some equipment, the library can produce local programs as well as play back commercial software. Videocassette recorders (VCRs) allow people to perform a variety of recording and playback functions, most of which (like freeze frame) no one uses. Knowing community needs and use patterns may save the library money. Special VCR features may be necessary, nice, or merely gimmicks, depending on the local situation. Ease of operation is very important: Can a person quickly learn to operate the equipment, or does it take extensive training to use it properly?

Once one's library decides to develop a media collection, how does one select appropriate items? There are four sets of factors to consider—programming, content, technical aspects, and format—with criteria related to each factor. The following paragraphs highlight major selection criteria.

Programming Factors

Programming (that is, use of material) is important in deciding what to acquire. Many articles and books about this topic are available (see the bibliography at the end of this chapter). Programming questions include:

- Will the medium be used in formal instructional situations?
- Is it only for recreational use?
- Who is the primary audience: adults, children, or all ages?

- Will the item circulate, or will it be available only for in-house use? If used in house, will it be available to individuals or only to groups? Will group use involve a library staff member or an expert in the field to guide group discussions before or after the item's use?

- Will the library be a member of a resource-sharing network? If so, will the item become part of the shared material pool?

Answers to these questions will affect the type of media purchased and the prices paid. For example, many videos for home use are less expensive than videos for instructional use, even when both packages are the same title.

Content Factors

Content is the next concern in the selection of any format. In the past, audiovisual selection was a group process rather than the sole responsibility of one selector. This was especially true in the case of expensive formats. Today, with the prices of videos dropping and increasing numbers of titles needed for the collection, the selection process is more like book selection, that is, an individual process. School media centers still emphasize the group process, in part because of limited funds but also because the possibility of someone objecting to an item's presence in the collection is higher than in other types of libraries. Whether selection is a group or individual process, using an evaluation form is useful. Keeping the forms for several years, for titles rejected as well as those purchased, can save selectors' time in the long run. Unlike print material, most media are sequential in nature; this means that it takes 50 minutes to review a 50-minute program. An evaluation form indicating that the library reviewed and rejected an item three years ago should help selectors decide whether the item is worth reconsidering. No matter what questions are on the form—and not all items listed in this chapter will be on any one form—one ought to consider all of the following points:

1. What is the primary purpose of the item? If there is a user's guide, does it provide a specific answer to this question?

2. Given the purpose(s) of the item, is the length of the program appropriate? Items can be too short, but more often than not, they are too long.

3. Is the topic a fad, or is it likely to have long-term interest? Long-term interest and lasting value are not always the same.

4. Is the material well organized?

5. Is the story line easy to follow?

6. If the item is of relatively short duration and is an attempt to popularize a subject, does it do this with sufficient accuracy? (That is, does the simplification cause misunderstandings or, worse, create a misrepresentation?)

7. When was the material copyrighted? Copyright information can be difficult to find for some formats. Films usually provide this information somewhere in the credits, often in roman numerals. There is no national bibliographic description standard for this information. Sales catalogs may or may not provide the date of production. Unfortunately, a large number of dated products are, or have been, sold as if they were current.

8. Will the visuals or audio date quickly? In many educational films, the subject matter is important but the actors' dress makes the film appear old-fashioned. If one does not present the material as historical, many viewers may miss its true purpose. Audience attention is easily drawn away from the real subject. Needless to say, this ties into the need for accurate copyright information.

9. Are there multiple uses for the item, in addition to those identified by the producer? If there are a number of ways to use the format (with various types of programs or audiences), it is easier to justify spending money on the item.

Technical Factors

Technical issues vary in importance from format to format, but some general considerations apply to several formats. In most instances, judging technical matters is less subjective than judging many other selection criteria. Nevertheless, it will take time and guidance from experienced selectors to develop a critical sense of these factors. Most individuals entering the field of library and information work are more attuned to good literature, well-manufactured books, and the various methods of literary review and criticism than the average person. Though our exposure to television, film, and video recordings may be greater than to books, few of us have the background to assess the technical aspects of these formats. This fact is evident during film and television awards ceremonies—the public interest is in the best film or program and performance categories. It is the rare individual who can name the winners in the technical areas (direction, production, special effects, cinematography, and so forth). Following are some questions to consider regarding technical features:

1. Are the visuals, assuming that there are visuals, necessary?

2. Are the visuals in proper focus, the composition effective, the shots appropriate? (These questions must be asked because out-of-focus shots, strange angles, and jarring composition may be used to create various moods and feelings.)

3. Is the material edited with skill?

4. Does the background audio material contribute to the overall impact?

5. Is there good synchronization of visuals and audio?

6. How may the format be used—can it be viewed by small or large groups or by both? Can it be viewed in a darkened, semi-lighted, or fully lighted room?

Format Factors

Questions to consider about format are:

1. Is the format the best one for the stated purposes of the producer?

2. Is the format the least expensive of those that are appropriate for the content?

3. Will the carrier medium (the base material that supports the image or sound layer) stand up to the amount and type of use that library patrons would give it?

4. If damage occurs, can it be repaired (locally or by the producer), or must one buy a replacement copy? Does it require maintenance? If so, what kind?

5. What equipment is needed to use the medium? How portable is the equipment and how heavy?

Additional Considerations

It is possible to group all audiovisual materials into six broad categories: still images (filmstrips, slides, microformats, transparencies); moving images (film and video); audio recordings; graphic materials (maps, charts, posters, etc.); three-dimensional materials (models, realia, dioramas); and other formats (games, software, etc.). Each type has some equipment or storage implications that one needs to take into consideration. For example, microform storage cabinets are heavy when empty and become even heavier as they are filled. Until one knows that the floor was designed to carry such weight, which is greater than book stacks, one should be cautious about starting a major collecting program in that format.

Microforms

Where do microformats belong—with books or with audiovisuals? Probably in both places. Most of the guides to microform materials cover microfilm and microfiche that contain previously published information; it is rare for a microformat title to contain original (new) material. The major exception to this is technical reports, which may be available only in microform.

One problem for people doing retrospective selection is finding paper copies of all of the items they might wish to add to the collection. Usually, if one waits long enough (perhaps years), the book or periodical will turn up in an out-of-print shop. Sometimes the need for the item is too great to wait. If reprint dealers do not have the item, then a microform copy may be the answer. Anything printed that occupies substantial space and that one can photograph is convertible to a microformat, including items for which color is a factor.

Microforms are also a means of access to primary research material or to items that are very rare and may be available, in their original form, in only one or two libraries in the world. Thus, though many librarians and most of the public view microforms with some degree, or a great deal, of displeasure, they do serve a useful function in providing access to materials that would not otherwise be available locally.

Another reason for using microformats is to save space, especially with low-use backfiles of serials. (A *backfile* or *back run* is a set of older volumes of a current serial subscription; for example, if a library's current issues of *Newsweek* begin with volume 92, then volumes 1–91 constitute the backfile for that library's *Newsweek* collection.) When a library has long runs of low-use material, it is wasting valuable shelf space by keeping the physical volumes in the library. A serial that occupies several hundred feet of shelving may be reduced to less than a foot of space when converted to a microformat. Naturally, there is a tradeoff in space: the more material there is in microformat, the more equipment the library needs to meet user demand. Some serials librarians use a microformat for backfiles of popular titles that have a high incidence of mutilation or a habit of disappearing. If the library has a reader-printer (a device that allows a person to read the microform and receive a hard copy of the page on the screen at the push of a button), loss and mutilation rates tend to drop.

One major drawback to using microforms to any major degree is user resistance. Many persons claim that they cannot read anything in a microformat, that it gives them headaches and causes eyestrain and other problems. Occasionally, someone will complain that it causes nausea. To date, none of these concerns is supported by research. Usually when the only source for the information is microform, an individual is able to use the material without a problem. Admittedly, it takes time to get used to using microforms; it is more difficult in some formats, such as reels, to locate a specific portion of text than in the traditional book format. Without proper maintenance, the image quality will be poor, and that will cause eyestrain. Equipment breaks down and malfunctions at times, causing user and staff frustration.

Despite these problems, it will become necessary to use more and more microformats as time goes on. The major factor in increased use will be economic in nature. New library buildings will be harder to secure; the prices of hard copies of older materials keep rising; and library book and materials budgets remain about the same or increase at a rate less than the rate of inflation. Also, the thought that the older material will be digitized is more a hope than a practical expectation, due to the low market potential for some materials. If there were a viable commercial market, the material would still be in print. Libraries may join together to digitize material, but such projects will most likely be for materials that are on paper and not in microform (for example, JSTOR; see pp. 190–94). Again the reason is economic: the labor costs are high and getting paper material that is in need of preservation into some other format is the goal rather than having multiple formats. Thus, it is important to know the guides to microformats. Two guides to in-print microformats are *Guide to Microforms in Print* (Microform Review) and *National Register of Microform Masters* (Library of Congress). Both titles try to be international in scope, include both commercial and noncommercial sources of supply (for example, libraries and historical associations), and cover more than 16 types of microformats. The *National Register* includes only U.S. suppliers, but the material available is international in scope. *Microform Market Place* (Microform Review) is an international directory of micropublishing, which includes microform jobbers. A major source of reviews of microform series, both current and retrospective, is *Microform Review* (Microform Review). Major producers offer extensive catalogs of what they have available. It is necessary to keep a file of their catalogs, because it is even less common for micropublishers than for book publishers to contribute information to the in-print guides.

The two most common microforms formats in libraries are reels and fiche. Reel formats are the older of the two and are still widely used for newspapers and serials. Reel microfilms are long strips of film on reels that come in several sizes: 16, 35, and 70mm. The film can be positive (clear with black text) or negative (dark with white text). Library staff and selection officers need to know about these different types because microfilm readers require adjustment for different film sizes and types. Failure to use the correct size take-up reel can damage film. Failure to adjust the reader for positive or negative film will make it difficult to produce a readable paper copy on a reader-printer machine. (Most people prefer not to read at the machine, but rather to make paper copies and leave the machine as quickly as possible.)

Most libraries try to confine the microfilm collection to one or two sizes (35mm and 70mm) and one type (positive). With any large-scale collection, however, more variety is inevitable—inevitable because the information needed by the library is only available in a particular size and type of microfilm. The choice is often either not to get the information or to accept yet another variation in format. Individuals who regularly use microforms are aware of many of the problems and can make the proper machine adjustments without staff assistance. Most individuals, however, will avoid microforms and use them only as a last resort; these people will need assistance.

Microfiche are sheets of film with the images of the original document arranged in columns and rows. Fiche tend to be used for materials that are likely to have many people needing access at the same time or with multiple means of access. The COM (computer output microfiche, a common format in the recent past) catalog is a good example of both these qualities. Although it is possible to reduce a large card catalog to 15 to 20 full reels of 70mm microfilm, it would also mean that only 15 to 20 people could consult the material at any one time. Fiche can be a great space-saving device while providing much greater access by breaking up the file into smaller units, somewhat like drawers in the card catalog. A microfiche with *headers* legible to the unassisted eye is illustrated by the photo in figure 10.1, page 284. Such legible titling helps patrons locate the desired material and helps the staff keep the fiche in order. The most useful headers are those with numbers and different colors to distinguish content (for example, a COM catalog with white headers for author entries, blue for title entries, and yellow for subject entries). The card catalog that could have been reduced to 10 to 15 reels becomes 500 to 600 fiche. That does mean more material for the staff to keep in order, but it also means better service.

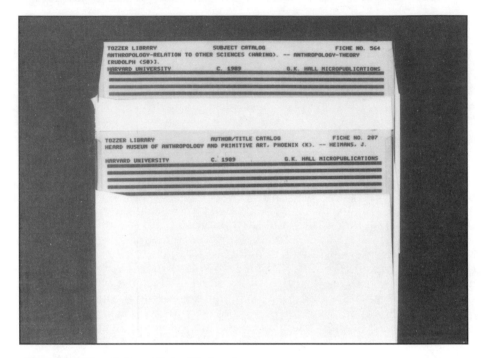

Fig. 10.1. Microfiche with legible header.

Like other media, microfiche comes in a variety of sizes as well as reduction ratios. Common sizes are 3 by 5 inches, 3 by 6 inches, and 6 by 7 inches; reduction ratios range from 12 to more than 200. The greater the reduction ratio, the more information the producer can fit on a single fiche. An item marked *10x* means the image is 1/10th the size of the original. Currently, producers use five categories of reduction: low (up to 15x), medium (16–30x), high (31–60x), very high (61–90x), and ultra high (greater than 91x). Reduction ratios are important because one must, in most cases, change lenses in the reader as one uses microforms at various reduction ratios. Most microform collections contain materials produced using various reduction ratios.

Some of the most expensive readers have a lens capable of "zooming" from 10 to 75x. Such units tend to be very costly, in the tens of thousands of dollars. Most libraries must get along with readers that have interchangeable lenses; that is, one lens for each of the common reduction ratios. These lenses must be available at a public service desk and the staff needs to know how to change them. Using the wrong lens with the wrong type fiche will not damage the equipment or the fiche, but it will increase customer resistance to microforms. A 16x lens with a 48x fiche will produce a very fuzzy image that, with effort, a determined individual can read, but that person will be certain that microforms are a form of library torture! A 48x lens with a 16x fiche will produce a very sharp image of a very small part of the text. Reading such a text image will tax the patience of even the most friendly reader, as very small shifts of the fiche carrier result in substantial shifts in the text. One unfortunate characteristic of fiche is that they do not indicate on the eye-legible header what the reduction ratio is. If they did, it would be a great help to the library staff in assisting the public.

Again, libraries try to limit the variation in fiche size and reduction ratio but, like microfilm, a variety of types is inevitable. Lacking an accepted standard, commercial vendors select the size and ratio most convenient for them, and that will perhaps increase their income if they produce enough material libraries believe they must own. The lack of standardization in creating combination of format packages (filmstrips with sound or sound slide sets with sound, for example) is a problem area between media producers and libraries, especially with producers who sell both equipment and the software for that equipment. Changing lenses is one reason patrons are uncomfortable using microforms. Selectors should try to keep the variations in reduction ratios to a minimum, although there may be few options when it comes to a particular title or collection of titles. One either accepts what the producer selected or forgoes purchasing the item.

Another concern is whether the film treatment is silver halide, diazo, or vesicular. The latter two are less expensive but have relatively short shelf lives, even with good storage and handling conditions. Silver halide, though more expensive, is the option to choose when there is a choice and long-term retention is an issue. A related issue is the polarity of the film (positive or negative). A negative film produces a black image on a white background (the traditional image people expect) in hard copy. Some of the more expensive reader-printers automatically produce the traditional image, regardless of polarity, and most require the user to select the film's polarity before printing. This is yet one more step that many users resent having to undertake.

As noted earlier, there is strong user resistance to microforms. Microformats are best for low-use materials, for older materials that need only a black-and-white image, and as second copies of materials with high demand or high loss and mutilation rates. Backfiles of journals are excellent candidates for storage on microfilm. Color microforms are expensive, and few libraries have equipment capable of making hard color copies from color microforms.

Moving Pictures (Film and Video)

We include film and video in this section because video has taken over most of the role films used to play in libraries. Most educational/instructional films are now available on videocassettes. Almost all individuals using a library now know how to operate a VCR, which means less staff time spent in assisting in equipment set-up.

Some years ago, in 1990, Pamela Hancock wrote a short article about 16mm film service in public libraries.[4] (*Note:* Until the 1980s, most of the libraries with film collections were schools, community colleges, and public libraries. All of the films were educational/documentary in character, and public libraries tended to use them for programming purposes rather than circulation.) Hancock noted that, at that time, film usage was increasing by 20 percent per year and the video collection had even higher numbers. She made the point that there are similarities and differences in the two formats and that they complement rather than compete with one another. There are reasons to have the title in both formats, in order to meet different needs.

Hancock listed several strengths of 16mm film, starting with portability in the sense that it serves *group* needs. Another strength is that it provides better quality images in a large room setting (current video projection systems are changing that) and the film image is (or was) vastly superior to a video image (high-definition television/video may change this). Finally, the cost of the equipment is less than for a video projection system. She believed the weakness for the format was isolation from other library services. She might have included that film can be more easily damaged and more often than not more expensive to replace. One of the challenges for film collections is that many items are available only in that format. Also, it is still the best format for teaching cinema studies. The threats to the film format were two. First is a lack of understanding about the differences between film and video, on the part of librarians as well as the public—video has replaced film and videos only cost $24.95. Hancock's second threat was that even producers/distributors have the idea that libraries are not interested in buying films.

Our point in covering the Hancock material is to emphasize the fact that the two formats are related but different. Both can play an important role in meeting the community information needs for some time to come.

Films

Films also come in a variety of sizes; the 8, Super 8, 16mm, and 35mm formats are, or were, common in libraries. The 70mm format is collected primarily by film archives or universities with degree programs in cinematography, as it is the size most often used for distribution of so-called theatrical films (the type shown in movie theaters). Most film producers now provide a choice of film or video for titles intended for the educational market. Even if libraries no longer acquire the film-format media, some retain their existing films because replacement videos are unavailable and some people still use the films. As a result, the staff will need to understand and work with films, perhaps in several size formats. If the motion picture collection is primarily intended for presentation to large groups, say, 100 or more persons, the film format (16mm or 35mm) is recommended. As the picture quality of projection video/television improves, the need for film, which still produce clearer large images, will decrease.

The 8mm film (the home movie size) is common in school and community college media centers. Compared to other film formats, there are several advantages to this size when the viewing group is small. First, the unit cost per film is very low, so a library can have a larger collection of 8mm films than if it buys 16mm titles. Second, the format works well with rear-screen projection equipment and headsets, so one or two people can view and hear a film in the same room with other people without creating a disturbance. Third, producers have developed short *single-concept* loop cassette films that are almost as simple to use as videocassettes. The loop cassette eliminates the rewinding problem for the public service staff. Most of the 8mm projectors sold for institutional use are capable of showing both silent and sound films; however, the "Super" 8mm films do require a different projector. Not knowing the difference between the two formats can result in a reel of ruined film.

Film can be silent or have sound, and there are two different types of sound tracks, optical and magnetic. Each type requires a different projector. Normally the sound track is optical on 16mm and 35mm and magnetic on 8mm, but not always. Nothing creates ill will more quickly than providing the wrong or inoperative equipment. Again, there is nothing to indicate the type of sound track on the film. When the library has films with different sound tracks, the storage cans *and* the film reels should indicate the type of sound track.

Video Recordings

A number of video recording formats exist. In March 1999, Mika Iisakkila's *Video Recording Formats* Website (<http://www.hut.fi/~iisakkil/videoformats.html>) listed 15 different formats. (This site provides more than adequate technical information about each format, at least for library purposes.) The good news about this is that library staff need only know a few formats: VHS, laser disc, U-Matic, DVD, and perhaps Beta. Without question today, and for the next few years, VHS is the format most libraries are collecting and providing service for.

Video recordings, in the cassette format, reduce the equipment problems associated with motion picture collections. More and more people own videocassette player-recorders and, therefore, know something about how to operate the equipment—unlike the situation with motion picture projectors.

As stated earlier, most film producers offer both film and video formats, sometimes 8mm and 16mm, VHS, and very rarely 35mm. Anyone who has had a home VCR for any length of time is aware of the marketing battle that occurred between the VHS and Beta formats and knows they were not compatible. A few individuals still own Beta machines and a few libraries still have some Beta cassettes. The 3/4 inch format, sometimes called U-Matic, was/is yet another option for video collections in the library. Intended for institutional use, the design of both cassette and player was intended to withstand the heavy use, and sometimes abuse, that occurs in schools, colleges, and business settings. A few libraries still have collections of reel-to-reel videotapes and one or two players, but most of the tapes are in-house productions and seldom used. More often than not, these are transferred to a cassette if there is any expectation of real use.

Initially some public libraries charged a fee for each cassette that circulated out of the library. (Hence Will Manley's point about unnecessary competition with video stores, at least in a sense.) The fee, though low compared to those charged by commercial stores, was still a charge. The purpose was, in the early days, based on the idea that tapes would be damaged easily and have to be replaced. Another stated reason was to provide funds to expand the video collection—perhaps a reflection of the idea that the format was marginal and not worthy of operating funds? In time, at least in some cases, videos became a source of revenue during times of budget cuts.

Generally, today few libraries charge for videos. We know of one library system that has a policy of charging for "popular" titles and not for others, with *popular* defined as titles shown in movie theatres.[5] In such a case, colored stickers can help the circulation staff know which titles are free. Charging a fee for high-demand titles is not unheard of in public libraries, even for books. Often there is a fee for the current bestsellers for those patrons who do not wish to put their names on a waiting list. Occasionally there is even a small charge for putting one's name on the waiting list, something more than the cost of postage to inform one that the item is now available.

Depending upon the purpose of the video collection—circulation or instruction—the access issues vary. In many ways the circulating collection creates the greatest number of concerns, ranging from reserving or not reserving tapes for individuals to maintaining some listing of cassette titles available. Although the Beta format no longer exists commercially, some people still own such units and libraries did collect the format. This means that a video collection designed to circulate had to provide both VHS and Beta copies of the same title. Having multiple copies, in different formats, of the same title can create headaches for staff operating any booking or reserve system. If possible, the library should not reserve videos if there are copies of the same title in different formats. Even if the OPAC records clearly differentiate the formats, not all the staff or public will remember to think about format issues. However, this is difficult not to do if you have a reserve system for in place for highly popular books.

One problem with video collections, of whatever format, is the cost of replacing damaged cassettes. People expect to see fairly recent (six to ten months old) theater films released on videocassette and often priced well under $30. Video clubs, like book clubs, seldom offer single cassettes at more than $80 or $90. When confronted with a replacement bill of $150 or $200 for a damaged instructional cassette, people get angry. They often are not aware that the size of the potential market plays a major role in pricing, just as with books and journals. A novel that is expected to sell several hundred thousand hardcover copies, which is also released in paperback and also becomes a book club selection, can sell at a relatively low price compared to a scholarly book that sells fewer than 2,000 copies. Theatrical movie releases and a small percentage of educational and instructional videos are distributed widely enough to be low-cost items. The majority of educational and instructional videos, however, are usually well over $100 each and often as high as $300 to $500.

A relatively new format for theatrical releases, which is gaining in popularity, is the laser disc. At present it is a play-only technology, which has slowed its growth in the home market. If and when it seriously cuts into the videocassette player-recorder market, libraries will need to consider adding this format to their video collections. The manufacturers claim that laser disc technology produces a much sharper, clearer picture with better color. People who have seen both the cassette and disc versions of a movie agree. Currently one disc plays for approximately 60 minutes and is about the size of a 33-1/3 rpm sound recording disk. Thus, there is some space saving for libraries with film collections, from film cans 1/2 inch to 2 inches thick to cassettes 3/4 inches to 1 inch thick to laser discs less than 1/4 inch thick. As of 1999, only a few libraries have laser discs and even fewer have circulating collections of them. Another format that is appearing commercially for home use is DVD, which may have an impact on library collections; 11 percent of the public libraries surveyed in 1998 had DVD or laser disc collections.[6]

One of Will Manley's concerns, increased potential for complaints and censorship challenges, can be an issue with video collections. Other than special libraries, there is probably no library with a video collection that has not had at least one person question the suitability of a title or two in the collection. School libraries have somewhat less exposure to challenges, due to the instructional nature of the collections; however, even here it is possible to have a parent complain about a video (such as one dealing with evolution).

Academic libraries also have their challenges. The senior author of this book has worked at a private Catholic university for a number of years. That university has a strong film and television degree program. Because of this program's strength, the library has a substantial film and video collection, especially in the area of theatrical movies. Nonuniversity individuals (there are no restrictions on the general public's use of the library) have raised questions about the suitability of some of the titles in the collection, especially as it is a Catholic institution. Such complaints take staff time to address, if the library's goal is not to create a major problem. Following the ALA guidelines for handling such complaints is the best approach, but staff need some training in how to handle the situation when complaints arise (see chapter 19 for a fuller discussion of intellectual freedom issues and collection development).

Public libraries face the greatest challenge. Their public is in fact anyone, children to seniors. Very often the individuals who raise a question about the suitability of certain titles will do so in the context of "protecting the children."

In addition to the broad service community, public library video collections have, in general, a high percentage of theatrical titles. As most people know, for better or worse, the Motion Picture Association of America (MPAA) has a rating system for its releases—the familiar G, PG, PG-13, R, and NC-17 one sees in the movie section of the newspaper. The Classification and Rating Administration (CARA) handles the rating of each title. Although these ratings have no legal force and, in fact, are based on the somewhat subjective opinions of the 11-member CARA board, the general public accepts them as appropriate. The key is the content of the film in terms of its suitability for children. The 1998 *LJ* survey of public library media collections indicated that some libraries do not purchase R-rated videos. Others do so on the ground that R-rated films are not that different from many of the novels in their collections. Still others avoid the entire issue by purchasing only educational and documentary videos.[7]

Although ALA has a statement opposing labeling, the majority of public libraries that responded to a national video survey indicated that the MPAA/CARA ratings did influence acquisition decisions.[8] The unfortunate fact is that even a collection of G- and PG-rated titles would not ensure that there would be no complaints. One possible way to handle the situation, though not always easy to accomplish, is to create two sections for video, one in the children's/young adult area and another in the adult area. Again, this will not forestall all complaints, but it could help. From the staffing point of view, making certain that the videos are in the proper section will be something of a challenge, unless the cassette boxes are clearly color-coded or marked in some way that makes sorting easy.

The Indianapolis-Marion County Library reaffirmed its video policy in 1996 after a customer's concerns about "potential effect on minors."[9] The library formed a "Community Video Task Force" to review the current policy and make recommendations, if any, for changes. The task force's report concluded that the policy should retain the parents' right to restrict a child's borrowing to the juvenile videos, and that the staff should continue to receive training in the current policy. The basic policy is that anyone can borrow any video, unless the person is a child with a card stamped "JV," which indicates a parental restriction. The person who raised the issue wanted the policy to require parents to give written permission for a child to borrow anything but juvenile titles.

Perhaps the greatest problem with videocassettes is copyright. What can and cannot a library do with videocassettes? For example, can one use a video sold for home use in a classroom? What is meant by *public performance*? Public performances are any performances the public may attend, even when there is no fee. Library programs, including story hours and senior discussion groups, as well as programs by any formal group (such as Scouts, churches, and service organizations), are public performances. To be safe, in library programs one should not use any video for which the library has not purchased performance rights.

The issue of performance rights is important for classroom use, and this is a growing area of use. According to Lillian Gerhardt, classroom use of videos in educational institutions, elementary through graduate school, is the steadiest growing area of video use.[10]

Many special libraries are also finding a growing demand for videos. Publications like Ellen Miller and Timothy Hallahan's dated but still valuable *Media Guide for Lawyers*[11] and Bowker's *Law Books and Serials in Print*[12] and *Legal Video Review*[13] indicate a high level of interest in one profession. The same is true of the medical field, where, among other titles, one finds *Media Profiles: The Health Sciences*.[14] In addition, the visual arts, such as architecture, interior design, fashion design, and commercial art, make extensive use of video materials.

Selection of videos is very much like book selection, at least for lower-priced titles. More often than not, one person makes the decision about titles costing less than $100. The decision may be based on information in a producer's catalog or a journal review, as well as a preview of the item. Identifying potentially useful videos is becoming easier and easier. *Bowker's Complete Video Directory*,[15] *Video Source Book*,[16] *Educational Film and Video Locator*,[17] and *Film and Video Finder*[18] all provide long lists of available video titles. Unfortunately, no one source is comprehensive, so one must consult several sources when building a subject collection.

Access to theatrical films is reasonably easy because of the number of retail video stores and their need to have bibliographic control. Documentary film access also is fairly good, in the sense that a number of guides are available. However, independent filmmakers come and go with great speed; many "indie" films never appear in a guide, and others remain in the guides long after the producers are out of business. Keeping current with changes in the independent filmmakers' field could become a full-time occupation for a person, if serious collecting is a goal.

Reviews of videos are becoming common, appearing alongside book reviews in professional journals. *Library Journal, School Library Journal,* and *Booklist* cover a number of formats. However, remember that these publications tend to cover items that have broad appeal, and they do not cover many titles in the course of a year. A sampling of journals that cover a wide range of subjects and levels of treatment includes: *American Film Magazine, AV Video, Educational Technology, Educators Curriculum Product Review,*

EFLA Evaluations, Media and Methods, Photographic Trade News, Sightlines, and *Videography.*

Some questions to bear in mind when selecting videos and films are:

- Does the motion add to the message?
- Are variable speed capabilities (fast, normal, slow, and stop) used effectively?
- Is the running time appropriate to the content? Too long? Too short?
- Do recreational films using performers or animation present an accurate picture of the events depicted?
- Is the sound properly synchronized with the visuals?

Still Pictures (Filmstrips, Slides, Photographs, and Other Graphic Material)

A related film format is the filmstrip. A filmstrip (usually 16mm or 35mm) is a series of single-frame still photographs on a strip of film. Though it is a somewhat dated format, educational libraries and public libraries still have filmstrip collections. In the public library, they are usually in the children's department or area and are film versions of books in the collection, often with accompanying audiocassettes containing the story. In essence, a child can have a book read to him or her while viewing the pictures—all without much assistance from the library staff. The popularity of the library's story hour in the children's department is well known. Minimum story-hour staffing is one, but it may require the presence of two or more staff, depending upon the program and number of children in attendance. Audio filmstrips extend a form of this service to individual children with almost no staffing requirements. Rewinding the filmstrip and making certain the film is in the proper container is about the extent of staff time needed to handle this format.

Educational libraries, schools, and colleges often have a broader range of filmstrips. Schools do collect audio filmstrips based on picture books, but most of the collection is of a more instructional nature. Many instructional needs call for pictorial material, but there is no need for motion. Filmstrips are less expensive than motion picture film and the user has the advantage of being able to stop the film at any image for careful study. In essence, one can think of filmstrips as an uncut set of slides. Almost all commercial filmstrips in a library's collection could have been produced as a slide set. A major advantage of the filmstrip over a set of slides, from a library point of view, is that it is easier to handle one filmstrip can than it is to keep track of 75 to 100 individual slides that should be in a prescribed sequence.

The filmstrip format for instructional use is probably the area with the greatest variety of proprietary versions. You can find vendors offering 16mm half-frame strips, 16mm half-frame with sound track, 16mm half-frame strip with audiocassette with an embedded signal that will advance the film at the proper time (assuming you have the vendor's special projector), and 16mm half-frame with an audio disc (the recording may or may not use a standard speed so that you can use one of your existing record players). The variations go on with 16mm full frame, 35mm half-frame, and 35mm full frame. Clearly, few libraries can afford to acquire all the variations and their attendant equipment. Most try to deal with vendors that stock a wide selection of titles in nonproprietary formats.

Filmstrips come in either sound or silent format. Sound products consist of the filmstrip and an audio recording (usually a cassette tape). Many of the sound tapes have an electronic signal indicating that it is time for the user to advance the filmstrip to the next frame. There are also sound packages that can automatically advance the filmstrip as the recording plays. Such packages require the use of special, more expensive equipment.

Reviews of filmstrips appear in several standard review sources, such as *Booklist*, *Library Journal* (*LJ*), and *School Library Journal* (*SLJ*). More specialized review sources that cover filmstrips with some regularity are *Landers' Film Review*, *Media and Methods*, *Media Review Digest*, and *Science Teacher*.

In today's electronic environment, it may be difficult to believe that filmstrips have any future; perhaps they do not. However, companies are still producing them and apparently managing to stay in business. The future for the format may be brighter than many of us imagine, at least for younger children's materials. Dea Roberts wrote the following in late 1995: "I love using filmstrips with kindergartners and first graders. They think it is a new and wonderful invention with Big Pictures—much better than the dinky TV screen. When the lights go out (another novel attraction not associated with videos) voices and movement are hushed in anticipation."[19]

Slides

For most people, the term *photographic slides* brings to mind the traditional family collection of 35mm slides from various vacation trips and family events. Indeed, the common 35mm slide is a part of many library collections, but it is not just a matter of collecting the garden-variety, paper-mounted 2-by-2-inch 35mm slide. Like all the other media formats, there are several variations on a common theme. Large slide collections are likely to consist of 2 x 2-inch, 2-1/4 x 2-1/4-inch, and 3 x 4-inch slides, perhaps with even a few old glass lantern slides. In a sense, slides are simply filmstrips cut into individual frames and mounted for projection onto a screen. The larger the size, the better the image will project for large audiences. Like filmstrips, there are combined sound and slide packages, primarily for the educational market.

Slide mountings vary from paper to plastic to metal to glass. Each type of mounting material results in a different thickness for the final slide, which may create some projection and projector problems. Many projectors are capable of handling the various thicknesses, but are better with one or two types of mounts (paper and plastic). Problems of jamming, with potential damage to the slide, and the need to adjust the focus for each type of mount are common.

Although the 35mm slide is satisfactory for most general purposes, high-definition slides require a larger film format. Such slides are commonly found in special libraries, especially those supporting scientific, medical, and art museum work. Historical picture collections may include stereo slides as well as a variety of still photographs and negatives. Stereo slides and photographs may also be part of a map collection. (Stereo slides or photographs are slightly overlapping images that, with special viewers, give the illusion of three dimensions.)

Only special and academic libraries collect extensively in the slide format. Special libraries (museums, medical, technical, art, and architecture) will have working slide collections. It is rare for a public library to have a slide collection, even in the standard 35mm format, despite the number of homes that have slide projectors. Some high school and most academic libraries will have instructional collections. Anyone teaching an art appreciation course will want slides for classroom use as well as for students to view independently. A constant problem for the staff members who are responsible for the slide collection is keeping track of thousands of small, thin, square and rectangular pieces of film and mounting material. Another problem is loss of color when slides are exposed to light, including the projector's lamp (more about this later in the chapter, when we discuss preservation issues). Efforts to "copy" slides into a digital database—via scanning—can result in a well-preserved collection, but may violate copyright.

Perhaps the greatest problem in collecting slides is the large number of sources, which may produce packages of highly variable quality. A major issue with slides is color quality and the quality of lighting and exposure. Slow exposure using a fine-grained film produces the best quality slides, assuming that the photography (focus, composition, and so forth) and film processing were performed competently.

Reviews of slide sets appear, irregularly at best, in such standards as *Booklist*, *LJ*, and *SLJ*. Two more-or-less regular sources of review are *Art and Activities* and *International Bulletin for Photographic Documentation of the Visual Arts*. The latter publication provides updates for Norine Cashman's *Slide Buyers' Guide,* 6th edition (Englewood, Colo.: Libraries Unlimited, 1990). See also Sandra C. Walker and Donald W. Beetham, *Image Buyers' Guide*, 7th edition (Englewood, Colo.: Libraries Unlimited, 1999).

Transparencies

Transparencies and opaque projector materials are used primarily in education. Of all the media choices available, this form is the most group-oriented, designed to aid in the presentation of graphic material to small- and medium-sized groups. Though an individual can use the material, it has no advantage over flat pictures. A library could obtain materials in this format related to adult education classes, especially in the science fields. Plainly, this format has limited value to the individual user, and public libraries seldom collect it. There are a number of guides to educational transparencies, including Mary Sive's *Complete Media Monitor* (Scarecrow Press, 1981) and *Elementary School Library Collection*, 21st edition (Brodart, 1998).

School media centers may collect overhead transparencies. As with the picture files, the transparency collection focuses on the teaching units of the school district and normally supplements the teachers' personal collections. Commercial sources produce quantities of transparencies geared toward supplementing major text series. Textbook publishers often offer their own series of transparencies based on or using illustrations from their books.

Flat Pictures

Flat pictures, such as paintings, posters, postcards, photographs, and other pictorial materials, are often part of a library's collection. School libraries often have a collection of pictures from magazines and other sources that teachers use to supplement their personal collections. The collection focuses on the teaching units in the particular school district. Some public libraries have a circulating collection of art reproductions, both paintings and sculptures. Museums and academic libraries often have extensive collections of posters, usually housed in special collections in the case of academic libraries. Photographic archives, museums, and academic libraries often have collections of photographs and occasionally postcards. The archive normally focuses on historic photographs. In 1989, the photography industry celebrated 150 years of photography. Museums frequently have both historical photographs and extensive collections of contemporary photographs, as well as motion pictures and, of late, videos, taken during museum-sponsored expeditions. Academic libraries that serve as the institutional archive will, over time, develop a photograph collection and hold a few films and videos relating to major institutional events. The special collections department may receive gifts of photographs, or more commonly, will find photographs mixed in with other gift material. A few libraries have major postcard collections (200,000 or more cards).

Aside from a few UNESCO publications, there is little bibliographic control in this field. Selectors and acquisition staff must learn about producers and maintain files of catalogs to secure these materials in a timely fashion. Once in a great while there are reviews of these formats in *LJ, Booklist,* and *SLJ.*

Providing access to pictorial material is a longstanding problem. Users complaints about where the library has classified a book or serial title are uncommon, because they have good access to the material through the OPAC. If people had similar access to pictorial material, complaints would be nonexistent. However, bibliographic control for a great many photographs, posters, pictures, and postcards is difficult to achieve, as there is little or no information about the photographer or artist who created the work. In the worst cases, there is no information on the picture about the person(s) or place. Pictures generally include a number of people or objects as well as background scenery. Identifying the main feature and organizing the collection for use present a challenge for the library. Whatever system is in place, the public service staff will need to understand it to assist patrons in using the pictorial files effectively. Keeping the files in proper order, though not a major problem, is important for efficient service.

Scanning images is one approach to keeping pictorial materials in order. However, unless one does a great deal of coding, access by different subject/content categories is not improved by scanning. Certainly images on the Internet are searchable to a point, but mounting a large number of scanned images requires staff commitment and equipment and is still not too accessible. The process of scanning is more complicated than placing the item on a scanner and clicking "scan/save." One needs to verify that there is a match between the scanned and original images. Images also require substantial amounts of disk memory and high-end computers to make effective use of scanned images. Perhaps in a few years these factors will be less important, but for now they are very real concerns.

Maps

Maps are a form of pictorial material and most libraries have at least a small collection, in addition to atlases in the reference collection. Small collections of local-area maps pose no particular problem other than having them disappear into an individual's books or briefcase. Large public libraries, academic libraries, and many business and industrial libraries have extensive map collections. Maps, as graphic representations of geological, physical, and natural features, take many forms and shapes, from folded road maps to raised relief globes. Any major map collection must determine its scope and define what to collect. Most would include aerial photographs, including satellite photographs—but should they also house the remote sensing data from satellites? Are raised relief maps worth including in a collection, or are they a commercial product of no real information value? Clearly the users' needs will determine the answers to these and many other questions about the collection.

Depending on the collection's purpose, maps can be organized in a simple geographic location sequence or by some more complex system. An individual's, "Do you have a map of X ?" may (and usually does) mean a map showing streets, roads, and other manmade features. It could mean a topographic map that provides elevation information in addition to cultural features. Or the individual may really want a soils map to get information for agricultural or construction purposes. Most map users who want a contour map, however, will ask for "the topo map of X." Normally, persons with specialized maps needs are knowledgeable about maps and will be precise in their requests. In a large collection it is common to keep types of maps together, for example, topographic, cultural, political, and geologic maps. In addition to map content, factors such as projection and scale may be important in their organization and storage. Staff working with large map collections will need special training to properly handle this format.

Globes and maps, although different in form and requiring different handling, usually are available from the same sources as flat pictures. Most libraries have always had a small collection of local maps and atlases, along with a globe or two. Increased leisure time and increased interest in outdoor recreational activities have generated a demand for maps of recreational areas for boaters, campers, and hikers. However, the control of map production is very uneven. There are not many commercial sources of maps, and these are easy to identify. Unfortunately, the largest producers of maps are government agencies. Though federal agency maps are reasonably well controlled, state and local agencies have little central control. Acquisition departments need to develop and maintain their own lists, if map collecting becomes a significant activity.

Some of the selection issues for maps and globes are:

1. Is the level of detail presented appropriate, or is it confusing given the scale of the map?

2. If a color map, are the colors aligned (registered) properly with the lines outlining an area?

3. Are the symbols clearly defined?

4. For world political maps, do the names on the map reflect the current or appropriate names of the countries represented?

5. Will the map or globe be able to withstand the type of use that the library anticipates it will receive?

A variety of professional journals publish reviews to assist selection officers. *American Cartographer, Cartographic Journal* (British), *Canadian Cartographer, Geographical Review* (United States), and *Geographical Journal* (Britain) are but a few of the professional journals that publish evaluative reviews. The *Information Bulletin of the Western Association of Map Libraries* also publishes reviews and is a useful source for selection.

An interesting development is the growing use of computer-based (CD-ROM and tape) geographic and demographic data. Geographic Information Systems (GIS) opens a new and challenging area of image collecting for many libraries. (GIS is a computer-based tool for analyzing and mapping features. It combines database operations, such as statistical analysis, with unique visualization and geographic analysis capability to create maps.) However, it requires equipment that is capable of handling the images and color graphics these products contain. Another option for maps, at least for general information or recreational use, is an Internet-based service called *MapQuest* (<http://www.mapquest.com>). Though this will not replicate the physical map collection, it will allow individuals to find information about places for which the library does not collect maps.

There are some general questions the selector should consider when working with material that features still pictures, whether the format is filmstrips, flat pictures, slides, or transparencies:

1. Does the lack of movement cause the viewer to misinterpret the meaning?

2. How accurate is the color reproduction? Is the color necessary?

3. Are the mountings and holders compatible with existing library equipment?

4. For filmstrips, is the sequence of frames logical and easy to follow?

5. If there is an audio track, does it aid in understanding the materials?

6. Is the ratio of pictures to narration appropriate? (A frequent problem with slide or tape programs or narrated filmstrips is too few illustrations; this often results in a product that seems to last too long.)

Audio Recordings: Discs and Tapes

Returning to a widely held format, audio recordings, we again encounter great diversity and incompatibility. Sound recordings were among the first nonprint formats collected by libraries. In public libraries, the recordings are usually part of the circulating collection. For educational libraries, the purpose is usually instructional, with limited use outside the library. As we will show, this is the media category that most clearly reflects the long-term influence of a changing technology on a library collection.

Although a few music libraries and archives have collections of early cylinder recordings, by the time most libraries began actively collecting recordings the standard format was the flat disk. Many libraries built up extensive collections of 78 rpm (revolutions per minute) records by the end of the 1950s. For a period of time there were four common playing speeds for records: 16-1/2, 33-1/3, 45, and 78 rpm. Although the 16-1/2 rpm speed was not widely used, most record players had that setting as well as the other "standard" speeds. From a library point of view this was fine; record speed was not a consideration in building the collection. Then in the late 1950s and early 1960s, the recording industry shifted to 33-1/3 rpm "long play" records and the 45 rpm speed for popular, "single" recordings (that is, one track per side).

The substantial investment in 78 rpm albums was not lost because the newer equipment still played the recordings, even if you could not buy new 78-speed albums and records. One problem with the older format was that the sound quality was not as good as that of the 33-1/3. Also, more material would fit on a single side of the new recording. The public began to expect the newer format to be in the library's collection, just as it was in their personal collections.

Eventually, equipment manufacturers stopped including 78 rpm as a standard speed. As older players wore out and could not be repaired, some libraries attempted to transfer the 78 rpm recordings to tape format; others sold or, in some cases, gave away the records. At almost the same time, the "new" 33-1/3 format had a challenger in the form of tape formats, mostly reel-to-reel, because of tape's better sound reproduction qualities and the ability to record on the tape.

Tape and CDs are today's most popular formats for sound recordings. With increased portability of radios and tape or CD players, the popular music industry dropped the 45 rpm recording in favor of cassette tapes and, later, CDs and CD mini-disks. The lifespan of each new and better recording method (except possibly the CD) is getting shorter and shorter and most are not compatible with other forms. An old sound recording collection could consist of cylinders, disks (16-1/2, 33-1/3, 45, 78 rpm, and compact), tapes (reel-to-reel, with both acetate and wire recordings recorded at a variety of speeds), and cassettes (both dual-track and 8-track, and recorded on tapes with different characteristics that may or may not cause equipment problems). Each format uses its own equipment, or older, more flexible equipment, either of which requires special skills to maintain. And, now there is another change taking place, digital tapes, which will probably mean yet one more format to collect.

A circulating collection will need to keep closer pace with changing technology than will an instructional collection. Part of the problem, from a library point of view, is that the recording industry focuses on the individual and home markets rather than the institutional market. The new technologies tend not to be too expensive. They cannot be if mass sales are the goal. Most individuals do not invest as heavily in sound recordings as libraries and can switch to a new format and equipment more easily; libraries, however, may have collections of several thousand titles in a particular recording format. The librarian who finds that she or he suddenly has a "historical" collection, or to whom the music department chairperson says, "Get rid of the 33-1/3s, they are dinosaurs. Replace them with CDs," may wonder where to find the funds. Also, how soon will the CD become the next dinosaur? The library with an instructional collection may be able to move slowly into the new format, as long as the old equipment is serviceable. The shift for the circulating collection will have to be faster and perhaps more frequent.

The variety of formats and equipment may provide a slight challenge for the public service staff. Most homes have some type of sound recording equipment; therefore, staff members will probably be more familiar with this equipment than other media equipment. Probably the biggest problem is keeping the very thin records, tapes, or CDs in proper order and being able to locate the desired item quickly.

For public libraries, spoken-word tapes (the preferred trade term is *audio books*) have become almost as important as the video collection. (*Audio books* is actually the best term to use, as many of the other shorthand labels people use are in fact copyrighted names: Books on Tape, Talking Book, Recorded Book, BookCassette, and Talking Tape, for example.) Automobile and portable handheld tape players have created a market for audio books. Even reading a small paperback book on a crowded subway or bus can be difficult. "Popping a tape" into a small player that fits in one's jacket pocket and has a small headset allows one to close out the noise, to some degree, and enjoy a favorite piece of music or listen to a current bestseller book. The same is true for those commuting in cars or just out for their "power walk."

The audio book format has substantial sales to individuals as well as libraries. In a 1996 article in *Publishers Weekly*, one of the titles on tape passed the 1 million copy mark (*The Seven Habits of Highly Effective People,* by Stephen R. Covey, from S&S Audio).[20] This same article listed 29 titles that had surpassed the 175,000 sales mark. An interesting feature of the list was that 17 of the titles were nonfiction. The fact that *PW* has a regular section on audio books is an indication of their importance to the trade.

Donna Holovack wrote an article outlining the popularity of audio books in *Public Libraries*. She suggested that audio books are "a good marketing aid, a loss leader extraordinaire."[21] She noted that libraries have supplied recorded books (and, we note, current magazines as well) for the visually impaired for some time. (The Library of Congress's service for the visually and physically impaired is a most valuable program and one that perhaps led publishers to think there was a bigger market for audio books.) The question of the "suitability" of libraries making abridged versions of works of fiction available is one for the profession; some people prefer abridged versions. The idea that people are only looking for the latest work of fiction is belied by the data from Holovack's *PW* article.

One of the drawbacks of audiocassettes, whether spoken word or music, is that they have a relatively short lifespan, five to six years, even under optimal usage conditions. They are also small objects that have few places upon which a library can attach a security strip/device, so their loss rate (shrinkage in retail terms) can be rather high. Nor, for that matter, is there much room to apply barcodes or other property markings. Replacing lost items can be costly. The fact that a single unabridged audio book can have as many as four to six cassettes means that keeping every thing sorted in its proper order can be a problem, from both the public's and staff's point of view. Certainly the staff must check each title that has multiple cassettes each time it is returned. If in fact a person is listening to the cassettes in the car and is using more than one title, there is a very good chance that a cassette will end up in the wrong container. No one wants to have the ending of a "whodunit" delayed because the last cassette is for Shakti Gawain's *Creative Visualization Meditations* (New World Library).

On the technical side, because of different tape types, there can be problems. Some companies attempt to reduce the amount of tape required for a title, thus reducing the number of cassettes, by recording using multichannel technology. The user needs good "balance control" capability for this to work; few portable players or car tape decks have such control, and lacking such control, one hears two tracks, neither of which is clear. Often when a person returning an item complains that something is wrong with the tape, it is a multichannel recording. The tape is fine but the necessary balance control was lacking. However, the staff must still listen to the tapes to be certain that they are in fact all right. Another aspect of the multiple-cassette question is, given a choice, what approach is better for the library? Some companies offer the same title on different lengths of tape, perhaps a choice between six and eight cassettes. There is a tradeoff for the library. The fewer the cassettes, the less checking staff will need to do on returning materials. The fewer the cassettes, the thinner the tape used; the thinner the tape, the greater the chances are that a player will "eat" the tape. That is, the tape stretches and may become stuck in part of the player, or it simply breaks and really becomes entangled in the deck's mechanisms.

Before ending our coverage of audio recordings, we should say a word or two about musical recordings. Some of the same issues covered earlier about tape length, etc., apply to music recordings as well. We noted that libraries have had music recording collections for a great many years. Some have also collected music scores; a question for the library is whether the scores and recordings should be together. Certainly, in the case of academic institutions, the music department, if it does have a separate library, would like the two together. The reality for most libraries is that if the two are combined, scores probably will get moved to the media department. First, because that is where the equipment to play back the recordings is located and where the staff has the training to assist the public in using the equipment. Second, few libraries have the resources to buy additional playback equipment and find space for it where the scores are located (usually in the main book collection stacks). And third, the storage needs of the formats are very different. In the 1997 edition of *A Basic Music Library*, the editors make the following statement:

> differences reflect inherent, practical distinctions between print and recordings: printed music is typically sought by players or students of a particular instrument (bassoon) or medium (choral), while recordings tend to be thought of in relation to a stylistic category (salsa) with less concern towards details of instrumentation.[22]

This view may or may not help libraries that are attempting to provide both recordings and scores for their service population, at least in terms of deciding whether to integrate the two formats.

Many audio recording collections that have been in place for any length of time contain a wide variety of formats, including vinyl disks, reel-to-reel tapes, cassette tapes, and compact discs. No other format more clearly demonstrates changing technology. In little more than 40 years, the technology has evolved from 78-rpm disk recordings to 45-rpm and 33-1/3-rpm disks to tape cassettes of various kinds to the compact disc. Each change required new equipment and new recording formats. In libraries that support music programs, it is not uncommon to find fairly large collections of two or three different formats that more or less duplicate content. That is, a library may have all of Bach's cantatas on 33-1/3-rpm vinyl disks, on audiocassette, and on compact disc. The cost of duplicating the information can be substantial; however, users demand the newer format because of the improved quality of sound. (At Loyola Marymount University, a new music department chair demanded that the library replace all the 33-1/3-rpm albums and the audiocassettes with compact discs. To have done so would have cost the library more than $20,000. The library has been replacing the recordings slowly over the last five years but still has about 25 percent of the collection on what the music department chair calls "the dinosaurs.") Unlike secondhand books, there is not a strong used recording trade, making it more difficult to resell or give away materials in the old format. The commercial music and spoken-book trade is reasonably well controlled in a bibliographic sense; certainly there is more control than in any other nonbook format. Where will it go from here? At this writing, tape cassettes and compact discs are the major formats. However, music videos are gaining in popularity and there is talk of CD-ROM or laser disc music videos.

Audiotapes have a special value in teaching languages. Language learning is always facilitated by hearing the proper sounds and is further enhanced when the student can practice pronouncing words. Dual-track tapes, with an instructor's voice on a nonerasable track and a learner's recording track, allow this type of use. Schools and academic libraries supporting language instruction often house the language learning laboratory. Many of these centers, to supplement the program, develop a collection of spoken-book titles in the languages taught.

Reviews of popular music recordings are relatively easy to locate in both mass-market and professional publications. *Booklist, LJ, SLJ,* and *Notes* are a few of the professional sources that review sound recordings. *High Fidelity, Stereo Review, Billboard,* and *Downbeat* are mass-market publications one can consult for music reviews. For audiobooks, *PW* publishes a regular section of reviews; *Audio File* magazine is also an excellent source for reviews and announcements, and occasionally one can find such reviews in *Booklist* as well.

Regardless of the format, there are some general questions to keep in mind during the selection process:

1. How much use can the format withstand without distorting the quality of the sound?

2. How easily damaged is the format? Can people erase it by mistake?

3. Does the recording cover the full range of sound frequencies?

4. Is there any distortion of the sound?

5. Is the recording speed constant? (This is seldom a problem with major producers, but it can be significant with smaller producers.)

6. If the recording is multiple-channel, were the microphones properly placed to ensure a balanced recording?

7. Was the recording site suitable for the purposes? (For example, if the goal is to produce an excellent recording of a musical composition, then a recording studio or a concert hall with excellent acoustics and no audience, rather than a concert, is the best location. Live performances do not produce the best sound quality.)

Other Media

Printed Music

One rather surprising void in public and academic libraries is sheet music. When both recorded music and books about music are available, why is it so difficult to secure the score? Cost is one explanation, but most other media cost more than books. Difficulty in handling (storage and checking in the parts) may be another aspect of the problem, but other media are also difficult to handle in some ways. Libraries ought to reconsider this format; music publishers' catalogs are available, and there is frequently a community need.

Most academic music departments would like the library to collect both full-size scores (also called complete, open, or performance scores) and miniature scores (pocket or study scores). Music accreditation groups expect to find scores on campus, and because of the problems in maintaining them and controlling their use, the library is the location of choice. One of the biggest factors limiting the growth of score collections, other than cost, is that scores are unbound and need special handling. Because they are and must remain unbound, pages easily get lost and damaged, usually requiring the purchase of another full score. Information about scores appears in the Music Library Association's *A Basic Music Library*[23] guide, and one can find reviews in *Notes*, *Music Review*, *Music and Letters*, and other journals.

Models, Realia, and Dioramas

Models have a long history of use in education, especially in the sciences. Libraries have not been active collectors, in part because instructors want to keep the models in the laboratories and classrooms for regular use. Students do need to have access to these items for study at times when the labs and classrooms are unavailable. Perhaps computer-generated virtual reality models providing a satisfactory three-dimensional alternative, such as *A.D.A.M.*, will be more widely used in the future. For the present, one needs to consider physical models.

One factor limiting the collecting of models is their cost. Good models are expensive, and small institutions may be able to afford only one model for classroom use. Storage of models is another limiting factor, because most are bulky and of variable sizes, making it difficult to store them on standard library shelving. Some questions to consider are:

1. Are objects of less than life size reproduced in an appropriate scale?

2. Is the scale sufficient to illustrate the necessary details? Would a two-dimensional representation work just as well?

3. When horizontal and vertical scales must be different, is the distortion so great as to create a false impression?

4. Are the colors accurate?

5. Are the objects durable enough to withstand the type of handling that they will receive?

Reviews of these materials are few and far between. *Booklist* occasionally reviews models. Three curriculum journals—*Curator, Instructor*, and *Curriculum Review*—also publish model reviews. Libraries usually purchase models from educational supply houses.

Games

Games and Realia

Although schools are the primary collectors of games and realia, some public and a few academic libraries have small collections. Public libraries sometimes have loan collections of games and toys that may attract new people to the library. The loaning of games often proves to be a problem for the circulation department, as staff need to go through each returned game to be sure all the pieces are still there. Naturally, it also means there must be some easily available record of what should be there. All this takes time and effort away from other activities. When the staff view the process as getting in the way of their "real" work, check-in becomes perfunctory. That view usually results in games with missing pieces and a "service" that is no longer a service. School libraries collect educational games for use in the classroom or in the media center. Though checks for missing parts must still take place, the losses are usually minimal and the learning value of the game far outweighs the cost of staff time in checking the returned games.

Teaching realia and models can range from samples of materials, such as rocks or insects, to working models to large take-apart anatomical models. Scientific and technical supply houses offer a variety of useful large-scale models for use in the classroom. Because the models are expensive, few teachers can afford to buy them and the instructional media center is the usual source, except when a large biology or physics department acquires the items. Even in the case of large departments, students get better service if the models are in the media center where they can examine the material any time.

The idea of buying educational games for library collections is relatively new in the United States, yet libraries in the Scandinavian countries have been lending recreational games for years. Libraries serving teacher education programs and, of course, school media centers usually engage in some game collection building. Teachers, rather than library staff, do almost all of the game selection. One exception is when the school media center staff selects games to assist in bibliographic instruction programs. Until more institutions enter the games market, there will be little incentive to improve bibliographic control. This means that a library wanting to buy games must develop its own file of sources and catalogs.

Simulation learning materials find their greatest use at opposite ends of the educational spectrum: primary and secondary schools and specialized postgraduate programs (e.g., government agencies, especially military, and advanced management training). Some simulations are computer-based and others are paper-based. Today there is frequent discussion in both the popular and professional press about interactive media and learning. In many ways, this discussion is like the discussions about programmed (self-paced) learning that took place in the 1960s and 1970s. Perhaps interactive materials will succeed where programmed learning failed. Simulations are likely candidates for incorporation into the interactive marketplace. If that happens, perhaps prices will come down (good programs are expensive) and more reviews will appear in print. At present, *Simulations and Games, Simulation/Games for Learning,* and *Simgams* are the most consistent sources of review. Once in a great while *T.H.E., Creative Computing,* and *Man, Society & Technology* publish announcements of new products and, even more infrequently, reviews.

Laser technology, and its place in the library and information field, are only beginning to be explored. Promises of major developments made in the 1980s have not materialized. Though laser-disc video recordings offer higher quality picture with no wear to the disc, the format has not grown in popularity as predicted. One reason given is that the technology is playback only and, as long as the videocassette recorder can both play and record a reasonably good picture, buyers will not switch. As a storage unit of printed information, the laser hologram far surpasses microformats. A few technical and research libraries now have small collections of holograms, and most, if not all, of these have been produced in research and development units of companies or in engineering departments of universities. Again, the promise of the perfect storage solution has not materialized. Perhaps the hologram's greatest potential is in combination with other formats, rather than as a separate form. Currently, most of the holograms are scientific or artistic in character. There is nothing resembling a commercial market for holograms at present. Therefore, locating information about them is difficult. One source of information is the Museum of Holography in New York City.

Working models, specimen collections, and realia are primarily for the educational market. A few items are useful for adults who are studying a subject independently, but most public libraries acquire them only to supplement school library resources. A number of catalogs and guides to these items exist.

These are but a few of the considerations that must go into the selection of audiovisual formats. As there are few, if any, universal questions to raise when selecting books, so it is with audiovisuals. Selectors will develop their own selection criteria as they gain experience in the field.

Previewing

The actual process of selecting audiovisual materials is often a group rather than an individual activity. This is particularly true of films and expensive video sets. To some degree, the cost of the material under consideration, rather than the usual collection development factors, drives the issue. In essence, making a mistake about a 20-minute sound, color, 16mm film or educational video has more serious economic consequences for the library budget than most single mistakes with a book, transparency, or sound recording. Educational videos cost $200 to $500 per cassette; in a multiple-cassette package, the total cost is substantial. The criteria for selection are highly subjective. Having multiple opinions about a prospective purchase helps avoid costly mistakes. In public libraries and school media centers, an audiovisual selection committee is the typical mechanism employed for securing multiple points of view. In academic libraries, often a single faculty member makes the recommendation, assuming that the purchase will be made with departmental funds, or the head of the library's media program selects titles on the basis of reviews and a knowledge of instructional needs.

How does the audiovisual selection committee differ from the book selection committee? Audiovisual selection committees usually function as a true group decision-making body. Normally, the group previews audiovisual materials under consideration, as a group. They view the material from beginning to end. (With book selection, the typical approach is for committee members to divide the items among group members and have individuals give oral reports about each item. Thus, only one member of the committee reviews the item completely.) A group discussion usually takes place after each screening, and each person expresses a reaction to and evaluation of the item. Everyone sees the same material, and group interaction ends in a decision to buy or not to buy. Sometimes the product is rerun several times, when there are strong differences in opinion.

An important difference in the two formats affects the selection process. This is the sequential nature of films and video formats. It is not possible to effectively skim a film as one does a book. One must view films and videos at their normal speed to get the proper impression. A 20-minute running time means 20 minutes of previewing time. Simple arithmetic indicates that a group previewing 20-minute films could view only 24 films in an 8-hour work day. A book selection committee meeting would be a disaster if only 24 titles were discussed in 8 hours. Realistically, no group can preview 24 titles in 8 hours, as the figure does not provide for discussion time or breaks. Finally, it is not feasible to expect people to view materials for four hours straight; they need a break. All of this means, more realistically, that the group could preview 10 to 12 items per day.

Not only do audiovisual formats cost more to buy, they also cost more to select. Combined, these two cost factors can be significant. Thus, one cannot conclude that, because a library does not have a collection of films or videos, it is reluctant to accept new formats. A significant difference exists between reluctance and a lack of money and qualified staff to select the newer formats. The only question is whether the library is using the monetary factor as an excuse to avoid trying out nonprint formats.

Additional Selection Aids

Despite the desirability of previewing audiovisual materials, published evaluations (especially when combined with previewing) are important in this field. Each year, there is a little more progress toward bibliographic control of the field, including reviews of most formats. Perhaps when multiple published reviews of a majority of formats are available, there will be less and less need for hundreds of audiovisual librarians to spend hours and hours in preview screening rooms.

At this time, no comprehensive source for audiovisual materials similar to *Book Review Digest* or *Book Review Index* exists. *Media Digest* (National Film and Video Center) has developed into the best source for locating reviews in all formats.

Identifying potentially useful audiovisual materials also presents a problem. The National Information Center for Educational Media (NICEM) focuses on educational materials; however, because NICEM employs a rather broad definition of education, the publications are useful to all types of libraries. NICEM Net (<http://www.nicem.com>) allows one to search the entire database by subject, age level, and media type. The 1999 subscription was $900 for a single-user license for a year. (One can also get online access to the database through *DIALOG*, *SilverPlatter*, and *EBSCOHost*. CD-ROM, tape load, and print versions are available.) The database contains almost 500,000 records in English and 60 other languages. Its primary strengths lie in the video, film, audio recording, filmstrip, and CD-ROM formats, although there are records for almost every format discussed in this chapter. NICEM also has a 300-page thesaurus of terms used to index the database, which is a great help in formulating accurate searches. This database is as close as one can come to an audiovisual equivalent of *Books in Print*.

Although the preceding list of sources provides a general overview, there is a slight emphasis on films. One reason for this is historical. After microforms and phonograph records, motion picture films and videos are the most commonly held audiovisual forms in libraries. Also, 16mm films and educational videos cost significantly more than either of the other two formats, making previewing all the more important. Because of film's popularity, cost, and longer history of use, film review and evaluation have had more time to become established. Increased popularity of other formats will, in time, make it economically feasible to publish journals covering other audiovisual formats.

Some of the most active nonprint discussion lists are: <videolib@library.berkely.edu>, <VIDEONEWS@library.berkeley.edu>, and <MEDIA-L@BINGVMB.CC.BINGHAMTON.EDU>. These provide information on how to handle various media issues as well as information about sources. We list additional guides in the "further readings" section at the end of the chapter.

Ordering Media

For all practical purposes, the process of ordering materials in the formats discussed in this chapter is the same as for ordering books and serials, with a few exceptions. One difference is that libraries place most of the orders directly with the producer, because there are no general audiovisual jobbers as there are for books and serials. Some book jobbers, such as Baker & Taylor, handle some of the most widely collected formats (for example, videos and audiotapes), but they do not handle the full range of audiovisual materials. Another difference is the need to secure preview copies.

There is a major difference between review copies of books and preview copies of other media. With books, if the purchasing librarian likes what he or she sees, the library keeps it, pays the invoice, and perhaps orders multiple copies at the same time. With audiovisual materials, for a number of reasons (risk of loss, damage, and so forth), the library usually requests a preview copy from the supplier, views the copy, and then returns the item. (Some producers now send a new copy—especially for videos—and expect the library to keep the copy if it decides to buy the item. Other producers charge for previewing, but deduct the charge from the purchase price. A few film vendors ship an approval copy with a 10 percent discount if the library buys the film.) One must request the preview copy well in advance of the preview date. Normally, a librarian writes to the producer or supplier asking for preview copies of certain titles and listing a number of alternative dates. This becomes an issue when previewing with a group, because of scheduling problems. One also must know when specific items will be available for previewing. A preview file thus becomes a very important aid in the selection process; it contains a listing of each title requested, the dates requested, scheduled preview dates, and the result of the preview.

One should keep in mind several other factors for previewing as well. A preview copy may have had some prior use; therefore, the quality may not be as high as that of a new copy. If one can determine from the supplier how often the item went out for previewing, it is possible to gain insight into the durability of the product. In assessing this information (assuming one can get it), the librarian must remember that the preview copy's use was by individuals who know how to properly handle the material (unlike many library users).

Upon receiving the purchased copy, a staff member should view the item to be certain it is (1) a new print, (2) the item the library ordered, and (3) technically sound (checking for breaks, sound quality, and quality of processing). Checking for technical soundness upon receipt should be standard procedure for all audiovisual items, not just for previewed items. Generally, other media are not mass-produced in the same manner as are books. Many are produced on demand, that is, in response to orders. The producer has several preview copies and a master copy; when an order arrives, the producer uses the master copy to produce a new print.

One issue to decide before ordering is that of performance rights. Does the library pay an additional fee for public performance rights, or are they part of the quoted price? (This is a typical issue for videos.) There may be some justification for paying a somewhat higher price for performance rights in an educational setting, but there is hardly any when the videos are for circulating home use. The classic example of the confusion between "the home market" and "the library market" was Public Broadcasting System's release of its series *The Civil War* in 1990. Initially it was available to libraries for $450; only a few months later, PBS released it to the "home market" for just under $200. Another example, from 1995, was *Malcolm X: Make It Plain:* $99.95 from PBS Video (with public performance rights) and $29.95 from MPI Home Video (with home video rights).[24] Failure to have public performance rights and using a film or video in a "public performance" setting could lead to a very costly lawsuit. Knowing how the item is most likely be used, acquiring the appropriate rights, and maintaining a record of what was purchased can be important in building media collections.

With some formats, there may be still another decision: to buy or rent. Normally, the rental fee is 10 percent of the list price. If there are doubts about the level of demand, it may be best to rent a copy. (Ten uses in five years would be more than enough to justify buying the item.) Remember, when calculating the cost, that it will be necessary to include staff time for preparing rental forms, as well as time for mailing and handling activities. In many cases, with film, video, and software, the library is not buying an item in the same sense that it purchases books and serials. Often the library must sign an agreement that outlines what the library may or may not do with the item. These agreements cover duplication and resale and, in some cases, place restrictions on where performances are possible. Vendors do enforce these agreements, which are legal contracts, so the librarian must understand what he or she is signing. If something is not clear, or if a clause should be modified, the librarian should discuss it with the vendor and the library's legal counsel before signing.

Summary

Building a media collection for the library is a time-consuming and expensive undertaking, but it is important and worthwhile for both the library and its service population. Each new format is capable of doing certain things that no other format can do, but each also has its limitations; as a result, they supplement rather than replace each other. It is clear that patrons have various preferences in seeking, using, and enjoying information. If the library is to be responsive to the community, it must build a collection of materials that reflects that community's various interests and tastes.

Notes

1.   Will Manley, "Facing the Public," *Wilson Library Bulletin* 65 (June 1991): 89–90.

2.   Sally Mason, "Libraries, Literacy and the Visual Media," in *Video Collection Development in Multitype Libraries,* edited by G. P. Handman (Westport, Conn.: Greenwood Press, 1994), 12.

3.   Norman Oder, "AV Rising: Demand, Budgets, and Circulation Are All Up," *Library Journal* 123 (November 15, 1998): 30–33.

4.   Pamela Hancock, "16 MM Film Services in Public Libraries: A S.O.W.A.T. Analysis," *Sightlines* 23 (Fall 1991): 29.

5.   Anne Menard, "Videocassette Collections: The Fee or Free Debate Revisited," *Public Libraries* 35 (July/August 1996): 249.

6.   Oder, "AV Rising," 32.

7.   Pat Lora, "Public Library Video Collections," in *Video Collection Development in Multitype Libraries,* edited by G. P. Handman (Westport, Conn.: Greenwood Press, 1994), 25.

8.   Oder, "AV Rising," 32.

9.   "Inidanapolis PL Reviews Video Policy," *Library Journal* 121 (June 1, 1996): 20.

10.   Lillian Gerhardt, "Sharpening the AV Focus," *School Library Journal* 37 (April 1991): 4.

11.   Ellen Miller and Timothy Hallahan, eds., *Media Guide for Lawyers* (Owings Mills, Md.: National Law Publishing, 1982).

12.   *Law Books and Serials in Print 1999* (New York: R. R. Bowker, 1999).

13.   *Legal Video Review* (Boston: Lawrence R. Cohen Media Library, 1985–).

14.   *Media Profiles: The Health Sciences* (Hoboken, N.J.: Olympic Media Information, 1983–).

15.   *Bowker's Complete Video Directory* (New York: R. R. Bowker, 1999).

16.   *Video Source Book* (Syosset, N.Y.: National Video Clearinghouse, 1979–).

17.   Consortium of University Film Centers and R. R. Bowker, *Educational Film and Video Locator* (New York: R. R. Bowker, 1990).

18.   *Film and Video Finder,* 5th ed. (Medford, N.J.: Plexus Publishing, 1997).

19.   Dea Ann Roberts, "The Shadowy World of Filmstrips," *School Librarians Workshop* 16 (December 1995): 10.

20.   "*Seven Habits* Reaches Million-Selling Milestone for S&S," *Publishers Weekly* 243 (September 2, 1996), 43.

21.   Donna Holovack, "The Popularity of Audiobooks in Libraries," *Public Libraries* 35 (March/April 1996): 115.

22.   The Music Library Association, comp., *Basic Music Library: Essential Scores and Sound Recordings,* 3d ed. (Chicago: American Library Association, 1997), xii.

23. Ibid.

24. Randy Pitman, "The Outer Limits of Video Pricing," *Library Journal* 120 (May 15, 1995): 34.

Further Reading

General

Annicharies, M. "Playing for Time: Delicate Art of Abridging Audio Books." *Library Journal* 117 (November 15, 1992): 41–44.

Audio Video Market Place. New York: R. R. Bowker, 1984–. Annual.

Dickinson, G. K. *Selection and Evaluation of Electronic Resources*. Englewood, Colo.: Libraries Unlimited, 1993.

Hoffert, B. "Books into Bytes." *Library Journal* 117 (September 1, 1992): 130–35.

Hudson, A. "Spoken Word: The Book of the Future?" *Assistant Librarian* 89 (March 1996): 44–46.

Kaye, S., and B. Baxter. "Breaking the Sound Barrier." *Library Journal* 119 (May 15, 1994): 34–36.

Langstaff, M. "Selling the New Media." *Publishers Weekly* 238 (May 10, 1993): 42–45.

Luchs, K. *Developing and Managing Audio Collections in Libraries: A How-to-Do-It Manual*. New York: Neal-Schuman, 1995.

Mason-Robinson, Sally. *Developing and Managing Video Collections*. New York: Neal-Schuman, 1996.

Pitman, Randy. *The Video Librarian's Guide to Collection Development and Management*. New York: G. K. Hall, 1992.

Robinson, S. "Copyright or Wrong: The Public Performance Dilemma." *Wilson Library Bulletin* 66 (April 1992): 76–77.

Rorick, W. C. "Discometrics: A System for Acquiring Scores and Sound Recordings." *Library Journal* 112 (November 15, 1987): 45–47.

Salce, J. "Video Distribution: The Maze Made Manageable." *Library Journal* 115 (July 1990): 42–43.

Scholtz, J. C. *Video Acquisitions and Cataloging: A Handbook*. Westport, Conn.: Greenwood Press, 1995.

Stokell, A., and A. H. Thompson. "In the Crystal Ball." *Audiovisual Librarian* 20 (February 1994): 36–41.

Video Collection Development in Multi-Type Libraries: A Handbook. Edited by G. P. Handman. Westport, Conn.: Greenwood Press, 1994.

Zimmerman, B. "The Tangle of Multimedia Rights." *Publishers Weekly* 238 (November 22, 1991): 17–19.

Academic

Bierman, E. G. "Beyond Print: Object Collections in Academic Libraries." *Collection Building* 10, nos. 1/2 (1989): 7–11.

Breen, T. H. "Keeping Pace with the Past." *Microform Review* 10 (Spring 1991): 57–60.

Briody, E. "Microforms: A Brief Narrative of Primary Research in a Secondary Place." *Microform Review* 29 (Spring 1991): 61–66.

Butchart, I. "Management of Collections of Non-Print Materials." In *Collection Management in Academic Libraries.* Edited by C. Jenkins and M. Morely. Brookfield, Vt.: Gower, 1991.

"College and University Media Centers News & Views." *Sightlines* 22 (Fall 1989): 4–6.

Cullen, P. "Acquisition of AV Materials in a Higher Educational Institution." *Audiovisual Librarian* 17 (August 1991): 153–57.

Dick, J. "Documentary Delivery." *Library Journal* 119 (May 15, 1994): 38–40.

Renwick, K. "Acquiring A/V in the Academic Arena." *Audiovisual Librarian* 17 (May 1991): 14–18.

Rooker, J. "Federal Copyright Law: How It Affects Academic Video Services." *Indiana Media Journal* 14 (Winter 1992): 23–25.

Thompson, A. H. "University Libraries and Multimedia Development." *Audiovisual Librarian* 15 (November 1989): 203–5.

Tomczyk, C. B. "Academic Media Selection." In *Operations Handbook for Small Academic Libraries.* Edited by G. B. McCabe, 269–76. Greenwich, Conn.: Greenwood Press, 1989.

Video Collections and Multimedia in ARL Libraries: Changing Technologies, edited by K. Brancolini. Washington, D.C.: Association of Research Libraries, 1997.

Public

Ahmad, N. "Collection Development Tools for Media Centres." *Public Library Quarterly* 11, no. 4 (1991): 29–41.

Doran, M. "Libraries or Video Shops? The Need for an Acquisition Policy." *Audiovisual Librarian* 17 (August 1991): 158–61.

Hoppe, D. "Paradise Lost? A Brief History of Alternative Media in Public Libraries." *Wilson Library Bulletin* 68 (March 1994): 26–30.

Kay, K. "Satellite Television and the Public Library." *Audiovisual Librarian* 17 (November 1991): 212–16.

Koepp, D. P. "Map Collections in Public Libraries: A Brighter Future." *Wilson Library Bulletin* 60 (October 1985): 28–32.

Kreamer, J. T. "The Format War." *Wilson Library Bulletin* 67 (November 1992): 38–40.

Palmer, J. B. *KLIATT Audiobook Guide.* Englewood, Colo.: Libraries Unlimited, 1994.

Rankin, K. L., and M. L. Larsgaard. "Helpful Hints for Small Library Collections. (Basic information to start and maintain a map collection)." *Public Libraries* 25 (May/June 1996): 173–79.

Sager, D. J. "Evolution of Public Library Audiovisual Services." *Public Libraries* 31 (September/October 1992): 263–69.

Thibodeaux, A. "Audiovisual Selection." *Book Report* 10 (November/December 1991): 40.

Wund, B. "Talking Books." *Small Press* 10 (Spring 1992): 16–17.

School

Considine, D., and G. E. Haley. *Visual Messages: Integrating Imagery into Instruction*. Englewood, Colo.: Libraries Unlimited, 1992.

Dewing, M. *Beyond TV: Activities for Using Video with Children*. Santa Barbara, Calif.: ABC-CLIO, 1992.

Kerman, M. "Making Friends with Audiovisuals." *Book Report* 10 (September/October 1991): 16–17.

Knirk, F. G. "New Technology Considerations for Media Facilities." *School Library Media Quarterly* 20 (Summer 1992): 205–10.

Lenz, M., and M. Meacham. *Young Adult Literature and Non-Print Materials: Resources for Selection*. Metuchen, N.J.: Scarecrow Press, 1994.

Sales, G. C. "Computer Cache: Videodiscs: An Exciting Resource in School Media Centers." *School Library Media Activities Monthly* 8 (December 1991): 255–75.

School Library Media Annual. Englewood, Colo.: Libraries Unlimited, 1983– .

Triche, C. "Video and Libraries: Video in the School." *Wilson Library Bulletin* 67 (June 1993): 39–40.

Warden, J. M. "Making Tough Decisions About All Those Video Programs." *Ohio Media Spectrum* 43 (Fall 1991): 36–39.

Weaver, C. K. "Captivate the MTV Generation." *School Library Journal* 38 (April 1991): 50.

Special

Bixler, L. S. V. *Evaluation of Criteria for Weeding Non-Print Materials in Health Sciences Libraries*. Master's thesis, Texas Women's University, 1991.

McCormack, T. E. "Media Equipment Selection Methods for Law Libraries." *Law Library Journal* 83 (Spring 1991): 283–88.

———. "Video Technology in the Law Library." *Legal Reference Service Quarterly* 11, nos. 1/2 (1991): 5–37.

Miller, E. J. "Video Collection: Selection and Evaluation." *Law Library Journal* 85 (Summer 1993): 591–98.

Rydeskey, M. M. "Audiovisual Media: Special Library Asset or Bane?" In *Special Librarianship*. Edited by E. B. Jackson, 521-29. Metuchen, N.J.: Scarecrow Press, 1980.

Singarella, T., et al. "Videodisc Technology Trends in Academic Health Sciences Libraries." *Bulletin of Medical Library Association* 79 (April 1991): 59–67.

Wagers, R. "Online Sources of Competitive Intelligence." *Database* 9 (June 1986): 28–38.

Walters, S. G. "Playing Now at the Law Library." *Legal Reference Service Quarterly* 10, nos. 1/2 (1990): 29–39.

11
Acquisitions

"Morphing," if that is a valid word, is something moviegoers and television watchers frequently see. Computers and other technologies allow filmmakers to easily cause objects and people to change shape before our eyes. Those same technologies are changing, if somewhat more slowly than in a film, the way we structure and operate acquisition units in libraries and information centers. Change is a natural aspect for any dynamic organization and we believe that most libraries and information centers are such dynamic organisms. (S. R. Ranganathan's fifth law of librarianship was "a library is a growing organism."[1] A growing organism is a changing one.) Though change has always been part of the field, the 1990s has been a period of very rapid change in the nature and character of collections and how one goes about developing them.

One outcome of these changes is that some people in the acquisition area have begun questioning the role and character of their work. A surprising amount of time has gone into exploring the question "Is acquisitions a profession?" Some people—for example, Alex Bloss[2]—believe strongly that it is; others, such as Ron Ray,[3] do not. Although a number of significant changes have been taking place in collection development, everyone agrees that the basic function of the acquisitions unit remains as it has been for the past 30 years: that is, acquisitions work involves locating and acquiring the items identified as appropriate for the collection.

Changing Environment of Acquisitions Work

As one might expect, it is the electronic materials—more specifically the networked/Web materials that are creating the most changes in the environment for library acquisitions units. Carol Diedrichs reported that between 1995 and 1998, the Ohio State University libraries' serials librarian shifted her time commitment to almost 50 percent conducting licenses reviews and negotiations for electronic products.[4] Electronic products, as we have noted in several earlier chapters, call for a different acquisitions approach, such as having trial periods and leasing rather than owning materials. While one might think of a trial period as somewhat like an approval plan for books, previewing other media—in other words, looking before buying—is very different, especially when you consider who needs to be involved and the communication process followed.

Collection development and acquisitions have always been closely coordinated, if not integrated, in libraries and information centers with successful programs. In today's increasingly electronic environment, that coordination/integration becomes vital. Joyce Ogburn made the point that managing an acquisitions program calls for a special set of skills and activities—assessment, prediction, control, choice, validation, and quantification. In doing so, libraries:

> [a]ssess the risk and feasibility of acquisition, the availability of the resources, and the chances of success, control the system and methods needed, the choice of the source, the supporting services, and the resources themselves; and quantify the resources, work, and costs involved to conduct the business of acquisitions and measures of success.[5]

We believe that these skills and activities are a constant, but today libraries may need to draw on the expertise of a number of staff members to acquire the desired electronic resources. Further, we fully agree with Ron Ray's concluding comment: "Library administrators cannot afford to leave acquisitions expertise out of their considerations as libraries navigate into new technology environments and unconventional patterns of information distribution. But neither should they feel constrained to continue organizing acquisitions expertise as it historically developed in libraries."[6]

To be fully effective, selection and acquisitions personnel must have a close, cooperative work relationship. Poor coordination will result in wasted effort, slow response time, and high unit costs. Achieving coordination requires that all parties understand the work processes, problems, and value of each other's work. Beyond the obvious purpose of supporting overall library objectives, the acquisitions department has both library-wide goals and departmental goals. One can group the library-wide goals into five broad areas of purpose:

- assist in developing a knowledge of the book, media, electronic resources trade
- assist in the selection and collection development process
- assist in processing requests for items to be added to the collection
- assist in monitoring the expenditure of collection development funds
- assist in maintaining all the required records, and produce reports regarding the expenditure of funds

By disseminating material from the various information producers and vendors, the acquisitions department aids in the selection process, even if there is duplication, as there is likely to be. (Most information producers are uncertain who in the library makes purchasing decisions. With electronic materials, the process is generally more complex, with two or more persons involved in the decisionmaking. Thus, it is not surprising that producers buy a number of mailing lists to use when promoting a new or revised product, and that several copies of the promotional literature will thus be sent. However, you should never assume that the item in hand is a duplicate unless you are the only person to decide on the item in question.)

Traditionally, acquisitions departments maintained collections of publishers' catalogs, prepublication announcements, and vendors' catalogs. It is reasonable to expect to have a location where such items are kept. Such a location, when properly maintained, can help assure that selectors have the opportunity to review all the appropriate items, regardless of whose name appeared on the mailing label. Acquisitions units also collect information regarding changes in publishing schedules, new publishers, and new services. Many departments serve as clearinghouses for this type of information for the entire library. Indeed, in larger libraries, the department sometimes operates a limited selective dissemination of information (SDI) system by routing information to selectors based on each individual's subject or area of responsibility. Despite the changing environment, there is no particular reason to change the location of such activities unless there is a major reorganization, and even then the activities ought to be retained in some form somewhere.

Processing requests for materials involves several activities to ensure that the library acquires the needed items as quickly and inexpensively as possible. Libraries would waste time and money if they simply forwarded requests to the appropriate publisher or vendor. Inaccurate information, duplicate requests, unavailable material, and similar problems would generate unacceptable costs for both the library and the supplier (and would probably cause considerable ill will). Each acquisitions department develops its own set of procedures to reduce such problems. Though there are hundreds of variations, the basic process is the same: preorder searching, ordering, receiving, fiscal managing, and recordkeeping.

Acquisitions departments also have internal goals. Four common goals are:

1. To acquire material as quickly as possible.

2. To maintain a high level of accuracy in all work procedures.

3. To keep work processes simple, to achieve the lowest possible unit cost.

4. To develop close, friendly working relationships with other library units and with vendors.

Internal goals are important to the achievement of the broader, library-wide goals, because all of the department's decisions regarding internal goals will have some impact on other operating units in the library.

Speed is a significant factor in meeting user demands and determining user satisfaction. An acquisitions system that requires three or four months to secure items available in local bookstores will create a serious public relations problem. A system that is very fast but has a high error rate will increase operating costs, and will waste time and energy for both departmental staff and suppliers. Studies have shown that, in many medium-sized and large libraries, the costs of acquiring and processing an item are equal to or greater than the price of the item. By keeping procedures simple, and by periodically reviewing workflow, the department can help the library provide better service. Speed, accuracy, and thrift should be the watchwords of acquisitions departments. Certainly, online ordering, electronic invoicing, and credit card payments greatly enhance the speed with which the department can handle much of the traditional paperwork. What has not changed very much is the speed with which items actually arrive. The label "snail mail" is still all too often appropriate for the shipping speed, unless one is willing to pay a premium price for faster service.

Staffing

The rapidly changing electronic environment also has an impact on staff. New technologies and applications put pressure on the staff to quickly learn new skills because the workload seldom decreases and there is a need to maintain a steady flow of materials into the library. Acquisitions is but the first step in the technical services process of making the materials ready for the users. Keeping a flow of materials as even as possible allows other units, such as cataloging, to plan their work more effectively.

One popular label for the technology pressure on staff is *technostress*. Technology pressures exist for all the library staff, not just in acquisitions. Kalin and Clark suggested that:

> The rapid change of technology necessitates a different approach to training. … Staff also have to make a commitment to learn new skills. Training must become an integral part of their work life, not an adjunct.[7]

Given the need for training, as well as time to become reasonably comfortable in using the new skill(s) and have such activities become integral to daily work activities, there is a need to rethink duties. Certainly many of the new technologies and applications make the process of acquisitions less paper-based and in some ways more efficient. Funding sources are more willing to spend money on technology than they are to commit resources to additional positions. What this means is that one must not just move the traditional paper-based methods over to a computer system. One must rethink activities and duties which, more often than not, leads to still more change for the staff to handle. In addition, one must also factor in time for the staff to get training and develop new skills. It is a challenge for all concerned.

Efficient staffing usually involves using four classes of employees: professionals, library media technical assistants (LMTAs), other support staff, and part-time help. Persons in each category supply certain skills and knowledge required for optimum operation of the department.

Librarians provide in-depth knowledge of library operations and the information trade, in all its various guises. They set departmental objectives and goals, prepare operating plans, develop policies, and supervise departmental operations. They also carry out tasks requiring special skills or knowledge, such as negotiating license agreements, monitoring and forecasting possible price increases for budget requests, and working with vendors to secure discounts. If the acquisitions department does not have any selection responsibility (and few do), only the largest departments need to have many professionals. With properly planned procedures, support staff (LMTAs and clerks) can handle a large percentage of the department's activities.

Library media technical assistants are staff who have had some training in librarianship. Many LMTAs are graduates of community college library technician training programs and also hold a bachelor's degree. On the surface, this background appears similar to that of a library school graduate. Acquisitions departments make considerable use of LMTAs in conducting departmental activities. Acquisitions work requires some knowledge of librarianship, yet its structured nature makes it possible to employ LMTAs for most of the work. LMTAs have enough background to perform most functions effectively. Acquisitions typing and filing activities are appropriate for clerical and part-time staff.[8]

Several surveys indicate that this staffing pattern is typical of U.S. libraries. One of the more comprehensive studies was that done by Karen Schmidt.[9] Her data showed that support staff perform at least 75 percent of each of the major acquisitions activities (preorder searching, ordering, claiming, and receiving). Another study, by James Coffey, reviewed personnel costs of library acquisitions. His message was that there is a need to carefully consider staffing patterns when one tries to control the cost of acquisitions work.[10] Similar studies done today would have much the same results, despite the changes brought about by technology.

An interesting aspect of the Schmidt article is her data showing the continuing division of acquisitions and serials work in the majority of the responding libraries.[11] (We did not identify any similar later study, but our sense is that more merged units exist today.) A somewhat dated, but still sound, review of technical service reorganization efforts, including merging acquisitions and serials departments, is by Gomez and Harrell.[12] There is a trend toward merging the departments, as Loyola Marymount University did, when the library installs an integrated automation system. After nine years, we can say with confidence that the merger at LMU works well. (A reflection of the ease of securing funds for collections and technology but not people is found in the LMU acquisitions/serials department. In the nine years since the merger, collections development funds went from just under $400,000 to $1.7 million and went through two generations of automation systems, all without a single new staff member.)

As noted earlier, few acquisitions departments have any selection responsibility. Most libraries divide selection responsibility among all librarians and, in some instances, users. Many large public and research libraries employ full-time subject specialists for collection development work. Even in such libraries, the individuals involved in the process must cover broad subject areas or select materials published in many countries. Chapter 1 outlined the six major collection development functions; each function has many elements. Beyond those basic functions, excluding acquisitions, selectors perform ongoing liaison activities with their primary user groups:

- Review gift and exchange materials
- Review acquisition programs, such as approval plans and standing orders
- Take part in fund allocation discussions

- Conduct various user and circulation studies
- Be involved in deselection decisions
- Plan and implement collection evaluation studies
- Identify needed retrospective materials.

When one adds these duties to other full-time activities, as is typical in most libraries, it is not surprising to find that not all the duties are performed as often as everyone might wish. The result is that some activities receive little attention; deselection and user studies are two areas commonly given less time and effort than is desirable. This chapter covers only the basic functions of the acquisitions department staff (see fig. 11.1).

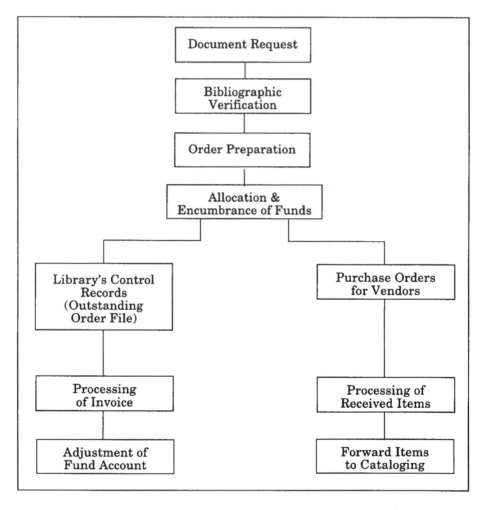

Fig. 11.1. Acquisition process. From *Introduction to Technical Services*, 6th ed., by G. Edward Evans and Sandra M. Heft. Englewood, Colo.: Libraries Unlimited, 1994, p.23.

Before leaving the discussion of staffing, we should provide a few comments about outsourcing, as it has also become a staff stress factor, especially in the area of technical services. If one only read the 1998–1999 literature about library outsourcing, one might think this was a radical departure for libraries. To the degree it is being done to reduce staff ("downsizing" in current management jargon), it is relatively new. However, libraries have outsourced a variety of activities for many years—using jobbers/vendors to consolidate order placement for books and/or serials, for example. When used for what Arnold Hirshon and Barbara Winters labeled "strategic reasons"[13]—that is, to supplement existing staff efforts or to handle ever-increasing workloads without benefit of additional staff—outsourcing can be a useful tool in the acquisitions department.

Acquisitions Processing

Acquisitions departments, merged with serials or not, acquire materials using several methods, each carrying with it somewhat different processing. Essentially, there are eight standard methods of acquisition: firm order, standing order, approval plans, blanket order, subscriptions (for serials departments), leases (increasing in use), gifts, and exchange programs. A *firm order* is the usual method for acquiring many titles that the library *knows* it wants—one or two copies of an item sent to either a vendor or the producer of the item sought. One employs this method when ordering most items requested on a title basis. Ordering directly from the individual producers takes substantially more time than placing an order for a number of titles, from different producers, with a jobber/wholesaler. The major drawback of this method is the time it takes to prepare the individual orders.

Standing orders work best for items that are somewhat serial in nature. That is, they appear on an irregular basis, as an annual or biannually. Some are a numbered or unnumbered series from a publisher that deals with a single subject area. The library places the order for the series/items rather like one places a journal subscription. The supplier (vendor or producer) automatically sends the items as they appear, along with an invoice. *If* the library knows it wants all the items, then a standing order will save staff time and effort due to the automatic shipments. However, especially in academic libraries, standing orders are often the result of one person's request, and if the library does not periodically review its standing orders it may find that the requestor (who may have been the lone user) left the institution years ago. The result is money spent on less useful items. The greatest drawback to standing orders is their unpredictable nature in terms of both number and cost. Certainly there is no problem about numbers for the regular series, but their cost per item may vary. When it comes to publishers' series or irregular series, one may go several years without receiving a title, and then receive several in one year. This is one of the areas where Joyce Ogburn's (see p. 314) prediction skills come into play, as one must "questimate" how much money to set aside at the start of the budget year to cover standing order expenses. Looking at past experience and using an average amount is a safe approach; however, one is seldom able to set aside exactly the right amount. Committing (encumbering) too money much for too long may result in lost opportunities to acquire other useful items. Committing too little can result in having invoices arrive and not having the funds available to pay them. Standing orders are a valuable acquisition method, but one that requires careful monitoring throughout the year.

Approval plans are, in a sense, a variation of the standing order concept. They involve automatic shipment of items to the library from a vendor, along with automatic invoicing after the library accepts the items. The differences are that the approval plan normally covers a number of subject areas and the library has the right to return any items it does not want. Approval plans are usually available from book jobbers, for example Yankee Book Peddler, Academic Book Center, and Coutts. It may be possible to arrange for some type of video- or audiocassette approval program, but we were unaware of any such programs at the time we wrote this chapter. Saving of staff time and effort is one of the major advantages of such plans. Another advantage is the right to return unwanted items; the underlying assumption is that selectors can make better decisions about an item's appropriateness by looking at the item before committing to its purchase. However, research evidence indicates that the approval plan can result in a higher number of very low or no-use items being added to the collection.[14]

The key element in making the approval plan a cost-effective acquisition method is in developing a sound "profile" with the plan vendor. A profile outlines the perimeters of the plan and covers issues such as subjects wanted, levels of treatment (undergraduate, graduate, etc.), countries covered, no reprints, no collections of reprinted articles, and so forth. The greater the time spent in preparing the profile, as well as in monitoring the actual operation of the plan and making adjustments, the greater the value of an approval plan to the library and the acquisitions unit. The monitoring of operations and actually review of items are also an obvious key to success. Given today's staffing situation in most libraries, there is a real danger that the plan will shift from approval to blanket order, simply because the staff has to attend to more pressing duties.

Blanket order is a combination of firm order and approval plan. It is a commitment on the library's part to purchase all of something, usually the output of a publisher, or a limited subject area, or from a country. In the case of a subject area or country, a profile is developed between the library and the blanket order vendor. The materials arrive automatically along with the invoice, thus saving staff time. Another advantage, for country blanket order plans, is that they ensure that the library acquires copies of limited-print-run titles. (It is not uncommon to have very limited print runs of scholarly items in most countries. Waiting for an announcement or a listing in a national bibliography may mean that there are no copies available to purchase.) Like the standing order, the major drawback of blanket order plans is predicting how much money one should reserve to cover the invoices. There is even less predictability with blanket order plans because there are more variables.

We covered subscriptions and leases in earlier chapters (Chapters 7 to 9) and will cover gifts and exchange programs later in this chapter.

Request Processing

The first step in the acquisitions process is to organize the incoming requests. The form of requests ranges from oral requests or a scrawled note on a napkin to a completed formal request card. Eventually, the staff organizes all requests so they can carry out an efficient checking process. Each library will have its own request form, typically a card produced by a library supply firm such as Gaylord or Brodart. Requests arriving in other forms usually are transferred to a request card, making it easier to conduct the necessary searches. Sometimes, when selectors use a trade or national bibliography (such as *Booklist*), they simply check desired items in the publication, and the searchers work with the entire publication rather than transferring everything to request cards. (Despite all the electronic aspects of today's acquisitions work, there is a rather large dependence on paper-based forms. It may be a long time before that dependence disappears.)

Commercially produced request cards cover all the categories of information called for in the *Guidelines for Handling Library Orders for In-Print Monographic Publications*,[15] that is, author, title, publisher, date of publication, edition, ISBN or ISSN, Standard Address Number (SAN), price, and number of copies. Many provide space for other information that is of interest only to libraries, such as requester's name, series, vendor, funding source, and approval signature. For any person not familiar with library or book trade practice, the most confusing item on the request card is the space labeled "date/year." Many nonlibrary requesters often assume that the library wants the date they filled out the form, rather than the items' copyright or publication date. Anyone with acquisitions department experience knows how often this confusion takes place. If the form specifically calls for the date of publication, there will be no problem.

Many patrons request items already in the collection because they do not know how to use the public catalog. People occasionally combine or confuse authors' names, titles, publishers, and so on. Therefore, bibliographic searching is the next step in acquisitions work.

Preorder Work

Bibliographic verification or searching consists of two elements. First is establishing the existence of a particular item, that is, *verification*. Second is establishing whether the library needs to order the item, that is, *searching*. In verification, the concern is with identifying the correct author, title, publisher, and other necessary ordering data. Searching determines whether the library already owns the item (perhaps received, but not yet represented in the public catalog), whether there is a need for a second copy or multiple copies, and whether the item has been ordered but not received. Integrated automated library systems make searching quick and easy, except for determining the need for additional copies. Many systems show ordered and received status in the online public catalog, which tends to reduce the number of requests that duplicate existing orders. (Some vendors are now offering this type of service, for a fee of course. Some vendors may be able to Telnet, or otherwise gain access, to the library's OPAC and determine if the item already appears in the catalog. A potential problem with this is when the library wants a second copy or the item is to be a replacement copy. If a vendor is used for this activity, a system must be in place to handle such situations.)

Where to begin the process? The answer depends on the collection development system employed by the library. Though it is true that all requests require searching, it also is true that not all request cards have sufficient correct information to search accurately. If the majority of information comes from bibliographies, dealers' catalogs, publishers' flyers, or forms filled out by selection personnel, then searching may be the most efficient way to start. A survey by Karen Schmidt of preorder searching indicated that between 30 percent and 40 percent of nonlibrarian requests are duplicates or for items already in the collection.[16] When a large percentage of the selections are from nonlibrarians, it is advisable to start with the verification process.

One of the major activities for preorder searchers is establishing the correct author (main entry). Some selectors, usually nonlibrarians, know little about cataloging rules of entry. Even bibliographers may not keep up-to-date on rule changes. Knowing something about main entry rules, as well as how the standard bibliographic sources list titles, will save search time.

As can be expected, corporate authors, conference papers, proceedings, or transactions are the most troublesome to search. If the department maintains its order files by title rather than main entry order, it may be possible to reduce bibliographic training to a minimum while improving accuracy. Titles generally do not change after publication. However, catalogers' decisions about the proper main entry may change several times between the time of selection and the time the item is on the shelf. Main entry searching requires a greater knowledge of cataloging rules, which, in turn, requires more time for training searchers and more time spent searching.

If the author main entry search procedure does not verify 60 to 90 percent of the items, the staff should review the procedure. It is probable that either the requests lack adequate information (requiring additional education or training of requesters), or the staff is searching the wrong verification tools. A title search should verify most, if not all, the requests that cannot be verified by author main entry. Occasionally, it is impossible to verify an item using the submitted information. All the department can do is contact the requester to try to acquire additional information. If the requestor cannot provide additional information, a subject search may produce a verification. The success rate of subject searches is low for several reasons. First, some bibliographies do not provide subject access, making it impossible to search all the commonly used bibliographies. A more critical reason is that the assignment of subject is somewhat arbitrary. Even with a work in hand, two individuals may well provide two different subject categories for the same title. Searchers must look under as many subjects as seem likely and still can never be certain that they have examined all the appropriate headings. Because of its low success rate, subject verification is a last resort for urgently needed items.

Occasionally, it is necessary to examine three or four sources to establish all of the required order information. One may quickly find the author, title, publisher, date of publication, and price, but it may be difficult to find information determining whether the item is in a series. Failure to identify series information may lead to unwanted duplication; for example, one copy received on a series standing order and another copy from a direct order. *Books in Series* was helpful, but is no longer published. The 1991 edition covered only the United States (37,619 series with more than 326,688 titles).[17] There is no good single source for this information today.

Both verification and searching procedures involve using several bibliographic tools, the major categories of which are described in chapter 4. Book dealers' catalogs are another helpful source (see chapter 12).

There are several files to check when establishing the library's need for an item; this is true whether the file is paper or electronic. The most obvious starting point is the OPAC. A searcher should look first under the assumed main entry; if the results are negative and there is some doubt as to validity of the main entry, then a title search is appropriate. Many librarians suggest that checkers begin with the title, because there tends to be less variation and doubt. In some libraries, even if there is an online public catalog, there may be several other public catalogs to search (for example, special collections or a nonprint catalog), and all should be part of the checking process, if appropriate. Audiovisual materials, government documents, serials, and collections in special locations often are not fully represented in the online system or card catalog. Other public service files that searchers need to examine are those for lost, missing, or damaged items (replacement files). The searcher would not examine all of these files for all items, but merely for those popular items not marked "added copy" or "replacement."

There are files that are unavailable to the public that searchers may have to examine to determine whether the item is already somewhere in the acquisitions/cataloging process. If the library has a manual system, normally there are three files to consult: the in-process file, the verified requests file (items awaiting typing on order forms), and the standing order file. The in-process file represents books on order, books received but not yet sent to cataloging, and books in the cataloging department. The standing order file represents items that will arrive automatically from a supplier, and that may end the search.

Online systems are available in many libraries to speed preorder checking. *Books in Print* is available in both online and CD-ROM formats, as well as in the traditional print version. Other commercial bibliographic selection aids are also available in electronic formats. Bibliographic utilities such as OCLC and RLIN provide large bibliographic databases that are useful in verification and searching. Integrated automation systems have eased the workload on acquisitions. For example, it is possible to download bibliographic data from a bibliographic utility. With some systems, the staff can use the downloaded data to prepare a computer-generated order form, provide an online status report, and create the basis for local cataloging work. In some libraries, a person responsible for preorder activities may be able to do 90 percent or more of the work at one terminal merely by logging on and off the integrated system and the bibliographic utility.

Ordering

We noted earlier in this chapter that libraries employ several acquisitions methods (see p. 319). Each method has a useful role to play in developing a collection in an efficient, cost-effective manner. Today the majority of libraries use computer-generated orders and store the data electronically, thus reducing the volume of paper associated with ordering activities. For a few libraries, there is no order form for current trade books, because the libraries handle the entire order process electronically, storing the transaction in both the library's and the supplier's computers. In the future, this may be the way all libraries place their orders; however, for thousands of libraries, the paperless order is far from reality.

Regardless of the method used to order material, the vendor must receive enough information to assure shipment of the correct materials: author, title, publisher, date of publication, price, edition (if there are various editions), number of copies, order number, and any special instructions regarding invoicing or methods of payment. Also, more suppliers are asking for the International Standard Book Number (ISBN) or International Standard Serial Number (ISSN). In time, International Standard Numbers (ISNs) may be all the library needs to send, because ISNs are unique numbers representing a specific journal or a specific edition of a specific title.

A useful publication for all aspiring collection development officers is *Guidelines for Handling Library Orders for In-Print Monographic Publications.* Prepared by the Book Dealer–Library Relations Committee of the Resources and Technical Services Division of ALA, it reflects the needs of both groups and contains recommendations for establishing and maintaining good working relationships. One suggestion is that libraries use the American National Standards Institute (ANSI) Committee Z39 single-title order form, which measures 3 x 5 inches.

At present, there is no equivalent standard for electronic order transmission; however, ANSI Committee Z39 is working on such a standard, "Computerized Book Ordering Standard."

Another standard of ANSI Committee Z39 is the Standard Address Number (SAN). Like the ISBN, the SAN is a unique number (of seven digits) that identifies each address or organization doing business in the American book trade. For example, the SAN of the Charles Von der Ahe Library at Loyola Marymount University is 332-9135; Brodart is 159-9984; and Libraries Unlimited is 202-6767. Perhaps, in time, all that will be necessary to order a title electronically will be three sets of unique numbers: the ISBN or ISSN and the SANs for the supplier and the buyer. Again, such ease of ordering will take some time off the process, if it ever becomes reality. Nevertheless, these unique numbers are useful as a cross-check for accuracy. Keys to SANs appear in a variety of sources, such as the *American Library Directory*, which includes library SANs in its entries.

With a manual system, libraries commonly use a multiple-copy order form for placing orders. (Almost any computer-based acquisition system handles all of the following tasks with little or no paper.) These forms are available in a number of formats and contain from four to as many as twelve copies. The 3-x-5-inch size is standard in the United States. Normally, each copy is a different color, for easy identification. There is no standard dictating a particular color for a certain purpose. A minimum of four copies is typical: (1) outstanding order copy, (2) dealer's copy, (3) claiming copy, and (4) accounting copy. Only the librarians' imagination limits the number of potential uses of additional copies. A few libraries still use ten copies. Some libraries mail two copies to the dealer and keep three or four in the in-process file. In some larger systems, where selectors are not in close contact with the acquisitions department (as in research libraries, where faculty members do much of the selecting), an information copy goes to the selector.

The in-process file may contain several copies of the order form. For example, after sending the order, the staff might place five copies in the in-process file. One copy represents on-order status, two are available for possible claims, one is forwarded to cataloging with the item when it arrives, and the final one remains in the file, indicating that the item is being processed but is not yet ready for public use. Upon receipt, a staff member pulls all slips except the in-process slip. When the item is ready for circulation, the cataloging department returns a slip to acquisitions to prompt the removal of the in-process slip. Presumably, at this point a set of entries are in the public catalog indicating that the item is available for use.

Claiming and handling supplier reports is one of the more time-consuming and frustrating aspects of the order function. Most multiple-copy order forms have slips for these purposes. Purchasers have every reason to expect American commercial publishers, or vendors supplying titles from such publishers, to deliver or report on the status of the order within 90 days. For American noncommercial publishers (for example, university presses or professional associations), an additional 30 days (120 days total) is common for delivery or a report. Western European titles delivered to the United States normally require 180 days, but for items from countries with a developing book trade, a year or more is not uncommon. When there is an active collecting program from developing countries, one must expect a certain percentage of nonresponse. Learning how long to wait for delivery or a status report takes experience.

When dealing with an American publisher, allowing for the normal two-way postal time, it is reasonable to send a second claim in 60 days, if there has been no response. Many order forms have a printed note stating "cancel after x days." Although such statements are legally binding, most libraries send a separate cancellation notice. Certainly, cancellation should not take place until after the normal response time passes, unless there are unusual circumstances, such as unexpected reductions in the budget. Unfortunately, over the past 20 years, many such cuts have taken place, and most vendors have been cooperative about making the adjustments. By establishing a regular cancellation timeline, libraries that must expend funds within a fixed period can avoid or reduce the last-minute scramble of canceling outstanding orders and ordering materials that the vendor can deliver in time to use the funds.

Vendors should respond with a meaningful report when they cannot fill an order within a reasonable period. One less-than-helpful report that vendors did and occasionally still do use is "temporarily out of stock" (TOS). How long is "temporarily"? What has the vendor done to secure the item? Poor or inaccurate reporting costs the library money, as Audrey Eaglen pointed out in "Trouble in Kiddyland: The Hidden Costs of O.P. and O.S."[18] In periods of rapid inflation, each day the funds remain committed but unexpended erodes buying power, because producers and suppliers raise prices without notice. Recommended vendor reports are "not yet received from publisher" (NYR); "out-of-stock, ordering" (OS, ordering); "claiming"; "canceled"; "not yet published" (NYP); "out-of-stock, publisher" (OS, publisher); "out-of-print" (OP); "publication canceled"; "out-of-stock indefinitely" (treat this one as a cancellation); "not our publication" (NOP); "wrong title supplied"; "defective copy"; and "wrong quantity supplied." After one learns how long a vendor takes to supply items first reported in the recommended manner, it is possible to make an informed decision regarding when to cancel and when to wait for delivery.

Before placing an order, the staff must make three important decisions:

1. Which acquisition method to use.

2. What vendor to use.

3. Where to get the money.

The remainder of this chapter explores the methods of acquiring materials. Chapter 12 discusses vendors—when and how to use them and what to expect from them. Chapter 13 covers the fiscal side of acquisitions work.

For most current items, the firm order is the only logical method to use. It is often the best method for the first volume in a series, even if the selectors are thinking about ordering all the items in the series. There is a distinction between "thinking about" and "planning on" when considering series items. When the selectors know that the reputation of the publisher or editor of the series is sound, it is probably best to place a standing order. If there is some question about suitability or content of the series, a firm order or approval copy order for the first volume is the better choice. In late 1993, there were a number of e-mail messages on one of the collection development discussion lists regarding an article in *Lingua Franca* about a publisher that appears to be a vanity house but markets books as part of a series.[19] Getting to know publishers and editors is an important activity for selectors.

Deciding to use the gift or deposit method of acquisition will almost always result in a long delay in receiving the desired item. Verification may establish that the item is a government publication that is part of the library's depository program, or it may be a new government series that should become part of the program. In either case, one would not issue a firm order, but would notify the requester so he or she can decide what to do. Sometimes a library user or board member donates certain materials on a regular basis, making it unnecessary to order the item if there is no immediate demand for the material. Occasionally, an appropriate series or set costs so much that a library cannot buy it with regular funding sources. Seeking out a donor to assist with funding or to pay for the purchase is not unheard of, but again, there may be substantial delays in acquiring the item. Most often, this takes place with rare books and special collections items. An active (and well-to-do) Friends of the Library group may be the answer to a special-purchase situation. Friends groups, used judiciously, can significantly expand the collection and stretch funds.

Gifts and Deposits

Usually, acquisitions departments are the ultimate recipients of unsolicited gifts of books, serials, and other materials (including a variety of molds and insects) that well-meaning people give to the library. Both solicited and unsolicited gifts can be a source of out-of-print materials for replacement, extra copies, and the filling of gaps in the collection. The collection development policy statement on gifts will help acquisitions personnel process the material quickly. A good article outlining all aspects of handling gifts is Mary Bostic's "Gifts to Libraries: Coping Effectively."[20] Another excellent survey of both gift and exchange programs, by Steven Carrico,[21] covers all management aspects of the work.

Reviewing gifts is important, as a library cannot afford to discard valuable or needed items that arrive as gifts. However, one must keep in mind the fact that a library should not add unnecessary items just because they were "free." Processing and storage costs are the same for a gift as for a purchased item. Older books require careful checking, as variations in printings and editions may determine whether an item is valuable or worthless. (Usually, a second or third printing is less valuable than the first printing of a work.) Searching must be done by persons with extensive training and experience in bibliographic checking.

There are some legal aspects about gifts that staff must be aware of. Essentially, these issues are related to tax deductions and Internal Revenue Service regulations, which we address in chapter 18 on legal issues. At a minimum, staff should make a count of the gift items, noting hardcover, softcover, and, if magazines are included, the number of issues and if any are bound. Beyond the minimum, there are several steps to take, which we cover in chapter 18.

There are two basic types of exchange activity: the exchange of unwanted duplicate materials, and the exchange of new materials between libraries. Usually, only large research libraries engage in exchanging new materials. In essence, cooperating institutions trade institutional publications. Tozzer Library (Harvard University's anthropology library) has exchange agreements with several hundred organizations. These organizations send their publications to Tozzer which, in turn, sends them Peabody Museum publications. Often this method is the only way a library can acquire an organization's publications. Occasionally, libraries use this system to acquire materials from countries in which there are commercial trade restrictions. Where government trade restrictions make buying and selling of foreign publications difficult or impossible, the cooperating libraries acquire (buy) their local publications for exchange. Exchanges of this type are complex and difficult to manage, and this is a method of last resort. Libraries can exercise better quality control when they trade for known organizational series or titles than when the choice of publications from the organization is more or less left to chance. Exchanges of this type exist on the basis of formal agreements between the cooperating organizations. They play an important role in developing comprehensive subject collections.

Libraries normally add only a small percentage of gifts to the collection. This means that the library must dispose of a great many unwanted items. In some libraries, a separate unit handles unneeded material; this unit usually is called the *exchange unit*. In most cases, the gift unit handles disposal work.

Disposition of unwanted gift materials is an activity that almost every library engages in at some time. One method is to list the unwanted items and mail the list to exchange units in other libraries; the first library to request an item gets it for the shipping cost (usually book-rate postage). This method is time-consuming. Another method is to arrange with an out-of-print dealer to take the items, usually as a lot rather than for a per-item price. It is unusual to receive cash; instead, the dealer gives the library a line of credit. The library uses the credit to acquire materials from the dealer.

This system works well when the library has specialized materials the dealer wants and when the dealer stocks enough useful material that the library can use its credit within a reasonable time (less than 18 to 24 months). Holding a book sale is yet another method of disposing of unwanted material, one that is gaining in popularity as dealers resist the credit memo system. However, this is not a "free" venture, as staff must select the items for sale, establish a fair price, find a suitable location, and monitor the sale. Depending on the volume of gifts, annual, semiannual, or monthly sales are appropriate. Sales can be an excellent Friends of the Library project that can save some staff time. A few libraries use an ongoing sale tactic, especially when they have limited staff and space and a high volume of unwanted gifts. There is, as one might expect, a Web site devoted to listing book sales (<http://www.book-sales-in-america.com>).

Order Placement and Receiving

After selecting a vendor, a staff member assigns an order number and decides which fund to use for payment. Order numbers assist the staff in tracking the order. The assignment process is simply a matter of checking the last order number and using the next number in the sequence. As soon as the department head signs the orders, they are ready for mailing.

Receiving orders, though not difficult, requires careful planning. If not handled properly, receiving can be more complex and time-consuming than ordering. As strange as it may seem, proper unpacking of shipments will save everyone in the department a great deal of time, energy, and frustration. Finding the packing slip or invoice is the key first step in the process. A *packing slip* lists all the items in a particular shipment. An *invoice* is an itemized bill, which business offices require before they will issue a voucher or check. For receivers' convenience, most vendors attach a clearly marked envelope containing the packing slip to the outside of one of the boxes. Unfortunately, a few vendors seem to delight in hiding the slip in strange places. One technique is to enclose the slip inside one of the items, and another favorite hiding place is under a cardboard bottom liner on the bottom of the box. If no packing slip is found, it is essential to keep the items separated from other materials in the receiving area. Mixing shipments can create seemingly endless problems.

A second important step is to check each item against the packing slip as it comes out of the box. This serves as a check on what the shippers think they sent against what the library actually received. After all, boxes go astray in shipment, shipping room clerks overlook items, and sometimes, items disappear from the library before processing. Checking the physical condition of each item is another step in the receiving process. Defective materials may be returned for credit or replacement without prior approval from the vendor. Imperfections can be of many kinds. With books, typical problems are missing or blank pages or improperly collated texts. Staff members need to check audiotapes and videotapes for gaps, blank or fogged sections, and proper recording speed. Microforms must be examined to assure that the producer processed them properly; sometimes they have fogged, streaked, or spotted areas, and occasionally there is hypo (developing solution) residue, which can ruin the film. The following list highlights some common receipt problems:

- The wrong edition sent. (*Note:* The checker must be aware of the difference between an edition and a printing. A new edition means that there are substantial changes—material added or deleted; a new printing merely indicates that the publisher sold out the previous printing and reprinted more copies with no changes in the text.)
- Items ordered but not received.
- Items not ordered but shipped.
- Too many or not enough copies sent.
- Imperfect copies received.

Vendors usually are good about accepting returns of unwanted items, even when it turns out to have been the fault of the library—as long as the library has not property-marked them.

After determining that the shipment is complete, property marking (such as stamping or embossing) takes place. As noted earlier, sometimes items disappear, so the sooner property marking takes place the more difficult it will be for materials to vanish without a trace. Property marking takes many forms. Stamping the fore edge and the title page of books is a common practice. (Rare books are handled differently.) Another method is to *accession* items, that is, to give each item a unique number. A staff member records the number and title of the item in an accessions book. Today, linking the barcode in an item to its item record in a database accomplishes the same type of inventory control with much less effort.

The last step in processing is approving the invoice for payment. Normally, this requires the signature of the head of the department or that person's representative. Usually, only a completely filled order may be approved for payment. The library bookkeeper passes the approved invoice on to the agency that actually issues the check. Rarely does a library itself write such checks; it is done by the governing agency.

Serials Processing

To a large extent, the preceding material applies to intake of serials. We covered many of the processing issues—check-in and claiming, for example—in the serials chapters. However, we do want to point out that e-serials are an example of how technology changes the process of acquisitions. Ellen Duranceau's excellent article spelled out the differences between print and electronic serials acquisitions.[22] Her major points are that more teamwork is required, more higher-level personnel are involved, it takes more time because it is not a linear process (in most cases), and it requires input from legal and technical staff that may not be part of the library staff. Further, she noted that the concept of "Til Forbidden" does not work well for e-serials, as producers and aggregators change the "product" all the time, even during a subscription period.

Future Developments

What about the future of automated acquisition systems? One does not have to be a prophet to predict greater growth in the functionality of the systems. Furthermore, it is likely that in our lifetime the technical service aspects of the hypothetical total library system will exist with a national online bibliographic database. Steps are being taken in that direction, and some movement has been made toward an international system. The merger of OCLC and the Western Library Network is but one example of the trend toward an ever-larger integrated bibliographic database. Such trends will make the work of searching for retrospective materials much easier and more efficient.

Undoubtedly, hardware and software technology, especially in the area of small, relatively inexpensive home computer systems, will make it increasingly possible for the smallest libraries to benefit from technology, as well as to tie into regional and national systems. The idea that all homes and offices will have terminals that connect to a library's online catalog is no longer a daydream. With each new subsystem bringing the total integrated library system closer to reality, collection development can become more effective and efficient. But, despite the marvels of technology, there will always have to be intelligent, widely read, humanistic, and service-oriented information professionals making the decisions and planning the systems.

Summary

This chapter touched on only the basic activities and problems in acquisitions work. The following three chapters cover vendors and suppliers, fiscal management related to collection development, and an overview of how materials are removed from collections once they have outlived their usefulness.

Notes

1.   S. R. Ranganathan, *The Five Laws of Library Science* (Bangalore, India: Sarada Ranganathan Endowment for Library Science, 1988), 326.

2.   Alex Bloss, "The Value-Added Acquisition Librarian: Defining Our Role in a Time of Change," *Library Acquisitions: Practice and Theory* 19 (Fall 1995): 321–30.

3.   Ron L. Ray, "Where Is the Future of Acquisitions Expertise Written in the Future of Libraries?," *Journal of Academic Librarianship* 24 (January 1998): 80–82.

4.   Carol Diedrichs, "Acquisitions: So What and Where?," *Journal of Academic Librarianship* 24 (January 1998): 74.

5.   Joyce L. Ogburn, "T2: Theory in Acquisition Revisited," *Library Acquisitions: Practice and Theory* 21 (Summer 1997): 168.

6.   Ray, "Where Is the Future of Acquisitions Expertise," 82.

7.   Sally Kalin and Katie Clark, "Technostressed Out?," *Library Journal* 121 (August 1996): 32.

8. The details regarding support staff acquisition duties are discussed in G. Edward Evans and Sandra Heft, *Introduction to Library Technical Services,* 6th ed. (Englewood, Colo.: Libraries Unlimited, 1994).

9. Karen Schmidt, "Acquisition Process in Research Libraries," *Library Acquisitions: Practice and Theory* 11, no. 1 (1987): 35–44.

10. James Coffey, "Identifying Personnel Costs in Acquisitions," in *Operational Costs in Acquisitions,* edited by J. Coffey (New York: Haworth Press, 1990), 55–74.

11. Schmidt, "Acquisition Process in Research Libraries."

12. Joni Gomez and Jeanne Harrell, "Technical Services Reorganization: Realities and Reactions," *Technical Services Quarterly* 10, no. 2 (1992): 1–15.

13. Arnold Hirshon and Barbara Winters, *Outsourcing Library Services: A How-to-Do-It Manual* (New York: Neal-Schuman, 1996).

14. G. Edward Evans, "Book Selection and Book Collection Usage in Academic Libraries," in *Library Quarterly* 40 (July 1970): 297–308; G. Edward Evans, "Approval Plans and Collection Development in Academic Libraries," *Library Resources & Technical Services* 18 (Winter 1974): 35–50.

15. *Guidelines for Handling Library Orders for In-Print Monographic Publications,* 2d ed. (Chicago: American Library Association, 1984).

16. Karen Schmidt, "Cost of Pre-Order Searching," in *Operational Costs in Acquisitions*, edited by J. Coffey (New York: Haworth Press, 1990), 5–20.

17. *Books in Series* (New York: R. R. Bowker, 1991).

18. Audrey Eaglen, "Trouble in Kiddyland: The Hidden Costs of O.P. and O.S.," *Collection Building* 6 (Summer 1984): 26–28.

19. Warren St. John, "Vanity's Fare: The Peripatetic Professor and His Peculiarly Profitable Press," *Lingua Franca* 3 (September/October 1993): 1, 22–25, 62.

20. Mary Bostic, "Gifts to Libraries: Coping Effectively," *Collection Management* 14, nos. 3/4 (1991): 175–84.

21. Steven Carrico, "Gifts and Exchanges," in *Business of Acquisitions*, 2d ed., edited by K. Schmidt (Chicago: American Library Association, 1999).

22. Ellen F. Duranceau, "Beyond Print: Revisioning Serials Acquisitions for the Digital Age," *Serials Librarian* 33, nos. 1/2 (1998): 83–106.

Selected Websites and Discussion Lists*

"Acquisitions, Serials, and Collection Development." From the *Internet Library for Librarians.*
<http://www.itcompany.com/inforetriever/acqsercd.htm>.

ACQNET.
<mailto: acqnet-l@listserv.appstate.edu>.

ACQWEB.
<http://www.library.vanderbilt.edu/law/acqs/html>.

Association for Library Collections and Technical Services: Acquisitions Section:
Statement on Principles and Standards of Acquisitions Practice.
<http://venus.twu.edu/~f_bohannan/techservices/acquisitions.htm>.

Back Issues & Exchange Services.
<http://www.uvm.edu/%7ebmaclenn/backexch.html>.

BACKMED.
<mailto:listserv@sun.blackwells.com>.

BACKSERV.
<mailto:listserv@sun.readmore.com>.

EUROBACK.
<mailto:euroback@lists.ulg.ac.be>.

"Resources for Acquisitions Librarians."
<http://venus.twu.edu/~f_bohannan/techservices/acquisitions.htm>.

SERIALST.
<mailto:serialst@listuvm.edu>.

*These sites were accessed 15 October 1999.

Further Reading

General

Alldredge, N. S. "Doing Business in the West." *Library Acquisitions: Practice and Theory* 15, no. 1 (1991): 21–27.

American Library Association. *Acquisitions Guidelines Series.* Nos. 1–10. Chicago: American Library Association, 1994.

———. Association for Library Collections and Technical Services. *Statement of Standards and Principles of Acquisitions Practice*. Chicago: American Library Association, 1994.

Baker, J. W. "Acquisitions Principles and the Future of Acquisitions." *Library Acquisitions: Practice and Theory* 17, no. 1 (1993): 23–32.

Buis, Edward. "Killing Us with Kindness or What to Do with Those Gifts." *Collection Building* 11, no. 2 (1991): 10–12.

Bushing, M. C. "Acquisitions Ethics." *Library Acquisitions: Practice and Theory* 17, no. 1 (1993): 47–52.

Cargille, D. "Acquisitions and Collection Development." *Library Acquisitions: Practice and Theory* 20 (Spring 1996): 41–47.

Case, Beau David. "Approval Plan Evaluation Studies." *Against the Grain* 8, no. 4 (1996): 18–21, 24.

Conant, Roy B. "Libraries Are Businesses: Not! A Citizens Response." *Library Acquisitions: Practice and Theory* 215, no. 2 (1997): 158–59.

Dickinson, Dennis W. "Free Books: Are They Worth What They Cost?" *Library Issues: Briefings for Faculty and Administrators* 17 (May 1997): 1–4.

Dilys, E. Morris, et al. "Monographs Acquisitions: Staffing Costs and the Impact of Automation." *Library Resources & Technical Services* 40 (October 1996): 301–18.

Dugger, L. J. "Fundamentals of Acquisitions." *Serials Review* 23, no. 3 (1997): 85–87.

Fisher, W. "Libraries Are Businesses." *Library Acquisitions: Practice and Theory* 215, no. 2 (1997): 151–55.

Forsyth, J. H. "Monitoring a Business Approval Plan for Balance and Numbers." *Library Acquisitions* 22, no. 3 (Fall 1998): 335–40.

Kennedy, G. A. "Relationships Between Acquisitions and Collection Development." *Library Acquisitions: Practice and Theory* 7, no. 3 (1983): 225–32.

Miller, H. S. "Monographic Series Approval Plan: An Attempt to Refine Purchasing of Books in Series." *Library Resources & Technical Services* 42 (April 1998): 133–39.

Ogburn, Joyce L. "An Introduction to Outsourcing Library Acquisitions." *Library Acquisitions: Practice and Theory* 18, no. 4 (1994): 363–416.

———. "Theory in Acquisitions: Defining the Principles Behind Practice." *Library Acquisitions: Practice and Theory* 17, no. 1 (1993): 33–40.

O'Neill, A. L. "Evaluating the Success of Acquisitions Departments." *Library Acquisitions: Practice and Theory* 16, no. 3 (1992): 209–19.

———. "How Richard Abel Co., Inc., Changed the Way We Work." *Library Acquisitions: Practice and Theory* 17, no. 1 (1993): 41–46.

Samore, T. *Acquisition of Foreign Materials for U.S. Libraries.* 2d ed. Metuchen, N.J.: Scarecrow Press, 1982.

Saunders, L. M. "Transforming Acquisitions to Support Virtual Libraries." *Information Technology and Libraries* 14, no. 1 (March 1995): 41–46.

Schmidt, K. A., ed. *Business of Library Acquisitions.* 2d ed. Chicago: American Library Association, 1999.

Vickery, J. E. "Library Acquisitions 1986–1995: A Select Bibliography." *Collection Management* 22, nos. 1/2 (1997): 101–86.

Academic

Archer, J. D. "Preorder Searching in Academic Libraries." *Library Acquisitions: Practice and Theory* 7, no. 2 (1983): 139–44.

Atkinson, R. "Acquisitions Librarian as Change Agent in the Transition to the Electronic Library." *Library Resources & Technical Services* 39 (January 1992): 7–20.

Association of Research Libraries. *Gifts and Exchange Function in ARL Libraries.* Washington, D.C.: Association of Research Libraries, 1997.

Bucknall, C. "Mass Buying Programs." In *Collection Management: A New Treatise.* Edited by C. B. Osburn and R. Atkinson, 337–50. Greenwich, Conn.: JAI Press, 1991.

Diodato, L. W., and V. P. Diodato. "Use of Gifts in a Medium-Sized Academic Library." *Collection Management* 5 (Summer 1983): 53–71.

Hewitt, J. A. "On the Nature of Acquisitions." *Library Resources & Technical Services* 33 (April 1989): 105–22.

Jasper, R. P. "Challenge, Change, and Confidence: The Literature of Acquisitions." *Library Resources & Technical Services* 36 (July 1992): 263–75.

Ladizesky, K., and R. Hogg. "To Buy or Not to Buy—Questions About the Exchange of Publications Between the Former Soviet Bloc Countries and the West in the 1990s." *Journal of Librarianship and Information Science* 30 (September 1998): 185–93.

Pritchard, S. M. "Foreign Acquisitions." In *Collection Management: A New Treatise.* Edited by C. B. Osburn and R. Atkinson, 351–72. Greenwich, Conn.: JAI Press, 1991.

Walpole, M. G. "The Meta-Exchange Pilot Project: A New Way to Organize Book Exchanges with Russia." *Library of Congress Information Bulletin* 58 (February 1999): 21+.

Zager, P. A., and O. A. Samadi. "A Knowledge-Based Expert Systems Application in Library Acquisitions." *Library Acquisitions* 16, no. 2 (1992): 145–54.

Public

Bullard, S. R. "Acquisitions-Ache and Its Relief." *American Libraries* 18 (November 1987): 857–60.

Gambles, B. R. "Which Supplier?" *Public Library Journal* 6 (November/December 1991): 153–56.

Hoffert, B. "Paperback Bind." *Library Journal* 116 (July 1991): 51–55.

McLachlan, R. W. "Public Libraries—Shrinking Dollars, Increased Demands." *OCLC Micro* 7 (December 1991): 19–22.

Montgomery, J. G. "Issues in Public Library Acquisitions." *Library Acquisitions* 22, no. 2 (1998): 206–7.

Steinbrenner, J. "Cost-Effectiveness of Book Rental Plans." *Ohio Library Association Bulletin* 49 (April 1979): 5–6.

Strand, Benita. "How to Look a Gift Horse in the Mouth, or How to Tell People You Can't Use Their Old Junk." *Collection Management* 14, no.2 (1995): 29–30.

Vertrees, L. S. "Foreign Acquisitions: Frustration and Fun!" In *Vendors and Library Acquisitions*, edited by W. Katz, 75–81. New York: Haworth Press, 1991.

School

Bertland, Linda. "Circulation Analysis as a Tool for Collection Development." *School Media Quarterly* 19 (Winter 1991): 91–93.

Brodie, C. S. "Promotional 'Hotlines.' " *School Library Media Activities Monthly* 7 (April 1991): 42–44.

Kemp, B. *School Library and Media Center Acquisitions Policies and Procedures.* 2d ed. Phoenix, Ariz.: Oryx Press, 1986.

"Ordering Procedures." In *Media Program in the Elementary and Middle Schools,* edited by J. J. Delaney, 126–44. Hamden, Conn.: Shoe String Press, 1976.

Pretorius, M. "Strengthen Your Buying Power Through Reviews." *Ohio Media Spectrum* 42 (Spring 1990): 18–22.

Roback, D. E. "Checking out Children's Books." *Publishers Weekly* 238 (May 31, 1991): 38–39.

Tucker, C. "Selection Power." *Ohio Media Spectrum* 42 (Spring 1990): 26–29.

Special

Ali, S. N. "Acquisition of Scientific Literature in Developing Countries." *Information Development* 5 (April 1989): 151–68.

Byrne, N. "Selection and Acquisition in an Art School Library." *Library Acquisitions: Practice and Theory* 7, no. 1 (1983): 7–11.

Cooper, E. R. "Options for the Disposal of Unwanted Donations." *Bulletin of the Medical Library Association* 78 (October 1990): 388–94.

Dickson, L. E. "Law Library Book Orders." *Law Library Journal* 73 (Spring 1980): 446–50.

Moore, E. "Acquisitions in the Special Library." *Scholarly Publishing* 13 (January 1982): 167–73.

Myers, A. K. "Acquiring Minds Want to Know." *Law Library Journal* 83 (Summer 1991): 479–91.

St. Clair, G., and J. Treadwell. "Science and Technology Approval Plans." *Library Resources & Technical Services* 33 (October 1989): 82–92.

Schaffer, E. G. "Georgetown University's Developing Foreign Law Policy." *Legal Reference Service Quarterly* 9, nos. 1/2 (1989): 121–26.

Wineburgh-Freed, M., et al. "Library-Wide Use of a dBase Acquisition System." *Bulletin of the Medical Library Association* 76 (January 1988): 73–74.

12
Distributors and Vendors

Like all other organizations involved in the information business, library vendors and distributors are facing a changing environment, in large measure due to technology. Another factor in their changing environment is what has been happening to the majority of libraries; the past 20 years or so have not been the best of times for library funding and support in general. Library staffs are under pressure to do more with less, including personnel. Because they want to continue to do business with libraries, as well as take advantage of new business opportunities, many vendors and suppliers are offering a wider range of services to libraries. This is one of the places for libraries to consider outsourcing some of their traditional in-house activities. We mention a few of these new "services" later in this chapter.

In chapter 5, we identified three major problems for materials producers: economics, copyright infringement, and distribution. Knowledge of the information product distribution system is essential for developing the most cost-effective collection of information materials. Wholesalers, retailers, and remainder houses are major sources of material for the library collection. Often, several different sources can supply the same item. Is there an important difference among these sources? What services does each provide? For example, if one is looking for a book published last year, it is possible to acquire a copy from many of the sources. Would it matter which source is used? How likely is it that all would have the book? For that matter, what function does each source perform?

Jobbers and Wholesalers

Librarians refer to *jobbers* or *vendors* rather than wholesalers. There is a technical difference between a wholesaler and a jobber,[1] but for libraries, the difference is insignificant. Jobbers purchase quantities of books from various publishers, then sell the copies to bookstores and libraries. Because they buy in volume, they receive a substantial discount from publishers.

When the jobber sells a book, the purchaser receives a discount off the producer's list price, but it is much lower than the discount that the jobber received. For instance, if the jobber received a 40 percent discount from the producer, the discount given the library will be 15 to 20 percent. If the library or bookstore orders the book directly from the publisher, the discount may be just as high or perhaps even higher.

Discounting is a complex issue in any commercial activity, and it is highly complex in the book trade. Every producer has a discount schedule that is slightly different, if not unique. Some items are *net* (no discount); usually, these are textbooks, science/technology/medical (STM) titles, or items of limited sales appeal. *Short discounts* are normally 20 percent; these are items the producers expect will have limited appeal, but with more potential than the net titles. *Trade discounts* range from 30 to 60 percent or more; items in this category are high-demand items or high-risk popular fiction. Publishers believe that by giving a high discount for fiction, bookstores will stock more copies and thus help promote the title. Jobbers normally receive 40 to 50 percent discounts, primarily because of their high-volume orders (hundreds of copies per title rather than the tens that most libraries and independent bookstore owners order).

Recently, jobbers have encountered financial problems in the form of rising costs and declining sales. A number of publishers are requiring prepayment or have placed jobbers on a *pro forma* status. Pro forma status requires prepayment, and suppliers extend credit on the basis of the current performance in payment of bills. Much of the credit and order fulfillment extended by publishers depends on an almost personal relationship with a jobber. This means that libraries must select a jobber with care. It is not inappropriate to check a prospective jobber's financial status (through a rating service, such as Dun & Bradstreet).

One very pertinent question for the library is how many vendors to use. There are pros and cons to consolidating one's business with only one or two vendors, just as there are to using a number of vendors for the same type of product. Consolidation usually means that the vendor gains a better sense of the library's requirements, perhaps a better discount for the library and some "free" services from the vendor. The primary danger is the vendor's viability. Today's environment requires substantial investment in technology on a regular basis, which, combined with libraries' budget woes, means that smaller firms may not be able to survive—or at the least not be able to keep up with technological developments in the field. In contrast, having several vendors for one type of product may also yield a higher discount, because there is a degree of competition for the library's business. On the downside, the service may not be as good, and perhaps the vendors will not have the resources to invest in newer technology. The primary concern should be service followed by financial strength (serials librarians may recall the scare that occurred when a major serials vendor had a serious financial problem). As stated earlier, privately held companies can be checked in a service such as Dun & Bradstreet, and publicly held firms file 10K reports that one can see.

What Can Jobbers Do?

Why buy from an indirect source that charges the same or a higher price than the direct source would? Service! Jobbers provide an important service in that they can save a library a significant amount of time and money. Although jobbers do not give high discounts, the time saved by placing a single order for 10 different titles from 10 different publishers (instead of 10 different orders) more than pays for the slightly higher price. Other savings can result from the batch effect of unpacking only one box and authorizing only one payment. Most jobbers also promise to provide fast, accurate service. It is true that a few publishers, if they accept single-copy orders (and most do), handle these orders more slowly than they do large orders. But it is also true that jobbers do not always have a specific title when the library wants it, which means that the library must allow additional time to secure the desired item.

Many jobbers promise 24-hour shipment of items in stock. Do they make good on such claims? Generally, yes; however, the key phrase is *in stock*. Frequently, there can be delays of three to four months in receiving a complete order because some titles are not in stock. When talking with jobbers, do not be impressed by numbers quoted in their advertising, for example, "more than 2 million books in stock." What is important is how many titles and which publishers they stock. For various reasons, from economic to personal, some publishers refuse to deal with a particular jobber. Four important questions to ask any jobber before a library contracts for that firm's services are:

1.   Will you give me a list of all the publishers that you do not handle?

2.   How does your firm handle a request for a title not in stock?

3.   Will you give me a list of series that your firm does not handle?

4.   Do you have any service charges on any category of material? (If so, ask if the charge is indicated on the invoice as a separate cost.)

Often the answer to the first question is difficult to obtain. Sales representatives want to say they can supply any title from any publisher, with only minor exceptions. However, libraries in the same system may simultaneously receive different lists from various representatives of the same firm. The issue is important, and the acquisitions department must resolve the question if it is to operate effectively. Sending an order for a title from a publisher that the jobber cannot handle only delays matters. In some cases, the jobber will report that it is trying to secure the item; this often leads to a later report of failure, making the acquisition process even slower. Buying directly from the publisher is the best approach to this problem, if one knows which publishers the jobber cannot handle.

The second question relates to the speed of service. Some jobbers order a single title from a publisher when it is not in stock. Others say they will do this, but they may actually wait until they have received multiple requests before placing the order. By placing a multiple-copy order, the jobber receives a better discount. For the library, the delay may be one to several months, because it will take that long for the jobber to accumulate enough individual requests for the title to make up an order of sufficient size. Usually, jobbers that place single-copy orders for a customer offer a lower discount on those items. Again, the acquisitions staff must weigh service and speed against discount. Occasionally, a jobber will have a title in stock after the publisher has listed the item as out-of-print (OP). On occasion, a jobber can supply out-of-print material, and a few jobbers will even try to find out-of-print items for their best customers. This is a special service that is never advertised and is offered only to favored customers.

Beyond fast, accurate service, jobbers should provide personal service. A smooth working relationship is based on mutual understanding and respect. When those are present, it is much easier to solve problems, even the difficult ones. The jobber, because of the smaller base of customers, normally can provide answers more quickly than a publisher's customer service department. Even the small-account customer receives a jobber's careful attention (in order to hold the account), something that seldom happens with publishers.

No single jobber can stock all of the in-print items that a library will need. However, most large firms do carry the high-demand current and backlist items. Book trade folklore says that 20 percent of the current and backlist titles represent 80 percent of total sales. All of the good jobbers try to stock the right 20 percent of titles. Some are more successful than others. Bookstores find this useful for maintaining their stock of bestsellers. Libraries, however, must acquire a broader range of titles. Thus, the opinion of bookstore owners about the best jobbers is useful only if librarians and bookstores agree about whether 20 percent of all titles will fill 80 percent of all needs.

One problem with a jobber that has limited stock is in invoicing and billing procedures. A small jobber may ship and bill for those items in stock, then backorder the remainder of the titles. In this case, the jobber expects to receive payment for the partial fulfillment of the order. However, some funding authorities allow payment only for complete orders. That is, the library must receive or cancel every item on an order before the business office will issue a check. This procedure can cause problems for small jobbers and libraries alike. Few small vendors are able or willing to wait for payment until a particular order is complete. For small libraries with small materials budgets, the challenge is to find a jobber that will accept complicated procedures and delays despite low volume. It is becoming harder to find such firms, and libraries are attempting to persuade their funding authorities to simplify ordering and payment procedures.

Jobbers may handle thousands of different publishers and may maintain an inventory of more than 200,000 titles. One useful service that many large jobbers offer is a periodic report on the status of all of a library's orders. Many provide a monthly report on all items not yet shipped. They provide a list of backordered items along with the reason why each item is unavailable. A timely and complete status report will save both library and jobber unnecessary letter-writing campaigns and telephone calls. Most large jobbers offer a flexible order and invoicing system; that is, they try to adapt to the library's needs, rather than force the library to use their methods.

Status reports are an area of concern for both the acquisitions and collection development staff. Almost everyone in the field has been frustrated by these reports. Does a report stating that a book is out of print mean that the book is *really* out of print? It should, but occasionally, by contacting the publisher, the library may have the item in hand in less than 30 days. This happens often enough to keep alive doubts about the quality of jobber reports. Perhaps two of the most frustrating reports are out-of-stock (OS) and temporarily out-of-stock (TOS) reports. Exactly what these two reports mean varies from jobber to jobber. The basic meaning is clear: the book is not available at present. Beyond that, however, doubt exists. How long will the title be out of stock? Some cynics suggest that these reports really mean: "We are waiting until we get enough orders from buyers to secure a good discount from the producer." The cynics propose that the difference between the two reports is that TOS means "We expect to have enough soon," and OS means "Don't hold your breath." Those interpretations are much too harsh, but they do indicate some problems with the quality and content of the reporting system. (*Note:* Not all blame for faulty reporting lies with jobbers; sometimes producers change their plans after reporting a status to a jobber.) An article in a 1989 issue of *School Library Journal* reported that 10 percent of all school library orders and 7 percent of public library orders are unavailable for some reason.[2] This figure has likely not changed over the years.

Does it really matter how accurate the reports are? Yes, it does matter, and the result can have an impact on collection development. An item on order encumbers (sets aside) the necessary funds for payment. The acquisitions staff cannot determine the precise cost of the item until the invoice arrives; the price may change, the exact discount is unknown, and shipping and handling charges vary. One hopes to set aside slightly more than the total cost. Most libraries and information centers have annual budgets and operate in systems where any monies not expended at the end of the fiscal year revert to the general fund (that is, the funds do not carry forward into the next fiscal year). In essence, the library loses the unspent money. Having large sums of money tied up (encumbered) in outstanding orders that are undeliverable before the end of the fiscal year can result in a real loss for the collection. In a sense, the library loses twice: wanted items go unreceived, and the library loses funds.

Another problem commonly encountered is the paperwork involved in cancellations and reordering. Many people have estimated the cost of normal library paperwork; these estimates range from $4 for a simple, two-paragraph business letter, to more than $21 for placing an order, to even more, depending on the complexity of the task, the organization, and the cost elements included in the calculation. Regardless of how one calculates the costs, one must consider the staff time, forms, letters, and postage involved in each transaction. Though these costs do not come out of the acquisitions budget, they represent a loss in the sense that the order did not result in the library receiving the desired material.

Finally, the library does lose some buying power as funds remain encumbered. Unlike money in a savings account, which earns a small amount of interest each day, encumbered funds lose a small amount of purchasing power each day. If inflation is rapid or if one is buying foreign books and the currency's value is fluctuating widely, losses can be large. Producers raise prices without notice, and in times of inflation one can count on regular price increases. The less time funds remain encumbered, the more purchasing power the library has. Thus, the accuracy of vendor reports is important. If the vendor cannot supply an item (OP, OS, or TOS) in time, and so informs the library, the library can cancel the order and use the funds for something that is available for delivery. Monitoring of vendor performance in report accuracy and speed of delivery can help control the problem.

Where does one learn about vendors and services? One method that allows one to talk directly with a variety of vendors in a short time is to attend an American Library Association summer or winter meeting. Here one will find just about every major vendor doing business with U.S. libraries; and yes, firms from many other countries are also present. In addition to "majors," there are always a surprising number of smaller firms present that are trying to break into the library market.

Beyond library association conference contacts and word-of-mouth suggestions from one's peers, several guides are available. General publications such as *Literary Market Place, International Literary Market Place, International Subscription Agents*, or specialized lists by format, region of the world, and subject matter will provide a long list of possibilities. One can also post questions about who uses who on acquisitions discussion lists.

A number of jobbers offer their services to U.S. libraries. Some of the larger firms that are active in marketing their programs are Brodart, Baker and Taylor, Ingram, Yankee Book Peddler, Ballen, Coutts, and Blackwell North America. There are also specialized jobbers, such as Majors, a leading firm for medical, science, and technical books. Serials jobbers include EBSCO, Faxon, and Readmore.

When selecting a vendor, one should keep several factors in mind. We have mentioned them earlier, but a summary list is useful.

- Service—a representative, toll-free numbers, Websites, etc.
- Quality of service—ask for and check references, ease of handling "problems"
- Speed of fulfillment—this includes accuracy
- Discounts and pricing
- Vendor's financial viability
- Vendor ability to work with the library's automation system
- Special services available—free and at a cost

Needless to say, these are the same factors one should use to evaluate the vendor(s) after selection.

Vendor-Added Services

Today, most vendors offer services beyond the basics of supplying books, serials, media, and electronic resources at "wholesale" prices. Some of the more common services are:

- Acquisition assistance—searches and verification, for example
- Automated selection assistance programs (some including book reviews)
- Book rental plans

- Cataloging and shelf-ready processing
- Customized management data
- Electronic financial transactions beyond the basics
- More than one information format
- Provision of electronic tables of contents or machine-readable data
- Library furniture
- Library supplies

As this list suggests, vendors are entering the outsourcing market and some are attempting to offer most of the supplies and services necessary for library operation.

Many small libraries, and today more and more large libraries, find it beneficial to buy books shelf-ready. Future studies may show this approach to be very cost-effective, if the public service staff and users find that the material supplied is adequate. Normally, the technical services offered by vendors allow the library a number of choices. Processing kits that include catalog cards, pockets, labels, jackets, and so forth are available for purchase; the library staff uses the kit to complete the processing routines. Some firms offer completely processed, ready-for-shelf products and in cooperation with OCLC provide records for the library's OPAC. Flexibility is essential in these services; yet, to make them cost-effective or profitable for the vendor, there are limits on the variations allowed or, at least, a high sales volume for each variation. Thus, one can expect to receive a degree of personalized customer service but not custom processing.

One jobber, Brodart, offers a rather unusual service, the McNaughton Plan, to help solve the problem of providing an adequate number of high-demand titles for both books and audiobooks. Most libraries have suffered the problem of high demand for a popular book, with the demand lasting only a few months. Should the library buy many copies and discard all but one or two after the demand subsides, or buy only a few copies and take reservations? The McNaughton Plan offers another alternative: rent multiple copies for the duration of the title's popularity. Brodart describes the plan as a leasing program. The plan offers high-demand items that Brodart's staff selects. One cannot order just any book; it must be on Brodart's list of high-demand titles. Savings occur in several areas. There are no processing costs, because the books come ready for the shelf, and the leasing fee is considerably lower than the item's purchase price. Patrons will be happier about shorter waiting times for the high-interest books. All in all, anyone involved in meeting recreational reading interests will find the program worth investigating. College and university libraries may use it to stock a variety of materials for recreational reading without taking too much money out of the book fund.

Other services many vendors offer are electronic ordering and, especially useful for serials, electronic invoicing. Access to an electronic version of *Books in Print* is often part of the service as well. With electronic ordering, acquisitions staff have dial-in access to the vendor's inventory database. This allows one to learn the availability of a title, place an order, receive confirmation of receipt of the order, and receive the invoice electronically, with the entire process taking only a few seconds. One problem with electronic ordering is that most acquisitions departments use many different vendors, and each vendor offering this type of service seems to have a number of variations in the system. This is an area where standards could be beneficial to everyone. Learning and remembering, or consulting manuals for several different electronic ordering systems, cuts into the time that could be saved by using such systems. Some vendors offer useful management reports based on their electronic systems. An example from a book vendor is illustrated in figure 12.1, page 344; figure 12.2, pages 346–47, is a report from a serials vendor. Such reports assist the library in making budget requests and estimating encumbrances for standing orders and blanket orders.

We discussed Brodart's TIPS program (<http://www.brodart.com/BOOKS/b_tips.htm>) in the chapter on selection and mention it again here as an example of vendor-assisted selection.

What Should Jobbers and Librarians Expect from Each Other?

Librarians are responsible for helping to maintain good working relationships with vendors. Simply stated, a vendor's profits are the difference between the price it pays producers and the resale price. Is this any different than for any other type of business? Not in the fundamentals, but there are some special aspects to the book trade and library market. One such variation is that any buyer can buy directly from the materials producer. This is seldom true in other fields. Another difference is that, to a large degree, libraries can find out the maximum price of any item by checking in-print lists, such as *Books in Print*, or by consulting the producer. When every buyer knows the maximum price, as well as any producer discount, vendors must at least match the maximum price and provide superior service to hold customers.

Volume buying and selling is the only way a jobber can make a profit. Efficient plant operations and low overhead can help, but no matter how efficient the operation, it will fail without high volume. One order for 15 or 20 titles in quantities will yield a high discount for the jobber, perhaps as high as 60 percent. Even after giving a 20 to 25 percent discount to the library, the jobber has a comfortable margin with which to work. In the library market, such orders are usually the exception rather than the rule. More often, the jobber's discount is 50 percent. A smaller margin is still acceptable if all the items sell—but not all of them do! Many publishers have a return policy (in which a publisher buys back unsold books). However, many producers are changing or dropping the return policy, thus increasing the risk for the vendor. Returns normally result in credits against the current account or future purchases. They seldom result in a cash refund for book jobbers.

Jobbers, being dependent on volume sales, must know their markets very well to project sales and maintain proper stock in their warehouses. When a vendor representative stops by, the purpose is not mere public relations or, necessarily, an attempt to sell more books. Rather, it is an attempt to determine the library's plans for collection development. It is not curiosity nor an attempt to make conversation that generates questions like "How does next year's materials budget look?" The collection development librarian should take time to explain new programs and areas to be worked on

MIDWEST LIBRARY SERVICE
University Press Publications Analysis by Subject
FOR THE PERIOD 5/1/98 TO 4/30/99

NUMBER OF TOTAL AVERAGE

LC Classification			Number	Total	
#		Description	of Titles	Price	Price
AC	1-195	Collections of monograph	2	54.95	27.48**
AG	1-90	Dictionaries. Minor encyc	2	38.90	19.45**
AM	10-101	Museography. Individual	1	32.50	32.50**
AM	111-160	Museology. Museum methods	1	25.00	25.00**
AS		Academies & learned soc.	4	322.00	80.50**
AZ		History of scholarship	2	55.00	27.50**
		A'S SUBTOTALS	12	528.35	44.03***
B		Philosophy (General)	7	409.90	58.56**
B	69-5739	History & systems	13	679.70	52.28**
B	108-708	Ancient	25	1,361.10	54.44**
B	720-765	Medieval	2	119.00	59.50**
B	770-785	Renaissance	1	54.95	54.95**
B	790-5739	Modern	24	1,197.20	49.88**
B	850-5739	By region or country	40	2,042.25	51.06**
B	1801-2430	France	23	1,319.70	57.38**
B	2521-3396	Germany. Austria(German)	48	2,382.25	49.63**
BC		Logic	12	809.25	67.44**
BD		Speculative philosophy	1	35.00	35.00**
BD	10-41	Gen'l philosophical wks.	2	122.00	61.00**
BD	95-131	Metaphysics	2	129.95	64.98**
BD	143-236	Epistemology	14	705.30	50.38**
BD	300-450	Ontology	20	849.18	42.46**
BD	493-701	Cosmology	2	124.90	62.45**
BF		Psychology	17	704.65	41.45**
BF	173-175	Psychoanalysis	17	684.25	40.25**
BF	180-210	Experimental psychology	2	97.00	48.50**
BF	231-299	Sensation. Aesthesiology	4	222.40	55.60**
BF	309-499	Cognition. Perception	27	1,214.15	44.97**
BF	501-504.3	Motivation	1	64.95	64.95**
BF	511-593	Emotion	16	675.20	42.20**
BF	608-635	Will. Choice	2	129.95	64.98**
BF	636-637	Applied psychology	4	169.85	42.46**

Fig. 12.1. Sample book vendor management report. Reprinted by courtesy of Midwest Library Services.

or describe how budget prospects look for the next year. This type of information helps vendors plan their buying policies for the coming months.

Selection officers should ask jobbers' representatives about what is available in any field the library is developing, even if the selection officers think they know. The answers may be surprising. One should ask what the vendor could do to supply the items. Is it a field the vendor carries as part of the normal inventory, or is the field one for which the jobber has listed publishers? (Listed publishers indicate that the vendor has an established relationship with the publisher but does not stock its titles. If the library uses a vendor for listed publishers, there will be a delay in receiving the material, because the jobber must forward the order to the publisher.) Such discussions take time but result in better service.

To get the maximum discount, some librarians dump their "problem" orders on vendors and order easy items directly from the publishers. Nothing could be more shortsighted. Without the income from easy, high-volume items, no jobber can stay in business. Someone has to handle the problem orders, and most vendors will try to track down the difficult items, especially for good customers. However, libraries should give jobbers easy orders as well. Almost all of the problems facing jobbers involve cash flow. Lack of cash has been the downfall of many businesses, and it becomes critical for jobbers when they handle only problem orders; staff expenses go up, but income does not. Failure of jobbers would lead to higher labor costs for most acquisitions departments, as a result of having to place all orders directly with publishers.

Whenever possible, the library should use the order format preferred by the vendor and not plead legal or system requirements for a particular method of ordering, unless it is impossible to change the requirement. Most vendors and publishers go out of their way to accommodate the legal requirements of library ordering procedures. If libraries could come closer to a standardized order procedure, jobbers could provide better service, because they would not have to keep track of hundreds of variations. If libraries keep all paperwork to a minimum, everyone will benefit.

Though most jobbers accept a few returns from libraries, even if the library is at fault, returns create a lot of paperwork. If an item serves no purpose in a library's collection, perhaps it would save time and money to accept the mistake and discard it rather than return it, assuming mistakes are infrequent. Frequent mistakes signal a problem in the acquisitions department or selection procedures. (*Note:* This discussion refers to items sent in error; the library should return any defective copy received for replacement.)

Finally, libraries should process invoices promptly; the acquisitions department should not hold them longer than necessary. Most library systems require at least two approvals before issuing a payment voucher: the library's approval and the business office's approval. Some systems have three or more offices involved in the approval process. The collection development officer should know the system, from approval to final payment. If payment takes longer than six weeks, the library should inform any new jobber of that fact so the firm can decide whether it can do business with the library. There is also a need to inform jobbers of any changes in the system that may affect the speed of payment. Most jobbers would like to receive payment within 30 days, because they are on a 30-day payment cycle with publishers.

Office	Acct	Title Number	Title Name	ISSN	LCC
LA	xxxx	000792002	AB Bookmans Yearbook	00650005	Z990
LA	xxxx	009259003	ACTA Musicologica	00016241	ML5
LA	xxxx	019928829	Aerospace America	0740722X	TL501.A68
LA	xxxx	043255009	American Journal of Botany	00029122	QK1
LA	xxxx	479766693	Journal of Forecasting	02776693	H61.4
LA	xxxx	586273005	Modern Language Journal	00267902	PB1
LA	xxxx	969344001	Writers Market	00842729	PN161
LA	xxxx	969539659	Writing on the Edge	10646051	PE1404

Fig. 12.2. Based on data from EBSCO for the Charles Von der Ahe Library.

Jobbers provide a valuable service to libraries. Given a good working relationship, both parties benefit. Following is a summary of the basic factors at work in establishing such a relationship.

What Do Libraries Expect from Jobbers?

A collection development officer has reason to believe that a chosen jobber will provide:

- A large inventory of titles
- Prompt and accurate order fulfillment
- Prompt and accurate reporting on items not in stock
- Personal service at a reasonable price

What Do Jobbers Expect from Libraries?

By the same token, jobbers should be able to expect:

- Time to get to know what the library needs
- Cooperation in placing orders
- Paperwork kept to a minimum
- Prompt payment for services

DDC	Retail Year 4	Retail Year 3	Retail Year 2	Retail Year 1	Retail Curr	Subscriber	Country of Origin
015	2500	2500	2500	2500	2500	AA	US
781	11000	0	0	0	0	AA	GE
625	8500	9500	13000	13000	13000	AA	US
585	15500	16500	16500	16500	19500	AA	US
005	35500	41500	49500	57500	69500	AA	EN
805	4500	4700	5200	5900	5900	AA	US
825	2995	3099	3149	3149	3149	AA	US
825	1500	1500	1500	1500	1500	AA	US

Vendor Evaluation

The trend in the 1990s has been toward making a contract between vendor and library. The contract is the result of either a formal bidding process or a response to a Request for Proposal (RFP). If one has a choice—and often public libraries have to employ a bidding process—the RFP is the better option. Often the bid process is out of the library's hands, and is conducted by business officers who do not fully understand that information materials are *not* the same as pencils, paper, or even computers. With the RFP there should be at least some library input to the requirements, if the library is not solely responsible for the document. An RFP will or should contain all the elements and aspects the library will use to evaluate the vendor's performance and often specifies performance parameters. The "Further Readings" section in this chapter provides references to resources that will assist in preparing an acquisitions RFP.

Even without a formal contract, acquisitions departments and collection development officers should monitor vendor performance. In the past, monitoring vendors was time-consuming and difficult, and it still is if one is working with a manual acquisitions system. However, today's automated acquisitions systems can produce a variety of useful management/vendor reports very quickly and in various formats. Knowing what to do with the quantity of data the systems can produce is another matter. (*Note:* there are two types of evaluation that acquisitions staff undertake. One is more a monitoring of vendor performance, with an eye to identifying small concerns that left unnoticed could become a major issue. The other is a formal assessment of the vendor, with an eye toward changing vendors or renewing a contract.)

One obvious issue that arises in evaluation is which vendor performs best on a certain type of order (examples are conference proceedings, music scores, or video recordings). The first thing to do is to decide what *best* means. Highest discount? Fastest delivery? Most accurate reports? Highest percentage of the order filled with the first shipment? All of the above? The answer varies from library to library depending on local needs and conditions. Once the library defines *best*, it knows what data to get from the system. This is an example where the RFP process is of assistance, because the answers to these questions should be in that document. Other questions to consider are:

- Who handles rush orders most efficiently?

- Who handles international orders most effectively—a dealer in the country of origin or a general international dealer?

- Are specialty dealers more effective in handling their specialties than are general dealers?

Figure 12.3, on pages 349–51, is a systems report covering three years' performance of some of Loyola Marymount University Library's book vendors on some typical areas of concern. It shows quantities of titles ordered; total expended; average delivery time; percentage of the order received; average cost of each order; what, if any, shipping/handling charges; and the discount for each of the vendors. In addition to system reports based on normal operating procedures, one can conduct some experiments by placing a random sample of a type of order with several vendors to assess their performance. When doing a test or experiment, one must be certain that each vendor receives approximately the same mix of titles so that no vendor receives more or less easy or hard items to handle. Often, the normal procedure data reflects the use of a particular vendor for only one type of order. This makes comparing vendor performance rather meaningless because one is not comparing like groups. One can use the test method to select a vendor for a particular type of order and use the operating data approach to monitor ongoing performance.

Checking on the performance of serials vendors is more difficult. Most libraries use only domestic serials vendors, because of the complexity of changing ongoing subscriptions. A library that is just establishing a current subscription list, or is starting a large number of new subscriptions, might consider splitting the list between two or more vendors for several years to determine which would be the best sole source for the long term.

Vendor Performance Statistics - Delivery Time
Processed Record # : 1583591 to 1984433
Count Orders Placed in Period 06-01-96 to 04-20-99

Ave Del Time			# orders received in					
		02 wks	04 wks	08 wks	12 wks	16 wks	17+ wks	
1	a&e	7.7	0	2	5	0	0	1
2	abc	10.3	21	323	3020	1506	369	622
3	abca	0.0	5208	1	3	1	0	1
4	abcc	3.1	115	3	11	0	1	7
5	abcr	6.2	1	8	10	3	1	1
6	aip	3.0	0	1	0	0	0	0
7	ala	0.6	54	1	1	1	1	0
8	alss	6.7	1	1	5	2	0	0
9	ama	0.0	1	0	0	0	0	0
10	amazc	3.4	10	3	5	1	0	0
11	amb	13.5	9	31	1194	831	252	370
12	ambr	4.0	0	8	0	0	0	0
13	amdfv	4.2	0	3	2	0	0	0
14	ams	15.1	0	0	1	5	18	2
15	ann	2.3	3	3	0	0	0	0
16	ared	0.0	28	0	0	0	0	0
17	arl	8.8	0	0	4	0	0	1
18	asce	5.6	0	0	5	0	0	0
19	asme	2.0	1	0	0	0	0	0
20	astm	?	0	0	0	0	0	0
21	auerp	3.0	0	1	0	0	0	0
22	aufo	3.9	0	7	4	0	0	0
23	bakea	156507.6	1335	0	3	0	0	2
24	bakec	0.0	2	0	0	0	0	0
25	bakep	0.0	1	0	0	0	0	0
26	baker	3.2	318	190	85	2	0	6
27	balpr	13.0	0	0	0	0	1	0
28	banc	0.0	1	0	0	0	0	0
29	barni	0.0	11	0	0	0	0	0
30	berna	0.5	10	2	0	0	0	0
31	bfrog	2.3	2	4	0	0	0	0
32	bh	7.0	10	170	370	37	18	39
33	bigwo	1.0	3	0	0	0	0	0
34	bilrp	5.0	0	0	2	0	0	0
35	blk	16.2	0	0	17	24	5	17
36	bna	0.0	1	0	0	0	0	0

Fig. 12.3. Vendor performance statistics.

(Figure 12.3. continues on page 350.)

Fig. 12.3—*Continued.*

Vendor Performance Statistics - Percentages
Processed Record # : 1583591 to 1984433
Count Orders Placed in Period 06-01-96 to 04-20-99

		# Orders	Ave Est Price/ Order	Ave Est Price/ Recd Order	Ave Amt Paid/ Order	% Orders Recd	% Orders Canc	% Orders Claim	Total Claims
1	a&e	11	$27.68	$33.70	$32.63	72.72	9.09	0.00	0
2	abc	6687	$45.96	$46.81	$41.75	87.64	1.85	0.00	0
3	abca	5226	$162.50	$47.78	$139.94	99.77	0.09	0.00	0
4	abcc	144	$57.74	$59.59	$104.72	95.13	0.69	0.00	0
5	abcr	24	$43.52	$43.52	$48.57	100.00	0.00	0.00	0
6	aip	2	$0.00	$0.00	$259.06	50.00	0.00	0.00	0
7	ala	58	$32.48	$32.48	$42.66	100.00	0.00	0.00	0
8	alss	10	$249.50	$253.88	$295.88	90.00	0.00	0.00	0
9	ama	1	$0.00	$0.00	$0.00	100.00	0.00	0.00	0
10	amazc	21	$25.44	$27.59	$26.71	90.47	4.76	0.00	0
11	amb	3399	$41.32	$41.56	$40.74	79.05	1.26	0.20	7
12	ambr	8	$74.96	$74.96	$82.64	100.00	0.00	0.00	0
13	amdfv	5	$60.00	$60.00	$79.70	100.00	0.00	0.00	0
14	ams	28	$56.11	$55.39	$41.59	92.85	0.00	0.00	0
15	ann	6	$155.65	$155.65	$180.94	100.00	0.00	0.00	0
16	ared	28	$44.62	$44.62	$0.00	100.00	0.00	0.00	0
17	arl	5	$41.60	$41.60	$52.19	100.00	0.00	0.00	0
18	asce	6	$124.93	$122.12	$117.39	83.33	0.00	0.00	0
19	asme	1	$74.00	$74.00	$87.00	100.00	0.00	0.00	0
20	astm	4	$517.75	?	?	0.00	0.00	0.00	0
21	auerp	2	$164.00	$175.00	$202.39	50.00	0.00	0.00	0
22	aufo	12	$29.79	$32.50	$39.36	91.66	8.33	0.00	0
23	bakea	1342	$44.13	$44.16	$39.27	99.85	0.00	0.00	0
24	bakec	2	$54.10	$54.10	$56.99	100.00	0.00	0.00	0
25	bakep	1	$45.00	$45.00	$51.46	100.00	0.00	0.00	0
26	baker	623	$42.01	$43.20	$39.24	96.46	2.24	0.00	0
27	balpr	2	$15.45	$12.95	$15.13	50.00	0.00	50.00	1
28	banc	2	$132.50	$265.00	$662.53	50.00	0.00	0.00	0
29	barni	11	$20.29	$20.29	$0.00	100.00	0.00	0.00	0
30	berna	15	$551.90	$23.20	$707.58	80.00	6.66	0.00	0
31	bfrog	6	$313.95	$313.95	$344.03	100.00	0.00	0.00	0
32	bh	772	$35.69	$38.17	$38.93	83.41	4.40	0.00	0
33	bigwo	5	$355.00	$370.66	$643.81	60.00	0.00	0.00	0
34	bilrp	2	$9.75	$9.75	$12.59	100.00	0.00	0.00	0
35	blk	88	$41.81	$42.65	$55.85	71.59	2.27	0.00	0

Vendor Performance Statistics - TOTAL
Processed Record # : 1583591 to 1984433
Count Orders Placed in Period 06-01-96 to 04-20-99

Average Estimated Price per Order:	$2,517,010.67 / 39060 = $64.43
Average Paid Amount of Receipts:	$2,235,412.84 / 35270 = $63.38
Average Estimated Price for Received Orders:	$1,682,515.20 / 35270 = $47.70
Average Delivery Time:	219988034 / 35270 = 6237
% Orders Received in 2 weeks:	2663 / 35270 = 35.90 %
% Orders Received in 4 weeks:	3839 / 35270 = 10.88 %
% Orders Received in 8 weeks:	10920 / 35270 = 30.96 %
% Orders Received in 12 weeks:	4700 / 35270 = 13.32 %
% Orders Received in 16 weeks:	1341 / 35270 = 3.80 %
% Orders Received in 17+ weeks:	1807 / 35270 = 5.12 %
% Cancelled:	577 / 39060 = 1.47 %
% Claimed:	9 / 39060 = 0.02 %
Average Claims per Claimed Order:	9 / 9 = 1.00
Average Claims per Order:	9 / 39060 = 0.00

A limited amount of checking is possible through comparisons with other libraries. Often, this type of checking is done in a casual manner, that is, by merely asking a colleague in another library, "Do you use vendor X? How do you like them?" or "How much is your service charge?" To make valid and useful comparisons, one needs to know the other library's title mix. Recent developments of union catalogs based on OPAC data suggest that collections, even in apparently similar libraries, have surprisingly different holdings. At one time a comparison was made of the monograph holdings of Loyola Marymount, Santa Clara, University of San Francisco, and the University of San Diego libraries for a 10-year period, using the AMIGOS CD-ROM collection analysis software. The university librarians thought the collections would have a large percentage of overlap because the institutions are similar in size and programs. All were surprised to learn that more than 80,000 titles of the 159,000 titles in the database were unique; that is, only one of the four schools held the title. Although the results were not as striking for serials holdings, the number of titles held by just one library was a surprise. These discoveries reinforced the idea that casual, impressionistic assessments are suspect.

One way to compare serials vendors is to take a sample of commonly held titles. Items to investigate include the service charges on those titles, the effectiveness of claims processing, and other issues such as vendor follow-up and handling of credit memos.

In any vendor evaluation, keep in mind some of the problems vendors have with producers. These bear repeating:

- Changes in title, or not publishing the title
- Not being informed when publishing schedules change or when publishers suspend or cease publication
- Incorrect ISBNs or ISSNs
- Producers refusing to take returns
- Producers refusing to sell through vendors
- Producers reducing discounts or charging for freight and handling when those were free in the past
- Poor fulfillment on the producer's part
- Constantly changing policies on the producer's part
- Producer price increases without prior notice

We provide references to several "models" for conducting vendor evaluation studies in the "Further Readings" section.

Several years ago, a student in one of Dr. Evans's collection development classes asked, during a discussion of vendors, "Why are you so pro-vendor? They are our enemies, with all their high prices and low discounts." Perhaps being somewhat more aware of vendors' problems, having had work experience in both publishing and libraries, is a factor in the senior author's not being highly negative about vendors. However, it is not a matter of being "pro-vendor," but rather recognition that there are at least two sides to most stories. Libraries depend on vendors; they offer services that save libraries time, effort, and staffing. Libraries need vendors and need to understand the vendors' problems.

That said, one must monitor their performance, question charges, and challenge charges that seem inappropriate. Maintaining good relations is everyone's business. If librarians, vendors, and producers take time to learn about one another's businesses, working relationships will be better. The senior author met a new regional manager of our serials vendor who had no prior experience in the library marketing sector. He asked if he could spend a week in our library learning how we handle journals and how our customers use the journals. We said yes, and he spent three days in technical services with the serials acquisition staff and two days in public services. Even if our operations are not completely typical, his experience made him more aware of the problems libraries face in handling serials. Another outcome has been that several of our staff have spent two or more days observing the vendor's operations. Increased understanding of one another's problems solidified an already good working relationship. It is not necessary to go to such lengths, but reading about developments in each other's fields and asking informed questions helps build mutual understanding and respect. Having realistic expectations for one another is the key, just as it is in personal relationships. Be professional and ethical in working with vendors and publishers; expect and demand the same from them.

Retail Outlets

Several articles appeared in the late 1990s about the potential competition between bookstores and libraries, in particular public libraries.[3] Essentially the articles suggested that bookstores have a great advantage over libraries. In some ways, this message is surprising, as one often hears that public libraries in particular hurt the sales of bookstores because they offer large quantities of popular titles for free. Authors and bookstores have both made such claims in the past. Why buy a copy of the latest bestseller that everyone is talking about, especially if it is not a topic one has a long-term interest in, when one can get a copy for free in the library? For some countries this claim, at least from authors, has given rise to legislation that compensates authors for "lost income" due to the presence of their books in libraries—public lending right laws (we cover this topic in chapter 18).

Public libraries and bookstores have existed side by side in communities for close to 200 years. Both have been in the book and magazine business and now both see themselves as being in the information business. Both generally stock a variety of formats, not just print-based materials. Despite the long association and similarity in activities, neither side seems to have taken much time to learn about the other. We believe that libraries can learn some useful lessons from bookstores and, further, that there are potentially useful library/bookstore partnership opportunities. Certainly bookstores can be and often are a source for acquisitions units, especially when the item is popular and has to be in-house today.

How Do New Bookstores Operate?

New bookstores—stores selling new books, not stores that just opened—are interesting places to visit, whether or not one is responsible for collection development. Many librarians started haunting bookstores long before they became librarians. (If there is a bibliographic equivalent of alcoholism, many librarians have it.) *Bibliomania* is defined as "excessive fondness for acquiring and possessing books."[4] Most bibliomaniacs (librarians included) cannot stay out of bookstores, and consider it a great feat of willpower and self-control if they manage to leave one without buying a book or two.

Bookstore owners would be happy if a large percentage of the general population suffered from bibliomania. In the United States, however, they do not. In fact, the general population appears to have a high level of immunity. On a percentage basis, book buyers are a minority group in most countries, although their actual numbers are large. As a result, bookstores generally exist in somewhat special environments and operate in a certain way. Though most librarians have undoubtedly visited many bookstores innumerable times, each one should make a special visit to at least two stores to answer some specific questions. What are the environmental and operating conditions necessary for a good bookstore? How does the store display and market its materials? What is for sale? How wide a range of materials is available? Could this shop be of any value in developing the collection?

One consideration for any bookstore owner is location. Many owners live and work in the community for a long time before they open their stores. Just as the person responsible for library collection development needs to know the community, so does the bookstore owner. Bookstores, like libraries, must face the "Law of Least Effort," which means having a location that is easy to find and convenient to use.

A few librarians harbor the dream of finding a quaint little town where they will retire and then open up a small bookstore. Most use it as a nice day-dream on the occasional "bad library day." Of those who go further and try to implement the idea, few succeed. Those who *do* succeed do so by locating the store in a community they know, and the community knows them as a result of frequent visits and extended stays. A successful bookstore is a busy, people-oriented organization. It is not a quiet retreat for persons who do not like working with people, any more than a library is. Furthermore, owning a bookstore requires physical work on the part of the owner and a fairly large population base to support the required volume of sales, assuming that one hopes to live off the income.

Population base is a key consideration in determining where to locate a bookstore. The American Booksellers Association suggests that a minimum population to support a books-only store is 25,000 persons. Thus, large cities are the most likely locations for books-only stores. The smaller the community, the less likely it is that a books-only store will survive. Cultural activities in a large city help stimulate interest in reading. In major cities, it is even possible to find a variety of specialized bookstores (foreign language and subject matter). Smaller communities adjoining a good-sized academic institution, or having a high level of tourism, provide the primary exceptions to the rule.

The educational level of the population is another factor in store location. As the average level of education in a community rises, so do the chances of a bookstore's succeeding with a smaller population base. College graduates represent the largest segment of book buyers. Where one finds a high concentration of college-educated people living near a large shopping center, one is also likely to find a bookstore.

A shopping center is a desirable location for a bookstore, if there is a lot of foot traffic. A store tucked away in a remote corner of the busiest center is not likely to do well. If bookstore owners had to survive solely on sales to individuals seeking a particular book, there would be even fewer stores than now exist. Catering to the tastes of middle- and upper-income persons increases a store's chance of success, because a large percentage of book sales result from impulse buying, which requires a location where the bookseller can stimulate the impulse in persons who can afford to indulge themselves. It frequently happens that one goes into a bookstore looking for just one book or something to read and walks out with three or four books. Bookstore owners depend on such impulse buying.

There are striking similarities between a successful bookstore and a successful library. Both require solid knowledge of the community. If librarians could select sites as do bookstore proprietors, library circulation would skyrocket. A public library branch in the center of Stockholm provides an example of an almost ideal bookstore location: on a shopping mall in the center of the main business district, with a high volume of foot traffic, and near a concourse to a major subway station. This branch is the most active of all the service points in a system where high use is the norm. Atlanta, Georgia, also has a branch of its public library located in a subway station, and it too has very heavy usage.

Store owners attempt to stimulate buyers through a variety of sales methods. Owners employ store window and entryway displays to provide clues about the basic stock before customers enter. Only very large stores can afford to purchase newspaper advertisements on a weekly basis, and radio and television advertising costs are prohibitively high for most owners. An occasional newspaper advertisement and a good storefront display are the best they can do to promote business.

One can make a fair assessment of a bookstore merely by looking through its windows, without even walking in the door (of course, this is an assessment of the type of material sold, not the level of service). Observing is not the same as casually looking. One can look closely, but without some guidelines one may not know what to look for or how to interpret what is seen. The following broad generalizations can serve as the most basic guidelines, providing a foundation on which to build as one gains experience. One can use retail store marketing techniques in a variety of library settings.

An owner has two basic methods for promoting a store through its windows: One is to focus on a particular topic or on a few bestsellers; the other is a "shotgun" approach, that is, displaying a wide variety of titles appealing to a wide range of interests. Using a little imagination, some nonbook props, and a good supply of books, successful store owners can create interesting window displays. Such windows can stimulate the inactive reader to come in and buy the promoted title, but such buyers seldom pause to examine other titles in the store. Typically, the display leads to good sales of the promoted title or subject. Unfortunately, most buyers, especially those interested only in a certain topic, will not return to the store until the store has another equally striking window display on that topic.

Shotgun window displays are less likely to attract the inactive reader. If they are well done, however, such displays will stop a reader. A jumble of books in the window will not do the job, but a wealth of titles using some basic graphic techniques will. Store owners know that this type of window attracts the steady book-buying customer. Such individuals are as likely to buy four or five titles as one, and all of the titles may be impulse purchases, in the sense that the buyer did not come into the store looking for the specific titles purchased.

If a store has consistently striking windows featuring the latest top sellers, this likely reflects the orientation of the total book stock. Almost everything in such a store will have a proven track record. Backlist titles that have had steady sales (dictionaries, cookbooks, home reference items, and classics) will comprise the majority of items in stock, plus stacks of faddish titles and tables piled high with discount and gift books. Though shops of this type may be willing to order single titles, there will be little advantage for the library. Almost the only reason for a library to patronize such stores is for the discount (remainder) books they offer.

There is a remote chance that an independent (non-chain) store owner would special-order items for the library. In smaller communities, this may be the only type of store available. If the library were to buy $10,000 worth of books each year from the store, this would probably be an adequate incentive for the owner to shift emphasis. (For many small libraries, $10,000 would be 10 years' purchases.) It will still be possible for the store's regular patrons to find their favorite types of books there, and perhaps it will draw in some new steady customers as a result of the change.

If a store's windows do not provide enough clues to its stock, looking in the door can provide another quick visual check. Tables of books with banners such as "Top 20!," "55% to 75% Off!" or "Giant Discounts!" are almost certain signs of a store that will be of limited value to a library, especially if most of the window displays have favored the latest and best sellers. A store with a good, wide range of stock cannot afford to devote much floor area to such sales methods. All stores have sales from time to time—books that have not sold and may be past their return date, some remainders—and of course, there is always the pre-inventory sale. However, the store that is always having a sale is never really having a sale and is seldom of value to libraries.

Another quick visual check is for sideline items. A new bookstore selling only new books needs a minimum community population of 25,000, but almost all bookstores now sell some sidelines: greeting cards, stationery and office supplies, posters, art supplies, audio and video recordings, magazines and newspapers, calendars, games, and so forth. Why the sideline? It is difficult to make a good living just selling books, because there are few buyers and the margin of profit on books is much smaller than the margin on sideline items.

The possible profit on books is a complex subject given the various discount arrangements available to booksellers. Publishers offer the same general discounts (trade, long, short, new, mass-market) to bookstores that they offer to jobbers. Bookstores receive long discounts (40 percent or more) on most trade hardback books. In the case of large orders (multiple copies), discounts of 50 percent or more are possible. Normally, the discount is 40 percent, and even then the store may have to buy a required minimum number of copies (five or more) to receive this amount. A few publishers offer 33 to 40 percent off an order of 10 different single titles under the Single Copy Order Plan (SCOP). Librarians ordering a sizable number of single copies from one publisher may find bookstores eager to place such orders. However, it is important to remember that such an agreement requires the bookseller to prepay and to do all the paperwork. Thus, if the library is slow in issuing payments, only large bookstores can afford to carry its accounts.

Some stores will order short-discount (20 to 25 percent) items but add a service charge. If the order contains enough short-discount items from a single publisher, most stores will handle the order without a service charge. On a $20 book with a 25 percent discount, the bookstore has only a $5 margin with which to work. After covering the clerical time and recordkeeping costs, the owner is lucky if the transaction has not cost the store more money than it received from the customer, so a service charge is not unreasonable.

There are two classes of paperbacks: quality and mass-market. Quality paperbacks (the term does not necessarily apply to the content of the book) generally sell for more than $15 and are found only in bookstores. Mass-market books are those in drugstores, grocery stores, airports, and so forth, that usually sell for $6 to $8. Most publishers give a long discount on quality paperbacks when ordered in groups of five to ten or more. A store must order

25 to 50 assorted titles of the mass-market type to begin to approach a 40 percent discount. Orders for less than that amount will get discounts of 25 to 35 percent.

The book distribution system in the United States is cumbersome and frequently adds to the cost of books. A simplified system would benefit everyone. Perhaps the best illustration of the complexity of the system is in the area of discounts, returns, billings, and so forth. Each year the American Booksellers Association (ABA) publishes a 500-page guide titled *ABA Book Buyer's Handbook* (New York: American Booksellers Association, 1947–). Pity the poor bookseller, confronted with all the other problems of a bookstore, who also must work through a mass of legal forms and sales conditions for purchasing from various publishers. It does create extra work for both bookseller and publisher, and they undoubtedly pass their costs on to the buyer.

Thus, when a sideline item offers a 70 to 80 percent discount, it is not surprising to find a mixed store; as much as 30 to 40 percent of the total store income comes from nonbook sales. A store that devotes more than one-third of the available floor space to nonbook items probably will not be of much use to a library for developing collections, so the librarian should be sure to observe the percentage of floor space devoted to sidelines. In addition to quick visual checks, some acquaintance with the store's personnel will provide additional information about a store. Although more and more stores must use a self-service arrangement as labor costs rise, getting to know what staff there is can pay dividends in getting service. Most self-service operations emphasize paperbacks, sidelines, and popular trade books. Obviously, such stores offer little that will be of value to the library.

In general, bookstores can be a valuable means of acquiring new books. Carrying out visual inspection of local stores and discussing the library's needs with their owners can form an important link in the selection and acquisition program. Only a few libraries, in large metropolitan areas, have good bookstores nearby. Many libraries are lucky if there is one bookstore in the community. Although most libraries will spend only a small part of the materials budget in such stores, the possibility is worth exploring. Though most bookstores have limited potential as a major source of supply for collection development, when a general bookstore exists nearby, the library ought to talk to the owner to determine what, if any, business relationship might be possible. It may take time for the relationship to fully develop, but it can prove mutually beneficial. (*Note:* Most of the preceding discussion does not apply to the large national chains, such as Borders, Barnes & Noble, and Waldenbooks. Their operations are very different.)

We cannot leave this section without making a few comments about Internet bookstores. When Amazon.com went online in 1995, it was the only e-store that was "independent." An early 1999 check of Yahoo!'s "Books" page had links to more than 270 online stores (both new and out-of-print sources). Certainly these stores are popular, but not always the quickest means of getting book in hand, at least not during holiday periods.

The Loyola Marymount University library has been using Amazon.com for several years for the purchase of some popular items. (We should note that it did take some effort to develop a workable means of payment.) Monica Fusich wrote a brief article on the use of Amazon.com and other e-stores that appeared in *College & Research Libraries News*.[5] She outlined several services that she had found useful, in her role as a collection development officer who has other duties as well. (Being a reference librarian or some other "full-time" assignment as well as having selection responsibilities is very common in today's library environment.) The features she mentioned were:

- Cumulated book reviews (one must remember that some of the reviews are from the general public)
- Search and browsing capability
- Size of the database(s)
- Coverage of both in- and out-of-print titles, as well as recorded music
- Notification services (a rather limited SDI service as of mid-1999)

Certainly e-stores are not *the* answer to the challenges facing busy librarians with a number of duties besides collection development; however, they are of assistance.

Out-of-Print, Antiquarian, and Rare Book Dealers

Retrospective collection building is one of the most interesting and challenging areas of collection development work. It was also one of the last to experience the impact of technology and the Internet. Libraries buy retrospectively for two reasons—to fill in gaps in the collection and to replace worn-out or lost copies of titles. There has been a steady decline in retrospective buying on the part of libraries over the past 20 years, due to limited budgets, as well as the need to increase purchases of nonprint formats. Another factor in the decline has been the ever-growing bibliographic databases, such as OCLC, that make locating a copy of an out-of-print title to borrow through ILL much easier. As a result, acquisitions staff and selectors have less and less experience to draw upon when they need to work in this field. (Dealers in this field are a special breed, unlike other vendors with which the library has more experience.) One outcome of the decline is that this field, which was always very dependent on collectors, is now even more driven by collector interests.

Allowing for overlap, there are two broad categories of out-of-print (OP) dealers. (It should be noted that most of these dealers dislike the label "secondhand dealer.") One category focuses primarily on general OP books, that is, with buying and selling relatively recent OP books. Often, these books sell at prices that are the same as, or only slightly higher than, their publication price. The other category of dealer focuses on rare, antiquarian, and special (for example, fore-edge-painted, miniature, or private press) books. Prices for this type of book range from around $10 to several thousand dollars per item.

There is a changing face to the field. Margaret Landesman provided an excellent, detailed outline of the current types of dealers:

- Book scouts, working part-time or full-time, searching out desirable books and selling them to dealers and collectors.

- Neighborhood stores that operate part- or full-time from low-cost facilities and depend primarily on walk-in trade and a few very loyal customers. They seldom issue catalogs or engage in searching except for their best customers.

- Specialized dealers that often issue catalogs and do searching in their specialty; more and more often, these firms operate only by mail or electronically (via an e-mail or Internet Website).

- General out-of-print dealers who have a rather large stock in varied areas; many have specialties as well. Some offer search services, some issue catalogs.

- Mixed in-print and out-of-print stores—often a store that was an independent new bookshop that is trying to survive the competition from the "superstores" by diversifying.

- Academic library book vendors that also offer out-of-print search services.

- Rare book dealers specializing in rare and expensive titles. Most established rare book dealers do not handle the more ordinary scholarly out-of-print titles, but many general out-of-print dealers also handle some rare books.[6]

The vast majority of such dealers have small shops in low-rent areas or operate out of their homes. Because of this diversity, it is difficult to make many generalizations about this group. Sol Malkin painted a cheery picture of at least part of the out-of-print trade:

> Imagine a separate book world within the world of books where dealers set up their businesses where they please (store or office, home or barn); where the minimum markup is 100 percent; where they can call upon 5,000 fellow dealers throughout the world and a stock of over 200 million volumes, practically from the beginning of the printed word; where books are safely packed and mailed with no extra charge for postage; where there is no competition from the publishers and discount houses; where colleagues help one another in time of need to provide fellow dealers with a unique service that makes customers happy all the time—an ideal imaginary book world that never was nor ever will be? Perhaps ... but the above is 99 percent true in the antiquarian book trade.[7]

Most libraries will have occasion to use the services of these dealers. Collection development officers working with large research collections spend much of their time, or did in the past, engaged in retrospective collection development. Changes in organizational goals and programs may result in developing whole new areas of collecting, of both current and retrospective materials. Public libraries also buy from OP dealers, especially for replacement copies and occasionally for retrospective collection building. School libraries make limited use of this distribution system, and when they do, it is for replacement copies; scientific and technical libraries rarely need to worry about acquiring retrospective materials.

Several directories to antiquarian or rare book dealers provide information about specialties (for example, *American Book Trade Directory* from R. R. Bowker), and anyone concerned with selection and acquisition needs to get to know these directories. Some major metropolitan areas have local directories or guides to special bookstores. In any case, a person will find it worthwhile to develop a listing of the local shops. This can provide quick information about search services, hours, and true specialties. One can go to a shop that advertises itself as a Western Americana store only to find the specialty stock very limited or overpriced. Nevertheless, one should examine the shop's stock to identify its true specialties and assess its general pricing polices. Maintaining this private directory can prove well worth the time required to keep it up-to-date. This is not to say that the published sources are worthless. However, owners change emphasis, and their stock turns over and is subject to local economic conditions that often change faster than published sources can monitor.

Many acquisitions librarians and book dealers classify OP book distribution services into three general types: (1) a complete book service, (2) a complete sales service, and (3) a complete bookstore. The first two may operate in a manner that does not allow, or at least require, customers to come to the seller's location. All contact is by mail, e-mail, and telephone. The owner may maintain only a small stock of choice items in a garage or basement. In a complete book service, a dealer actively searches for items for a customer even if the items are not in stock, by placing an ad in a publication like *AB Bookman's Weekly* (Antiquarian Bookman).

Sales service is just what the name implies: A dealer reads the "wanted" sections of book trade publications and sends off quotes on items in his or her stock. Such services seldom place ads or conduct searches for a customer. The complete bookstore is a store operation that depends on in-person trade. Stores of this type often engage in book service and sales service activities as well. Given the unpredictable nature of the OP trade, it is an unusual store that does not need to exploit every possible sales outlet.

AB Bookman's Weekly (*AB*) is a weekly publication devoted solely to advertisements from dealers offering or searching for particular titles. Publications of this type are an essential ingredient in the OP book trade, because they serve as a finding and selling tool. Without services like this, the cost of acquiring an OP item would be much higher (assuming the library could locate a copy without the service).

Selectors also use *AB* in their work. Other useful publications for both dealers and libraries are *AB*'s *Yearbook, Bookman's Price Index* (Gale), Bowker's *Books Out-of-Print*, Ruth Robinson and Daryush Farudi's *Buy Books Where—Sell Books Where* (Robinson Books), *American Book Prices Current* (Bancroft Parkman), and *Library Bookseller* (Antiquarian Bookman). We list some of the more useful Websites at the end of this chapter; however, one very good site is Bibliofind (<http://www.bibliofind.com>).

Both OP and rare bookstores require a high capital investment in a book stock that may not sell immediately. Most owners feel lucky if total sales for a year equal one times the total stock. Indeed, some items may never sell, and most will remain on a shelf for several years before a buyer appears. Lacking the return rights of the new bookstore owner, a used or rare bookstore owner must be careful about purchases and have inexpensive storage facilities available.

Factors like high investment and low turnover force most owners to locate their businesses in low-rent areas. Rare and antiquarian shops can sometimes exist in high-rent areas, but in such locations the buyer will pay a premium price for the books. Shops in high-rent areas often grew up with the area and seldom resulted from an owner's decision to move into a high-rent area. Several attempts to start antiquarian shops in high-rent areas in Los Angeles failed, despite locations that had a high volume of foot traffic, well-to-do customers with higher-than-average education, and a large university only a few blocks away.

One requisite for an OP dealer is a reputation for honesty, service, and fair prices. To gain such a reputation requires a considerable period of time in this field. Many newcomers to the business do not have adequate capital to carry them through this period, if they locate in a high-rent area. As a result, most OP shops operate in the less desirable areas of a community. This means that a person looking for such shops must make a special trip to visit them. Out-of-the-way, low-rent quarters for such a store also mean that there will be little walk-in trade. This means that most customers come looking for specific items and are unlikely to take an interest in nonbook items. Therefore, these stores do not stock sideline items, although a few may have selected used phonograph records, old photographs, or posters. Owners can only hope that they have the right items to spark some impulse book-buying in the true bibliophile.

One element in the OP trade is very mysterious to the outsider and even to librarians who have had years of experience with these dealers: How do dealers determine the asking price? As Malkin indicated, the markup is at least 100 percent, but how much more? One may find a book in an OP store with no price on it, take it to the salesperson (often the owner), ask the price, and receive, after a quick look, the answer, "Oh, yes. That is X dollars." Sometimes the amount is lower than one expects, other times much higher, but most of the time it is close to the price the library is willing to pay. Some salespersons seem to be mind readers, to know exactly how much a customer is willing to pay. Malkin summed up the outsider's feeling about pricing in the OP trade: "Many new book dealers think of the antiquarian bookseller as a second-hand junkman or as a weird character who obtains books by sorcery, prices them by cannibalistic necromancy, and sells them by black magic."[8]

It may appear that magic is the essential ingredient in successful OP operations. Actually, the mystery fades when one understands the interaction of three central issues concerning this trade: the source of supply, the predominant sales methods, and the way dealers set prices. Fortunately for those who enjoy the OP trade, the magic remains. With an excellent memory, a love for books, the ability and time to learn books, enough capital to buy a basic stock of books, and finally, the patience to wait for a return on capital, anyone can become an OP bookseller.

To a large degree, dealers set prices after they know the answers to the questions of supply and potential sales. The OP dealer has several sources of supply, but only two consistently produce new stock. One major source is personal or business collections. Placing an ad in the telephone directory (saying "I buy old books") will generate a number of inquiries. Two of the most frequent reasons a private collection comes onto the market are household moves and the settling of estates. Only when outstanding private collections of a well-known collector come on the market will dealers enter into a bidding contest. They may come to look at a collection, but only after determining by telephone that it is large and has potential value. After a quick review of the collection, they make a flat offer with a take-it-or-leave-it attitude. A person who has no experience with the OP trade is usually unhappy with what that person believes is too low an offer. After one or two such offers, a prospective seller might conclude that there is a conspiracy of OP dealers to cheat owners out of rare items.

Nothing could be further from the truth. Experienced OP dealers know how long most of the items they have bid on will occupy storage space in their shops. They also know how few of the seller's treasures are more than personal treasures. Grandfather's complete collection of *National Geographic* from 1921 to 1943 may be a family heirloom, but to most OP dealers it is only so much fodder for the 25-cent table.

Time is the central theme in the OP trade. In time, every edition of a book will become OP; in time, most of the world's printed materials should return to pulp mills for recycling. In time, the few valuable books will find a buyer. But when is that time? Knowing the time factor as well as they do, OP dealers must buy for as little as they can or they will go out of business. Knowledgeable dealers know the local and the national market; therefore, it should not be surprising that several bids on the same collection are almost identical. Dealers read the same trade magazines, they see the same catalogs, and to some extent, they see the same local buyers. If they are to stay in business, they must know the market.

Walk-in sales are only a small segment of OP sales income. Mail-order sales—buying and selling items through publications such as *AB* and catalogs—are the major source of income. Most dealers prepare catalogs of selected items in stock and mail them to other dealers, libraries, and book collectors. Often, the catalog will list only one type of material (for example, Western Americana, European history, first editions, or autographed books); at other times, it will list a variety of titles that the dealer hopes will appeal to many different buyers.

Just as the contents of catalogs vary, so does the quality of the item descriptions and the care taken in preparing the catalog. Some catalogs are nothing more than hard-to-read photocopies of text typed on a typewriter in need of cleaning. At most, one can decipher an author, title, and price. On the other end of the spectrum are catalogs that are so well done and contain so much bibliographic information that research libraries add these catalogs to their permanent bibliography collection. Catalogs of high quality are less and less common today, and the trend is likely to continue because of rising printing costs. To recover the cost, it is necessary to sell the catalog to buyers who are not regular customers, which also usually means that the prices for all the items in the catalogs will be rather high ($100 and up).

When a librarian sees a catalog or finds something on one of the OP Websites that contains something the library needs and can purchase, he or she should run, not walk, to the nearest telephone, fax, or e-mail computer and place the order. It will probably be too late, and the telephone offers almost the only chance of getting the order in quickly enough to secure the item. A mailed order is almost certain to arrive too late. Out-of-print folklore says that if one librarian wants an item, so do 30 others.

Dealer catalogs and magazines, such as *AB*, provide both a sales mechanism and a major means of establishing prices. If an OP dealer in London offers an autographed copy of the first edition of Richard Adams's *Watership Down* for £10, other dealers will use this information as a guide in setting prices for copies of the book that they have in stock. An unautographed copy of the first edition would be something less than £10, assuming that both copies were in approximately the same physical condition. Other editions, including foreign first editions, also would sell for less. The foreign first editions might come close to the English first edition in price, but the *first* first edition usually commands the highest price.

Prices are based on a number of interrelated factors:

1. How much it costs to acquire the item

2. The amount of current interest in collecting a particular subject or author

3. The number of copies printed and the number of copies still in existence

4. The physical condition of the copy

5. Any special features of the particular copy (autographed by the author or signed or owned by a famous person, for example)

6. What other dealers are asking for copies of the same edition in the same condition

Without question, the current asking price is the major determining factor—given equal conditions in the other five areas—thus making sales catalogs and *AB* major pricing tools.

A few additional facts about the condition of OP books are important for beginning librarians to know, because these bear directly on price. The condition of the book will affect its price. One may assume that most OP dealers sell their stock as described or "as is." If there is no statement about the item's condition, one may assume it to be in good or better condition. A common statement in catalogs is "terms—all books in original binding and in good or better condition unless otherwise stated." An example of such a condition statement appears in figure 12.4.

One should carefully study the examples of OP dealer catalog entries in figures 12.4 through 12.9. These are examples of the basic catalogs that a librarian concerned with retrospective buying would check. The sample from the William H. Allen catalog (fig. 12.4, p. 365) represents more expensive materials, but is still well within the limits from which a beginner might select. All the catalogs give information about the condition of the items offered. What does the "t.e.g." indicate about item 6438 in the Oriental and African Books catalog (fig. 12.5, p. 366)? What is the difference between "VG" (very good) (item 3) and "fine" (item 9) in the Janice Bowen catalog (fig. 12.6, p. 367), or between "exceedingly rare" (item 847) and "scarce" (item 852) from The Jenkins Company (fig. 12.7, p. 368)? "T.e.g." means "top edges gilt." Some of the meanings become clear only after one gets to know the particular dealer, but some guidance can be found in books like John Carter's *ABC for Book Collectors* and *The Bookman's Glossary*.[9] (New editions of such works appear periodically, but initially, any edition will be suitable.) Carter provides illuminating and entertaining notes about dealer adjectives describing the condition of a book:

> *General*—As new, fine, good, fair, satisfactory (a trifle condescending, this) good second-hand condition (i.e., not very good), poor (often coupled with an assurance that the book is very rare in any condition), used, reading copy (fit for nothing more and below collector's standard), working copy (may even need sticking together).
>
> *Of exterior*—Fresh, sound (probably lacks "bloom"), neat (implies sobriety rather than charm); rubbed, scuffed, chafed, tender (of *joints*), shaken, loose, faded (purple cloth and green leather fade easily), tired (from the French *fatigue*), worn, defective (very widely interpreted), binding copy (i.e., needs it).
>
> *Of interior*—Clean, crisp, unpressed, browned (like much later 16th century paper), age-stained, water-stained (usually in the depreciating form, "a few light water stains"), foxed (i.e., spotted or discolored in patches: often "foxed as usual," implying that practically all copies are), soiled, thumbed (in the more lyrical catalogue notes, "lovingly thumbed by an early scholar"), and (very rare in English or American catalogues, but commendably frank), washed.[10]

A careful review of the sample catalog pages in figures 12.4 to 12.9 reveals many terms, which are to a large degree subjective. What one dealer describes as fine another may call good. An experienced special collections librarian suggests that one buy on approval whenever possible, especially when buying from a dealer for the first time.

Because dealer catalogs are so important and the manner in which they describe an item's condition is central to a buying decision, a former student of Dr. Evans conducted a small "experiment" in describing some out-of-print books. The student worked for an antiquarian book dealer and helped prepare sales catalogs. The student selected three items that were to appear in a forthcoming catalog. The dealer's description of each book was one element in the study. Two other antiquarian dealers who worked in the same subject areas were then given the three items to describe as if they were going to list the books in one of their catalogs. In addition, the books were given to two librarians (both were in charge of large rare book collections in major research libraries), asking them to describe the condition of each item. Five major conditions (water stains, mildew, tears, and so forth) were previously identified in each book before the librarians and other dealers described the items. Both librarians noted all of the conditions for each book and gave precise information. All three dealers' descriptions had to be combined to have a complete list of all the conditions for each item. No one dealer described all the conditions for all the items. It was also interesting, but not surprising, to find that the dealer descriptions tended to downplay the faults. One would

(Text continues on page 371.)

No. 275 Autumn 1986

American & European History
Art, Science, Philosophy, Etc.

Unless otherwise noted, books are 12mo or 8vo, bound, and in good second-hand condition. Prices are net; carriage extra. **Send no money; you will be billed.** Pennsylvania residents are liable to the 6% sales tax. All bills are payable only in U.S. dollars, drawn on a U.S. bank, or by postal money order.

William H. Allen, Bookseller

2031 Walnut Street   Philadelphia, Pa. 19103
(Area Code 215) 563-3398

A.   Anderton, James. **The Protestants Apologie for the Roman Church, by John Brereley, Priest.** St. Omar 1608. 4to. New half morocco. Small piece out of corner of title-page. $150.00
The author, a Roman Catholic controversalist and probably a priest, quotes passages from the works of Protestants which admit the claims of the Roman church.

B.   Bacon, Sir Francis. **The Elements of the Common Lawes of England, branched into a double tract.** 1639. Old calf, one cover detached. Small piece torn from one margin. Name cut from title. $200.00
The third issue of this work, containing Bacon's proposed restatement of English law.

C.   Bible. Whole. **The Self-Interpreting Bible: containing the sacred text of the Old and New Testaments.** With marginal references by John Brown. New York 1792. Folio. 20 engr. pl. by Doolittle, A. Godwin, & others. Old leather, front cover detached, 2 leaves, the margins of which are quite frayed, supplied. Some tears into text. $300.00
The second illustrated Bible printed in America.

D.   ———. **Biblia, das ist: die ganze goettliche Heilige Schrift alten und neuen Testaments.** Reading, Pa. 1805. 4to. Old calf, quite worn, stitching on spine torn, leather partly covered with scotch tape. Contents very good. $65.00
The fourth edition of the Bible in German printed in America.

E.   Bilson, Thomas, Bp. **The True Difference betweene Christian Subjection and Unchristian Rebellion: wherein the princes lawful power to command for truth, and indeprivable right to beare the sword, are defended against the popes censures and the Jesuits sophismes.** 1586. Royal coat-of-arms on verso of title. Lacks first blank. Stamped leather of the 19th century. One joint starting. $200.00
A defense of the English Reformation and an assertion that the English Church is the true Catholic Chjurch.

F.   Bungus, Petrus. **Numerorum mysteria ex abditis plurimarum disciplinarum fontibus hausta.** Paris 1618. 4to. Vellum, one joint cracked, edges mouse-eaten. Worm-holes in corner of about 150pp. Title-page mounted. $125.00
The author, a Catholic theologian, devoted much of the work to the mystical number 666 which he equated with Luther, thus proving that he was the Antichrist. Other sections are devoted to other numbers in which he found mystical powers.

Fig. 12.4. William H. Allen, Bookseller catalog sample. Reproduced by courtesy of William H. Allen.

30

6431 (Cont.) with a full description of the Sudd, and of the measures which have been taken to clear the navigation of the river.'

6432 GIDEIRI, Y.B.A. A Guide to the Perciform Fishes in the Coastal Waters of Suakin. K.U.P., 1968. Oblong 8vo., pp. 52, illus., a v.g. copy. £8.50

6433 GLADSTONE, P. Travels of Alexine. Alexine Tinne 1835-1869. John Murray, 1970. Bds., pp. xii, 247, illus., 2 maps, v.g. in rubbed d.w. £12.50

6434 GREENER, L. High Dam over Nubia. Cassell, 1962. Illus., maps, v.g. in d.w. £5

6435 GWYNN, C.W. Imperial Policing. Macmillan, 1934. pp. ix, 366, 13 maps; a working copy only with front hinge weak and bds. spotted and creased; internally good. £8.50

6436 HAKE, A.E. The Story of Chinese Gordon. Remington, 1884 rep. (1884). Port. frp., plate, 2 folding maps, orig. dec. cloth gilt; 2 vols., and a very good set. £65

6437 Ditto, another set, both vols. first edn.; cloth rubbed and faded, o/w good. £45

6438 HAKE, A.E. The Story of Chinese Gordon. With additions, bringing the narrative to the present time. Worthington, N.Y., 1884. Orig. pict. cloth gilt, t.e.g., frp., illus., pp. 358, a v.g. copy. £25

6439 HALLAM, W.K.R. The Life and Times of Rabih Fadl Allah. Stockwell Ltd., Ilfracombe, 1977. Bds., pp. 367, 3 mpas, illus., a v.g. copy in d.w. £15

6440 HARTMANN, Dr. R. Reise des Freiherrn Adalbert von Barnim durch Nord-Ost-Afrika in den Jahren 1859 und 1860. Georg Reimer, Berlin, 1863. Lge. 4to., orig. cloth, pp. xvi, 651, XI, + appendix of 111 pp.; tinted lithographic frp., 28 woodcut illus. in the text, (some full-page), 2 other plates, sketch map, 2 folding maps; some foxing to text and fore-edge, faint waterstain to bottom margin, (but not affecting the text), and a v.g. clean copy. With the accompanying Atlas : Reise in Nordost Africa, 1859-1860. Skizzen nach der Natur gemalt von Adalbert Freiherrn von Barnim und Dr. Robert Hartmann. Oblong folio, (48 x 32 cms.), orig. cloth, cold. lithographic title-page, double page panorama, 23 other lithographic plates, (of which nine are cold.), by W. Loeillet after sketches by the author and von Barnim, an exceptionally fine copy. £2500
   Hartmann, a naturalist who ended his career as Professor of Anatomy at Berlin University, accompanied the young Baron A. von Barnim on the latter's journey to the Sudan. Crossing the Bayuda Desert from Old Dongola to Khartoum, they continued up the Blue Nile valley via Sennar to Fazughli. After von Barnim died of fever at Roseires, Hartmann took the body to Europe for burial. The work he later produced about this ill-fated tour ranks with those of Tremaux and Lejean as one of the most beautifully produced travel books relating to the Sudan in the mid-Nineteenth Century. Far from being a simple description of the tour, it is a primary source for the period, a major and immensely detailed contribution to the study of Sudan's natural history and ethnography, particularly regarding the Upper Blue Nile, Dar Funj and Sudan-Ethiopian borderlands. The quality of the text is matched by that of the accompanying plates, illustrating the natural history, landscapes and peoples en route, and of which this copy is an exceptional example.

6441 HASSAN, Y.F. & DOORNBOS, P. The Central Bilad Al Sudan. Tradition and Adaptation. Essays on the Geography and Economic and Political History of the Sudanic belt. K.U.P., Sudan Library Series No. 11, 1977. Sm. 4to., wraps, pp. v, 316, maps, tables etc., a v.g. copy. £15

6442 HENDERSON, K.D.D. Sudan Republic. Benn, 1965. Cloth, pp. 233, 2 maps, (1 folding), a v.g. copy. £22.50
   In the series 'Nations of the Modern World' ; provides a good general survey of the later Condominium period and early years of the independent Sudan.

Fig. 12.5. Oriental and African Books catalog sample. Reproduced by courtesy of Oriental and African Books, Shrewsbury.

ANTHROPOLOGY & TRAVEL

THEORETICAL & COMPARATIVE
AFRICA
MIDDLE EAST
ASIA
AUSTRALASIA & PACIFIC
AMERICAS & CARIBBEAN
POLAR REGIONS
EUROPE
ADDENDA

THEORETICAL & COMPARATIVE

1   BANTON (Michael) - Race Relations. Tavistock Pubs., 1967. Pp. xiv+434,
     brown clothgilt, d-j. (snagged). VG. (Analyses of the history and oper-
     ation of different patterns of racial tension.)   £10

2   BETTANY (G.T.) - Red, Brown & Black Men & Their White Supplanters / The
     Inhabitants of America & Oceania. Ward Lock, n.d. (c.1890.) Pp. xi+221,
     numerous ills., grey pictorial clothgilt. Lacks 1 page, o/w VG. Manners,
     customs, racial characteristics and drawings of many tribes.   £10

3   BINDER (Pearl) - Magic Symbols of the World. Hamlyn, 1972. Pp. 127, ills.
     (some coloured), cloth, silvergilt. VG in worn d-j. (Study by artist
     Fellow of the R.A.I. discussing fertility symbols, magical protection
     of body and dwelling, family and livelihood, death and afterlife.) £4.50

4   BOISSEVAIN (Jeremy) - Friends of Friends: Networks, Manipulators and
     Coalitions. Oxford, Blackwell, 1974. Pp. xv+285. Tan clothgilt. Fine,
     in d-j.   £9.50

5   CHAPPLE (Eliot Dismore) & Carlton Stevens Coon - Principles of Anthropology
     New York, Holt, 1947, reprint. Pp. xii+718, blue cloth, VG. (Includes
     operational method, development of personality, symbolism.)   £14

6   COON (Carleton S.) - The Hunting Peoples. Book Club Associates, 1974, rpt.
     Pp. 413, maps, ills., brown clothgilt. VG in chipped d-j.   £9

7   COTLOW (Lewis) - In Search of the Primitive. Robert Hale, 1967 (first Eng-
     lish edn). Pp. 454, col. & b/w plates. Green clothgilt. Bumped at base
     of spine. Good, in chipped d-j. (Ituri Forest pygmies, Watusi, Masai,
     Babira, Jivaro, Matto Grosso Bororo, Yaguas, Eskimo.)   £8

8   DOUGLAS (Mary) - Evans-Pritchard: His Life, Work, Writings & Ideas. Har-
     vester Press/Fontana, 1980. Blue clothgilt, d-j. Mint.   £6

9   DOUGLAS (Mary) - Purity & Danger / An Analysis of the Concepts of Pollution
     & Taboo. Routledge & Kegan Paul, Ark Paperback, 1984. (First pub. 1966.)
     Pp. 188. Paperback, fine.   £2.75

10   DOUGLAS (Mary) - Natural Symbols / Explorations in Cosmology. Barrie &
     Jenkins, 1978, 2nd edn, rpt. Pp. 218. Black clothgilt, d-j. VG.   £7.50

11   EPSTEIN (A.L.) Ed. - The Craft of Social Anthropology. Intro. Max Gluckman.
     Tavistock Pubs., 1969, rpt. Pp. xx+276. Contributors include Mitchell,
     Barnes, Turner, Marwick. Paperback; signature, some scuffmarks and
     scratched erasing on back cover - o/w clean and fresh.   £6

12   EVANS-PRITCHARD (E.E.) - Social Anthropology. Cohen & West, 1960, rpt.
     Pp. vii+134, blue cloth, d-j. (embrowned). Good.   £6.50

Fig. 12.6. Janice Bowen catalog sample. Reproduced by courtesy of Janice Bowen.

- Dec. 6, 1879.   Volume I, nos. 1-18 complete. Elephant folio, bound in original cloth, pictorial gilt on front cover. Illus. An interesting collection including military reminiscences of various wars, especially the Civil War, each issue 16 pages in length. Very scarce. (V27-20774)   125.00

MCKENNEY AND JACKSON ON INDIANS

847. [NEW YORK] McKenney, Thomas L. *DOCUMENTS AND PROCEEDINGS RELATING TO THE FORMATION AND PRO-GRESS OF A BOARD IN THE CITY OF NEW YORK FOR THE EMIGRATION, PRESERVATION, AND IMPROVEMENT OF THE ABORIGINES OF AMERICA.* N.Y.: Vanderpool & Cole, 1829. 48pp. Sewn. First printing. S. & S. 39083. Includes a lengthy address by McKenney, an address from Pres. Andrew Jackson to the Creek Indians, an address from John H. Eaton to John Ross and the Cherokees, the Constitution of the Indian Board for the Emigration, Preservation, and Improvement of the Aborigines of America, and a report by Eaton on the Indians in Georgia. Exceedingly rare, with very fine content. (V27-20797)   125.00

848. [NEW YORK] Murphy, William D. *BIOGRAPHICAL SKETCHES OF THE STATE OFFICERS AND MEMBERS OF THE LEGISLATURE OF THE STATE OF NEW YORK.* N.Y., 1861. 298pp. Original cloth. First edition. A nice copy of the principal reference work on the state legislature of the Civil War's first year. (V27-20731)   35.00

849. [NEW YORK] *THE NEW YORK DEMOCRACY AND VALLANDIGHAM: THEY ENDORSE THE TRAITOR AND WINK AT THE TREASON.* N.p., 1861. 4pp. First printing. "By the time of his return to Ohio he was suspected of treasonable intent and had become one of the most unpopular and most bitterly abused men in the North....Whatever his policy at any time, he advocated it with the ardor and sincerity of a fanatic. In 1871 he was retained as counsel for the defendant in a murder case and while demonstrating the way in which the victim had been shot he mortally wounded himself." (V27-20638)   20.00

850. [NEW YORK] [WEST POINT] *WEST POINT LIFE: AN ANONYMOUS COMMUNICATION, READ BEFORE A PUBLIC MEETING OF THE DIALECTIC SOCIEY, U.S. MILITARY ACADEMY, MARCH 5, 1859.* N.p., 1859. 16pp. Original printed wrappers. In verse form, this fascinating pamphlet details the intense social life at West Point on the eve of the Civil War with amusing accounts of balls and dances and courtships, as well as learning soldiering. George A. Custer and many other future generals were at the Point at this time. (V27-20811)   65.00

851. [NEW YORK] Wilkins, William, et al. *ADDRESS OF THE FRIENDS OF DOMESTIC INDUSTRY, ASSEMBLED IN CONVENTION, AT NEW YORK, OCTOBER 26, 1831, TO THE PEOPLE OF THE UNITED STATES.* Baltimore, 1831. 44pp. Much on developing American industry and on cotton mills. With a complete list of the delegates. S.& S. 5637. (V27-15106)   25.00

852. Nicollet, Joseph Nicolas. *REPORT INTENDED TO ILLUSTRATE A MAP OF THE HYDROGRAPHICAL BASIN OF THE UPPER MISSISSIPPI RIVER.* Wash.: SD237, 1843. 237pp. Calf and boards. First edition. Huge folding map in facsimile by J. C. Fremont. Holliday 820: "Scarce and most interesting." Howes N152. Buck 339: "The report contains also a sketch of the early history of St. Louis." Graff 3022. Wagner-Camp 98: "Nicollet gives many details regarding his expedition to the upper Missouri in 1839 with Fremont." Overlooked by Clark. (VW1-5101)   100.00

853. Noble, Samuel H. *LIFE AND ADVENTURES OF BUCKSKIN SAM, WRITTEN BY HIMSELF.* Rumford Falls, Maine, 1900. 185pp. Original cloth. Fine copy. Frontis. Recollections of his travels throughout the world. His hunting trips, being captured by Indians in South America, and his experiences with Custer during the Civil War. (VW5-12817)   100.00

854. [NORTH CAROLINA] *AN ACT TO INCORPORATE THE NORTH CAROLINA TRANSPORTATION COMPANY.* [Raleigh], 1866. Broadside, 1p., octavo. Creating a steamboat company for the Chesapeake Canal. (VW14-6601)   15.00

855. [NORTH CAROLINA] Alderman, Ernest H. *THE NORTH CAROLINA COLONIAL BAR [AND] THE GREENVILLE DISTRICT, BY E. MERTON COULTER.* Chapel Hill: Univ. of N.C., [1913]. 56pp. 1st ed. Orig.ptd.wrp. Articles in the Sprunt Historical Series (Vol.13 #1). (VW14-15868)   35.00

856. [NORTH CAROLINA] Arthur, John P. *WESTERN NORTH CAROLINA: A HISTORY (FROM 1730 TO 1913).* Raleigh, 1914. 709pp.+errata. First edition. Illus. An early scholarly survey. CWB II, 210: "Sheds light on civil and military affairs [during the Civil War]." Thornton 317. Howes A342. (VW14-9597)   100.00

857. [NORTH CAROLINA] *A BILL CONCERNING THE FAYETTEVILLE & CENTRE PLANK ROAD COMPANY.* Raleigh, 1854. 4pp. (VW14-2-6595)   15.00

858. [NORTH CAROLINA] *A BILL TO IMPROVE THE PUBLIC ROADS IN NORTH CAROLINA.* Raleigh, 1850. [8]pp. (VW14-6596)   15.00

859. [NORTH CAROLINA] *A BILL TO INCORPORATE THE FAYETTEVILLE AND NORTHERN PLANK ROAD COMPANY.* Raleigh, 1850. [8]pp. (VW14-6594)   15.00

860. [NORTH CAROLINA] Boyd, William K. [ed.]. *SOME EIGHTEENTH CENTURY TRACTS CONCERNING NORTH CARO-LINA.* Raleigh, 1927. 508pp. Illus. Facs. Index. An excellent scholarly edition of 14 early North carolina-related printed sources, including politics, religion, economics, Indians, and law. Boyd provides and introduction and good notes for each work. Scarce. (VW14-9598)   65.00

61

Fig. 12.7. The Jenkins Company catalog sample. Reproduced by courtesy of The Jenkins Company.

19. CALLIMACHUS. Callimachi Cyrenæi Hymni (cum scholis Græcis) & Epigrammata. Eivsdem Poemativm Decoma Berenices, a Catullo versum. Nicodemi Frischlini Balingensis interpretationes duæ Hymnorum . . . Henrici Stephani Partim emendatione partim Annotationes . . .
[*Geneva*] *Excudebat Henricus Stephanus, 1577.*
Tall quarto, nineteenth century vellum, soiled, light waterstain to edges, title dust soiled, quite decent.
As noted on the title, the translation of the Coma Berenices is by Catullus; both Frischlin and Estienne edited the text, though some work was done by others including Florido. This important edition includes a number of fragments for the first time and because of its completeness and scrupulous editing, became the basic text for all subsequent editions.
Renouard 1,145, =3; Brunet I, 1480; not in Schreiber. $475.

20. CANNING (Stratford, *Viscount* Stratford de Redcliffe). Shadows Of The Past. In Verse.
London, MacMillan, 1866.
Octavo, original red morocco gilt presentation binding, corners and edges a bit worn, all edges gilt, complete with the half title. Inscribed by the author to Lady Alford, the brilliant spouse of the Bridgewater heir: "For the Lady Marian Alford from her grateful neighbor and servant the author, Stratford de Redcliffe. October 15th, 1866."
His first full-length book of poems; the uncommon first edition. $150.

21. COOPER (Thomas). Thesavrvs Lingvae Romanae & Britannicae . . . Accessit Dictionarivm Historicum & poeticum . . .
Londini, In AEdibus quondam Berthelet, per Henricum Wykes, 16 March 1565.
Folio, neat new half calf, title cut close and mounted, no text lost, title and following leaf somewhat soiled and worn but not badly so. In all, a decent example of a work rarely found in acceptable condition.
Cooper, the tutor of William Camden, first gained fame for his continuation of Thomas Lanquet's *Chronicle*; indeed that work usually is better known as "Cooper's Chronicle." But it was his great dictionary, the *Thesaurus*, which brought him his greatest fame and the recognition of Queen Elizabeth. For scholars, the greatest interest lies in the English idioms of the Elizabethan period. The *Thesaurus* was the standard reference work during the formative years of Spenser, Marlowe, Sidney, Shakespeare, and Jonson, and a copy of the 1573 edition exists with notes identified by Collier as in the hand of Milton. Adapted to the needs of its time, the *Thesaurus* was unique and its influence on English lexicography far reaching.
STC 5686. The rare first edition. $1250.

Fig. 12.8. G. W. Stuart, Jr. Catalogue 49. Reprinted with permission.

1 AUDEN, WYSTAN HUGH

ABOUT THE HOUSE.
London: Faber & Faber, 1966.

FIRST ENGLISH EDITION. 8vo. Pp. [viii],
[9-12]13-94. With the four-line errata slip
tipped in on the Acknowledgements page.
Bloomfield & Mendelson A495.

Original light purplish-blue cloth with gold
lettering down the spine, in dust-jacket.

Excellent copy. $85

2 AUDEN, WYSTAN HUGH

CITY WITHOUT WALLS, AND OTHER
POEMS.
New York: Random House, 1969.

FIRST EDITION. 8vo. [x], [1-2]3-
124[125-126]. NCBEL Vol IV, 209.

Fine copy in the original cloth, in very
good dust-jacket with tape-closed tear
on the inside of front cover. $50

3 AUDEN, WYSTAN HUGH

EPISTLE TO A GODSON AND OTHER
POEMS.
London: Faber & Faber, 1972
FIRST EDITION. 8vo. Pp. [viii], 9-72.

Fine copy in the original brown cloth-backed
stiff boards; spine lettered in gold. In fine
dust-jacket. $75

4 AUDEN, WYSTAN HUGH

HOMAGE TO CLIO.
London: Faber & Faber, 1960.

FIRST EDITION. 8vo. Pp. [viii], 9-91[92].
NCBEL Vol IV, 208.

Fine copy in the original purple cloth
lettered in gold along the spine, in fine
price-clipped dust-jacket. $100

5 AUDEN, WYSTAN HUGH

THANK YOU FOG.
London: Faber & Faber, 1974.
FIRST EDITION. 8vo. Pp. [vi], 7-57[58].

Fine copy in the original blue cloth-
backed stiff boards lettered in gold
along the spine, in fine price-clipped
dust-jacket.

These are Auden's last poems, completed
after his return to England in the Spring
of 1972. Also included is his last piece for
the stage, "The Entertainment of the
Senses," written in collaboration with
Chester Kallmann in 1963. He died in
September 1973. $75

6 BATES, HERBERT ERNEST

SEVEN TALES AND ALEXANDER.
London: The Scholartis Press, 1929.

FIRST EDITION. 8vo. Pp. [xii], [1-2]3-
166[167-168]. One of 1,000 copies,
printed on *Antique de Luxe* paper.
NCBEL Vol IV, 520.

Fine copy in the original white stiff
boards and blue cloth spine lettered
in gold, in very good plus dust-jacket.

An early book of stories published three
years after the author's first book. $100

7 BELLOC, HILAIRE

THE POSTMASTER GENERAL BY
HILAIRE BELLOC WITH THIRTY
DRAWINGS BY G. K. CHESTERTON.
London: Arrowsmith, 1932.
FIRST EDITION. 8vo. Pp. [viii]9-10, 11-286.

Original green cloth with gold-lettering on
the spine. Fine copy in near-fine pictorial
dust-jacket.

Another delightful Chester-Bellow satire
with a futuristic plot about the 1960s
television age. $275

8 BETJEMAN, JOHN

A FEW LATE CHRYSANTHEMUMS.
London: John Murray, 1954.
FIRST EDITION. 8vo. Pp. [vi], [1-2]3-95[96].
NCBEL Vol IV, 233.

Fine copy of one of the late poet laureate's
best titles, in the original purple cloth, in
near-fine lightly soiled dust-jacket. $100

T.S. VANDOROS
RARE BOOKS

Fig. 12.9. T. S. Vandoros. Rare Books—British Modern Firsts. March 1994.

expect this, because their goal is to sell the items. Professional associations (such as ALA) and antiquarian dealer associations attempt to develop guidelines to help reduce the tensions that often arise between libraries and dealers as a result of catalog descriptions.

Overall, working in this area can be fun and frustrating at the same time. Clearly there is a need for experience with dealers to know if the descriptions of their offerings are good enough for the library. There is also the nagging question of fair market price for what is often a one-of-kind offering, at least at that moment. There are commercial guides that can help one judge the asking/quoted price—*Bookman's Price Index* (Detroit, Mich.: Gale Research, 1964–), *American Book Prices Current* (New York: Bancroft-Parkman, annual, 1930–), and *Book-Auction Records* (London: W. Dawson, annual, 1902–) are three examples.

This section, like the one on new bookstores, can only briefly outline some of the more significant points about the OP book trade. It provides some basic information upon which one can continue to build while buying and collecting books for oneself or a library.

Other Media Retail Outlets

Because of the variety of their formats and purposes, it is not possible to generalize about retail outlets for other media. In most cases, libraries acquire most of the formats directly from their producers or from an educational media jobber.

The most common retail outlets for media other than books are the music shop and video store. Many small communities that do not have a bookstore have a music store and a video outlet. One reason for their popularity is that each tape or CD has a relatively low sales price (videocassettes are often rented), and a fairly large market exists for both formats. The top 20 recordings (tapes and CDs) of popular music may outsell the top 20 books by a 20-to-1 margin, at least in the United States.

Other than music and video stores, it is almost impossible to describe other media retail outlets, primarily because there are so few that it is hard to generalize. There are a few map shops in larger cities, most metropolitan areas have at least one sheet music store, and there are museums that sell slides and art reproductions. Sometimes, one can locate needed educational models and games at a teacher supply store. Libraries frequently purchase microforms from the producers.

Summary

The distribution system for books and other library materials is varied and complex. One must know something about the system before beginning to develop a library collection. This chapter merely highlighted what one needs to know; it portrays just the beginning of a long, challenging, but enjoyable learning process. Jobbers, book dealers, and media vendors are more than willing to explain how they modify their operations to accommodate library requirements, when they know that a librarian has taken time to learn something about their operations.

Notes

1. A *jobber* buys merchandise from manufacturers and sells it to retailers. A *wholesaler* is a person or business that sells large quantities of goods to a retailer. A *drop shipper* is a person or company that orders materials from manufacturers after receiving an order from a retailer (or library). Unlike jobbers and wholesalers, a drop shipper does not have a stock of materials, just a telephone.

2. Lotz Wendall, "Here Today, Here Tomorrow: Coping with the OP 'Crisis,' " *School Library Journal* 35 (July 1989): 25–28.

3. Renee Feinberg, "B&N: The New College Library?," *Library Journal* 123 (February 1, 1998): 49–51; Steve Coffman, "What If You Ran Your Library Like a Bookstore?," *American Libraries* 29, no. 3 (March 1998): 40–46; J. Raymond, "Libraries Have Little to Fear from Bookstores," *Library Journal* 123 (September 1998): 41–42.

4. *Random House Dictionary of the English Language* (New York: Random House, 1996), 153.

5. Monica Fusich, "Collectiondevelopment.com: Using Amazon.com and Other Online Bookstores for Collection Development," *College & Research Libraries News* 59 (October 1998): 659–61.

6. Margaret Landesman, "Out-of-Print and Secondhand Market," in *The Business of Library Acquisitions*, edited by K. A. Schmidt (Chicago: American Library Association, 1990), 186–88.

7. Sol Malkin, "Rare and Out-of-Print Books," in *A Manual on Bookselling* (New York: American Booksellers Association, 1974), 208.

8. Ibid.

9. John Carter, *ABC for Book Collectors,* 4th ed. (New York: Knopf, 1970); *The Bookman's Glossary,* 6th ed. (New York: R. R. Bowker, 1983).

10. Carter, *ABC for Book Collectors,* 67–68.

Selected Websites*

Advanced Book Exchange.
    <http://www.abebooks.com>.

ALIBRIS.
    <http://www.alibris.com/cgi-bin/texis/bookstore>.

Antiquarian Booksellers Association of America.
    <http://www.abaa-booknet.com>.

Biblio Magazine.
    <http://www.bibliomag.com>.

BookFinder.Com.
    <http://www.bookfinder.com>.

Books.COM.
    <http://www.books.com>.

International League of Antiquarian Booksellers.
    <http://www.lila-ilab.org/ilab/index.html>.

Internet Bookshop.
   <http://www.bookshop.co.uk/>.

UMI Book Vault.
   <http://www.UMI.com/ph/Support/BOD/bkvault.htm>.

Yahoo: Books: Booksellers.
   <http://www.yahoo.com/Business_and_Economy/Companies/Books/Booksellers/>.

*These sites were accessed 15 October 1999.

Further Reading

General

Alessi, D. L. "Me and My Shadow: Vendors As the Third Hand in Collection Evaluation." *Journal of Library Administration* 17, no. 3 (1992): 155–60.

American Library Association, Collection Development and Management Committee. *Guide to Performance Evaluation of Library Materials Vendors. Acquisitions Guidelines No. 5.* Chicago: American Library Association, 1993.

Anderson, R. "How to Make Your Book Vendor Love You." *Against the Grain* 10
   (1998): 68–70.

Association for Library Collections and Technical Services, Collection Management
   and Development Committee. *Guide to Performance Evaluation of Library
   Materials Vendors.* Chicago: American Library Association, 1988.

Barbato, J. "Small Press Struggle for Distribution." *Publishers Weekly* 238 (November 15, 1991): 25–34.

Barker, J. W., et al. "Organizing Out-of-Print and Replacement Acquisitions for Effectiveness, Efficiency and the Future." *Library Acquisitions: Practice and Theory* 14, no. 2 (1990): 137–63.

———. "Vendor Studies Redux." *Library Acquisitions: Practice and Theory* 13, no. 2
   (1989): 133–41.

Barker, J. W., D. Tonkery, and C. Flansburg. "Unbundling Vendor Costs." *Library
   Acquisitions: Practice and Theory* 15, no. 3 (1991): 399–406.

Basch, N. B. "Department Stores to Boutiques: How Many Serial Vendors and What
   Kind of Services Does Your Library Need?" *Serials Librarian* 12, nos. 3/4 (1990):
   81–85.

Bottomley, L. "Changing Role of the Vendor." *Serials Librarian* 23, nos. 3/4 (1993):
   245–47.

Brown, Linda A. "Approval Vendor Selection—What's the Best Practice?" *Library Acquisitions* 22, no. 3 (Fall 1998): 341–51.

Brown, Lynne C. "Vendor Evaluation." *Collection Management* 19 (1995): 47–46.

Demaris, N. "Electronic Book and Serials Acquisitions: The Medium Is the Message."
   Computers in Libraries 13 (January 1993): 25–27.

Gammon, J. A. "Partnering with Vendors for Increased Productivity." *Library Acquisitions Practice and Theory* 21, no. 4 (1997): 229–35.

Gaskell, Philip. *A New Introduction to Bibliography.* Oxford: Oxford University
   Press, 1972.

Gilbert, D. L. *Complete Guide to Starting a Used Book Store*. Chicago: Chicago Review Press, 1986.

Grant, J. "Librarian and the Purchasing Function." *Library Acquisitions: Practice and Theory* 9, no. 4 (1985): 305–6.

Hirshon, Arnold, and Barbara Winters. *Outsourcing Library Technical Services: A How-to-Do-It Manual*. New York: Neal-Schuman, 1996.

Hubbard, W. J., and J. Welch. "An Empirical Test of Two Vendors' Trade Discounts." *Library Acquisitions* 22, no. 2 (1998): 131–37.

Ivins, O. "Library Acquisitions: Budget Strategies, Vendor Selection, Vendor Evaluation." *Library Acquisitions: Practice and Theory* 16, no. 3 (1992): 257–63.

Kent, P. "How to Evaluate Serial Suppliers." *Library Acquisitions: Practice and Theory* 18, (Spring 1994): 83–87.

McQueen, J., and N. B. Basch. "Negotiating with Subscription Agencies." *American Libraries* 22 (June 1991): 532–34.

Miller, Heather S. *Managing Acquisitions and Vendor Relations*. New York: Neal-Schuman, 1992.

Morris, J. H. "Library Sales and Wholesalers." *Small Press* 11 (Summer 1993): 20–27.

National Acquisitions Group. *The Value to Libraries of Special Services Provided by Library Suppliers: Developing a Costing Model*. Leeds, England: National Acquisitions Group, 1996.

Phelps, D. "Publishers' Discounts But at What Price?" *Library Acquisitions: Practice and Theory* 14, no. 3 (1990): 289–93.

Presley, R. L. "Firing an Old Friend, Painful Decisions: Ethics Between Librarians and Vendors." *Library Acquisitions: Practice and Theory* 17, no. 1 (1993): 53–59.

Richards, D. T. "Library/Dealer Relationships: Reflections on the Ideal." *Journal of Library Administration* 16, no. 3 (1992): 45–55.

Serebnick, J. "Selection and Holding of Small Publishers' Books in OCLC Libraries: A Study of the Influence of Reviews, Publishers, and Vendors." *Library Quarterly* 62 (July 1992): 259–94.

Shabb, C. H. "Partnership: Reality or Myth." *Library Acquisitions* 20, no. 3 (1996): 387–89.

Shafa, Z. M., et al. "Regional Study of Vendor Performance for In-Print Monographs." *Library Acquisitions: Practice and Theory* 16, no. 1 (1992): 21–29.

Shrik, G. M. "Contract Acquisitions." *Library Acquisitions: Practice and Theory* 17 (Summer 1993): 145–53.

Stankus, T. "Death of a Salesman: The Decline in Library Visits from Serial Marketers." *Technicalities* 17 (July/August 1997): 11–13.

Walther, James. "Assessing Library Vendor Relations: A Focus on Evaluation and Communication." *Bottom Line* 11, no. 4 (1998): 149–57.

Wilmering, Bill. "Using the RFP Process to Select a Serials Vendor." *Serials Librarian* 28, nos. 3/4 (1996): 325–29.

Wingen, Peter V. *Your Old Books*. Chicago: American Library Association/ACRL—Rare Books and Manuscripts Section, 1994.

Academic

Anderson, J. "Order Consolidation: A Shift to Single Vendor Service." *Serials Librarian* 17, nos. 3/4 (1990): 93–97.

Brunet, Patrick J., and Lee Shiflett. "Out-of-Print and Antiquarian Books: Guides for Reference Librarians." *RQ* 32 (Fall 1992): 85–101.

Calhoun, J., et al. "Modelling an Academic Approval Plan." *Library Resources & Technical Services* 34 (July 1990): 367–79.

Ferguson, A. W. "British Approval Plan Books: American or British Vendor?" *Collection Building* 8, no. 1 (1988): 18–22.

Flood, Susan, *Evaluation and Status of Approval Plans*. SPEC Kit 221. Washington, D.C.: Association of Research Libraries, 1997.

Kaatrude, P. B. "Approval Plan vs. Conventional Development." *Collection Management* 11, nos. 1/2 (1988): 145–51.

Kuo, Hui-Min. "Flat or Float? A Study of Vendor Discount Rates Applied to Firm Orders in a College Library." *Library Acquisitions* 22, no. 4 (1998): 409–14.

Womack, K., et al. "An Approval Plan Vendor Review." *Library Acquisitions: Practice and Theory* 12, nos. 3/4 (1988): 363–78.

Public

Anichiarico, M., and A. Boaz. "Distributor Connection: Responding to Demand." *Library Journal* 118 (February 1, 1993): 129–36.

Prete, B. "Publishing for Literacy." *Publishers Weekly* 237 (November 30, 1990): 27–28.

Schiller, J. G. "Appraising Rare and Collectible Children's Books." *AB Bookman's Weekly* 86 (November 1990): 1861–71.

Strickler, D. "What I Learned Working in a Bookstore." *Library Journal* 117 (June 15, 1992): 47–48.

Tuttle, M. "Magazine Fulfillment Centers." *Library Acquisitions: Practice and Theory* 9, no. 1 (1985): 41–49.

"Weathering the Storm: Publishers, Booksellers, and Wholesalers Discuss the Effect of the Recession on Children's Books." *Publishers Weekly* 239 (February 12, 1992): 7–9.

School

Eaglen, A. B. "Book Wholesalers: Pros and Cons." *School Library Journal* 25 (October 1978): 116–19.

———. "Shell Game: Publishers, Vendors and the Myth of the Backlist." *School Library Journal* 38 (November 1992): 24–28.

Hass, E. "Librarians and Booksellers Working Together in the Year of the Young Reader." *School Library Journal* 35 (January 1989): 24–27.

See, L. "Biting the Hand That Feeds You." *Publishers Weekly* 238 (December 13, 1991): 28–29.

Stafford, P. "One-Stop Shopping with Your Paperback Wholesaler." *School Library Journal* 32 (September 1985): 39–41.

Stefani, J. "Using Vendors as Educational Resources." *Southeastern Librarian* 40 (Spring 1990): 9–11.

"Vendor Connections: Relations with School Media Specialists." *School Librarian's Workshop* 17 (May 1997): 1–2.

Special

Cather, J. P. "Librarians and Booksellers: Forming a Durable Bond." *AB Bookman's Weekly* 86 (June 18, 1990): 2624–32.

Front, T. "Music as an Antiquarian Trade Specialty." *AB Bookman's Weekly* 86 (December 10, 1990): 2289–97.

Hook, W. J. "Approval Plans for Religious and Theological Libraries." *Library Acquisitions: Practice and Theory* 15, no. 2 (1991): 215–27.

Schwalb, R. "Distributors: Religious and General Wholesalers." *Publishers Weekly* 237 (October 5, 1990): 58–64.

St. Clair, G., and J. Treadwell. "Science and Technology Approval Plans Compared." *Library Resources & Technical Services* 33 (October 1989): 382–92.

Stave, D. G. "Art Books on Approval: Why Not?" *Library Acquisitions: Practice and Theory* 7, no. 1 (1983): 5–6.

13

Fiscal
Management

When faced with limited funding, a library must make the money go as far as possible. In the area of collection development, fiscal management is a joint activity involving everyone who participates in the process—selectors, acquisitions staff, and senior management. Controlling expenditures and securing adequate funding are two key activities in collection management. Monies spent on materials for the collection constitute the second largest expense category for the majority of libraries and information centers. Traditionally, in United States libraries, salaries represent the largest percentage of the total budget, followed by the materials (book) budget, and finally, all other operating expenses. That order remains today, but the percentage spent on materials has decreased as salaries have risen. Although percentages vary, the order also remains the same in any type of information environment or any size collection. As is often the case, most of the literature on the topic of collection budgeting reflects a large research library orientation. However, the same issues exist in other libraries. Similarly, most of the ideas and suggestions contained in such articles apply equally well to other information settings.

In the recent past, there has been constant pressure on the materials budget of most libraries. This pressure resulted in a decline in the percentage of the total budget spent on acquiring items for the collection. The almost yearly double-digit inflation of serials prices further skewed the traditional balance in collection fund allocations. In many libraries in the United States, serials expenditures exceed monographic purchases, even in institutions that have traditionally emphasized book collections.

If one compares the total amount of money expended on materials 30 years ago with the current funding levels, today's total is considerably higher. Unfortunately, the total expenditures do not tell the entire story. When one looks at the number of items acquired for the money, one sees that the increase in acquisitions is not proportional to the funding increases. We are spending more and acquiring less. Since the 1970s, many libraries, along with many other organizations, have dealt with budgets that some persons call "steady state," others call "zero growth," and still others call "static." At best, budgeting of this type uses the previous year's inflation rate as the base for the next fiscal year's increase. An average inflation rate, like all averages, contains elements that increase at both above and below the average rate. For libraries this is a problem, because the inflation rate for information materials has been running well ahead of the overall inflation rate.

Problems in Fiscal Management

Over the years, collection development staffs in the United States have faced several problems. Book and journal prices have generally increased, and continue to increase, at rates well above the country's average inflation rate as measured by the Consumer Price Index (CPI). As a result, most libraries have experienced some decline in acquisition rates. Serials prices increased even more rapidly than did monographic prices. To maintain serials subscriptions, libraries took monies from book funds, thus further reducing the number of monographs acquired. Eventually, libraries started canceling subscriptions. Thus, differential inflation rates and the use of national average rates as the basis for calculating budgets have contributed to declining acquisition rates for many libraries.

A second problem was, and still is, that the materials budget is vulnerable in periods of tight budgets. Expenditures on materials are somewhat discretionary in that (in theory) one could wait to buy an item until the next fiscal year. Institutions set staff salaries on an annual basis, and staff reductions are rare during the middle of a fiscal year, unless the organization faces a major financial crisis. In essence, salaries are the last item organizations cut when attempting to save money. Without heat, light, and water (utility bills), the organization cannot remain open, so those generally are not cut during a fiscal year. Some operating expenses are discretionary: pens, pencils, paper, typewriter ribbons, and other office supplies. Professional development and travel reimbursements may likewise be frozen, in an attempt to save funds. Institutions may achieve small savings, in terms of percentage of the total budget, by cutting back in such areas. Institutions with relatively large library collections view the materials budget as one of the largest available pools of funds that could be cut in an emergency. (Even a medium-sized library, such as the Von der Ahe Library at Loyola Marymount University, has a materials budget of well over $1.5 million. This amount is large enough to make the financial officers look at it as a source of significant funds if needed.) Further, the reality is that the monograph materials budget is the only place where significant cuts are easy to make, because of the non-ongoing nature of the material. All too often, the long-term impact of such decisions does not receive enough consideration, and the other choices appear, at least in the short run, to be even less acceptable. These issues are institutional and apply to corporate and special libraries as much as to publicly funded libraries.

What happened in collecting in the 1970s and 1980s was a shift in emphasis from monographs to maintaining periodical collections. Today, that shift is slowly reversing, and through careful library budget preparation and presentation, funding authorities appear to be more willing to accept differential budget increases that more closely reflect the actual expense experience. If nothing else, the problems of the past 30 years caused collection development officers to become better planners and to develop more accurate methods for calculating budgetary needs. As a result, they have more credibility with funding authorities.

This chapter covers several budget and fiscal topics: (1) a brief discussion of library accounting systems, (2) estimating costs of materials, (3) allocating available funds, (4) monitoring expenditures (encumbering), and (5) special budgeting problems.

Library Fund Accounting

The vast majority of libraries and information centers are part of not-for-profit (NFP) organizations. Being not-for-profit affects how the library maintains its financial records, particularly when contrasted with for-profit organizations. Libraries that are part of a governmental jurisdiction receive most revenues through an annual budget. Collection development officers must have accurate information about the monies available, and they need accurate data to assist in the preparation of budget requests. The funding authorities review the budget requests and authorize certain levels of funding for various activities. The three most common forms of income for libraries are appropriations (monies distributed by the governing body to its agencies to carry out specific purposes), revenue generated by the library as a result of service fees and fines, and endowment/donations.

Because of the nature of the financial activities, certain accounting terms and concepts are different for NFP organizations than for for-profit organizations. However, some general accounting rules and practices do apply. One special term for NFP accounting is *fund accounting*. (Fund accounting has been defined as a set of self-balancing account groups.) Another difference is that the profit-oriented bookkeeping system equation uses *assets, liabilities*, and *equity*; in NFP accounting, the elements used are assets, liabilities, and *fund balance*. One of the equations for NFP bookkeeping is that assets must equal liabilities plus the fund balance; another is that the fund balance is the difference between assets and liabilities. Substituting equity for fund balance would make the equation apply to for-profit organizations. A difference between these equations is that an increase in fund balance carries with it no special meaning, whereas an increase in equity is a positive signal in a for-profit organization. Other terms, such as *debit, credit, journalizing, posting*, and *trial balance*, have the same meaning, regardless of the organization's profit orientation.

In most libraries, the major fund is the operating fund. Other funds may be endowment and physical plant funds. The operating funds are the group of accounts used to handle the day-to-day activities of the library for a given time, usually one year, covering such items as salaries, materials purchases, and utility bills. Within the operating fund there may be two categories of accounts: restricted and unrestricted.

Restricted accounts require that one use the monies only for specific purposes. Collection development and acquisition staff often work with such accounts (frequently referred to as funds in the monetary rather than the accounting meaning of the term). More often than not, these accounts are the result of donations by individuals who have definite ideas about how the library may spend the money. Some libraries have endowments that are a combination of individual and corporate or foundation gifts; an example is endowments developed under the National Endowment for the Humanities Challenge Grant program. (Sometimes gifts are for current use, and sometimes they are for an endowment. Endowments should generate income for the library indefinitely. The normal procedure for endowments is to make available some percentage of the interest earned. The balance of the interest is returned to the endowment to increase its capital base. Private libraries, and an increasing number of publicly funded libraries, have one or more endowments.) Often the donor's restrictions are narrow. When the restrictions are too narrow, it is difficult to make effective use of the available monies. Most collection development officers prefer *unrestricted* book accounts (used for any appropriate item for the collection) or broad-based restricted accounts.

The purpose of the accounting system is to assure the proper use of monies provided and to make it possible to track expenditures. That is, one must record (charge) every financial transaction to some account, and keep a record of what the transaction involved. With a properly functioning fund accounting system, it is possible to tie every item acquired to a specific account and to verify when the transaction took place. With a good accounting system, one can easily provide accurate reports about all financial aspects of collection development activities. Furthermore, it is a great planning aid. It takes time to understand accounting systems, but one must understand them if one wishes to be an effective and efficient collection development officer. A good book to consult for accounting is G. Stevenson Smith's *Managerial Accounting for Libraries and Other Not-for-Profit Organizations*.[1] For budgeting, another very sound title is Richard S. Rounds's *Basic Budgeting Practices for Librarians*.[2]

Estimating Costs

Several factors influence the funding needs for collection development. Changes in the composition of the service community may have an important impact in either a positive or negative sense (see chapter 2). Another factor is changes in collecting activities, such as the scope or depth desired in a subject area (see chapter 3). The two cost factors that come up year in and year out are the price of materials and inflation.

From time to time, libraries have had some problems establishing the credibility of collection development funding requirements. Though a good accounting system will assist in justifying budget requests, additional data about book expenditures is often necessary. One example of the problems caused by inflation, stable budgets, and rapidly rising prices for materials (and perhaps limited credibility) is what happened to the expenditures and acquisition rates for academic libraries. Between 1993 and 1998, monograph prices rose just over 25 percent. For serials, the data was almost shocking, if one experienced it; between 1986 and 1996 prices rose 169 percent. Although the total amount of money expanded was higher in 1998 than in 1993, monograph purchases fell by 14 percent.[3] Libraries of every type and size experienced similar problems during this time. *Library Journal* periodically publishes surveys of spending and other activities of various types of libraries. Though the surveys do not appear predictably, when they become available they provide useful national data to compare where your library falls.

Data about price increases has been available for some time. During the 1970s, the profession made an all-out effort to create useful library price indexes that measure rates of change. A subcommittee of the American National Standards Institute, the Z39 Committee, was able to develop guidelines for price indexes.[4] By the early 1980s it was necessary to revise the guidelines. Another group effort was that of the Library Materials Price Index Committee (Resources Section, Resources and Services Division of ALA). That committee produced a price index for American materials and some international publications. These efforts provide consistent data on price changes over a long period, which, when averaged, is as close as one can come to predicting future price changes.

One finds the most recent data in journals; historical data appear in *The Bowker Annual*. Using *The Bowker Annual* may be adequate for some purposes, but one needs to be aware that the information appearing in the "current" volume is almost two years old. Preliminary data for books published during a calendar year appear in *Publishers Weekly* (often in late February or early March). Final data appear some months later (September or October). The major problem with the published indexes is that up-to-date data may not be readily available when one must prepare a budget request. Vendors can sometimes provide more current data. Some vendors will provide custom pricing information, and others may provide a general set of data based on their experience, such as the Yankee Book Peddler material illustrated in figures 13.1–13.2, pages 382–83. These information sheets contain price data about books handled in the firm. At the time of preparation of this chapter, the sheets covered titles processed between January 1997 and December 1998. Figure 13.3, page 384, illustrates custom information supplied by Academic Book Center for the same type of material but for a different time period.

It is also possible to secure information about serials subscriptions from a vendor. Figures 13.4, pages 385–93, reproduced from EBSCO's *Serials Price Projections—2000*, illustrates the differences among types of libraries as well as the relationship between subscription prices and exchange rates.

Just as libraries prepare budget requests at different times of the year, pricing data appears at various times during the year in a variety of sources. The challenge is to find the most current data, which may determine whether the library receives requested funding.

For libraries that purchase a significant number of foreign publications, there is a need to estimate the impact of exchange rates. Volatile exchange rates affect buying power almost as much as inflation. For example, in January 1985, the pound sterling was at $1.2963 (U.S.); in January 1988 it was up to $1.7813 (U.S.); in 1992 it was $1.7653 (U.S.); by January 1994 it was down to $1.4872 (U.S.), and in March 1999 had moved up to $1.6064 (U.S.). During the same period, the Canadian dollar went from $0.6345 to $0.7693 (U.S.), then to $0.7913 (U.S.), back to $0.736 (U.S.) and then to $0.5199 (U.S.). Although it is impossible to accurately forecast the direction and amount of fluctuation in the exchange rates for the next 12 months, some effort should

(Text continues on page 394.)

Annual Roundup of
Publisher Title Output: 1997 vs. 1998

The next six pages are YBP's traditional examination of the publishing harvest, in statistical terms and as captured in our U.S. Approval Plan coverage. The numbers usefully mirror some of the market forces that cause output and prices to go up and down. Note, however, that variations can occasionally be the result of mergers or distribution changes. Unusually expensive titles or sets can skew the average price per title for the year.

SELECTED UNIVERSITY PRESSES

| | JAN 1997 - DEC 1997 | | JAN 1998 - DEC 1998 | | PRICE |
	TITLES	AVG. LIST	TITLES	AVG. LIST	VARIANCE
Alabama	44	$32.38	40	$33.75	4.23%
Alaska	6	$23.66	4	$30.46	28.74%
Arizona	26	$32.63	80	$38.82	18.97%
Arkansas	23	$34.13	26	$26.42	-22.59%
Associated Univ. Presses	120	$40.55	138	$43.15	6.41%
Bowling Green	16	$45.58	11	$45.50	-0.18%
British Columbia	40	$55.70	34	$52.11	-6.45%
Brookings Institution	102	$24.79	156	$25.27	1.94%
California	212	$43.52	220	$38.27	-12.06%
Cambridge	1,078	$64.44	996	$64.79	0.54%
Carleton	16	$18.48	16	$27.33	47.89%
Carnegie-Mellon	11	$15.50	19	$16.53	6.65%
Catholic	20	$43.65	26	$44.45	1.83%
Chicago	196	$45.05	210	$42.99	-4.57%
Colorado	36	$36.31	30	$30.41	-16.25%
Columbia	219	$55.99	192	$49.74	-11.16%
Cornell	134	$38.26	185	$39.86	4.18%
Dist. de Livres (see note #1)	38	$27.22	75	$24.45	-10.18%
Duke	105	$47.12	103	$46.47	-1.38%
Florida	67	$40.34	77	$41.76	3.52%
Fordham	39	$28.33	39	$27.34	-3.49%
Georgetown	24	$45.05	22	$52.76	17.11%
Georgia	93	$35.55	80	$31.61	-11.08%
Harvard	145	$34.88	200	$35.82	2.69%
Hawaii	106	$38.30	147	$43.24	12.90%
Hoover	25	$9.31	3	$19.28	107.09%
Idaho	10	$33.46	8	$31.21	-6.72%
Illinois	103	$34.18	90	$37.66	10.18%
Indiana	147	$32.55	144	$34.16	4.95%
Iowa	38	$25.66	29	$29.81	16.17%
Iowa State	49	$49.26	57	$51.04	3.61%
Johns Hopkins	194	$33.75	192	$36.50	8.15%
Kansas	40	$33.08	46	$34.93	5.59%
Kent State	27	$31.74	27	$38.57	21.52%
Kentucky	56	$30.83	56	$28.53	-7.46%
Louisiana State	85	$26.14	69	$26.46	1.22%
Loyola	25	$29.34	22	$21.75	-25.87%
McGill-Queens	78	$49.60	34	$48.51	-2.20%
Manchester Univ. Press	59	$57.95	63	$64.79	11.80%
Massachusetts	41	$39.01	31	$37.12	-4.84%
Medieval Institute	6	$19.83	15	$38.60	94.65%
Mercer	40	$28.42	38	$27.97	-1.58%
Michigan	171	$40.69	147	$45.38	11.53%
Michigan State	26	$31.91	18	$30.46	-4.54%

(continued on next page)

Fig. 13.1. Annual roundup of publisher title output: 1997 vs. 1998.

SELECTED SCHOLARLY TRADE AND PROFESSIONAL PRESSES

	JAN 1997 - DEC 1997		JAN 1998 - DEC 1998		PRICE
	TITLES	AVG. LIST	TITLES	AVG. LIST	VARIANCE
A.H.A. Press (Amer. Hosp. Assoc.)	28	$86.06	39	$97.60	13.41%
Abbeville	69	$48.66	72	$46.01	-5.45%
ABC-CLIO	67	$67.94	47	$83.29	22.59%
Abingdon Press	115	$18.92	90	$18.93	0.05%
Ablex	32	$73.64	45	$76.02	3.23%
Abrams	147	$47.87	161	$45.88	-4.16%
Academic	351	$105.23	344	$102.34	-2.75%
Addison Wesley Longman	499	$38.90	598	$42.41	9.02%
Africa World	40	$55.76	51	$63.83	14.47%
AMACOM	66	$37.40	71	$38.20	2.14%
Amer. Ceramic Society	25	$86.20	15	$103.93	20.57%
Amer. Chemical Society	103	$125.92	46	$105.22	-16.44%
Amer. Enterprise Institute (AEI Press)	19	$17.32	20	$21.25	22.69%
Amer. Institute of Aeronautics (AIAA)	17	$73.52	35	$74.13	0.83%
Amer. Institute of Architects	15	$33.32	3	$25.63	-23.08%
Amer. Library Association	26	$50.46	61	$38.66	-23.38%
Amer. Psychiatric Press	43	$38.26	42	$44.17	15.45%
Amer. Psychological Assoc.	55	$34.47	54	$40.60	17.78%
Amer. Soc. of Civil Engineers	79	$46.94	59	$68.14	45.16%
Amnesty International USA	27	$6.11	34	$6.20	1.47%
Anthroposophic Press	21	$18.66	43	$21.30	14.15%
Antique Collectors Club	139	$64.20	182	$53.07	-17.34%
Applause Theatre Book	30	$21.12	18	$15.06	-28.69%
Appleton & Lange	41	$58.98	56	$66.59	12.90%
Ariadne Press	13	$23.02	13	$25.56	11.03%
Jason Aronson	179	$33.22	124	$39.13	17.79%
Arte Publico	20	$13.95	20	$14.00	0.36%
Artech	58	$76.95	50	$79.26	3.00%
Ashgate (ex-Gower)	594	$77.57	531	$79.40	2.36%
ASM International	19	$123.32	17	$137.58	11.56%
Asme Publications	5	$186.99	66	$150.01	-19.78%
Aspen Pub.	88	$65.56	78	$61.50	-6.19%
ASQC (Amer. Soc. Quality Control)	27	$28.77	15	$31.17	8.34%
Augsburg Fortress	70	$19.75	39	$23.74	20.20%
Avon Books	49	$22.24	61	$21.69	-2.47%
Baker Book House	125	$19.33	73	$22.73	17.59%
A.A. Balkema	76	$108.82	105	$97.43	-10.47%
Ballantine/Fawcett/Del Rey	125	$17.50	258	$19.52	11.54%
Bantam Doubleday Dell	394	$21.09	409	$20.82	-1.28%
Barron's Educational	163	$12.28	148	$13.00	5.86%
John Benjamins	71	$81.22	81	$74.43	-8.36%
Berghahn Books	23	$54.10	24	$48.60	-10.17%
Bernan Associates	106	$40.82	52	$49.29	20.75%
Black Sparrow	12	$28.33	9	$27.50	-2.93%
Blackwell	227	$60.28	205	$63.69	5.66%
Blackwell Science	201	$84.56	155	$101.01	19.45%
BNA Books	22	$138.64	11	$102.27	-26.23%
Books Nippan	59	$64.77	18	$69.69	7.60%
Boydell & Brewer	113	$75.35	83	$73.91	-1.91%
Brassey's	70	$45.56	50	$30.48	-33.10%
George Braziller	15	$28.31	21	$28.37	0.21%
Brill Academic Publishers	169	$123.45	189	$112.40	-8.95%
Broadview Press	26	$18.07	6	$16.78	-7.14%
Brookes	28	$38.26	31	$37.60	-1.73%
David Brown Book Co.	43	$46.31	33	$46.37	0.13%
Butterworth-Heinemann	392	$52.78	413	$51.29	-2.82%
Camden House	27	$48.99	33	$55.96	14.23%
Carol Publishing	91	$18.71	85	$16.42	-12.24%
Carolina Academic Press	21	$42.30	41	$36.32	-14.14%
Frank Cass	71	$41.43	82	$45.26	9.24%

(continued on next page)

Fig. 13.2. Selected scholarly trade and professional presses.

37248 *LOYOLA MARYMOUNT U.
CHAS. VON DER AHE LIB

MIDWEST LIBRARY SERVICE
MAP REPORT - RETURNS BY SUBJECT
FOR THE PERIOD 5/01/98 TO 4/30/99

AP6600   PAGE   1
REPORT DATE 5/03/99

LC CLASSIFICATION#	DESCRIPTION	QTY SHIPPED BOOKS	FORMS	TOTAL	$'S	QTY RETURNED BOOKS	FORMS	$'S	TOTAL	$'S	REASON FOR RETURN	RETURN % BOOKS	FORMS	TOTAL
AM 10-101	Museography. Individual	0	1	1	.00	0	0	.00	0	.00		0	0	-0
A'S SUBTOTAL		0	1	1	.00	0	0	.00	0	.00		0	0	0
B 69-5739	Philosophy (General)	3	0	3	120.35	2	0	.00	2	120.35	40-2;	67	0	67
B 108-708	History & systems	7	1	8	.00	0	0	.00	0	.00		0	0	0
B 720-765	Ancient	17	1	18	209.46	4	0	.00	4	209.46	11-1; 40-3;	24	0	22
B 790-5739	Medieval	2	1	3	20.75	1	0	.00	1	20.75	40-1;	50	0	33
B 850-5739	Modern	15	1	16	171.36	4	0	.00	4	171.36	40-3; 60-1;	27	0	25
B 1801-2630	By region or country	13	9	22	.00	0	0	.00	0	.00		0	0	0
B 2521-3396	France	13	2	15	148.54	4	0	.00	4	148.54	40-4;	31	0	27
B	Germany. Austria(German)	30	9	39	157.62	4	0	.00	4	157.62	40-3; 60-1;	13	0	10
BC	Logic	2	0	2	.00	0	0	.00	0	.00		0	0	0
BD 143-236	Epistemology	10	1	11	239.38	5	0	.00	5	239.38	20-1; 21-1; 40-3;	50	0	45
BD 240-260	Methodology	0	1	1	.00	0	0	.00	0	.00		0	0	0
BD 300-450	Ontology	11	4	15	159.66	5	0	.00	5	159.66	10-1; 40-3; 60-1;	45	0	33
BD 493-701	Cosmology	0	1	1	.00	0	0	.00	0	.00		0	0	0
BF	Psychology	8	0	8	.00	0	0	.00	0	.00		0	0	0
BF 175-175	Psychoanalysis	8	1	9	132.72	3	0	.00	3	132.72	40-2; 60-1;	38	0	33
BF 180-210	Experimental psychology	2	0	2	.00	0	0	.00	0	.00		0	0	0
BF 231-299	Sensation. Aesthesiology	4	0	4	.00	0	0	.00	0	.00		0	0	0
BF 309-499	Cognition. Perception	14	3	17	.00	0	0	.00	0	.00		0	0	0
BF 501-504.3	Motivation	1	0	1	.00	0	0	.00	0	.00		0	0	0
BF 511-593	Emotion	10	1	11	173.81	5	0	.00	5	173.81	10-1; 40-3; 90-1;	50	0	45
BF 608-635	Will. Choice	2	0	2	.00	0	0	.00	0	.00		0	0	0
BF 636-637	Applied psychology	3	0	3	49.39	1	0	.00	1	49.39	40-1;	33	0	33
BF 698-698.9	Personality	2	0	2	.00	0	0	.00	0	.00		0	0	0
BF 699-711	Genetic psychology	1	0	1	.00	0	0	.00	0	.00		0	0	0
BF 712-724.85	Developmental psychology	3	1	4	.00	0	0	.00	0	.00		0	0	0
BF 721-723	Child psychology	1	0	1	.00	0	0	.00	0	.00		0	0	0
BF 724.8	Old age. (General works)	1	0	1	.00	0	0	.00	0	.00		0	0	0
BF 795-839.5	Temperament. Character	0	1	1	.00	0	0	.00	0	.00		0	0	0
BF 1001-1389	Parapsychology	2	1	3	.00	0	0	.00	0	.00		0	0	0
BH	Aesthetics	2	1	3	65.95	2	0	.00	2	65.95	40-2;	100	0	67
BJ	Ethics. Social usages	2	1	3	.00	0	0	.00	0	.00		0	0	0
BJ 71-1185	History and systems	7	0	7	.00	0	0	.00	0	.00		0	0	0
BJ 1188-1295	Religious ethics	6	0	6	.00	0	0	.00	0	.00		0	0	0
BJ 1518-1697	Individual ethics. Charac	3	0	11	.00	0	0	.00	0	.00		0	0	0
BL	Religions. Mythology	2	0	2	.00	0	0	.00	0	.00		0	0	0
BL 74-98	Religions of the world	3	0	3	49.76	2	0	.00	2	49.76	40-2;	67	0	67
BL 175-290	Natural theology	1	0	1	.00	0	0	.00	0	.00		0	0	0
BL 300-325	The myth. Comparative	1	0	1	.00	0	0	.00	0	.00		0	0	0
BL 425-490	Religious doctrines(Gen)	1	0	1	.00	0	0	.00	0	.00		0	0	0
BL 500-547	Eschatology	1	0	1	.00	0	0	.00	0	.00		0	0	0

10-Duplicate; 11-Firm Order; 12-Standing Order; 13-Exclude this series from our profile; 20-Readership level; 21-Highly specialized; 22-Entry level; 30-Geographic area;
31-Limited interest in this area; 32-Local interest; 40-Limited interest in this topic; 50-Popular treatment; 60-Library has adequate coverage in this subject; 70-Out of profile;
80-Defective. No replacement; 81-Defective. Send replacement; 90-No reason given by customer; 91-Budget or too costly;

Fig. 13.3. Loyola Marymount returns by subject. Reprinted courtesy of Midwest Library Service.

SERIALS PRICES 1995-1999
WITH PROJECTIONS FOR 2000

University Research Library Cost History

	Average # Titles	1995 Average Cost Per Title	1996 Average Cost Per Title	Change from 1995-1996	1997 Average Cost Per Title	Change from 1996-1997	1998 Average Cost Per Title	Change from 1997-1998	1999 Average Cost Per Title	Change from 1998-1999	Change from 1995-1999
UNIVERSITY RESEARCH LIBRARY											
U.S. TITLES	3,367	$195.67	$214.28	9.51%	$233.86	9.14%	$255.19	9.12%	$280.10	9.76%	43.15%
NON-U.S. TITLES	1,537	$472.78	$567.99	20.14%	$634.28	11.67%	$675.89	6.56%	$724.04	7.12%	53.15%
ALL TITLES	4,904	$282.51	$325.12	15.08%	$359.34	10.53%	$387.03	7.71%	$419.22	8.32%	48.39%

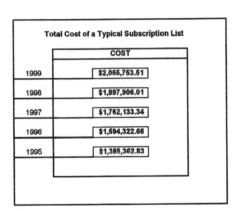

Total Cost of a Typical Subscription List

	COST
1999	$2,055,753.51
1998	$1,897,906.01
1997	$1,762,133.34
1996	$1,594,322.66
1995	$1,385,362.83

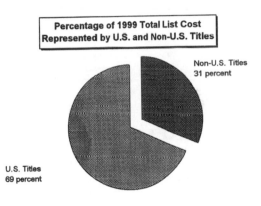

Percentage of 1999 Total List Cost Represented by U.S. and Non-U.S. Titles

Non-U.S. Titles
31 percent

U.S. Titles
69 percent

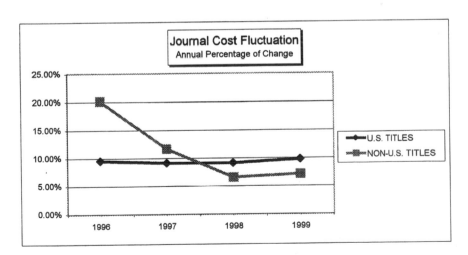

Journal Cost Fluctuation
Annual Percentage of Change

Fig. 13.4. Serials prices, 1995–1999, for various types of libraries.

(Figure 13.4 continues on page 386.)

Fig. 13.4—Continued.

College/University Library Cost History

	Average # Titles	1995 Average Cost Per Title	1996 Average Cost Per Title	Change from 1995-1996	1997 Average Cost Per Title	Change from 1996-1997	1998 Average Cost Per Title	Change from 1997-1998	1999 Average Cost Per Title	Change from 1998-1999	Change from 1995-1999
COLLEGE/UNIVERSITY LIBRARY											
U.S. TITLES	2,016	$152.88	$167.62	9.64%	$182.46	8.85%	$198.74	8.92%	$217.28	9.33%	42.12%
NON-U.S. TITLES	600	$411.32	$488.27	18.71%	$543.17	11.24%	$583.39	7.40%	$629.68	7.93%	53.09%
ALL TITLES	2,616	$212.17	$241.18	13.67%	$265.21	9.96%	$286.98	8.21%	$311.88	8.68%	47.00%

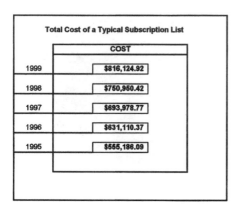

Total Cost of a Typical Subscription List

	COST
1999	$816,124.92
1998	$750,950.42
1997	$693,978.77
1996	$631,110.37
1995	$555,186.09

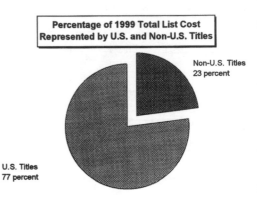

Percentage of 1999 Total List Cost Represented by U.S. and Non-U.S. Titles

Non-U.S. Titles
23 percent

U.S. Titles
77 percent

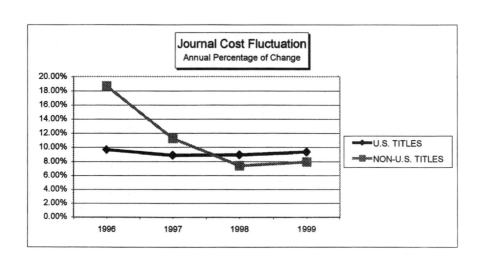

Journal Cost Fluctuation
Annual Percentage of Change

U.S. TITLES
NON-U.S. TITLES

SERIALS PRICES 1995-1999
WITH PROJECTIONS FOR 2000

Academic Medical Library Cost History

	Average # Titles	1995 Average Cost Per Title	1996 Average Cost Per Title	Change from 1995-1996	1997 Average Cost Per Title	Change from 1996-1997	1998 Average Cost Per Title	Change from 1997-1998	1999 Average Cost Per Title	Change from 1998-1999	Change from 1995-1999
ACADEMIC MEDICAL LIBRARY											
U.S. TITLES	933	$269.30	$305.76	13.54%	$341.06	11.55%	$380.41	11.54%	$425.03	11.73%	57.83%
NON-U.S. TITLES	516	$610.91	$725.40	18.74%	$814.99	12.35%	$870.36	6.79%	$927.75	6.59%	51.86%
ALL TITLES	1,449	$390.99	$455.25	16.44%	$509.89	12.00%	$554.94	8.84%	$604.12	8.86%	54.51%

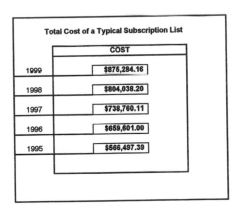

Total Cost of a Typical Subscription List

	COST
1999	$875,284.16
1998	$804,038.20
1997	$738,760.11
1996	$659,601.00
1995	$566,497.39

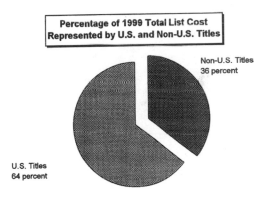

Percentage of 1999 Total List Cost Represented by U.S. and Non-U.S. Titles

Non-U.S. Titles
36 percent

U.S. Titles
64 percent

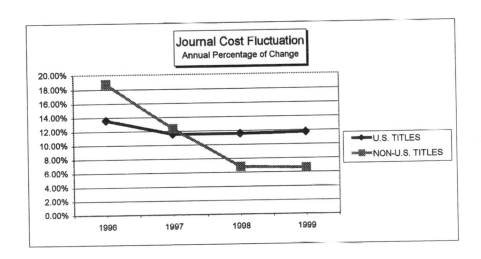

Journal Cost Fluctuation
Annual Percentage of Change

U.S. TITLES
NON-U.S. TITLES

(Figure 13.4 continues on page 388.)

Fig. 13.4—*Continued.*

Hospital Library Cost History

SERIALS PRICES 1995-1999
WITH PROJECTIONS FOR 2000

	# Titles	1995 Average Cost Per Title	1996 Average Cost Per Title	Change from 1995-1996	1997 Average Cost Per Title	Change from 1996-1997	1998 Average Cost Per Title	Change from 1997-1998	1999 Average Cost Per Title	Change from 1998-1999	Change from 1995-1999
HOSPITAL LIBRARY											
U.S. TITLES	105	$162.45	$182.82	12.54%	$207.31	13.40%	$226.21	9.12%	$251.49	11.18%	54.81%
NON-U.S. TITLES	15	$278.74	$295.27	5.93%	$323.95	9.71%	$357.14	10.25%	$392.15	9.80%	40.69%
ALL TITLES	120	$176.99	$196.88	11.24%	$221.89	12.70%	$242.58	9.32%	$269.07	10.92%	52.03%

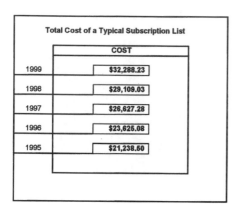

Total Cost of a Typical Subscription List

	COST
1999	$32,288.23
1998	$29,109.03
1997	$26,627.28
1996	$23,625.08
1995	$21,238.50

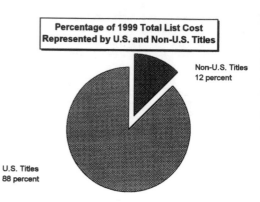

Percentage of 1999 Total List Cost Represented by U.S. and Non-U.S. Titles

Non-U.S. Titles 12 percent

U.S. Titles 88 percent

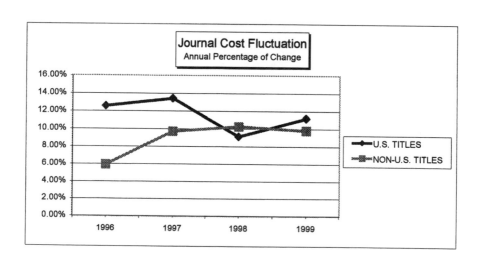

Journal Cost Fluctuation
Annual Percentage of Change

SERIALS PRICES 1995–1999
WITH PROJECTIONS FOR 2000

Law Firm Library Cost History

	Average # Titles	1995 Average Cost Per Title	1996 Average Cost Per Title	Change from 1995-1996	1997 Average Cost Per Title	Change from 1996-1997	1998 Average Cost Per Title	Change from 1997-1998	1999 Average Cost Per Title	Change from 1998-1999	Change from 1995-1999
LAW FIRM LIBRARY											
U.S. TITLES	138	$246.02	$258.69	5.15%	$268.52	3.80%	$277.63	3.39%	$290.66	4.69%	18.14%
NON-U.S. TITLES	7	$366.06	$391.08	6.83%	$414.60	6.01%	$423.01	2.03%	$441.99	4.49%	20.74%
ALL TITLES	145	$252.07	$265.36	5.27%	$275.88	3.96%	$284.96	3.29%	$298.28	4.67%	18.33%

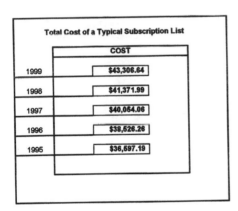

Total Cost of a Typical Subscription List

	COST
1999	$43,306.64
1998	$41,371.99
1997	$40,054.06
1996	$38,526.26
1995	$36,597.19

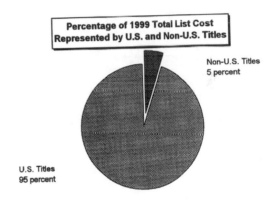

Percentage of 1999 Total List Cost Represented by U.S. and Non-U.S. Titles

Non-U.S. Titles
5 percent

U.S. Titles
95 percent

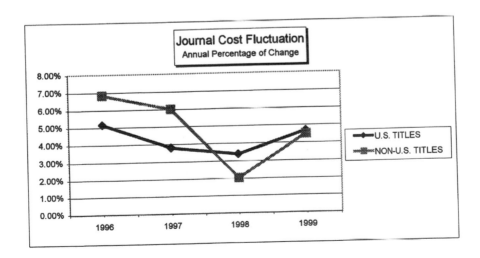

Journal Cost Fluctuation
Annual Percentage of Change

U.S. TITLES
NON-U.S. TITLES

(Figure 13.4 continues on page 390.)

Fig. 13.4—Continued.

Law School Library Cost History

SERIALS PRICES 1995–1999
WITH PROJECTIONS FOR 2000

	Average # Titles	1995 Average Cost Per Title	1996 Average Cost Per Title	Change from 1995-1996	1997 Average Cost Per Title	Change from 1996-1997	1998 Average Cost Per Title	Change from 1997-1998	1999 Average Cost Per Title	Change from 1998-1999	Change from 1995-1999
LAW SCHOOL LIBRARY											
U.S. TITLES	427	$59.95	$63.86	6.52%	$66.85	4.68%	$70.20	5.01%	$73.41	4.57%	22.45%
NON-U.S. TITLES	59	$166.64	$186.27	11.78%	$204.62	9.85%	$212.32	3.76%	$227.64	7.22%	36.61%
ALL TITLES	486	$72.90	$78.72	7.98%	$83.56	6.15%	$87.44	4.64%	$92.13	5.36%	26.38%

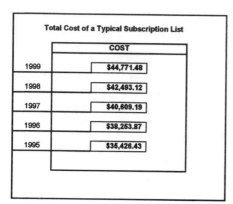

Total Cost of a Typical Subscription List

	COST
1999	$44,771.48
1998	$42,493.12
1997	$40,609.19
1996	$38,253.87
1995	$35,426.43

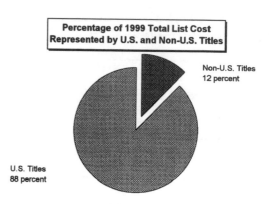

Percentage of 1999 Total List Cost Represented by U.S. and Non-U.S. Titles

Non-U.S. Titles
12 percent

U.S. Titles
88 percent

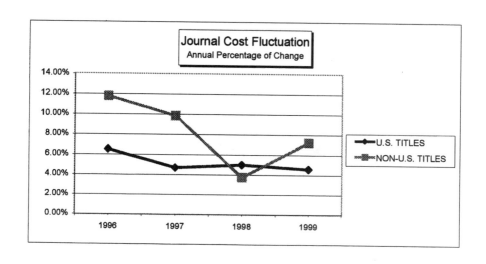

Journal Cost Fluctuation
Annual Percentage of Change

SERIALS PRICES 1995-1999
WITH PROJECTIONS FOR 2000

Public Library Cost History

	Average # Titles	1995 Average Cost Per Title	1996 Average Cost Per Title	Change from 1995-1996	1997 Average Cost Per Title	Change from 1996-1997	1998 Average Cost Per Title	Change from 1997-1998	1999 Average Cost Per Title	Change from 1998-1999	Change from 1995-1999
PUBLIC LIBRARY											
U.S. TITLES	2,508	$48.36	$50.82	5.09%	$52.88	4.05%	$54.81	3.65%	$57.03	4.05%	17.93%
NON-U.S. TITLES	116	$143.78	$158.47	10.22%	$170.18	7.39%	$179.72	5.61%	$191.51	6.56%	33.20%
ALL TITLES	2,624	$52.59	$55.59	5.70%	$58.08	4.48%	$60.34	3.89%	$62.98	4.38%	19.76%

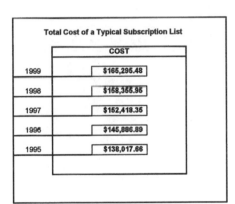

Total Cost of a Typical Subscription List

	COST
1999	$165,295.48
1998	$158,355.95
1997	$152,418.35
1996	$145,886.89
1995	$138,017.66

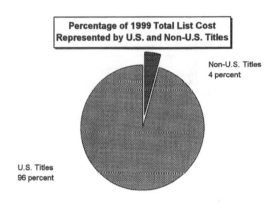

Percentage of 1999 Total List Cost Represented by U.S. and Non-U.S. Titles

Non-U.S. Titles
4 percent

U.S. Titles
96 percent

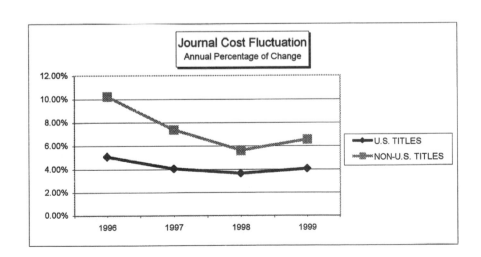

Journal Cost Fluctuation
Annual Percentage of Change

U.S. TITLES
NON-U.S. TITLES

(Figure 13.4 continues on page 392.)

Fig. 13.4—*Continued.*

Corporate Library Cost History

	Average # Titles	1995 Average Cost Per Title	1996 Average Cost Per Title	Change from 1995-1996	1997 Average Cost Per Title	Change from 1996-1997	1998 Average Cost Per Title	Change from 1997-1998	1999 Average Cost Per Title	Change from 1998-1999	Change from 1995-1999
Corporate Library											
U.S. TITLES	1,018	$179.15	$192.29	7.33%	$204.89	6.55%	$217.40	6.11%	$232.81	7.09%	29.95%
NON-U.S. TITLES	172	$622.26	$726.42	16.74%	$811.53	11.72%	$872.24	7.48%	$930.50	6.68%	49.54%
ALL TITLES	1,190	$243.29	$269.61	10.82%	$292.71	8.57%	$312.19	6.66%	$333.81	6.93%	37.21%

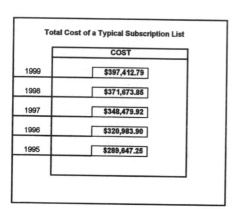

Total Cost of a Typical Subscription List

	COST
1999	$397,412.79
1998	$371,673.85
1997	$348,479.92
1996	$320,983.90
1995	$289,647.25

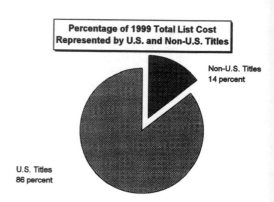

Percentage of 1999 Total List Cost Represented by U.S. and Non-U.S. Titles

Non-U.S. Titles
14 percent

U.S. Titles
86 percent

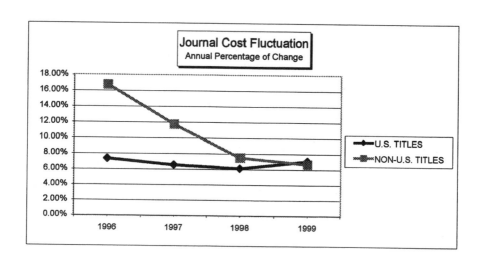

Journal Cost Fluctuation
Annual Percentage of Change

SERIALS PRICES 1995–1999
WITH PROJECTIONS FOR 2000

Other Library Cost History

	Average # Titles	1995 Average Cost Per Title	1996 Average Cost Per Title	Change from 1995–1996	1997 Average Cost Per Title	Change from 1996–1997	1998 Average Cost Per Title	Change from 1997–1998	1999 Average Cost Per Title	Change from 1998–1999	Change from 1995–1999
Other Library											
U.S. TITLES	223	$134.22	$144.14	7.39%	$154.14	6.94%	$163.16	5.85%	$174.85	7.16%	30.27%
NON-U.S. TITLES	45	$342.67	$405.02	18.20%	$449.27	10.93%	$483.77	7.68%	$533.45	10.27%	55.67%
ALL TITLES	268	$168.97	$187.62	11.04%	$203.34	8.38%	$216.61	6.53%	$234.63	8.32%	38.86%

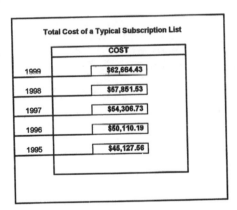

Total Cost of a Typical Subscription List

	COST
1999	$62,664.43
1998	$57,851.53
1997	$54,306.73
1996	$50,110.19
1995	$45,127.56

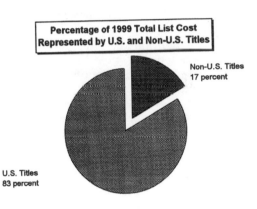

Percentage of 1999 Total List Cost Represented by U.S. and Non-U.S. Titles

Non-U.S. Titles
17 percent

U.S. Titles
83 percent

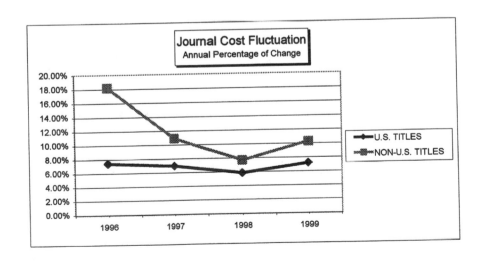

Journal Cost Fluctuation
Annual Percentage of Change

U.S. TITLES
NON-U.S. TITLES

go into studying the past 12 months and attempting to predict future trends. Naturally, one must have good data about the amounts spent in various countries during the past year. The country of publication may be less important than the country in which the vendor is located. For example, if the library uses the vendor Harrassowitz, prices will be in deutsche marks, regardless of the country of origin of the items purchased. After collecting the data, one can use them as factors in estimating the cost of continuing the current acquisition levels from the countries from which the library normally buys.

A new publication, started in 1999, may prove to be very useful for collection development budget planning. *BiblioData Price Watcher* is a twice-monthly newsletter, about four pages per issue, that tracks prices of information products in both print and electronic formats. Subscription information is available at the Bibliodata Website (<http://www.bibliodata.com>).

Allocation of Monies

As mentioned earlier, collection development funds may be restricted or unrestricted. For most libraries, the unrestricted allocation represents the majority of monies available for collection development. Libraries employ internal allocation systems in an attempt to match monies available with needs and to assure that all collecting areas have some funding for the year. These systems provide guidelines for selection personnel; the allocation sets limits on, and expectations for, purchases in subject areas or for certain types of material.

Ordinarily, the method selected reflects the collection development policy statement priorities. If the library employs a collecting intensity ranking system in the collection development policy, it is reasonable to expect to find those levels reflected in the amount allocated to the subject or format. Almost all allocation methods are complex, and how one goes about matching the needs and monies available requires consideration of several factors.

Among the factors one must consider are past practices, differential publication, unit cost and inflation rates, level of demand, and actual usage. Implementing a formal system takes time and effort. Some professionals question whether it is worthwhile allocating the monies. Opponents to allocation claim it is difficult to develop a fair allocation model, and it is time-consuming to calculate the amounts needed. They also claim that, because the models are difficult to develop, libraries tend to leave the allocations in place too long and simply add in the next year's percentage increase rather than recalculate the figures annually. They suggest that selectors may not spend accounts effectively because there is too much or too little money available. Finally, they argue that it is difficult to effect transfers from one account to another during the year. Proponents claim that allocations provide better control of collection development and are a more effective way to monitor expenditures.

Some allocation does take place, regardless of the presence or absence of a formal allocation process. When there is no formal system, selectors engage in informal balancing of needs and funds available for various subjects or classes of material. (In the worst case, the more influential selectors have greater access to the funds, regardless of actual collection or user needs.) It seems reasonable, if the process is going to take place one way or another, to have the formal process provide the best opportunity for achieving a fair balance.

A good allocation process provides at least four outcomes. Obviously, its overall purpose is to match available funds with needs. Second, it provides selectors with guidelines regarding how they should allocate their time. That is, if one is responsible for three selection areas with funding allocations of $15,000, $5,000, and $500, it is clear which area requires the most attention. (In some cases, it is harder to spend the smaller amount, because one must be careful to spend it wisely.)

Third, the allocation process provides a means of assessing the selector's work at the end of the fiscal year. Finally, it provides clients with a sense of collecting priorities, assuming the allocation information is made available to them. The library can communicate the information in terms of percentages rather than specific monetary amounts if there is a concern about divulging budgetary data.

The allocation process should be collaborative, with input from all interested parties. Two things are certain: Whether the library uses a formal or informal approach to gaining the input, the process has political overtones, and the outcome will invariably disappoint some individual or group. This is particularly true when introducing a revised allocation of a static budget. Those who receive more money will be happy, but those who lose funds will object to the method used to reallocate the funds. Unfortunately, sometimes the objectors are influential enough to get the allocations changed, which defeats the purpose of the process—matching funds to needs.

What allocation method the library selects is influenced, in part, by internal library practices, institutional needs, and extra-institutional requirements (such as those of accreditation agencies). Internal factors include operational practices that determine what type of information is readily available to those making the allocation decisions (vendor's country of origin, number of approval titles versus firm orders, format and subject data, and use are some examples). How the library organizes its services—centralized or decentralized—also plays a role in the selection decision. Other internal factors affecting which allocation method is used include past practices for allocation and the purpose of allocation (that is, its use as a control mechanism or guideline). Institutional factors, in addition to the obvious importance of the institution's mission and goals, include the type of budget control it employs, its organization, and its overall financial condition. Extra-institutional factors are the political atmosphere (for example, the degree of accountability), economic conditions, social expectations and values regarding information services (such as equal access and literacy levels), and outside agencies (such as accreditation bodies or governmental bodies) that monitor or control the institution.

One can think of allocation methods as being a continuum with impulse at one end and formula at the opposite end. Between the two extremes are several more-or-less structured methods. Impulse allocation can take the form of allowing active selectors to have greatest access to available funds or, with a slightly more structured approach, to allocate on the basis of perceptions of need. History of past use and some annual percentage increase for each allocation area is a little more formal; it is probably one of the most widely employed methods. Allocating on the basis of organizational structure (main and branch units) is still more formal (often, the allocation is a fixed percentage of the fund pool). If one adds to that method some incremental funding based on workload (such as circulation data), one moves even closer to the formula end of the continuum. Also, somewhere in the middle of the continuum is the format allocation method (including books, serials, audiovisual, electronic, and reference).

Format allocation may be as simple as dividing monies between monographic and serials purchase accounts. Even this "easy" division is no longer easy, because serials prices increase more rapidly than other materials costs. How long can one shift monies from other accounts to maintain serials subscription levels without damaging the overall collection? Libraries employ several category allocation methods in addition to format, such as subject, unit, users, language, and formula. Most libraries that use a format allocation system use several approaches. Many small libraries, including most school media centers, employ the format system using monographs, serials, and audiovisuals as the broad groupings. The library divides these funds by subject (language arts), grade level (fifth grade), or user group (professional reading). Occasionally, libraries divide monograph funds into current, retrospective, and replacement categories. In libraries using approval, blanket-order, or standing-order plans, it is normal practice to set aside monies for each program before making any other allocations. A typical approach would be to set aside an amount equal to the prior year's expenditure for the category with an additional amount to cover expected inflation. The reason for setting aside these funds first is that they are ongoing commitments.

Formula allocations have become more and more popular, especially in large libraries. Librarians have proposed many formulas over the years, but no one formula has become standard. Each library must decide which, if any, formula is most appropriate for its special circumstances. A 1992 article by Ian R. Young described a project that compared seven formulas.[5] His results showed that, though each formula employed one or more unique variables, there were no statistically significant differences among the formula results in terms of a single institution. He concluded that there was a high degree of similarity among the seven formulas, at least when applied to his institutional setting. Based on our experience with formulas and the selection of a formula in several institutional settings, we would say the library selects the formula that contains all the variables necessary to satisfy all interested parties. (Thus, political rather than practical considerations dictate which formula is used.) Only quantifiable factors (for example, average price, number of titles published, and use data) can be used as variables in formulas. This does not mean that subjective judgments do not play a role, but the allocation process as a whole depends on weightings, circulation data, production figures, inflation and exchange rates, number of users, and so forth. Figure 13.5 shows the allocation formula used at Loyola Marymount University.

ALA's *Guide to Budget Allocation for Information Resources* indicates that there are six broad allocation methods: historical, zero-based (no consideration of past practice), formulas, ranking (a variation of formulas), percentages, and other modeling techniques.[6] The book also outlines some of the variations in formulas by type of library. For example, academic libraries

Department	Use	Average Cost	Cost-Use	Percent Cost-Use	Formula Allocation	Present Allocation
Psychology (BF& RC 435-577)	4,674	$38.55	180,183	0.07	$12,693	$15,033
Sociology (HM-HX)	5,311	$37.85	201,021	0.09	$14,542	$6,587
Theater Arts (PN 1600-1989, 2000-3310)	144	$38.14	5,492	0.003	$361	$3,908
Theology (BL-BX)	6,503	$36.49	237,294	0.1	$16,258	$7,409
Totals			2,491,436		$181,342	$180,652

Use = Circulated use of the class numbers associated with the department
Average Cost = Price listed as average for that discipline in *Choice*
Cost-Use = Average cost times use for the field
Percent Cost-Use = Percentage of library's total cost-use for the field
Formula Allocation = Amount of new allocation under new formula
Present Allocation = Amount of current allocation

Fig. 13.5. Loyola Marymount University library book allocation formula. Courtesy of Loyola Marymount University.

might consider enrollment by major or degrees granted in a field (the factors used in figure 13.5 are widely used in academic libraries as well). Public libraries might factor in differences in the service communities being served, the ratio of copies per title of bestsellers to general titles, or the demand (in terms of use or requests) in popular subject fields. Special libraries employ factors like delivery time expectations of the clients, service chargebacks, and the number of clients or departments served. Many school media centers use factors like changes in curriculum, number and ability of students by grade level, and loss and aging rates of various subject areas in the collection. The guide provides a starting point for anyone thinking about changing the allocation process a library uses.

Allocating funds is an involved process, and changing an existing method is almost more difficult than establishing a new method. Often, past practices and political issues keep the process from moving forward or evolving. Serials inflation rates (almost 700 percent since 1970[7]) make it difficult to provide both ongoing subscriptions and a reasonable level of monographic acquisitions. How much to allocate to current materials and how much to allocate to retrospective purchases is related, in part, to the serials inflation rate. If the decision is to maintain serials at the expense of monographs, in time, there will be a significant need for retrospective buying funds to fill in gaps in the monograph collection. Subject variations also complicate the picture: Science materials are very expensive; social science materials are substantially less costly but are more numerous. Electronic access, rather than local ownership, also clouds the picture, especially because electronic access often involves cost at the individual level, something with which allocation models have not dealt. Although allocation work frequently involves political issues and occasionally involves upset individuals, in the long run careful attention to this process will produce a better collection for the organization the library or information center serves.

Encumbering

One aspect of accounting and financial management in collection development that differs from typical accounting practice is the process of *encumbering*, which allows one to set aside monies to pay for ordered items. When the library waits 60, 90, or 120 or more days for orders, there is some chance that the monies available will be over- or underspent if there is no system that allows for setting aside monies.

The following chart shows how the process works. Day 1, the first day of the fiscal year, shows the library with an annual allocation of $1,000 for a particular subject area. On day 2, the library orders an item with a list price of $24.95. Though there may be shipping and handling charges, there probably will be a discount. Because none of the costs and credits are known at the time, the list price is the amount a staff member records as encumbered. The unexpended column reflects the $24.95 deduction, though there is still nothing in the expended category. Sixty-two days later, the item and invoice arrive; the invoice reflects a 15 percent discount ($3.74) and no shipping or handling charges. The bookkeeper records the actual cost ($21.21) under expended and adds the $3.74 to the unexpended amount. The amount encumbered now is zero.

	Unexpended	Encumbered	Expended
Day 1	$1,000.00	0	0
Day 2	$ 975.05	$24.95	0
Day 62	$ 978.79	0	$21.21

Needless to say, this system is much more complex than the example suggests, because libraries place and receive multiple orders every day. With each transaction the amounts in each column change. *One seldom knows the precise balance, except on the first and last day of the fiscal year.* If the funding body takes back all unexpended funds at the end of the fiscal year (a cash accounting system), the collection development staff will want to know their fund(s) balances as they enter the final quarter of the year.

Several factors make it difficult to learn the exact status of the funds, even with the use of encumbrance. One factor is delivery of orders. Vendors may assure customers that they will deliver before the end of the fiscal year, but then fail to do so. Such a failure can result in the encumbered money being lost. With a cash system, the collection development staff must make some choices at the end of the fiscal year if there are funds in the encumbered category. The main issue is determining if the items still on order are important enough to leave on order. An affirmative answer has substantial implications for collection development. Using the foregoing example and assuming that day 62 comes after the start of a new fiscal year and that the new allocation is $1,000, on day 1 of the new fiscal year, the amount unexpended would be $975.05 ($1,000 minus $24.95), encumbered $24.95, and expended zero. In essence, there is a reduction in the amount available for new orders and the library lost $24.95 from the prior year's allocation. (The senior author once took over as head of a library on June 25, and on July 1 the system financial officer reported that the entire acquisitions allocation was encumbered for the coming fiscal year. To have some funds for collection development over the next 12 months, it was necessary to cancel 347 orders.)

With an accrual system, the unexpended funds carry forward into the next fiscal year. Under such a system, using the example, the day 1 figures would be unexpended $1,000, encumbered $24.95, and expended zero.

The staff also needs to consider how reliable the vendor or producer is, because occasionally an item never arrives. How long should one wait? The answer varies from producer to producer and country to country. If the library buys substantial amounts from developing countries, waiting several years is not unreasonable. Because print runs tend to be very close to the number of copies on order, the chance of never being able to acquire the item makes it dangerous to cancel the order.

There is a problem in leaving funds encumbered for long periods under either system, especially when there is rapid inflation or exchange rates are unfavorable. These are two reasons why a firm but reasonable date for automatic cancellation of unfilled orders is important.

Other factors making it difficult to know the precise fund balance during the year are pricing and discounts. Prices are subject to change without notice on most library materials, particularly online resources, which means that the price may be higher on delivery than when ordered. In addition, discounts are unpredictable. Because of the uncertainty, most libraries encumber the list price without freight charges and just hope that the amount will be adequate. Exchange rates enter the picture for international acquisitions, and the question of when the rate is set can be a critical issue. Certainly, the rate is not firm on the date the order is placed, but is it firm at the time of shipment? The date of the invoice? The date the library receives the invoice and items? The date the financial office makes out the check? Possibly even the date the supplier deposits the check? With international orders, one can expect four months or more to elapse between order placement and delivery. In periods of rapid rate changes, even a four-month difference can significantly affect the amount of money available for purchases.

Moving monies back and forth, especially in a manual system, can lead to errors, so the acquisitions department needs a good bookkeeper. Automated accounting systems speed the recording activities and provide greater accuracy, as long as the data entry is correct. Despite the uncertainty that exists with the encumbering system, it is still better than having unexpended and expended categories, because without it one would not know how much of the unexpended balance was actually needed for items on order.

Special Problems

Shipping and handling rates and taxes on items purchased have taken a toll on the funds available for additions to the collection. Vendors that in the past paid for shipping now pass the cost to customers. The U.S. Postal Service has reduced the difference between postal rates such as the library rate and parcel post. For example, in 1970 it cost $0.18 to ship a 2-pound book; in 1980 it cost $0.80; by 1999 the rate was $1.54. There are suggestions in the press that the Postal Service will request a 47 percent increase in the rate in the near future. All the charges on the invoice (postage, handling, shipping, taxes, and so forth) must come from the acquisitions budget. As these charges mount, there is less money for the items the library wishes to add.

Some publishers and vendors employ a freight pass-through (FPT) charge. Originally, in 1981, publishers intended FPT to create a two-tier pricing system to enable bookstores to pass on freight charges to the customer. That is, the publisher charged the bookstore an invoice price and the dust jacket carried the higher FPT price. Some publishers used a percentage of the invoice price (3 or 4 percent), and others used a flat fee ($0.50). The problem for libraries buying from jobbers is determining what price the jobber used in calculating the library discount. Most contracts with jobbers call for discounts on list price. What is the list price: the invoice price or the FPT price printed on the dust jacket? Jobber practice varied from one extreme to the other. Though the percentages are small, as are the amounts of money for any one title, the cumulative effect on an acquisition budget is great. The FPT problem is not as important today as it once was, but the growing cost of shipping and postage is an ongoing concern.

Audits

We have a favorite Robert Frost poem[8] about accounting that goes:

> Never ask of money spent
> Where the spender thinks it went.
> To remember or invent
> What he did with every cent.
>
> Robert Frost,
> "The Hardship of Accounting"

One outcome of having the power to manage and expend substantial amounts of money is fiscal accountability. Actually, the amount of money need not be "substantial," if they are public or private funds. Only a few librarians have the opportunity to expand the medium amount of an ARL library for collection development purposes ($5.48 million in 1998).[9] The process of establishing how well one has handled the monies one is responsible for expending is the audit.

A rather legalistic definition of an *audit* is the process of "accumulation and evaluation of evidence about quantifiable information of [an] economic entity to determine and report on the degree of correspondence between the information and established criteria."[10] More simply put, it is the process of assuring that the financial records are accurate and that the information is presented accurately, using accepted accounting practices; and of making recommendations for improvements in how the process is carried out. The basic questions and required records relate to: Was the purchase made with proper authorization? Was it received? Was it paid for in an appropriate manner? Is the item still available? (If the item is not still available, there should be appropriate records regarding its disposal.) Today, with auto-mated acquisitions systems, undergoing an audit is less time-consuming than in the past, where the "paper trail" was in fact a number of different pa-per records that had to be gathered up and compared. At least now the sys-tem can pull up the necessary material fairly quickly.

Are audits really necessary in libraries? Must we remember how, where, on what, and when we spent every cent? Unfortunately, the answer is yes. Not many years ago Herbert Synder and Julia Hersberger published an article outlining embezzlement in public libraries.[11]

Summary

One must be constantly aware of changes in prices and in invoicing practices to gain the maximum number of additions to the collection. Watch for changes, and demand explanations of freight and handling charges, inap-propriate dual-pricing systems, or other costs that may place additional strain on the budget. By understanding basic accounting principles and us-ing the reports and records generated by the library's accounting system, one will be better able to monitor the use of available monies and to use them ef-fectively to meet the needs of the public.

Notes

1.   G. Stevenson Smith, *Managerial Accounting for Libraries and Other Not-for-Profit Organizations* (Chicago: American Library Association, 1991).

2.   Richard S. Rounds, *Basic Budgeting Practices for Librarians*, 2d ed. (Chicago: American Library Association, 1994).

3.   Barbara Hoffert, "Book Report, Part 2: What Academic Libraries Buy and How Much They Spend," *Library Journal* 123 (September 1, 1998): 144–46.

4.   American National Standards Institute, Z39 Committee, *Criteria for Price In-dexes for Library Materials* (New York: American National Standards Institute, 1974) (ANSI Z39.20).

5.   Ian R. Young, "A Quantitative Comparison of Acquisitions Budget Allocation Formulas Using a Single Institutional Setting," *Library Acquisitions: Practice and Theory* 16, no. 3 (1992): 229–42.

6.   Edward Shreeves, ed., *Guide to Budget Allocation for Information Resources* (Collection Management and Development Guides No. 4) (Chicago: American Li-brary Association, 1991).

7.   Frank W. Goudy, "Academic Libraries and the Six Percent Solution: A Twenty-Year Financial Overview," *Journal of Academic Librarianship* 19 (September 1993): 212–15.

8.   Robert Frost, "The Hardship of Accounting," in *Collected Poems, Prose and Plays* (New York: Library of America, 1995), 282.

9.   Hoffert, "Book Report, Part 2," 144.

10.   Alvin Arens and James Loebbecke, *Auditing: An Integrated Approach* (Englewood Cliffs, N.J.: Prentice Hall, 1994), 1.

11.   Herbert Synder and Julia Hersberger, "Public Libraries and Embezzlement: An Examination of Internal Control and Financial Misconduct," *Library Quarterly* 67 (January 1997): 1–23.

Selected Sources for
Library Materials Price Information

"Average Book Prices." *School Library Journal.* Annual article, usually March, author varies (in the mid-1990s it was L. N. Gerhardt).

"Book Title Output and Prices, Final Figures 19*XX.*" *Publishers Weekly.* Annual article, September or October, title varies.

"British Book Production, 19*XX.*" *The Bookseller.* Annual review of British book production and prices; various issues, usually in the January issue.

"College Book Price Information 19*XX.*" *Choice.* Annual article, in the April or May issue.

Higher Education Prices and Price Indexes: 19XX. Washington, D.C.: Research Associates of Washington. Annual publication listing a variety of higher education costs, including library costs.

"Periodical Prices 19*XX*–19*XX.*" *Serials Librarian.* Annual survey of serial prices; author and issue vary.

"Prices of U.S. and Foreign Published Materials." In *The Bowker Annual: Library and Book Trade Almanac.* New York: R. R. Bowker.

"The Year in Review. Title Output and Prices." *Publishers Weekly.* Annual article, usually in the March issue.

Further Reading

General

Alley, B. "Increasing Demands, Shrinking Budgets and the Alice's Restaurant Mentality." *Technicalities* 12 (November 1992): 1.

Barker, J. W. "What's Your Money Worth?" *Journal of Library Administration* 16, no. 3 (1992): 25–43.

Barnes, Marilyn. "Managing with Technology: Automating Budgeting from Acquisitions." *Bottom Line* 10, no. 2 (1997): 65–73.

Berger, Sharon. "The First Audit." *Bottom Line* 5 (Summer 1991): 28–30.

Budd, J. "Allocation Formulas in the Literature." *Library Acquisitions: Practice and Theory* 15, no. 1 (1991): 95–101.

Bustion, M., et al. "Methods of Serials Funding: Formula or Tradition?" *Serials Librarian* 20, no. 1 (1991): 75–89.

Campbell, J. D. "Getting Comfortable with Change: A New Budget Model for Libraries in Transition." *Library Trends* 42, no. 3 (Winter 1994): 448–59.

Carrigan, D. P. "Improving Return on Investment: A Proposal for Allocating the Book Budget." *Journal of Academic Librarianship* 18 (November 1992): 292–97.

Christianson, E. "When Your Parent Dictates Your Accounting Life." *Bottom Line* 7 (Summer 1993): 17–21.

Christianson, E., and S. Hayes. "Depreciation of Library Collection: Terminology of the Debate." *Bottom Line* 5, no. 3 (1991): 35–37.

Cline, N. M. "Staffing: The Art of Managing Change." In *Collection Management and Development: Issues in an Electronic Era*. Edited by P. Johnson and B. MacEwan, 13–28. Chicago: American Library Association, 1994.

Cubberly, C. "Allocating the Materials Funds Using Cost of Materials." *Journal of Academic Librarianship* 19 (March 1993): 16–21.

Dannelly, G. "Justifying Collection Budgets: Indexing Materials Costs." *Journal of Library Administration* 19, no. 2 (1993): 75–88.

Enikhamenor, F. A. "Formula for Allocating Book Funds." *Libri* 33 (June 1983): 148–61.

Farrell, D. "Fundraising for Collection Development Librarians." In *Collection Management and Development: Issues in an Electronic Era*. Edited by P. Johnson and B. MacEwan, 133–42. Chicago: American Library Association, 1994.

Granskog, K. "Basic Acquisitions Accounting and Business Practice." In *Business of Acquisitions* 2d ed. Edited by K. Schmidt. Chicago: American Library Association, 1999.

Guide to Budget Allocation for Information Resources. Collection Management and Development Guides, no. 4. Edited by Edward Shreeves. Chicago: American Library Association, 1991.

Hamon, P., et al. *Budgeting and the Political Process in Libraries*. Englewood, Colo.: Libraries Unlimited, 1992.

Hawks, C. P. "The Audit Trail and Automated Acquisitions." *Library Acquisitions: Practice and Theory* 18 (Fall 1994): 333–39.

Johnson, P. "Preparing Materials Budget Requests." *Technicalities* 15 (April 1995): 6–10.

Lee, S. H. *Budget for Acquisitions: Strategies for Serials, Monographs and Electronic Formats*. New York: Haworth Press, 1991.

Lowry, C. B. "Reconciling Pragmatism, Equity, and Need in the Formula Allocation of Book and Serial Funds." *College & Research Libraries* 53 (March 1992): 121–38.

Lynden, F. C. "Impact of Foreign Exchange on Library Materials Budgets." *Bottom Line* 9, no. 3 (1996): 14–19.

———. "Strategies for Stretching the Collection Budget." *Journal of Library Administration* 16, no. 3 (1992): 91–110.

MacEwan, B. "Projecting Increases Needed to Maintain the Serials Budget: One Library's Story." In *Collection Management and Development: Issues in an Electronic Era*. Edited by P. Johnson and B. MacEwan, 121–25. Chicago: American Library Association, 1994.

McPheron, W. "Quantifying the Allocation of Monograph Funds." *College & Research Libraries* 44 (March 1983): 116–27.

Murray, M. S., and M. T. Wolf. *Budgeting for Information Access: Managing the Resource Budget for Absolute Success.* Chicago: American Library Association, 1998.

Niemeyer, M., et al. "Balancing Act for Library Materials Budgets: Use of a Formula Allocation." *Technical Services Quarterly* 11, no. 1 (1993): 43–60.

O'Neill, A. L. "Evaluating the Success of Acquisitions Departments." *Library Acquisitions: Practice and Theory* 19, no. 3 (1992): 209–19.

Park, L. M. "Endowed Book Funds." In *Library Fund Raising* (annual). Chicago: American Library Association, 1995.

Rein, L. O., et al. "Formula-Based Subject Allocation: A Practical Approach." *Collection Management* 17, no. 4 (1993): 25–48.

Schmitz-Veitin, G. "Literature Use as a Measure for Funds Allocation." *Library Acquisitions: Practice and Theory* 8, no. 4 (1984): 267–74.

Sellen, M. "Book Budget Formula Allocations: A Review Essay." *Collection Management* 9 (Winter 1987): 13–24.

Stanley, N. M. "Accrual Accounting and Library Materials Acquisitions." *Bottom Line* 7, no. 2 (1993): 15–17.

Vickery, J. E. "Library Acquisitions 1986–1995: A Select Bibliography." *Collection Management* 22, nos. 1/2 (1997): 101–86.

Academic

Allen, F. R. "Materials Budgets in the Electronic Age: A Survey of Academic Libraries." *College & Research Libraries* 57 (March 1996): 133–43.

Dannelly, G. "Indexing Material Budgets at Ohio State University." In *Collection Management and Development: Issues in an Electronic Era.* Edited by P. Johnson and B. MacEwan, 126–32. Chicago: American Library Association, 1994.

Jones, P. A., and C. L. Keller. "From Budget Allocation to Collection Development: A System for the Small College Library." *Library Acquisitions: Practice and Theory* 17 (Summer 1993): 183–89.

Kohut, J. "Allocating the Book Budget: Equity and Economic Efficiency." *College & Research Libraries* 36 (September 1975): 403–10.

Werking, R. H. "Allocating the Academic Library's Book Budget: Historical Perspectives and Current Reflections." *Journal of Academic Librarianship* 14 (July 1988): 140–44.

Public

Bender, A. "Allocation of Funds in Support of Collection Development in Public Libraries." *Library Resources & Technical Services* 23 (Winter 1979): 45–51.

Call, J. R. "Changing Acquisitions at Detroit Public Library." *Library Resources & Technical Services* 41 (April 1997): 155–57.

Gray, R. "Evolution or Extinction: The Current State of Library Supply." *Public Library Journal* 13 (September/October 1998): 70–72.

McCabe, G. B., and R. N. Bish. "Planning for Fund Management in Multiple System Environments." *Library Administration and Management* 7 (Winter 1993): 51–55.

McGarth, S. "A Pragmatic Book Allocation Formula for Academic and Public Libraries." *Library Resources & Technical Services* 19 (Fall 1975): 356–69.

Missineo, L. "Supply-Side Measurement: A Formulation for the Allocation of Book Funds in Public Libraries." *Technical Services Quarterly* 2 (Spring/Summer 1985): 61–72.

Smith, M. I. "Using Statistics to Increase Public Library Budgets." *Bottom Line* 9, no. 3 (1996): 4–13.

Waznis, Betty, "Materials Budget Allocation Methods at San Diego County Library." *Acquisitions Librarian* 20 (1998): 25–32.

School

Callison, D. "A Review of the Research Related to School Media Collections, Part 1." *School Library Media Quarterly* 19 (Fall 1990): 57–62.

———. "A Review of the Research Related to School Media Collections, Part 2." *School Library Media Quarterly* 19 (Winter 1991): 117–21.

Miller, M. L., and M. L. Schontz. "Small Change: Expenditures for Resources in School Library Media Centers." *School Library Journal.* [These authors compile biennial reviews of acquisitions and price data. In 1997, the article appeared in the October issue on pages 28–37.]

Wright, R. J. "Selected Acquisition Statistics." *School Library Media Annual* 10 (1992): 222–23.

Special

Burdick, A. J. "Citation Patterns in the Health Sciences: Implications for Serial/Monograph Fund Allocation." *Bulletin of the Medical Library Association* 81 (January 1993): 44–47.

Norton, R., and D. Gautschi. "User-Survey of an International Library's Resource Allocation." *ASLIB Proceedings* 37 (September 1986): 371–80.

Weimers, R. F. E. "Archives and the New Information Architecture of the Late 1990's." *American Archivist* 57 (Winter 1994): 20–34.

14
Deselection

We have mentioned, in more than one section of this book, the fact that libraries have faced collection development budget problems. Further, there has been little increase in staff for most libraries during the past 15 years. Thus, it should be no surprise to read that libraries have had, and continue to have, serious problems with collection storage space. If one cannot get money for collections or staff, one can imagine how difficult it is to secure funding for additional space for either users or collections. The result is many libraries have had to engage one or more deselection projects in the recent past. Even if there has been a decline in the number of items acquired, there has been a steady growth of the collections; it has just been slower than in the past.

"Selection in reverse" is one way to think about weeding or collection control. Deselection, or weeding, is something most librarians thought about but seldom did in the past. However, this process is as important as the other steps in collection development. Without an ongoing weeding program, a collection can quickly age and become difficult to use. Although the major function of a library is to acquire, store, and make available knowledge resources, it is obvious that no library can acquire and store the world's total production of knowledge resources for any current year.

Some of the world's largest libraries (the Library of Congress, the British Library, Bibliothèque Nationale, and others) do acquire most important items. Nevertheless, even these giants of the library world cannot do it all. Eventually, when they reach the limit of their growth, they confront, as the smallest library does, three alternatives: (1) acquire new physical facilities, (2) divide the collection (which also requires space), or (3) weed the collection (which may or may not require new space). Only with new, adequate storage area can a librarian avoid selecting items for relocation.

The need to find space for collections is a problem almost as old as libraries themselves. One of the earliest references to the problem in the United States was a letter from Thomas Hollis to Harvard College's Board of Governors in 1725. He wrote, "If you want more room for modern books, it is easy to remove the less useful into a more remote place, but do not sell them as they are devoted."[1] More than 100 years passed before Harvard followed Hollis's advice; today, like most major research libraries, remote storage is part of everyday collection development activities at Harvard.

What Is Deselection, or Weeding?

H. F. McGraw defined *weeding* (called *stock relegation* in the United Kingdom) as "the practice of discarding or transferring to storage excess copies, rarely used books, and materials no longer of use."[2] He defined *purging* as "officially withdrawing a volume (all entries made for a particular book have been removed from library records) from a library collection because it is unfit for further use or is no longer needed."[3] The word *purging* applies more to the library's files than to items in the collection. Libraries seldom destroy purged items. Slote's definition of *weeding*, from the fourth edition of his book, is "removing the noncore collection from the primary collection area [open stack area]."[4] Disposal takes several forms: gifts and exchange programs, Friends of the Library book sales, or sale to an out-of-print dealer for credit against future purchases. Occasionally, the material goes into a recycling program. The result is that a patron who may later request a purged item will have to use interlibrary loan to secure a copy.

Storing, in contrast, retains the item at a second level of access. Second-level access normally is not open to the client and is frequently some distance from the library. Most second-level access storage systems house the materials as compactly as possible to maximize storage capacity. Compact shelving for low-use material is coming into widespread use as libraries attempt to gain maximum storage from existing square footage. Generally, a staff member retrieves the desired item from the storage facility for the user. Depending on the storage unit's location and the library's policy, the time lapse between request and receipt ranges from a few minutes to 48 hours. Nevertheless, this arrangement is normally faster than interlibrary loan.

Before implementing a deselection program, the collection development staff should review deselection policies and goals. This review should include an analysis of the present staffing situation, consideration of alternative approaches, the feasibility of a weeding program in terms of other library operations, user interest and cooperation in such a project, types of materials collected, and cost. Some of the data for the program should come from collection evaluation projects that the selection officers and others undertake on a regular basis. An active (i.e., ongoing) deselection program should be part of the library's collection development policy.

Selection and weeding are similar activities: first, they are both necessary parts of an effective collection development program; and second, both require the same type of decision-making rules. The same factors that lead to the decision to add an item lead to a later decision to remove the item. Book selection policy should determine deselection activities.

Collection policies, if properly prepared, help reduce space problems by controlling growth. Nevertheless, the time eventually comes when collection space no longer accommodates additional material. When this happens, some hard, costly decisions confront the library: build a new building, split the collection and use remote storage, or reduce the collection size. All three alternatives involve time-consuming and expensive processes. A policy of continuous deselection is more effective in the long run. Lazy librarians, like lazy gardeners, will find that the weeding problem only gets larger the longer they wait to do the job.

One piece of library folklore helps slow or stop many deselection programs. That is, no matter how strange an item may seem, at least one person in the world will find it valuable—and that person will request the item 10 minutes after the library discards it. We have never met anyone who has had it happen, but everyone agrees that it does.

One of collection development's proverbs is: one person's trash is someone else's treasure. This is the fundamental problem confronting collection development staffs every day. When the library bases its collection building on current user needs, deselection can be a major activity, because those needs change.

Some years ago, in *Current Contents*, Eugene Garfield noted that weeding a library is like examining an investment portfolio. Investment advisors know that people don't like to liquidate bad investments. Just like frustrated tycoons, many librarians can't face the fact that some of their guesses have gone wrong. They continue to throw good money after bad, hoping, like so many optimistic stockbrokers, that their bad decisions will somehow be undone. After paying for a journal for 10 years, they rationalize that maybe someone will finally use it in the eleventh or twelfth year.[5]

Deselection by Type of Library

Because different types of libraries have significantly different clientele and goals, they approach deselection from different points of view. Although the basic problems, issues, and methods of deselection apply to all libraries, variations occur in how they select the weeds and what they do with the weeds after pulling them.

Public Libraries

Public libraries may be viewed as supplying materials that meet the current needs and interests of a diverse community of users. In the public library, user demand is the important factor influencing selection and deselection. Therefore, materials no longer of interest or use to the public are candidates for storage or disposal. Usually, only large municipal public libraries consider storage, because their collections include research materials. As for discarding, a public library rule of thumb is that collections should completely turn over once every 10 years. Actual practice probably falls far short of that goal. Storage, when undertaken, usually involves separating little-used books from the high-use working collection and discarding duplicates, worn-out volumes, and obsolete material. Some people claim that a collection containing many items of little interest is less useful, because high-demand items are not readily visible or accessible. Costs involved in maintaining a large collection are also a consideration.

Certainly there are differences due to size. Small and branch public libraries generally focus on high-demand materials, with little or no expectation that they will have preservation responsibilities. (An exception would be in the area of local history, where the library may be the only place one might expect to find such material.) Large public libraries have different responsibilities that often include housing and maintaining research collections.

Thus they have to consider a wider range of issues, more like those confronting academic libraries, when undertaking a deselection program.

Sometimes a deselection project can have unexpected results; an example was the Free Library of Philadelphia. In chapter 13, we noted that auditors expect to find items purchased still available. When the Philadelphia City Controller's office conducted its review of the library, it concluded that the library was in violation of the city charter by "destroying hundreds of thousands of books." Although the report acknowledged that weeding was a generally accepted practice in libraries, it also stated that "this practice had gone awry."[6] At issue was the library's failure to try to find takers for the worn books it had withdrawn (admittedly the numbers involved were substantial—360,000 volumes).

Two books are especially useful in planning public library weeding projects: Stanley J. Slote's *Weeding Library Collections* (actually this book can be considered *the* book for planning and implementing a deselection project in any type of library) and Joseph P. Segal's *Weeding Collections in Small and Medium-Sized Libraries: The CREW Method.*[7] Both authors emphasize the use of circulation data, with Slote's system relying on circulation data (shelf-life) to identify candidates for weeding. Segal's system uses age of the publication, circulation data, and several subjective elements he labels MUSTY (M = misleading, U = ugly [worn out], S = superseded, T = trivial, and Y = your collection no longer needs the item). The CREW in Segal's title represents Continuous Review Evaluation and Weeding. Ideas and methods described in both books are useful in all types of small libraries, especially school media centers.

Special Libraries

The category "special libraries" encompasses such a range of libraries as to make the category almost meaningless. Nevertheless, special libraries have to exercise the most stringent deselection programs, because of strict limits on collection size, usually the result of fixed amounts of storage space. Paula Strain examined the problem of periodical storage and cost of industrial floor space and found, not surprisingly, that the cost is so high that libraries must make efficient use of each square foot.[8] The special library must operate with the businessperson's eye toward economy and efficiency. Also, the collections of such libraries usually consist of technical material, much of it serial in character and often with a rapid and regular rate of obsolescence, at least for the local users.

The major concern of special libraries is meeting the current needs of clients. In such a situation, deselection is easier because of comparatively straightforward and predictable use patterns, the small size and homogeneous nature of the clientele, and the relatively narrow service goals for the library. Deselection takes place with little hesitation because costs and space are prime considerations. Many of the bibliometric measures described in chapter 6 can be valuable in establishing deselection programs in special libraries. A book addressing the special requirements of weeding in some types of special libraries is Ellis Mount's *Weeding of Collections in Sci-Tech Libraries.*[9] An article that describes an actual special library weeding project is

Richard Hulser's "Weeding in a Corporate Library as Part of a Collection Management Program."[10]

Academic Libraries

Traditionally, the purposes of the academic research library have been to select, acquire, organize, preserve (this has had special emphasis), and make available the full record of human knowledge. Collection development officers in these institutions seldom view demand as a valid measure of an item's worth. Potential or long-term research value takes highest priority. This being said, why are deselection programs part of academic library collection development?

The role of the college and university library is evolving. Whenever librarians discuss the changing role, they cite the information explosion as one cause. It is clear to most collection development staffs that it is futile to expect any one institution to locate and acquire all of the printed matter that comes into existence. Nor can they organize it, house it, or make it readily accessible to their public. No one person can manage to absorb all the relevant material that would be available, even if libraries could collect and preserve everything.

School Media Centers

School libraries and media centers employ highly structured collection development practices. In most schools and school districts, the media center expends its funds with the advice of a committee consisting of teachers, administrators, librarians, and, occasionally, parents. The need to coordinate collection development with curriculum needs is imperative. Typically, media centers lack substantial floor space for collections. Thus, when there is a major shift in the curriculum (new areas added and old ones dropped), the library must remove most of the old material. To some degree, the media center's deselection problems are fewer because there usually are other community libraries or a school district central media center that serve as backup resources.

In addition to the Slote and Segal books, two excellent articles about weeding school media collections are Anita Gordon's "Weeding: Keeping up with the Information Explosion," and the Calgary Board of Education, Educational Media Team's "Weeding the School Library Media Collection."[11] Gordon's article, though short, provides a good illustration of how one may use some standard bibliographies (*Senior High Catalog*, for example) in a deselection program. The Calgary article provides a detailed, step-by-step method for weeding the school collection.

Reasons for Deselecting

Four reasons for implementing a deselection program appear regularly in the literature:

* to save space
* to improve access
* to save money
* to make room for new materials

If the volume of literature on the subject reflected the degree to which libraries practiced deselection, there would be no need for conferences and workshops on the subject. Librarians spend more time writing about deselection than they do implementing the concepts. In part, this is because theory and the real world do not coincide. Often, from a realistic point of view, no other solution to space problems suggests itself except thinning the collection. When existing space fills up, and there is no additional collection space, the staff must do something.

In 1944, Fremont Rider determined that between 1831 and 1938, American research libraries doubled the size of their collections every 16 years, an annual growth rate of 4.25 percent.[12] Since then, studies have shown a gradual decrease in the annual growth rate (to 2.85 percent); nevertheless, libraries often quickly reach their limits of growth. The implications of an annual growth rate are obvious. In addition to the problem of limited shelf space, rapid growth of library collections leads to several other problems: (1) existing space is often not used efficiently, (2) obtaining additional space is expensive, and (3) servicing and using the collections become difficult.

Do theory and practice concerning space-saving coincide? Definitely! Compact storage systems save space. The conventional rule of thumb allows 15 volumes per square foot (500,000 volumes would require more than 33,000 square feet). A compact shelving system using a sliding shelf arrangement can store 500,000 volumes in slightly more than 14,000 square feet (an average of about 35 volumes per square foot)—a savings of more than 50 percent. Using a rail system of moving ranges, such as Space Saver, some libraries achieve savings of more than 80 percent. Less than 7,000 square feet can be used to house 500,000 volumes. The compact system recently installed at Loyola Marymount University will store 92,000 volumes in the same area that contained 24,000 volumes on conventional shelving.

Obviously, one pays a price for saving space, such as the extra cost of the compact system. However, Ralph Ellsworth, in *Economics of Book Storage in College and Research Libraries*, noted that conventional systems are also very expensive.[13] Although his 1969 cost figures have not been updated, the relationships still hold: conventional shelving costs $1.31 per volume; sliding shelves, $1.24; and a moving range system, $0.91. Thus, one can lower the unit cost for stored items by using a compact storage system. However, the cost cited covers only the building and shelving; one must also consider several other cost factors.

One basic theme of this book is that libraries exist to provide service. Archival libraries provide service, so our discussion naturally includes them, as they, too, eventually run out of space. However, service and size frequently do not go together. Anyone who has used a major research library knows that it takes time and effort to locate desired items. Often, such a library is the only location for certain materials, which is clearly an important service. However, few clients claim that such libraries are easy or convenient to use. Most people still like everything to be convenient and easy to use. Thus, it is possible for a smaller, well-weeded collection to provide better service than a larger collection—as long as the smaller collection contains popular items.

Does deselection improve access? Here theory and practice start diverging. Some staff members and customers give enthusiastically positive answers. Others give equally definite negative responses. For those who require quick, easy access to high-use, current materials, the thoughtfully maintained collection becomes the ideal. However, for older, seldom-used materials housed in a remote storage facility, it may take some time to determine whether the library even owns the item, in addition to the time needed to retrieve it. Thus, the answer to the question of whether weeding improves access is sometimes yes, sometimes no.

Finally, does weeding save money? Here the answer is probably no. Theory and reality are far apart at this point. As indicated, the cost per volume stored is usually lower using a compact storage system. However, one should consider several other important costs. For example, it is possible to quickly reduce the size of a collection by some arbitrary figure (5,000 volumes) or percentage (20 percent). One method of weeding in a public library would be to withdraw all books published before 1920 (or some other date) that have not circulated in the past five years. Just withdrawing the items from the shelves does not, however, complete the process. Staff must also change all the public and internal records to reflect the new status of the withdrawn books. Though online catalogs and databases allow rapid record updating, there are still labor costs to consider.

In addition to the cost of record modification, one must consider:

- the cost of deciding which items to remove;
- the cost of collecting and transporting them to their new location; and
- the cost of retrieving items when needed.

Even if the storage system is less expensive per volume than conventional stacks, these hidden costs can quickly overtake the apparent savings.

Another cost, often overlooked, is the cost to customers. Delayed access to desired materials carries a user cost, if nothing more than negative public relations. Almost every customer wants items now, not in a few hours, much less days. In a research and development environment, retrieval delays may cost researchers valuable time and, perhaps, cost the organization money. Though difficult to determine or measure accurately, customer cost should be taken into account when evaluating the costs of deselection.

Gary Lawrence's "A Cost Model for Storage and Weeding Programs" detailed a cost model for an academic storage program at the University of California.[14] Anyone planning a large-scale deselection and storage project should read the article.

Barriers to Deselection

A story of questionable veracity, but highlighting the major deselection barrier, concerns a collection development teacher. The teacher insisted that there was only one possible test to determine a person's suitability for becoming a collection development officer. Candidates would visit a doctor's office, where office staff would immediately take the candidate's blood pressure. The doctor would then hand the candidate a new book and tell the person to rip out one page and throw the book in a wastebasket. If the candidate's blood pressure rose above the initial reading, he or she would fail the test. True or not, the story does emphasize one of the most significant barriers to deselection—the psychological one.

Parents and teachers teach most of us to treat books and magazines with respect. In fact, we learn a great respect for anything printed. The idea of tearing pages or otherwise damaging a book goes against all we have learned. The problem is that we are again confusing the information contained in a package with the packaging. Some material becomes dated and must go, or people will act on incorrect information (prime examples are a loose-leaf service with superseding pages or dated medical or legal information). Travel directories and telephone books are other examples of materials that should go. Long-term value of other materials is less clear, and it is easy to find reasons to save them. In essence, our childhood training adds to the difficulties in removing items from a collection. If the library's goal is to purge rather than store the item, the problem is even bigger.

Some of the more common excuses for not thinning a collection are:

- lack of time
- procrastination
- fear of making a mistake
- fear of being called a "book burner."

These reasons are, to a greater or lesser extent, psychological. No matter how long the candidate for storage or removal has remained unused, a collection development officer's reaction is, "someone will need it tomorrow." Also, an unused book or audiovisual raises two questions: "Why wasn't it used?" and "Why did the library buy it?" Like anyone else, collection officers are reluctant to admit to mistakes. The possibility of erroneously discarding some important items always exists. But to use fear of making a mistake as the reason for not engaging in deselection is inexcusable.

Another barrier, which is political as well as psychological, is created by patrons and governing boards. An academic library staff may feel that it needs to institute a weeding and storage program, but fails to do so because of faculty opposition. If experience is any indication, one can count on everyone being in favor of removing the dead wood—but not in their areas of interest.

Sometimes, librarians never suggest deselection because they assume that there will be opposition from faculty, staff, general users, board members, or others. Naturally, there will be opposition. However, if no one raises the issue, there is no chance of gaining customer support. The possibility also exists that the assumed opposition will never materialize and that customers from whom one least expects help turn out to be strong supporters. Fear of possible political consequences has kept libraries from proposing a deselection program.

Loyola Marymount University's library recently completed an extensive deselection project, reviewing 82,000 volumes still classified in Dewey class numbers (DDC) and in the collection for at least 14 years. The librarians responsible for collection development had solid working relationships with the academic departments, and so had no trouble gaining support for the project. Gaining active participation in the process was another matter. Because the library was running out of collection space, the collection development staff hoped to remove at least four years' growth space (40,000–50,000 volumes). Three categories were identified for the DDC volumes: (1) high-use—reclass to Library of Congress Classification as soon as possible; (2) low-use—store; and (3) discard. To gain faculty involvement, the librarians told them that all material that had circulated at least four times would be reclassed as quickly as possible. The faculty were asked to recommend what should be done with the other materials (see fig. 14.1). As an additional incentive, the librarians warned the faculty that, after a certain date, the librarians would decide what to store and what to toss. Needless to say, every department claimed that nothing in its subject area should go. The library was able to discard fewer than 20,000 volumes and garnered less than 25 percent faculty participation—but there was no faculty opposition to the project.

Related to the political barrier is the problem of size and prestige. Many librarians, library boards, and customers rate libraries by size: the bigger the better. This brings us back to the epigraph of this book: "No library of a million volumes can be all BAD!" Quantity does not ensure quality. Collecting everything and throwing away nothing is much easier than selecting and deselecting with care. Librarians risk no political opposition, their prestige remains high, and only the taxpayers and customers pay the price of maintaining everything the library ever acquired.

Practical barriers to deselection also exist. Time can be a practical as well as a psychological barrier. The processes of identifying suitable deselection criteria, developing a useful program, and selling that program require significant amounts of time. Beyond those steps, time is required for staff training, as is time to identify and pull the candidate items, to change the records, and, finally, to dispose of the weeds. (Loyola Marymount University estimates indicated that the library committed a minimum of 2.5 FTE (full time equivalent) staff for 10 months to its deselection project. That estimate covers all staff time; no staff member was full-time on the project.)

With a small library staff, it is difficult to mount a major deselection project because there are too many things to do with too few people. Starting a program is, inevitably, a major project for any size library. After completing the first project, the library should establish an ongoing deselection procedure and incorporate it into the normal workflow. The ideal approach to a major project is to seek special funds and temporary staff to support the work.

Charles Von der Ahe Library, Loyola Marymount University
Deselection Project Faculty Letter

TO: ALL FACULTY
FROM: Marcia Findley, Head, Collection Development

RE: Weeding Library Books

As you know, the Library has been planning a large scale weeding project affecting books still classified in the Dewey Decimal system. A copy of the twenty-page report outlining the rationale and procedures for this project was sent to each department head and each dean in early December. The Library Committee approved the report in their meeting of February 12 and set the dates for its implementation from March 15 to May 15, 1992.

The faculty will play an important part in weeding these books. Your expertise is necessary in deciding whether they will be kept for storage or discarded. The procedure for faculty is as follows: stop at the Circulation Desk in the Library to pick up boxes of colored adhesive dots; proceed to the subject area to review books (outline of Dewey class attached); examine each book, noting circulation use, and indicate whether to keep, store, or discard it on the brief Book Review Form stapled to each date due card; put the appropriate colored dot on the book spine: blue = keep, yellow = store, red = discard. Books which have circulated during the past 5 years will already have blue dots and will not require examination.

It is important that all faculty participate in this project, so that your decisions reflect your present and future resource needs. Although a university library collection the size of LMU should have a significant number of retrospective materials, these titles should also have a recognized value. At present we have many old, outdated, inappropriate books that have never circulated which should be weeded out to make room for new books. Even for those books you wish to keep, the costs of storage are high: up to $50,000 per year in rent alone to store in a temperature and humidity-controlled building. This money will be taken from the acquisitions budget for the coming year. Also, remember that some books may be discarded with the knowledge that, if needed, they may be borrowed on Inter Library Loan. These are some of the things to keep in mind as you are making weeding decisions.

Sections not reviewed by faculty will be weeded by librarians.

Attached is a copy of the Book Review Form found in each book. Please call me about any questions you may have.

Thank you,

Fig. 14.1. Deselection project faculty letter.

Occasionally, libraries encounter legal barriers. Although not common problems, when they do arise, they are time-consuming. The problem arises in publicly supported libraries where regulations may govern the disposal of any material purchased with public funds. In some cases, the library must sell the material, even if only to a pulp dealer. Any disposal that gives even a hint of government book-burning will cause public relations problems; this stems from general attitudes toward printed materials. The library should do all it legally can to avoid any such appearance.

Deselection Criteria

Deselection is not an overnight process, and it is not a function that one performs in isolation from other collection development activities. Persons involved in deselection must consider all library purposes and activities. Some of the most important issues are library goals, the availability of acquisition funds for new titles, the relationship of a particular book to others on that subject, the degree to which the library functions as an archive, and potential future usefulness of an item. Only when one considers all the factors can one develop a successful deselection program.

After the staff recognizes the need for a deselection project, several lists of criteria can help in the deselection process. H. F. McGraw developed the following fairly comprehensive list:

- duplicates
- unsolicited and unwanted gifts
- obsolete books, especially science
- superseded editions
- books that are infested, dirty, shabby, worn out, juvenile (which wear out quickly), and so forth
- books with small print, brittle paper, and missing pages
- unused, unneeded volumes of sets
- periodicals with no indexes[15]

The mere fact that a book is a duplicate or worn out does not necessarily mean that one should discard it. Past use of the item should be the deciding factor. Also, consider whether it will be possible to find a replacement copy. The books and articles cited earlier provide additional criteria.

Three broad categories of deselection criteria exist, at least in the literature: physical condition, qualitative worth, and quantitative worth. Physical condition, for most researchers, is not an effective criterion. In most cases, poor physical condition results from overuse rather than nonuse. Thus, one replaces or repairs books in poor physical condition. (There is little indication in the literature on deselection that poor condition includes material with brittle paper. As discussed in chapter 17, brittle paper is a major problem.) Consequently, if the library employs physical condition as a criterion, it will identify only a few items, unless brittle paper is part of the assessment process.

Qualitative worth as a criterion for deselection is highly subjective. Because of variations in individual value judgments, researchers do not believe that this is an effective deselection method. Getting people to take the time to review the material is difficult. As noted earlier, Loyola Marymount University's library staff were only moderately successful in enlisting faculty input. Also, the faculty did not always agree about what to reclass and what to store, and few faculty recommended that the library discard anything. When all is said and done, the same factors that govern the buying decision should govern deselection judgments.

Any group assessment will be slow. Researchers have shown that a library can achieve almost the same outcome it would from specialists' reviewing the material by using an objective measure, such as past circulation or use data, if one wishes to predict future use. Also, the deselection process is faster and cheaper when past-use data are available.

C. A. Seymour summed up the issues regarding deselection as follows:

When the usefulness and/or popularity of a book has been questioned, the librarian, if the policy of the library permits discarding, must decide:

a.   If the financial and physical resources are present or available to provide continuing as well as immediate housing and maintenance of the book;

b.   If the book can be procured, within an acceptably short time, from another library at a cost similar to, or lower than, the cost of housing and maintenance within the library;

c.   If allowing the book to remain in the collection would produce a negative value.[16]

The problems that plague monograph weeding also apply to serials. A major difference, however, is that journals are not homogeneous in content. Another difference is that the amount of space required to house serial publications is greater than that required to house monographs. Thus, cost is often the determining factor in weeding (that is, although there may be some requests for a particular serial, the amount of space that a publication occupies may not be economical or may not warrant retaining the full set in the collection).

Of course, one should not forget the customer. Considering the benefits and disadvantages, in terms of customer service, that result from an active deselection program is a step in the process. Based on personal research projects, the percentage of librarians who think that a customer should be able to decide which materials to use out of all possible materials available (that is, no deselection) is much smaller than the percentage of librarians who strongly believe that a no-weeding policy is detrimental to the patron. Even academic faculty members lack complete familiarity with all the materials in their own subject fields; faced with a million volumes or more in a collection, how can we expect a student to choose the materials most helpful to his or her research without some assistance?

Criteria for
Deselection for Storage

Large libraries, particularly research libraries, deselect for storage rather than for discarding. These are two different processes. Often, criteria useful in making discard decisions do not apply to storage decisions. It is important to recognize that the primary objective of these two different forms of treatment is not necessarily to reduce the total amount of money spent for library purposes. Instead, the primary objective is to maximize, by employing economical storage facilities, the amount of research material available to the patron. The two main considerations for a storage program are: (1) What selection criteria are most cost-effective? and (2) How will the library store the items?

Although it is more than 30 years old, a Yale University Library project, the Selective Book Retirement Program, has value for today's deselection project planners. The project funding came from the Council on Library Resources, with the expectation that the results would be useful to other libraries. Project staff were to determine how best to cope with the problem of limited shelf space while continuing to build quality research collections and provide good service. The council outlined the following objectives for Yale in Yale's Selective Book Retirement Program:

a.   To expedite the Yale University Library's Selective Book Retirement Program (from 20,000 to 60,000 volumes per year) and to extend it to other libraries on the campus;

b.   To study (in collaboration with the faculty) the bases of selection for retirement for various subjects and forms of material;

c.   To study the effects of the Program on library use and research by faculty, graduate and undergraduate students;

d.   To ascertain what arrangements may compensate for the loss of immediate access caused by the program;

e.   To explore the possible effectiveness of the Program toward stabilizing the size of the immediate-access collection;

f.   To publish for the use of other libraries the policies, procedures, and results thus discovered.[17]

According to the report, the project staff fulfilled all the objectives but "d."

The Yale staff based their decisions about which books to move to storage on several factors:

1. A study of books on the shelves.
2. Value of a title as subject matter.
3. A volume's importance historically in the field.
4. Availability of other editions.
5. Availability of other materials on the subject.
6. Use of a volume.
7. Physical condition[18]

Clearly, the selection process depended upon the subjective judgment of individual librarians, some of whom were subject bibliography specialists. The librarians determined that general policies regarding weeding were easier to formulate than those that applied to specific fields; that it was easier to recommend weeding of specific titles than groups or kinds of books in specific fields; and that unanticipated mechanical problems greatly affected weeding procedures. These last problems included:

1. Lack of regularity in weeding (i.e., finding an adequate number of faculty and staff members and the time to keep the process going satisfactorily).
2. Diminishing returns over the long period (i.e., the longer the program existed, the more difficult the weeding process became).
3. The "Ever-Normal-Granary" theory (one of the purposes of the selective retirement program was to discover whether a library can control the growth of its collection by annually removing from the stacks the same number of volumes it adds). It was discovered that for the theory to be practical, either fragmentation into department libraries must occur, or the library administration must be willing to manage its collection and facilities solely on the principle of stabilization—neither of which Yale was willing to do.
4. Disagreement among weeders (i.e., the narrower viewpoint of faculty because of subject specialty versus the broader viewpoint of the librarian).[19]

Another unforeseen problem was a general feeling of discontent among faculty members and students. Neither group really understood the storage problem, and both objected to any change. Students particularly disliked the fact that they could not browse in the storage area.

In *Patterns in the Use of Books in Large Research Libraries*, Fussler and Simon reported some interesting ideas and statistical findings concerning the use factor in selective weeding of books for storage.[20] Although they recognized that frequency of circulation or use of books is not always an accurate measure of the importance of books in large research libraries, Fussler and Simon hoped to determine whether some statistical method could identify low-use books in research library collections. One of their goals was to sort the collection into high- and low-use materials. High-use items would remain in the local collection, and low-use items would go to a remote storage facility. They found that use and circulation data was effective for the first cut, that is, to identify potential materials. The final judgment of what to send to storage or discard remained with the collection development staff and other interested persons. Blindly following use data can create more problems than it solves.

The authors concluded that past use of an item was the best predictor of future use. Given the nature of a large research library, they thought a 15- to 20-year study period provided the best results, but a 5-year period provided adequate data.

Fussler and Simon's study is valuable because it outlines the factors that affect the validity of comparing criteria (for example, between two research collections) for removing books for storage, and because of their findings concerning the advantages of libraries devising similar rules.

These factors are helpful reminders to any library considering a deselection program:

1. Differences among libraries in composition of the collection in specific subject areas.

2. Differences in size of collections.

3. Differences in size of university populations.

4. Differences in nature of university populations.

5. Differences in kind of record-of-past-use.[21]

In addition to factors that affect comparisons, Fussler and Simon's findings indicate that their methods would produce similar percentages of use in libraries regardless of type, clientele, and collection size. They concluded that scholars at various institutions have similar reading interests. Finally, they identified three practical alternatives for selecting books for storage:

1. Judgment of one or a few expert selectors in a field.

2. An examination of past use of a book and/or its objective characteristics.

3. A combination of these two approaches.[22]

Of these alternatives, they concluded that an objective system (that is, a statistical measure) ranks books more accurately in terms of probable value than does the subjective judgment of a single scholar in the field. They did recommend, however, that subject specialists and faculty review the candidate books identified using objective means before moving the books to remote storage.

Richard Trueswell quantitatively measured the relationship between the last circulation date of a book and user circulation requirements, and their effect on weeding.[23] He hoped to determine a quantitative method of maintaining a library's holdings at a reasonable level while providing satisfactory service to the user. (One can also use his method to determine the need for multiple copies, thus increasing the probability of a user's finding the needed books.)

Trueswell's basic assumption was that the last circulation date of a book is an indication of the book's value. He determined the cumulative distribution of the previous circulation data, which he assumed represented the typical circulation of a given library. Next, he determined the 99th percentile, which he used as the cutoff point for stack thinning. By multiplying the previous monthly circulation figures and the distribution for each month after establishing the 99th percentile, he was able to calculate the expected size of the main collection.

In applying this method to a sample from the Deering Library at Northwestern University, Trueswell predicted that a library could satisfy 99 percent of its circulation requirements with just 40 percent of its present holdings. That is, the library could move 60 percent of its collections to storage without significantly affecting the majority of users.[24] Trueswell did admit that many of his basic assumptions were questionable and that future research would yield more reliable data. Additional research, including that by Trueswell, supported his initial results.

Another study of note is Aridamen Jain's *Report on a Statistical Study of Book Use*.[25] This quantitative study of book use is based on extremely different assumptions from the two studies described previously. Though his statistical manipulations may completely baffle a nonstatistician, the theory behind Jain's method of measuring book use is easy to understand. The purpose of his study was to examine mathematical models and statistical techniques for determining the dependence of circulation rate on a book's age and on certain other characteristics. He hoped to indicate that the age of a book is the most significant variable both in predicting rates of monograph usage and in deciding which books to transfer to storage. He reviewed other studies concerned with determining whether the frequency with which groups of books with defined characteristics were likely to show use in a research library when identified through statistical methods. He hoped to establish, through comparative methods, that the probability of a book not being used is an efficient method of predicting use by taking into account the age of the book.

Jain's model seems to be particularly valuable in deselection projects, for two reasons. One is that, contrary to the total library collection sampling method used by Fussler and Simon, Jain, like Trueswell, derived his data from all of the books checked out for a specific time period (that is, without regard to the total library collection). Jain felt that this method was superior to that used by Fussler and Simon. Although their method ensures the gathering of information on the same books over a longer time, Jain's method is much more conducive to a statistical design and data collection—missing data and lack of control are no longer problems. A second reason for this model's importance is that by using the specific time period sampling method, one can determine relative use of books within the library. With Fussler and Simon's method, this is not possible. Jain felt that the relative use concept was more efficient in studying the usage of books than the collection method.

Many other deselection studies exist, and they all generally agree that deselection based on past-use data provide the most cost-effective results. Although most of the studies were from academic libraries, Stanley Slote found that the method also worked in public libraries. (A British study by J. A. Urquhart and N. C. Urquhart has taken exception to these findings, especially for serials.[26]) Past use is a reasonable criterion if one is selecting for storage. However, the questions raised by the Urquharts indicate that librarians should go slowly in applying the past-use criterion when selecting items for purging.

Researchers have investigated almost every conceivable combination of objective criteria at one time or another in hope of finding the best. For example, they have examined language; date of publication; subject matter; frequency of citation; and listing in bibliographies, indexes, and abstracting services. Citation analysis and presence or absence of indexing or abstracting are most effective for serials and periodicals.

An interesting method for deselecting periodicals is to calculate a density-of-use value. The method requires establishing a unit of space occupied (perhaps one linear foot of shelf space) for each periodical title. Next, one determines the number of uses the title receives during a fixed time (perhaps one month). A ranking of the titles by use will produce one list, whereas a ranking by space occupied will probably result in a different list. Because one common objective of deselection programs is cost-effective use of existing collection space, calculating a ratio of space occupied to use (density of use) will help determine which periodicals to move to storage. An interesting article about weeding journals in a special library environment is by Richard Hunt.[27]

The preponderance of evidence points to the past-use criterion as the one most reliable for storage purposes. If the library has a circulation system that leaves a physical record of use in each book or in a database, one can easily collect the needed data. Today's automated circulation systems can provide detailed information about items, including frequency of circulation, class of borrower, use by class number, age of the item, language, and producer, as well as almost any other physical or intellectual content characteristic.

Though circulation data is as sound a predictor of future use as one can find, it does rest upon several assumptions that staff must understand and accept. One assumption is that circulated use is proportional to in-house use. What that proportion is depends on local circumstances. A second assumption is that current use patterns are similar to past and future patterns. (Trueswell restudied the same library over a period of 10 years with the same results from each study. Of course, that does not mean that the patterns would be the same 50 or 100 years from now.) A third assumption is that statistically random samples provide an adequate base for determining use patterns. A known limitation of circulation data is that a few customers can have a major impact on circulation (otherwise known as the 80/20 rule). Failure to take in-house use into account in a deselection program dependent on use data as the main selection criterion will have skewed results.

One factor to keep in mind is that the automated circulation systems now in use in many libraries will make it possible to collect valuable data for a project. With many systems, it is possible to collect data about in-house use by using a handheld reader and then downloading the data to the system. In the past, in-house use data was particularly time-consuming to collect. The fourth edition of Slote's book has an excellent chapter on using computer data in a deselection project.

Records Retention

Some information professionals in a special library or information center environment find themselves in charge of the organization's paper files, or archive. Some academic libraries also have responsibility for the campus archive. Just as print and audiovisual collections eventually exceed the space available, so do company files. When this happens, the equivalent of the library environment deselection process takes place.

In the business setting, and when dealing with the organization's records, the term used for the process is *retention*. A records retention program, developed by the person in charge of the files (who may be an information specialist, librarian, or records manager) is designed to meet several objectives:

- assure protection of the organization's vital records
- retain records of value or historical interest for the appropriate amount of time, meeting both legal and business needs for the records to be available
- restrict storage equipment and floor space, in expensive areas, to active records
- store inactive records in inexpensive storage facilities
- release reusable materials—audiotapes, magnetic tapes, or floppy disks—as quickly as possible
- destroy records that have served their purpose and are no longer useful.

With only slight rewording, these objectives apply to almost any library setting.

Records managers classify documents in several ways: as record or nonrecord, as active or inactive, and by value or use. A *record* is an official document of the organization; nonrecords are convenience copies. With a multiple-part order form, the original, or top copy, of the order is a record and all the other copies are nonrecords. Photocopies and carbon copies are almost always nonrecord items. *Active records* are those needed for current operating activities and consulted on a regular basis. The organization determines the cutoff period between active and inactive. (Perhaps one consultation in six months keeps a record active.) Factors influencing the organization's decision include the amount and cost of available storage space and the cost of active space. Storage of inactive records normally occurs away from the main facilities of the organization in special warehouses designed to store the inactive records of many organizations. Records managers determine value by the way people use the records. Typical categories of value are legal, operating, administrative, fiscal, research, and historical.

In many cases, the determination of when the organization may destroy a record is a function of various federal and state laws. In other cases, the retention period is related to business or needs. Records managers estimate that only about 10 to 20 percent of all records retained are in storage for legal reasons. Determining the laws and regulations covering record retention can be a challenge. Several guides assist in making retention decisions: *Guide to Record Retention Requirements* (Government Printing Office, irregular–); *Disposition of Federal Records* (College Park, Md.: National Archives and Records Administration, Office of Records Services, rev. ed, 1997); and *Recordkeeping Requirements* and *Records Retention Procedures*, both by Donald Skupsky (Englewood, Colo.: Information Requirements Clearinghouse, 1994). An organization develops a master retention schedule that lists the record series, where it comes from (that is, the office of record), how long to retain it, where to store it, in what form (according to law, some records must be originals, but others may be copies), and how and when the organization may dispose of it (either by destroying it or transferring it to an archive).

Though not all the issues are the same, there are some striking parallels between records retention and collection deselection. The Association of Records Managers and Administrators (ARMA; <http://www.arma.org/>) and the National Archives and Records Administration (NARA; <http://www.nara.gov>) are the best sources for further information about records management.

Summary

One way to overcome some of the psychological barriers to deselection is to develop cooperative programs like that of the Center for Research Libraries (see chapter 16). As long as there is a continuing emphasis on independence and size, customers suffer. Too much material to buy, too little money to spend, too little space to service and store adequately what we do buy, too few staff members to help bewildered patrons find what they need, and too little time and money to maintain collections on a human scale—these are but a few of the problems that librarians face. Clearly, any solution will require cooperation.

Notes

1.   Kenneth E. Carpenter, *The First 350 Years of the Harvard University Library* (Cambridge, Mass.: Harvard University Library, 1986), 122.

2.   H. F. McGraw, "Policies and Practices in Discarding," *Library Trends* 4 (January 1956): 270.

3.   Ibid.

4.   Stanley J. Slote, *Weeding Library Collections,* 4th ed. (Englewood, Colo.: Libraries Unlimited, 1997), 228.

5.   Eugene Garfield, "Weeding," *Current Contents* 15 (June 30, 1975): 26.

6.   Evan St. Lifer, "City Rebukes Philadelphia Library on Weeding Practices," *Library Journal* 121 (May 15, 1979): 12.

7.   Stanley J. Slote, *Weeding Library Collections*, 4th ed. (Englewood, Colo.: Libraries Unlimited, 1997); Joseph P. Segal, *Evaluating and Weeding Collections in Small and Medium-Sized Public Libraries: The CREW Method* (Chicago: American Library Association, 1980).

8.   Paula M. Strain, "A Study of the Usage and Retention of Technical Periodicals," *Library Resources & Technical Services* 10 (Summer 1966): 295.

9.   Ellis Mount, ed., *Weeding of Collections in Sci-Tech Libraries* (New York: Haworth Press, 1986).

10.   Richard Hulser, "Weeding in a Corporate Library as Part of a Collection Management Program," *Science and Technology Libraries* 6 (Spring 1986): 1–9.

11.   Anita Gordon, "Weeding: Keeping up with the Information Explosion," *School Library Journal* 30 (September 1983): 45–46; Calgary Board of Education, Educational Media Team, "Weeding the School Library Media Collection," *School Library Media Quarterly* 12 (Fall 1984): 419–24.

12.   Fremont Rider, *The Scholar and the Future of the Research Library* (New York: Handen Press, 1944), 17.

13.   Ralph Ellsworth, *Economics of Book Storage in College & Research Libraries* (Washington, D.C.: Association of Research Libraries, 1969).

14.   Gary S. Lawrence, "A Cost Model for Storage and Weeding Programs," *College & Research Libraries* 42 (March 1981): 139–41.

15.   McGraw, "Policies and Practices in Discarding," 269–82.

16.   C. A. Seymour, "Weeding the Collection," *Libri* 22 (1972): 189.

17.   L. Ash, *Yale's Selective Book Retirement Program* (Hamden, Conn.: Archon, 1963), ix.

18.   Ibid., 66.

19.   Ibid.

20.   H. H. Fussler and J. L. Simon, *Patterns in the Use of Books in Large Research Libraries*, rev. ed. (Chicago: University of Chicago Press, 1969), 4.

21.   Ibid., 125.

22.   Ibid., 208.

23.   R. Trueswell, "Quantitative Measure of User Circulation Requirements and Its Effects on Possible Stack Thinning and Multiple Copy Determination," *American Documentation* 16 (January 1965): 20–25.

24.   Ibid., 20.

25.   Aridamen Jain, *Report on a Statistical Study of Book Use* (Lafayette, Ind.: Purdue University, 1968).

26.   J. A. Urquhart and N. C. Urquhart, *Relegation and Stock Control in Libraries* (London: Oriel Press, 1976).

27.   Richard Hunt, "Journal Deselection in a Biomedical Research Library," *Bulletin of the Medical Library Association* 78 (January 1990): 45–48.

Further Reading

General

Barnett, L. "The Enemy Is Us." *Collection Building* 11, no. 3 (1991): 25–27.

Broadus, R. N. "Materials of History: Saving and Discarding." *Collection Building* 10, nos. 1/2 (1989): 3–6.

Carpenter, E. "Depreciation of Library Collections." *Library Administration and Management* 5 (Winter 1992): 41–43.

Egghe, L., and I. K. Ravichandra Rao. "Citation Age Data and the Obsolescence Function." *Information Processing Management* 28, no. 2 (1992): 201–17.

Guide to the Review of Collections: Preservation, Storage and Withdrawal. Edited by L. Clark. Chicago: American Library Association, 1991.

Kennedy, J. R., and G. Stockman. *The Great Divide: Challenges in Remote Storage*. Chicago: American Library Association, 1991.

Miller, E. P., and A. L. O'Neill. "Journal Deselection and Costing." *Library Acquisitions: Practice and Theory* 14, no. 2 (1990): 173–78.

Nolan, C. W. "Lean Reference Collection." *College & Research Libraries* 52 (January 1991): 80–91.

Pao, M. L., and A. J. Warner. "Depreciation of Knowledge." *Library Trends* 41 (Spring 1993): 545–709.

Wezeman, F. "Psychological Barriers to Weeding." *ALA Bulletin* 52 (September 1958): 637–39.

Academic

Fang, X. "A Study of the Problems of Aging Books in University Libraries." *Journal of the American Society of Information Science* 43 (August 1992): 501–05.

Farber, Evan I. "Books Not for College Libraries." *Library Journal* 122 (August 1997): 44–45.

Miller, J. W. "Problem Librarians Make Problems for Humanists." *Collection Building* 10, nos. 3/4 (1989): 11–19.

Milne, S. J. "Periodicals and Space Constraints." *Indiana Libraries* 9, no. 2 (1990): 55–58.

Osheroff, S. K., and M. C. Knittel. "Team Weeding in a University Library." *College & Research Library News* 51 (September 1990): 723–25.

Rhodes, J. A. "Sentimentality? An Exercise in Weeding in the Small College Library." *Christian Librarian* 40 (January 1997):16–17+.

Rider, F. *The Scholar and the Future of the Research Library*. New York: Handen Press, 1944.

Sam, S., and J. A. Major. "Compact Shelving of Circulating Collections." *College & Research Library News* 54 (January 1993): 11–12.

Seaman, S., and D. DeGeorge. "Selecting and Moving Books to a Remote Depository." *Collection Management* 16, no. 1 (1992): 137–42.

Turner, S. J. "Trueswell's Weeding Technique: The Facts." *College & Research Libraries* 41 (March 1980): 134–38.

Public

Albsmeyer, B. "Danger—Our Books Contain Outdated Information." *Unabashed Librarian* 73 (1989): 5–6.

Bazirjiian, R. "Ethics of Library Discard Practices." In *Legal and Ethical Issues in Acquisitions*. Edited by K. Strauch and B. Strauch, 213–34. New York: Haworth Press, 1990.

Donovan, C. A. "Deselection and the Classics." *American Libraries* 26 (December 1995): 110–11.

Ehrlich, M. "Criteria for Not Discarding from a Public Library." *Unabashed Librarian* 78 (1991): 26.

Futas, E., and J. S. Tryon. "Scheduled Reference Collection Maintenance." *Reference Librarian* 29 (1990): 69–76.

Mahoney, K. "Weeding the Small Library Collection." *Connecticut Libraries* 24 (Spring 1982): 45–47.

Roy, L. "Weeding Without Tears." *Collection Management* 12, nos. 1/2 (1990): 83–93.

Slote, S. J. *Weeding Library Collections*, 4th ed. Englewood, Colo.: Libraries Unlimited, 1997.

Tuchmayer, H. "Why Let the Dust Settle?" *North Carolina Libraries* 52 (Spring 1994): 15–16.

Wallace, D. P. "The Young and the Ageless: Obsolescence in the Public Library Collection." *Public Libraries* 29 (March/April 1990): 102–5.

School

Brown, C. "Selection for Rejection." *School Librarian* 40 (November 1992): 135–36.

Cerny, R. "When Less Is More: Issues in Collection Development." *School Library Journal* 37 (March 1991): 130–31.

Gordon, A. "Weeding—Keeping up with the Information Explosion." *School Library Journal* 30 (September 1983): 45–46.

Kahler, J. "Dated, Tattered, and Ugly." *Texas Library Journal* 65 (Fall 1989): 100–102.

Vogel, B. D. "The Adventures of Molly Keeper, A Cautionary Tale." *School Library Journal* 38 (September 1992): 136–42.

"Weeding Media." *School Library Workshop* 14 (November 1993): 8–9.

"Weeding the School Library Media Collection." *School Library Media Quarterly* 12 (Fall 1984): 419–24.

"Weeding Woes." *School Library Workshop* 17 (November 1996): 10.

Special

Bedsole, D. T. "Formulating a Weeding Policy for Books in a Special Library." *Special Libraries* 49 (May 1958): 205–9.

Burdick, A. J. "Science Citation Index Data as a Safety Net for Basic Science Books Considered for Weeding." *Libraries & Technical Services* 33 (October 1989): 367–73.

Diodato, V. P., and F. Smith. "Obsolescence of Music Literature." *Journal of the American Society of Information Science* 44 (March 1993): 101–12.

Drake, C. S. "Weeding of a Historical Society Library." *Special Libraries* 83 (Spring 1992): 86–91.

Fisher, W. "Weeding the Academic Business/Economics Collection." *Behavioral and Social Sciences Librarian* 4 (Spring 1985): 29–37.

Goldstein, C. H. "Study of Weeding Policies in Eleven TALON Resource Libraries." *Medical Library Association Bulletin* 69 (July 1981): 311–16.

Hulser, R. P. "Weeding in a Corporate Library as Part of a Collection Management Program." *Science and Technology Libraries* 6 (Spring 1986): 1–9.

Hurt, R. K. "Journal Deselection in a Biomedical Research Library." *Bulletin of the Medical Library Association* 78 (January 1990): 45–48.

Index to Federal Record-Keeping Requirements. New York: National Records Management Council, 1981.

"Jury Rules Corporate Library Willfully Destroyed Documents." *Library Journal* 118 (February 1, 1993): 14.

Kidd, Y. M. "New Regulation Relaxes Federal Records Management Requirements." *Inform* 5 (March 1991): 9–10.

Mount, Ellis, ed. *Weeding of Collections in Sci-Tech Libraries*. New York: Haworth Press, 1986.

Oberhofer, C. M. A. "Information Use Value." *Information Processing and Management* 29 (September/October 1993): 587–600.

Triolo, V. A., and D. Bao. "A Decision Model for Technical Journal Deselection with an Experiment in Biomedical Communications." *Journal of the American Society for Information Science* 44 (April 1993): 148–60.

Williams, R. F. "Document Disposition of Optically Stored Records." *Inform* 7 (February 1993): 35–45.

———. "Is It Legal?" *Document Image Automation* 12 (Fall 1992): 10–12.

15
Evaluation

Sheila Intner and Elizabeth Futas stated that the 1990s was the decade of evaluation.[1] Whether it was *the* decade of evaluation may be debatable; what is not debatable is that *evaluation, assessment, outcomes*, and *accountability* were words frequently found in library literature in the 1990s. Certainly, accreditation bodies were demanding evidence that institutional expenditures were more than just expenditures; that is, they wanted to know what was the result. No longer acceptable were long statistical lists of books added, journal subscriptions started, and items circulated. Accreditation visiting teams were saying things like, "So you added x thousands of books, have x hundreds of subscriptions, and your users check out an average of x items per month. Have you any evidence that this has made any difference and helped meet the institutional mission and goals?" "What evidence of quality do you have and how do you and your institution define that concept?"

Answering such questions is difficult unless you have collected a body of data with those types of questions in mind. What this means is that some of the measures of evaluation we have employed in the past, such as collection size, will not be acceptable in some circumstances when outcome and accountability are at issue. Certainly the questions go beyond just our collections, both physical and virtual, but having carefully evaluated our collections will help us address the broader issues (such as, is the library worth the money expended on it?).

What are the strengths of the collection? How effectively have we spent our collection development monies? How useful are the collections to the service community? How do our collections compare to those of our peers? These are but a few of the questions one may answer by conducting a collection evaluation assessment project. Evaluation completes the collection development cycle and brings one back to needs assessment activities. Though the term *evaluation* has several definitions, there is a common element in all of them related to placing a value or worth on an object or activity. Collection evaluation involves both objects and activities, as well as quantitative and qualitative values.

Dozens of people have written about collection evaluation—Stone, Clapp-Jordan, Evans, Bonn, Lancaster, Mosher, McGrath, Broadus, and Hall, to name a few. Though the basics remain unchanged, the application of the basics has become more and more sophisticated over the years. Computers make it possible to handle more data, as well as a wider variety of data. Bibliographic and numeric databases can provide valuable data that in the past would have been exceedingly difficult, if not impossible, to obtain (see, for example, Metz's older but still interesting *Landscape of Literatures*[2]). Bibliographic utilities, such as WLN, and regional groups, such as AMIGOS, offer CD-ROM products for assessing and comparing collections. Despite the assistance of technology and increasingly sophisticated systems of evaluation, as Betty Rosenburg, a long-time teacher of collection development, repeatedly stated, the best tool for collection evaluation is an intelligent, cultured, experienced selection officer with a sense of humor and a thick skin. Because there are so many subjective and qualitative elements involved in collection development, Rosenburg's statement is easy to understand and appreciate. Though this chapter will not help one develop the personal characteristics she identified as important, it does outline the basic methods available for conducting an evaluation project and provides a few examples.

Background

Before undertaking any evaluation, the library must carefully define the project's purposes and goals. One definition of *evaluation* is "a judgment as to the value of X, based on a comparison, implicit or explicit, with some known value, Y." If the unknown and the (presumably) known values involve abstract concepts that do not lend themselves to quantitative measurement, there are bound to be differences of opinion regarding the value. There are many criteria for determining the value of a book or of an entire collection: economic, moral, religious, aesthetic, intellectual, educational, political, and social, for example. The value of an item or a collection fluctuates depending on which yardstick one employs. Combining several measures is effective as long as there is agreement as to their relative weight. So many subjective factors come into play in the evaluation process that one must work through the issues before starting. One important benefit of having the goals defined and the criteria for the values established ahead of time is that interpretation of the results is much easier. It may also help to minimize differences of opinion about the results.

Libraries and information centers, like other organizations, want to know how they compare with similar organizations. Comparative data can be useful, but it can also be misleading. Like all other aspects of evaluation, comparative data presents significant problems of definition and interpretation. What, for example, does library A gain by comparing itself with library B, except, perhaps, an inferiority complex—or a delusion as to its own status? Without question, some libraries are better than others, and comparisons may well be important in discovering why this is so. Two key issues in interpreting comparisons are: (1) one assumes a close approximation of needs among the comparative groups and (2) one assumes the existence of standards or norms that approximate optimum conditions. Neither assumption has a solid basis in reality. If the library or its parent organization is considering starting a new service or program, comparative data from libraries already supporting similar services can provide valuable planning information.

Though comparisons are interesting and even helpful in some respects, one should be cautious in interpreting the significance of the findings.

Based on many years of experience in surveying library resources, Robert Downs suggested:

> From the internal point of view, the survey, if properly done, gives one an opportunity to stand off and get an objective look at the library, to see its strengths, its weaknesses, the directions in which it has been developing, how it compares with other similar libraries, how well the collection is adapted to its clientele, and provides a basis for future planning.[3]

Downs believed that, in addition to their internal value, surveys are an essential step in preparing for library cooperative acquisitions projects and resource sharing.

Organizations conduct evaluations for several reasons, including:

- To develop an intelligent, realistic acquisitions program based on a thorough knowledge of the existing collection.

- To justify increased funding demands or for particular subject allocations.

- To increase the staff's familiarity with the collection.

Accreditation standards usually address the library, and many of the evaluative criteria apply to collection evaluation. J. H. Russell, in his article "The Library Self-Survey," stated that a survey provides "a check of the effectiveness of the library; ... a kind of psychological security for the library staff and for the college faculty; ... a valuable instrument in public relations for the library; ... [and that it will] force the library staff to formulate clearly the objectives of the library itself."[4] By changing the environmental context, the statement could apply to any library.

It is possible to divide collection evaluation purposes into two broad categories: internal reasons and external reasons. The following lists provide a variety of questions or purposes for each category.

Internal Reasons

Collection development needs

- What is the true scope of the collections (that is, what is the subject coverage)?

- What is the depth of the collections (that is, what amount and type of material comprise the collection)?

- How does the service community use the collection (that is, what is the circulation and use within the library)?

- What is the collection's monetary value? (This must be known for insurance and capital assessment reasons.)

- What are the strong areas of the collection (in quantitative and qualitative terms)?
- What are the weak areas of the collection (in quantitative and qualitative terms)?
- What problems exist in the collection policy and program?
- What changes should be made in the existing program?
- How well are collection development officers carrying out their duties?
- Provide data for possible cooperative collection development programs.
- Provide data for deselection (weeding) projects.
- Provide data to determine the need for a full inventory.

Budgetary needs

- Assist in determining allocations needed to strengthen weak areas.
- Assist in determining allocations needed to maintain areas of strength.
- Assist in determining allocations needed for retrospective collection development.
- Assist in determining overall allocations.

External Reasons

Local institutional needs

- Is the library's performance marginal, adequate, or above average?
- Is the budget request for materials reasonable?
- Does the budget provide the appropriate level of support?
- Is the library comparable to others serving similar communities?
- Are there alternatives to space expansion (for example, weeding)?
- Is the collection outdated?
- Is there sufficient coordination in the collection program (that is, does the library really need all those separate collections)?
- Is the level of duplication appropriate?
- Is the cost/benefit ratio reasonable?

Extra-organizational needs

- Provide data for accreditation groups.
- Provide data for funding agencies.
- Provide data for various networks, consortia, and other cooperative programs.
- Provide data to donors.

Having undertaken numerous evaluation projects, as staff members and consultants, the authors have found that these reasons inevitably surface in one form or another. Not all the reasons apply to every type of information environment, but most have wide applicability.

After the library or evaluators establish the purposes for carrying out the evaluation, the next step is determining the most effective methods of evaluation. A number of techniques are available, and the choice depends, in part, upon the purpose and depth of the evaluation process. George Bonn's "Evaluation of the Collection" lists five general approaches to evaluation:

1. Compiling statistics on holdings.

2. Checking standard lists—catalogs and bibliographies.

3. Obtaining opinions from regular users.

4. Examining the collection directly.

5. Applying standards [which involves the use of various methods mentioned earlier], listing the library's document delivery capability, and noting the relative use of a particular group.[5]

Most of the methods developed in the recent past draw on statistical techniques. Some of the standards and guidelines of professional associations and accrediting agencies employ statistical approaches and formulas that give evaluators some quantitative indicators of what is adequate. Standards, checklists, catalogs, and bibliographies are other tools of the evaluator.

Some years ago, Dr. Evans was part of a team that reviewed the effectiveness of library evaluation through the literature. The team examined more than 750 articles and research reports. From that pool, the team established six categories of measures employed to evaluate library effectiveness: accessibility, cost, user satisfaction, response time, cost/benefit ratio, and use.

Four surprising features emerged from the examination. First, almost none of the 750-plus studies provided a clearly stated purpose for the project. The team also found evidence of dissatisfaction with the outcome of some of the studies; where dissatisfaction existed, there was also a lack of a clear statement of purpose.

Second, none of the methods employed was sufficiently sensitive to both quantitative and qualitative issues. No method was completely satisfactory from either the librarians' or nonlibrarians' point of view. (Perhaps part of the problem was that there had been no agreement as to the purposes of the projects before they were begun.) Third, most methods placed high value on circulation and accessibility. Often, this high value was at the expense of quality and breadth. The method that generated the most questioning was document delivery time. Finally, a most surprising finding was that none of the measures then in use, even in combination, took into account a total service program—this is more or less true today. For example, none of the measures took conservation and preservation issues into account. (Chapter 17 discusses preservation, a major issue in collection management.)

The ALA's *Guide to the Evaluation of Library Collections*[6] divides the methods into collection-centered measures and use-centered measures. Within each category are a number of specific evaluative methods. The *Guide* summarizes the major techniques currently used to evaluate information collections. These methods focused on print resources, but there are elements that one can employ in the evaluation of electronic resources.

Collection-Centered

- Checking list, bibliographies, and catalogs
- Expert opinion
- Comparative use statistics
- Collection standards

Use-Centered

- Circulation studies
- User opinion/studies
- Analysis of ILL statistics
- Citation studies
- In-house use studies
- Shelf availability
- Simulated use studies
- Document delivery tests

Each method has its advantages and disadvantages. Often it is best to employ several methods that will counterbalance one another's weaknesses. We will touch on each of these; however, the use-centered methods all share the same broad characteristics as circulation studies. Each is valuable in its own way to evaluate some aspect of use, but due to space limitations, we will not address all of the variations. One should also consult items listed in the "Notes" and "Further Readings" sections before planning an evaluation project.

Collection-Centered Methods

List Checking

The checklist method is an old standby for evaluators. It can serve a variety of purposes. Used alone or in combination with other techniques—usually with the goal of coming up with some numerically based statement, such as "We (or they) have X percentage of the books on this list"—it provides objective data. Consultants frequently check holdings against standard bibliographies (or suggest that the library do it) and report the results. Checklists allow the evaluator to compare the library's holdings against one or more standard lists of materials for a subject area (*Business Journals of the United States*), for a type of library (*Books for College Libraries*), or for a class of customer (*Best Books for Junior High Readers*).

When asked to assess a collection, we use checklists as part of the process, if appropriate lists are available. Whenever possible, we ask a random sample of subject experts at the institution to identify one or two bibliographies or basic materials lists in their specialty that they believe would be reasonable to use in evaluating the collection. The responses, or lack of responses, provide information about each respondent's knowledge of publications in her or his field and indicate the degree of interest in the library collection. When appropriate, we also use accreditation checklists, if there is doubt about the collection's adequacy.

Accreditation committees frequently use checklists in evaluation, particularly for reference and periodical collections. Such committees strive to apply standards for various kinds of libraries. The College Library Standards Committee's "Standards for College Libraries" recommends, "Library holdings should be checked frequently against standard bibliographies, both general and subject, as a reliable measure of their quality. A high percentage of listed titles which are relevant to the program of the individual institution should be included in the library collections."[7]

As collections increase in size, there is less need to worry about formal checking or standard bibliographies. However, it is worthwhile for selectors to occasionally take time to review some of the best-of-the-year lists published by various associations. Such reviews will help selectors spot titles missed during the year and serve as a check against personal biases playing too great a role in the selection process. Selectors quickly identify items not selected and can take whatever steps are necessary. Often such lists appear in selection aids; it takes little extra time to review the list to conduct a mini-evaluation.

Self-surveys by the library staff frequently make use of checklist methods. M. Llewellyn Raney conducted the first checklist self-survey, at least the first reported in the literature, in 1933 for the University of Chicago libraries. This survey used 300 bibliographies to check the entire collection for the purpose of determining future needs. There is little question that this pioneering effort demonstrated the value of using checklists to thoroughly examine the total collection.

Obviously, one can use a variety of checklists in any situation. The major factor determining how many lists to employ is the amount of time available for the project. Today's OPACs make checking an easier process, but it still requires a substantial amount of time. Many evaluators have their favorite standard lists, but there is a growing use of highly specialized lists in an effort to check collection depth as well as breadth. Most evaluators advocate using serials and media checklists in addition to book checklists. Large research libraries (academic, public, or special) seldom use the basic lists; instead, they rely on subject bibliographies and specially compiled lists. One of the quality control checks employed by the RLG/ARL conspectus project uses the specially prepared checklist technique. Specially prepared bibliographies are probably the best checklist method. However, preparing such lists takes additional time, and many libraries are unwilling to commit that much staff effort to the evaluation process.

Using any checklist requires certain assumptions; one is that the selected list reflects goals and purposes that are similar to those of the checking institution. Normally, unless an examination of a collection is thorough, the checklist method merely samples the list. Thus, the data are only as good as the sampling method employed.

The shortcomings of the checklist technique for evaluation are many, and eight criticisms appear repeatedly:

- Title selection was for specific, not general, use.
- Almost all lists are selective and omit many worthwhile titles.
- Many titles have little relevance for a specific library's community.
- Lists may be out of date.
- A library may own many titles that are not on the checklist but that are as good as the titles on the checklist.
- Interlibrary loan service carries no weight in the evaluation.
- Checklists approve titles; there is no penalty for having poor titles.
- Checklists fail to take into account special materials that may be important to a particular library.

To answer these criticisms, the checklist would have to be all things to all libraries. All too often, there is little understanding that not all works are of equal value or equally useful to a specific library. Though some older books continue to be respected for many years, an out-of-date checklist is of little use in evaluating a current collection.

Obviously, the time involved in effectively checking lists is a concern. Spotty or limited checking does little good, but most libraries are unable or unwilling to check an entire list. Checklist results show the percentage of books from the list that is in the collection. This may sound fine, but there is no standard proportion of a list a library should have. How should one interpret the fact that the library holds 53 percent of some list? Is it reasonable or necessary to have every item? Comparisons of one library's holdings with another's on the basis of percentage of titles listed is of little value, unless the two libraries have similar service populations. In a sense, the use of a checklist assumes some correlation between the percentage of listed books held by a library and the percentage of desirable books in the library's collection. This assumption may or may not be warranted. Equally questionable is the assumption that listed books not held necessarily constitute desiderata, and that the proportion of items held to items needed (as represented on the list) constitutes an effective measure of a library's adequacy.

This lengthy discussion of the shortcomings of the checklist method should serve more as a warning than a prohibition. There *are* benefits from using this method in evaluation. Many librarians feel that checking lists helps to reveal gaps and weaknesses in a collection; that the lists provide handy selection guides if the library wishes to use them for this purpose; and that the revelation of gaps and weaknesses may lead to reconsideration of selection methods and policies. Often, nonlibrary administrators respond more quickly and favorably to information about gaps in a collection when the evaluators identify the gaps by using standard lists than when they use other means of identifying the weaknesses.

Expert Opinion

As its name implies, this method depends on personal expertise for making the assessment. What are the impressionistic techniques used by experts? Some evaluators suggest examining a collection in terms of the library's policies and purposes and preparing a report based on impressions of how well the collection meets those goals. The process may involve reviewing the entire collection using the shelf list; it may cover only a single subject area; or, as is frequently the case, it may involve conducting shelf examinations of various subject areas. Normally, the concern is with estimating qualities like the depth of the collection, its usefulness in relation to the curriculum or research, and deficiencies and strengths in the collections.

Very rarely is this technique used alone. It occurs most frequently during accreditation visits, when an accreditation team member walks into the stacks, looks around, and comes out with a sense of the value of the collection. No consultant who regularly uses this technique limits it to shelf reading. Rather, consultants prefer to collect impressions from the service community. Though each person's view is valid only for the individual's areas of interest, in combination, individuals' views should provide an overall sense of the service community's views. (This approach falls into the category of user satisfaction.) Customers make judgments about the collection each time they look for something. They will have an opinion even after one brief visit. Thus, the approach is important, if for no other reason than that it provides the evaluator with a sense of what the customers think about the collection. Further, it encourages customer involvement in the evaluation process.

Frequently, an outside consultant, an experienced librarian, or an accrediting committee uses this approach. The evaluation draws on information compiled from various sources—personal examination of the shelves, qualitative measures, and the impressions of the service community. Subject specialists give their impressions of the strengths and weaknesses of a collection. Sometimes, the evaluator employs questionnaires and interviews to collect the data from many people. Less frequently, specialists' impressions may constitute the entire evaluation. Library staff member opinions about the collection add another perspective to the assessment; often, these views differ sharply from those of the users and those of an outsider.

Library self-studies make effective use of the impressions of subject specialists and librarians in combination with list checking and other evaluative methods. An example of application of the impressionistic method was a project undertaken by the librarians at the State University of New York at Buffalo. The library's subject bibliographers formed an evaluation team that developed an impressive set of project guidelines. The bibliographers prepared a preliminary evaluative statement for their areas of responsibility. They then checked the collection holdings against various bibliographies. They were to use their ingenuity in approaching the research collection, and they were to evaluate the book selection procedures, as well as faculty interest and assistance in the selection process. After gathering the objective data (that is, the results of bibliography checks), the evaluators reexamined their original statements. They found that though some adjustments were necessary, their initial assessment was reasonably close to the checklist results.

Because many large public libraries employ subject specialists, most special libraries have in-depth subject specialists available, and school libraries can draw on teachers for subject expertise, this method is viable in any library environment.

The major weakness of the impressionistic technique is that it is overwhelmingly subjective. Obviously, the opinions of those who use the collection regularly and the views of subject specialists are important. Impressions may be most useful as part of an evaluation when used in connection with other methods of examining a collection, but their value depends on the objectives of the individual evaluation project, and their significance depends on their interpretation.

Comparative Use Statistics

Comparisons among institutions can offer useful, if sometimes limited, data for evaluation. The limitations arise due to institutional differences in objectives, programs, and service populations. For instance, a junior college with only a liberal arts program requires one type of library, whereas a community college with both a liberal arts curriculum and strong vocational programs requires a much larger collection. Comparing the first library to the second would be like comparing apples and oranges. There simply is no basis for comparison, and no point in it unless one can effectively isolate the liberal arts components.

Comparing libraries is difficult because of the way some libraries generate statistics about their collections and service usage. On paper, two libraries may appear similar, yet their book collections may differ widely. Some years ago, Eli Oboler documented this problem:

> One library, without any footnote explanation, suddenly increased from less than twenty-five thousand volumes added during 1961-62 to more than three times that number while the amount shown for books and other library materials only increased approximately 50 percent. Upon inquiry the librarian of this institution stated that, "from storage in one attic we removed forty thousand items, some of which have been catalogued, but in the main we are as yet unsure of the number which will be added. The addition of a large number of volumes also included about one-fourth public documents, state and federal, and almost fifty thousand volumes in microtext."[8]

No one suggests that it is possible to determine the adequacy of a library's collection solely in quantitative terms. Number of volumes is a poor measure of the growth of the library's collection in relation to the programs and services it provides. However, when standards fail to provide quantitative guidelines, budgeting and fiscal officers, who cannot avoid quantitative bases for their decisions, adopt measures that seem to have the virtue of simplicity but are essentially irrelevant to the library's function. Therefore, it is necessary to develop quantitative approaches for evaluating collections that are useful in official decisionmaking and that retain the virtue of simplicity while being relevant to the library's programs and services.

Some useful comparative evaluation tools have been developed as a result of technology and growth of bibliographic utilities. Two widely used products were produced by AMIGOS and WLN. The AMIGOS product employed data from OCLC, and the WLN product uses its own bibliographic database. Due to the recent merger of OCLC and WLN, only the product that WLN developed is currently available. What such products do is allow one to compare one collection against one or more other collections in terms of number of titles in a classification range. One could, with either product, identify "gap" titles, items not in the collection but in the collection(s) of the other libraries.

The product that still exists, at the time we prepared this edition, is OCLC/WLN's "Automated Collection Analysis Service." There are four possible analyses. One analysis is a useful benchmarking and planning tool that analyzes the collection by subject, age, language, and format, and for public libraries breaks the data down between adult and juvenile materials. This analysis is for a library or consortium. The second and third services are comparisons of two or more libraries—overlap analysis and gap analysis. The last analysis is a comparison of an academic library's holdings against the third edition of *Books for College Libraries*.

Loyola Marymount University used the AMIGOS product for several years to evaluate various subject areas and work with the appropriate academic department to strengthen the collection in that area. We used two CD-ROMs, one disk containing data from a "peer group" consisting of 40 libraries that are comparable to the LMU library or to which we wished to compare ourselves. The other disk contained data for the four California Catholic universities. The disks were used for several projects. One project was to explore the possibilities for resource sharing and cooperative collection development among the California Catholic universities. Another use was to assist in assessing the collection to support proposed new academic programs. The library also used the material, in combination with other data, to respond to various accreditation and self-study reports that were done every year.

Using these products took time, because the manual was large and learning how the product worked and how to interpret the results had a steep learning curve. It also took time to teach the recipients of the data how to use the material effectively. Table 15.1 presents a sample of the type of data one can secure from such a product. An article by Marcia Findley (LMU's collection development officer) described in detail a project assessing the art history collection.[9]

Table 15.1. Subcollection counts, proportions, and gaps from OCLC/AMIGOS Collection Analysis CD.

Subcollection Counts
Peer Group: PEER GROUP 1 (40)
LC Division: BL-BX Religion

NATC	Peer Group Titles	Peer Group Holdings	Evaluator Unique	Evaluator Titles	Overlap Titles	Overlap Holdings
BL1-BL9999	2,821	18,774	922	672	647	8,520
BM1-BM9999	1,157	6,680	324	204	189	2,242
BP1-BP9999	746	4,539	274	94	88	1,359
BQ1-BQ9999	710	3,293	284	93	89	976
BR1-BR9999	2,626	16,205	862	643	626	8,529
BS1-BS9999	4,166	23,597	1,274	946	914	10,564
BT1-BT9999	3,194	17,957	1,239	760	737	8,785
BV1-BV9999	3,341	12,412	1,447	458	444	4,314
BX1-BX0799	344	1,323	153	36	36	382
BX0800-BX4795	4,144	20,951	1,635	924	903	10,368
BX4800-BX9999	1,774	7,904	752	287	277	3,012
Totals	25,023	133,635	9,166	5,117	4,950	59,051

Subcollection Proportions
Peer Group: PEER GROUP 1 (40)
LC Division: B-BJ Philosophy/Psychology

NATC	Titles Evaluator	Titles Avg Mbr	Comparative Size	Comparative Peer Group	% of Subcollection Evaluator
B1-B68	80	54	148.15	2.23	2.09
B69-B789	386	241	160.17	9.96	10.08
B790-B5739	937	606	154.62	25.00	24.47
BC1-BC9999	60	49	122.45	2.01	1.57
BD1-BD9999	336	196	171.43	8.08	8.78
BF1-BF1000	1,500	939	159.74	38.71	39.17
BF1001-BF1400	48	37	129.73	1.54	1.25
BF1401-BF1999	38	37	102.70	1.51	0.99
BH1-BH9999	68	44	154.55	1.81	1.78
BJ1-BJ1800	372	217	171.43	8.95	9.72
BJ1801-BJ2195	4	5	80.00	0.19	0.10
Totals	3,829	2,425	157.88	100.00	100.00

Subcollection Proportions
Peer Group: CALIFORNIA CATHOLIC (3)
LC Division: D-DZ History: General & Old World

NATC	Titles Evaluator	Avg Mbr	Size	Comparative Peer Group	% of Subcollection Evaluator
D1-D0899	470	823	57.11	15.62	16.50
D0900-D2009	16	37	43.24	0.70	0.56
DA-DA9999	469	654	71.71	12.41	16.47
DAW1001-DAW	1051	0	0	0.00	0.00
DB-DB9999	31	53	58.49	1.01	1.09
DC-DC9999	133	262	50.76	4.96	4.67
DD-DD9999	152	191	79.58	3.62	5.34
DE-DE9999	20	19	105.26	0.36	0.70
DF-DF9999	140	103	135.92	1.95	4.92
DG-DG9999	137	183	74.86	3.47	4.81
DH-DH9999	4	8	50.00	0.15	0.14
DJ-DJ9999	5	0	100.00	0.09	0.18
DJK-DJK9999	7	50	14.00	0.94	0.25
DK-DK9999	130	373	34.85	7.07	4.56
DL-DL9999	9	22	40.91	0.42	0.32
DP1-DP0500	39	94	41.49	1.78	1.37
DP0501-DP0900	3	8	37.50	0.15	0.11
DQ-DQ9999	2	1	200.00	0.03	0.07
DR-DR9999	14	60	23.33	1.13	0.49
DS1-DS0040	31	69	44.93	1.30	1.09
DS0041-DS0329	278	659	42.19	12.50	9.76
DS0330-DS0500	67	211	31.75	4.00	2.35
DS0501-DS0937	368	857	42.94	16.25	12.92
DT-DT9999	294	433	67.90	8.21	10.32
DU-DU9999	28	96	29.17	1.81	0.98
DX-DX9999	1	3	33.33	0.05	0.04
Totals	2,848	5,271	54.03	100.00	100.00

Subcollection Gap
Peer Group: CALIFORNIA CATHOLIC (3)

Division	Holdings Range	Gap Titles In Range	Cumulative	Comparative Size
D1-D0899	90-100%	0	0	57.09%
History: General	80-89%	131	131	73.00%
	70-79%	0	131	57.09%
Current:	60-69%	0	131	57.09%
LMU Titles 470	50-59%	300	431	93.52%
Comparative Size	40-49%	0	431	57.09%
	30-39%	0	431	57.09%
	20-29%	0	431	57.09%
	10-19%	0	431	57.09%
	1-09%	0	431	57.09%
Unique		718	1,149	144.29%
Total	0-100%	1,149	1,149	196.64%

The term *peer* in table 15.1 refers to the group LMU is comparing itself to; the term *evaluator* refers to LMU. The Subcollection Counts notes that in the areas denoted BL1-BL9999, the peer group of 40 libraries holds 2,821 titles with a total 18,774 copies. There are 922 unique titles (that is, only one library has a copy); of those, 672 are at LMU. In addition, LMU has 647 titles that other libraries in the peer group hold. For the Subcollections Proportions for B1-B68, LMU has 80 titles; the average peer library holds 54. LMU's collection is 48.15 percent larger than the average size for these class numbers. The Subcollection Gap Table shows that LMU does not own 131 books that 80 to 89 percent of the peer libraries (in this case, three libraries) hold. If LMU were to buy the 131 titles, its comparative rank would increase to 73 percent of that of the peer group. The Bibliographic Lists portion of the CD-ROM program allowed LMU to generate a list of the 131 books it did not own.

Collection Standards

There are published standards for almost every type of library. The standards cover all aspects of a library, so there is at least one section that addresses collections. Additionally, some standards have one section about print collections and another dealing with other formats. The standards vary over time, and sometimes shift from a quantitative to qualitative approach and back again. These shifts make long-term comparisons problematic.

Quantitative standards have proven useful, in some instances, for libraries that do not achieve the standard or that have a low "score" or "grade." For example, the *Standards for College Libraries* has a grading method for collection size based on the percentage held of the ideal size. The ideal size is a calculation using so many books per category such as undergraduate majors and minors, with another number for each master's degree program. Meeting or exceeding the ideal is an "A" grade, anything less is a lower grade. For some funding authorities, such standards are important; for others, such standards are of little or no interest unless failure to achieve the standard has clear consequences for the institution.

The standard lists developed for opening-day collections operated on the premise that a certain critical mass of material (collection size) was necessary for any library of a given type, regardless of the size of the service population. When J. W. Pirie first compiled *Books for Junior Colleges,* he stated that a junior college library needed 20,000 volumes to support a liberal arts curriculum.[10] *Books for College Libraries* assumes that a four-year college must have a minimum of 150,000 volumes, 20 percent of which should be bound periodical volumes and the other 80 percent monographic titles.[11] Similar assumptions appear in the ALA Public Library Association's shorter list, *Books for Public Libraries: Nonfiction for Small Collections.*[12]

Use-Centered Methods

Circulation Studies

Studying collection use patterns as a means of evaluating collections is increasingly popular. Two basic assumptions underlie user/use studies: (1) the adequacy of the book collection is directly related to its use by students and faculty, and (2) circulation records provide a reasonably representative picture of collection use. Such pragmatic evaluations of collections or services are distasteful to some professionals. As L. Carnovsky stated:

> In general surveys of college and university libraries, where surveyors have devoted attention to use, they have focused on rules and regulations, physical convenience of facilities, and stimulation of reading through publicity, browsing rooms, open stacks and similar matters. They have not been concerned with circulation statistics, and in fact, the statistics for college and university libraries issued by the Library Services Branch do not include them at all. This is tacit recognition of the fact that circulation is largely a function of curriculum and teaching methods, and perhaps also of the realization that the sheer number of books a library circulates is no measure at all of its true contribution to the educational process. In spite of the fact that Wilson and Tauber advocated the maintenance of circulation records, Wilson and Swank, in their survey of Stanford University reported: "Because statistics of use are kept for only a few of the University libraries and those that are kept are not consolidated and consistently reported, it is impossible for the surveyors to present any meaningful discussion or evaluation of this significant aspect of the library program."[13]

Use data, normally viewed in terms of circulation figures, are objective, and the legitimate differences in the objectives of the institution that the library serves do not affect the data. They also serve as a useful check on one or more of the other evaluation methods. They are helpful in deselection projects. An important factor is to have adequate amounts of data on which to base a judgment. With today's computer-based circulation systems, use data becomes relatively easy and inexpensive to gather. An example of an early study that made extensive use of circulation data is the aforementioned *Landscape of Literatures: Use of Subject Collections in a University Library*, by Paul Metz.[14]

Certainly, there are problems in interpreting circulation data in terms of the value of a collection. Circulation data cannot reflect use generated within the library, such as reference collections and noncirculating journals. Even for circulating items, there is no way of knowing how the material was used; perhaps the volume was used to prop open a window or press flowers. Also, the value derived by a customer from a circulated item is unknown, making it difficult to accurately assess the collection's worth. Use factors are only a small part of the overall mission of research and archival libraries.

In the public library setting, circulation and use data can be useful in determining the need for multiple copies as well as subject areas of high use in which the library has limited holdings. Automated circulation systems allow one to gather such data quickly with little staff effort. The staff time goes to assessing the data and deciding what to do about the results.

Customer Perceptions

Surveys of users' opinions about collection adequacy, in terms of quantity, quality, or both, have been staples in evaluation programs for many years. On the positive side, users know, or think they know, if the material in the collection has met their needs. On the negative side, past experiences will affect their assessment. A person who has used material from only one collection may be more positive about the collection than it warrants because of lack of experience with any other collection. Likewise, a person who has experience with a large research collection may be overly critical of anything less. Knowing something about the individuals' past library experiences can help evaluators assess the responses more accurately. One must also be careful in interpreting self-selected samples; those volunteering information are a small but vocal segment of the user population and may unduly influence the evaluation.

If there is a high percentage of users with a negative attitude toward the collection, there may or may not be a problem with the collection. Certainly, if the results are from a proper random sample, there is a good chance it is a collection problem. However, other factors may be more significant; for example, poor marketing or ineffectual bibliographic instruction may be the more pressing issue. When developing a survey one should ask one or two questions that will help "sort out" such variables. Only sampling actual users may leave out a large number of people in the service population and fail to discover basics: Why are nonusers nonusers? Is it because of collection inadequacies?

Use of Other Libraries (ILL Statistics)

One factor that is sometimes overlooked in the assessment process is the service population's use of other libraries. Heavy use of other libraries may or may not signal a collection issue for the users. There are at least three aspects to use of "other resources"—physical access to other facilities, traditional ILL, and document delivery services. People often use several libraries to meet their various information requirements: educational libraries for academic needs, special libraries for work-related information, and public libraries for recreational materials. They may also use such libraries for a single purpose, because no one type to which they have access can or does supply all the desired data. It is this latter group that has implications for collection development officers. Just knowing that some segment of the service population is using two or more libraries is not enough. The issue is why they are doing so. Again, the reasons may be something other than collection adequacy—closer proximity to where they live or work, different or more convenient service hours, more or better parking, and so forth. However, it is also possible that the problem *is* the collection, and learning from the users their reasons for securing information from other libraries will be of assistance in thinking about possible adjustments in collecting activities.

Collection development officers should periodically review ILL data for journal articles, if for no other reason than copyright compliance. There should be a careful consideration of whether it is better to add a paper subscription or depend upon a commercial service that pays a royalty fee for each item delivered. An overall review of ILL data may reveal areas of the collection that are too weak to meet all the demands or that may need greater depth of coverage.

Likewise, document delivery data may also provide useful clues for collection development officers, assuming one employs a broad definition that includes electronic full-text materials mounted on remote databases. The library needs to review/assess the use of the databases. Who is using what and for what purpose? The key issue is long-term versus short-term needs and how the archiving of the electronic information is or is not handled by the vendor(s).

As we noted earlier in chapter 7 on e-serials, aggregators add and drop titles with little or no notice. (It is important to note that the dropping is usually at the request of the producer of the title, not the aggregator.) Who is responsible for the loss is not an issue for end users; only the fact that it is no longer available matters. Unfortunately, most libraries have had to face one or more cuts in the acquisitions budget and there is little reason to believe that such cuts are a thing of the past. Electronic resources will eventually be considered suitable for possible reductions, if they are not yet in that category. Vendors try to assure librarians that there will be adequate archiving. At present it is too early to say whether such assurances are warranted, but past experience suggests some valid room for doubt. (One electronic resource vendor, in a nationwide video conference, basically stated that a library would have access to backfiles for which that library had had a current subscription *at a reasonable per-item rate*. Certainly there are storage costs, and upgrade/migration costs to consider as systems change, as well as a record-keeping system for tracking what library subscribed to what title for what years.) When we drop a paper-based subscription, we have the volumes we paid for and do not pay for later use of those volumes. Thus, it may be more cost-effective, for high-use titles, either to acquire a microform backfile or to keep or even start a paper-based subscription. It is not likely that libraries and vendors will agree on what is "a reasonable per-item price."

Citation Studies

We touched on citation studies in chapter 4 (selection practice) in particular for journal selection purposes. One can use this method to assess the collections of academic and STM libraries by using a sample of research publications appropriate to the library's overall purpose(s). Compiling a sample of appropriate studies often takes time as well as the cooperation of some scholars to assist in the identification process. One then checks the works cited against the library's catalog to determine how many of the items are in the collection. Essentially this is a variation on the checklist method, but for research-level materials. The authors employ this method or suggest it to an academic department considering a new graduate degree program. Although a dissertation or thesis is normally original in character, it is expected to draw on some body of important literature in the broader field of interest. If the collection lacks a substantial percentage of a sample of "typical research" in the area of interest, the collection will be inadequate in its support of a program.

Citation studies are relatively easy to conduct and over time provide good measures of changes in strength of the collections. We outlined the downside of this method in chapter 4. A relatively recent article by Margaret Sylvia[15] provided a good example of how one may use citation analysis for collection development purposes.

One other evaluation technique is worth mentioning, although it is not primarily a collection development tool. Some years ago T. Saracevic and others reported on a study of the causes of customer frustration in academic libraries.[16] Since that time, many researchers have used variations of the original methodology in a variety of institutional settings. Whatever form the project takes, it requires substantial staff effort as well as customer cooperation. This method requires a staff member or researcher to look over the customer's shoulder as she or he searches for material. The focus is on material availability and reasons for its not being available.

One studies two types of searches with this method: a search for a specific item (called a *known search*) and a search for material on a topic (a *subject search*). Within each search there are six decision points, or errors:

- Bibliographic error. (Customer has incorrect citation; the correct citation is verifiable in some source and the item is correctly listed in the catalog.)

- Acquisition error. (Customer has correct citation and library does not own the title.)

- Catalog use error. (Customer has correct citation but fails to locate the call number that is in the catalog or fails to record the number properly.)

- Circulation error. (The desired item is identified but it is in circulation or being held for someone else.)

- Library malfunction error. (Library operations or policies block access to the desired item; such errors include items that are lost or missing and no replacements are on order, or the items are misshelved, at the bindery, or waiting to be reshelved.)

- Retrieval error. (Customer has correct call number or location but cannot find the properly shelved item.)

For the subject search, instead of acquisition and bibliographic errors, there are:

- Matched query error. (This occurs at the start of the search when the customer fails to find a match between search topic and library subject headings, or matches the topic to Library of Congress subject headings but the library has no listings under that heading.)

- Appropriate title error. (This occurs at the end of the search when the customer does not select any of the items listed under the matched subject heading or does not borrow any items after examining them.)

Clearly, this technique goes well beyond collection assessment, but it has obvious collection development implications in terms of specific titles needed, subject area weakness, and the issue of how many copies to have of a title.

Electronic Resources

Although we are only beginning to develop electronic information collections, it is not too soon to begin to think about evaluating those collections. It seems likely that over time we will develop as many, if not more, methods for evaluating e-collections as we have for print-based collections. In fact, many of the "print-based" methods apply just as much to electronic collections— usage data, end-users' assessments, and citation studies, for example.

At present, the work of Charles McClure and his colleagues provides the most comprehensive approach for evaluating e-resources.[17] They suggest a matrix approach that incorporates many of the elements one uses in the electronic selection process: technical infrastructure, information content, support issues, and management issues. To that they add that one should assess those elements in terms of their extensiveness, efficiency, effectiveness, service quality, impact, usefulness, and adoption. (One should read their publications, as we can only very briefly outline their major ideas here.) Efficiency and effectiveness elements are what they sound like. *Extensiveness* is how much of the electronic service users access; this can be a major factor with aggregator packages. *Service quality* is how well the activity is accomplished; McClure et al. suggest that one measure would the percentage of users who find what they need. *Impact* is a measure of what, if any, difference the service makes to other activities. *Usefulness* is a measure of how appropriate the service is for a class of users or an individual. *Adoption* is a measure of how much, if at all, users incorporate the service into individual or organizational activities.

As we noted in chapter 8, many electronic products provide, as part of the package or as an optional addition, report software that allows one to easily monitor who is using what when. One can and should load management report software onto the servers that provide access to electronic resources. Management reports will provide some of the data needed to evaluate electronic resources and the "value" of different products and services to local as well as remote users.

Summary

There is much research to do before collection evaluation becomes an objective science. Everyone agrees that collection evaluation is a difficult task, and the results are highly subjective. Thus, the evaluator must be willing to live with what are, at best, tentative results.

Because no one evaluation method is adequate by itself, a combined approach is most effective. Most evaluation projects employ several methods, to take advantage of the strengths of each technique. Karen Kruger prepared a guide for the Illinois State Library to aid in cooperative collection development activities; it also provides an effective evaluation technique.[18] D. V. Loertscher and M. L. Ho's *PSES: Computerized Collection Development for School Library Media Centers* offers a multiple approach for examining school media center collections.[19] A comprehensive plan is outlined in Blaine Hall's *Collection Assessment Manual*.[20]

When we serve as consultants on collection evaluation projects, we employ the following steps after determining the library's goals and objectives:

1. Develop an individual set of criteria for quality and value.

2. Draw a random sample from the collection and examine the use of the items (shelflist sample).

3. Collect data about titles wanted but not available (ILL requests).

4. Keep a record of titles picked up from tables and in stack areas (in-house use).

5. Keep a detailed record of interlibrary loan activities.

6. Find out how much obsolete material is in the collection (for example, science works more than 15 years old and not considered classics).

7. If checklists have some relevance to the library, check them; but also do some research concerning the usefulness of these checklists.

8. Relate findings to the library's goals and objectives.

Collection evaluation is time-consuming, but only after completing the task does the staff know the collection's strengths and weaknesses. With this knowledge, the collection development staff can formulate a plan to build on the strengths and correct the weaknesses. This assumes that the assessment of strengths and weaknesses took place in the context of the library's goals, objectives, and community needs. After the first effort, if the process is ongoing, the work will be less time-consuming, and with each assessment the judgments will come closer to accurately assessing the collection's true value.

Notes

1.   Sheila Intner and Elizabeth Futas, "Evaluating Public Library Collections," *American Libraries* 25 (May 1994): 410–13.

2.   Paul Metz, *Landscape of Literatures: Use of Subject Collections in a University Library* (Chicago: American Library Association, 1983).

3.   Robert B. Downs, "Techniques of the Library Resources Survey," *Special Libraries* 23 (April 1941): 113–15.

4.   J. H. Russell, "The Library Self-Survey," *College & Research Libraries* 17 (March 1956): 127–31.

5.   George Bonn, "Evaluation of the Collection," *Library Trends* 22 (January 1974): 265–304.

6.   B. Lockett, ed., *Guide to the Evaluation of Library Collections* (Chicago: American Library Association, 1989).

7.   Association of College & Research Libraries, College Library Standards Committee, "Standards for College Libraries," *College & Research Libraries News* 47 (March 1986): 189.

8.   Eli Oboler, "Accuracy of Federal Academic Library Statistics," *College & Research Libraries* 25 (September 1964): 494.

9.   Marcia Findley, "Using the OCLC/AMIGOS Collection Analysis Compact Disk to Evaluate Art and Art History Collections," *Technical Services Quarterly* 10, no. 3 (1993): 1–15.

10.   J. W. Pirie, comp., *Books for Junior Colleges* (Chicago: American Library Association, 1969).

11.   *Books for College Libraries,* 4th ed. (Chicago: American Library Association, 1998).

12.   C. Koehn, ed., *Books for Public Libraries: Nonfiction for Small Collections,* 3d ed. (Chicago: American Library Association, 1981).

13.   L. Carnovsky, "Survey of the Use of Library Resources and Facilities," in *Library Surveys*, edited by M. F. Tauber and I. R. Stephens (New York: Columbia University Press, 1967), 68.

14.   Metz, *Landscape of Literatures.*

15.   Margaret J. Sylvia, "Citation Analysis as an Unobtrusive Method for Journal Collection Evaluation Using Psychology Student Research Bibliographies," *Collection Building* 17, no. 1 (1998): 20–28.

16.   T. Saracevic et al., "Causes and Dynamics of User Frustration in an Academic Library," *College & Research Libraries* 38 (January 1977): 7–18.

17.   John Carlo Bertot and Charles McClure, "Measuring Electronic Services in Public Libraries," *Public Libraries* 37 (May/June 1998): 176–80; Charles McClure, John Carlo Bertot, and Douglas Zweizig, *Public Libraries and the Internet: Study Results, Policy Issues, and Recommendations* (Washington, D.C.: National Commission on Libraries and Information Science, 1994); John Carlo Bertot, Charles McClure, and Douglas Zweizig, *The 1996 National Survey of Public Libraries and the Internet* (Washington, D.C.: National Commission on Libraries and Information Science, 1996); John Carlo Bertot, Charles McClure, and Patricia D. Fletcher, *The 1997 National Survey of Public Libraries and the Internet* (Washington, D.C.: National Commission on Libraries and Information Science, 1997).

18.   Karen Kruger, *Coordinated Cooperative Collection Development for Illinois Libraries* (Springfield, Ill.: Illinois State Library, 1982).

19.   D. V. Loertscher and M. L. Ho, *PSES: Computerized Collection Development for School Library Media Centers* (Castle Rock, Colo.: Hi Willow Publishing, 1986).

20.   Blaine Hall, *Collection Assessment Manual for College and University Libraries* (Phoenix, Ariz.: Oryx Press, 1985).

Further Reading

General

Aguilar, W. "Application of Relative Use and Interlibrary Demand in Collection Development." *Collection Management* 8 (Spring 1986): 15–24.

Baughman, J. C., and M. E. Kieltyka. " Farewell to Alexandria: Not Yet!" *Library Journal* 124 (March 15, 1999): 48–49.

Born, K. "Using Your Serials Vendor in the Collection Assessment and Evaluation Process." In *Serials Collection Development*. Birmingham, Ala.: Vantage Point/EBSCO, 1995.

Bremer, T. A. "Assessing Collection Use by Surveying Users at Randomly Selected Times." *Collection Management* 13, no. 3 (1990): 57–67.

Britten, W. A. "A Use Statistic for Collection Management." *Library Acquisitions: Practice and Theory* 14, no. 2 (1990): 183–89.

Dannelly, G. N. "National Shelflist Count: A Tool for Collection Management." *Library Acquisitions: Practice and Theory* 13, no. 3 (1989): 241–50.

Evans, G. E. "Review of Criteria Used to Measure Library Effectiveness." In *Reader in Library Management.* Edited by R. Shimmer. London: Clive Bingley, 1976.

Francq, C. "Bottoming out the Bottomless Pit with the Journal Usage/Cost Relational Index." *Technical Services Quarterly* 11, no. 4 (1994): 13–26.

Hacken, R. D. "Statistical Assumption-Making in Library Collection Assessment: Peccadilloes and Pitfalls." *Collection Management* 7 (Summer 1985): 17–32.

Holleman, C. "Study of the Strengths, Overlap, and National Collection Patterns: The Uses of the OCLC/AMIGOS Collection Analysis CD and Alternatives to It." *Collection Management* 22, nos. 1/2 (1997): 57–69.

Lancaster, F. W., and S. L. Baker. *The Measurement and Evaluation of Library Services.* Arlington, Va.: Information Resources Press, 1991.

Lee, S. H. *Collection Assessment and Acquisitions Budgets.* New York: Haworth Press, 1992.

Lockett, B., ed. *Guide to the Evaluation of Library Collections.* Chicago: American Library Association, 1989.

Miller, A. H. "Do the Books We Buy Get Used?" *Collection Management* 12, nos. 1/2 (1990): 15–20.

Nisonger, T. E. "Collection Assessment in the Library Without Walls." *Library Acquisitions* 21 (Winter 1997): 478–81.

O'Connell, J. B. "Collection Evaluation in a Developing Country." *Libri* 34 (March 1984): 44–64.

Osburn, C. B. "Collection Evaluation and Acquisitions Budgets: A Kaleidoscope in the Making." In *Collection Assessment and Acquisitions Budgets.* Edited by S. H. Lee, 3–11. New York: Haworth Press, 1992.

Paskoff, B. M., and A. H. Perrault. "A Tool for Comparative Collection Analysis." *Library Resources &Technical Services* 34 (April 1990): 199–215.

Rao, S. N. "Meeting Modern Demands of Collection Evaluation." *Collection Building* 13, no. 1 (1992): 33–36.

Rossi, P. H., and H. E. Freeman. *Evaluation: A Systematic Approach.* Beverly Hills, Calif.: Sage Publications, 1985.

Sandler, M. S. "Quantitative Approaches to Qualitative Collection Assessment." *Collection Building* 8, no. 4 (1987): 12–17.

Vellucci, S. L. "OCLC/AMIGOS Collection Analysis CD: Broadening the Scope of Use." *OCLC Systems and Services* 9, no. 2 (1993): 49–53.

Weber, J., and Ridley, D. "Assessment and Decision Making: Two User-Oriented Studies: Borrowing/Browsing Patterns in Academic Libraries." *Library Review* 46, nos. 3/4 (1997): 202–9.

Wood, R. J. "Building a Better Library Collection." *Library Software Review* 15 (1996): 22–24.

Academic

Barstow, S. "Quickly Selecting Serials for Cancellation." *Technical Services Quarterly* 10, no. 4 (1993): 29–40.

Gaylor, R. H. "Collection Analysis at a Junior College Library." *OCLC Systems and Services* 10, no. 1 (1994): 9–12.

Harloe, B. "Achieving Client-Centered Collection Development." *College & Research Libraries* 50 (May 1989): 344–53.

Hyman, F. B. "Collection Evaluation in the Research Library." *Collection Building* 9, nos. 3/4 (1989): 33–37.

Lucas, T. A. "Verifying the Conspectus: Problems and Progress." *College & Research Libraries News* 46 (March 1990): 199–201.

Mosher, P. H. "Collection Evaluation in Research Libraries." *Library Resources & Technical Services* 23 (Winter 1979): 16–32.

Nisonger, T. E. *Collection Evaluation in Academic Libraries: A Literature Guide and Annotated Bibliography.* Englewood, Colo.: Libraries Unlimited, 1992.

Porter, M. A., and F. W. Lancaster. "Evaluation of a Scholarly Collection in a Specific Subject Area by Bibliographic Checking." *Libri* 38, no. 2 (1988): 131–37.

Siverson, S. E. "Fine-Tuning the Dull Roar of Conspectors." In *Collection Assessment.* Edited by R. J. Wood and K. Strauch, 45–64. New York: Haworth Press, 1992.

Stebelman, S. "Using Choice as a Collection Assessment Tool." *Collection Building* 15, no. 2 (1996): 4–11.

Sylvia, M., and Lesher, M. "What Journals Do Psychology Graduate Students Need?" *College & Research Libraries* 56 (May 1995): 313–18.

Walch, D. B. "1986 College Library Standards: Applications and Utilization." *College & Research Libraries* 54 (May 1993): 217–26.

Public

Baker, S. L. "Quality and Demand: The Basis for Fiction Collection Assessment." *Collection Building* 13, nos. 2/3 (1994): 65–68.

Davis, B. "How the WLN Conspectus Works for Small Libraries." *Acquisitions Librarian*, no. 20 (1998): 53–72.

D'Elia, G., and E. Rodger."Customer Satisfaction with Public Libraries: Surveys in Five Urban Library Systems with 142 Libraries." *Public Libraries* 35 (September/October 1996): 292–97.

Koehn, C., ed. *Books for Public Libraries*. 3d ed. Chicago: American Library Association, 1981.

Kruger, K. *Coordinated Cooperative Collection Development for Illinois Libraries.* Springfield, Ill.: Illinois State Library, 1982.

Moore, C. M. "Taking the Measure: Applying Reference Outputs to Collection Development." *Public Libraries* 25 (Fall 1986): 108–11.

Senkevitch, J. J., and J. H. Sweetland. "Evaluating Public Library Adult Fiction: Can We Define a Core Collection?" *RQ* 36 (Fall 1996): 103–17.

Smith, M., and G. Rowland. "To Boldly Go; Searching for Output Measures for Electronic Services." *Public Libraries* 36 (May/June 1997): 168–72.

Stielow, F. J., and H. R. Tibbo. "Collection Analysis in Modern Librarianship: A Stratified, Multidimensional Model." *Collection Management* 11, nos. 3/4 (1989): 73–91.

Weber, M. "Effects of Fiction Assessment on a Rural Public Library." *Collection Building* 13, nos. 2/3 (1994): 83–86.

Zweizig, D. "So Go Figure It: Measuring Library Effectiveness." *Public Libraries* 26 (Spring 1987): 21–24.

Zweizig, D., and B. Dervin. "Public Library Use, Users, Uses." In *Advances in Librarianship*. Edited by M. J. Voigt and M. H. Harris, 231–55. New York: Academic Press, 1977.

School

Aaron, S. L. "Current Research." *School Library Media Quarterly* 10 (Winter 1982): 185–89.

Bell, G. "System-Wide Collection Assessment Survey (Birmingham Public School System)." In *School Library Media Annual 10,* 135–47. Englewood, Colo.: Libraries Unlimited, 1992.

Bertland, L. H. "Collection Analysis as a Tool for Collection Development." *School Library Media Quarterly* 19 (Winter 1991): 90–97.

Bruggeman, L. " 'Zap! Whoosh! Kerplow!' Build High-Quality Graphic Novel Collections with Impact." *School Library Journal* 43 (January 1997): 22–27.

Doll, C. A. "Quality and Elementary School Library Media Collections." *School Library Media Quarterly* 25 (Winter 1997): 95–102.

Garland, K. "Circulation Sampling as a Technique for Library Media Program Management." *School Library Media Quarterly* 20 (Winter 1992): 73–78.

Kachel, D. E. *Collection Assessment and Management for School Libraries: Preparing for Cooperative Collection Development.* Westport, Conn.: Greenwood Press, 1997.

Latrobe, K. H. "Evaluating Library Media Programs in Terms of 'Information Power,' " *School Library Media Quarterly* 21 (Fall 1992): 37–45.

Loertscher, D. V., and M. L. Ho. *PSES: Computerized Collection Development for School Library Media Centers.* Castle Rock, Colo.: Hi Willow Publishing, 1986.

"Performance Measures for School Librarians." In *Advances in Librarianship*. Edited by M. J. Voigt and M. H. Harris, 1–51. New York: Academic Press, 1976.

Roy, L. "Collection Evaluation as Research." *Journal of Youth Services* 5 (Spring 1992): 297–300.

Thomason, N. W. "Evaluating a School Media Center Book Collection." *Catholic Library World* 53 (Spring 1981): 87–88.

Special

Berger, M., and J. Devine. "Serial Evaluation: An Innovative Approach." *Special Li braries* 81 (Summer 1990): 183–88.

Carlson, B. A. "Collection Development Assessment for Biomedical Serials Collections." *Serials Librarian* 23, nos. 3/4 (1993): 289–92.

Carpenter, K. H. "Evaluating Library Resources for Accreditation." *Bulletin of the Medical Library Association* 80 (April 1992): 131–39.

Gottlieb, J., ed. *Collection Assessment in Music Libraries.* New York: Music Library Association, 1994.

"Health Libraries: Checklist Will Boost Quality." *Library Association Record* 100 (December 1998): 620.

Kehoe, K., and E. B. Stein. "Collection Assessment of Biotechnology Literature." *Science and Technology Libraries* 9 (Spring 1989): 47–55.

McClure, C. R., and B. Reifsnyder. "Performance Measures for Corporate Information Centers." *Special Libraries* 75 (July 1984): 193–204.

O'Connor, D. O., and E. R. Dyer. "Evaluation of Corporate Reference Collections." *Reference Librarian* 29 (1990): 21–31.

Rashid, H. F. "Book Availability as a Performance Measure of a Library: An Analysis of the Effectiveness of a Health Science Library." *Journal of the American Society for Information Science* 41, no. 7 (1990): 501–7.

Rhine, L. "Development of a Journal Evaluation Database Using *Microsoft Access*." *Serials Review* 22, no. 4 (1996): 27–36.

Richards, D. T. *Collection Development and Assessment in Health Sciences Libraries.* Lanham, Md.: Medical Library Association, 1997.

Snow, M. "Theatre Arts Collection Assessment." *Collection Management* 12, nos. 3/4 (1990): 69–81.

Urquhart, C. "Comparing and Using Assessment of the Value of Information to Clinical Decision-Making." *Bulletin of the Medical Library Association* 84 (October 1996): 482–89.

Zachert, M. J. K. "Qualitative Evaluation of Law School Library Services." *Law Library Journal* 81 (Spring 1989): 269–76.

16

Cooperative Collection Development and Resource Sharing

Library literature is full of discussions about cooperative collection development. Based on the volume of material, a newcomer to the field might think that libraries have been successfully engaged in such activities for a long time. However, just the opposite is the case. Libraries have tried mounting everything from local to national programs, with modest success[1] at best; most of the success has come at the local and regional levels. What has changed in the last few years is a rapid growth of consortia that purchase electronic resources. Some people believe that electronic materials will change the picture of cooperative collection development from being modestly successful to very successful. We think that may be the case, if one changes the label to "cooperative purchasing." We see little on the horizon leading us to believe that paper-based cooperative collection development will change for the better. Rather, there will be a different form of resource sharing, which we will discuss later in this chapter.

Shortly after the beginning of World War II, U.S. research libraries began to learn that their collections were not as strong as they had believed. The weakness lay in publications from other countries and in all formats, not just books. After the war there was an effort, the Farmington Plan, to get research libraries across the United States to divide up the collecting responsibility for *all* of the knowledge from most countries. The plan was ambitious, to say the least, and in the end it failed for a variety of reasons, not just because of its scale. However, that elusive goal of comprehensiveness remains, to many, a desirable mission for research libraries. Smaller-scale efforts to reduce duplication and expand breadth of coverage grew out of early efforts such as Farmington. Regional and local groups with various types of resource-sharing arrangements exist, but there has been little progress in establishing a coordinated national program that will assure that one copy of almost any research item will be available somewhere in the United States. Technology helps us know who has what, and other tools, such as the RLG conspectus, help librarians know who thinks they have strong collections in various subject fields. However, many barriers exist when it comes to developing a workable plan. As Edward Shreeves stated, "There is, however, widespread belief that cooperation in building collections can significantly improve the quality of library service by broadening and deepening the range of materials collectively available."[2]

Webster's Third New International Dictionary defines *cooperative* in part as "given to or marked by working together or by joint effort toward a common end"; it defines *coordinate* as "to bring into a common action, movement, or condition; regulate and combine in harmonious action."[3] Cooperative resource-sharing programs are likely to grow, but the future of coordinated collection development appears dim. Some years ago, John Berry wrote an editorial in *Library Journal* about how the then-current tight funding situation was causing cooperative ventures to cease. Unfortunately, the situation has changed little since Berry wrote:

> The pressure is reported by public, academic, and school librarians from across the United States. One state's fine multitype systems are near collapse. Cooperative county systems in another have been reduced to bickering disarray from years of no-growth funding. Consortia members are scrapping over slices of a shrinking pie. New, harsh limitations on interlibrary loan crop up. Stiff nonresident fees and interlibrary charges proliferate. Old battles between small and large libraries in shared jurisdictions flare anew. State agency and cooperative system operating budgets are openly attacked by constituent librarians. ... Librarians, torn between professional commitment to library cooperation and local pressure to provide service with deeply diminished resources, have to make the choice to cut service to outsiders.[4]

Today, what seems to be the most likely outcome of e-resources and cooperative efforts is best described as "resource sharing." ALA's *Glossary* defines *resource sharing* as "activities engaged in jointly by a group of libraries for the purposes of improving services and/or cutting costs. Resource sharing may be established by informal or formal agreement or by contract and may operate locally, nationally, or internationally. The resources shared may be collections, bibliographic data, personnel, planning activities, etc."[5] That definition is wide-ranging enough to encompass almost any activity.

Essentially, we are looking at three concepts in this chapter:

1. *Cooperative collection development,* a mechanism whereby two or more libraries agree that each one will have certain areas of "primary collecting responsibility" and that they will exchange such materials with one another free of charge (the Farmington/Scandia models).

2. *Coordinated acquisitions,* whereby two or more libraries agree to buy certain materials, and/or share the associated cost(s), and one or more of the members houses the material (LACAP/CRL model).

3. *Joint acquisitions,* whereby the members place a joint order for a product or service and each member receives the product/service.

All three can, and generally do, lead to resource sharing among the members.

There is another element, which involves cooperative networks that link OPACs and has some form of document delivery system in place to speed up the traditional ILL borrowing process. Even if there is no formal agreement among the member libraries regarding collection development activities, collection development officers frequently check the holdings of the member libraries when considering the possible purchase of an item they think will be low use in their library. If another member has the item, they often do not purchase the item, depending on the document delivery system to supply the item when the need arises.

The Nature of Cooperative Systems

In library cooperation, a primary reason efforts fail is that we do not really understand what we are trying to accomplish. Figure 16.1 presents a general overview of the possible combinations of cooperative collection development.

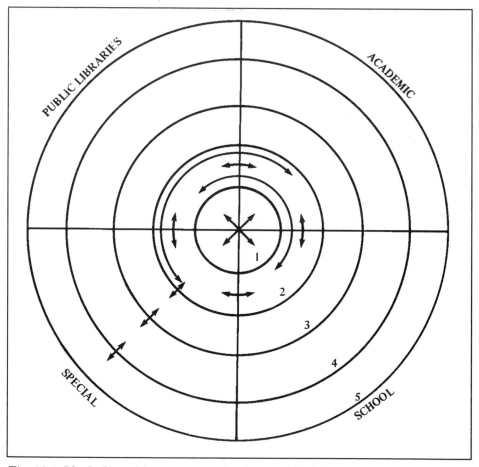

Fig. 16.1. Ideal of interlibrary cooperation (networking). Adapted from Mary Dugan, "Library Network Analysis and Planning," *Journal of Library Automation* 2, no. 9 (1969): 157–75. Reprinted with permission from the American Library Association.

This figure represents the hope we all have of reaching the librarian's utopia of total cooperation among libraries and access to all of the world's information resources. (See discussion of UNESCO's Universal Availability of Publications [UAP] project on page 482.) This ideal is a long way off, even at the local level. Many classes of users still get different levels of service in various libraries in the same community. Even personality differences among chief librarians can create minor but real barriers to effective cooperation at any level. As one moves farther afield, it is harder to work out major cooperative programs. No longer do only library and community needs decide the issue of whether to cooperate. Legal, political, and economic issues tend to dominate the decision-making process.

Models of Cooperative Activity

Michael Sinclair, in his article "A Typology of Library Cooperatives," proposed four theoretical models of cooperative activity (see fig. 16.2, p. 458).[6] Although the concepts are Sinclair's, the following interpretation is ours. (One should read Sinclair's article in its entirety to gain a full understanding of his model.)

Type A is a bilateral *exchange model,* in which two participating libraries exchange materials. In practice, libraries calculate the exchange rate according to some agreed-upon value (for example, one for one, two for one); frequently, there is an annual review of the actual results as part of the formal exchange agreement. All of Loyola Marymount University's reciprocal borrowing agreements contain the annual review clause. A number of existing regional resource-sharing plans employ this model; OHIOLink and LINK+ (a California program) are two examples, as is the traditional interlibrary loan program.

Type B, a multilateral development of Type A, is the *pooling model.* In this model, more than two libraries contribute to and draw from a common pool of materials. Many of the early cooperative library systems were of this type; in a sense, OCLC started as a pool.

In Type C, the *dual-service model,* two or more participating libraries take advantage of the facilities of one of the participants to produce a common output—for instance, a shared online public access catalog (OPAC). The term *dual service* distinguishes this model from the next and emphasizes the fact that *all* participants, including the facilitator, contribute to the common output. Many of the early library systems evolved into this type; frequently, they refer to the facilitator as the *flagship library.* An example of this type of model is the Research Library Information Network (RLIN).

In type D, the *service center model,* a number of libraries employ the services of a facilitating organization to input and process materials for the individual libraries, rather than for common output. Today's OCLC/WLN is this type. These four types are adequate to cover all existing systems; however, new systems under consideration may not fit this classification system.

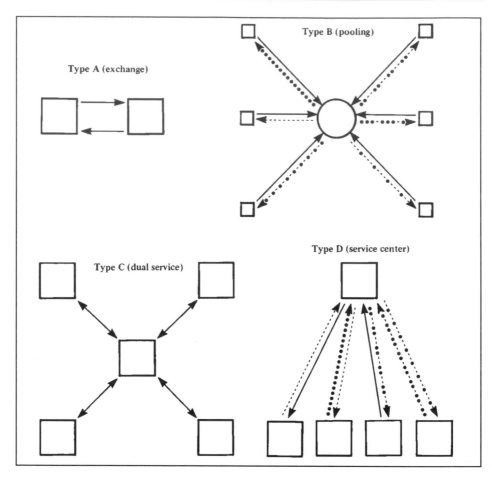

Fig. 16.2. Models of library cooperative activities. A graphic interpretation of M. P. Sinclair, "A Typology of Library Cooperatives," *Special Libraries* 64, no. 4 (April 1973): 181–86.

The Something-for-Nothing Syndrome

Library cooperative systems operate on a series of assumptions that one should examine with considerable care. Perhaps the most important assumption, although the one least often stated, is that all of the participants in the system are or will be equally efficient in their operations involving the cooperative activities. No one assumes that every member will achieve the same benefits or contribute materials that are equally valuable. Rather, the assumption is that each library is somewhat unusual, if not unique (that is, each library has different clientele, collections, and service programs). Why assume that each is equally efficient? It is clear that one cannot legitimately make such an assumption. However, if libraries do not make that assumption, it is difficult to believe that every library will gain something, or at least receive a value equal to its contribution. Each library hopes that it will be the one to receive more than it puts into the system. If a library enters into a cooperative program with the "something for nothing" goal in mind, there is little hope of success. During periods of low funding from outside sources, libraries have a tendency to not cooperate. According to Boyd Rayward, "Networks (cooperatives) are a phenomenon of relative affluence. They cannot be created unless each member at the local level has sufficient resources of time, staff, materials, and basic equipment and supplies to participate."[7]

Librarians seldom consider client costs; the assumption is that cooperation will result only in increased benefits for them. Cooperative planners sometimes factor in the extra work of a staff member filling out one or more forms or answering extra questions for the library, but almost never do so for the customer. Too often, the planners think of these as small, insignificant increases for an individual to absorb. However, though a single increase may be small, in time or in aggregate such increases become significant. Nevertheless, a true cooperative collection development program can provide customers with a much broader range of materials than would be possible for one library working in isolation.

Two examples of these problems will illustrate the point. First, in the United States, the traditional Postal-Service-based interlibrary loan (ILL) system is becoming slower and more costly to operate. The early ILL assumption was that everyone would gain as a result of the free exchange of resources. In the 1970s, larger libraries started charging for ILL services because of the workload it involved. Today, librarians discuss developing agreements to allow free ILL services to one another. (One interesting outcome of more and more libraries having OPACs and being part of regional or statewide networks is that large libraries are actually borrowing more material from smaller institutions than they are lending. This suggests that in the past it was lack of information rather than weak collections that led to the imbalance of ILL activity.) In 1993, the library directors at U.S. Jesuit colleges and universities completed such an agreement after three years of discussion. It was doing well in 1999, and the amount of borrowing was not a burden for any member. That is interesting given that the primary stumbling block to reaching an agreement was concern about the workload.

The second example is from Denmark. Copenhagen's public library established a system for reciprocal borrowing rights with suburban public libraries. A high percentage of the persons living in the suburbs work in the central city. Danes are avid readers, and, like anyone else, prefer to use a convenient rather than an inconvenient service. So, it was not surprising to find them using the most convenient public library for their general library needs. Apparently, for a great many suburbanites, the most convenient location is the Copenhagen public library, with its branches near bus and train stops, and not their local libraries. The cost of providing this free service rose so much that several politicians suggested either dropping the arrangement or charging a nonresident fee. We see similar problems in the United States with reciprocal borrowing agreements and a growing trend to impose substantial fees on nonresident borrowers. The original planning projections assumed that it would be possible to expand service without increasing costs (something for nothing). That assumption has been proven false.

What Can Be Gained
Through Cooperation?

One can identify six general benefits that could arise from any library cooperative effort. First is the potential for improving access—improving in the sense of making available a greater range of materials or better depth in a subject area. We noted earlier that lack of information about holdings was a problem in the past for ILL "resource sharing." That becomes less and less of a problem as libraries automate their catalogs and join various networks. Some networks are statewide (for example, OHIOLink and LINK+ in California) and include both public and private institutions. Loyola Marymount University library joined LINK+ in 1999, with the result that its service population went from having access to a collection of just under 400,000 volumes to having online access to a collection of more than 4 million titles and 6 million copies. Although the LMU collection was the smallest added to the database up to that time, more than 37 percent of the items were unique additions to the system. (The experience has been that each new member contributes between 30 and 40 percent unique titles, according to the firm that handles both OHIOLink and LINK+. This suggests that, to some degree, the claim that each library is "special" is true, at least in terms of its collections.)

A second benefit is that it may be possible to stretch limited resources. One danger in suggesting that cooperation may benefit the public or the professional staff is that the idea of getting something for nothing becomes ingrained. Too often, people view cooperation as a money-saving device. In truth, cooperation does not save money for a library. If two or more libraries combine their efforts, they will not spend less money; an effective cooperative program simply divides the work and shares the results.

Sharing results leads to some benefits, such as greater staff specialization. A person can concentrate on one or two activities rather than on five or six. The resulting specialization should produce better overall performance. Naturally, better performance should lead to better service, and thus greater customer satisfaction. Reducing unnecessary duplication is a second result of sharing work. The reduction may be in work performed or materials purchased, but planners should study just how much duplication they can eliminate before developing a formal cooperative agreement. Vague discussions about reducing duplication, without an in-depth study of the situation, usually lead to high expectations and, all too often, dashed hopes. Nevertheless, reduced duplication of low-use items is a real potential benefit.

By actively advertising its presence and services, a cooperative program may reduce the number of places a customer will need to go for service. However, in most systems, this benefit is more theoretical than real. In the past, a lack of union lists generally negated this potential benefit. Today, networked OPACs provide a real benefit in terms of better directing clients to the correct source of information.

A final benefit, one not frequently discussed, is the improvement in the working relationships among cooperating libraries. This is particularly true in a multitype system. Persons can gain a better perspective about others' problems as a result of working together on mutual problems. Also, learning about the special problems that another type of library encounters helps one to know what its staff can or cannot do. Some systems have found this to be so important that they have set up exchange internships for staff members, both professional and nonprofessional.

As for many other areas of collection development, ALA's Resources and Technical Services Division has created a set of guidelines for cooperative collection development. Paul H. Mosher and Marcia Pankake discussed these guidelines in "A Guide to Coordinated and Cooperative Collection Development."[8] The guidelines provide specific details about benefits, problems, and recommendations that fit easily into this chapter's more general concepts.

In terms of collection development, cooperative programs force libraries to have better knowledge of their collections. In a cooperative program, a library must know both what it has and what the other member libraries have. The RLG conspectus and ARL's National Collection Inventory Project (NCIP), which uses the conspectus model, attempt to identify who has what and in what strength. Although developed for academic library use, the conspectus concept is now in use in all types of libraries. When most libraries complete their conspectus work, they should have the information they need to begin to develop meaningful cooperative collection development programs. If there is to be a division of collection responsibility by subject area, each library must have an in-depth knowledge of its own collection before entering into a meaningful cooperative agreement. And that is but the first step in the process of developing a workable program. Even if there is no final agreement, the process of examining the collection will be of great value. Also, the opportunity to share problems and solutions should improve each participant's capabilities.

Figure 16.3, page 462, is an example of how a cooperative program using the conspectus approach might draw together data from a variety of libraries. How a library uses and interprets the data is another matter, but using some form of standardized subject list to identify collection strength is a first step toward possible cooperative or coordinated collection development.

We now turn our discussion to six broad categories of cooperation issues: (1) institutional; (2) legal, political, and administrative; (3) technological; (4) physical; (5) people; and (6) knowledge-based. This section reviews the changes that have or have not taken place in cooperative collection development in the past 15 years. In 1992, Richard Hacken suggested that perhaps the changes were not as great as one might expect. He described the results of a study of the use of the conspectus among RLG libraries:

> Although small efforts have been made in light of the Conoco Study findings, acquisitions in the vast majority of institutions, both inside and outside RLG, proceed in the traditional manner. When requests for interlibrary loan materials are made, it is overwhelmingly on the basis of "somebody somewhere must have this title," rather than from foreknowledge of pre-planned cooperative or collaborative collecting.[9]

PAGE 2 OF 11

SUBJECT AREA	SPECIFIC SUBJECT	COLLECTION SIZE		BUDGET	CIRCULATE		MACHINE READABLE		CATALOGED		WILL PARTICIPATE		LIBRARY
		BOOKS	OTHER		YES	NO	YES	NO	YES	NO	YES	NO	
Art	Fiber arts	700		n/a	x		x		x		x		JeffCo-Arvada
	Drawing and decorative	1040		Gen. b.	x		x		x		x		Arapahoe Reg.
	Geo. E. Burr		etching etc.	n/a		x		x		x			Denver Public
	Blunt Art Print		1250 prints	n/a				x		x	x		Canon City Pub.
	Fore-edge Pnt	55		Gen. b.		x							Univ. Col. -B
Asian Studies	Model coll.	275	misc.	LSCA		x	x		x		x		JeffCo-Villa
Bibles	Foreign lang.	246		Gen. b.		x							Univ. Col. -B
Blind/Deaf	Large print	430		Gen. b.	x			x	x		x		Canon City Pub.
	Hearing impaired	40		Gen. b.	x		x		x		x		Arapahoe Reg.
	Large print	1000		n/a	x		x		x		x		JeffCo-Arvada
	n/a	700		Endowed	x			x	x			x	Colo. School Deaf & Blind
Botanical	n/a	10760		Sales, etc.	x			x	x		x		Denver Bot. Garden
Business	n/a	4000		Gen. b.	x		x		x		x		JeffCo-Villa
	n/a - tax	456		Gen. b.	x		x		x		x		Weld Co.
	& career info	350		Gen. b.	x		x		x		x		Englewood

Fig. 16.3. Colorado State Library subject strength survey.

Institutional Issues

A traditional goal for libraries, especially academic libraries, has been to be locally self-sufficient. While that remains a goal, librarians know it is impossible to achieve. Bendik Rugaas, the national librarian of Norway, presented a paper titled, "The End of All and Forever"[10] at a meeting of national librarians. In that paper, Rugaas outlined the reasons why no national library can hope to collect and preserve all the information materials created within its country's boundaries. All the participating librarians agreed that it was an impossible task. Evidence that national libraries are coming to act on this knowledge appeared in the front-page article of the September 19, 1994, issue of *Library Hotline*. (The article stated that the British Library is giving up collecting every edition of every book, magazine, and journal printed in Great Britain.)

If the "giants" of the library world are giving up local self-sufficiency, what can other libraries of more modest means hope to accomplish? Librarians know there always will be items a client will someday need but the library does not have the funds to buy. As a result, librarians look to interlibrary loan or some form of document delivery to fill most of the gaps.

Customers have never been fond of ILL, and thus they are a constant source of pressure on the library to be self-sufficient. User pressure is particularly strong when there is a proposal to share collection development responsibilities among libraries. A frequent customer reaction to such a proposal is, "What will happen to my area of interest? I do not want the library to stop buying my materials. I cannot afford to wait months for ILL!" If the library has developed the collection carefully in terms of service community needs, what can be given up? How does one respond to customer inquiries about the impact of the proposed cooperative? How can a library be an effective member without giving up some areas? Almost always, the library's level of funding will be insufficient to buy as much as was purchased before, while it takes on new cooperative obligations. Therefore, some areas will have to be given up or sharply reduced.

Happily, today there are some ways to address some of these concerns. Earlier we cited projects like OHIOLink and LINK+; in both of those cases member libraries have a courier service that picks up and delivers items every day. Based on LMU's experience, we can affirm that the promise of delivery of an item within 24 hours is kept by the courier service—and that can be from a library in San Diego to one in Sacramento. The process begins by a person looking up an item in the local OPAC; if that library does not own the item, the person may, with a keystroke, search the LINK+ database. If a copy of the item is available in a member library, the person can fill out a request form online. The system first verifies that this is a valid user. The holding library then receives the request, locates the item, checks the item out to that user in her or his home system, and places the item in a pouch for the courier to pick up. It is essentially a self-service ILL process with a 24-hour turnaround time. Given the system's performance to date, many of the traditional issues about local self-sufficiency are no longer major factors. Perhaps by the time of the next edition we will have started some true cooperative collection development activities.

Tom Ballard's provocative article, "Public Library Networking: Neat, Plausible, Wrong," raised a number of points regarding the primary service population.[11] He made a strong case, with data supporting his arguments, that for public libraries and others in a multitype library system, the idea of cooperative collection development with an eye toward resource sharing (ILL, generally) is fine—but it does not work. Drawing on data from a number of systems across the United States, he showed that interlibrary lending accounts for very little of the total circulation, almost always representing less than 2 percent of the total. He cited studies indicating that people tend to select from what is available at the time they come in, even if it is a second or third choice, rather than seek the desired material. (This is another clear example of the "law of least effort" we described in chapter 2.) It would be interesting to see what the results would be if such a study were done today, when many more libraries have their holdings more readily available online.

Although Ballard emphasized public libraries and provided examples relating to them, his statements hold some truth for anyone who works in a school media center or an academic library serving undergraduates. Undoubtedly, part of the explanation is that many people are not aware of the possibility of getting needed items somewhere else, so more active marketing by the library may be necessary. A more important factor is that people tend to wait until the last minute to seek out needed information, and so cannot wait even a few days to get the precise information. Perhaps a third factor is that most people do not really need or want the material enough to pay the price for delivery. If it is "immediately" available (LMU is finding that 24-hour availability is acceptable), fine; if not, forget it. All these make a strong case for local self-sufficiency.

In academic institutions, even small ones, there are two primary collecting goals: curriculum and research support. At smaller institutions, though faculty seldom face pressure to engage in research, peers and administrators tend to have greater regard for those faculty who do take on some research activity. Usually, there is the expectation that the library will provide some support for scholarly activities beyond the classroom. Today, for many schools, that support is more moral than substantive. Occasionally, the motivated faculty member will slip through purchase requests for items that are more research than instructional in character. This is especially true when the teaching departments control the bulk of the materials budget. They do this because other means of access—ILL, document delivery, or reciprocal borrowing—are too slow for them.

For ARL libraries, low-use material forms a large percentage of the collection. It also consumes a significant portion of the materials budget. For most other libraries, the vast majority of the collection is devoted to reasonably high-use material, at least compared to research library collections. As the funding gets tighter, the amount of potentially useful, as opposed to known-to-be-useful, material any library can buy becomes smaller and smaller. Tight budgets also mean that there is less money to offer for pooling or sharing collecting categories; low-use items have been the staple of shared collecting projects. Hacken indicated that interest in considering, much less implementing, shared collection building was for items thought to be of potential research interest as opposed to demonstrated interest.[12] Although his comments focused on ARL libraries, the idea of sharing high-demand items is not a common part of any resource-sharing proposal.

Some accrediting agencies (for example, the Western Association of Schools and Colleges [WASC]) include statements in their standards regarding ownership of the instructional collection. The following is from the WASC *Handbook of Accreditation*:

> 6.B.1 Basic collections *held* by the institution are sufficient in quality and quantity to meet *substantially all* of the needs of educational programs on and off campus.
>   and
> 6.B.2 Interlibrary loan or contractual use arrangements may be used to *supplement* basic holdings *but are not* to be used as the main source of learning resources.[13]

Though such statements do not preclude cooperative collection building, they certainly add another layer of complexity to an already complex issue.

Twenty years ago, the pressure was strong among all customers to maintain self-sufficiency. Today, many are willing to let electronic services provide some access, if that access is more convenient than going to the library. In contrast, funding officials pressure libraries to find ways to cooperate and reduce the costs of collection building. Unfortunately, as noted in John Berry's editorial (see page 455), given current economic conditions, what libraries and customers mean by local self-sufficiency is more and more restricted in scope. Libraries are lucky to meet all the local high-demand needs, much less acquire material for low-demand areas. That, in turn, reduces the pool of low-use material that might be fodder for a cooperative program. In such circumstances, it is not surprising to find libraries having a difficult time identifying areas that they can forgo having locally available.

In a pre-agreement stage, two institutions may have overlapping low-use material and overlapping interests in some areas in which neither is currently collecting. A post-agreement study might show how the two institutions could share their collecting activities in such a manner that they not only cover their current low-use areas, but also expand slightly into new areas. That is the theory, which makes it seem simple, logical, and reasonable to engage in such projects; in practice, it is not at all simple.

Other institutional issues are size and status. These are less important in cooperative collection building than in selection. They were more a factor in the past than they are today; however, they do arise. Today, most librarians think they are doing well if the library receives enough funding to maintain last year's buying strength. Librarians seldom need to concern themselves with worries about gaining enough size to surpass another library that they consider comparable but slightly ahead in terms of collection size. Where status, size, and cooperative collection building cross is that not all subject areas grow at the same rate. If a library gives up an area of moderate growth for one that is slow-growing, there may be a decline in the overall collection growth. In addition to the growth rate within a subject area, one must consider the cost of materials. Many science and technology items cost 25 to 50 percent more than social sciences and humanities items, so a library can acquire fewer titles for the same amount of money; this basic fact obviously affects the growth rate. For some institutions, this can be a problem, because for many individuals, bigger is better, which also means higher status. That may then make it difficult, if not impossible, to find an agreeable breakdown of collecting responsibilities. Realistically, today status and size are minor issues for groups attempting to develop an agreement for a cooperative or co-ordinated collection building program.

Institutional history and past and current practices also affect efforts to develop a cooperative venture. Examples of historical and traditional barriers that may arise are: institutional competition, special access rules (who may use the service), funding problems, library operating practices, and inability to satisfy local needs. The last problem has been and always will be there. No matter how much money is available to develop local collections, some imaginative customer or staff member will think of a new collecting area that will use up all available funding. A variation of both Maslow's needs hierarchy and one of Parkinson's laws is that organizations, like people, always have wants slightly in excess of their ability to satisfy those wants. If local need combines with the desire for local self-sufficiency, librarians will never be able to agree to any cooperative effort.

One obvious historical library practice is the library's classification system. Early in any effort toward developing a cooperative collection building program, the planners must face the task of determining who has how much of what. A common way of doing that is to use existing, or to undertake developing, conspectus data (see chapters 3, 14, and 15) for the libraries. Anyone who has done a conspectus project knows the time and effort it takes. The commitment increases when the libraries use different classification systems. The RLG conspectus is built on the LC system, with conversion tables for DDC. Based upon personal experience of doing a conspectus at Tozzer Library at Harvard, which used its own classification system at the time, the senior author knows the problems of converting shelflist data from one classification scheme to another. For many libraries, in today's tight budget and staffing environment, the cost of converting the data is too high.

Another library practice or regulation is who has access to the collection. Many private institutions employ restricted access to help control operating costs. Outsiders, when they are allowed to use the library, are charged a fee. Charging the outside customer was started by the "privates" (that is, privately held institutions). In many cases, the private library must include an expected revenue from outsider use in its budget request; some libraries must make up any shortfall from operating funds. This tends to make the library firm about enforcing fees and reluctant to give up a source of income for an unknown benefit from a cooperative project. Today, larger public libraries are following suit with often substantial use fees. In 1992, the University of California (UC) campus libraries started charging non-UC and nonstate college and university system students a minimum of $100 a year for a borrowing card; the fee goes up to $500 for a card that provides the full range of use privileges (borrowing more than five books at a time and ability to recall or place holds on a desired item). Even without fees, there will be questions about loan periods, who can borrow what, and fines, all of which probably vary with each potential participant.

The fee issue brings up the issue of competition for funding and, secondarily, for customers. Traditional practice was that public institutions received their funding from taxes and government grants. Private institutional fund-raising "turf" was individuals, foundations, government granting agencies, and private business. Today that division no longer exists. Public institutions are very active in raising funds from what were primary sources for the privates. One sees this trend most clearly in higher education; however, it is occurring in all areas. The *Chronicle of Higher Education* from time to time publishes lists of the top fund-raising higher education institutions. Fifteen years ago, it would have been unusual to see a public institution appearing on the list, much less in the first position. Over the past six years, more often than not, large public institutions occupy most of the top 10 positions. As the publics become increasingly dependent on such funding, it becomes difficult for the smaller privates to get a hearing, much less funding. Most cooperatives require some start-up capital, and foundations and government granting agencies are the most likely source of support, if one can get one's foot in the door.

The issue of never being able to completely satisfy local needs with local resources is also an institutional competition and funding problem. Often, at the local level, public, school, and community college libraries compete for the same local tax money. Each type of library may have a certain legal minimum due to it, but beyond the minimum, the situation is very competitive. In some manner, though, the community will establish a maximum total amount that it is willing to devote to library services. If the allocation process does not use a formula or weighting system, the politics of the budgetary process will determine the final allocation; that is, the best library politician will get the largest share. Furthermore, each type of library will count as customers a large number of persons who also use other types of libraries. Though the count of users is correct, the duplication in counting distorts the actual number in the service population. Collections, in fact, reflect the multiple activities and interests of customers. Educational libraries have recreational materials and recreational (public) libraries have educational materials. The competition in trying to meet the needs of the same customer causes a sizable duplication of materials in some cases. In turn, that can result in significant funding problems. Attempts to extract additional monies for cooperative activities from local funding authorities are not likely to be successful unless the funding authorities see the request as a device for stabilizing, if not reducing, total local funding.

Returning to issues related to library practice, incompatibility of procedures is a fact that all cooperatives must address at some point. "We have *always* used *this* procedure, and it works" is a statement heard over and over again in cooperative planning meetings. Some of these compatibility problems are reasonably easy to overcome if everyone is really interested in forming a system. Not so easy to resolve are certain other operational problems, such as differences in classification systems used.

Finally, there are problems of rules and regulations to be overcome— usually a matter of who may use a certain type of library. As long as the cooperative membership consists of one type of library, there are few problems of this kind. However, when several different types of libraries join a system, there may be significant problems. Archival and special-collection libraries may have a number of restrictions on who may use the material, just as some professional libraries do (for example, law and medicine). Normally, this is not a major barrier, although it is time-consuming to make certain that the agreement takes into account all the rules and regulations.

Legal, Political, and Administrative Barriers

Legal, political, and administrative barriers to resource sharing can be complex and unique. One can imagine some of the legal and political barriers that may arise by referring to figure 16.1 (page 456).

Each circle in the figure represents a different level of government and political concern. To develop a library system that combines all four major types with the least amount of waste, in the sense of not duplicating resources and services unnecessarily, planners must cross several jurisdictional lines. Crossing such lines raises questions such as:

- Where do the funds come from for a multi-jurisdictional system?
- Who will control the funds?
- Will there be a lessening of local control?
- Is it legal to take money from one jurisdiction to spend in another?
- What are the politics of securing enabling legislation for such a system?

Attempts to start at the local level and work upward in the hierarchy of government sometimes succeed because the persons involved are more familiar with the way local programs relate (for example, levels of funding and interest) to the political system.

Crossing governmental jurisdictional lines can mean that the project will have to develop one or more joint power agreements, which allow using funds from two or more jurisdictions for a joint purpose. Usually, this process is a matter of time rather than of getting the agreement, but it involves politicians, and one never really knows how long it will take them to act.

Starting at the national level usually reduces the number of jurisdictional questions and results in better funding. Although the national approach has some major advantages, it also has significant disadvantages. One of the most frequent responses to a national plan from the local authorities is: "What do the bureaucrats in the capital know about our problems? No one on the planning committee ever asks us what we need, much less comes to see our program." Suspicion is the key word here, followed by possessiveness. ("What is the real motive for this project, and why should we give up local control?") These problems, of course, are not just library problems; they are part of the political process. Another problem is that the many national plans, to allow for local variation, do not contain enough detail to make them functional. At times it seems as if reporting results to national authorities consumes more administrative time than the library saves through cooperative activities. Finally, regional jealousies and a desire for political gain may dominate the entire process, thus negating most of the advantages that the project could achieve for library customers across the country.

As mentioned earlier, there can be problems when the project involves public and private institutions, particularly when the funding comes from public sources. Certainly, a major concern of the directors of private academic libraries in California (California Private Academic Libraries [CAL

PALS]) about a proposed statewide cooperative relates to administrative control and the amount of influence privates will have. Apparently, because the funds would be state or federal, legally only public institutions may decide how to expend the money. Several CAL PALS directors have stated that they could not agree to participate unless there were greater sharing of administrative and policy decisionmaking.

Accrediting bodies may play a role in the process because of their standards. For small and medium-sized educational institutions (secondary as well as higher education), the accrediting agencies can play a significant role in institutional decisionmaking. Top administration can change their minds almost overnight about funding priorities based on an accreditation report.

The role of the WASC as an institutional accrediting body has had a mixed influence on cooperative collection building. WASC's accreditation standards, particularly 6.B.1 (see page 465), were designed, in part, to control institutions that were establishing widely scattered off-campus programs. One concern was that students were not receiving proper support—in particular, library support—at the off-campus sites. This standard has proven to be a two-edged sword for cooperative collection building. In a few instances, it motivated the library and its parent institution to enter into formal agreements with the libraries near the off-campus instructional sites. Usually, such agreements state that the institution needing access to material will pay an annual fee, which the receiving library agrees to use to subscribe to certain journals or to buy books about certain subjects. Given that most libraries do not have large amounts of excess collection growth space, it appears clear that the receiving library believes its primary customers will also benefit from the acquired material. This form of cooperative collection building is often overlooked.

On the negative side, the standard also resulted in libraries acquiring technologies that would allow the remote sites to have access to the main campus library. Undoubtedly, for many of the libraries, the accreditation pressure regarding off-campus students having access to library support resulted in funding for online catalogs, fax machines, CD-ROMs, and networking capabilities. In many cases, most of the technology would have been much slower in arriving in the library had it not been for the accreditation concerns. The technologies, in essence, reduced the need to enter into cooperative agreements. The standard also resulted in lost opportunities to work at developing true cooperative collection building programs. Perhaps with the technologies in place, it will be easier to undertake a cooperative project.

In some cases, there is a need to maintain two systems for a time. Dual operations are always a part of the start-up procedure in any cooperative system, but normally the two systems operate simultaneously for only a short period of time. However, even two or three months of dual operation may create a real economic burden for some members with tight operating budgets. All the cooperative can do is to keep the transition period as short as possible. Finally, complex systems require extensive staff training; thus, some loss of normal productivity will occur while the staff is in training. In addition, a complex system usually means that more mistakes will occur and necessitates a longer transition period.

Technological Issues

Faith that new technological developments will vastly increase the storage capacity of a library is an important issue. In some instances, pressure for cooperative collection development comes from a lack of physical space in which to store the collection. Eliminating unnecessary duplication of low-use items can result in more space for high-use materials. However, if new technology allows storage of the equivalent of the Library of Congress or British Museum Library collections in space no larger than an office desk or less, why worry about running out of space? In addition, the potential for local self-sufficiency may again arise. If one can purchase microfiche collections for less than hard copies, the book budget will stretch farther. Increased acquisition rates will increase the title count and thus raise the status of the library. Increased depth and scope in the collection, plus almost immediate satisfaction of patron needs, are what libraries are all about, right?

Technological developments (for example, CD-ROM) that were mere speculations 15 years ago hold out the hope of being able to store large quantities of full-text material in little space. Long-term costs of such technology, however, are a serious consideration. Most of the new technologies are costly, and many require additional fees when a library wishes to provide simultaneous user access, or in some cases even to print a screen. In the past, the only major high-density format was microforms that were (and are) unpopular with customers. For some reason, people are willing to sit for much longer periods at a computer than they are willing to sit at a microform reader. (This is most probably because of the greater flexibility in accessing the desired information.) If the primary reason for exploring cooperative collection building is slowing collection growth, then the new technologies teasingly revive the hope for self-sufficiency while not running out of storage space. However, most librarians desire to expand access for customers while not expending more money. (If the same program buys the library or institution time before having to face a remodeling or construction project, so much the better.)

For some, the new technologies invite a new form of cooperative collecting, if a group of libraries shares full-text database costs. In all likelihood, the cost of such an arrangement would be greater than the combined material budgets of the cooperating libraries. This is because the vendors base their charges on the total number of potential simultaneous users. For example, LMU explored mounting a scientific indexing and abstracting service on a local area network (LAN). The database owner wanted a fee for every university student, faculty, and staff member, rather than a more realistic number of likely simultaneous users. The difference was more than 5,000 users.

Twenty years ago, it was difficult to know who held what material. Bibliographic utilities (such as OCLC, WLN, and RLIN) were still developing, and their databases were small compared to actual library holdings. Union catalogs had proven to be expensive to develop and maintain as well as cumbersome to use. The utilities were slowly replacing the union catalogs, but few libraries could afford the costs of membership and equipment to belong to more than one such service. Today, with the utilities and libraries allowing dial-in access to their OPACs, it is much easier to determine who owns what.

New technologies provide additional ways of expanding access for the customer. Are they also a form of resource sharing? If two or more neighboring libraries agree to share some journal titles, that is a form of cooperation. When several libraries engage in online recording of the journals' tables of contents, is this resource sharing? Probably not. However, if there is the added element of delivering the indexed articles to any customer of the cooperating libraries, resource sharing is clearly present. CARL (Colorado Alliance of Research Libraries) does just that, and the CARL Corporation markets its efforts to other libraries with CARL *UnCover*. Is the *UnCover* product a form of resource sharing or a sound entrepreneurial move? Does the view change when a purely commercial entity offers a similar service?

Technology is blurring the lines of what constitutes resource sharing. Does one really care, as long as the customer's access expands to material the library cannot afford to acquire? A short-term answer is probably not. However, taking a longer view, perhaps librarians should care. As discussed in chapter 5, information pricing practices, like other commodities, factor in the number of units sold or likely to sell. Shared resources projects may in fact drive prices up, thus negating any financial gain from cooperating.

Without question, technology offers us more opportunities to cooperate than it presents barriers to cooperation. The major concern is what the ultimate costs will be.

Physical Issues

Physical concerns (for example, lack of seating capacity, lack of parking) were moderately important in the past. In a sense, staffing was another physical barrier; one public service person can handle only so many people in a given time. Today, these problems are as great, if not greater, than they were 15 years ago. This may make it more difficult to establish reciprocal borrowing agreements.

Local customers use the collection and the reader stations to the maximum, so acquiring additional customers would result in long waits or no service. Small archival libraries and special libraries, where patrons must use the materials in the library, often face this problem. Even large facilities, especially academic libraries, often experience this phenomenon. For example, not long ago UC-Berkeley decided to close its undergraduate library to outsiders, including non-UC students and faculty. This will mean that resource sharing will have to focus on ways of supplying the needed information to the customer at his or her home institution. Without question, this will raise the cost of cooperation.

Insufficient storage space for materials is not easy to resolve. Cooperative collection development proposals may reduce the need for storage space in some subject areas in the future, but they will add demands in other areas. Normally, such proposals do not address the issue of older materials already in a collection. If there is to be a new central storage unit for low-use items (for example, the Center for Research Libraries), then libraries may gain some space, but this usually does not solve the long-term space problem.

Geographic and transportation issues also can create problems, although technology is making distance less of a problem. Distance is a well-known issue in collection building. As we have mentioned before, people are prone to follow the "law of least effort." Often, this translates into using what is easily accessible as opposed to what is most appropriate. When thinking about distance, especially in urban areas such as Los Angeles, think about time rather than distance. Saying that item X is available at a library only 10 miles away means one thing to a person in Boston or Los Angeles and quite another to someone in Peoria or Colorado Springs. Depending on the time of day and day of the week, that 10-mile drive can turn into a lengthy and challenging commute. The distance issue and the "law of least effort" force librarians to think and plan in terms of document delivery in any cooperative project.

People Issues

Perhaps the biggest barrier to cooperative collection building is people. Avoiding (but not discounting) such factors as ego, the need to control discussion, or the need to get (or take) credit for a successful project, this discussion focuses on institutional people issues.

The planners of a cooperative program must overcome a variety of psychological barriers. Change is almost always threatening to at least a few people. Both customers and staff become uneasy when talk of cooperative collection building begins. During the early exploratory discussions, no one knows whether the program will start or what its precise form will be; thus, almost everyone raises a concern or an open objection. Sometimes, the sum total of the concerns is such that heeding all of them would mean no project.

A related issue is the potential loss of autonomy. Staff, and sometimes faculty, worry abut this, and their concerns take the form of questions such as: Who will decide? What voice will we have? Won't X dominate the process? Certainly, when it comes to multitype cooperatives or public/private ventures, there are some reasonable grounds for concern. The larger libraries probably would dominate, unless the governance arrangements were carefully thought out. When the bulk of the funding is from public sources, there is a danger that the public institutions may have—or may want—too much control for private institutions to take part in the project. Carefully formulated agreements can handle these problems in most cases.

Passive resistance, as well as inertia and indifference, can be a serious problem at both the planning and implementation stages. Staff may view the project as resulting in more work with little or no benefit to themselves. For such individuals, passive resistance is the easiest course of action. As with selling any change, planners must be honest and forthright about possible modifications in the workload. If an increase in work is likely, the planners should try to identify some project benefit that will come directly to the affected person or unit. An abstract benefit for the library, library customers, or institution all too often is insufficient to effectively combat resistance.

Like staff, customers can also engage in passive resistance. An academic library should not undertake a cooperative collection building program without gaining tacit faculty approval. This may require more than just a library committee's blessing. Securing approval by the faculty governing body is wise, even if it is not required. Lacking such prior approval, any faculty opposition to the plan is likely to delay the project because of the need to consult widely with all the faculty. A related obstructionist tactic is, "This is a wonderful idea, but we need assurance that there is an equitable distribution of funds for our instructional needs before ... ." In any situation, consulting with customers during the planning process is wise. By carefully planning and taking the time to consult and inform all interested parties as the work progresses, planners have an excellent chance of overcoming user resistance.

Because selection decisions are subjective, there are concerns about how the process will take place in the cooperative system. Who will and how will they make the decision to buy? Certainly a carefully formulated joint collecting policy statement will help allay worries on this count, but interpretation of the policy is still subjective. In the University of California shared acquisitions program, individual campuses suggest titles to acquire, but a committee representing some of the campuses makes the final decision. (Committee membership rotates, so all campuses have representation from time to time.) Such a process can help overcome worries about losing control over the funds and the collection. It does not completely remove subjectivity, but it is based on group discussion and decision.

A final obstructionist tactic is questioning the quality or reliability of one or more of the proposed cooperative partners. This is a strategy some staff members may employ to slow down the planning process. Errors, especially in an electronic database, present problems for everyone. One of the long-standing complaints about OCLC has been that its quality control is too lax. A point like that is certain to be made by staff members who oppose the project. Sharing access to any database is likely to raise concerns about quality control. However, with proper planning and control, this should not be a major stumbling block.

The bottom line in cooperative collection building should be better service to customers. If customers fight the project and the library staff has doubts as well, there is little reason to think the project will succeed. These issues existed 15 years ago, and they remain strong today.

Knowledge or
Lack of Knowledge Issues

Lack of knowledge about customer use patterns can present a barrier to coordinated collection development. As librarians, perhaps we thought we would have time someday to collect use data, but just have not found the opportunity to do so. Do we have adequate knowledge about what patrons need and want? Furthermore, even if we know the current situation, needs and wants can change quickly. Certainly, selection officers deal with these two issues every day. Why is it any greater a problem for a cooperative? Lacking knowledge about the customer base, we have little or no basis for accurately projecting how the proposed cooperative would affect service. Every member of the cooperative faces the same issues. Collecting data about customer needs can delay the project indefinitely.

A major difficulty with cooperative plans is the speed with which one can make adjustments to changing needs in a network of more than two members. It is much easier to respond to changing local needs when one does not have to worry about the impact the adjustments will have on other libraries. Of course, any proposed change may require modification of the original agreement. Though most changes would be minor, each requires discussion with other member libraries.

The specter of the failure of the Farmington Plan may haunt planners. However, people learn from past projects and mistakes. Most people who studied the rise and fall of the Farmington Plan suggest that one factor that caused it to fail was constantly changing institutional needs. Though librarians might hope things have improved, given today's need to control growth and effectively manage limited collection building funds, institutions are seldom willing to make long-term commitments. Experience tells us that institutions change and their libraries must change as well. The problem is that no one knows when the change will take place or what form it will take. As a result, each institution tries to protect its right to respond to unknown, but inevitable, changes.

Another problem is that the literature seldom fully reports how and why a cooperative project failed. Usually, journals publish articles about successful projects. Although this is understandable, information about failed efforts might be even more useful to planners. Announcements about new cooperative projects may appear in the news section of journals like *Library Journal, Wilson Library Bulletin,* or *College & Research Libraries News.* If the project succeeds, an article explaining how and why the project succeeded may appear at a much later date. More likely, there will be no follow-up article. Did the project ultimately succeed or fail? Short of tracking down someone from one of the libraries involved in the project, if that information exists, there is no way to know. Most libraries do not have the time or staff to engage in this type of investigation. Thus, lack of knowledge about past efforts is a barrier to success.

Even projects that are reported change over time. Such changes almost never appear in print, but often these changes, especially during the first two or three years of operation, are key elements in a successful project. About the only way to learn about such changes is to conduct a survey. Locating individuals who have detailed knowledge about how and why the changes occurred is time-consuming. Using a questionnaire for this type of information is a waste of time, energy, and money. The only effective way to obtain the information is through in-person or telephone interviews; even then, one senses that critical data is missing. (Ten years ago, the senior author served as co-advisor for a doctoral student studying innovation and change in academic libraries. He spent more than $3,000 attempting to get information from 45 individuals through telephone interviews. In addition, he went to eight conferences and conventions to conduct interviews. By the time he completed his research, we both knew he had all the data anyone could collect, yet neither of us felt satisfied that all the critical data was available.)

One other important piece of information is almost impossible to collect: the actual costs of the project. Because a major motivation in initiating a cooperative project is to stretch limited funding, knowing project costs is important. When there is a special grant to start the project, it is easy to get that cost information. What one does not find is information about staff costs not covered by the grant. Anyone with grant experience knows that, even with cost-sharing grants, the institutional contribution is always larger than what appeared in the grant proposal. Getting start-up cost information is simple compared to getting ongoing operational cost data. With excellent contacts in a successful cooperative project, you may be able to get some sense of the direct costs. However, it is often the indirect costs that ultimately eat up the savings that the cooperative generates in other areas. For example, tracking the extra cost in ILL staff time, buried in the overall ILL operations, or calculating ILL indirect costs becomes so burdensome that few institutions undertake such studies. When one does get cost data, one must remember to factor in regional differences in salary. One will also want to know whether there was any consideration of overhead costs and, if so, what the group included as overhead.

Thus, 15 years ago librarians had problems with lack of knowledge. There is little change in the situation today. Pressures to cooperate are perhaps stronger than ever before, yet libraries do not have an adequate base of knowledge about what did and did not work.

Despite what may seem to be a litany of problems, it is possible to establish cooperative projects, and it is becoming more and more a matter of economic necessity.

What to Avoid When Establishing a Resource-Sharing Program

The following seven points about what to avoid in order to establish a successful cooperative program come from the literature on the topic. Avoid these pitfalls, and your system has an excellent chance of succeeding:

- Avoid thinking of the cooperative as "supplementary" and an "add-on"; instead, consider it as something it is impossible to do without.

- Have planners spend time working out operational details.

- Realize that the system *should* cause major operational changes in the member libraries.

- Avoid thinking of the system as providing the library with something for nothing.

- Have the cooperative's funding and operation handled by an independent agency.

- Realize that it takes time; careful, complete communication; and one or two persons who take on the leadership role with patient understanding for such a project to succeed.

- Remember that above all else, forming a cooperative is a political process.

An indication of the difficulties associated with developing resource sharing is found in a classic article by Maryann Dugan, "Library Network Analysis and Planning."[14] She asked a group of 109 head librarians to indicate what type of cooperative activities would be appropriate to develop. Based on the responses, she identified 10 important activities, which the librarians ranked by their desirability and the need to develop cooperatives. Their ranking is indicative of the attitudes we have been discussing:

1. Union list
2. Interlibrary loan

3. Facsimile transmission

4. Networking

5. Reference service

6. Regional centers

7. Central facility

8. Type of library centers

9. Central processing

10. Collection management

In one sense, resource sharing was both first and last; union lists, interlibrary loan, and facsimile transmission are all forms of resource sharing. However, for these to be most useful, in terms of both cost-effectiveness and gaining access to the full universe of knowledge, coordinated collection management must occur. Without cooperative collection management, the situation is the same as it has always been. Certainly today, with hundreds of OPACs available on the Internet, customers can locate material quickly. However, if everyone is buying basically the same materials, is there any useful gain? For years we have used interlibrary loan and variations of facsimile transmission. The attitude in 1969 (when Dugan's survey was conducted) was to cooperate, so long as doing so did not have a negative impact on local autonomy and self-sufficiency. To a large extent, that attitude remains strong today.

The ALA guidelines identify seven models for cooperative collection development: the Farmington Plan, the National Program for Acquisitions and Cataloging (NPAC) system, the Library of Congress system, the Center for Research Libraries model, the mosaic overlay of collection development policies, the status quo, and the combined self-interest models.

As we saw earlier, the Farmington Plan, a valiant but unsuccessful effort, was an attempt by major American research libraries to have one copy of any currently published research work available somewhere within the United States. After years of effort, it was abandoned in the 1970s. The plan originally assigned acquisition responsibility on the basis of institutional interests. In 20 years, those interests changed, but the goal of one copy remained. Another problem was that some areas were not of major interest to any institution. Sufficient national interest existed to warrant coverage, but deciding which institution should have the responsibility for buying such materials was a constant problem. A careful study of why the Farmington Plan failed provides invaluable data for future cooperative ventures. In the final analysis, it failed as a result of not avoiding the pitfalls discussed earlier.

A European example was the Scandia Plan, implemented in the Scandinavian countries, which experienced similar problems. This plan never achieved the same level of activity as the Farmington Plan, primarily because of problems of changing needs and the assignment of responsibilities.

The NPAC system was another attempt at acquiring quantities of research materials from outside the United States and assuring that cataloging data would be available for the material. (Cataloging was a stumbling block to the Farmington Plan.) The Library of Congress was the focal point in NPAC, but there was consultation with other research libraries in the United States about what subjects to include in the program. Public Law 480[15] was an element of the NPAC program in which the Library "was authorized by Congress to acquire books abroad by using U.S.-owned non-convertible foreign currency under the terms of the Act."[16] Again, the Library of Congress was responsible for operating the program, including cataloging, and distributing the materials to participating academic libraries. Public Law 480 was not a cooperative collection development project in the usual sense of the term; it was a centralized acquisition and cataloging program.

A related, joint acquisition program that also failed was the Latin American Cooperative Acquisition Plan (LACAP). LACAP was a commercial undertaking designed to share costs and problems of acquiring quantities of research material, on a regular basis, from Latin American countries. Although some research libraries in the United States still collect extensively from Latin America, they could not sustain the program. Three factors played an important role in the demise of LACAP. First, most of what the libraries acquired was low-use material. Tight funding requires hard choices, and low-use items are always a prime area for cuts. Second, the plan started in a period when many institutions were developing area study programs, and there was an expectation that this would be a growing field. Economic conditions changed; institutions stopped planning for new programs and often cut some of the most recently established programs. As a result, not as many institutions were interested in participating in LACAP. Finally, the book trade in many Latin American countries matured, and it was no longer as difficult to locate reliable local dealers. If one can buy directly and reliably at a lower cost, it is reasonable to buy the most material possible with the funds available.

The ALA guidelines describe the Library of Congress system as "a variation of the Farmington Plan." In general terms, it is a centralized (coordinated) system in which the national library and the research libraries in a country work together to ensure that at least one copy of all relevant research material is available.

Two of the most successful cooperative programs are the Center for Research Libraries (CRL) in the United States and the British National Lending Division (BLD). One reason for their success is that they operate as independent agencies. Their purpose is to serve a diverse group of member libraries; in essence, they have no local constituency to serve. Another major difference for CRL is that there is no attempt to acquire high-use items; in fact, just the opposite is true. With no local service population, the fiscal resources can go to acquiring low-use items of national interest.

The CRL does face some major decisions regarding its collection policies. One issue is whether it should build a broad-based selective collection, with many subjects and areas, or whether it should attempt to be comprehensive in a few areas. A second issue relates to the need for a single source of low-use periodicals (the "National Periodicals Center" concept) and what role CRL should play. An interesting article by Sarah E. Thomas, "Collection Development at the Center for Research Libraries," suggests that the number of the Center's periodical holdings is not as unique as many members would like (only 20.66 percent of the Center's titles were unique).[17] Local needs of member libraries would account for some of the duplication. Also, the project looked at title holdings in the United States, not just at CRL member libraries, so some of the duplication undoubtedly occurred in nonmember libraries. What of the future? One would hope that the Center will continue to develop as the holder of unique materials. With better delivery systems, perhaps libraries can supply low-use items quickly enough from CRL and let patrons know about the system, which would allow less duplication of low-use items.

A "mosaic overlay of collection development policies" is what the RLG conspectus and ARL National Collection Inventory Project (NCIP) are trying to accomplish. The purpose is to assure national coverage; to identify collection gaps nationally; to serve as a basis for libraries taking on collecting responsibilities (primary collecting responsibility, or PCR); to assist in directing scholars to strong collections; to create a consistent basis for collection development policies; to function as a communication device signaling changes in collection activities; to serve as a link among collecting policies and processing and preservation policies; to serve as a possible fund-raising tool; and finally, to stimulate interest in and support for cooperative programs. Whether NCIP and RLG efforts will succeed in achieving that long list of purposes, only time will tell. The final product will be an assessment of collection strength in almost 7,000 subject categories by the participating libraries, giving each appropriate subject category a value of 0 to 5. When that is done, we shall know which libraries think they have strong or weak collections in each area, but we will not know exactly what is in each collection. The assessment will identify gaps and will be useful for referral purposes, and perhaps for ILL if the library is online and the library seeking the information can tap that database. The possibility of each of some 200 or so research libraries (a generous estimate of potential participants) accepting its share of the potential 5,000 PCRs, about 25 PCRs each, is grand. Will it happen? It would be wonderful if it did; however, it has not happened yet.

The "status quo" approach, as the label implies, would keep things as they are. This model assumes that the sum total of current collecting activities, primarily by research libraries and archives, achieves the comprehensiveness needed. By sharing in-process and catalog files, online of course, adequate access is available to allow individual purchase decisions with the knowledge of who has or has not ordered an item. It is doubtful that many research librarians really believe that the current system is achieving the needed level of coverage.

The combined self-interest plan is something of a multitype system, in that a significant number of libraries would combine with one or more major libraries. In a sense, this is what the Collection Development Committee of the Colorado Council on Library Development attempted to create, with the Denver Public Library and the University of Colorado Library System serving as the major libraries. The committee goals and objectives, as outlined in "Developing Collections in Colorado," were:

GOALS:

1. To work toward coordinated collection development policies for all libraries in the state to give greater access to materials for all Colorado citizens.

2. To assess budgetary constraints affecting local and statewide collection development and to work for increased funding and resources to overcome restraints.

OBJECTIVES:

1. To have individual libraries recognize their role in collection development and to prepare their own collection development policy in terms of their own clientele and role within the state.

   A. Each library should define who it serves as its primary client.

   B. Each library should determine and define the needs of that client.

   C. Each library should have a mission statement or goal.

   D. Each library should establish written priorities for allocation of resources.

2. To raise the awareness of individual librarians about collection development, including an understanding of what collection development is and the training needed for it.

3. To determine what materials the state does not have and to make recommendations for providing those needed resources within [Colorado].

4. To encourage preparation of regional and statewide collection development plans.

   A. Identifying local and state responsibilities.

   B. Assisting libraries to delineate responsibilities for materials.

5. To coordinate current collection development activities within the state and provide a clearinghouse for collection development information.[18]

Again, the RLG conspectus and the ALA policy guideline concepts were the basis for the combined policy statements. With all types of libraries involved, problems developed and, in some cases, remain unresolved, and not everyone views the concept with enthusiasm.

Another Colorado cooperative is CARL. Donnice Cochenour and Joel Rutstein's article provides an excellent description of how the project came into being and operates today.[19] Any group thinking about undertaking the development of a proposal for coordinated or cooperative collection building should read this article.

Yet another good paper to consult is Sue Medina's description of the Network of Alabama Academic Libraries.[20]

On a more limited scale is the University of California Library System's "Shared Purchase Program." The program has a 15-year history of shared buying; its purpose being

> to acquire materials which, because of their high cost (or antici-
> pated frequency of use), should be shared among the campuses
> without unnecessary duplication. The program has also been in-
> stituted to reduce competition for, and to promote sharing of,
> manuscript and subject area collections among the various cam-
> puses of the University of California. Stanford University is a full
> member of the program. However, state funds will not be used to
> acquire materials housed at Stanford (except for necessary in-
> dexes). Materials acquired with shared funds are to be shared
> among the campuses either statewide or on a regional (North and
> South) basis.[21]

Any campus library can recommend items for the committee to acquire, and membership on the committee rotates so that every campus has representation from time to time.

Local and International Projects

A current project illustrates most of the points discussed in this chapter. Los Angeles County has a number of libraries with theology collections that support one or more degree programs. None of the libraries is well-off finan-cially, and combining acquisition budgets would be of assistance to all cus-tomers. Certainly, there is interest in cooperative work at the directors' level. Thus, there is enough institutional and library support to at least explore co-operative ventures. It is still much too early to know how many, if any, of the specific institutional barriers will arise.

Because all of the schools are private institutions, they should not en-counter any legal barriers. Because we are in the "what-if" stage, it is un-known whether any administrative barriers may appear. However, it seems likely that administrative barriers could be quickly resolved.

Technology is on our side, at least so far. A year ago, those of us from the 23 theology libraries who use EBSCO as our serials agent agreed to have the firm produce a union list of our serials subscriptions (quarterly or more fre-quent titles). The listing is comprehensive, not just theology and philosophy titles, so we have a fairly sound knowledge of our joint serials holdings. Naturally, there are a few direct-order titles that do not appear on the list. We could use this listing as the starting point for cooperative serials collec-tion management. We have agreed to an annual update of the listing. This could not have been done 15 years ago without the expenditure of large sums of money. The next step will be to agree that any theology or philosophy title held by only one of us would not be cancelled without first consulting the other libraries.

Most of us have a fax machine, and for those that do not, an investment of a few hundred dollars would provide a Los Angeles-area theological li-brary fax network. Assuming that the libraries could agree to giving member libraries priority ILL fax service for theology or philosophy articles, they would achieve a journal document delivery service that should satisfy most customers.

All but a few of the libraries have OPACs. For a relatively modest cost, each could provide dial-in access, at least by member library staff. This would allow the libraries to share information about what each library has in its monograph collections. Certainly, it would be ideal to have a union OPAC, but that is unrealistic at this time. Without question, having to dial into 10 or more individual OPACs to determine whether a library owns a desired title would be time-consuming. Nevertheless, it would appear that such an approach would provide better service than the libraries now provide. Even without entering into formal subject buying agreements, this approach would allow the libraries to make some selection decisions on the basis of knowing who has what in the local area. Some of the libraries have automation systems that reflect information about items on order in the OPAC. This would provide additional data for selectors, if all the libraries could agree to activate such a capability in their systems.

Though making the OPACs available to individual faculty members would be ideal, such a move would probably overload dial-in access ports. (Most of the libraries did not plan on heavy off-campus dial-in access.) There would be problems in educating faculty members about the capabilities of five or six different types of OPACs. In the case of LMU, where the law school is in downtown Los Angeles and the main campus is in Westchester, 12 miles away, the library has a simple but difficult problem to solve. Both libraries have the same automation systems. We want the faculty on both campuses to have access to both systems. Currently, access is via telephone dial-in, but there are plans to link the two campuses with a fiber optic network. Our problem is this: How do we make certain that the person accessing a catalog knows whether she or he is looking at the law school or the Westchester campus catalog? Both menu screens look very much alike, and, when one views a specific record, nothing on the screen indicates in which library the item is located. Reprogramming is expensive, and so far we have not come up with a cost-effective solution. Although various OPAC systems do format the screens in a variety of distinctive ways, only the experienced user is likely to remember that *this* screen is LMU or *that* one is the University of Judaism. With proper planning, these problems should be overcome.

The lack of a union catalog will make it more difficult for the L.A.-area theology libraries to determine strengths, weaknesses, and, perhaps of greatest importance, degree of overlap. One option that exists to solve this problem, for the libraries using OCLC, is to use one of the existing CD-ROM products, such as the OCLC/AMIGOS CD-ROM, for collection evaluation. This system provides data about comparative holdings, unique titles, and overlap. The major drawback to the AMIGOS product as it now stands is that one cannot determine which library in the peer group holds which titles. Nevertheless, it could be a useful tool if the project goes forward.

As noted in the discussion of barriers, document delivery (distance) is a stumbling block in developing satisfactory (from the customer's point of view) cooperative collections of books, monographs, and audiovisual materials. Immediate, or at least quick, access is what every customer desires. We may have something of a solution to this problem. The LMU library has a courier service program for faculty to receive research material from UCLA.

A person who works 26 hours a week makes the trip (12 miles) to UCLA three times a week to pick up and return material. The person uses a library-owned station wagon. It is possible, with support from proposed member libraries, that this courier service could be expanded to five or six days a week among the libraries. Using this approach, we might be able to promise—and deliver on the promise—a maximum delay of 48 hours between request and book-in-hand.

Thus, we have most of the necessary pieces available to set up a cooperative collection building program:

- managerial interest
- institutional interest (unknown as to strength)
- union list of serials
- OPACs
- collection assessment tool
- document delivery capability
- fax capability
- courier service
- limited geographic service area

Why are we not very optimistic about our chances of success? Lack of knowledge and people are to blame. We have not progressed far enough in our thinking to know exactly what we do and do not know. It is doubtful that many of us have much data about our collection use patterns. We probably would be hard-pressed to produce much data about our core collections, much less our high- and low-use research material. There is no sense of the costs involved. Thus, lack of knowledge and the time and money to collect the information are serious barriers.

However, the people concerns will pose the major problems. Customer resistance will be particularly hard to overcome. During the early spring of 1993, the senior author approached a member of the LMU faculty library committee, who is in the theology department, about this project. He was given a brief outline of the major points, which was presented to his department colleagues at their last meeting of the academic year. His report on the outcome of the discussion was depressing. The faculty said that they would prefer a mediocre collection in all areas at LMU, rather than having certain areas of great strength while depending on other libraries in the area for in-depth, noncurriculum, or course subjects. If other institutional faculty respond in a similar way, it will be difficult to get the project off the ground, even if the library staffs are fully supportive. Will it succeed? It will depend on how much we want it to work and how well we market the idea to our customers and our funding authorities.

At the international level, there is the ambitious UNESCO program, Universal Availability of Publications (UAP). Although it is not actually a cooperative collection development plan, it must be mentioned. In concept, UAP is grand. It proposes that all published knowledge, in whatever form it is produced, should be available to anyone whenever he or she wants it.

Every information professional knows there is a long way to go in achieving that goal, even in countries with strong library systems and economies, let alone in developing countries. As Maurice Line stated,

> One of the main reasons why the situation with regard to UAP is so unsatisfactory is that availability has been approached piece-meal; particular aspects such as acquisitions and interlending have been tackled by individual libraries or groups of libraries, but uncoordinated piecemeal approaches can actually make things worse. ... UAP must ultimately depend on action with individual countries.[22]

If the concept is to succeed, it will be necessary to develop coordinated collection development plans in all countries and develop effective delivery systems, because everyone cannot buy, process, and store everything everywhere.

Summary

A midsummer 1994 electronic list discussion summed up the major points about cooperative collection development. First, the concept of cooperation is subject to many varying interpretations, even among the library staff—public service staff see it as more access, selection officers have both positive and negative views, and, often, top administrators see it as a way to save money. Second, status and budgets are still major issues, if there is a chance that cooperating might have a negative impact on size. Finally, multitype or multisize library efforts are unlikely to succeed because of the libraries' different goals and what each library can contribute to the cooperative venture.
Cooperative collection development is not an easy task. Local needs often seem to be at odds with broader needs of the area or nation. However, problems of funding and local practices can be overcome. As new delivery systems become available, we may be able to break down the need for local self-sufficiency, and expand resource-sharing programs beyond levels currently seen. It will be a long, slow process, but it is necessary to keep striving for this goal.

Notes

1.   J. J. Branin, "Cooperative Collection Development," in *Collection Management: A Treatise* (Greenwich, Conn.: JAI Press, 1991), 87.

2.   Edward Shreeves, "Is There a Future for Cooperative Collection Development in the Digital Age?," *Library Trends* 45 (Winter 1997): 373–91.

3.   *Webster's Third New International Dictionary* (Springfield, Mass.: G & C Merriam, 1976), 501.

4.   John Berry, "Killing Library Cooperation: Don't Let Professional Principles Become the Economy's Next Victim," *Library Journal* 117 (August 1992): 100.

5.   *ALA Glossary of Library and Information Science* (Chicago: American Library Association, 1983), 194.

6.   Michael P. Sinclair, "A Typology of Library Cooperatives," *Special Libraries* 64, no. 4 (April 1973): 181–86.

7.   Boyd Rayward, "Local Node," in *Multiple Library Cooperation*, edited by B. Hamilton and W. B. Ernst (New York: R. R. Bowker, 1977), 66.

8.   Paul H. Mosher and Marcia Pankake, "A Guide to Coordinated and Cooperative Collection Development," *Library Resources & Technical Services* 27 (October/December 1983): 417–31.

9.   Richard Hacken, "RLG Conoco Study and Its Aftermath: Is Resource Sharing in Limbo?," *Journal of Academic Librarianship* 18 (March 1992): 22.

10.   Bendik Rugaas, "The End of All and Forever," paper presented at IFLA Conference, Sydney Australia, 1988.

11.   Tom Ballard, "Public Library Networking: Neat, Plausible, Wrong," *Library Journal* 107 (April 1, 1982): 679–83.

12.   Hacken, "RLG Conoco Study and Its Aftermath," 21–22.

13.   Western Association of Schools and Colleges, *Handbook of Accreditation* (Oakland, Calif.: Western Association of Schools and Colleges, 1988), 62.

14.   Maryann Dugan, "Library Network Analysis and Planning," *Journal of Library Automation* 2, no. 9 (1969): 157–75.

15.   Pub. L. No. 480, The Agricultural Trade Development and Assistance Act, *codified at* 7 U.S.C. § 41.

16.   *A Historical Guide to the U.S. Government,* edited by George T. Kurian et al. (New York: Oxford, 1998), 366.

17.   Sarah E. Thomas, "Collection Development at the Center for Research Libraries: Policy and Practice," *College & Research Libraries* 46 (May 1985): 230–35.

18.   "Developing Collections in Colorado," *Colorado Libraries* 8 (December 1982): 7–8.

19.   Donnice Cochenour and Joel Rutstein, "A CARL Model for Cooperative Collection Development in a Regional Consortium," *Collection Building* 12, nos. 1/2 (1993): 34–53.

20.   Sue O. Medina, "The Evolution of Cooperative Collection Development in Alabama Academic Libraries," *College & Research Libraries* 53 (January 1992): 7–19.

21.   University of California, Library Council, Collection Development Committee, *Guidelines for University of California Library Acquisitions with Shared Purchase Funds* (Berkeley, Calif.: University of California, 1984), 1.

22.   Maurice Line, "Universal Availability of Publications: An Introduction," *Scandinavian Public Library Quarterly* 15 (1982): 48.

Further Reading

General

Dunn, R. T. "Sharing the Wealth." *PNLA Quarterly* 57 (Fall 1992): 25.

Dykeman, A. "True Cooperative Collection Development: Is It Possible?" In *Serials Collection Development*. Birmingham, Ala.: Vantage Point/EBSCO, 1995.

Ferguson, A. W. "Conspectus and Cooperative Collection Development." In *Collection Assessment*. Edited by R. J. Wood and K. Strauch, 105–14. New York: Haworth Press, 1992.

Hannesdottir, S. K. *Scandia Plan*. Metuchen, N.J.: Scarecrow Press, 1992.

Johnson, M. A. "When Pigs Fly: Or When Access Equals Ownership." *Technicalities* 12 (February 1992): 4–7.

Luquire, W., ed. *Coordinating Cooperative Collection Development: A National Perspective*. New York: Haworth Press, 1986.

Lynden, F. C. "Will Electronic Information Finally Result in Real Resource Sharing?" *Journal of Library Administration* 24, nos. 1/2 (1996): 47–72.

Miller, K. L. "Library Consortia Change the Rules." *Computers in Libraries* 16 (November/December 1996): 20–21.

Morgan, E. L. "Resource Sharing and Consortia, or, Becoming a 600-Pound Gorilla." *Computers in Libraries* 18, no. 4 (1998): 40–41.

Mosher, P. H. "A National Scheme for Collaboration in Collection Development." In *Coordinating Cooperative Collection Development*. Edited by W. Luquire, 21–35. New York: Haworth Press, 1986.

Networks for Networkers: Critical Issues in Cooperative Library Development. New York: Neal-Schuman, 1980.

Schroeder, P. "Consortial Arrangements: The Real Deal." *Library Acquisitions* 21, no. 4 (Winter 1997): 525–28.

Shirk, G. M. "Lee Tzu's Pit: Partnering in Dangerous and Chaotic Times." *Library Acquisitions* 22, no. 4 (Winter 1998): 415–21.

Shreeves, E. "Is There a Future for Cooperative Collection Development in the Digital Age?" *Library Trends* 45, no. 3 (1997): 373–91.

Sohn, J. "Cooperative Collection Development: A Brief Overview." *Collection Management* 8 (Summer 1986): 1–10.

Thompson, A. "Getting into a Cooperative Mode." In *Collection Management for the 1990s*, 127–34. Chicago: American Library Association, 1993.

Walters, D. H. "Distributed National Collection, Conspectus, Resource Sharing and Cooperative Collection Development." *Australian Academic and Research Libraries* 23 (March 1992): 20–24.

Weech, T. L. "Networking and Cooperative Collection Management." *Collection Building* 10, nos. 3/4 (1989): 51–57.

Academic

Brill, P. J. "Cooperative Collection Development." In *Collection Management in Academic Libraries*. Edited by C. Jenkins and M. Morley, 235–58. London: Gower, 1991.

Edelman, F. "Death of the Farmington Plan." *Library Journal* 98 (April 15, 1973): 1251–53.

Erickson, R. "Choice for Cooperative Collection Development." *Library Acquisitions: Practice and Theory* 16, no. 1 (1992): 43–49.

Glicksman, M. "Some Thoughts on the Future of the Center for Research Libraries." *Journal of Academic Librarianship* 10 (July 1984): 148–50.

Higginbotham, B. B., and S. Bowdowin. *Access Versus Assets*. Chicago: American Library Association, 1993.

Hightower, C., and G. Soete. "The Consortium as Learning Organization: Twelve Steps to Success in Collaborative Collection Projects." *Journal of Academic Librarianship* 21, no. 2 (1995): 87–91.

Holickey, B. H. "Collection Development vs. Resource Sharing." *Journal of Academic Librarianship* 10 (July 1984): 146–47.

Munn, R. F. "Cooperation Will Not Save Us." *Journal of Academic Librarianship* 12 (July 1986): 166–67.

Potter, G. "Recent Trends in Statewide Academic Library Consortia." *Library Trends* 45, no. 3 (1997): 416–33.

Rutstein, J. "Cooperative Collection Development Among Research Libraries: The Colorado Experience." In *Coordinating Cooperative Collection Development.* Edited by W. Luquire, 65–79. New York: Haworth Press, 1986.

Schwartz, C. A. "Social Science Perspective on Cooperative Collection Development." In *Impact of Technology on Resource Sharing.* Edited by T. C. Wilson, 47–60. New York: Haworth Press, 1993.

Shales, N. C. "Cooperative Collection Management Succeeds in Illinois." *Resource Sharing and Information Networks* 12, no. 1 (1996): 49–53.

Thomas, S. E. "Collection Development at the Center for Research Libraries." *College & Research Libraries* 46 (May 1985): 230–35.

Public

Abbott, P., and R. Kavanagh. "Electronic Resource Sharing Changes Interlibrary Loan Patterns." *Library Journal* 111 (October 1986): 56–58.

Atkinson, H. "Resource Sharing." In *Collection Management in Public Libraries.* Edited by J. Serebnick, 38–48. Chicago: American Library Association, 1986.

Ballard, T. H. *Failure of Resource Sharing in Public Libraries and Alternative Strategies for Service.* Chicago: American Library Association, 1986.

———. "Public Libraries and Resource Sharing." *Encyclopedia of Library and Information Science* 44, supplement 9 (1989): 257–74.

Devenish-Cassell, A. "Electronic Impacts on Library Resource Sharing." *Catholic Library World* 57 (March/April 1986): 221–24.

English, J. "Resource Sharing: A Promise Worth Fulfilling." *American Libraries* 22 (May 1991): 446.

Fiels, K. M. "Coordinated Collection Development in a Multitype Environment." *Collection Building* 7 (Summer 1985): 26–31.

Grabill, C. "Children's Materials: Resource Sharing in Action." *Public Libraries* 25 (Winter 1986): 135–36.

Hanson, C. D. "Commitment to Access: Resource Sharing in Public and School Libraries." *Library Administration and Management* 6 (Winter 1992): 21–25.

Rayward, W. B. "Local Node." In *Multitype Library Cooperation.* Edited by B. Hamilton and W. B. Ernst, 60–66. New York: R. R. Bowker, 1977.

Scott, S. "Cooperative Collection Development: A Resource Sharing Activity for Small Libraries." *Colorado Libraries* 18 (June 1992): 27–28.

Turlock, Betty S. *Public Library in the Bibliographic Network.* New York: Haworth Press, 1986.

Yelland, M. *Local Library Co-Operation.* London: British Library, 1980.

School

Bright, S. K. "New York City School Library System: Resource Sharing Network." *Bookmark* 50 (Fall 1991): 54–55.

Dickinson, G. K. "Effect of Technology on Resource Sharing in a School Media Program." In *Advances in Library Resource Sharing*. Edited by J. S. Cargill and D. J. Graves, 97–105. Greenwich, Conn.: Meckler, 1992.

Doan, J. K. "School Library Media Centers in Networks." *School Library Media Quarterly* 13 (Summer 1985): 191–99.

Dyer, Ester R. *Cooperation in Library Service to Children*. Metuchen, N.J.: Scarecrow Press, 1978.

Guthrie, D. "Experience in Resource Sharing." *Illinois Libraries* 72 (October 1990): 556–57.

Kulleseid, E. "Cooperative Collection Development in the School Library Revolution." *Bookmark* 50 (Fall 1991): 21–23.

Meizel, J. "High School Education and the Internet." In *Impact of Technology on Resource Sharing*. Edited by T. C. Wilson, 127–40. New York: Haworth Press, 1993.

Special

Cotter, G. A., R. W. Hartt, and D. J. O'Connor. "Integrated Bibliographic Information System: Concept and Application for Resource Sharing in Special Libraries." *Information Reports and Bibliographies* 17, no. 5 (1988): 12–20.

Freitag, W. M. "Cooperative Collection Development Among Art Libraries." *Art Libraries Journal* 11, no. 2 (1986): 19–32.

Klimley, S. "Taking the Next Step: Directions and Requirements for Cooperative Collection Development Among Academic Geology Libraries." In *User and Geoscience Information*. Edited by R. A. Bier, Jr., 69–76. New York: Geoscience Information Society, 1987.

Ladner, S. J. "Effect of Organizational Structure on Resource Sharing in Sci-Tech Libraries." *Science and Technology Libraries* 12 (Winter 1991): 59–83.

Lanier, D., and K. H. Carpenter. "Enhanced Services and Resource Sharing in Support of New Academic Programs (medical libraries)." *Journal of Academic Librarianship* 20 (March 1994): 15–18.

Millson-Martula, C. A. "Greater Midwest Regional Medical Library Network and Coordinated Cooperative Collection Development." *Illinois Libraries* 71 (January 1989): 31–39.

Roberts, E. P. "Cooperative Collection Development of Science Serials." *Serials Librarian* 14, nos. 1/2 (1988): 19–31.

Ward, S. M. "Resource Sharing Among Library Fee-Based Information Services." In *Advances in Library Resource Sharing*. Edited by J. S. Cargill and D. J. Graves, 124–38. Greenwich, Conn.: Meckler, 1992.

17

Protecting
the Collection

Every year libraries around the world expend large sums of money on information resources for their users. Most of that money goes to acquiring materials the library owns, although each year the amount spent on leased electronic resources increases substantially. A small percentage of material has a short useful (shelf) life and everyone knows this at the time of purchase. However, the vast majority of the acquisitions have a substantial, if not indefinite, expected shelf life. To realize a long-term shelf life, the staff must take steps to preserve the material.

A major premise of this book is that collection development is the central function of collection management. However, collection management involves several other functions as well, including preservation and conservation of the collection. As there should be a concern for preservation and conservation throughout the collection development process, it is appropriate to place responsibility for preservation with the collection managers. More and more libraries are placing preservation and binding under the direction of the chief collection development officer.

There are several aspects to protecting the collection, including proper handling of materials, environmental control, security (to protect against theft and mutilation) and disaster preparedness planning, conservation (binding and preservation), and insurance. Most of these issues are broad concerns, and detailed discussion of them is beyond the scope of this book; however, this chapter briefly touches on each topic. In a sense, all these factors work together to prolong the useful life of the materials in the collection. Even insurance fulfills this function, because claims payments help the library replace lost or damaged items.

Problems of acidic paper have long been the major concern of those involved in conservation activities in the library. There is now a new challenge that may be more difficult to resolve than neutralizing the acid in paper. (In fact, many books are now printed on nonacid paper.) The challenge is electronic resources and their long-term preservation. We explore this issue later in the chapter.

Two terms that we used in the preceding paragraphs are in common use, but have different meanings for different people. A 1998 article by Joseph Settanni addressed terminology definition issues.[1] Settanni made the point that there is a hierarchy of activity in protection of collections: conservation to preservation to restoration. He defined *conservation* as "the overall or general attempt to prevent further damage and deterioration,"[2] and *preservation* as "the specific effort to not merely stop but reverse the various negative and unwanted effects of destructive chemical and other agents that can destroy."[3] His definition of *restoration* is "the ideal goal of attempted reconstruction toward achieving the entire renovation of documents, artifacts, or physical structures to their original condition."[4]

We take just a slightly broader view of the term *conservation*. If we were to modify Settanni's definition, it would be as follows: "attempt to prevent damage and deterioration, or further damage and deterioration." Essentially we see most "good housekeeping" practices as part of the conservation program. Our discussion starts with print materials and follows the conservation to preservation concept. (It is beyond the scope of this book to explore restoration in any detail.) In the last sections of this chapter we look at nonprint and electronic resources.

Conservation

Proper Handling

Storage and handling are the two first steps in protecting a collection. Neither step requires extra expenditures on the part of the library. Libraries purchase storage units from time to time; the purchaser needs to give some thought to what is the most appropriate type of storage unit for the format. (This does not necessarily translate into the most expensive unit.)

Too narrow and/or shallow a shelf will result in items being knocked off and damaged. Filling shelves and drawers too tightly is a poor practice. Equally harmful is allowing the material to fall over on the shelf (because proper supports are lacking) or slide around in a drawer, because either practice will lead to damage in time. Buying adjustable storage units provides the library a measure of flexibility.

Anyone with extensive experience in shelving books (except a conservation specialist) probably has found a way to squeeze "just one more book" onto a shelf when good practice calls for shifting the material to provide proper space. This often happens when shelvers are under pressure to finish shelving a full book truck within a certain time period. Having sound performance standards is proper management; however, libraries must be certain that the shelving standard includes time for shifting materials. Not factoring that in will result in cracked and damaged book spines, as well as torn headbands resulting from patrons' attempts to pull books out from a fully packed shelf. Books should be vertical or horizontal on the shelf, not leaning this way and that. Fore-edge shelving should be avoided because it places undue strain on the binding (which is designed for horizontal or vertical storage). Proper supports and bookends help to keep materials in good order. Poorly constructed or finished supports can be more damaging to materials than having none at all.

Teaching people how to handle material properly is important. Training public service staff is an ongoing task; teaching proper handling techniques, if not already taught, will cost some time but will pay off in longer-lasting materials. One should make an effort to educate users in proper handling of materials as well. Some librarians regard housekeeping issues as bad for the library's image. If the library effectively communicates the fact that monies spent on repair and replacement of materials damaged through improper handling ultimately means less money to buy new material, people will understand the importance of housekeeping. It does not take more than two or three items sent for rebinding to equal the cost of a new book. And, like everything else related to collection development, bindery fees are constantly increasing.

Environmental Control

Climate control in the library is essential to any successful conservation program. Few libraries are able to follow the example of the Newberry Library in Chicago, where a stack area 10 stories high is double-shelled, windowless, and monitored by a computerized environmental system. Something less complex, however, will still help extend the useful life of most materials. The major concerns for environmental control are humidity, temperature, and light. Architects and librarians should take these issues into account when planning a library building. This is often easier said than done, because the ideal environmental conditions for human comfort and for preserving materials don't match. For example, the design of the book stacks for the Newberry Library storage facility calls for a constant temperature of 60°F +/- 5°F.

Few people would be happy to engage in sedentary work all day in a room with a 60-degree temperature. Most library designs place human comfort ahead of material preservation. The only time designers can effectively meet both sets of requirements is in situations like the Newberry, where the stacks are closed to the public and even employees are in the stacks for only short periods. Still, this arrangement does not answer all concerns about the environment for preserving materials. There also are differences in the ideal conditions for preserving various types of materials. Thus, building design characteristics may present some problems for implementing a good conservation program.

Institutional emphasis on energy conservation can lead to cooler winter temperatures and warmer summer temperatures. Cooler winter temperatures are better for materials, but normally the temperature is still well above 65 degrees. The greatest damage occurs in summer, when reducing air conditioning costs becomes an institutional priority. (A related problem is that changes in air temperature affect relative humidity.) One way to reduce air conditioning costs is to turn off the system when the library is closed, but overnight shutdowns are damaging to materials. When the system is off for some time, such as the weekend, the temperature can rise dramatically. When the air conditioning is turned back on, the temperature falls fairly quickly. This "roller coaster" temperature swing is more damaging to materials than storing them at a steady, somewhat higher temperature. Temperature cycling is damaging (it ages paper prematurely), but so are high temperatures. For every rise of 10°C, book paper deteriorates twice as fast. With rapid fluctuations in temperature, the primary problem is the humidity level, which causes damage to the materials.

The Library of Congress Preservation Leaflet no. 2 recommends a temperature of 55°F in book storage areas and a maximum of 75°F (below 70°F, if possible) in reading areas, all with a 50 percent relative humidity. Paul Banks, a well-known preservation specialist who set the standards for the Newberry storage area, also recommended 50 percent relative humidity. For most libraries constructed after World War II, there is little chance of having temperature differentials in storage and reading areas, because the design concept called for integrating readers and materials. Also, in most libraries, the temperature and humidity range is much greater than +/- 5°F.

Why are conservationists concerned with humidity? Because changes in humidity can physically weaken materials, which, in turn, can create added costs for repair or replacement. Books (including bound periodicals) consist of a number of different materials—paper, cloth, cardboard, thread, man-made fabrics, adhesives, and sometimes metal (for example, staples). Often, a single book is made up of several different types of material from each category; for example, heavy endpapers, a moderate-weight paper for the text, and coated paper for illustrations. Each component absorbs and loses water vapor (humidity) at a different rate. Materials expand as they absorb moisture and shrink as the humidity falls. As the amount of water vapor in the air goes up or down, there is constant shrinking and swelling of the materials. With each expansion and contraction, the material weakens slightly. Overall, paper deterioration is the main problem with cycling. Humidity and heat combine to accelerate deterioration from paper acidity.

The differences in the rates of expansion and shrinkage for the different components in the book weaken the bonds between the components, making the book more likely to fall apart. (Humidity is also an issue with photographic materials.) Constant humidity stabilizes the materials. How much water vapor is normally present is important; paper fibers are subject to deterioration when humidity is somewhere below 40 percent. At 65 percent or higher, the chances of mildew and mold formation increase. The musty smell of the antiquarian bookshop may contain more than a hint of mildew or mold, something one does not want in the library.

Other materials (microfilms, videotapes, photographs, and so forth) have somewhat different ideal temperature and humidity storage requirements. The ideal range for microforms is 70°F +/- 5° with humidity at 40% +/- 5%. The same ranges apply to still photographs and safety motion picture film. In contrast, nitrate-based motion picture film must be stored below 55°F but can tolerate humidity up to 45 percent. Videotapes do best at 65°F +/- 5° and no more than 45 percent humidity. Audiodiscs (LPs, 45s, and so forth) can handle temperatures up to 75°F and 50 percent humidity. However, the upper limits for audiotapes are 70°F and 45 percent humidity.

The National Archives has set even higher standards for its new facility in College Park, Maryland. Text and map storage areas call for 70°F and 45 percent relative humidity. Black-and-white film, audiotapes, and sound recordings have a 65°F and 30 percent relative humidity limit. Glass negative, black-and-white photographs, slides, negatives, posters, and electronic materials will be in areas with 65°F temperature and 35 percent relative humidity. Storage areas for color photography film, slides, and photographs will be still cooler—38°F and 35 percent relative humidity. Coldest of all will be storage areas for color motion picture film and color serial film, at 25°F and 30 percent relative humidity.

Recalling basic chemistry, we know that increasing the temperature also increases chemical activity. Roughly, chemical reactions double with each 10°C increase in temperature. Freezing books would be the best way to preserve them; however, it is not likely that readers would be willing to sit about in earmuffs, overcoats, and mittens. One is fortunate to achieve a controlled temperature below 70°F in areas where people work for extended periods. One reason for wanting the lower temperatures is to slow down the chemical decomposition of wood pulp paper, which the majority of books and journals contain. However, lower temperatures only slow the process; they do not stop it. All formats are sensitive to temperature variations, and the ideal storage condition is an environment with minimal changes.

Lighting, both natural and artificial, influences conservation in two ways. First, it contributes to the heat buildup in a building. Naturally, designers take this into account when specifying the building's heating, ventilating, and air conditioning system. Fluorescent lighting is not a major heat contributor, but in older libraries where incandescent fixtures exist, the heat generated by the fixtures can be a problem. If the light fixtures are close to materials (i.e., in exhibit cases), there can be significant temperature differentials from the bottom to the top shelf in a storage unit. Windows and sunlight generate heat as well, and they create mini-climates. The Newberry Library's windowless storage unit eliminates the sunlight problem. Many libraries have designs featuring numerous windows to provide natural lighting (thus reducing electric costs) and to satisfy users' desire to see outside. The cost of these designs has been high in terms of money spent after a few years to reduce the sunlight problem and to repair damaged materials.

The second concern is ultraviolet radiation, a result of sunlight, fluorescent, and tungsten lights. Ultraviolet light is the most damaging form of light because it quickly causes materials to fade, turn yellow, and become brittle. Windows and fluorescent light fixtures should have ultraviolet screens or filters built in or installed. Tungsten lighting has the lowest levels of ultraviolet radiation, but even these lights should have filters. The longer one exposes materials to unfiltered light, the more quickly damage occurs. Nonprint materials are even more sensitive and they require greater protective measures than do print materials.

Air filters that reduce the gases in the air inside the library are useful, if expensive. Urban activities pump a variety of harmful gases into the air every day. Some enter the building as people come and go. Few buildings have airlocks and ventilating systems that remove all harmful gases. Whenever it is economical, the ventilation system should remove the most harmful substances. Sulfur dioxide is a major air pollutant and a concern for library conservation programs, because it combines with water vapor to form sulfuric acid. Hydrogen sulfide, another common pollutant, also forms an acid that is harmful to both organic and inorganic materials. In addition to gases, air filters can also reduce the amount of solid particles contained in the building air. Dust and dirt include mold spores, which can cause problems if the air conditioning fails in warm, humid weather. Solid particles act as abrasives, contributing to the wearing out and wearing down of materials.

Dusty, gritty shelves wear away the edges of bindings—and, all too often, dusting book shelves is not in anyone's job description.

Mold can be a serious problem for paper-based collections and people as well. For example, *Aspergillas furnigatus* can be toxic, in sufficient quantities, and many molds can cause serious (even debilitating) allergy problems for some people. A good source of information about controlling mold is the Northeast Document Conservation Center's "Technical Leaflet: Protecting Books and Paper Against Mold" (<http://www.nedcc.org/mold.htm>).

Finally, insects contribute to the destruction of books and other items in the collection. Silverfish enjoy nothing more than a feast of wood pulp paper, flour paste, and glue. Cockroaches seem to eat anything, but have a particular taste for book glue. Termites prefer wood, but wood pulp paper is a good second choice. Larder beetle larvae (book worms), though lacking intellectual curiosity, can devour *War and Peace* in a short time. Finally, book lice enjoy the starch and gelatin sizing on paper. Other, less destructive insects can infest collections in the temperate zones; in a tropical setting, the numbers and varieties increase dramatically. Control of insects presents a few challenges, because pesticides create pollution problems. Naturally, the best control is to keep the insects out. One way to control insects, especially cockroaches, is to keep food and drink out of the library. A second step is to keep the temperature and humidity as low as possible, because insects multiply faster and are more active at higher temperature and humidity levels. If the library faces a significant insect infestation, it is better to call on a commercial service rather than attempt to handle the problem with library staff.

What are the signs of insect infestation? Most of the insects that cause damage prefer the dark and to stay out of sight. When one sees them, it is a signal that the population may be so large that there is nowhere to hide. Obviously, if one finds "remains" of insects on shelves, windowsills, or the floor, it is a sign of potential trouble. Unusual dust, "sawdust," or colored powder on bookshelves is likely to be "frass" (insect droppings), and is a clear indication of a problem. A good source of information about pest management in libraries and archives is Chicora Foundation, Inc.'s *Managing: Pest in Your Collection* (<http://palimpsest.stanford.edu/byorg/chicora/chicpest.html>).

Gifts to the library require careful examination before being stored in any area where insects could get into the general collection. Shipments that arrive by sea mail also need careful study. As the concern for the environment increases, many in-library fumigation units have ceased to operate or been extensively (and expensively) modified. This may mean using commercial systems, with additional costs and delays in getting and keeping material on the shelf.

Security

We include physical security of the collection in our discussion of conservation because some of the issues are conservation issues—for example, mutilation and water/smoke damage.

A full library security program involves several elements. Broadly, the program's goals are to assure the well-being of people and to protect the collections and equipment from theft and misuse. This discussion emphasizes the collections, with only passing mention of the people and equipment issues;

topics covered include theft, mutilation, and disaster preparedness. (For a fuller discussion of security programs, see chapter 14 in *Introduction to Library Public Services,* 5th edition.[5])

We tell people, only half in jest, that if a library wishes to identify its true core collection, all it has to do is prepare a list of all the lost and missing books and mutilated journal titles. Normally, these are the items that, for one reason or another, are (or were) under pressure from users, including high-use or, in the case of missing books, potentially high-use materials.

Every library loses books each year to individuals who, if caught by the security system, say they forgot to check the material out. Journals and other noncirculating material are subject to some degree of mutilation. Each incident of theft and mutilation means some small financial loss for the library, if nothing more than the cost of the material and the labor expended to make the item available. Other costs are the cost of staff time to search for the item, to decide how or whether to replace it, plus actual replacement and processing costs. Though a single incident seldom represents a significant cost, the total annual cost may be surprising, even if one calculates only the amount paid for replacement materials. The Loyola Marymount University library spends about $10,000 per year on replacement materials, and few of those replacements are for items that have become too worn to remain in circulation. This rate of loss occurs despite a high-quality electronic security exit system and targeting every book and every issue of every journal that goes into the collection. Needless to say, time and money expended to prevent theft or replace materials is time and money not spent on expanding the resources available to customers.

There are several givens to any security program. First, there will be some level of loss no matter what the library does. Second, the systems help basically honest people stay honest. A professional thief will circumvent almost any library security system, as Stephen Blumberg and David Siegelman demonstrated a few years ago.[6] Therefore, the library must decide how important the problem is and how much loss it can tolerate. The goal is to balance the cost of the security program against the losses. The less loss the library will accept, the higher the security costs, so finding the proper balance is important.

Most libraries employ some mix of people-based elements and electronic systems for security. Door guards or monitors who check every item taken from the library are the most effective and most costly option. This method works well only when the person doing the checking is not a peer of the people being checked. That is, using students to check fellow students, much less their teachers, does not work well. Retired individuals are very effective. They interact well with users but also do the job without favoring anyone. The major drawback to exit monitors, after the cost, is, when there are peaks and valleys in the exit flow, there can be long queues during the peaks.

Electronic systems are common and may give a false sense of security. Every system has a weakness that the person who regularly "forgets to check out books" eventually discovers, and the professional thief knows. Also, some materials (for example, magnetic tape and videotape) cannot have the "target" deactivated without damaging the content, and some materials simply do not have a place for a target. Such systems are susceptible to electronic interference, such as frequencies generated by computers or even fluorescent light ballasts. Finally, the inventive thief can jam the operating frequency and no one on the staff will know the difference.

Mutilation is another ongoing problem, which, during a year, can generate a surprisingly large loss for the library. There are few cost-effective options for handling this problem. Having copy services available and at competitive prices will help. Monitors walking through the building will solve or reduce many other security problems, but will do little to stop mutilation. Studies suggest that even customers who see someone mutilating library materials will not report the activity to library staff.[7] One option that customers do not like, but that does stop the mutilation of journals, is to supply only microform backfiles of journals that are subject to high mutilation. This option does not safeguard the current issues, and it requires providing microform reader-printers, which are more expensive than microform readers. There is also the occasional title that does not make its backfiles available in a microformat. Full-text CD-ROMs or Web-based services are a partial answer to some of the problems, because there is little user resistance to electronic material. However, if the person is seeking a color photograph or any color image there may still be a problem, especially if the library does not provide color printing or copier service. Another option is to acquire multiple copies of high-use titles. Here again, one trades some collection breadth for a possible reduction in mutilation. Theft and mutilation are a part of doing business. How much they cost the library depends on the local situation. Those costs come at the expense of adding greater variety to the collections and, in the long run, they hurt the customer.

Disaster preparedness planning is vital for the protection of people, collections, and equipment. Planners must think in terms of both natural and manmade disasters. Earthquakes, hurricanes, tornadoes, heavy rains, and floods are the most common natural disasters for which one should plan. The most common manmade disaster is water damage, which can be caused by a broken water pipe or sprinkler head, a faulty air conditioning system, or broken windows. In the case of a fire, water may cause more damage than the flames.

The following are the basic steps to take in preparing a disaster plan:

1. Study the library for potential problems. Often, the institution's risk management officer (insurance) is more than willing to help in that assessment.

2. Meet with local fire and safety officers for the same purpose.

3. Establish a planning team to develop a plan. This team may become the disaster handling team.

4. Establish procedures for handling each type of disaster and, if appropriate, form different teams to handle each situation.

5. Establish a telephone calling tree, or other fast notification system, for each disaster. A *telephone tree* is a plan for who calls whom in what order.

6. Develop a salvage priority list for the collections. If necessary, mark a set of floor plans and include them in the disaster planning and response manual. Most plans do not have more than three levels of priority: first priority is irreplaceable or costly materials, second priority is materials that are expensive or difficult to replace, and third priority is the rest of the collection. The LMU plan includes a category for hand-carrying one or two items from the immediate work area, if the disaster strikes during normal working hours. Establishing priorities can be a challenge for planners, because everyone has some vested interest in the subject areas with which they work.

7. Develop a list of recovery supplies the library will maintain on site (for example, plastic sheeting and butcher paper).

8. Include a list of resources—people and companies—who may assist in the recovery work.

Needless to say, after the planners finish the disaster plan, the library must put copies in the hands of each department and in the homes of the disaster team. It is also important to practice some of the procedures before disaster strikes. The LMU plan has been in place since 1991 and has been used three times, twice for water problems and once for an earthquake. With the water problems, the library was able to save all but eight books out of more than 15,000 that got wet. Had the staff not practiced its disaster response plan ahead of time, the loss rate would have been much higher. The library did not fare as well in the earthquake, because it is impossible to practice having book stacks collapse. Though LMU certainly fared better than libraries closer to the epicenter, it lost 1,237 books. Unfortunately, these losses could have been avoided if the shelving had been properly braced. The library staff knew where the problem stacks were and was waiting for funds to have the stacks retrofitted; however, the earthquake was quicker than the funding authorities.

Locating water, gas, and electrical system shut-offs is a good starting point for training the disaster team. Next, the team should check fire extinguisher locations to determine whether the units are operational and are inspected regularly. The team also should implement a program to train staff in use of the extinguishers. Usually, the local fire department will do this at no charge. There are three types of fire extinguishers: "A" for wood and paper fires, "B" for oil and electrical fires, and "C" for either type of fire. Match type to location and anticipated problems. Prepare floor plans, clearly identifying locations of shut-offs and extinguishers.

Salvage operations require careful planning and adequate personnel and materials. It is a good idea to develop a list of potential volunteers if the situation is too large for the staff to handle within a reasonable time. Keep in mind that the library can count on only about 72 hours of assistance from volunteers—that is, 72 hours from the time the first request for assistance goes out. Thus, there should be planning for what to do after 72 hours, if the disaster is major.

Water damage is a potentially destructive problem, as is the development of mold and mildew. Mold can develop in as little as 48 hours, depending on the temperature. What basic steps should one follow in a water emergency? The best way to handle large quantities of water-soaked paper is to freeze it and process the material as time and money allow. Planners should identify companies with large freezer facilities and discuss with them the possibility of using or renting their freezers in case of emergency. Often, such companies are willing to do this at no cost, because of the good publicity they gain from such generosity. Large grocery store chains and meat packing plants are possible participants. Refrigerated trucks can be most useful, if costly to rent. Getting wet materials to the freezing units is a problem: milk crates, open plastic boxes, or clothes baskets work well, because they allow water to drain. Cardboard boxes absorb water. Plastic interlocking milk crates are ideal, because they are about the right size for a person to handle when three-fourths full of wet material. Sometimes, local dairies are willing to assist by supplying free crates for the duration of the emergency. Freezer or butcher paper is best for separating the materials; never use newsprint, because it tends to stick and the ink comes off. Finally, find some drying facilities. There are three primary methods of drying wet books: (1) freezing/ freeze-drying, (2) vacuum drying, and (3) vacuum freeze-drying. Vacuum freeze-drying is the best way to handle wet items. Often, vacuum drying facilities are difficult to locate and can handle only a small volume of material at a time, so materials may be in the freezer for a long time while a small quantity is done whenever the source and funding permit. A variety of disaster-related online information, including Peter Waters's *Procedures for Salvage of Water-Damaged Library Materials*, is available from Conservation OnLine (CoOL, <http://palimpsest.stanford.edu>).

Two other steps are important when designing a disaster preparedness plan. One is to identify the nearest conservation specialist(s). Most are willing to serve as a telephone resource, and often they will come to the scene. A second important step is to arrange for special purchasing power. Although some groups, organizations, and companies may be willing to assist free of charge, many will not, and the library may need to commit quickly to a specific expense. Having to wait even a few hours for approval may cause irreversible damage.

Although most disasters are minor—a few hundred water-damaged items—a large disaster is always possible. One example was the April 1986 fire that struck the Los Angeles Public Library. For more than 10 years, there had been concern about the fire danger, but the hope that a new building would be constructed forestalled major modifications in the existing building. According to *Library Hotline,* it took 1,700 volunteers working around the clock to shrink-wrap and freeze the 400,000 water-soaked books (about 20 percent of the Central Library's collection).[8] In addition, the city paid a salvage contractor $500,000 for his firm's services. One can only speculate what the costs and problems might have been with no disaster preparedness plan.

Preservation

By having the collection properly stored and handled in a controlled climate, and with sound security practices as well as a disaster preparedness plan in place, the library will lengthen the useful life of its materials and reduce preservation problems. However, if the library fails to employ good preservation methods, much of what it gains from those practices will be lost as items fade, decompose, or become unusable. Conservation should start with the purchase decision (which ought to include consideration of how well the material will stand up to the expected use) and should end with the question of what to do about worn, damaged materials and items identified in the weeding process.

One element in a library's conservation program is the basic binding and repair program. In-house repairs are fine as long as they employ good conservation methods and use materials that will not cause more harm. Repairers should do nothing that cannot be undone later, if necessary. For example, one should avoid using any adhesive tape other than a reversible adhesive, nonacidic tape to repair a torn page.

Most commercial binderies follow sound practices and employ materials that will not add to an already serious problem of decomposing books. An excellent overview of library binding practices, in a commercial setting, is Paul Parisi's "An Overview of Library Binding."[9] Selecting a commercial binder should involve the chief collection officer, if the bindery operation is not under the supervision of that person. Most libraries spend thousands of dollars on bindery and repair work each year, and having a reliable and efficient binder, who uses the proper materials, benefits the library and its customers. Knowing something about bindery operations and the process the materials undergo can help the library staff responsible for selecting materials for binding to make better judgments about the type of binding to order, given the probable use of the material. Most commercial binders are pleased to explain their operations and give customers and new library employees tours of their plant.

At present, the source of many conservation and preservation problems is acidic wood pulp paper. William J. Barrow is the person most often associated with identifying acid as the cause of the deterioration of wood pulp paper. The problem is not new, but people are now seeing the full implications of the findings of Barrow and other researchers. Estimates vary as to just how big the problem is. One project estimated that there were more than 600,000 brittle or moderately brittle books in a collection of 2 million books in the UCLA library system in 1979. (A *brittle book* is one in which a corner of a page breaks off when folded back and forth two or fewer times.) The estimate was based on a random sample of books in the collection. An estimated 1 million volumes in Widener Library (Harvard University) are in similar condition.[10] In the early 1980s, the Library of Congress estimated that it had 6 million brittle volumes.[11] According to Richard Dougherty, the Commission on Preservation and Access estimated that "more than 25 percent of the world's greatest monographic collections are already embrittled beyond redemption."[12] The problem grows with each passing day and nothing is done to stop the process. Unfortunately, few libraries have sufficient funding to do more than address a small percentage of the items needing attention.

Deanna Marcum published a short article in the *New York Times* in 1998 about the ever-growing problem of preservation. She outlined the stark facts and made a strong case that technology may be a greater problem than acidic paper. In the article, she noted that the U.S. National Archivist had advised government agencies that they "could delete certain computer files *if they kept paper copies*" (emphasis added).[13] She also noted that the acidic paper issue was still a problem.

In the case of brittle books, short fibers and chemical residues from the paper manufacturing process are the culprits. The longer the fibers in the paper, the stronger it is. When ground wood pulp became the standard source for paper manufacturing, the long-term strength of paper dropped sharply. A weak paper combined with the acidic residue from sizing and bleaching, as well as lignin (a component of the wood used for paper), creates self-destructing material. At one end of the scale is newsprint, which is very acidic; at the other end is the nonacidic paper that more and more publishers are using in books. The Council on Library Resources' efforts to establish some guidelines for publishers, manufacturers, and librarians regarding the use of alkaline paper in book production are paying off. The CLR report stated that "alkaline paper *need not be more expensive* than acidic paper of the quality normally used in hardbound books."[14]

The guidelines provide standards for both performance (acid content) and durability (folding and bending), as well as long-term book binding for the initial commercial binding. Though the guidelines will reduce future problems, they cannot help the present situation. Each year, the number of brittle items already in the collection increases. What can be done about materials that are self-destructing in the stacks? Maintaining environmental factors (temperature, humidity, and light) at the recommended levels slows the chemical processes; thus, this is a first step to take. For the already-brittle materials in the collection, the two concerns are permanence (shelf life) and durability (use). Permanence is the first issue, and there are several ways to stop the acidic activity. After the acidic action is under control, several options exist to enhance durability.

Several mass deacidification systems on the market are designed to process large numbers of books at one time. The only one with a reasonably long history of use is the Wei T'o process developed by Richard Smith. Probably the second best known system is the DEZ system. Developed with the support of the Library of Congress, the process received widespread press coverage after it encountered several problems, the most notable being an explosion at the test site.[15] A good review of the history of deacidification systems is found in Michèle V. Cloonan's "Mass Deacidification in the 1990s."[16]

Options for Handling Brittle Materials

Given the magnitude of the acid paper problem, almost every library will be faced with a variety of decisions on what to do. Here, if nowhere else, collection development staff must enter the preservation picture. When an item in the collection deteriorates to the point that it cannot be rebound, what should one do? Ten options exist:

- Ignore the problem and return the item to storage.
- Withdraw the item from the collection and do not replace it.
- Seek a reprint edition on alkaline paper.
- Convert the material to microfilm and decide what to do with the original.
- Convert the material to an electronic format.
- Photocopy the material on alkaline paper and decide what to do with the original.
- Seek a replacement copy through the out-of-print trade.
- Place it in an alkaline protective enclosure made for the item and return it to the collection.
- Withdraw the item from the main collection and place in a controlled access storage facility.
- Deacidify and strengthen the item and return it to use.

Ignoring the problem is the most reasonable alternative for materials about which one is confident that long-term retention is unnecessary or undesirable and only a limited amount of use is probable. If there is little or no probability of use in the near future, withdrawing the item is probably the most effective option.

Seeking a reprint edition printed on alkaline paper is the least expensive option for materials that are worth long-term storage and probably will experience moderate to heavy use. Reprints are not available for all the items that are self-destructing; only the high-demand titles are reprinted. Several companies exist to serve the reprint market, for example, AMS, Scholarly Reprints, Kraus, Harvester Press Microform Publications, and Research Publications. *Guide to Reprints* (Guide to Reprints, Inc.), *Books on Demand* (University Microfilms), and *Guide to Microforms in Print* (Microform Review) are three sources of information about a broad range of titles. (*Note:* Just because an item is a reprint does not mean that it is printed on alkaline paper. Be certain to specify alkaline paper when ordering.)

Microformat and electronic storage of the brittle material are other options. Until the mid-1980s, microfilming was the most common way of storing the content of brittle materials in a secondary format. The cost of making the master negative is high, but once made, duplicate copies are relatively inexpensive to produce. Thus, if the primary collection development concern is with preserving the intellectual content of the brittle material and not with the item as an artifact, a microformat is a good solution. It may be possible to locate a master copy of an item, thereby reducing costs. Two places to check are the *National Register of Microforms Masters* (Library of Congress) and *Guide to Microforms in Print* (Meckler). The *Register* covers more than 3,000 library and publisher holdings worldwide and is produced by the Library of Congress. *Guide to Microforms in Print* is similar to *BIP*; it lists titles from commercial publishers around the world.

The Directory of Library Reprographic Services (Meckler) can be of assistance in identifying libraries with the capability of making a master. The

Library of Congress has the most experience in working with analog video-disc technology as a preservation format. The advantages of the technology are high-density storage (54,000 graphic images stored on one disc) and random access to those images. In contrast, optical discs are used to store print material. A disc can hold about 3,000 pages of text or 200,000 catalog cards. Both technologies have potential for assisting in solving preservation problems. As one might expect, there is a relatively high cost associated with these systems, but as more organizations use optical or analog disc technology, it is reasonable to expect the cost to decline. However, it is now clear that digitization does not necessarily translate into long-term preservation.

Some publishers (and even the Copyright Office) have questions about the legality of converting copyrighted material to a disc format. How this differs in principle from microfilming, which no one seems to question, is unclear. Under U.S. copyright law (§ 108(e)), it is legal for a library to make a single complete copy of an out-of-print item after making a reasonable search for the item.

A photocopy of the original may be the best option when the library anticipates moderate use and cannot locate a reprint. There are commercial firms that will produce a bound photocopy on alkaline paper from an individual volume on demand. This is an especially good alternative when it is not necessary to preserve the original item. Photocopying and microfilming cause physical wear on bound materials, and a bound item may have to be taken apart to be duplicated properly. Generally, in the photocopy process, there is some loss in image quality; obviously, this may not be acceptable for items with high-quality photographs and illustrations. Several paper manufacturers (for example, Hollinger, Process Materials, and Xerox) offer buffered (alkaline) paper for use in photocopy machines. When binding the photocopies, it is necessary to specify that the binder use buffered materials. If alkaline paper or deacidified paper comes into contact with acidic material, the acid will migrate into the alkaline paper and start the process all over again.

The staff should think carefully before going to the out-of-print market for replacement copies. Although a replacement copy may be available at the lowest price of any of the options, will the replacement be in any better condition than the one it is to replace? Unless the replacement copy had better storage conditions than the library's copy, both will be in about the same state of deterioration. It is probable that the replacement copy will be less worn (as long as it is not an ex-library copy), but there will be little difference in the acidic state. Normally, the replacement copy's storage history is worse than the library's copy, and thus the replacement copy will be in greater need of preservation. Locating a replacement copy in the out-of-print market will take months or even years. During the search, the library must decide what to do with the item in hand. If it is brittle, should customers continue to use it while the library is waiting for a replacement copy that may or may not exist? Additional use may make it difficult, or perhaps impossible, to exercise other options, if the library fails to find a replacement. Although the out-of-print market is a frequent first choice, it is probably the least suitable for long-term preservation purposes.

Protective enclosures or containers provide a stopgap treatment. Enclosing the brittle item in an alkaline container (made of paper, plastic, or cardboard) protects it from unnecessary handling and light. This is a common method of storage for the original (hopefully deacidified) item when a surrogate copy is available for general use. The most common approach is to make custom-sized phase boxes for the item using alkaline cardboard. Bindery/archival supply firms and commercial binderies offer a wide range of prefabricated standard-sized phase boxes, as well as materials for constructing custom-sized boxes. Unfortunately, the materials, including alkaline mending tapes and adhesives, are expensive. To save a small amount of money, some libraries decide not to use the proper materials. Certainly, there is no need to use expensive mending materials on items that the library is likely to discard in time, but, all too often, librarians do not know which items will be kept and which will be discarded.

Secondary storage is a stopgap measure in most cases. It may become the most common first option when the quantity of brittle materials escalates beyond the library's ability to handle it. A controlled environment with limited handling would slow the destructive process and buy some time to determine which of the more permanent solutions to implement. The essential element is controlling the storage environment; merely placing the materials in a remote storage area with the same or worse climate control accomplishes little and may cause further deterioration. Another danger of remote storage is that the adage "out of sight, out of mind" frequently applies. Without a preservation officer or someone on the staff charged with supervising preservation activities, the storage area can become a dumping ground for materials that no one wants to think about. Even in a controlled environment, the disintegration continues day and night until something is done to stop it.

The following are some basic guidelines for preparing materials for storage:

1. Remove extraneous materials, such as paper clips, rubber bands, wrapping material, old folders, and any other material that is not pertinent. If foreign matter, such as pressed flowers, must be saved as documentary evidence, place it in a separate enclosure.

2. Unfold and flatten papers wherever possible without causing damage to the folds. If the paper is brittle or inflexible, it may have to be humidified before unfolding. Remove surface soil with a soft brush.

3. Isolate newsprint because it is highly acidic and will stain adjacent paper. Newspaper clippings can be replaced with photocopies on alkaline paper or placed in a separate envelope. Fax copies are similarly unstable and should be reproduced or isolated, unless they are plain-paper faxes.

4. Note any badly damaged items; place them within individual folders and set them aside for professional conservation treatment. Do not undertake any first aid unless you have received training and are qualified to do so.

5. If it is necessary to place identifying information on the object itself, use a soft (no. 2) pencil and write on the verso or in the lower right margin. Repeat the identification on the storage folders and envelopes in pencil or typing. Never use ballpoint or felt-tip pens that might stain or bleed.

6. Identify boxes with labels that contain adequate information about the contents. This curtails unnecessary browsing and rifling through documents.[17]

If materials should be humidified (see step 2), consult Mary Lynn Ritzenthaler's *Preserving Archives and Manuscripts.*[18]

Restoration is expensive, and libraries will never be able to restore all or even most of the brittle items they own. As noted earlier, the deacidification process is also expensive, and added to that are costs of restoring strength to the individual pages and binding. For a good description of the advantages and disadvantages of the various methods of preservation, see Robert Mareck's "Practicum on Preservation Selection."[19]

To end this section on an upbeat note, in 1996 the Library of Congress (LC) began a major program to deacidify books in its collection. Prior to 1996 LC had had a series of evaluation programs, one of which led to the destruction of its test facility in 1986. Between 1996 and 1998, more than 100,000 books had gone through the process, and Congress authorized a contract through October 2001 that will involve another 275,000 volumes.[20] For additional information about the program, check <http://cweb.loc.gov/perserv/>.

Nonpaper Preservation Issues

Although this chapter emphasizes books and paper, other library materials also require conservation and preservation. In many cases, librarians, as well as technicians, do not fully understand how long a format may last without loss of information, or what problems may arise. However, various groups, such as the Council on Library Resources (CLR), the Mellon Foundation, and the National Endowment for the Humanities, are actively exploring the issue.

Like paper products, all photographic products (microfilm, photographs, motion picture films) are self-destructing on the shelves and in the cabinets of libraries and archives. There was some hope that electronic technologies would prove a more stable storage medium for older materials, but little testing has been done on their longevity. Already we know that there are serious concerns about the long-term value of digitization of print materials. The Library of Congress is using analog videodiscs to store images from old glass lantern slides, photographs, motion picture publicity stills, and architectural drawings.

Current estimates are that CD-ROMs will have a 30-year life. This may not be a major problem, because one can restore digital information. However, no one can predict what it will cost to periodically check the data and restore it as necessary. One major question is who will be responsible and have the necessary funding to carry out the work.

A 1998 article in *U.S. News & World Report* had a title that sums up current concerns about electronic data: "Whoops, There Goes Another CD-ROM."[21] The author of the article described the frustration of NASA's Jet Propulsion Laboratory scientists when, in 1996, they tried to read magnetic data from the 1976 Viking Mars mission. What they found was that 10 to 20 percent of the data was missing—this in spite of the fact that the laboratory had tried to maintain the tapes according to "standard guidelines."

Anyone who has been a computer user for more than a few years knows something of the problem. Just try opening a word processing document that was created two or more versions before the current version, one that had not been opened in later versions. Even when one does open all the old documents in the newer version, one usually sees a warning message about the danger of possible loss of formatting and other information. Though the loss due to the migration from one version to the next may be small, the cumulative loss over 10 or more versions could be significant. Given the speed with which software and hardware companies "improve" their products, it does not require too many years to reach potentially troubling losses.

Gerd Meissner wrote an article for the *New York Times* about problems in preserving data in the German Federal Archives.[22] In that piece he touched on many of the problems. "While shellac records or damaged microfilms can still be put to use today, one faulty data bit on a 10-year-old magnetic tape or a scratched optical disk often renders the rest of the stored information useless." Tracking down documentation, even from the company that produced the software or hardware, for old versions is difficult and sometimes impossible.

One of this book's authors had first-hand experience with the problem of digitized data and "long-term" preservation. LMU's campus has been growing in size over the last 20 years. The university acquired 20 acres of vacant land adjacent to the campus. Environmental impact reports are now part of any development plan. During part of the assessment, it was determined that there were at least two archeological sites within the boundaries of the projected campus expansion. Thus, in 1984 archeological field work was undertaken to assess the scope, character, and significance of the sites. More than five tons of material were carefully mapped, collected, and recorded. Each item had a unique (accession) number that would, in conjunction with the field notes, place the object vertically and horizontally in relation to all the other objects, as well as the surrounding matrix. The firm doing the work used an aging Tandy computer to generate the paper report (one copy) and "stored" the floppy disks.

Lacking an anthropology or archeology department, the paper copy of the report was handed over to various people in the university's facilities planning unit. In 1996, Dr. Evans was asked to develop a plan for handling the tons of material stored in the facilities and maintenance warehouse. Upon reading the narrative report, it became clear that there should be at least one more paper document—the list of accession numbers and the provenance data. Without that data, the five tons of cultural material were really just so much junk, from a research point of view. No one knew, or even remembered, a second volume being part of the file. A call to the archeological firm confirmed that there should be a very large second, or perhaps three or four, volume(s). The call also confirmed that the only other source was the old Tandy floppies, and they had no idea of where one could find a Tandy machine capable of reading the files. When Dr. Evans and some members of the local Native American community suggested, in light of the problem, that the material be reburied, the archeological firm began what turned out to be a 28-month effort to find a way to retrieve the data. We have no idea how much it cost the firm to recover the data, but in November 1998 they delivered four large volumes with the information. (Today, all the original volumes are in the LMU library's Archives and Special Collections department.)

The NASA Jet Propulsion Laboratory, the German Federal Archives, and LMU cases are just a sample of the problems that can arise with electronic data, and serve as cautionary examples of the dangers in committing to digitization as *the* preservation solution. We have doubts about the effectiveness of digitization—"long-term" in the preceding cases was less than 25 years. We agree with Roy Tennant's assessment: "Digital libraries are sitting on a time bomb. Yes, libraries are already familiar with deteriorating materials, but digital libraries face an even graver threat."[23]

Librarians do have some recommended guidelines for checking some of these special formats. Staff should inspect and rewind motion picture film once every three years, inspect and rewind videotapes and audiotapes every two years, and inspect still photographs every three years. Peter Graham's paper dealing with electronic preservation is an excellent source of information about the issues related to preserving intellectual content in an electronic environment.[24] The Commission on Preservation and Access published a mission and goals statement for digital consortia that should help resolve some of the unanswered questions about digitized data and long-term retention. The goals are:

1. Verify and monitor the usefulness of digital imagery for preservation and access.
    a. Establish the convertibility of preservation media.
    b. Foster projects to capture special types of documents.
    c. Insure the longevity of digitized images.
    d. Cultivate research on the application of intelligent character recognition.
2. Define and promote shared methods and standards.
    a. Sponsor forums to define production quality standards.
    b. Promote the development and use of the document structure file.
    c. Create appropriate bibliographic control standards.
    d. Address copyright issues.
    e. Organize a document interchange project.
3. Enlarge the base of materials.
    a. Encourage the involvement of service bureaus.
    b. Focus on the conversion of thematically related materials.
    c. Mount a large inter-institutional collaborative project.
4. Develop and maintain reliable and affordable mechanisms to gain access to digital image documents.
    a. Involve a broad base of constituents in technology development.
    b. Forge effective support structures for end users.
    c. Determine the efficacy of access to digital materials in the context of traditional library collections.[25]

These goals are very similar to those for the paper preservation efforts that started almost 10 years ago. If these goals are as successful as the earlier ones, there is reason to think that the profession will resolve the digital preservation problems in time to save at least many valuable materials.

Cooperation

Because of the magnitude of the problems confronting libraries and scholars, it seems clear that cooperative preservation is essential. In the mid-1980s, under the leadership of CRL, the profession created the Commission on Preservation and Access. Two groups, ARL and RLG, have been collecting statistics on research library preservation activities and developing guidelines. The National Endowment for the Humanities has provided funding for microfilming projects. A program for educating preservation librarians was started at the Columbia University Library School; after that school closed, the preservation program was transferred to the University of Texas Library School. Many large libraries are hiring full-time preservation specialists. Two newsletters that allow one to keep up to date on conservation matters are *The Abbey Newsletter* (7105 Geneva Drive, Austin TX 78723) and *CAN: Conservation Administration News* (Graduate School of Library and Information Science, University of Texas, Austin, TX 78712). The American Institute for Conservation of Historic and Artistic Works (AIC) provides a forum for concerned individuals to discuss preservation and conservation issues. Naturally, ALA and many of its divisions have an active interest in this area, as do most other library associations around the world. One online source of information is Conservation OnLine (CoOL). We list some additional Websites at the end of this chapter.

In addition to national efforts, several regional preservation cooperatives exist. One such group project is the University Center of Georgia. This group started by educating staff members and raising awareness of preservation issues and concerns and what to do to help reduce the problems. The group's operating premises reflect the message this chapter attempts to convey:

> There are some areas in preservation that do not require a team of experts. Self-reliance should be developed in these areas. One area in which this could be done is basic housekeeping.
>
> Prevention is more cost-effective than treatment. Prevention will be stressed as a priority. (For example, preservation thinking will be built into the collection building process.)
>
> Preservation is an ongoing activity that is part of normal work flow. Awareness of this, and a sense of individual responsibility, will be fostered. (Again, this emphasizes the basic activities each staff [member] can perform that will help protect the collections.)
>
> Library and archival collections represent an investment that preservation can protect. (Preservation is an essential function, like cataloging or acquisitions, and should be funded as such.)
>
> Low-cost preservation activities are possible and desirable, but no-cost preservation is unrealistic.[26]

Another example of a regional cooperative is MAPS (MicrogrAphic Preservation Service), a service established by Columbia, Cornell, and Princeton, the New York Public Library, and the New York State Library.

> MAPS' focus is to assist libraries, archives, museums, and historical societies prepare their preservation microfilm for the digital present and future. ... To simply reformat endangered materials into a form resistant to scanning or one that complicates scanning is a serious disservice to scholars and researchers of the future.[27]

Efforts like these will help solve future preservation problems. All library professionals should do their part to avoid adding to these problems.

Insurance

Careful planning, proper handling, and the other elements discussed in this chapter will help prolong the useful life of collections. A good disaster preparedness plan will help reduce the scope of loss when disaster strikes. Because the odds are rather high that a disaster will strike eventually, where will the library get the funds to replace the materials damaged beyond salvaging? In fact, where will the library get the funds to salvage what it can? The obvious answer is some type of insurance. The section on developing a disaster preparedness plan suggests that one early contact for the planning team should be the institution's risk manager. This is the person who monitors safety conditions in the workplace and oversees the insurance programs that cover various loss situations, from fires to slippery floors to actions of the institutional officers. The risk manager for LMU visits the library once a year to discuss any new or outstanding problems, as well as to review the values assigned to the collections, equipment, and building.

The LMU risk manager and library staff have discussed and clarified the fact that there will be insurance coverage for salvage operations, after the institution's deductible limit is surpassed. Discussions regarding the collection valuation have been interesting, especially when it comes to what to do about coverage for special collections and archives materials. If a Shakespeare folio is stolen or destroyed by fire, it is highly unlikely that the library could ever replace it, even if the library insured each folio for several million dollars. The risk manager sees no point in paying an extra premium for something that cannot be replaced. That moved the discussion to facsimile works and the appropriateness of replacing an original with a top-of-the-line facsimile. To date, this is a topic of ongoing debate. Anyone who has dealt with homeowners' or renters' insurance representatives and policies can understand the complexities involved. Does the collection valuation increase or decrease over time? What does *replacement* mean? Will there be funds to process the material, or merely to acquire it? What damage is covered? In 1989, 12 ranges of shelving containing 20,000 volumes collapsed at the Columbia University library annex. Many, if not most, of the volumes were brittle, so the fall was very damaging. However, the embrittlement was a pre-existing condition. After some long negotiations, the insurer agreed to pay for volumes with damage to the cover or text block attachments, but not for volumes with broken pages. There were questions about serial runs as well; this was finally resolved with the insurer paying for the entire run of backfiles, if more than one-third of the run was damaged.[28]

A relatively recent and major disaster took place in late July 1997 at Colorado State University. After an unusually heavy rainstorm, major flooding occurred on the campus, with much of the water damming up against the wall of the lower level of the library. The wall collapsed as result of the water pressure and a huge wave of water poured into the building. All of the materials on the lower level became water-soaked; more than 500,000 items, with an estimated value of more than $100 million.[29] Recovery was still under way in 1999. Although insurance helped cover some of the costs, the final recovery was being assisted by donations of materials from libraries and publishers.[30]

Working out reasonable arrangements in advance, such as who pays for salvage work, will reduce the pressure on everyone during a disaster. One cannot anticipate everything, but some issues are bound to arise, and, to the extent one can deal with those concerns ahead of time, there will be fewer distractions during recovery operations. Another element that bears predisaster discussion is how to value the collection. One common way is to use averages, such as one finds in *The Bowker Annual*, and multiply that figure by the number of units held. The problem with that approach, as was noted in an unsigned comment on the collection development listserv, is that local circumstances also determine the value of an item; "a single volume of *JAMA* from 1952 is probably worth $2.00, but as part of a set that is missing from 1952, it's worth $500!"[31]

For a good discussion about replacement, actual cash value, average replacement cost, valuable papers, and records coverage, as well as other basic insurance topics and libraries, see Judith Fortson's "Disaster Planning: Managing the Financial Risk."[32] Having insurance is a sound practice, because almost every library at some time will have a disaster of some type and size. Having insurance is one more step in protecting the library's and institution's investment.

Summary

This chapter highlights the many aspects of protecting the collections on which libraries and information centers expend large sums of money. Many of the issues raised are ones that virtually any library staff member can implement without major changes in duties or in training. Preparing for trouble always makes it easier to handle the trouble when, or if, it happens. Knowing what type of financial help one can expect to assist in recovering from a disaster can provide some peace of mind, if nothing else. Long-term preservation, though the primary responsibility of the large libraries, is also a concern, or should be, of all libraries and information centers. Working together, we will solve preservation problems, even if it takes a long time and great effort.

Notes

1. Joseph Settanni, "Conservation, Preservation, Restoration: Terminology Should Assist Clarity," *Archival Products News* 6 (Spring 1998): 1–2, 4–7.

2. Ibid., 1.

3. Ibid., 2.

4. Ibid., 4.

5. G. Edward Evans, Anthony Amodeo, and Thomas Carter, *Introduction to Library Public Services*, 5th ed. (Englewood, Colo.: Libraries Unlimited, 1992).

6. Susan Allen, "The Blumberg Case: A Costly Lesson for Librarians," *AB Bookman's Weekly* 88 (September 2, 1991): 769–73; "Rare Document Thief Sentenced," *Library Journal* 123 (June 1, 1998): 20.

7. Terri L. Pederson, "Theft and Mutilation of Library Materials," *College & Research Libraries* 51 (March 1990): 120–28.

8. *Library Hotline* (May 12, 1986): 2.

9. Paul A. Parisi, "An Overview of Library Binding: Where We Are, How We Got Here, What We Do," *New Library Scene* 12 (February 1993): 5–9.

10. *Harvard Crimson* (October 23, 1986): 1.

11. *Book Longevity* (Washington, D.C.: Council on Library Resources, 1982).

12. Richard Dougherty, "Redefining Preservation and Reconceptualizing Information Service," *Library Issues* 13 (November 1992): 1.

13. Deanna Marcum, "We Can't Save Everything," *New York Times,* Op-Ed section, July 6, 1998, at 11.

14. *Book Longevity*, 9.

15. "LC's Mass Deacidification Facility Destroyed," *Wilson Library Bulletin* 60 (May 1986): 8–9.

16. Michèle V. Cloonan, "Mass Deacidification in the 1990s," *Rare Books and Manuscripts Librarianship* 5, no. 2 (1990): 95-103.

17. *Gaylord Preservation Pathfinder No. 2, Archival Storage of Paper* (Syracuse, N.Y.: Gaylord Brothers, 1993), 5.

18. Mary Lynn Ritzenthaler, *Preserving Archives and Manuscripts* (Chicago: Society of American Archivists, 1993).

19. Robert Mareck, "Practicum on Preservation Selection," in *Collection Management for the 1990s*, edited by J. J. Brain (Chicago: American Library Association, 1993), 114–26.

20. Kenneth Harris, "Library of Congress Mass Deacidification Program," *New Library Scene* 17 (September 1998): 8–9.

21. Laura Tangley, "Whoops, There Goes Another CD-ROM," *U.S. News & World Report* (February 16, 1998): 67–68.

22. Gerd Meissner, "Unlocking the Secrets of the Digital Archive Left by East Germany," *New York Times*, March 15, 1999, at D5.

23. Roy Tennant, "Time Is Not on Our Side: The Challenge of Preserving Digital Materials," *Library Journal* 124 (March 15, 1999): 30–31.

24. Peter Graham, *Intellectual Preservation: Electronic Preservation of the Third Kind* (Washington, D.C.: Commission on Preservation and Access, 1994).

25. *Digital Preservation Consortium: Mission and Goals* (Washington, D.C.: Commission on Preservation and Access, 1994).

26.   Laurel Bowen and Nan McMurry, "How Firm a Foundation: Getting Cooperative Preservation Off the Ground," *Collection Building* 13, no. 4 (1993): 28.

27.   "MAPS—Preservation for the Future," *PAC-News* 45 (June 1993): 2.

28.   Janet Gertz, "Columbia Libraries Annex Disaster," *Archival Products News* 1 (Summer 1992): 2.

29.   Leonard Kniffel, "Flood Toll at Colorado State Could Reach $100 Million," *American Libraries* 28 (September 1997): 16.

30.   Thomas Delaney, "The Day It Rained in Fort Collins, Colorado," *Journal of Interlibrary Loan, Document Delivery and Information Supply* 8, no. 4 (1998): 59–70.

31.   "Number 570—Collection Valuation (Summary of Responses)," COLLD-LUSCVM, August 8, 1994 [listserv].

32.   Judith Fortson, "Disaster Planning: Managing the Financial Risk," *Bottom Line* 6 (Spring 1992): 26–33.

Selected Websites*

Conservation OnLine.
    <http://www.palimpsest.stanford.edu>.

Conserve O Grams.
    <http://www.cr.nps.gov/csd/publications>.

Digital Library Federation.
    <http://www.clir.org/diglib/d/homepage.htm>.

Preservation and Access International Newsletter.
    <http://www.clir.org/pubs/pain/pain.html>.

Preserving Access to Digital Information.
    <http://www.nla.gov.au/dnc/tf2001/padi> *and*
    <http://www.nla.gov.au/nica/digital/princ.html>.

RLG DigiNews.
    <http://www.rlg.org/preserv/diginews>.

Strategic Policy Framework for Creating and Preserving Digital Collections.
    <http://ahds.ac.uk/manage/framework.htm>.

*These sites were accessed 14 October 1999.

Further Reading

Conservation

Baird, B. J. "Brittle: Replacing Embrittled Titles Cooperatively." *College & Research Libraries News* 58 (February 1997): 83–84+.

Bansa, H. "New Media: Means for Better Preservation or Special Preservation Problem?" *Restaurator* 12, no. 4 (1991): 219–32.

Brittle Books: Reports of the Committee on Preservation and Access. Washington, D.C.: Council on Library Resources, 1986.

Child, M. *Directory of Information Sources on Scientific Research Related to the Preservation of Sound Recordings, Still and Moving Images and Magnetic Tape.* Washington, D.C.: Commission on Preservation and Access, 1993.

———. "Preservation Issues for Collection Development Staff." *Wilson Library Bulletin* 67 (November 1992): 20–21.

Clark, L., ed. *Guide to Review Library Collections: Preservation, Storage and Withdrawal*. Chicago: American Library Association, 1991.

Cloonan, M. V. "Preservation of Knowledge." *Library Trends* 41 (Spring 1993): 594–605.

Demas, S. G. "What Will Collection Development Do?" *Collection Management* 22, nos. 3/4 (1998): 151–59.

Dvoriashina, Z. P. "Biodamage to Book Collections in the USSR: Some Aspects of Organization of Insect Control." *Restaurator* 8, no. 4 (1987): 182–88.

Eden, P., J. Feather, and L. Graham. "Preservation Policies and Conservation in British Academic Libraries." *British Journal of Academic Librarianship* 8, no. 2 (1993): 65–88.

Fortson, J. *Disaster Planning and Recovery*. New York: Neal-Schuman, 1992.

Fox, L. L. *A Core Collection in Preservation*. Chicago: American Library Association, 1988.

Gertz, J. E., C. B. Brown, and J. Beebe. "Preservation Analysis and the Brittle Book Problem." *College & Research Libraries* 54 (May 1993): 227–39.

Graham, P. S. "Long-Term Intellectual Preservation." *Collection Management* 22, nos. 3/4 (1998): 81–98.

Henderson, K. L., and W. T. Henderson. *Conserving and Preserving Materials in Nonbook Formats*. Urbana, Ill.: University of Illinois, Graduate School of Library and Information Science, 1991.

Higginbotham, B. B., and M. E. Jackson, eds. *Advances in Preservation and Access*. Greenwich, Conn.: Meckler, 1992.

Kenny, A. R., and P. Conway. "From Analog to Digital: Extending the Preservation Tool Kit." *Collection Management* 22, nos. 3/4 (1998): 65–79.

Kueppers, B., and C. Coleman. "Preservation of Performing Arts Materials in Los Angeles." *Conservation Administration News* 54 (July 1993): 12–13.

Lienardy, A. "Evaluation of Seven Mass Deacidification Treatments." *Restaurator* 15, no. 1 (1994): 1–25.

Lowry, M. D. "Preservation and Conservation in the Small Library." *Public Library Quarterly* 11, no. 3 (1991): 58–60.

Lynn, M. S. "Digital Preservation and Access." *Collection Management* 22, nos. 3/4 (1998): 55–63.

Manns, B. "The Electronic Document Format." In *Preservation of Electronic Formats and Electronic Formats for Preservation*. Edited by J. Mohlhenrich, 63–81. New York: Highsmith Press, 1993.

Matthews, G. "Surveying Collections: The Importance of Condition Assessment for Preservation Management." *Journal of Librarianship* 27 (December 1995): 227–36.

McCabe, C. "Photographic Preservation." *Restaurator* 12, no. 4 (1991): 185–200.

Merrill-Oldham, J., and P. Parisi. *Guide to the Library Binding Standard for Library Bindings*. Chicago: American Library Association, 1986.

Mohlhenrich, J., ed. *Preservation of Electronic Formats and Electronic Formats for Preservation*. New York: Highsmith Press, 1993.

Nelson-Strauss, B. "Preservation Policies and Priorities for Record Sound Collections." *Notes* 48 (December 1991): 425–36.

O'Neill, E. T., and W. L. Boomgaarden. "Book Deterioration and Loss." *Library Resources & Technical Services* 39, no.4 (1995): 394–408.

"Preservation Treatment Options for Law Libraries." *Law Library Journal* 84 (Spring 1992): 259–79.

Reilly, B., and J. Porro, eds. *Photograph Preservation and the Research Library*. Stanford, Calif.: Research Library Group, 1991.

Silberman, R. M. "Mandate for Change in the Library Environment." *Library Administration and Management* 7 (Summer 1993): 145–52.

Sitts, M. *A Practical Guide to Preservation in School and Public Libraries*. Syracuse, N.Y.: Information Resources Publications, 1990.

Slide, A. *Nitrate Won't Wait*. New York: McFarland, 1992.

Waters, D. J. "Transforming Libraries Through Digital Preservation." *Collection Management* 22, nos. 3/4 (1998): 99–111.

Disaster Preparedness

Abifarin, A. "Library Stock Security." *Library and Archival Security* 14, no. 1 (1997): 11–19.

Cunha, G. M. "Disaster Planning and a Guide to Recovery Resources." *Library Technology Reports* 28 (September/October 1992): 533–623.

Eden, P., and G. Graham. "Disaster Management in Libraries." *Library Management* 17, no. 3 (1996): 5–12.

Ezennia, S. E. "Flood, Earthquakes, Libraries and Library Materials." *Library and Archival Security* 13, no. 1 (1995): 21–27.

Greene, H. "Build It and They Will Come: Libraries and Disaster Preparedness." *North Carolina Libraries* 52 (Spring 1994): 6–7.

Matthews, G., and P. Eden. "Disaster Management Training in Libraries." *Library Review* 45, no. 1 (1996): 30–8.

Morris, J. *Library Disaster Preparedness Handbook*. Chicago: American Library Association, 1986.

Owens, B. M., and C. Brown-Syed. "Not in Our Stars: University of Windsor Archives and Library Disaster Plan." *Library and Archival Security* 14, no. 2 (1998): 61–66.

Environmental Control

Applebaum, B. *Guide to Environmental Protection of Collections*. Madison, Conn.: Sound View Press, 1991.

Davis, M. "Preservation Using Pesticides: Some Words of Caution." *Wilson Library Bulletin* 59 (February 1985): 386–88.

Dean, S. T., and S. R. Williams. "Renovation for Climate Control." *Conservation Administration News* 56 (January 1994): 12–13.

Foot, M. "Housing Our Collections: Environment and Storage for Libraries and Archives." *IFLA Journal* 22 (1996): 110–14.

Gwin, J. E. "Preservation and Environmental Control Issues." In *Academic Libraries in Urban and Metropolitan Areas.* Edited by G. McCabe, 187–94. Westport, Conn.: Greenwood Press, 1992.

Stranger, C., and L. Brandis. "Insect Pests and Their Eradication." *Australian Library Journal* 41 (August 1992): 180–83.

Swartzburg, S., H. Bussey, and F. Garretson. *Libraries and Archives: Design and Renovation with a Preservation Perspective.* Metuchen, N.J.: Scarecrow Press, 1991.

Thomson, G. *Museum Environment.* 2d ed. Stoneham, Mass.: Butterworths, 1986.

Valentin, N., and F. Preusser. "Insect Control by Inert Gases in Museums, Archives and Libraries." *Restaurator* 11, no. 1 (1990): 22–33.

Weaver-Meyers, P. L., W. A. Stolt, and B. Kowaleski. "Controlling Mold on Library Materials with Chlorine Dioxide." *Journal of Academic Librarianship* 24 (November 1998): 455–58.

Housekeeping

Baird, B. J. "Motivating Student Employees: Examples from Collection Conservation." *Library Resources & Technical Services* 39 (October 1995): 410–16.

Dibble, B. "Conservation in the Stacks." *Idaho Librarian* 42 (January 1990): 7–8.

Promoting Preservation Awareness in Libraries: A Sourcebook for Academic, Public School and Special Libraries. Edited by J. M. Drewes and J. A. Page. Westport, Conn.: Greenwood Press, 1997.

Ristau, H. "Keep Your Shelves in Order." *School Library Journal* 35 (May 1988): 39–43.

Insurance

Berges, C. "Risk Management: The Unrecognized Necessity." *Rural Libraries* 13, no. 1 (1993): 53–66.

Brawner, L. B. "Insurance and Risk Management for Libraries." *Public Library Quarterly* 13, no. 1 (1993): 5–15.

Delong, L. R. "Valuating Library Collections." In *Conference on Acquisitions, Budget, and Collections,* 89–95. St. Louis, Mo.: Genaway & Associates, 1990.

Parsons, J. "Insurance Implications of Crime and Security." In *Security and Crime Prevention in Libraries.* Edited by M. Chaney and A. P. MacDougall, 203–16. New York: Ashgate, 1992.

Ungarelli, D. L. "Are Our Libraries Safe from Losses?" *Library and Archival Security* 10, no. 1 (1990): 55–58.

———. "Insurance and Prevention: Why and How?" *Library Trends* 33 (Summer 1984): 57–67.

Security

Association of College Research Libraries. "Guidelines for the Security of Rare Book, Manuscript, and Other Special Collections." *College & Research Library News* 60 (April 1999): 304–11.

Bahr, A. H. "Electronic Collection Security Systems Today." *Library and Archival Security* 11, no. 1 (1991): 3–22.

———. "The Thief in Our Midst." *Library and Archival Security* 9, nos. 3/4 (1989): 69–74.

Collver, M. "Subsequent Demand for Ripped-off Journal Articles." *Reference Librarian* 28, nos. 27/28 (1989): 347–66.

Dane, W. J. "A Major Challenge to Security." *Art Documentation* 10 (Winter 1997): 179–80.

Harris, C. L. "Preservation Considerations in Electronic Security Systems." *Library and Archival Security* 11, no. 1 (1991): 35–42.

Hulyk, B. R. "Rare and Valuable Documents: Identification, Preservation, and Security Issues." *North Carolina Libraries* 48 (Summer 1990): 118–21.

Lilly, R. S., B. F. Schloman, and W. L. Hu. "Ripoffs Revisited." *Library and Archival Security* 11, no. 1 (1991): 43–70.

McDonald, A. C. "Book Detection Systems." In *Security and Crime Prevention in Libraries*, edited by M. Chaney and A. P. MacDougall, 289–97. New York: Ashgate, 1992.

Newman, J., and C. Wolf. "The Security Audit." *Colorado Libraries* 23 (Spring 1997): 19–21.

Smith, F. E. "Door Checkers: An Unacceptable Security Alternative." *Library and Archival Security* 7 (Spring 1985): 7–13.

Stoker, D. "The Case of the Disappearing Books." *Journal of Librarianship and Information Science* 23 (September 1991): 121–24.

Wall, C. "Inventory: What You Might Expect to Be Missing." *Library and Archival Security* 7 (Summer 1985): 27–31.

Wyly, M. "Special Collections Security." *Library Trends* 36 (Summer 1987): 258–59.

18
Legal Issues

With the passage of the Digital Millennium Copyright Act in October 1998, much has changed for libraries and collection development officers. One issue that, at the time we prepared this chapter, remains unknown is just what the concept of "fair use" will mean in the future. Another legal issue that is becoming ever more important for libraries and collection managers is license agreements.

National laws and regulations influence collection development activities. Two of the topics discussed in this chapter are of concern only to U.S. libraries. However, most of the chapter addresses copyright, lending rights, licensing agreements, and other concepts of interest to libraries around the world. Two additional legal issues relating to U.S. libraries concern Internal Revenue Service (IRS) regulations.

IRS Regulations

We noted in earlier chapters that libraries of all types receive gifts from time to time. Some gifts are useful and occasionally even very valuable; however, much of the time they are of little interest to the library. Nevertheless, the individuals giving the material generally believe that it is very valuable. People often expect, want, and/or request a document from the library indicating the value of their gift.

Valuing Gifts

One of the IRS regulations relevant to libraries has to do with gifts and donations to a library or not-for-profit information center. Any library, or its parent institution, that receives a gift-in-kind (books, journals, manuscripts, and so forth) with an appraised value of $5,000 or more must report the gift to the IRS. A second regulation forbids the receiving party (in this case the library) to provide an estimated value for a gift-in-kind. A third disinterested party or organization must make the valuation. The latter requirement grew out of concern that recipients were placing unrealistically high values on gifts. The donor received a larger tax deduction than was warranted, and it did not cost the receiving organization anything to place a high value on the gift. Normally, an appraiser charges a fee for valuing gifts, and the donor is supposed to pay the fee. Most often, the appraisers are antiquarian dealers who charge a flat fee for the service unless the collection is large or complex. If the appraisal is complex, the appraiser charges either a percentage of the appraised value or an hourly fee.

Typically, with gifts thought to be less than $4,999 in value, the library may write a letter of acknowledgment indicating the number and type of items received. For gifts of less than $250, the IRS does not require a letter. The donor can set a value on the gift for tax purposes. (The best practice is to provide a letter for any accepted gift.) If asked, the library can provide dealer catalogs so that donors can review retail prices for items similar to their donation. However, the final value of the gift is established by the donor and her or his tax accountant. *Note:* The collection development staff should be involved in the acceptance of gifts and must have a sound knowledge of material prices. Just because the gift is small in terms of number of items does not mean that the fair market value is below $5,000. Recently, Loyola Marymount University (LMU) received a gift of 483 books about Japanese art, architecture, and landscape design; its appraised value was $39,743. The donor might well have accepted a letter simply stating the number of books given and thus have lost a substantial tax deduction. (For additional discussion about gifts, see chapter 11.)

To meet IRS requirements, an acknowledgment letter must contain the library's name, the date of the contribution, and the location or place of the gift. At a minimum, that description should state the number and kind of gift (100 mass-market paperbacks, 40 hardcover books, 6 complete and 20 unbound volumes of *National Geographic*).

Publishers' Inventories

Another IRS regulation or ruling (the *Thor Power Tool* decision[1]) had some influence on acquisition practices in the 1980s and early 1990s. The ruling overturned a longstanding practice common in business (including the publishing industry), which was writing down the value of inventories to a low level each year. The practice produced a paper loss that the firm deducted from its income, thus reducing tax liability. The U.S. Supreme Court, deciding that this was taking a current deduction for an estimated future loss, said the practice was inappropriate. Only if the inventory is defective or if there is objective evidence that the firm offered the inventory for sale below cost could it employ the write-down.

What does the *Thor* decision have to do with collection development? Publishers who followed the write-down practice claimed it was the only way they could afford to publish small runs of books expected to sell slowly (four to five years to sell out the first printing). Publishers talked about destroying some of their stock, and some did. In 1981 and 1982, jobbers indicated that they had received increased OP and OS reports from publishers. Blackwell North America stated in a promotional flyer in mid-1981, "[We] are receiving more o.p., o.s. and generally non-reports, than ever before. In fact, our reports to libraries on unavailable titles have increased 47 percent over a year ago."

There was some hope that the U.S. Congress might pass some legislation exempting publishers. What probably helped resolve the concern was the 1987 tax reform act. Though it did not address the question of inventories, the act did reduce corporate tax rates, thus reducing the need to find deductions. Concern has decreased, but publishers appear to declare items out of print more quickly now than before the *Thor* decision. No one is certain whether there has been a decline in short-run titles published or whether such a decline, if it exists, is the result of the *Thor* decision or of a changing economy. The decision does mean that librarians should not count on finding this year's imprints available in a year or two. In the past, a library might well have decided not to buy some current items, thinking that they could be ordered in a year or two, when funding would be better. Today, it is probably best to buy materials now rather than wait.

In 1990, Ambassador Book Service (a book jobber located in New York state), in response to librarian concerns about the increasing problem of OP and OS reports, issued some fact sheets. One sheet, based on data from the online version of *Books in Print* (*BIP*), showed books published, in print and out-of-print for an 11-year period (1979–1989). The table illustrated what everyone knows: the percentage of out-of-print materials increases the farther back in time one goes. However, 81.9 percent of the titles listed in the 1979 *BIP* were available in 1984, and 46.9 percent were available in early 1990. Acquisition or collection development common knowledge was that most books go out of print within four to five years.

Which was right, the vendor's data or librarians' common knowledge? Both are right and wrong. The vendor's data is correct, as far as it goes—that is, items listed in *BIP*. When one considers that libraries acquire a wide range of items not in *BIP*, including small and regional press titles, report literature, scholarly society publications, and so forth, the picture changes. Without doubt, there has been an increase in items going OP. In many cases, the slowing economy and library cutbacks on monographic purchases caused small publishers (private or professional) to reduce press runs. An article by Margaret McKinley, "The *Thor* Inventory Ruling,"[2] provided a good review of the issue. It leaves the reader with the impression that there was and still is some impact of the *Thor* decision, but not nearly as much as librarians believed.

Copyright

Is copyright an issue in collection development? Yes. Cooperative collection development efforts depend on sharing resources through interlibrary loan or other reciprocal borrowing agreements. There are also questions about how many photocopies one can use for course reserve purposes in educational institutions. What about making a copy of an out-of-print work for preservation purposes: how does the copyright law affect these programs? Clearly, libraries have modified copying policies as well as interlibrary loan practices. For example, under the present law, a library in a not-for-profit setting may borrow no more than five articles per year from any given journal. If the library borrows more than five articles, the assumption is that the borrowing is in lieu of placing a subscription and thus is a violation of the law. If libraries may not freely exchange books, periodicals, or photocopies of copyrighted items, it will be difficult to develop effective cooperative systems.

Copyright grants the creators of works certain rights that protect their interest in the work. Originally, copyright's purpose was to provide protection against unauthorized printing, publishing, importing, or selling of multiple copies of a work. In essence, it was protection from the unauthorized mass production and sale of a work. It was a straightforward and seemingly reasonable method of encouraging individuals or businesses to take a financial risk to produce and distribute information. Libraries, in contrast, exist to disseminate information on a mass, usually free, basis. Until photocopiers appeared on the scene, the relationship between copyright holders and libraries was cordial, if not always friendly.

With the development of fast, inexpensive photocopying, problems arose. Though the library might make only a single copy for a customer, the aggregate number of copies could be very high. By the mid-1960s, the volume of copying was so great that copyright holders became convinced that libraries, schools, and individuals were violating their rights—and in some cases they were correct.

In the past, copying printed matter for personal use was no problem. Word-for-word hand-copying of extensive sections of books or complete magazine articles was uncommon—people took notes. Today, quick, inexpensive copy services, as well as the ability to download digitized copyrighted material, exist everywhere. All of us have made photocopies of complete journal articles or printed many pages of Internet material rather than take notes; some of those items were from current issues of periodicals that we could have purchased for not much more than the cost of the copied item. All of us have done it and, if we thought about it at all, we thought that just one copy isn't going to hurt anyone. Unfortunately, as the number of such copies and printing increases, so does the problem.

With audiovisual materials (for example, videotapes and audiotapes), the problem is acute. Institutions and individuals who own the hardware to play these materials also have copying capabilities. Control of copying is even more difficult to achieve for audiovisual materials than for books or journals. Preview copies help control the institutional buying situation, because they tend to show wear to such an extent that many persons would not want to reproduce a copy. If the preview copy shows too much wear, however, the library's buyer may decide not to buy the item because it lacks technical quality.

The public still does have some rights to gain access to and to use copyrighted material. Where to draw the line between creators' and users' rights is a complicated problem, and has become more so with digitization of material and scanning devices. An old but still valid editorial by J. Berry in *Library Journal* summed up the complex issues involved in fair use. Today, the issues are even more complicated than they were when he wrote the editorial.

> Here at *LJ* we are often asked why the magazine has not come out strongly on one side or the other of the copyright issue. We are after all a library magazine. ... In the case of copyright, however, our library-mindedness is somewhat blunted by the facts of our existence as a publication which is in copyright and is published by an

independent, commercial publisher. Not only is copyright protection fundamental to our continued fiscal health, [but] we believe that authors and publishers deserve compensation for their creative work and for the risks taken to package and deliver that creative effort to users of it.

Like any magazine publisher we have winced when it was obvious our rights in our published material have been violated. ... Yet there is the other side, the flattery in the notion that people want to read what we print, and the gratification that so many share our view of its importance.

So the issue of copyright, particularly of library copying, is deeply complicated for us. ... We don't believe that "fair use" should be eliminated, but we can't subscribe to the view that wholesale copying should be allowed for "educational purposes." The answer has to be compromise.[3]

Several points about copyright bear emphasis. First, the problem of how to handle the rights of creators and users is worldwide, in the sense that each country has to deal with both its own copyright problems and international copyright issues. Second, in the past much of the controversy centered on educational and library copying. Today, with computer technology so readily available, the problem has increased far beyond libraries and educational institutions. Third, copyright disputes divide authors, publishers, and producers from libraries, schools, and users, almost destroying what were once friendly working relationships. The relationship has not yet deteriorated to the point of hostility, but unless true compromises emerge, hostility may be the result.

Most librarians agree that creators' rights need and deserve protection and that those rights have occasionally been violated in and by libraries. However, direct daily contact with users and their needs tempers that recognition.

There is no question that some people copy materials for commercial purposes, especially music and video products. However, much of the "improper" usage is a function of not understanding the nature of copyright and what fair usage may be in various circumstances. There are many misconceptions about copyright and we can only touch on a few of them. *Note: None of the following discussion of copyright or licensing should be thought of as legal advice. When in doubt, contact a legal specialist in the field of copyright, intellectual property, or contract law.*

One of the most common misunderstandings of copyright concerns notice of copyright. ("It did not indicate that it was copyrighted, so it must be public domain.") Part of the reason for confusion about the need to have a notice of copyright is because, in the United States, it *was* necessary until April 1, 1989. After that date, the United States joined most of the rest of the world as a signatory to the Berne copyright convention, which grants copyright with or without notice. Thus, the only safe assumption now is that everything is copyrighted, unless one has definite knowledge that it is not covered.

A related technical misconception is that if an item is on Usenet, it is public domain. For anything to be in the public domain, the creator or owner must include a statement putting the material into the public domain.

There is also a common belief that if one does not charge for or gain financially from the usage, there is no violation of copyright. We noted earlier that libraries should also purchase performance rights for the films and videos they purchase, if they are to be used in library programming. Even a free "public performance" during a children's program requires permission, if one did not pay for performance rights. Use in face-to-face instruction has been thought to be "fair use," but even that idea is questioned by many copyright holders. As we mentioned, it is better to acquire performance rights if at all possible.

Fair use is an area full of "yes, you can/no, you can't." Now that the United States has passed the Digital Millennium Copyright Act, the issue of what will and will not deemed fair use is unclear, as of mid-1999. (We explore this concept further later in this chapter.) Older guidelines seem to be under scrutiny and the goal appears to be a further lessening of fair use rights.

Another aspect of the situation seems to be peoples' attitudes. There appears to be a sense that infringing copyright is not really a crime. The attitude is rather like drivers who know that the speed limit is 65 miles per hour but think that it *really is okay to drive* 70 miles per hour. Related to that belief, which is inaccurate, is the notion that copyright holders are greedy and that the cost for permission to use copyrighted material is much too high. Therefore, using the material without permission is reasonable. Legally, it is not okay either to exceed the speed limit or to infringe copyright, even if no one is looking.

Libraries are caught in the middle of these issues. Librarians may agree that prices are high, but they also know that if there was no income and profit for the producers there would be no information. They believe in free access to information, especially for educational purposes, once the library acquires the material or information. Finding the balance, or John Berry compromise, is the challenge. In many ways, the only organized voice for users is library and educational associations.

Historical Background

As noted earlier, producers need encouragement to risk creating something new and making it available. Without adequate incentives, the producer will not produce. For publishers and media producers, copyright is one of the most important incentives. In essence, copyright states: "Person(s) X owns this creation; if you are not person(s) X, before you make copies of this creation for more than your own personal use, you must get written permission from person(s) X."

England was the first country to legalize creative ownership; in 1710, the English Parliament passed the Statute of Anne, the first copyright bill. This law did two things: it gave parliamentary recognition to a royal decree of 1556, and it gave legal recognition of a work's author as the ultimate holder of copyright. Whereas contemporary copyright laws exist to encourage the creation of new, original works and to encourage their wide public distribution, the 1556 decree had a less noble purpose: repression of the freedom of religion—in this case, the Protestant Reformation. Censorship, rather than free public dissemination of information and thought, was the goal. Without question, the Statute of Anne was a notable piece of legislation that did more than merely give legal sanction to censorship. Although by 1710 authors and publishers were allies in the fight to retain or gain more control over the use of their creations, it was an uneasy alliance, because the authors were the true creators of the copyrighted works. As the creators, authors thought they should have a greater share and say in the distribution of their works, and they thought the profits should be more evenly divided. Before 1710, all rights resided with the publisher. With the enactment of the Statute of Anne, authors received a 14-year monopoly on the publication of their works. An additional 14-year monopoly was possible if the author was still living at the end of the first term. Thus, for 28 years, the creator of a work could benefit from its publication.

The British colonies in North America developed a copyright concept based on the English model. Indeed, the concept was so much a part of American legal thought that it became part of the U.S. Constitution, wherein Congress was given the power "to promote the Progress of Science and Useful Arts, by securing for limited Times to Authors and Inventors the exclusive Right to their Respective Writings and Discoveries." Starting in 1790 and ending in 1891, Congress passed legislation granting exclusive rights to American authors and their representatives, but it refused to grant copyright to nonresident foreign authors. In 1831, Congress passed an act extending the copyright term: the new first term was for 28 years, though the second term remained 14 years. Extension of the exclusive rights has been of concern in all countries since the start of the nineteenth century.

By 1870, copyright also covered art prints, musical compositions, photographs, "works of fine arts," translation rights, and the right to dramatize nondramatic works. In 1887, performance rights for plays and musical compositions received coverage. The Chace Act of 1891 finally granted copyright to nonresident foreign authors, if their work was published in English and was printed in the United States.

In 1909, Congress passed a new copyright act that was a matter of extended debate from 1905 to 1909. (Since 1909, each time a revision in copyright law has been put forward, the length of debate time has increased, as has the number of groups wanting to have their voices heard.) Several important issues remained unresolved in 1909, including libraries' rights to import books printed in foreign countries and the use of copyrighted music on mechanical instruments, such as phonograph records and piano rolls. After considerable debate, libraries and musicians received the desired rights. Libraries could import a limited number of copies of a foreign work, and copyright owners were to receive payment for the use of their music in mechanical devices. (The later development of jukeboxes, not covered by the 1909 law, caused another problem. When a new technology, the jukebox, appeared on the scene, there was no legal mechanism for requiring payment to copyright owners for the repeated use of their works in the new devices, which were making substantial profits for jukebox owners.) Composers worried about technological developments in 1909; in the 1970s, authors and publishers worried about technological developments. Today, everyone worries about technology and copyright.

Other provisions of the 1909 law (as passed and amended over the years) included coverage of motion pictures; allowance to the owner of a nondramatic literary work to control public renditions of the work for profit and to control the making of transcriptions or sound recordings of the work; granting of full copyright protection to foreign authors (this was done so the United States could join the Universal Copyright Convention in 1954); coverage of all sound recordings; extension of copyright terms to two terms of 28 years each, with a renewal requirement for the second term; and requirement of a notice of copyright to be displayed on all works. Several of these provisions created barriers for American and foreign producers and made it difficult for the United States to be an effective member of a worldwide copyright program. The three major stumbling blocks have been term of protection, the renewal requirements, and the manufacturing clause (i.e., the requirement that works of foreign authors be printed in the United States in order to be protected).

International Copyright Conventions

At the international level, there have been two important copyright conventions: the Berne Convention (1886) and the Universal Copyright Convention (1952). Until the signing of the Berne Convention in 1886, international copyright was in chaos, with reciprocity only on the basis of bilateral treaties. Some countries, like the United States, made no such agreements. As a result, during the nineteenth century, a new form of piracy appeared: literary piracy. Some countries signed the Berne Convention, with notable exceptions being the United States and Russia. Basically, the signatories agreed to give one another the same copyright protection they provided their own citizens. A 1908 revision required this coverage to be automatic—copyright owners did not have to file any forms to secure coverage. The Internet brought chaos back to copyright, as different countries have very different concepts of fair use (U.S.) or fair dealing (U.K.).

The United States did sign the Universal Copyright Convention (UCC) in 1954. How is it that the United States was able to sign one international convention but not the other? There were two important differences between the conventions. First, the UCC did not provide automatic copyright without formalities. The formalities, however, were that a work carry the copyright symbol (©), the name of the owner, and the date of first publication. That satisfied the U.S. notice requirement and, presumably, made life easier for American librarians. The second difference was that the term of copyright could be whatever term the country granted its citizens at the time of signing; the only minimum was 25 years for all works other than photographs and applied arts. (Photographs and applied arts must have at least 10 years' protection.)

In 1971, modifications to both the Berne Convention and the UCC ensured that developing countries would receive certain licensing rights. The revisions provided a mechanism for forcing a copyright owner to grant use rights to developing countries under certain conditions—in effect, it was compulsory licensing. Most of the signatories to the two conventions approved the revisions by 1990. Certainly, the revisions helped control what was becoming the second era of international piracy of literary and creative works. Nevertheless, some countries are not party to any copyright agreement, nor do the publishers in those countries bother to seek a license; hence, piracy is still alive in the 1990s.

To understand current U.S. copyright law, it is also necessary to look at and understand the international aspects of intellectual property protection.

This is because the 1998 Digital Millennium Copyright Act (DMCA) was in part motivated by the need to conform to new international requirements.

As noted earlier, there were two major international conventions. The Berne Convention members set up an administrative group to handle its activities. That group evolved into today's World Intellectual Property Organization (WIPO), which is also one of the United Nation's specialized agencies. WIPO has 171 member countries and administers 21 treaties. Two of its goals are to "harmonize national intellectual property legislation and procedures," and to "marshal information technology as a tool for storing, accessing, and using valuable intellectual property information."⁴ (*Intellectual property* in the case of WIPO means industrial property, such as inventions, trademarks, and industrial design; and copyright covering such material as literary, musical, artistic, photographic, software [as a literary work] databases, and audiovisual works.)

A WIPO meeting in Geneva in December 1996 led to the approval of two treaties: the WIP Copyright Treaty and the WIPO Performances and Phonograms Treaty. A third proposed treaty, dealing with databases, was held over for later discussion. In part because of the lack of WIPO discussion, the matter of databases was not part of the DMCA either.

Digital Millennium Copyright Act

The purpose of the DMCA was to update existing U.S. copyright law in terms of the digital world, as well as to conform to the 1996 WIPO treaties. Congress also passed a Copyright Term Extension Act in 1998, which added 20 years to the protection term for both individuals and corporate bodies. The old protection terms were life plus 50 years for individuals and 75 years for corporate entities. (There was an exception for libraries, archives, and nonprofit educational institutions during the last 20 years of protection. Essentially, these groups would have greater fair usage during the last 20 years, if the work was not commercially available. One must wonder just how often that will be necessary. How many requests do libraries receive for special fair usage of material that is 70 years old?)

The 1978 copyright law is still in force, but changed dramatically as a result of amendments and the DMCA. The fair use doctrine is given statutory recognition for the first time in the 1978 law. Traditionally, fair use has been a judicially created limitation on the exclusive rights of copyright owners, developed by the courts because the 1909 copyright law made no provision for any copying. In the law, fair use allows copying of a limited amount of material without permission from, or payment to, the copyright owner, when the use is reasonable and not harmful to the rights of the copyright owner (§ 107).

The law extends copyright protection to unpublished works. Instead of the old dual system of protecting works under common law before publication and under federal law after publication, the law establishes a single system of statutory protection for all works, whether published or unpublished (§ 301).

A five-member Copyright Royalty Tribunal exists to review royalty rates and to settle disputes among parties entitled to several specified types of statutory royalties in areas not directly affecting libraries (§ 801).

Every librarian should have some knowledge of all of the following sections of the law. The sections of the law and the content of handbooks on the law can be helpful in developing a collection; however, when questions arise, the best source of information is an attorney who handles copyright cases. What follows *is not* legal advice—merely an outline of the sections and their content:

§§ 102–105 define works protected by copyright.

§ 106 defines the exclusive rights of the copyright owner.

§ 107 establishes the basis of the right of fair use.

§ 108 authorizes certain types of library copying.

§ 108(g) identifies library copying not authorized by the current law.

§ 602(a)(3) relates to the importation of copies by libraries.

Works Protected by Copyright

Copyright protection extends to *literary* (including computer software) works; *dramatic* works; *pantomimes* and *choreographic* works; *pictorial, graphic,* and *sculptural* works; *motion pictures* and other *audiovisual* works; and *sound recordings* (§ 102).

Unpublished works by U.S. and foreign authors receive protection under the copyright statute, as do published works by U.S. authors. The published works of foreign authors are subject to copyright under certain conditions, including coverage under national treaties such as the Universal Copyright Convention (§ 104) and now the WIPO Copyright Treaty.

United States government works are not copyrightable. The law did not change the basic premise that works produced for the U.S. government by its officers and employees are not subject to copyright (§ 105).

Exclusive Rights of Copyright Owners

Section 106 states the exclusive rights of copyright owners. Subject to §§ 107 through 118, the owner of copyright under this title has the exclusive rights to do and to authorize any of the following:

1. To reproduce the copyrighted work in copies or phonorecords.

2. To prepare derivative works based upon the copyrighted work.

3. To distribute copies or phonorecords of the copyrighted work to the public by sale or other transfer of ownership, or by rental, lease, or lending.

4. In the case of literary, musical, dramatic, and choreographic works, pantomimes, and motion pictures and other audiovisual works, to perform the copyrighted work publicly.

5. In the case of literary, musical, dramatic, and choreographic works, pantomimes, and pictorial, graphic, or sculptural works, including the individual images of a motion picture or other audiovisual work, to display the copyrighted work publicly.

It is important to understand the significant limitations on the exclusive rights stated in § 106, which are stated in §§ 107 through 118.

Fair Use

In the last edition of this book we wrote, "Even the most adamant copyright holder advocate acknowledges that at least some kinds of copying are fair and permissible. The problem lies in defining what constitutes fair use."

Although the existing law did recognize fair use, copyright holders have become less and less happy with the concept. Reading statements from representatives of copyright holders over the decade makes one wonder how long "fair use" will exist. For example, in 1992, the Association of American Publishers asserted:

The copyright law provided the copyright holder with the exclusive right to control the making of copies of a copyrighted work. Exceptions to the exclusive right are intended to permit limited, occasional copying for individuals in particular circumstances which will not impair the rights of the copyright holder, nor generate regular business-like activities based upon usurpation of copyright owners' rights, markets, or materials.[5]

Richard Schockmel commented about the AAP statement in a 1996 article on fair use and use fees:

[T]his 1992 AAP statement ... in effect nullifies fair use: Copyright holders have exclusive rights to control all copying and no exceptions are allowed which would impair these rights. It is difficult to imagine any copying made without permission and/or fee which would not impair the exclusive right to control making copies.[6]

Perhaps a more worrisome statement is that of Marybeth Peters, U.S. Register of Copyrights, in a 1998 interview with *Library Journal* staff. She was asked about ALA's concern that proposed changes in the law would mean that fair use would not exist in the twenty-first century. Her response was, "I disagree. What the library community is arguing is that if a copyright owner employs technological protection measures to safeguard his work, they may never be able to get around that protection to exercise their fair use rights. My point is you can't argue fair use to get access to a work."[7] Later in the interview she said, "Fair use is a defense to copyright infringement to the unauthorized exercise of any of the exclusive rights of a copyright owner."[8] We are not clear how exercising the permission given in § 107 for fair use is a defense against infringement, but then we are not lawyers. She went on to say, in relation to what was to become the DMCA, "That is why the act of circumventing a technological protection measure that prevents unauthorized exercise of any of the copyright owners' rights *is not* prohibited. For example, if a librarian obtained legal access to a work."[9]

If all of that seems confusing, it is because the matter is confusing. It is also the reason there are ongoing discussions about the concept. Attempts have been made to help define what really constitutes fair use. After passage of the 1976 law, the Conference on Technological Use (CONTU), drawing on the House Judiciary Committee report, developed some guidelines. Though helpful, neither users nor owners have been pleased with its results as technology evolved. Another effort, in 1994, by the Conference on Fair Use (CONFU), attempted to resolve some of the technological concerns. (Several groups—for example, the American Association of University Professors and Association of American Law Schools—had opposed the existing guidelines as not representing the needs of higher education well.) CONFU negotiators spent two years developing the report they issued in1996.[10] The proposed guidelines generated expressions of concern from a substantial number of educational organizations, unlike the earlier guidelines. Perhaps the most important point to keep in mind is that the fair use guidelines do *not* have the force of law. They are only interpretations of the law and they are not the only possible interpretation. A good article on this issue is Kenneth Crews's "Fair Use and Higher Education: Are Guidelines the Answer?"[11]

Fair use doctrine was codified in general terms in § 107. That section refers to such purposes as criticism, commentary, news reporting, teaching, scholarship, or research, and it specifies four criteria to use in determining whether a particular instance of copying or other reproduction is fair. The statutory criteria in § 107 are:

1. the purpose and character of the use, including whether such use is of a commercial nature or is for nonprofit educational purposes.

2. the nature of the copyrighted work.

3. the amount and substantiality of the portion used in relation to the copyrighted work as a whole.

4. the effect of the use upon the potential market for or value of the copyrighted work.

Depending on the circumstances, fair use might cover making a single copy or multiple copies. For example, multiple copying for classroom use may be considered fair use under certain circumstances. In deciding whether any particular instance of copying is fair use, one must always consider the statutory fair use criteria.

Guidelines for Copying

The 1976 Guidelines developed by educators, publishers, and authors provided some indication of what various parties believe is reasonable fair use. The guidelines are not part of the statute, but they are part of the House Judiciary Committee's report on the copyright bill.[12] They are *Guidelines for Classroom Copying in Not-for-Profit Educational Institutions* and *Guidelines for Educational Uses of Music.* As noted earlier, there is much debate about fair use and use of the guidelines as "safe harbors." However, until there is a clear court decision or Congress clarifies the meaning of fair use, the guidelines are all that users have to go by.

Library Copying Authorized by Section 108

In addition to copying that would fall within the fair use section of the statute, certain types of library copying that may not be considered fair use are authorized by § 108. Section 108 in no way limits the library's fair use right (§ 108(f)(4)).

Section 108(a) contains general conditions and limitations that apply to the authorized copying outlined in the rest of the section. These general conditions apply:

1. The copy is made without any purpose of direct or indirect commercial advantage.

2. The collections of the library are open to the public or available not only to researchers affiliated with the library but also to other persons doing research in a specialized field.

3. The copy includes a notice of copyright.

The House Judiciary Committee's report clarified the status of special libraries in for-profit institutions with respect to the criterion "without direct or indirect commercial advantage" (§ 108(a)(1)). It is the library or archives within the institution that must meet the criteria, not the institution itself.

In addition to the general conditions of § 108(a), it is possible for contractual obligations between a publisher or distributor and a library to limit copying that would otherwise be permissible under § 108. Furthermore, the limited types of copying authorized by § 108 can be augmented by written agreement at the time of purchase (§ 108(f)(4)).

Possible Contractual Limitations on Section 108

Section 108(f)(4) states that the rights of reproduction granted to libraries do not override any contractual obligations assumed by the library when it obtained a work for its collection. In view of this provision, librarians must be especially sensitive to the conditions under which they purchase materials. Before executing an agreement that would limit their rights under the copyright law, they should consult with legal counsel. *This is the key section with regard to licensing agreements.*

Single Copy of Single Article or Small Excerpt

Section 108(d) authorizes the making of a single copy of a single article or a copy of a small part of a copyrighted work in the library's collections, provided that (1) the copy becomes the property of the user; (2) the library has no notice that the use of the copy would be for any purpose other than private study, scholarship, or research; and (3) the library both includes on its order form and displays prominently at the place where users submit copying requests a warning about copyright in accordance with requirements prescribed by the Register of Copyrights.

On November 16, 1977, the *Federal Register* published the new regulation and provided the form for the warning signs that the library must post near all library copy machines (see fig. 18.1).

NOTICE: WARNING CONCERNING COPYRIGHT RESTRICTIONS

The copyright law of the United States (Title 17, United States Code) governs the making of photocopies or other reproductions of copyrighted material.

Under certain conditions specified in the law, libraries and archives are authorized to furnish a photocopy or other reproduction. One of these specified conditions is that the photocopy or reproduction is not to be "used for any purpose other than private study, scholarship, or research." If a user makes a request for, or later uses, a photocopy or reproduction for purposes in excess of "fair use," that user may be liable for copyright infringement.

This institution reserves the right to refuse to accept a copying order if, in its judgment, fulfillment of the order would involve violation of copyright law.

Fig. 18.1. Official text of the required copyright warning sign. From *Federal Register* (November 16, 1977).

The *Federal Register* (February 26, 1991) printed the text for a second warning sign for computer software. The warning is similar to the first warning, but the wording differs (see fig. 18.2).

NOTICE: WARNING CONCERNING COPYRIGHT RESTRICTIONS

The copyright law of the United States (Title 17, United States Code) governs the reproduction, distribution, adaptation, public performance, and public display of copyrighted material.

 Under certain conditions specified in law, nonprofit libraries are authorized to lend, lease or rent copies of computer programs to patrons on a nonprofit basis and for nonprofit purposes. Any person who makes an unauthorized copy or adaptation of the computer program, or redistributes the loan copy, or publicly performs or displays the computer program, except as permitted by Title 17 of the United States Code, may be liable for copyright infringement. This institution reserves the right to refuse to fulfill a loan request if, in its judgment, fulfillment of the request would lead to violation of the copyright law.

Fig. 18.2. Official wording of the required copyright notice for computer software. From *Federal Register* (February 26, 1991).

Copying for Interlibrary Loan

Section 108(d) authorizes the making of a single copy of a single article or a copy of a small part of a copyrighted work for purposes of interlibrary loan, provided that it meets all the conditions previously listed regarding a single copy of a single article from the library's own collections, and further provided (§ 108(g)(2)) that requests for interlibrary loan photocopies are not in such aggregate quantities as to substitute for purchases or subscriptions. The wording of the statute places responsibility for compliance on the library requesting the photocopy, not on the library fulfilling the request. The National Commission on New Technological Uses of Copyrighted Works (CONTU), in consultation with authors, publishers, and librarians, developed guidelines to assist libraries in complying with this provision. A library or archive may receive no more than five photocopies per year of articles published in the restricted issues of a periodical. (They may be five copies of one article or single copies of five different articles.) The restriction applies only to issues published within the last five years. Duplication of older issues is limited only by the broad provisions of § 108(g)(2), which prohibit copying that by its nature would substitute for a subscription. We should note that not all journal publishers agree with those guidelines. Also, in 1997 there was a ruling that has clouded the picture, at least for document delivery services.

UnCover, as of mid-1999, was facing a serious legal ruling in a copyright lawsuit. UnCover provides copies of journal articles as part of a document delivery service. One reason for using such a service for ILL requests is that part of the fee goes to cover royalty charges, based on a negotiated rate between UnCover and the various journal publishers. A San Francisco United States District Court judge issued a summary judgment in favor of the five freelance authors who filed the suit. Daniel Reidy, attorney for the plaintiffs, said, "In essence, the lawsuit's a copyright infringement action because UnCover typically only seeks permission from publishers, without seeking permission from freelance authors. Our position is that unless the authors have either assigned their copyrights or given the publisher express permission to sell individual copies of their articles, UnCover would need to get permission from authors."[13] He also indicated that the law firm was working on developing the case into a class action suit. If successful against UnCover, other document delivery firms might face similar suits; because libraries are also providers of such items, they too might be named in future lawsuits of this type. One wonders why the suit was not filed against the publishers in order to receive a share of the revenue the publishers received from UnCover.

Coin-Operated Copying Machines

Section 108(f)(1) and (2) make it clear that *neither libraries nor library employees* are liable for the unsupervised use of reproducing equipment (this does include microform reader/printers) located on library premises, if the machine displays the required notice (see fig. 17.1). The person making the copy is, of course, subject to liability for copyright infringement, if his or her copying exceeds the provisions of § 107.

Library Copying Not Authorized by Section 108

With the exception of audiovisual news programs, § 108 does not authorize a library to make multiple copies. Two general types of library copying that are not clearly defined in the statute are specifically not authorized by § 108. Stated only in the most general terms, the definitions of these types of library copying are susceptible to many interpretations.

The first is "related or concerted reproduction or distribution of multiple copies." This related or concerted copying by libraries is illegal, whether the library makes the copies all on one occasion or over a period of time, and whether the copies are intended for aggregate use by one individual or for separate use by individual members of a group (§ 108(g)(1)).

The second type of library copying not authorized by § 108 is "systematic reproduction or distribution of single or multiple copies." Because many librarians feared that this term might preclude a wide range of interlibrary lending systems, Congress amended this section of the bill to clarify that whatever may be meant by the term *systematic,* copying for purposes of inter-library loan as specifically authorized by § 108(d) is not illegal under § 108(g)(2) as long as it does not substitute for purchases or subscriptions. The wording of the statute places responsibility for copyright compliance on the library requesting the photocopy, not on the library filling the request (§ 108(g)(2)).

It is important to remember that the copyright law does not establish licensing or royalty payment schemes for library copying. It focuses primarily on the kinds of copying that libraries can do without such schemes. Section 108(g) merely states the two types of library copying that are *not* authorized by § 108.

Importation of Copies by Libraries

In general, the law prohibits the importation of copies of works without the permission of the copyright holder. There are, however, certain exceptions to this general prohibition, one of which directly relates to libraries. Section 602(a)(3) states that a nonprofit scholarly, educational, or religious organization may import no more than one copy of an audiovisual work for archival purposes only, and no more than five copies of any other work "for its library lending or archival purposes, unless the importation of such copies or phonorecords is part of an activity consisting of systematic reproduction or distribution, engaged in by such organization in violation of the provisions of Section 108(g)(2)."

Infringement

A person who violates the rights of the copyright owner is a *copyright infringer*. Remedies available to the copyright holder for infringement include damages (actual or statutory; the latter set by statute at from $100 to $100,000 per infringement), injunction, and recovery of court costs and attorney's fees. There is also criminal infringement (done willfully for commercial advantage or private financial gain), which is subject to a $10,000 fine and/or one year imprisonment per infringement.

There is a waiver of statutory damages for a library or nonprofit educational institution when the institution, or one of its employees acting within the scope of his or her employment, "believed or had reasonable grounds for believing that his or her use of the copyrighted work was a fair use under Sec. 107" (§ 504(c)(2)).

Librarians and media specialists have a professional responsibility to learn about provisions of the copyright law that relate to libraries and to frequently review their practices in light of such provisions. If current practices seem likely to constitute infringement, librarians should plan now for needed changes and make sure that library users understand the reason for such changes. Above all, it is important to take the time and trouble to master the basic provisions of the statute, so the library will fully exercise the rights it has under the copyright law. Anything short of this would be a disservice to library users.

DMCA and Technology Issues

Earlier we noted that the DMCA amended U.S. law to comply with WIPO treaties. It did more than that; it also addressed a great many of the technology aspects of copyright.

One of the education/library community's concerns about the decline of fair use rights related to § 1201. This section prohibits gaining unauthorized access to material by circumventing any technological protection measures a copyright holder may have put in place. The implementation of this section is to begin two years after the legislation became law—about the end of 2000. During this two-year period, the Library of Congress is to conduct a rule-making procedure to determine what, if any, exceptions would be appropriate. LC then must conduct similar proceedings every three years.

Section 1201 is not intended to limit fair use, but fair use is *not* a defense to circumventing technological protection measures. These other elements in the section have limited implication for collection development, at least at the time we wrote this chapter.

Section 1202 prohibits tampering with "Copyright Management Information" (CMI). The DMCA identified the following as constituting copyright management information:

- Information that identifies the copyrighted work, including title of the work, the author, and the copyright owner.

- Information that identifies a performer whose performance is fixed in a work, with certain exceptions.

- In the case of an audiovisual work, information that identifies the writer, performers, or director, with certain exceptions.

- Terms and conditions for use of the work.

- Identifying numbers or symbols that accompany the above information or links to such information; for example, embedded pointers and hypertext links.

- Such other information as the Register of Copyrights may prescribe by regulation, with an exception to protect the privacy of users.[14]

One aspect of the DMCA that will probably be very important to libraries is "Title II: Online Service Provider Liability." The reason for this is that the DMCA defines "online service provider" (OSP) very broadly, and libraries that offer electronic resources or Internet access could be considered OSPs. The law creates some "safe harbors" for certain specified OSP activities. When an activity is within the safe harbor, the OSP qualifies for an exemption from liability. One should read the most current material available about this title, as it is complex and legal interpretation of it is likely to evolve.

Title IV provides some clarification about library and archival digitization activity for preservation purposes. It allows the creation of up to three digital preservation copies of an eligible copyrighted work and the electronic loan of those copies to qualifying institutions. An additional feature is that it permits preservation, including in a digital form, of an item in a format that has become obsolete.

Distance education activities are also addressed in Title IV. The Register of Copyright is to provide Congress with a report on "how to promote distance education through digital technologies." Part of the report is to address the value of having licenses available for use of copyrighted works in distance education programs. (The DMCA was only six months old at the time we prepared this chapter.)

Enforcement

Copyright holders are quick to enforce their rights. One of the early suits was instituted just four years after the 1976 legislation became law. A group of book publishers filed a complaint against the Gnomon Corporation for alleged copyright infringements. Gnomon operated a number of photocopy stores in the eastern United States, many located near academic institutions. The publishers claimed that the company encouraged copyright violations by promoting its Micro-Publishing service with university and college teachers. By May 1980, publishers had their first favorable ruling and announced that their next target would be large for-profit corporations with libraries that did not use the Copyright Clearance Center (see page 534 for more about the Copyright Clearance Center). Although the publishers won their case against Gnomon, many photocopy service firms continued to promote similar services. By the early 1990s, publishers and commercial copy services had worked out a system for providing academic institutions with custom readers. The system uses an electronic copyright approval procedure that permits a copying service or other company to quickly secure the requisite permissions and legally produce the reader in the needed quantities. Many academic campus bookstores offer similar services, and most of them use the services of the Copyright Clearance Center. However, issues regarding "course packages" and copyright remain. A recent case involved the University of Michigan.[15]

In 1982, various publications carried announcements that the Association of American Publishers (AAP) had moved forward with infringement suits against several corporate libraries. The AAP had an out-of-court settlement with E. R. Squibb and Sons Corporation, a large pharmaceutical company, after filing suit. Squibb agreed to pay royalty fees when copying articles from technical journals, including ones to which the corporation library subscribed. Before the Squibb suit, the publishers had also been successful in a suit against American Cyanamid Company. More recently, Texaco lost a copyright suit.[16]

After their success against for-profit organizations, the AAP focused on the not-for-profit sector. On January 5, 1983, the *Chronicle of Higher Education* published an article about an AAP suit in the New York district court against New York University, nine faculty members, and a photocopy shop near the university. New York University settled out of court, agreeing to follow the 1976 guidelines and agreeing that faculty members who did not do so would not receive legal assistance from the institution if they were named as parties in a future copyright infringement suit. At about the same time, a Los Angeles secondary school teacher lost an infringement suit on the same grounds, namely, failure to follow the 1976 guidelines. In 1984, the National Music Publishers Association persuaded the University of Texas at Austin to stop allegedly illegal photocopying of music by its music department.

Though it is true that copyright holders do have rights, the law clearly states that libraries and other users do too. As Scott Bennett wrote:

> We should respect the copyright law. This means understanding the law so that we can obey it and benefit from it. It means a refusal to wink at violations of the law, however widespread, just as it means advancing no untenable claims either to copyright protection or to fair use. Most important, it means acknowledging there are many genuinely debatable issues before us that will need to be resolved through negotiation, legislation, and litigation. Respecting the copyright law means making judicious use of these methods of resolving differences.
>
> We should keep the Constitutional purposes of copyright in view; honor those purposes; and work to give them vitality.[17]

Without question, the most contentious issue is the electronic environment and who owns what, where, and how. The professional literature is full of articles exploring this or that aspect of the problem. Certainly, licensing of information, be it a CD-ROM, an online service, or an electronic journal, is at issue. Sometimes changes in the law assist in library operations, such as the amendment that authorizes libraries to make backup copies of computer programs (for example, programs on disks, which accompany more and more books).[18] Then one reads articles asking: "Will electronic journals fulfill the current role of assessment that print-on-paper does?" and "How are electronic journal publishers to make money out of document delivery?" These articles leave one wondering how the voice of the user can be heard.[19] One speculates whether librarians ever read licensing agreements, much less ask the institution's legal counsel to review such documents. Some agreements come in wrapped packages, so that one cannot read the full text until after one has opened the package, but the package carries words to the effect that "opening this package constitutes acceptance of the licensing agreement." A particularly good article discussing these issues is Laura Gasaway's "Copyright in the Electronic Era."[20] Both "shrinkwrap" and "click-wrap" licenses have been deemed legal by the courts.

Contractual Compliance

Following the various guidelines is one obvious way to achieve a limited form of compliance. (To date, there have been no suits in which the defendants claimed that they followed the guidelines; however, that does not mean there will not be such a suit.) For some libraries, the guidelines are too narrow and the cost of acquiring, processing, and housing the needed copyrighted material is high. Are these libraries and information centers cut off from needed information? Not if they have enough money.

The Copyright Clearance Center (CCC) is a not-for-profit service designed to serve libraries and other users of copyrighted material by providing a central source to which to submit copying fees. It is, in a sense, a licensing system; CCC does not copy documents, but functions as a clearinghouse. Several thousand organizations are members; many, if not most, of these are libraries and information services. The CCC handles both U.S. and foreign publications (it can grant permission to use more than 1.75 million publications).

The address/contact information for CCC is 222 Rosewood Drive, Danvers, MA 01923; telephone (978) 750-8400, and <http://www.copyright.com>. There is also a Canadian equivalent, the Canadian Copyright Licensing Agency (CANCOPY). Contact information for CANCOPY is 6 Adelaide Street East, Suite 90, Toronto, ON M5c1h6, Canada; telephone (416) 868-1620, and <http://www.cancopy.com>. Another service is the Television Licensing Center, which assists in legal off-the-air videotaping, an area of concern for school media centers as well as other educational institutions.

The fees can be substantial when one realizes that the charge is for one article; however, the cost of a lawsuit would be higher, and if the organization lost, it could be forced to pay as much as $50,000 plus other costs and fees.

When in doubt, ask for permission. The process can be complicated when one must go directly to the copyright owner, but that is often the only option. Libraries can help make it easier in various ways. Tom Steele reported on a project at Wake Forest University that has helped make the process easier, if not painless.[21] Two library staff members designed a Website with a list of publishers, a list of journals, a set of form letters for permission requests, and links to sites that provide information about copyright. (An online tutorial about copyright that the LMU library suggests to users with copyright questions is <http://www.utsystsem.edu/ogc/intellectualproperty/cprti/index.htm>. This site is to assist in securing permission; it does itself not grant permission.)

Licensing Agreements

Licensing is another method to achieve compliance. The CCC offers an annual license for publications it handles. Robert Oakley suggested a potentially useful approach to some of the copyright and preservation concerns in terms of journals.[22] His suggestion was based on the idea that many, if not most, publishers do not have significant backfiles in a digital format. (Perhaps one could go further and suggest that they do not want to commit too many resources to maintaining very-low-revenue material in either print or digital formats.) According to Oakley, this situation presents an opportunity for joint ventures between libraries and publishers. Libraries engage in what they have always done, preserve information, and publishers produce it. In return, libraries would receive access to the backfile materials. Such arrangements would probably be through a contract or license.

What is the relationship between copyright and licenses? Perhaps the best short description of the similarities and differences was written by Ann Oakerson:

- Copyright represents a set of general regulations negotiated through statutory enactment. The same laws and guidelines apply to everyone in the country.

- Licenses are contracts ... [that] represent [a] market-driven approach to such regulation. Each license is arranged between a willing surveyor and willing licensee, resource by resource. The owner of a piece of property is free to ask whatever price and set whatever conditions the market will bear.[23]

More and more producers and libraries are turning to contracts or licenses to handle access and use.

Typical licensing agreements outline the lessee's responsibility for such things as security, customer service, payment and delivery, limitations and warranties, termination, indemnification, and assignment. All of these factors can affect the expected use. Though having to add attorney fees to the cost of building a collection is unappealing, the fact is that most of the producers will negotiate changes, and librarians should demand changes that benefit or at least do not create unreasonable demands on libraries and customers.

The library should maintain a master file of copies of all the licensing agreements and contracts. There should be a contact person who is responsible for knowing the terms of these documents as well as for being able to answer or secure answers to questions about the agreements. Compliance is a key issue, and the library or information center must do what it can to ensure compliance. However, some licensing agreements contain language that places responsibility on the library (subscriber) to monitor what users do with material after they leave the premises. Such clauses are beyond any library's or information center's ability to handle, and librarians should insist that they be deleted from the agreement.

The key is knowing what is in the agreement before purchasing. As with computer software, the licensing agreement often comes with the product, that is, after the purchase. It is sealed in a package with a warning message to the effect that opening the package constitutes accepting the terms of the agreement inside the package. When considering a product from a new vendor, ask for a copy of the licensing agreement before making a final decision to purchase. This gives the staff an opportunity to review the document. It also provides an opportunity to request changes that the vendor may or may not be willing to make. In any event, it will give the library a chance to consider whether it can live with the conditions of the licensing agreement before committing to the purchase.

Because licensing is becoming a major and ever-growing issue for libraries, we include the "Principles" for licensing electronic resources as proposed by a number of library associations in North America in 1997.

PRINCIPLES

1. A license agreement should state clearly what access rights are being acquired by the licensee—permanent use of the content or access rights only for a defined period of time.

2. A license agreement should recognize and not restrict or abrogate the rights of the licensee or its user community permitted under copyright law. The licensee should make clear to the licensor those uses critical to its particular users including, but not limited to, printing, downloading, and copying.

3. A license agreement should recognize the intellectual property rights of both the licensee and the licensor.

4. A license agreement should not hold the licensee liable for unauthorized uses of the licensed resource by its users, as long as the licensee has implemented reasonable and appropriate methods to notify its user community of use restrictions.

5. The licensee should be willing to undertake reasonable and appropriate methods to enforce the terms of access to a licensed resource.

6. A license agreement should fairly recognize those access enforcement obligations which the licensee is able to implement without unreasonable burden. Enforcement must not violate the privacy and confidentiality of authorized users.

7. The licensee should be responsible for establishing policies that create an environment in which authorized users make appropriate use of licensed resources and for carrying out due process when it appears that use may violate the agreement.

8. A license agreement should require the licenser to give the licensee notice of any suspected or alleged license violations that come to the attention of the licenser and allow a reasonable time for the licensee to investigate and take corrective action, if appropriate.

9. A license agreement should not require the use of an authentication system that is a barrier to access by authorized users.

10. When permanent use of a resource has been licensed, a license agreement should allow the licensee to copy data for the purposes of preservation and/or the creation of a usable archival copy. If a license agreement does not permit the licensee to make a usable preservation copy,

a license agreement should specify who has permanent archival responsibility for the resource and under what conditions the licensee may access or refer users to the archival copy.

11.   The terms of a license should be considered fixed at the time the license is signed by both parties. If the terms are subject to change (for example, scope of coverage or method of access), the agreement should require the licenser or licensee to notify the other party in a timely and reasonable fashion of any such changes before they are implemented, and permit either party to terminate the agreement if the changes are not acceptable.

12.   A license agreement should require the licenser to defend, indemnify, and hold the licensee harmless from any action based on a claim that use of the resource in accordance with the license infringes any patent, copyright, trade-mark, or trade secret of any third party.

13.   The routine collection of use data by either party to a license agreement should be predicated upon disclosure of such collection activities to the other party and must respect laws and institutional policies regarding confidentiality and privacy.

14.   A license agreement should not require the licensee to adhere to unspecified terms in a separate agreement between the licenser and a third party unless the terms are fully reiterated in the current license or fully disclosed and agreed to by the licensee.

15.   A license agreement should provide termination rights that are appropriate to each party.[24]

Public Lending Right

Public lending right (PLR) is a system that allows an author to be compensated for the circulated use of his or her copyrighted work from libraries. Many Americans, including librarians, are not fully aware of this right. Elsewhere in the world it is better known, and in most countries where it exists, it operates successfully. In view of copyright owners' increasing attempts to charge a fee for types of usage that were free in the past, it may not be too long before the public lending right will come to the United States.

Authors are compensated in some manner for the circulated use or presence of their works in a library. Where does the money come from? There are only three logical sources: the user, the library, or the funding authority. In most countries, the money comes from a separate fund established for that purpose by the national government. Does the presence of a lending right program have any negative impact on library budgets? No one really knows, but it seems likely that there is some spillover that ultimately reduces library funding. However, a 1986 report from England indicated no adverse effects on library budgets as a result of PLR. Collections built using the demand principle will increase the pressure on the PLR fund, and a self-feeding cycle may begin which makes less money available to buy low-use titles.

The PLR system started in the Scandinavian countries after World War II. Initially, it was considered a way to encourage writers to write in languages that had a small number of native speakers (for example, Danish, Finnish, Icelandic, Norwegian, and Swedish). For more than 20 years, the concept did not spread beyond Scandinavia. Starting in the early 1970s, the idea spread to the Netherlands (1972), the Federal Republic of Germany (1972), New Zealand (1973), Australia (1974), the United Kingdom (1983), and Canada (1986). Although some legislation contains the provision that all libraries are to be included, in most countries only public libraries are involved in data collection. Details of the systems vary, but some form of sampling is used to collect the data, unless there is a single source from which the public libraries buy their books. A good but somewhat dated source of detailed information about PLR is a 1981 issue of *Library Trends*.[25]

In Canada, the system is called Payment for Public Use (PPU). A $2.5 million fund was established by the national government to compensate authors for the circulation of their books by Canadian public libraries. In 1985, the Council of Writers Organizations was able to get U.S. Senator Charles Matthias of Maryland to submit PLR-enabling legislation. Nothing has happened in the intervening years. Does such legislation have much chance of becoming law? Assuming that the plan would copy other countries' practice of federal funding, and as long as the federal deficit and budget cutting remain congressional priorities, establishment of a PLR system is unlikely. However, this assumption may not be valid, for several reasons. First, two other sources of funding are possible: the user and the library. Second, the worrisome § 106 of the copyright law lists as an exclusive right of the copyright owner "to distribute copies or phonorecords of copyrighted works to the public by sale or other transfer of ownership, or by rental, lease or *lending*" (emphasis added). Third is the attitude exemplified by a 1983 statement in *Publishers Weekly*: "The fate of a book after it is sold is an important one for the book industry, reflecting as it does the possibility of lost sales; pass-along readership of a book, unlike that of a magazine, does not translate into potential revenue."[26] If publishers, authors, and others, such as music producers (audio collections) and motion picture producers (video collections), join forces, we might well see another cost imposed on libraries and their users.

Summary

Copyright assures persons or organizations the right to seek tangible rewards from the production of creative or informative works. Without users of copyrighted materials, the producers would realize little or nothing from their efforts. Producers and users need to work together or everyone will lose. It would be desirable if once again we became partners in the dissemination of information and knowledge, rather than antagonists. Whatever does develop will not change the fact that it will not be possible to develop a library collection without considering the impact of copyright laws. Librarians should work to maintain a fair balance, but they must work primarily for the users because users have few spokespersons.

We agree with the ideas that Ann Prentice expressed in an article about WIPO, copyright owners, and users:

> Digital library projects are moving ahead in many libraries and much has been said about the benefits of being able to access information once it is in digital form. Because of copyright restriction, there are limitations on what can be digitized. ... What will happen when [we] look to digitize material[s] of greater mainstream interest that are under copyright? What kinds of charges will be suggested by copyright holders? Can libraries afford them?[27]

Notes

1. *Thor Power Tool Co. v. Commissioner of Internal Revenue*, 439 U.S. 522 (1979).

2. Margaret McKinley, "The *Thor* Inventory Ruling: Fact or Fiction," *Serials Librarian* 17, nos. 3/4 (1990): 191–94.

3. J. Berry, "Copyright: From Debate to Solution," *Library Journal* 100 (September 1, 1975): 1459.

4. World Intellectual Property Organization, "WIPO Today," <http://www.wipo.int/eng/infbroch/infbro98.htm>.

5. Association of American Publishers, *Statement of the AAP on Commercial and Fee-Based Document Delivery* (New York: Author, 1992).

6. Richard Schockmel, "The Premise of Copyright, Assaults on Fair Use, and Royalty Use Fees," *Journal of Academic Librarianship* 22 (January 1996): 17.

7. Evan St. Lifer, "Inching Toward Copyright Détente," *Library Journal* 123 (August 1998): 43.

8. Ibid.

9. Ibid.

10. *Conference on Fair Use: An Interim Report to the Commissioner* (Washington, D.C.: U.S. Patent and Trademark Office, 1996).

11. Kenneth Crews, "Fair Use and Higher Education: Are Guidelines the Answer?," *Academi* 83 (November/December 1997): 38–40.

12. U.S. Congress, House of Representatives, *Conference Report on General Revision of the Copyright Law 94-553* (September 29, 1976), 55.

13. Michael Rogers, "Judge Rules Against UnCover in Copyright Suit," *Library Journal* 123 (November 15, 1998): 19.

14. Title 17, U.S.C. § 1202(c) (1998).

15. Wiant, S. K., "Coursepack Copying," *Virginia Libraries* 43 (July/August/September 1997): 13–14.

16. Wiant, S. K. "Texaco Settles Suit," *Virginia Libraries* 42 (April/May/June 1996): 18–19.

17. Scott Bennett, "Copyright and Innovation in Electronic Publishing," *Library Issues* 14 (September 1993): 4.

18. Pub. L. No. 96-517, § 7(b), *amending* 17 U.S.C. § 117.

19. Jamie Cameron, "The Changing Scene in Journal Publishing," *Publishers Weekly* 240 (May 31, 1993): 24.

20.   Laura N. Gasaway, "Copyright in the Electronic Era," *Serials Librarian* 24, nos. 3/4 (1994): 153–62.

21.   Tom Steele, "The Copyright Permission Pages: Making a Frustrating Experience More Convenient," *Campus-wide Information Systems* 15, no. 2 (1998): 61–62.

22.   Robert Oakley, "The Copyright Context," *Collection Management* 22, nos. 3/4 (1998): 177–84.

23.   Ann Oakerson, "Copyright or Contract?," *Library Journal* 122 (September 1, 1997): 136–39.

24.   Association of Research Libraries, "Strategic and Practical Consideration for Signing Electronic Information Delivery Agreement," March 13, 1997, <http://arl.cni.org/scomm/licensing/licbooklet/html, conclusion>.

25.   "Public Lending Right," *Library Trends* 29 (Spring 1981): 565–719.

26.   "The Pass-Along Market for Books: Something to Ponder for Publishers," *Publishers Weekly* 224 (July 15, 1983): 20.

27.   Ann Prentice, "Copyright, WIPO and User Interests: Achieving Balance Among the Shareholders," *Journal of Academic Librarianship* 23 (July 1997): 309–12. See also University of California Libraries, Collection Development Committee, "Principles for Acquiring and Licensing Information in Digital Formats," <http://sunsite.berkeley.edu/Info/principles.html>.

Selected Websites*

CANCOPY
> <http://www.cancopy.com>
> Canadian Copyright Licensing Agency home page.

Copyright Clearance Center Online
> <http://www.copyright.com>
> Reference site for the CCC.

Information Policy: Copyright and Intellectual Property Resources
> <http://www.ifla.org/II/cpyright.htm>
> Website produced by the IFLA, with an international point of view.

Intellectual Property Home Page
> <http://www.utsystem.edu/home/OGC/intellectualproperty/INDEX.HTM>
> Website maintained by the Office of General Counsel at the University of Texas.

Licensing Electronic Resources
> <http://arl.cni.org/scomm/licensing/licbooklet.html>
> Website produced by the ARL.

Legal Information Institute: Law about ... Copyright
> <http://www.law.cornell.edu:80/topics/copyright.html>
> Cornell University's Legal Information Institute copyright home page.

SUL: Copyright & Fair Use
> <http://fairuse.stanford.edu>
> An extensive site maintained by the Stanford University Libraries.

U.S. Copyright Office, Registration Procedures
> <http://lcweb.loc.gov/copyright/reg.html>

Welcome to the Software Publishers Association
    <http://www.siia.net>
    The Website of the newly formed Software and Information Industry Association (SIIA), the trade association for this industry. The future URL of this site will be <http://www.siia.net>.

World Intellectual Property Organization
    <http://www.wipo.int>
    The Website of WIPO, an organization responsible for the promotion and protection of intellectual property throughout the world.

*These sites were accessed 14 October 1999.

Further Reading

Copyright

Bruwelheide, J. H. *Copyright Primer for Librarians and Educators*. Chicago: American Library Association, 1995.

Clark, C. "100 Years of Berne." *The Bookseller* 4209 (August 23, 1986): 788–92.

Crews, K. D. "Not the 'Last Word' on Photocopying and Coursepacks: The Sixth Circuit Rules Against Fair Use in the MDS Case." <http://www.iupui.edu~copyinfo/mdscase.html>.

"Digital Copyright Protection: Good or Bad for Libraries?" *Information Outlook* 3 (January 1999): 32–33.

Fields, H. "Congress Acts to Clarify the Fair Use Doctrine." *Publishers Weekly* 239 (October 19, 1992): 10. ·

Gasaway, L. *Growing Pains: Adapting Copyright for Libraries, Education and Society*. Littleton, Colo.: Fred B. Rothman, 1997.

Karlsen, G. "Copyright Reminder: PPR—Public Performance Rights for Video-tapes for Classroom Use." *School Libraries in Canada* 18, no. 2 (1998): 23–24.

Linke, E. "On Beyond Copyright." *Serials Libraries* 33, nos. 1/3 (1998): 71–81.

Marcon, T. "Electronic Reserves." *Library Acquisitions* 22 (Summer 1998): 208–9.

McDonald, D. D., E. J. Rodger, and J. L. Squires. *International Study of Copyright of Bibliographic Records in Machine-Readable Form*. Munich: K. G. Saur, 1983.

Okerson, A. "The Current National Copyright Debate: Its Relationship to Work of Collection Managers." *Journal of Library Administration* 22, no. 4 (1996): 71–84.

Rocca, J. "New Law Makes Copyright Renewal Optional." *Library of Congress Information Bulletin* 51 (September 7, 1992): 381–82.

Sievers, R. "Congress Passes Several Amendments to Copyright Act: Architecture, Software Rental, Visual Artist Rights Affected." *Library of Congress Information Bulletin* 49 (December 17, 1990): 437–38.

U.S. Congress, House of Representatives. *Conference Report on General Revision of the Copyright Law 94–553*. Washington, D.C.: Government Printing Office, 1976.

Weiner, R. S. "Copyright in a Digital Age." *Online* 21 (May/June 1997): 97–102.

Wiant, S. K. "Copyright and Government Libraries." *Information Outlook* 3 (February 1999): 38–39.

Wilson, P. "Copyright, Derivative Rights, and the First Amendment." *Library Trends* 39 (Summer/Fall 1990): 92–110.

Licensing

Davis, T. L. "Licensing in Lieu of Acquiring." In *Understanding the Business of Library Acquisitions,* 2d ed. Edited by K. A. Schmidt, 360–78. Chicago: American Library Association, 1999.

"License Agreements in Lieu of Copyright: Are We Signing Away Our Rights?" *Library Acquisitions: Practice and Theory* 21, no. 1 (1997): 19–27.

Okerson, A. "Copyright or Contract?" *Library Journal* 122 (September 1, 1997): 136–39.

Sanville, T. "A License to Deal." *Library Journal* 124 (February 15, 1999): 122.

Public Lending Right

Biskup, P. "Libraries, Australian Literature and Public Lending Right." *Australian Library Review* 11 (May 1994): 170–77.

"Britain's Public Lending Right Is Manna to Authors: Gets No Library Complaints." *American Libraries* 17 (May 1986): 362.

Hyatt, D. "Public Lending Right in the U.S.: An Active Issue." *Public Libraries* 27 (Spring 1988): 42–43.

Lariviere, J. "Le Droit de Pret Public au Canada." *Documentation et Bibliotheques* 37 (April/June 1991): 53–58.

Morrison, Perry D., and Dennis Hyatt, eds. "Public Lending Right." *Library Trends* 29 (Spring 1981): 565–719.

Poulain, M. "Le Droit de Preter." *Bulletin des Bibliotheques de France* 37, no. 3 (1992): 84.

"Public Lending Right." *Library Association Record* 99 (February 1997): 61.

Shimmon, R. "Public Lending Right Changes." *Library Association Record* 92 (August 1990): 540.

Shyu, J. "Preliminary Study on the Issue of Public Lending Right." *Journal of Library and Information Science* 17 (October 1991): 64–92.

Staves, T. "Pay as You Read: Debate over Public Lending Right." *Wilson Library Bulletin* 62 (October 1987): 22–28.

Swaffield, L. "Public Lending Right: Online Links for PLR." *Library Association Records* 100 (April 1998): 182.

Thor Inventory Decision

Biblarz, D. "Growing Out of Print Crisis." *Technical Services Quarterly* 7, no. 2 (1989): 3–12.

Habecker, J. "*Thor Power Tool* Decision and O.P. Rates." Master's thesis, University of North Carolina, 1988.

Loe, M. K. H. "Study Shows *Thor* Ruling Still Causes Book Dumping." *Publishers Weekly* 230 (September 5, 1986): 19.

————. *"Thor* Tax Ruling After 5 Years." *Library Acquisitions: Practice and Theory* 10, no. 3 (1986): 203–18.

Schrift, L. "After *Thor,* What's Next?" *Library Acquisitions: Practice and Theory* 9, no. 1 (1985): 61–63.

Selth, J. P. "My Say: OP Books: A Popular Delusion." *Publishers Weekly* 235 (January 6, 1989): 78.

19

Censorship, Intellectual Freedom, and Collection Development

In every chapter of this text, we have discussed the impact of digitization and technology. By this point, some readers might thinking, "At long last ... here is a chapter where there will be no references to technology." That thought will have to be fleeting at best, as technology is in fact as large an issue in this chapter as it has been in all the others. The question of "filtering" Internet access for children is a matter of national debate and interest. Filtering is both a national and an international concern, as is evidenced at "The Net Censorship Dilemma—The Hazard: Privatised Censorship" (<http://rene.efa.org.au/liberty/selfcens.html>) Website from Australia. We will address this topic later in the chapter.

All of the collection development topics discussed thus far are complex, and some touch on a wide variety of social issues and concerns. However, none is more complex than intellectual freedom and censorship. *Intellectual freedom, free speech, freedom to read,* and *open access to information* are alternative terms used for this topic. First Amendment rights are the cornerstones on which librarians and information managers build collections.

There is not enough space in this chapter to fully explore all the aspects of intellectual freedom and free speech. Although they are interesting and important concepts for anyone involved in collection development, they are so complex that each has been the subject of numerous books and articles. (The bibliography at the end of this chapter provides a starting point for exploring these topics in more depth.) All librarians must have an understanding of these areas, but it is essential that all selection personnel fully comprehend the issues relating to censorship.

Many library associations have membership-approved statements and public positions on the questions of free speech and intellectual freedom. The ALA's "Freedom to Read" statement (available online at <http://www.ala.org/alaorg/oif/freeread.html>) is a classic example. Most of the statements contain fine-sounding phrases. The statements *look* useful when one is discussing the theory or philosophy of intellectual freedom in the classroom or in a meeting. However, on a daily basis, these statements provide little assistance in collection development and provide only limited assistance in fighting off a censor.

Usually, intellectual freedom and free speech controversies revolve around interpretations of points of law and possible violations of existing law. Therefore, the fight normally involves attorneys and judges rather than librarians and the community. We hear about the cases that reach the courts, but seldom about daily local problems. Cases often start as local problems between the library and an individual or group from the community and are usually settled quickly. Most often, the problem arises when someone objects to an item already in the collection. Depending on the nature of the material, the level of emotional involvement, and the prior administrative actions (that is, policies), the library may be able to quickly resolve the issue, or the problem may escalate until it reaches the courtroom.

If the library successfully resolves a controversy without the aid of attorneys, it will be a result of having one or more of the following:

- Staff with an excellent background in interpersonal relations
- A plan of action for handling complaints
- A lack of strong feelings on the part of the person making the complaint
- A lack of concerted pressure from special-interest groups
- Available backup material from library associations

If the individual making a complaint believes very strongly in the matter, it is likely that the library's attorney will become involved. From that point on, depending on the emotional involvement and financial resources, the issue may go from the lowest to the highest court in the country before the problem is resolved.

The local issue usually is censorship. Charles Busha provided a satisfactory definition of *censorship* as it concerns the library: "The rejection by a library authority of a book (or other material) which the librarian, the library board or some person (or persons) bringing pressure on them holds to be obscene, dangerously radical, subversive, or too critical of the existing mores."[1] (Beginning selection officers should read the Busha article.) Censorship has been a problem for libraries as long as there have been libraries. Generally speaking, librarians attempt to resist censorship. (No one knows how many times a librarian or information officer responds to a complaint by removing the offensive item because he or she agrees that it is offensive.) Evidence suggests a difference between librarians' attitudes toward the concept of censorship and their behavior in handling censorship problems. An article by one of the gadflies of librarianship, Sandy Berman, outlined some of his ideas about "self censorship."[2] Librarians' success in fending off censors' efforts varies—there are both notable successes and spectacular failures. The sad truth is that there are no rules or guidelines that ensure success. It is possible to forestall many complaints and quickly resolve those that do occur; however, there is always a chance that the procedures and processes will fail and a legal battle will ensue.

Causes of Censorship

What causes or motives underlie the actions of a censor? Motives may be psychological, political, or social in nature. Psychological motives stem from the desire to restrain others from expressing ideas or creating works that the censor finds offensive. Political motivation underlies the actions of governments that attempt to maintain control over the communication systems that may threaten the government or its policies. Social motivations spring from a desire to preserve a wholesome social setting or to reduce crime, both of which the censor may consider related to the presence of objectionable material in the library. Frequently, the censor (government, groups, or an individual) claims to be acting for "protective" reasons. Censorship is a paternalistic act in that it limits the experiences of both adults and children and limits environments to influences acceptable to the censor·

Freedom and censorship exist in opposition. At one extreme, some persons believe there should be no controls; if they could, they would eradicate all laws, rules, and regulations. At the other extreme are those who think everyone needs protection and outside control. Between these extremes lies the necessary balance between freedom and restraint. Freedom must be restrained so that social institutions can intelligently protect citizens' rights and ensure individuals' free choice. Librarians work on a daily basis to achieve an appropriate balance in their collections and services.

The ALA adopted a Library Bill of Rights in 1948. ALA's Office for Intellectual Freedom (OIF) vigorously promotes and publicizes the concepts contained in that statement. Because the Library Bill of Rights is not law, the statement provides no legal protection for libraries or librarians. What legal protection exists is primarily in the freedom-of-speech provisions of the First Amendment to the United States Constitution. The First Amendment grants every U.S. citizen the right to freely express opinions in speech, writing, or with graphics; to distribute them; and to seek information from public sources without unnecessary restraint. The Library Bill of Rights outlines the basic freedom-of-access concepts that the ALA hopes will guide library public service. It states that persons should be able to read what they wish without intervention from groups or individuals—including librarians. Since its adoption in 1948, the provisions of the Library Bill of Rights have assisted librarians in committing their libraries to a philosophy of service based on the premise that users of libraries should have access to information on all sides of all issues. The text of the document, as amended February 2, 1961; June 27, 1967; and January 23, 1980; and reaffirmed in 1996 by the ALA Council, appears in figure 19.1. It is also available at the ALA Website (<http://www.ala.org/work/freedom/lbr.html>).

The Library Bill of Rights is an important guide to professional conduct in terms of intellectual freedom. It is a standard by which one can gauge daily practices against desired professional behavior in the realms of freedom of access to information, communications, and intellectual activity.

Despite the Library Bill of Rights, there is pressure to limit or exclude certain types of material from a library's collection. Occasionally, someone suggests labeling material with warnings or some kind of rating system rather than removing it. This practice usually takes the form of placing special marks or designations (stars, letters, and so forth) on certain classes of materials. The practice of labeling is prejudicial and creates bias.

The American Library Association affirms that all libraries are forums for information and ideas, and that the following basic policies should guide their services.

I.   Books and other library resources should be provided for the interest, information, and enlightenment of all people of the community the library serves. Materials should not be excluded because of the origin, background, or views of those contributing to their creation.

II. Libraries should provide materials and information presenting all points of view on current and historical issues. Materials should not be proscribed or removed because of partisan or doctrinal disapproval.

III. Libraries should challenge censorship in the fulfillment of their responsibility to provide information and enlightenment.

IV. Libraries should cooperate with all persons and groups concerned with resisting abridgment of free expression and free access to ideas.

V.   A person's right to use a library should not be denied or abridged because of origin, age, background, or views.

VI. Libraries which make exhibit spaces and meeting rooms available to the public they serve should make such facilities available on an equitable basis, regardless of the beliefs or affiliations of individuals or groups requesting their use.

Adopted June 18, 1948.
Amended February 2, 1961, and January 23, 1980,
inclusion of "age" reaffirmed January 23, 1996,
by the ALA Council.

Fig. 19.1. ALA Library Bill of Rights. Reprinted with permission from the American Library Association.

Labeling is a defensive method that says, in effect, "This item may not meet with full community approval." Labeling is contrary to the principles of intellectual freedom. It is not the librarian's duty to warn readers against such things as obscene language; descriptions of explicit sexual acts; or unorthodox political, religious, moral, or economic theories. Librarians are preservers and providers rather than censors. Librarians must always bear in mind that many intellectual advances, in all fields, involve controversy. A librarian's primary responsibility is to provide, not restrict, access to information. Thus, the ALA's position is against labeling materials, in the sense of warning people about the content of items. In 1951, ALA adopted an antilabeling statement, which it last amended on June 26, 1990; it is reproduced as fig. 19.2. As with the Freedom to Read statement, the Statement on Labeling is also available on the ALA Website, at <http://www.ala.org/alaorg/oif/labeling.html>.

The ALA statements provide a philosophical base for resisting censorship. However, in the long run, success or failure depends on the individual librarian's personal beliefs and attitudes. ALA's Office of Intellectual Freedom has a variety of publications and position statements that can assist libraries in handling issues of intellectual freedom, censorship, access to materials, and so forth. The OIF Website provides a number of the items in an electronic format (<http://www.ala.org/alaorg/oif/>).

Forms of Censorship

A librarian or information professional may encounter three forms of censorship: legal or governmental, individual or group, and self-censorship. The first two are easier to respond to than the third. For the first type, there are two choices: comply or fight. Usually, fighting to change a law or interpretation of a law is time-consuming and expensive. Because of the time and cost involved, a single librarian or library seldom attempts it. Even at the community level involving a local ordinance, if there is to be a modification, there must be community-wide support. The library staff working alone has little chance of success.

Literary censorship has existed for a long time. The United States has seen an interesting mix of individual and governmental censorship. Anthony Comstock was a person of strong beliefs and personality whose efforts to control the reading materials of Americans were so vigorous and successful that his name is now part of the lexicon of intellectual freedom and censorship discussions—Comstockery.

Indeed, Comstock was so vocal in his efforts that, in 1873, Congress passed a law that attempted to create a structure for national morality. For almost 75 years, this law went unchallenged, with the U.S. Postal Service designated as the government agency primarily responsible for enforcement at the national level. At the local level, several elements were at work. State and local governments passed similar regulations, and, thus, local police departments became involved in the control of vice. Law enforcement agencies had ample help from two citizen groups: the Society for the Suppression of Vice and the Watch and Ward Society. The "Society for the Suppression of Vice" was the vehicle Comstock used to gain popular support and to show the

Labeling is the practice of describing or designating materials by affixing a prejudicial label and/or segregating them by a prejudicial system. The American Library Association opposes these means of predisposing people's attitudes toward library materials for the following reasons:

1. Labeling is an attempt to prejudice attitudes and as such, it is a censor's tool.

2. Some find it easy and even proper, according to their ethics, to establish criteria for judging publications as objectionable. However, injustice and ignorance rather than justice and enlightenment result from such practices, and the American Library Association opposes the establishment of such criteria.

3. Libraries do not advocate the ideas found in their collections. The presence of books and other resources in a library does not indicate endorsement of their contents by the library.

A variety of private organizations promulgate rating systems and/or review materials as a means of advising either their members or the general public concerning their opinions of the contents and suitability or appropriate age for use of certain books, films, recordings, or other materials. For the library to adopt or enforce any of these private systems, to attach such ratings to library materials, to include them in bibliographic records, library catalogs, or other finding aids, or otherwise to endorse them would violate the Library Bill of Rights.

While some attempts have been made to adopt these systems into law, the constitutionality of such measures is extremely questionable. If such legislation is passed which applies within a library's jurisdiction, the library should seek competent legal advice concerning its applicability to library operations.

Publishers, industry groups, and distributors sometimes add ratings to material or include them as part of their packaging. Librarians should not endorse such practices. However, removing or obliterating such ratings—if placed there by or with permission of the copyright holder—could constitute expurgation, which is also unacceptable.

The American Library Association opposes efforts which aim at closing any path to knowledge. This statement, however, does not exclude the adoption of organizational schemes designed as directional aids or to facilitate access to materials.

Adopted July 13, 1951. Amended June 25, 1971; July 1, 1981; June 26, 1990, by the ALA Council.

Fig. 19.2. ALA Statement on Labeling: An Interpretation of the Library Bill of Rights. Reprinted with permission from the American Library Association.

depth of national support for his views. A primary activity of the society was checking on printed material available to local citizens, whatever the source (bookstores, newsstands, and libraries both public and private). Occasionally, when the society felt that local law enforcement officials were not moving quickly enough, it took matters into its own hands. Book burnings did take place, and the society applied pressure to anyone involved in buying or selling printed material to stock only items it deemed moral. The phrase "banned in Boston" originated as a result of the society's activity.

From 1873 until well into the twentieth century, the United States experienced a mix of all three types of censorship: official censorship because of the 1873 law; group pressure from organized societies concerned with the moral standards of their communities; and self-censorship on the part of publishers, booksellers, and librarians. A public or even a private stance by librarians against such censorship was almost unheard of; in fact, professional groups sponsored workshops and seminars to help librarians identify improper books. Most of the notable librarians of the past are on record (in ALA proceedings, speeches, or writings) in favor of this type of collection development. As E. Geller noted, Arthur Bostwick felt it was reasonable to purchase books like *Man and Superman* for the New York Library's reference collection (noncirculating), but not for branch libraries.[3] Bostwick's inaugural speech as president of the ALA (1908) was about the librarian as censor; as censor the librarian performed a positive act, if not an act of "greatness," Bostwick said.[4]

An interesting situation arose with foreign-language titles. Many authors were available in their own languages, but not in English. Apparently, if one could read French, German, Spanish, Russian, or any other language, one was reading a "moral" book—but that same work in an English translation was immoral. The censorial atmosphere caused a few American authors to live abroad, and some had a larger foreign readership than English-speaking readership. (Henry Miller is a prime example.) At the time, librarians were no more vocal in protesting this situation than anyone else in the country.

The period between 1873 and the mid-1950s exhibited all of the censorship problems one can encounter. From the 1930s to the mid-1950s, various federal court decisions, including several by the U.S. Supreme Court, slowly modified the 1873 law. The 1873 Comstock Act remains a part of the U.S. Code, but it is so modified as to be a completely different law. Most court cases dealing with censorship were between the government and publishers or booksellers. Librarians and their associations occasionally entered the suits as *amici curiae* (friends of the court) but seldom as defendants or plaintiffs.

Major changes in the interpretation of the law began with the U.S. Supreme Court's 1957 *Roth* decision.[5] This decision established a three-part test for obscenity. First, the dominant theme of the work as a whole had to appeal to a prurient interest in sex. Second, the work had to be patently offensive because it affronted contemporary community standards in its representation of sex. Third, the work had to be utterly without redeeming social value. With that interpretation, more sexually explicit material became available in the open market. Not unexpectedly, some people objected to the new openness, and in 1973, the Supreme Court, in deciding the *Miller* case,[6] modified the three-part test. The court suggested a new three-part test.

First, would an average person applying contemporary community standards find that the work as a whole appealed to prurient interest in sex? Second, does the work depict or describe in a patently offensive way sexual conduct specifically prohibited in a state's law? Third, does the work, as a whole, lack serious literary, artistic, political, or scientific value? The effect of the decision was to reduce the impact of national mores by employing tests that emphasize local standards. This test is in place today.

Does the shift in emphasis matter? Yes, especially in terms of production and distribution of materials. One example of what the changed interpretation could do to distribution occurred in 1982. *Show Me: A Picture Book of Sex for Children and Parents* (New York: St. Martin's Press, 1975), a children's book by Will McBride, was taken out of distribution by its American publisher/distributor, St. Martin's Press. It stopped distribution because the U.S. Supreme Court upheld a New York state child pornography law.[7] The book contained photographs of nude children. The New York law contained a strict provision barring the use of children in all sexually explicit films and photographs, obscene or not. St. Martin's had already successfully defended *Show Me* in Massachusetts, New Hampshire, and Oklahoma. However, the publisher decided that determining which of the 50 states it could legally ship the book to, as well as keeping track of individual orders, was much too difficult, so it stopped all distribution. Perhaps the most interesting aspect of this incident is that the book was written by a Swiss child psychologist (Helga Fleischhauer-Hardt) and the photographs were taken by an American photographer (Will McBride). They prepared the book for a Lutheran church-sponsored children's book company in West Germany in 1974. The English-language edition appeared in 1975, and St. Martin's stated that it had sold almost 150,000 copies in hardback and paperback before it ceased distribution.[8]

Some distributors and book clubs started using labeling systems in an attempt to protect themselves from lawsuits. For example, one book club used labels that state: "Warning: explicit violence" or "Warning: explicit sex and violence." A few people speculated that the purpose was to increase sales rather than avoid a lawsuit. Perhaps it served a dual purpose. For a time, one of the library distributors that serves many school media centers included warnings with "problem" books it shipped. For example, in children's books acquired for courses in children's literature, librarians at Loyola Marymount University have found slips bearing the warning, "This book is not up to our usual standards." (The standards referred to do not relate to the quality of the physical volume itself.) Such labeling violates the ALA Statement on Labeling; however, it also reflects the growing concern on the part of vendors with social values and with pressures to influence those values.

Today, just as during the period 1873–1950, most of the problems libraries encounter are with individual and group attempts to censor material. Although no active "Society for the Suppression of Vice" exists today, librarians increasingly face organized pressure groups. What may at first seem to be a person's objection to one book can become a major confrontation between a library and an organized pressure group. Much depends on the energy and time that the would-be censor is willing to devote to the issue. Influential persons may be able to organize a group to generate even greater pressure than the average person could. A librarian may encounter organized pressure groups based on local interests and views (often, views that are religious or politically oriented), but seldom does a librarian face a challenge from a local group with broad national support. If such a group were to exist, it would be extremely difficult to avoid at least an occasional debate (if not an all-out battle) over some materials in the collection. Policy statements about controversial materials, the ALA's Freedom to Read documents, and other support materials will help to slow the process, but they will not stop it. Local groups are particularly hard to resist, because they can have a fairly broad base of community support and their existence indicates some active interest in certain problems.

A few examples illustrate the problems that confronted many librarians in the United States during the 1990s. One example was found in a 1993 report about censorship in U.S. schools. The report, released by People for the American Way, indicated that in 41 percent of the 395 reported attempts at censorship, censors succeeded in having the objectionable material removed or restricted in some manner.[9] The report indicated that the majority of the reported attempts were by groups identified as religious right or "pro-family." It went on to report school personnel as acknowledging that they were being careful in what they added to the collections, a form of self-censorship. A 1983–1984 study indicated that school media centers resolved most challenges without removing the item or restricting access.[10] In 1992, ALA's Office for Intellectual Freedom recorded 653 incidents; however, it believes that libraries report less than 15 percent of all attempts.[11]

Much of the censorship pressure arises from a concern about children, and the concern is not limited to sex. Some parents do not believe they are capable of judging the materials that their children are exposed to in school or the library. As a result, several organizations review materials for worried parents. These groups include Educational Research Analysts, Inc.; Mr. and Mrs. Gabler; America's Future, New Rochelle, N.Y.; the John Birch Society; and Parents of New York United (PONYU). These reviewers are particularly active in the area of elementary school textbooks and required reading material, but they also assess what is in the general collections that support the curriculum.

Supporters of biblical creationism suggest that libraries are censoring Christian materials and especially creationism literature (or creation science). Anyone thinking about going into school media center work needs to be fully aware of what is taking place and to beware the dangers and pitfalls. The *Island Trees Union Free School District* decision of the U.S. Supreme Court,[12] which limited the power of school boards to limit access to materials, did not solve all the problems.

Not all censors are concerned about children's welfare. Challenges to materials based on their racist or sexist content arise fairly often. One of the more unusual cases was *"The Incredible Case of the Stack o' Wheat Murders"* photograph incident in 1980.[13] The case illustrates that censorship battles are not limited to public and school libraries. The Stack o' Wheat incident occurred in the special collections room at the University of California, Santa Cruz library. Ten 4-x-5-inch photographs, called *"The Incredible Case of the Stack o' Wheat Murders,"* were taken by photographer Les Krims. The collection was a parody of theme murders intended for use in a marketing project. Each photograph showed a "gruesomely" murdered nude woman dripping blood alongside a stack of wheat pancakes. The dripping blood was chocolate syrup; the chocolate represented the "epitome of the series humor," according to the text that accompanied the photographs. A young woman who viewed the photographs demanded their removal from the library's collection on the ground that they represented the sexploitation of women. When the library took no action, she went to the special collections room, ripped up the photographs and accompanying material, and poured chocolate syrup over the debris. The case quickly escalated into a significant problem for the campus, encompassing many complex issues, such as freedom of expression, censorship, status of women, vandalism, and social justice.

Another, more recent case involving photographs, one that gained national attention, was the Robert Mapplethorpe controversy. This case went to trial and led to the resignation of a museum director, as well as an individual who had once won ALA's intellectual freedom award.[14]

A variation on the censorship/intellectual freedom issue occurred in 1999 when the National Endowment for the Arts (NEA) withdrew funding for a book publishing project.[15] The publisher was a small press in El Paso, Texas, which had applied for and won a grant from the NEA to help cover the color publishing cost of $15,000 for 5,000 copies. *The Story of Color* is a children's book based on a Mexican folk tale about the gods that remade a gray world into one of many colors. The "problem" was the author, Subcomandante Marcos. Marcos is one the major leaders of the Zapatista guerrilla movement in Mexico. According to the newspaper article, William Ivey, chairmen of the NEA, cancelled the funding after learning about the book from a reporter. His decision overturned many levels of approval for the funding. The reason given for the reversal was concern that some of the funds might eventually reach the Zapatistas. "There was uncertainty about the ultimate destination of some part of the funds," according to Mr. Ivey.[16]

If nothing else, these cases illustrate how deeply a censorship issue can divide a community. When local pressure groups exist, the librarian may ask, "How will they react if I buy this item?" Thinking along these lines allows one to deal with one's worries. The real danger in the situation is when the thought is unconscious. At that point, the pressure group has almost accomplished its purpose, that is, control over what goes into the collection. Further, the group has accomplished it through the librarian's self-censorship.

Self-censorship is our greatest problem as librarians and information professionals. We all believe that we would never censor ourselves, but it is difficult to prevent. A few librarians would agree with Walter Brahm; it is better to retreat and fight another day.[17] He reasoned that censorship falls victim to the times; that public opinion can only dampen censorship; that over time, no one can lead society's mores in directions the population opposes. Certainly, libraries and librarians cannot accomplish this alone, and generally, libraries are not the main battleground of intellectual freedom. Most librarians would take a public stance against Brahm's position, when stated in a theoretical sense and when it does not affect them directly. When it becomes a real issue and there is personal involvement, it becomes another matter.

The following are but a few of the hundreds of attempts at censorship in libraries and information centers in the United States. ALA's *Newsletter on Intellectual Freedom* provides an ongoing source of news about this field.

Examples of Censorship

Journals

In the late 1960s, two periodicals, *Ramparts* and *Evergreen Review* (*ER*), caused libraries and librarians to confront the censorship issue head-on. These confrontations illustrate the variety of ways libraries deal with controversy. In Los Angeles, the public library had to fight a city council-man's efforts to have *ER* removed from the library.[18] The councilman was unsuccessful, but the library removed the current *ER* issues from public areas while the controversy raged. Eventually, the journal was returned to the open shelves after the parties reached a final decision. This was a short-term victory for censorship, but in the end, a victory for free access.

Not all librarians were so lucky. Richard Rosichan lost his position as director of the Kingston Area (New York) Public Library because he fought to keep *ER*, despite both library board and John Birch Society pressure to drop it.[19] At the same time, the American Legion demanded that he remove *Ramparts* because of what the Legion considered its un-American stance. Groton (Connecticut) Public Library managed to retain its staff but lost its subscription to *ER*; after a four-month fight, the library's board of trustees ordered the removal of all issues from the library and the subscription canceled. This was done under the threat of fines and jail sentences for both the library board and staff. Head librarian John Carey issued a statement to the effect that this decision would affect the general acquisition policy.[20] One can only hope that he was wrong.

Between keeping an item on the shelves and removing it is the compro-mise position to which librarians sometimes resort—restricted availability. The Philadelphia Free Library used this approach for *ER* when pressure be-gan to be applied. The library renewed the subscription for the main building and one regional branch, but it kept the issues in closed-stack areas and no one under the age of 18 could examine the title.[21] Emerson Greenaway, who was at that time the director of libraries for the Philadelphia Free Library, said this was done because *ER* was "important sociologically." Who was the winner here, the censor or the librarian?

The foregoing are a small sample of the problems that arose with *Evergreen Review* and *Ramparts*, and they are only two of hundreds of periodicals that have been attacked over the years. In fact, groups frequently question *Newsweek* and *Time*. Some other journals that have been questioned by an individual or group during the 1990s are: *Not-for-Profit* (a school magazine), *People*, *Playboy*, *Playgirl*, *Reader's Digest*, *Rolling Stone* (students under the age of 17 attending Kettle Moraine High School, since December 1998, must have written parental permission to read the library's copy), and *Young Miss*.

Books

The list of books that have caused trouble over the years is immense. The short list included at the end of this section illustrates the range of titles while indicating that one can never really tell what will cause trouble. Some topics are more sensitive than others, and one might expect difficulty with certain acquisitions but not encounter any. However, sex, religion, and politics are always potential problems.

Several school districts and public libraries faced complaints about *I Know Why the Caged Bird Sings* (Maya Angelou), because of passages dealing with child molestation and rape. In most instances, the objectors were successful in forcing its removal or restricting its use by requiring parental approval in writing.

The Adventures of Huckleberry Finn (Mark Twain) has a long history of complaints. The complaints are a perennial problem. The usual charge is that the book contains racist material. Complaints are also frequently filed over J. D. Salinger's *Catcher in the Rye*. Here the usual issue is profanity; occasionally, someone objects to sexual references. Another book that people claim contains inappropriate language is *One Hundred Years of Solitude* by Nobel prize-winner Gabriel Garcia Marquez.

Other books draw complaints because of the point of view they present— for example, Dee Brown's *Bury My Heart at Wounded Knee*. Still others encounter problems for reasons that are hard to understand. Try to find the offending nudity in *Where's Waldo?* or determine why some school media centers have *Snow White* on the list of books that may be read only with signed parental approval.

Some of the late 1990 "problem" titles are equally hard for many people to understand:

- *Twelfth Night* (due to a school district's ban on alternative lifestyle instruction)

- *Origin of the Species* (once again the Tennessee legislature attempted to limit the teaching of evolution)

- *Little Red Riding Hood* (because the basket of goodies included wine)

- *My Brother Sam Is Dead* (too much violence in a story about a family split apart by the American Revolution)

- *The Chocolate War* (due to language and sexual content—this book is beginning to catch up to *Catcher in the Rye* in terms of challenges)

- *My Friend Flicka* (due to cruelty to animals)

According to an ACLU survey in 1997, the most frequently challenged authors between 1995 and 1997 were Judy Blume, Robert Cormier, Christopher Pike, and R. L. Stine.[22] ALA's OIF indicated that the 1998 list of most challenged authors included all of the above, except Pike, and added Maya Angelou, James Lincoln Collier and Christopher Collier, Robie Harris, Lois Lowry, Katherine Paterson, and John Steinbeck.[23]

One early 1999 case involved a Wisconsin school district's banning of four books dealing with gay themes—*When Someone You Know Is Gay, The Drowning of Stephen Jones, Baby Be-Bop,* and *Two Teenagers in Twenty*.[24] What is interesting about this case is that the complaint that led to banning was filed by a parent of a former student in the school.

Music and Recordings

Although in the past there have been fewer problems with music than with other formats, that is no longer the case. Rap music, hard rock, and music lyrics in general now generate controversy quite regularly. In the late 1990s, 2 Live Crew recordings and performances drew national attention, and the concern continues to grow. Early in 1990, the recording industry instituted a labeling program similar to the motion picture rating system. This occurred after years of debate, even in Congress, and opposition from a variety of groups, such as the ALA. Anna Thompson's article, "Lyric Censorship," provides some good insights into this area.[25]

One older musical recording that still raises problems from time to time is *Jesus Christ, Superstar*. Some years ago, Rockford High School (Michigan) was the location of one such disagreement over both the music and the text. At the end of the debate, the school removed all materials relating to *Jesus Christ, Superstar* from the school system—both the library and the music department—because the musical was deemed "sacrilegious."[26] A good article that gives one a sense of how long people have been trying to censor music in the United States is Edward Volz's "You Can't Play That."[27]

Games

Nothing in the collection is immune from challenge, as several libraries have learned the hard way. Aurora Public Library (Colorado) had to deal with controversy over *Dungeons and Dragons* (D&D) players' books. (D&D is a popular role-playing game with an estimated 3 million players, mostly young people.) A woman presented an official complaint and a petition with 150 signatures supporting the complaint. She claimed the game promotes "violence, Satanism and blasphemy of Christian terms." The complaint was withdrawn a short time later because the woman said she feared reprisals against her and her widowed mother. However, the publicity sparked a rash of complaints about other items in the library, and a local evangelist began checking area public library collections for D&D players' books. He tried to pursue the Aurora complaint, but, because he did not live in the community, he could not file a complaint. At about the same time, in Hanover, Virginia, the parents of a 16-year-old who committed suicide sued a public school system. The parents alleged that the suicide was a direct result of his playing D&D in a school building. Wrongful death lawsuits related to games, movies, and television programs have been increasing. None has involved libraries, but there is no reason to suppose that libraries will be immune from such a suit, particularly when many collections have materials about suicide. The November 1983 issue of *American Libraries* published some responses to the ALA Ethics Committee question, "Should you give a student a copy of *Suicide Mode D'Emploi*?" The book is said to be linked to at least 10 suicides. If one believes in freedom to read, what should one do?

Film and Video

As library collections of theatrical videos grow, so do the odds that some-one will demand the removal of one or more titles. Educational videos, especially those dealing with reproduction, abortion, and alternative lifestyles, also present problems.[28] Even foreign-language videos, such as a Portuguese language film, can draw protests.[29] During the Gulf War, some libraries rejected an antiwar video, raising the question of whether the librarians were acting as censors and not providing both sides of an issue.[30] A short but informative article about issues of accessibility to video collections is by John Hurley.[31]

LMU's large video collection has drawn several complaints. None of the challenges have been serious enough to warrant attention outside of the library, as no one from the university has raised the issue. To date, the complaints have been from community users who think the collection should only contain "Christian if not solely Roman Catholic" materials. Films such as *Jesus Christ, Superstar* and *The Last Temptation of Christ* have drawn highly negative comments from several community members. What might happen if a student's parents or major donor were to complain is difficult to say. We rather expect the issue would go beyond the walls of the library.

Some years ago, librarians put on an amazing performance of self-censorship. The situation surrounding the film *The Speaker* includes almost every element one is likely to encounter in any censorship case. To fully understand all of the paradoxes that this event represents, one must review the background of the situation and view the film.

The problem with *The Speaker* began when ALA's Committee for Intellectual Freedom received funds to produce a film about the issues of censorship and intellectual freedom. Shown for the first time to membership at the June 1977 annual convention, the film generated one of the longer debates in ALA history. Seldom has there been as long or as bitter a debate within the ALA about an issue that is, presumably, an article of faith in the profession. Many of the African American members labeled the film racist. Many other members agreed that the film was a problem for that or other reasons. An attempt to have the ALA's name disassociated from the film failed, but not by much. Is that a move to censor? How does that differ from the definition given at the beginning of this chapter? Does that really differ from a publisher's deciding not to release a title because the work is found not to be in the best interest of the owner of the company?

As with every other problem of this type, we have no objective data on which to base a judgment. Not all African Americans or other persons of color who viewed the film saw it as racist. Just because one (albeit large) group claims that an item is this or that, does the claim make it so?

Is this really different from the Citizen's Committee for Clean Books saying that *The Last Temptation of Christ* is sacrilegious, or the John Birch Society claiming that *Ramparts* and the *Evergreen Review* are anti-American? One hopes that most librarians will agree with Dorothy Broderick regarding *The Speaker*:

> Let librarians across the country decide for themselves: If they find the film boring, let them not buy it. If they feel that using it will stir up trouble in their community—as if they had invited *"The Speaker"*—let them ignore its existence. If the film is as bad as its opponents claim, it will die the natural death of an inadequate work in the marketplace.[32]

Many persons believed that if the ALA removed its name from the film, the association would have taken the first step toward suppressing the film, thus practicing censorship, the very thing it tries to avoid.

Happily, the ALA has produced, or taken part in the production of, an excellent video, *Censorship vs. Selection: Choosing Books for Public Schools*.[33] Though the focus is on public schools, the issues covered are broad enough to make the film valuable for use with any group to generate a discussion of intellectual freedom and censorship.

Special Cases

Sometimes there are unusual circumstances surrounding a book or other item of controversy, and there are major efforts to suppress the distribution of the item by governments or other groups. An extreme example was that of Salman Rushdie's *The Satanic Verses*. Although Rushdie was alive and still in hiding at this writing, several translators and publishers around the world who played some role in publishing of the book are dead. Bookstores stocking the book received threats, as did those involved in distribution of the book. To the best of our knowledge, no library received threats for adding the title to the collection. OCLC holdings statements in 1995, when there was still significant concern, showed that only 218 OCLC libraries held a copy. As of April 1999, a check of OCLC showed that 2,334 libraries held the title.

A good review article about the Rushdie situation and why *The Satanic Verses* was condemned is John Swan's "Satanic Verses, the Fatwa, and Its Aftermath,"[34] which describes the major events through mid-1991.

One rather different situation came up in 1996 in a rather unexpected place—medical libraries. *Pernkopf Anatomy: Atlas of Topographic and Applied Anatomy* was a critically acclaimed anatomical atlas containing more than 800 detailed paintings of dissections that doctors, especially surgeons, used for many years. The first volume was published in Vienna in 1937, part two was printed in 1943, and the final volume appeared in 1952.[35] Urban & Schwarzenberg of Baltimore issued a two-volume set in 1989; later, Wavery Inc. acquired the rights to the title. Both the original and reissue volumes were (and still are) widely held by medical libraries. Reviewers in 1990 used phrases such as "in a class of its own" and "classic among atlases."[36] Anyone thinking about the date and place of the initial publication probably can guess why the controversy arose. Dr. Eduard Pernkopf was a Nazi Party member from 1933 forward, and was named dean of the medical school at the University of Vienna after the Anshluss of 1938. He also spent three postwar years in Allied prisoner of war camps, but was never charged with any war crimes. Some doctors in the 1990s wanted medical libraries to withdraw or at least not allow access to the work until there was an investigation into whether concentration camp victims had been used for the dissections upon which the paintings were based. To date, there is no word on the outcome of the investigation and, as might be expected, there were differing responses in medical libraries to requests to restrict access.

Librarians and Censorship

Realistically, all the situations discussed so far are of the type that one can easily identify and choose to fight or not. Given the foregoing sample of the problems that one may encounter, it should not be surprising to find librarians acting in a self-protective manner. Will knowing who the most challenged authors are in some way influence selection decisions? How great a problem is this? Several researchers have studied this phenomenon, but this discussion will explore the findings of only two of the more widely known studies, those of Fiske and Busha, and a recent study done in southern California.

Marjorie Fiske shook the library profession some years ago when she reported that a high percentage of librarians decided not to buy an item because it might cause a problem.[37] Some titles are likely to cause trouble, for example, *The Joy of Sex* or Madonna's *Sex*, and these are easy to identify. However, an examination of the sample list of titles that have caused trouble makes it evident that some problematic items are not easy to identify. After establishing the habit of not selecting a title that has the potential for controversy, it will be difficult to break the habit. Unfortunately, as with so many other habits, it is easy to slip into a behavior pattern without recognizing it.

Reasons like "lack of funds," "no demand," or "poor quality" may be true, or they may be rationalizations for not selecting an item that might make life troublesome. Other excuses, such as "I will buy it when someone asks for it" or "I don't like that author or producer; he or she never has anything worthwhile to say," clearly signal danger. Just because a librarian does not like an author or a subject does not mean that he or she has the right to keep others from access. This may not be self-protective in the sense of job security, but it may be self-protective in terms of one's own psyche. In any case, the result is the same—censorship.

One way to raise the level of self-awareness is to periodically check one's holdings against various lists of problem items. How many does the library have? Holdings of less than 50 percent should cause one to question what is happening in the selection process. There may be perfectly good reasons why there are so few of these items in the collection, but until the librarian can give good reasons, he or she cannot complacently say, "I am not a censor."

Charles Busha's study examined librarians' attitudes toward censorship and intellectual freedom. He compared his findings to scores on a standardized test that is an indirect measure of antidemocratic trends. His concluding sentence is probably a reasonable picture of all librarianship in the United States:

It is evident, as a result of opinion research, that Midwestern public librarians did not hesitate to express agreement with cliches of intellectual freedom but that many of them apparently did not feel strong enough as professionals to assert these principles in the face of real or anticipated censorship pressures.[38]

The data from a 1982 survey by Woods and Perry-Holmes indicated that the pattern of self-censorship continued, at least for small and medium-sized public libraries.[39] A 1996 study of selection practices in five southern California public libraries[40] suggested that little has changed since Fiske did her study more than 40 years ago.

A Sampling of Problem Books

It seems as if almost any book or other format can cause some person to complain. A list of the most frequently banned books in the 1990s, actually from 1990 to 1992, is available online at <http://www.cs.cmu.edu/People/spok/most-banned.html>. Some of the titles from that list also appear on the following list of books that have been attacked for a host of reasons:

Catcher in the Rye	Of Mice and Men
Daddy's Roommate	Limerick
Changing Bodies, Changing Lives	The Nancy Drew series
Exposing the AIDS Scandal	Rabbit Wedding
Forever	Robots of Dawn
The Hardy Boys series	Tom Sawyer
Intimacy Between Men	The Wizard of Oz
The Last Picture Show	Little Red Riding Hood
James and the Giant Peach	The Learning Tree
The Color Purple	In the Night Kitchen

What to Do Before and After the Censor Arrives

Knowing the dangers of censorship and having a commitment to avoid it is not enough in today's world. Information professionals must prepare for the censor long, long before there is a perceived threat or before the threat becomes real. The first step in preparing for the censor is to expect to have to face a censor. Prepare a policy statement about how the library will handle complaints, and have the policy approved by all the appropriate authorities. There is nothing worse than having no idea of what to do when facing an angry person who is complaining about library materials. Even with policies and procedures, the situation may escalate into physical violence; without procedures, the odds of violence occurring increase.

A typical procedure is to have the individual(s) file a formal complaint or fill out a form that specifies what is at issue. (Figure 19.3 is one such form.) Several organizations, such as the ALA and the National Council of Teachers of English, have recommended forms that are equally effective.

Since people differ, citizens may register their complaints by filling out the following form:

Author:

Title:

Publisher (if known):

Request initiated by _____
                              Name   Telephone No.

                              _____
                              Address

Complainant represents: Himself/Herself _____ Organization _____
If organization, give name:_____

1. Specify what you object to in the book (cite pages)_____
    _____

2. For what age group would you recommend this book?_____

3. What do you think might be the effects of reading this book?_____
    _____

4. What do you think is good about this book?_____
    _____

5. Did you read the whole book or just parts of it?_____

6. Do you know the literary critics' view of this book?_____

7. What is the theme of the book?_____

8. What action would you like the library to take about this book?
        Withdraw it from the shelves?_____
        Do not permit it in the children's room?_____
        Do not permit my child to sign it out?_____

9. What book would you recommend in its place?_____
    _____

                              _____
                              Signature of Complainant

                              _____
                              Date

Fig. 19.3. Patron's request for reconsideration of a book.

After the library develops the policies and procedures and they are approved, everyone working in public services needs to understand the system and receive training in implementing the system. (Sometimes role-playing is helpful in reinforcing the training.) ALA's Office for Intellectual Freedom has an excellent manual that provides details about what to do before censors arrive. Another good source is Frances Jones's *Defusing Censorship: The Librarian's Guide to Handling Censorship Conflicts.*[41]

The ALA's organizational structure for dealing with intellectual freedom concerns is somewhat confusing. The Intellectual Freedom Committee (IFC) is responsible for making recommendations to the association regarding matters of intellectual freedom. The Office for Intellectual Freedom (OIF), which has a full-time staff, has the charge of educating librarians and others about intellectual freedom and censorship matters. It also is the support service for the IFC, and it implements the association's policies related to intellectual freedom. As part of its educational function, the OIF produces several publications: *Newsletter on Intellectual Freedom* (news and current developments relating to intellectual freedom), *OIF Memorandum* (addressed to local library association intellectual freedom committees), and the *Intellectual Freedom Manual.*

Although the OIF does not provide legal assistance when a library faces a complaint, it does provide telephone consultation (occasionally with the addition of written statements or names of persons who might be able to testify in support of intellectual freedom). Very rarely, the OIF comes to the library to provide moral and professional support. Often, librarians are surprised to learn that the OIF does not provide legal aid. Legal assistance might be available from the Freedom to Read Foundation (FRF). The FRF is not part of the ALA (it is a separate legal entity), but the two are so closely affiliated that many people have difficulty drawing the line between the two. The executive director of the FRF is also the director of the OIF; with such an arrangement, it is not surprising that people think the FRF is part of the ALA. Be aware that there is no assurance of receiving financial or legal aid from the FRF; there are too many cases and insufficient funds to assist everyone.

Anyone interested in becoming involved in intellectual freedom activities should consider joining the Intellectual Freedom Round Table, which is the general membership unit of the ALA related to intellectual freedom. Although the ALA offers a variety of support services for handling censors' complaints, the best support is preparing before the need arises.

Filtering

We decided to place the discussion of filtering here because it is, in many ways, a very different concern than that of challenges to items that are part of one's collection(s). Filtering access to the Internet has been a recent "hot topic" for the general public, government officials, and libraries. As we enter the twenty-first century, libraries appear to be "caught between a rock and a hard place" on this issue, as long as they offer Internet access to the public. Some of the general public, governing boards, and elected government officials want libraries to use filter software that will deny access to certain types of sites. Others, believing in free speech (First Amendment), do not want filtering. The primary reason for filtering is to keep children from having access to "unacceptable" sites. An excellent article that describes how filtering works is Paul Resnick's article in *Scientific American*.[42]

Some of the cases involving libraries and filtering in 1999 reflect the problems that occur no matter which option is selected (filter or no filter). In Loudoun County, Virginia, the Public Library Board of Trustees adopted a policy in 1997 calling for the installation of filtering software on all public access computers that connected to the Internet. A citizens group (Mainstream Loudoun) filed suit against the board in 1998. Their basic argument was that (1) filters on all computers reduced everyone to the status of children, and (2) filters cannot block access just to sites deemed inappropriate for children. (As an example of the limits on filtering, some filters would deny a person access to sites relating to breast cancer, because the word *breast* is considered a "stop" word.) Although the court held in favor of the plaintiffs in late November 1998,[43] the board may appeal the decision. A former board member, now a Virginia state legislator, said he would introduce a bill that would require all public libraries to install filters.[44]

On the other side of the country the other side of the issue was also in court. The Pacific Justice Institute, an "organization dedicated to the defense of religious freedom" (<http://www.pacificjustice.org>), filed a lawsuit in 1998 against the city of Livermore, California, and its public library on behalf of a mother, because it did not have filtering software in place.[45] According to the complaint, the woman's son had, on at least 10 occasions, downloaded images of nude women using library computers connected to the Internet. The suit was dismissed in January 1999, for the second time in a few months, on the basis that filtering was too restrictive of free speech and the right to receive free speech. Michael Millen, the attorney for the plaintiff, announced that he was appealing the decision.[46] Thus, by mid-1999, there was no clear trend as to which way the issue will be decided.

The ALA prepared a statement about filtering in 1997, which is reproduced as figure 19.4, page 564. The statement is also available online at <http://www.ala.org/alaorg/oif/filt_stm.html>.

Not everyone in the ALA agreed with this statement, and by March 1999 there was some suggestion that ALA's policy might require modification.[47] A meeting was held in March 1999 at ALA headquarters; it was a first-time meeting of filtering software producers and ALA officers and members to discuss the issue of filtering. Ann Symons, then ALA President, suggested that perhaps the IFC should reconsider the policy. A February 1999 *Library Journal* report on library filtering[48] indicated that less than 20 percent of public libraries were using filtering software. How all these forces will play out is impossible to predict with any hope of accuracy. We suspect that by the time we prepare a new edition of this book, the issue will still be in the courts, as both sides challenge the presence or absence of policies or laws regarding access to the Internet and children.

American Library Association/
Intellectual Freedom Committee

July 1, 1997

On June 26, 1997, the United States Supreme Court issued a sweeping re-affirmation of core First Amendment principles and held that communications over the Internet deserve the highest level of Constitutional protection.

The Court's most fundamental holding is that communications on the Internet deserve the same level of Constitutional protection as books, magazines, newspapers, and speakers on a street corner soapbox. The Court found that the Internet "constitutes a vast platform from which to address and hear from a world-wide audience of millions of readers, viewers, researchers, and buyers," and that "any person with a phone line can become a town crier with a voice that resonates farther than it could from any soapbox."

For libraries, the most critical holding of the Supreme Court is that libraries that make content available on the Internet can continue to do so with the same Constitutional protections that apply to the books on libraries' shelves. The Court's conclusion that "the vast democratic fora of the Internet" merit full constitutional protection will also serve to protect libraries that provide their patrons with access to the Internet. The Court recognized the importance of enabling individuals to receive speech from the entire world and to speak to the entire world. Libraries provide those opportunities to many who would not otherwise have them. The Supreme Court's decision will protect that access.

The use in libraries of software filters which block Constitutionally protected speech is inconsistent with the United States Constitution and federal law and may lead to legal exposure for the library and its governing authorities. The American Library Association affirms that the use of filtering software by libraries to block access to constitutionally protected speech violates the Library Bill of Rights.

Fig. 19.4. ALA Statement on Internet Filtering. Reprinted with permission from the American Library Association.

Bibliotherapy

A common statement used when defending a book or other library material is that there is no definitive cause-effect relationship between reading or viewing and behavior. The ALA's Freedom to Read statements and the Educational Film Library Association's Freedom to View statements support this view. However, there is a body of literature about the use of reading in the treatment of illness. Some medical professionals believe there *is* a cause-effect relationship. In addition, a variety of lawsuits allege that reading or viewing caused someone to do something.

John Berry explored this area in a 1992 *LJ* editorial:

> If words don't incite action, I'm in the wrong line of work .... [I]f they don't motivate people to act, antisocially or otherwise, then our First Amendment is of little value and less importance. This is a tough contradiction for those of us who must argue the case against censorship .... We can't support free expression by saying it won't do any harm. It is obvious that action triggered by words and pictures can do harm and often does.[49]

Librarians frequently do not spend enough time learning about the circumstances in which reading or viewing may cause someone to harm a person or property. Perhaps a course or two in bibliotherapy should be required of any professional working in public service areas of a library or information center.

A standard definition of *bibliotherapy* is the "use of literature to bring about a therapeutic interaction between participant and facilitator."[50] Some believe that a healing process takes place through reading, that is, that "thoughtful suggestions provide a reader with just the right book, a book that triggers a significant and growth producing feeling in response to some need."[51] Most bibliotherapists operate on the basis of several assumptions:

- The process is interactive; it involves both participant and facilitator.
- Literature encompasses all forms of writing.
- The process is both clinical and developmental.
- The process can be one-on-one or group-based.
- The outcome is improved self-esteem and better assimilation of appropriate psychological or social values for the participant(s).
- The process is a therapy but draws heavily on the healthy aspects of the mind.
- The process depends on the facilitator's ability to select the appropriate material for the participant to read and consider.

To date, data about the effectiveness of bibliotherapy is inconclusive. (As a library intern in a Veterans Administration hospital while in library school, Dr. Evans took books and magazines to the locked psychiatric ward for patients to read. Before delivering the books, a psychiatrist examined every item on the book truck. Often, the doctor removed some items. One wonders:

was this an act of censorship? Was this violating the ALA's Freedom to Read statements?

There is much we do not know about reading or viewing and behavior. Perhaps when we know more, our freedom-to-read statements may need revision. In many ways, the issues of filtering are rather like this as well. If we need to protect children from Internet materials, is it not also likely that we need to protect them from printed materials as well? (*Note:* it is not just about "protecting children from pornography," despite what some people say.)

Determining the effectiveness of bibliotherapy, or the effect or lack of effect of reading, viewing, and listening on behavior, should be a high priority. The field makes the case for free and open access to all material for anyone at any time, yet there is some evidence that reading, viewing, and listening to certain items by certain people at certain times does affect behavior in a positive or negative way.

Summary

The problem of censorship is complex, and it is necessary to do extensive reading and thinking about this topic. A theoretical example may help to illustrate just how complex the issue can be. Assume that a librarian is responsible for selecting materials for a small public library. Naturally, the librarian needs this job to cover living expenses. A small group of persons in the community wants the librarian to buy certain items for the library collection; but the librarian also knows of a large group of vocal and influential persons who would be upset, and might even demand that the librarian be fired, if the items were purchased. Should the librarian buy the item and risk his or her family's welfare and own career over this? If the librarian does not buy the item, what can be said to the people who asked for its purchase? Does telling them they can get it somewhere else, or get it through interlibrary loan, really address that librarian's problem?

Finally, an article in *American Libraries* raised the question: "Is it censorship to remove all copies of *The Joy of Gay Sex* because it advocates sex practices that are now felt to be dangerous in light of the AIDS epidemic?"[52] Several librarians responded to the question, and there was some difference of opinion. One wonders how the respondents would have answered had the question been: Is it censorship not to buy copies of Madonna's *Sex*? As with all real problems, there is no simple, completely satisfactory answer.

Notes

1. Charles Busha, "Intellectual Freedom and Censorship," *Library Quarterly* 42 (July 1972): 283–84.

2. Sandy Berman, "Hot Stuff: Getting Sex in the Library," *Collection Building* 13, no. 1 (1994): 45–47.

3. E. Geller, "The Librarian as Censor," *Library Journal* 101 (June 1, 1976): 125.

4. A. Bostwick, "The Librarian as Censor," *ALA Bulletin* 2 (September 1908): 108.

5. Roth v. United States, 354 U.S. 476, 77 S. Ct. 1304 (1957).

6. Miller v. California, 413 U.S. 15, 93 S. Ct. 2607 (1973).

7. New York v. Ferber, 102 S. Ct. 3348 (1982).

8. "Children's Sex Book Removed from Sale," *Rocky Mountain News,* September 21, 1982, at 49.

9. "Censors Succeed in 41% of School Cases," *Library Hotline* 22 (September 27, 1993): 2.

10. *Library Hotline* 13 (March 12, 1984): 1.

11. "Besieged by Book Banners," *Los Angeles Times,* May 10, 1993, at 1, 20a.

12. Board of Education v. Pico, 457 U.S. 853 (1981).

13. "Stack o' Wheat Photos Uproar," *Los Angeles Times,* May 25, 1980, at 8, 1, 22–24.

14. "Director of Corcoran Resigns," *Newsletter on Intellectual Freedom* 39 (March 1990): 73; "Mapplethorpe Defender Wins Downs Award," *Newsletter on Intellectual Freedom* 41 (March 1992): 68.

15. Julia Preston, "N.E.A. Couldn't Tell a Book by Its Cover," *New York Times,* March 10, 1999, at A1, A8.

16. Ibid., A1.

17. Walter Brahm, "Knights and Windmills," *Library Journal* 96 (October 1, 1971): 3096–98.

18. *Wilson Library Bulletin* 48 (September 1969): 18.

19. Ibid.

20. *Wilson Library Bulletin* 50 (April 1971): 717.

21. *Newsletter on Intellectual Freedom* 18 (January 1969): 5.

22. "Banned Book Week, September 26–October 3, 1998," American Civil Liberties Union, <http://www.aclu.org/issues/freespeech/bbwind.html> (Accessed 13 May 1999).

23. "Banned Book Week: Challenged and Banned Books," American Library Association, <http://www.ala.org/bbooks/challeng.html> (Accessed 13 May 1999).

24. "ACLU Press Release: 10-06-98—ACLU of Wisconsin Fights School Censorship of Gay-Themed Books," American Civil Liberties Union, <http://www.aclu.org/news/1999/n021699a.html> (Accessed 13 May 1999).

25. Anna Thompson, "Lyric Censorship: The Risks of Dirty Disks," *Unabashed Librarian* 62 (1987): 5–7.

26. *Newsletter on Intellectual Freedom* 23 (May 1974): 54.

27. Edward J. Volz, "You Can't Play That: A Selective Chronology of Banned Music, 1850–1991," *Colorado Libraries* 19 (Summer 1993): 22–25.

28. Gordon Flagg, "Protesters Fail to Block Gay Videos at Tallahassee Library," *American Libraries* 23 (July/August 1992): 548–49.

29. L. Kniffel, "N.C. County Commissioner Defends Effort to Ban Video," *American Libraries* 24 (January 1993): 14.

30. B. Goldberg, "Librarians Called Censors for Declining Gulf War Video," *American Libraries* 22 (July/August 1991): 615–16.

31. John Hurley, "Free Access Issues and Video Collections," *New Jersey Libraries* 22 (Fall 1989): 8–10.

32. D. Broderick, "Son of Speaker," *American Libraries* 8 (October 1977): 503.

33. *Censorship vs. Selection: Choosing Books for Public Schools* (New York: Media and Society Seminars, 1982).

34. John Swan, "Satanic Verses, the Fatwa, and Its Aftermath," *Library Quarterly* 61 (October 1991): 429–43.

35. Howard Israel, "Nazi Origins of an Anatomy Text," *Journal of the American Medical Association* 276 (November 27, 1996): 1633.

36. Nicholas Wade, "Doctors Question Use of Nazi's Medical Atlas," *New York Times*, November 26, 1996, at C1.

37. Marjorie Fiske, *Book Selection and Censorship* (Berkeley, Calif.: University of California, 1958).

38. Busha, "Intellectual Freedom and Censorship," 300.

39. L. B. Woods and C. Perry-Holmes, "The Flak If We Had *The Joy of Sex* Here," *Library Journal* 107 (September 15, 1982): 1711–15.

40. Andrea E. Niosi, "An Investigation of Censorship and Selection in Southern California Public Libraries," *Public Libraries* 37, no. 5 (September/October 1998): 310–15.

41. Frances Jones, *Defusing Censorship: The Librarian's Guide to Handling Censorship Conflicts* (Phoenix, Ariz.: Oryx Press, 1983).

42. Paul Resnick, "Filtering Information on the Internet," *Scientific American* 276 (March 1997): 62–64.

43. Mainstream Loudoun v. Board of Trustees of the Loudoun County Library, 24 F. Supp. 2d 552 (D. Va. 1998).

44. "Loudoun County Library Loses Filtering Lawsuit," *American Libraries* 30 (January 1999): 14.

45. Mary Minow, "Internet Lawsuits," *California Libraries* 8 (September 1998): 1, 12–13.

46. Ibid.

47. "ALA's Symons Says IFC Should Revise Guidance on Filters," *Library Journal* 124 (April 15, 1999): 14–15.

48. Susan Hagloch, "To Filter or Not," *Library Journal* 124 (February 1, 1999): 50-51.

49. John Berry, "If Words Will Never Hurt Me, Then—?," *Library Journal* 117 (January 1992): 6.

50. Arleen M. Hynes and Mary Hynes-Berry, *Bibliotherapy: Interactive Process* (Boulder, Colo.: Westview Press, 1986).

51. Ibid., 10–11.

52. "Censorship in the Name of Public Health," *American Libraries* 17 (May 1986): 306.

Further Reading

General

Asser, P. N. "Freedom and Copyright." *Logos* 4, no. 1 (1993): 45–49.

Berman, S. "Hot Stuff: Getting Sex in the Library." *Collection Building* 13, no. 1 (1993): 45–47.

Bosmajian, H. A. *Freedom of Expression*. New York: Neal-Schuman, 1988.

——. *Freedom of Religion*. New York: Neal-Schuman, 1987.

——. *Freedom to Read*. New York: Neal-Schuman, 1987.

Brahm, W. "Knights and Windmills." *Library Journal* 96 (October 1, 1971): 3096–98.

Branin, J. J. "Collection Management and Intellectual Freedom." In *Collection Management for the 1990s*. Edited by J. J. Branin, 148–55. Chicago: American Library Association, 1993.

Broderick, D. "Son of Speaker." *American Libraries* 8 (October 1977): 503.

Busha, C. H. "Intellectual Freedom and Censorship." *Library Quarterly* 42 (July 1972): 283–84.

Bushman, J. "Librarians, Self-Censorship, and Information Technologies." *College & Research Libraries* 55 (May 1994): 221–28.

Cornog, M. "Is Sex Safe in Your Library?" *Library Journal* 118 (August 1993): 43–46.

de Grazia, E., and R. K. Newman. *Banned Films*. New York: R. R. Bowker, 1982.

Foerstel, H. N. *Banned in the U.S.A.: A Reference Guide to Book Censorship in School and Public Libraries*. Westport, Conn.: Greenwood Press, 1994.

Heckart, R. J. "The Library as a Marketplace of Ideas." *College & Research Libraries* 52 (November 1991): 491–505.

Manley, W. "Does Intellectual Freedom Protect the Politically Incorrect?" *American Libraries* 24 (December 1993): 1003–4.

Noble, W. *Book Banning in America: Who Bans Books and Why*. Middlebury, Vt.: Eriksson, 1992.

Pedersen, M. "They Censor, I Select." *Publishers Weekly* 241 (January 1994): 34–36.

Poppel, N., and E. M. Ashley. "Toward Understanding the Censor." *Library Journal* 111 (July 1986): 39–43.

Selth, J. P. *Ambition, Discrimination, and Censorship in Libraries*. Jefferson, N.C.: McFarland, 1993.

Shields, G. R. "Censorship, Social Violence, and Librarian Ethics." *Library Quarterly* 62 (April 1992): 217–22.

Smolla, R. A. "Freedom of Speech for Libraries and Librarians." *Law Library Journal* 85 (Winter 1993): 71–79.

Watson, D. J. "Love Among the Bookstacks." *Library Association Record* 99 (January 1999): 25–26.

West, C. "Secret Garden of Censorship: Ourselves." *Library Journal* 108 (September 1, 1983): 1651–53.

Wirth, E. "The State of Censorship." *American Libraries* 27 (September 1996): 44.

Woodward, D., ed. "Intellectual Freedom." *Library Trends* 39, nos. 1/2 (Summer/Fall 1990): 1–185.

Academic

Bosmajian, H. A. *Academic Freedom*. New York: Neal-Schuman, 1989.

Doyle, T. "A Millian Critique of Library Censorship." *Journal of Academic Librarianship* 24 (May 1998): 241–43.

Harmeyer, D. "Potential Collection Development Bias: Some Evidence on a Controversial Topic in California." *College & Research Libraries News* 56 (March 1995): 101–11.

Hippenhammer, C. T. "Patron Objections to Library Materials: A Survey of Christian College Libraries." *Christian Librarian* 37 (November 1993): 12–17.

Hood, E. "Academic Library Censorship in a Conservative Era." In *Association of College and Research Libraries, National Conference,* 4th ed., 15–17. Chicago: Association of College & Research Libraries, 1986.

Houbeck, R. L. "Locked in Conversation." *Journal of Library Administration* 17, no. 2 (1992): 99–131.

Metz, P., and B. Obenhaus. "Virginia Tech Sets Policy on Controversial Materials." *College & Research Libraries News* 54, no. 7 (July/August 1993): 386–88.

Peace, A. G. "Academia, Censorship, and the Internet." *Journal of Information Ethics* 6 (Fall 1997): 35–47.

Podrygula, S. "Censorship in an Academic Library." *College & Research Libraries News* 55, no. 2 (February 1994): 76–78.

Schrader, A. M., M. Herring, and C. De Scossa. "Censorship Phenomenon in College Libraries." *College & Research Libraries* 50 (July 1989): 420–32.

Public

Belk, N. "Know Your Community." *Public Libraries* 36 (September/October 1997): 280–81.

Bowen, C. F. "Preparing for the Censor's Visit." *Public Libraries* 36 (September/October 1997): 279–80.

Brawner, L. B. "Protecting First Amendment Rights in Public Libraries." *Public Library Quarterly* 16, no. 4 (1997): 3–7.

Bright, L. "Censorship in a Small Town." *Colorado Libraries* 19 (Summer 1993): 15–17.

Brown, C. M. "Collection Selection Challenges." *Unabashed Librarian* no. 102 (1997): 14.

Caler, S. L. "Library Will Soon Be Offering Sex." *Colorado Libraries* 19 (Summer 1993): 9–11.

Geler, E. *Forbidden Books in American Public Libraries.* Westport, Conn.: Greenwood Press, 1984.

Harrison, K. "Discussion About Ethics and the Community Connection of Utmost Importance." *Feliciter* 43 (February 1998): 6–7.

Katz, J. "Revisionist History in the Library." *Canadian Library Journal* 48 (October 1991): 319–24.

Kniffel, L. "Justify My Purchase: To Buy Madonna's *Sex* or Not." *American Libraries* 23 (December 1992): 902–4.

LaRue, J. "Reading with the Enemy." *Wilson Library Bulletin* 68 (January 1994): 43–45.

Robbins, L. S. "Fighting McCarthyism Through Film: A Library Censorship Case Becomes a Storm Center." *Journal of Education for Library and Information Science* 39 (Fall 1998): 291–311.

Sager, D. J. "Electronic Bowdlerites: Censorship in the Information Age." *Public Libraries* 36 (September/October 1997): 279–84.

Saunders, K. C. "Factors Affecting the Outcome of Challenges to Library Materials." *Texas Library Journal* 68 (Fall 1992): 84–86.

Schrader, A. M. "Why You Cannot 'Censorproof' Your Public Library." *Public Library Quarterly* 16, no. 1 (1997): 3–30. Also in *Australasian Public Libraries and Information Services* 10 (September 1997): 143–59.

Serebnick, J. "Book Reviews and the Selection of Potentially Controversial Books in Public Libraries." *Library Quarterly* 51 (October 1981): 390–409.

Short, A. M. "Internet Policies & Standards in Indiana Public Libraries." *Indiana Libraries* 16, no. 2 (1997): 48–56.

Sorensen, M. W. "Censorship and the Public Librarian." *Illinois Libraries* 78 (Summer 1996): 120–23.

Wirth, E. "The State of Censorship." *American Libraries* 27 (September 1996): 44+.

School

American Library Association, Office for Intellectual Freedom. *Censorship Litigation and the Schools*. Chicago: American Library Association, 1983.

Arbetman, L. "Reviewing the Books School Children Read: Censorship or Selection?" *Georgia Social Science Journal* 14 (Spring 1983): 1–4.

Burress, L. *Battle of the Books: Literary Censorship in the Public Schools (1950–1985)*. Metuchen, N.J.: Scarecrow Press, 1989.

Cornette, L. "A Censor: Do You Know One When You See One?" *Ohio Media Spectrum* 50 (Winter 1998): 13–14.

———. "Intellectual Freedom Is a Concern for All Media Specialists." *Ohio Media Spectrum* 50 (Fall 1998): 13–14.

———. "Who Do You Call?" *Ohio Media Spectrum* 49 (Fall 1997): 10–11.

Flagg, G. "Snow White Is the Latest Title Under Attack in Schools." *American Libraries* 23 (May 1992): 359–60.

Hamilton, C. "Censorship and Intellectual Freedom in Schools." *Book Report* 11 (March/April 1993): 5–29.

Hopkins, D. M. "A Conceptual Model of Factors Influencing the Outcome of Challenges to Library Materials in Secondary School Settings." *Library Quarterly* 63 (January 1993): 40–72.

Krug, J., and A. E. Penway. "School and Library Censorship." *Show-Me Libraries* 44 (Winter/Spring 1993): 3–6.

Mastroine, T. "Ten Good Things About a Censorship Challenge." *Ohio Media Spectrum* 50 (Spring 1998): 26–29.

McDonald, F. B. *Censorship and Intellectual Freedom: A Survey of School Librarians' Attitudes and Moral Reasoning*. Metuchen, N.J.: Scarecrow Press, 1993.

Mosley, M. "The School Library in Court." *School Library Journal* 27 (October 1981): 96–99.

Reichman, H. *Censorship and Selection: Issues and Answers for Schools*. Chicago: American Library Association, 1993.

Sorenson, G. P. "Removal of Books from School Libraries 1972–1982." *Journal of Law and Education* 12 (July 1983): 417–41.

Zapasnik, K. "Intellectual Freedom: TALK (Tolerance, Access, Literacy, Knowledge)." *Florida Media Quarterly* 23, no. 3 (1998): 25.

Special

Sherwill-Navarro, P. "Internet in the Workplace: Censorship, Liability and Freedom of Speech." *Medical Reference Services Quarterly* 17 (Winter 1998): 77–84.

Bibliotherapy

Allen, B., and L. O'Dell. *Bibliotherapy and the Public Library*. San Rafael, Calif.: San Rafael Public Library Bibliotherapy Project, 1981.

Anderson, M. "Literature in the Pediatric Setting." In *Many Faces, Many Voices*. Edited by A. L. Mana and C. S. Brodie, 79–86. Fort Atkinson, Wis.: Highsmith Press, 1992.

"Bibliotherapy Exchange." *Ohio Libraries*. [An ongoing column in various issues of the journal, each dealing with a different topic, such as death and dying, self-esteem, and divorce.]

Brett, D. *More Annie Stories: Therapeutic Storytelling Techniques*. Pasadena, Calif.: Magination Press, 1992.

Cecil, N. L., and P. Roberts. *Developing Resiliency Through Children's Literature*. Jefferson, N.C.: McFarland, 1992.

"Counseling in Public Libraries." In *Public Librarianship*. Edited by V. L. Pungitore, 115–32. Westport, Conn.: Greenwood Press, 1989.

Coville, B. "Magic Mirrors." *Bookmark* 49 (Fall 1990): 35–36.

Doll, B., and C. Doll. *Bibliotherapy with Young People*. Englewood, Colo.: Libraries Unlimited, 1997.

Gubert, B. K. "Sadie Peterson Delaney: Pioneer Bibliotherapist." *American Libraries* 24 (February 1993): 124–30.

Johnson, R. S. "Bibliotherapy: Battling Depression." *Library Journal* 124 (June 1, 1998): 73–76.

Lack, C. R. "Can Bibliotherapy Go Public?" *Collection Building* 7 (Spring 1985): 27–32.

Mohr, C., D. Nixon, and S. Vickers. *Books That Heal*. Englewood, Colo.: Teacher Ideas Press, 1991.

Pearl, P. *Helping Children Through Books*. Portland, Oreg.: Church & Synagogue Library Association, 1990.

Smith, A. G. "Will the Real Bibliotherapist Please Stand Up?" *Journal of Youth Services* 2 (Spring 1989): 241–49.

Steele, A. T. "Raising the Issue: Read Two Books and Call Me in the Morning." *Wilson Library Bulletin* 68 (June 1994): 65–66.

Trejos, N. "Healing the Pain, A Page at a Time," *Los Angeles Times,* April 18, 1999, at B2.

Epilogue:
The Future of
Collection Development

The best prophet of the future is the past.

—George Gordon, Lord Byron,
Letter, 28 June 1821

Throughout this volume, we have addressed the many aspects of collection development. We have reviewed the history of the field, and have looked at individuals associated with collection development, from the first key theorists to present-day practitioners. We have watched new formats emerge in our own libraries (such as Acrobat .PDF, .MP3, and DVD) as others (such as Betamax, phonorecords, and microcards) quietly retired to "antique" status.

Certainly, the "information explosion" is coloring the future of libraries and information centers. As it does so, the roles of librarians and information specialists have changed, particularly in the ways they develop and maintain collections. Virtually every aspect of library operations today is "morphing" or evolving, and collection development is no different. Though it would be impossible to predict the future with any great degree of accuracy, we do believe that certain trends and areas may be identified and watched in the coming months and years. These include:

- The changing role of print in a digital world
- Declining user rights in copyrighted material
- Digitization as both a preservation tool and another concern
- The growing need for resource sharing and consortia
- The future practice of collection development

The Future Practice
of Collection Development

Because we have addressed each of these issues throughout this volume, we will focus our closing remarks on this last point. Herbert Schiller viewed "information collection, organization, and dissemination as a neutral activity, absent of social direction .... [Thus it becomes] the equivalent of information for information's sake."[1] What is becoming alarmingly prevalent today is the steady increase in commercialization of information. The current view seems to be that any company has a right to charge what it wishes for information—often for information that in the past was free. As noted several times throughout this book, pricing practices, particularly for electronic (online and CD-ROM) materials, do not follow traditional pricing processes or, for that matter, any predictable pattern. This results in substantial costs for libraries and information centers and their customers.

How are we to combat this? This situation forces collection development specialists to be even more critical in their planning activities. Emphasis today is shifting from an evaluation of the cost of the *package* of information to the cost or value of the information contained within it. This indicates the level of importance attached to having an accurate needs assessment, as well as the necessity for libraries to seriously consider the benefits of cooperative collection development and resource sharing activities. It is impossible for any library today to be comprehensive in its print collection—let alone being able to afford access to even a majority of electronic resources available today. Electronic information will continue to garner a sizable share of the time, attention, and resources of present and future libraries. Issues of access versus ownership will likely remain, to one degree or another. Balancing these costs will be an ongoing challenge as we continually confront technologies that become outdated in less and less time. Consortia arrangements may very well become a necessity for a majority of library settings. In addition, our collections are aging as we write, and the need for a collection that is well preserved and has been properly weeded will continue to exist.

Closing Thoughts

Which of these aforementioned developments will make the largest strides in the time between this edition and the next is hard to say. Copyright, access to online information, preservation ... all are equally important issues. Certainly the development of the printing press did not spell the end of hand-lettered or handmade texts—no more than the onset of the Internet has spelled doom for the printed word. Perhaps in our lifetimes the "virtual library" will become a reality, but we would not want to hold our breaths that the library and information center of today will become tomorrow's "dinosaur" ... or even the horse.

The *printed* word plays such an important role in the lives of so many that it seems doubtful it will be left behind. As noted by Walt Crawford:

> Books matter, and will continue to matter, because people learn from them and enjoy reading them. Public and academic libraries will continue to rely heavily on printed collections because they work so well for the ideas of the future as well as the record of the past and present. Of course, libraries will extend those printed collections with in-house media collections, borrowed physical resources, and an ever-growing array of digital publications and on-line retrieval: that's neither revolutionary nor even new.[2]

The availability of this text in print format is but one example of this. What lies in the future is a need for effective, efficient, and systematic dissemination of an ever-growing world of information. This being the case, in the future there will be just as much need for selectors who are capable of building and preserving collections as there is today.

The challenge is yours. We wish you well.

Notes

1. Herbert Schiller, "Public Information Goes Corporate," *Library Journal* 116 (October 1, 1991): 43.

2. W. Crawford, "Paper Persists: Why Physical Library Collections Still Matter," *Online* (January/February 1998): 48.

Further Reading

Angileetta, A. "Collection Development in the Large American Research Library: At an End or at a Beginning?" In *Information Superhighway: The Role of Librarians, Information Scientists, and Intermediaries* (Publications of Essen University Library 18). Edited by A. H. Helal and J. W. Weiss, 337–48. Essen, Germany: Essen University Library, 1995.

Association of Research Libraries, Office of Management Services. *Organization of Collection Development*. SPEC Flyer 207. Washington, D.C.: ARL/OMS, 1995.

Atkinson, R. "Access, Ownership, and the Future of Collection Development." In *Collection Management and Development: Issues in an Electronic Era*. Edited by P. Johnson and B. MacEwan, 92–110. Chicago: American Library Association, 1994.

Demas, S. "What Will Collection Development Do?" *Collection Management* 22, no. 3/4 (1998): 151–59.

Holleman, C. "Collection Issues in the New Library Environment." *Collection Management* 57, no. 2 (1996): 47–64.

Maurer, R. "The View from Here." *Folio: The Magazine for Magazine Management* 26, no. 5 (April 1, 1997): 57, 59.

McCarthy, C. K. "Collection Development in the Access Age: All You Thought It Would Be and More." *Journal of Library Administration* 22, no. 4 (1996): 15–31.

Mosher, P. "The Coming of the Millennium: Is There a Future of the Research Library?" In *Collection Management and Development: Issues in an Electronic Era*. Edited by P. Johnson and B. MacEwan, 1–12. Chicago: American Library Association, 1994.

Rowley, G., and W. K. Black. "Consequences of Change: The Evolution of Collection Development." *Collection Building* 15, no. 2 (1996): 22–30.

Scholarship, Instruction, and Libraries at the Turn of the Century: Results from Five Task Forces Appointed by the American Council of Learned Societies and the Council on Library and Information Resources. Washington, D.C.: Council on Library and Information Resources, 1999.

Strangelove, M. "Current and Future Trends in Network-Based Electronic Journals and Publishing." In *The Evolving Virtual Library: Visions and Case Studies*. Edited by L. M. Saunders, 135–45. Medford, N.J.: Information Today, 1996.

Wulf, W. A. "Warning: Information Technology Will Transform the University." *Issues in Science and Technology* 11, no. 4 (Summer 1995): 46–52.

Index